communication
PRINCIPLES FOR A LIFETIME

Steven A. Beebe
SOUTHWEST TEXAS STATE UNIVERSITY

Susan J. Beebe
SOUTHWEST TEXAS STATE UNIVERSITY

Diana K. Ivy
TEXAS A&M UNIVERSITY–CORPUS CHRISTI

Shannon Watson
SENECA COLLEGE OF APPLIED ARTS AND TECHNOLOGY

CANADIAN EDITION

PEARSON
A and B

Toronto

This book is dedicated to all learners who seek to understand self and others, improve their relationships, and fulfil employment goals.

—S.L.W.

National Library of Canada Cataloguing in Publication

Communication: principles for a lifetime / Steven A. Beebe ... [et al.].—Canadian ed.

Includes bibliographical references and index.
ISBN 0-205-42667-0

1. Communication—Textbooks. I. Beebe, Steven A., 1950-

HM1206.C64 2004   302.2   C2004-901241-X

ISBN 0-205-42667-0

Vice President, Editorial Director: Michael J. Young
Executive Acquisitions Editor: Dave Ward
Executive Marketing Manager: Toivo Pajo
Supervising Developmental Editor: Suzanne Schaan
Production Editor: Joel Gladstone
Copy Editor: Susan Broadhurst
Permissions and Photo Research: Christina Beamish
Production Coordinator: Trish Ciardullo
Page Layout: Debbie Kumpf
Art Director: Mary Opper
Cover Design: Michelle Bellemare
Cover Image: Getty Images

1 2 3 4 5   09 08 07 06 05

Statistics Canada information is used with permission of the Minister of Industry, as Minister responsible for Statistics Canada. Information on the availability of the wide range of data from Statistics Canada can be obtained from Statistics Canada's Regional Offices, its World Wide Web site at www.statcan.ca, and its toll-free access number 1-800-263-1136.

Printed and bound in the United States.

Brief Contents

Contents

Appendix A: Interviewing   337

Appendix B: Sample Speeches for Discussion and Evaluation   356

Preface

The goal of *Communication: Principles for a Lifetime* is to provide a thorough presentation of what is fundamental about human communication by organizing the study of communication around five principles that are inherent in the process of communicating with others.

In this edition a Canadian context sets the backdrop for the principles of communication. For many students, this book may be the only one they will ever read that provides a comprehensive, research-based introduction to human communication. Consequently, they need a digest of classic and contemporary research and practice that will remain with them throughout their lives. Our goal is to present research conclusions and practical strategies in the framework of five fundamental communication principles.

THE CHALLENGE OF TEACHING A FUNDAMENTALS OF COMMUNICATION COURSE

Most introductory communication courses cover a lot of territory. There are many communication concepts, principles, and skills to learn. In fact, there may be too much of a good thing. The barrage of ideas, contexts, theories, and skills can leave students and instructors overwhelmed with a sometimes unrelated hodgepodge of information. Besides learning about several theories of communication, students are also presented with what may appear to them to be abbreviated courses in interpersonal communication, group communication, and public speaking. In addition to a conceptual understanding of communication, students are expected to master a cavalcade of communication skills, including group discussion and problem solving skills, listening and paraphrasing skills, conflict management skills, and public speaking competencies—both informative and persuasive presentation skills. When a typical hybrid or introductory communication fundamentals course is over, both students and instructors have breathlessly covered an astounding amount of information and skills; they may not, however, appreciate the coherence or superstructure of what is fundamental about human communication. They may end the course viewing communication as a fragmented area of study that includes a cornucopia of concepts and applications, but they may have little understanding of what is truly fundamental about how we make sense out of the world and share that sense with others.

OUR SOLUTION TO THE CHALLENGE: AN INTEGRATED APPROACH TO TEACHING AND LEARNING COMMUNICATION PRINCIPLES AND SKILLS

To help students and instructors stitch together the plethora of ideas and information typically found in an introductory communication course, we've organized the study of human communication around five fundamental communication principles. These five principles provide a framework for understanding the importance of communication in our lives. No, we don't claim that everything you need to know about communication is detailed in our five organizing communication principles. These principles do, however, synthesize essential research and wisdom about communication. They are designed to help introductory communication students see the "big picture" of the role and importance of communication, both as they sit in the classroom and as they live their lives. The communication principles we highlight should look familiar. Although they are included in some way in most introductory communication texts, they are not often used as a scaffolding to provide coherence to the entire course. In most texts, principles are typically presented in the first third of the book and then abandoned as material about interpersonal, group, and public communication is presented. We don't use a principled hit-and-run approach. As an alternative, using examples and illustrations to which students can relate, early in the book we carefully discuss each principle. Throughout the latter two-thirds of the book we gently remind students how these principles relate to interpersonal relationships and group and team discussions, as well as public presentations. We cover classic communication content but organize it around five principles so the information has coherence. What are the five fundamental principles?

- Principle One: Be aware of your communication with yourself and others.
- Principle Two: Effectively use and interpret verbal messages.
- Principle Three: Effectively use and interpret nonverbal messages.
- Principle Four: Listen and respond thoughtfully to others.
- Principle Five: Appropriately adapt messages to others.

An additional subtext for these five principles is the importance of communicating ethically with others. Throughout the book we invite students to consider the ethical implications of how they communicate with others, through the use of ethical probes and questions. As we discuss in Chapter 1, we believe that to be effective, a communication message must achieve three goals: It must be understood, achieve its intended effect, and be ethical. Our five communication principles for a lifetime are designed to help students achieve these three goals.

We illustrate with a pentagon model the relationships of the five communication principles that are the overarching structure of the book. When each principle is introduced or discussed, the model spotlights the principle by highlighting the appropriate part of the model in colour.

But in addition to identifying five communication principles, we want students to see how these principles relate to the classic communication contexts of interpersonal communication, group and team communication, and presentational speaking. We link the five communication principles with specific content by using a margin icon to note that a discussion in the text of a skill, concept, or idea is related to one or more of the five communication principles.

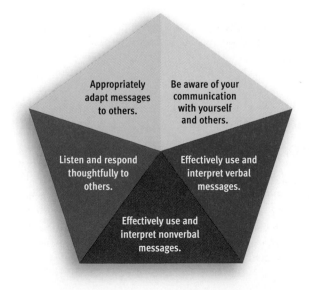

OVERVIEW OF THE BOOK

The book is organized into four units. In Unit I, the five principles are introduced in Chapter 1 and then each principle is explained in a separate chapter (Chapters 2 through 6). Each communication principle is discussed and illustrated to help students see the value and centrality of these principles in their lives. Chapter 2 discusses the principle of being self-aware. Chapter 3 focuses on using and interpreting verbal messages. Using and interpreting nonverbal messages is the focus of Chapter 4. Chapter 5 includes a discussion of the interrelated processes of listening and responding, giving special attention to the importance of being other-oriented and empathic. The last principle, appropriately adapting to others, is presented in Chapter 6; we use this principle to illustrate the importance of adapting one's behaviour to culture and gender differences among people.

Unit II applies the five communication principles to interpersonal relationships. Unlike many treatments of interpersonal communication, our discussion links the concepts and strategies for understanding interpersonal communication with our five communication principles for a lifetime. Chapter 7 presents information to help students better understand the nature and function of communication in relationships. Chapter 8 identifies strategies that can enhance the quality of our interpersonal relationships with others.

Unit III discusses how the five communication principles help us understand and enhance communication in small groups and teams. Chapter 9 helps to explain how groups and teams work. We offer more practical strategies for collaboratively solving problems, leading groups and teams, and running and participating in meetings in Chapter 10.

Our final unit, Unit IV, presents classic content to help students design and deliver a speech, with references to contemporary research and using the latest tools of technology. Based on our popular audience-centred approach to developing a speech, we emphasize the importance of adapting to listeners while also being an ethically vigilant communicator. Chapters 11 through 13 offer information and tips for developing presentation ideas, organizing and outlining messages, delivering a presentation (including the use of presentational and multimedia aids), crafting effective informative presentations, and developing ethically sound persuasive messages.

We conclude the book with two appendices designed to supplement our instruction about communication fundamentals. Appendix A offers practical strategies for being interviewed and for interviewing others. We continue to relate our discussion of interviewing to the five communication principles for a lifetime. Appendix B includes examples of actual speeches by prominent Canadians to illustrate what effective, principled speeches look like.

SPECIAL FEATURES TO HELP STUDENTS LEARN

A textbook is, in essence, a "distance learning" tool. The authors write the book separated by both time and space from the learner. To help shorten the distance between author and reader, we've incorporated a variety of learning resources and pedagogical features to engage students in the learning process. As we note in the text, information alone is not communication. Communication occurs when the receiver responds to information. Our special features help turn information into a responsive communication message that impacts students' lives.

Principles Model and Icons: Our pentagon model and margin icons help students see connections between the five principles and the various communication concepts and skills we present. Throughout the book we provide an integrated framework to reinforce what's fundamental about human communication. Long after the course is over and students have forgotten lists they memorized to cram for an exam, we want them to remember the five fundamental principles. These principles can also help them remember strategies and concepts to enhance their interpersonal relationships, improve group and team meetings, and design and deliver effective presentations.

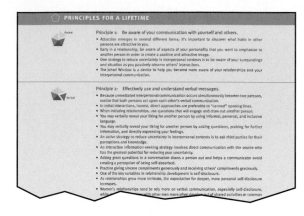

ETHICAL PROBE

Students in an interpersonal communication class were discussing cyber-relationships, when one said a surprising thing: "I got a break-up notice over the Internet once. I couldn't believe it; this girl actually had the nerve to break up with me through an e-mail message. We never ever discussed it face to face or over the phone." No one in the class had heard of a "Dear John" message being conveyed electronically.

Breakups are tough, but what is a person's ethical obligation when she or he wishes to terminate a relationship? Granted, the Internet allows for a certain level of impersonality, but is this the right way to "dump" someone? Would you want someone to break up with you in such a "high-tech" way?

COMMUNICATION and TECHNOLOGY

Finding Virtual Groups to Learn Online

Even with the increasing use of distance learning and Web-based or Web-assisted learning, most people have more experience in learning in live, real-time classrooms. One of the advantages to learning with others is the use of interaction and group association with other students to reinforce learning. When you are learning online, consider some of the following tips and strategies for recreating the advantages of learning with others in groups and teams.

- Seek out online courses that have real-time chat groups.
- Enrich your online class experience by joining a related Listserv, a group of people who receive information on related topics. You will then have a virtual support group to reinforce your learning.

- Read the e-mail postings from other students in your class to learn from the questions and comments of your classmates.
- Use e-mail or your membership in a Listserv to determine whether someone taking the same class lives near you and plan to meet for study sessions.

With thought and ingenuity, you can enjoy the advantages of distance-learning experiences while using the technology to work with others in groups to reinforce what you learn.

On the WEB

When you facilitate a meeting, you need all the help you can get. A Web site called The Virtual Meeting Assistant can give you some additional tips and tools for helping you prepare for and run a quality meeting:
www.ukans.edu/cwis/units/coms2/vma/vms.htm.

COMMUNICATION and DIVERSITY

Acknowledging Cultural Differences in Organizing Messages

What's the shortest distance between two points? Why, going in a straight line, of course. In organizing a message, it may seem that the most logical strategy is to develop a structure that moves from one idea to the next in a logical, "straight" way of thinking. But not every culture organizes ideas using that logic. In fact, each culture teaches its members unique patterns of thought and organization that are considered appropriate for various occasions and audiences. In general, Canadian speakers tend to be more linear and direct than do Semitic, Asian, Romance, or Russian speakers. Semitic speakers support their main points by pursuing tangents that might seem "off topic" to many Canadian listeners. Asians may allude to a main point only through a circuitous route of illustrations and parables. And

only gradually are related to a main point. The models in Figure 11.3 illustrate these culturally diverse patterns of organization. Of course, these are very broad generalizations. It should be noted that assigning characteristics by nationality is used as a general guideline to compare and learn from communication preferences when organizing messages. As an effective speaker who seeks to adapt to your audience, you should investigate and perhaps acknowledge or even consider adopting the customary organizational strategy of your particular audience. In addition, when you are listening to a presentation, recognizing the existence of cultural differences can help you appreciate and understand the organization of a speaker from a culture other

Chapter End Principles Summary (Principles for a Lifetime): In addition to the use of the margin icon to highlight material related to one or more communication principles in the text, we conclude each context chapter (Chapters 7–13) with a summary of the chapter content organized around the five communication principles. Miniature versions of our principles icon will serve as headings to highlight the five fundamental principles. The purpose of this chapter-end feature is to help students synthesize the material related to the context discussed (e.g. interpersonal communication) and the five principles that undergird the descriptive and prescriptive information presented in the chapter. This feature will help students see the link between the variety of ideas and skills we present and the five communication principles.

Ethical Probes: As we emphasized in Chapter 1 and reinforce throughout the book, effective communicators are ethical. To help students apply ethics as a dimension of learning about human communication, we provide brief case studies, termed "Ethical Probes," several places in each chapter. We ask students to ponder how they would respond to a specific ethical dilemma. The questions we pose are sure-fire class discussion starters, journal entries, or thought-provoking illustrations.

Communication and Technology: In each chapter we include special boxed material about technology and communication to help students become sensitive to the sometimes mind-boggling impact new technology has upon our communication with others. We also discuss the importance and role of technology in several chapters throughout the book.

On the Web: We do more than just talk about technology. We encourage students to reach out to the vast array of resources on the Internet by including Web resources that link to each chapter. All Internet addresses are included in the companion Web site that supports this book (www.pearsoned.ca/beebe).

Communication and Diversity: Because we believe diversity is such an important communication topic, especially when considering Canada's rich multicultural and multi-ethnic environment, we discuss diversity not only through our fifth principle of communication ("appropriately adapt messages to others") in a comprehensive chapter, but we also emphasize it throughout the book. Each chapter includes a "Communication and Diversity" box to help students see the importance of diversity in their lives.

Comprehensive Pedagogical Learning Tools: To help students master the material, we've built in a wealth of study aids, including:

- Learning objectives
- Chapter outlines
- Key terms in boldface with marginal glossary
- Recap Boxes
- Chapter-end narrative summaries of each chapter
- Chapter-end summaries of the five communication principles (Chapters 7–13)
- Chapter-end questions for review and discussion
- Skill-building activities and collaborative learning exercises

NEW TO THE CANADIAN EDITION

Reviewers have given us recommendations for this Canadian edition, and we listened and responded (principle four) to their suggestions. Throughout the text, material has been revised to provide a Canadian perspective on communication:

- *Canadian statistics and research* are included to provide a context for the discussion, with a specific focus on diversity. Key topics covered include Canada's linguistic diversity (Chapter 3) and Canada's ethnocultural portrait (Chapter 6).
- *Canadian examples and cultural references* appear throughout, to draw students into the discussion—everything from Newfoundland English to Aboriginal languages, from Preston Manning to Pierre Trudeau, and from winter storms to the SARS outbreak of 2003.
- *Canadian quotations and speeches* provide strong examples of good communication, especially the two sample speeches in Appendix B, by Jean Chrétien and Adrienne Clarkson.
- *Canadian Web sites* lead students to explore specific topics from a Canadian perspective, on sites such as the Self Esteem Institute of Canada, the Mediation and Restorative Justice Centre, and rabble.ca.

In response to market feedback, this Canadian edition also features streamlined coverage of presentational speaking in Unit IV, condensed from five chapters to three. This briefer treatment focuses on the essentials without sacrificing any of the key concepts required in most courses.

SUPPLEMENTS

STUDENT SUPPLEMENT

Companion Website (www.pearsoned.ca/beebe). Visit the Companion Website for this text for additional resources such as quizzes, essay questions, and Web links.

INSTRUCTOR SUPPLEMENTS

The Instructor's Resource CD-ROM includes the following supplements:

- *Instructor's Resource Manual.* This manual offers lecture outlines, discussion and journal questions, classroom assignments, student activities, and Internet exercises.
- *Test Item File.* This test bank contains over 1200 questions, including multiple choice, true/false, matching, fill-in-the-blank, short answer, and essay questions. It is offered in both Microsoft Word and TestGen formats (see below).
- *TestGen.* The Pearson TestGen is a special computerized version of the Test Item File that enables instructors to view and edit the existing questions, add questions, generate tests, and print the tests in a variety of formats. Powerful search and sort functions make it easy to locate questions and arrange them in any order desired. TestGen also enables instructors to administer tests on a local area network, have the tests graded electronically, and have the results prepared in electronic or printed reports.
- *PowerPoint Presentations.* These PowerPoint slides cover the key concepts in each chapter of the text.

Some of these resources can also be downloaded from Pearson Education Canada's Instructor Central Web site, a protected site for instructors only. An access code is required; apply online at www.pearsoned.ca/instructor or contact your local sales representative for details.

ACKNOWLEDGEMENTS

Although our four names appear on the cover as authors of the book you are holding in your hands, in reality hundreds of people have been instrumental in making this book possible. Communication scholars who have dedicated their lives to researching the importance of communication principles, theories, and skills provide the fuel for this book. We thank each author we reference in our voluminous endnotes for the research conclusions that bring us to our contemporary understanding of communication principles. We thank our students who have trusted us to be their guides in a study of human communication. They continue to enrich our lives with their enthusiasm and curiosity. They have inspired us to be more creative by their honest quizzical looks, and challenged us to go beyond "textbook" answers with their thought-provoking questions.

We are most appreciative of the outstanding editorial support we continue to receive from our colleagues and friends at Allyn & Bacon and Pearson Education. As the Canadian author, Shannon Watson would like to extend a special thank you to Pearson Education Canada for providing this opportunity to create educational materials that reflect the Canadian environment. Suzanne Schaan, my Developmental Editor at Pearson, has been particularly instrumental in the development and revision of the Canadian edition. Her unwavering guidance has been appreciated. My researcher, Rod Schmaltz, spent many hours searching for Canadian content—for this, I thank him.

We are grateful to the many educators whose comments on the two American editions helped shaped the core of this book. For the Canadian edition, we would particularly like to thank Zina Suissa of Dawson College, who completed an extensive review of the whole manuscript. The following reviewers also provided guidance:

Robert Bragg, Mount Royal College
Rita Halma, Lethbridge Community College
Tuula Heinonen, University of Manitoba
David Legg, Mount Royal College
Don McGavern, University of Calgary
Jason Novak, Mount Royal College
Kathy Pichora-Fuller, University of Toronto at Mississauga
Alexandre Sévigny, McMaster University
Zina Suissa, Dawson College
Bruce Watson, Southern Alberta Institute of Technology

Finally we express our appreciation to our families. Ivy thanks her ever-supportive family, parents Herschel and Carol Ivy, sister Karen Black (who supplied the permissions research and constant encouragement), and nephew Brian Black (whose humorous e-mails provided great comic relief). They have been constant and generous with their praise for her writing accomplishments. Ivy is especially grateful to her father, Herschel Ivy, for lovingly offering many lessons about living the highly ethical life.

Sue and Steve especially thank their parents, Herb and Jane Dye and Russell and Muriel Beebe, who taught us much about communication and ethics that truly are principles for a lifetime. We also thank our sons, Mark and Matthew Beebe, for teaching us life lessons about giving and receiving love that will remain with us forever.

Shannon would like to thank her husband, Tony Watson, for his continued support, guidance, and sense of humour throughout this writing process. She would also like to thank her children, Lauren, Brittany, and Blake Watson, for demonstrating the value of effective and appropriate communication. The unconditional love and support of her family provide constant sources of inspiration, motivation, and fulfillment.

Steven A. Beebe
Susan J. Beebe
San Marcos, Texas

Diana K. Ivy
Corpus Christi, Texas

Shannon L. Watson
Toronto, Ontario

A Great Way to Learn and Instruct Online

The Pearson Education Canada Companion Website is easy to navigate and is organized to correspond to the chapters in this textbook. Whether you are a student in the classroom or a distance learner you will discover helpful resources for in-depth study and research that empower you in your quest for greater knowledge and maximize your potential for success in the course.

[www.pearsoned.ca/beebe]

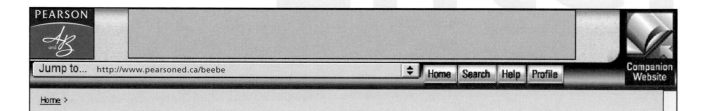

Jump to...   http://www.pearsoned.ca/beebe   Home   Search   Help   Profile

Home >

PEC Companion Website

Communication: Principles for a Lifetime, Canadian Edition, by Beebe, Beebe, Ivy, and Watson

The modules on this site provide students with tools for learning course material. These modules include:

- Multiple-Choice Questions
- True/False Questions
- Essay Questions
- Web Links
- Flashcards

In the quiz modules students can send answers to the grader and receive instant feedback on their progress through the Results Reporter. Coaching comments and references to the textbook may be available to ensure that students take advantage of all available resources to enhance their learning experience.

Jean Dubuffet, "Visage rouge et visage bleu" from the series "Le Metro," gouache on paper, 1943. Photo: Philippe Migeat. © 2003 Artists Rights Society (ARS), New York/ADAGP, Paris. © CNAC/MNAM/Dist. Reunion des Musees Nationaux/Art Resource, NY.

The purpose of all higher education is to make men aware of what was and what is; to incite them to probe into what may be. It seeks to teach them to understand, to evaluate, to communicate.

— OTTO KLEPPNER

1 Foundations of Human Communication

CHAPTER OUTLINE

AFTER STUDYING THIS CHAPTER, YOU SHOULD BE ABLE TO

1. Define communication and explain why it is an important course of study.

2. Describe three criteria that can be used to determine whether communication is competent.

3. Compare and contrast communication as action, interaction, and transaction.

4. Identify five characteristics of communication.

5. List and explain five fundamental principles of communication.

6. Define and describe communication in interpersonal, group, and presentational communication situations.

Communication is essential for life. Communicating is a fundamental aspect of being human. Even if you live in isolation from other people, you "talk" to yourself through your thoughts. Like life-sustaining breath, communication is ever-present in our lives. Understanding and improving how we communicate with others is a basic life skill.

Human communication is inescapable. Consider the number of times you have purposefully communicated with someone today, as you worked, ate, studied, shopped, or went about your daily duties. Most people spend between 80% and 90% of their waking hours communicating with others.[1] It is through the process of communication that we convey who we are, both to ourselves and to others; it is our primary tool for making our way in the world. Learning to communicate effectively will enhance our relationships with others and promote career success.

This book presents fundamental principles that undergird all aspects of communicating with others when both sending and receiving messages. In the course of our study of human communication, we will discuss a myriad of skills, ideas, concepts, and contexts. The number of terms, ideas, skills, and competencies can be overwhelming. To help you stitch together the barrage of ideas and information, we will organize our study around five fundamental communication principles. Together, these five principles will provide a framework for our discussion of the importance and pervasiveness of human communication.

Principle One: Be aware of your communication with yourself and others.
Principle Two: Effectively use and interpret verbal messages.
Principle Three: Effectively use and interpret nonverbal messages.
Principle Four: Listen and respond thoughtfully to others.
Principle Five: Appropriately adapt messages to others.

These five principles distil decades of research as well as the wisdom of those who have taught communication during the past century. We don't claim that everything you need to know about communication is covered by these five principles. They do, however, summarize considerable knowledge about the communication process and what constitutes effective communication.

We will provide an overview of these principles later in this chapter and devote a separate chapter to each principle. This book examines each fundamental principle in the context of three prevalent communication situations:

- interpersonal interactions
- group and team communication
- presentational speaking

Our goal is to present both classic and contemporary research conclusions about the role and importance of communication in our lives. In addition to discussing live, face-to-face human communication, throughout the book, in a feature called *Communication and Technology*, we will highlight the increasing importance of technology in our communication with others.

Before we elaborate on these principles, it is important to provide some background for our study of communication. The purpose of this first chapter is to provide that background. We will define communication, discuss why it is important to study, examine various models or perspectives of communication, and identify characteristics of human communication. With this background as prelude, we then discuss the five foundational principles of human communication that we will use throughout the book to help you organize the concepts, skills, and ideas we present in interpersonal, group, and presentational speaking situations.

COMMUNICATION DEFINED

Communication is one of those words that seems so basic you may wonder why it needs to be formally defined. Yet scholars who devote their lives to studying communication don't always agree on its definition. One research team counted more than 126 published definitions.[2]

In its broadest sense, **communication** is the process of acting on information.[3] Someone does or says something, and others think or do something in response to the action or the words as they understand them.

Communication is not unique to humans. It is possible, for example, for you to act on information from your dog. She barks; you feed her. This general definition also suggests that your dog can act on information from you. You head for the pantry to feed her; she wags her tail and jumps in the air, anticipating her dinner. Although researchers study communication between species as well as communication systems within a single animal species, these fields of study are beyond the scope of this book. The focus of our study is human communication: people communicating with other people.

Some scholars question whether *any* human behaviour is really communication. When you cross your arms while listening to your friend describe her day, this may indicate to your friend that you're not interested in what she's talking about. But it could just be that you're cold. While all human expression has the potential to communicate a message (someone may act or respond to the information they receive from you), it does not mean you *intentionally* are expressing an idea or emotion. Presenting information to others does not mean that effective communication has occurred: Information alone is not communication. "But I told you what to do!" "It's there in the memo. Why didn't you do what I asked?" "It's in the syllabus." These exasperated communicators assumed that if they sent a message, someone would receive it. However, communication does not operate in a simple, linear, what-you-send-is-what-is-received process. The receiver interprets and evaluates the information so that it creates meaning for him or her. However, people don't always accurately interpret the messages we express; this unprofound observation has profound implications. One reason we have communication courses, academic departments that focus on communication, and people who earn PhDs in communication is because of the challenge we have in understanding one another.

To refine our definition of communication, we can say that **human communication** *is the process of making sense out of the world and sharing that sense with others by creating meaning through verbal and nonverbal messages.*[4] We make sense out of the world by listening, observing, tasting, touching, and smelling, then sharing our conclusions with others using both words and unspoken expressions. As we've noted, the message sent may not be the message that is understood because meaning is *created* in the heart and mind of the listener. In reality, meaning is *co-created* by both the speaker and the listener. By this we mean that all individuals who are involved in the communication process shape how a message is understood by drawing upon their own experiences while attempting to make sense out of a message.

It is because of the ever-present potential for misunderstanding that effective and appropriate communication should be *other oriented*—it should acknowledge the perspective of others, not just of the creator of the message. Communication that does not consider the needs, background, and culture of the receiver is more likely to be misunderstood. We'll emphasize the importance of considering others or considering your audience throughout the book. Knowing something about the experiences of the person or persons you're speaking to can help you communicate more effectively and appropriately.

Human communication is complex and varied. It also emerges in many different forms: face-to-face conversations, speeches, radio and television programs, e-mail, Web sites, letters, books, and articles. Written communication is so complex that business writing courses have been developed to address its intricacies.

communication
The process of acting on information.

human communication
The process of making sense out of the world and attempting to share that sense with others by creating meaning through verbal and nonverbal messages.

COMMUNICATION COMPETENCE

What does it mean to communicate competently? Does it mean you are able to present a well-delivered speech? Or that you are able to carry on a brilliant conversation with someone? Is evidence of your competence the fact that you are usually asked to chair a committee meeting because you are so organized? Being a competent communicator is more than just being well liked, glib, able to give polished presentations, or able to smoothly interact with others one on one or in groups and teams. Although it is difficult to identify core criteria that are attributes of competent communication in all situations, we think certain goals of communication serve as measures of competent communication regardless of the setting. We suggest the following three criteria:[5]

- The message should be understood as the communicator intended it to be understood.
- The message should achieve the effect the communicator intended to achieve.
- The message should be ethical.

⤳ The Message Should Be Understood

A primary goal of any effective communication transaction is to develop a common understanding of the message from both the sender's and the receiver's perspectives. You'll note how the words "common" and "communication" resemble each other. We acknowledge the challenge of communicating with others; differences in culture, language, experience, gender, education, and background all contribute to sources of misunderstanding. The diversity of Canada's population, representing more than 200 ethnic groups, calls for a closer examination of how we can communicate successfully. One of the aims of the principles we discuss in this book is to create clarity of expression and a common understanding.

Message clarity is missing in the following headlines that have appeared in local Canadian newspapers:

High-flying loonie batters furniture firm
Include your children when baking cookies
The heads up on unseating your toilet
Talk turkey, Air Canada, unions told
Pain of broken heart is indeed in your head

Meanings are fragile, and messages can be misunderstood. An effective communication message is one that the receiver understands.

⤳ The Message Should Achieve Its Intended Effect

Often we communicate to achieve some goal or outcome. Typical goals of speaking in public are to inform, to persuade, or to entertain. In small groups we often communicate to solve problems and make decisions. In our interpersonal relationships we interact to build trust, develop intimacy, or just enjoy someone's company. Thus, another criterion for judging the effectiveness of communication is to gauge whether the intent of the message is achieved.

When you communicate intentionally with others, it is for a specific purpose: to achieve a goal or accomplish something. Because different purposes require different strategies for success, being aware of your purpose can enhance the probability of your achieving it.

Whether you are attempting to close a sale, get a date, give directions to the mall, or tell a joke, you should consider your goal. The purpose of our communication with others is not always to give or receive something tangible. Sometimes it is simply to make human contact, to establish a relationship, or just to be with someone. But one way to assess whether your communication was effective, regardless of the purpose, is to determine whether the outcome you sought is the outcome you got.

⤳ The Message Should Be Ethical

ethics
The beliefs, values, and moral principles by which we determine what is right or wrong.

Communication can be used to achieve good or bad objectives. A message that is understood and achieves its intended effect but manipulatively restricts the listener's choices or uses false information may be effective but is not appropriate or ethical. **Ethics** are the beliefs, values, and moral principles by which we determine what is right or wrong. Ethics and ethical behaviour have long been presented as critical components of human behaviour in a given culture. It is important to note that what may be appropriate or ethical in one culture may not be appropriate or ethical in another culture. Saying this, however, there appear to be some universal principles for ethical behaviour.

All religions of the world have a moral code that provides guidance for how people should treat others.[6] The Ten Commandments serve as ethical guidelines for those who adhere to Judeo–Christian ethical principles. In Christianity the Golden Rule—"Do unto others what you would have others do unto you"—is a fundamental value. Buddhism teaches a similar value: "One should seek for others the happiness one desires for one's self." Hinduism asks adherents to live by the precept, "Do nothing to others which would cause pain if done to you." Judaism teaches, "What is hateful to you, do not do to others." Islam suggests, "No one of you is a believer until he desires for his brother that which he desires for himself." The underlying ethic of how to treat others can clearly be seen across most if not all of the world's religions.[7] Our purpose is not to prescribe a specific religious or philosophical ethical code, but rather to suggest that humans from a variety of cultures and traditions have sought to develop ethical principles that offer a basis for how we should interact with others.

The Dalai Lama teaches an ethical code that, whether or not we believe in the Tibetan Buddhist religion, provides guidance for successful communication.

Religion is not the only realm that focuses on ethical behaviour. Most professions, such as medicine, law, and journalism, have an explicit code of ethics to provide a framework of what is appropriate and inappropriate behaviour. In 1999 the National Communication Association developed a Credo for Communication Ethics to emphasize the importance of being an ethical communicator:

> Ethical communication is fundamental to responsible thinking, decision making, and the development of relationships and communities within and across contexts, cultures, channels, and media. Moreover, ethical communication enhances human worth and dignity by fostering truthfulness, fairness, responsibility, personal integrity, and respect for self and others.[8]

Echoing the wisdom offered by others, we suggest that competent communication is grounded in an other-oriented ethical perspective that is fundamental to all human interactions.

For most people, being ethical means being sensitive to others' needs, giving people choices rather than forcing them to behave a certain way, keeping private such information as others wish to remain private, not intentionally decreasing others' feelings of self-worth, and being honest in presenting information. Unethical communication does just the opposite: It forces views on others and demeans their integrity.

Being honest is a key element of ethical communication. If you knowingly withhold key information, lie, or distort the truth, then you are not communicating ethically or effectively. For example, after Paul missed the test in his communication class, he mournfully told his professor that his grandmother had died and he had had to attend the funeral. Paul's professor obliged and allowed him to make up the test. Paul's professor understood the message, so Paul achieved the effect he wanted. Paul's grandmother, however, is alive and well. According to our criteria for effective communication, Paul's dishonesty would qualify his communication as inappropriate and unethical.

Throughout the book we will offer ethical questions, which we call *ethical probes*, to invite you to consider the ethical implications of the way we communicate with others.

WHY STUDY COMMUNICATION?

Why are you here? No, we don't mean why do you exist, or why you live where you do. Why are you taking a course about communication? Perhaps the short answer is: It's required. Or maybe your adviser, parent, or friend encouraged you to take the course. If it is a required course for you, what's the rationale for that requirement? If it's not required, what can a systematic study of human communication do for you?

Communication touches every aspect of our lives. To be able to express yourself to other people is a basic requirement for living in a modern society. From a practical standpoint, most of you will make your living with your mind rather than your hands.[9] Whatever job you do, you will need communication skills to work with others. The need to improve communication skills is echoed by the number of courses, books, databases, onsite corporate training programs, and coaches all ready and willing to provide guidance and information on the "how to" of effective communication. People with good communication skills are promoted within business and industry, maintain employment, and make good leaders. When you study communication, you are developing leadership skills. "The art of communication," said author Daniel Quinn, "is the language of leadership."[10]

The Canadian Association of Student Activity Advisors (CASAA) realizes the importance of good leadership and communication skills. It has sponsored leadership conferences to highlight skills such as self-awareness, public speaking, listening, and overall effective communication strategies across the country, including in Saskatchewan, Alberta, British Columbia, Yukon, and the Northwest Territories.[11]

Aren't some people just born to be better communicators than others? If so, why should you work to develop your communication skill? Just as some people have more innate musical talent, there is evidence that some people may have an inborn biological basis for communicating with others.[12] This does not mean you should not work to develop your communication ability. The Canadian Public Health Association's National Literacy and Health program provides workshops to youth across Canada highlighting literacy issues. Attention is given to the following elements of effective communication: listen; paraphrase; and ask questions to clarify, including the five Ws of who, what, when, where, and why. Listening barriers described include types of language (slang, etc.), stereotypes, body language, and preparedness.[13]

Throughout the book we will offer ample evidence that if you work to improve your skill, you will be rewarded with the benefits of enhanced communication competence. What are these benefits? Read on.

⋯⟩ To Improve Your Employability

Regardless of your specific job description, the essence of what you do when working at any job is to communicate; you talk, listen, relate, read, and write, whatever your job title. People who can communicate effectively with others are in high demand. Employers want employees who can communicate effectively, manage information, demonstrate positive attitudes, be responsible, and work with others. As shown in Table 1.1, the Conference Board of Canada developed an Employability Skills profile based on employer input regarding skills needed in the Canadian workforce. Three main categories identified are Fundamental Skills, Personal Management Skills, and Teamwork Skills. Under these categories it is noted that the ability to communicate, to demonstrate positive attitudes and behaviours, and to work well with others are essential skills if you are to progress in the world of work.[14]

Effective communication can promote employment opportunities.

TABLE 1.1

Employability Skills 2000+
The skills you need to enter, stay in, and progress in the world of work—whether you work on your own or as a part of a team. These skills can also be applied and used beyond the workplace in a range of daily activities.

Fundamental Skills
The skills needed as a base for further development
You will be better prepared to progress in the world of work when you can:

Communicate
- read and understand information presented in a variety of forms (e.g., words, graphs, charts, diagrams)
- write and speak so others pay attention and understand
- listen and ask questions to understand and appreciate the points of view of others
- share information using a range of information and communications technologies (e.g., voice, e-mail, computers)
- use relevant scientific, technological and mathematical knowledge and skills to explain or clarify ideas

Manage Information
- locate, gather and organize information using appropriate technology and information systems
- access, analyze and apply knowledge and skills form various disciplines (e.g., the arts, languages, science, technology, mathematics, social sciences, and the humanities)

Use Numbers
- decide what needs to be measured or calculated
- observe and record data using appropriate methods, tolls and technology
- make estimates and verify calculations

Think & Solve Problems
- assess situations and identify problems
- seek different points of view and evaluate them based on facts
- recognize the human, interpersonal, technical, scientific and mathematical dimensions of a problem
- identify the root cause of a problem
- be creative and innovative in exploring possible solutions
- readily use science, technology and mathematics as ways to think, gain and share knowledge, solve problems and make decisions
- evaluate solutions to make recommendations or decisions
- implement solutions
- check to see if a solution works, and act on opportunities for improvement

Personal Management Skills
The personal skills, attitudes and behaviours that drive one's potential for growth
You will be able to offer yourself greater possibilities for achievement when you can:

Demonstrate Positive Attitudes & Behaviours
- feel good about yourself and be confident
- deal with people, problems and situations with honesty, integrity and personal ethics
- recognize your own and other people's good efforts
- take care of your personal health
- show interest, initiative and effort

Be Responsible
- set goals and priorities balancing work and personal life
- plan and manage time, money and other resources to achieve goals
- assess, weigh and manage risk
- be accountable for your actions and the actions of your group
- be socially responsible and contribute to your community

Be Adaptable
- work independently or as a part of a team
- carry out multiple tasks or projects
- be innovative and resourceful: identify and suggest alternative ways to achieve goals and get the job done
- be open and respond constructively to change
- learn from your mistakes and accept feedback
- cope with uncertainty

Learn Continuously
- be willing to continuously learn and grow
- assess personal strengths and areas for development
- set your own learning goals
- identify and access learning sources and opportunities
- plan for and achieve your learning goals

Work Safely
- be aware of personal and group health and safety practices and procedures, and act in accordance with these

Teamwork Skills
The skills and attributes needed to contribute productively
You will be better prepared to add value and the outcomes of a task, project or team when you can:

Work with Others
- understand and work within the dynamics of a group
- ensure that a team's purpose and objectives are clear
- be flexible: respect, be open to and supportive of the thoughts, opinions and contributions of others in a group
- recognize and respect people's diversity, individual differences and perspectives
- accept and provide feedback in a constructive and considerate manner
- contribute to a team by sharing information and expertise
- lead or support when appropriate, motivating a group for high performance
- understand the role of conflict in a group to reach solutions
- manage and resolve conflict when appropriate

Participate in Projects & Tasks
- plan, design or carry out a project or task from start to finish with well-defined objectives and outcomes
- develop a plan, seek feedback, test, revise and implement
- work to agreed quality standards and specifications
- select and use appropriate tolls and technology for a task or project
- adapt to changing requirements and information
- continuously monitor the success of a project or task and identify ways to improve

The Conference Board of Canada
255 Smyth Road, Ottawa
ON, K1H 8M7 Canada
Tel. (613) 526-3280
Fax (613) 526-4857

Internet:
www.conferenceboard.ca/nbec

Source: "Employability Skills+Brochure 2000 E/F" (Ottawa: The Conference Board of Canada, 2000).

The Skills Solutions Forum has continued work done by the Conference Board of Canada and seeks to assist employers with corporate training. It has acknowledged that business success depends on employees' ability to communicate and to work independently and in teams. Among its many objectives, this organization identifies workplace skills, attitudes, and behaviours that employers are seeking.[15]

⸱⸱⸱⟩ To Improve Your Relationships

In addition to the practical, work-related rationale, enhancing your communication skills can significantly improve the quality of relationships with others in a variety of situations.

We don't choose our biological families, but we do choose our friends. For unmarried people, developing friendships and falling in love are the top-rated sources of satisfaction and happiness in life.[16] Conversely, losing a relationship is among life's most stressful events. Most people between the ages of 19 and 24 report that they have had from five to six romantic relationships and have been "in love" once or twice.[17] Understanding the role and function of communication can help unravel some of the mysteries of human relationships. At the heart of a good relationship is good communication.[18]

Virginia Satir, a pioneer in family enrichment, described family communication as "the largest single factor determining the kinds of relationships [we make] with others."[19] Learning the principles and skills of communication can give us insight into why we relate to other family members as we do. Our early communication with our parents had a profound effect upon our self-concept and self-worth. According to Satir, people are "made" in families. Our communication with family members has shaped how we interact with others today.

Many of us will spend as much or more time interacting with people in our places of work as we do at home. And although we choose our friends and lovers, we don't always have the same flexibility in choosing those with whom or for whom we work. Increasing our understanding of the role and importance of human communication with our colleagues can help us better manage stress on the job as well as enhance our work success.

⸱⸱⸱⟩ To Improve Your Physical and Emotional Health

Life is stressful. Having good friends and supportive family members helps maintain a healthy outlook on life. Research has clearly documented that the lack or loss of close relationships can lead to ill health and even death. Having a social support system seems to make a difference in our overall health and quality of life. Good friends and intimate relationships with others help us manage stress and contribute to both our physical and our emotional health. For example, physicians have noted that patients who are widowed

On the **WEB** ⸱⸱⸱⸱⸱●

Most colleges and universities offer courses in communication, and it is possible to select a major or minor in communication, speech communication, or communication studies. The study of human communication may also be included as part of a department that focuses on mass communication, speech communication, and theatre. Students who select communication as a major or minor pursue a wide variety of careers and professions, including business, law, government, education, and social services.

The World Communication Association (WCA) has developed a Web site that has links to many departments of communication and other professional communication associations, as well as a wide array of other communication-related topics. To find out more about the range of contemporary communication studies, visit the following information-rich site: **ilc2.doshisha.ac.jp/users/kkitao/organi/wca/**.

The Canadian Communication Association seeks to promote a better understanding of communication issues affecting Canadians. Its Web address: **www.acc_cca.ca**. The National Communication Association's (NCA) Web site also provides a wealth of information about the study of human communication. NCA's Web address is **www.natcom.org**.

or divorced experience more medical problems, such as heart disease, cancer, pneumonia, and diabetes, than do married people.[20] Grief-stricken spouses are more likely than others to die prematurely, especially around the time of the departed spouse's birthday or near their wedding anniversary.[21] Terminally ill patients with a limited number of friends or nonsocial support die sooner than those with stronger ties.[22] Without companions and close friends, our opportunities for intimacy and stress-managing communication are diminished. Studying how to enrich the quality of our communication with others can make life more enjoyable and enhance our overall well-being.

So again, we ask the question: Why are you here? We think the evidence is clear: People who are effective communicators are more likely to get the jobs they want; have better quality relationships with friends, family, and colleagues; and even enjoy a healthier quality of life.

COMMUNICATION MODELS

Our understanding of communication has changed over the past century. Communication was initially viewed as a transfer or exchange of information, but it evolved to include a more interactive give-and-take approach. It then progressed even further to today's view that communication is a process in which meaning is created simultaneously among people. The three models or representations of the communication process that we show here begin with the simplest and oldest perspective and then move to more contemporary models.

⋯⟩ Communication as Action: Message Transfer

"Did you get my message?" This simple sentence summarizes the communication-as-action approach to human communication. In this model, communication takes place when a message is sent and received. Period. It is a way of transferring meaning from sender to receiver. In 1948, Harold Lasswell described the process as follows:

Who (sender)	To whom (receiver)
Says what (message)	With what effect[23]
In what channel	

Figure 1.1 shows a basic model formulated in 1949, a year after Lasswell's summary, that depicts communication as a linear input/output process. Today, although researchers view the process differently, they still define most of the key components in this model in basically the same way.

Source

The **source** for communication is the originator of a thought or an emotion that expresses ideas or feelings. The transmitter (nowadays called the source), the originator of that thought or emotion, puts a message into a code that can be understood by a receiver.

source
Originator of a thought or emotion, who puts it into a code that can be understood by a receiver.

FIGURE 1.1 A Model for Communication as Action

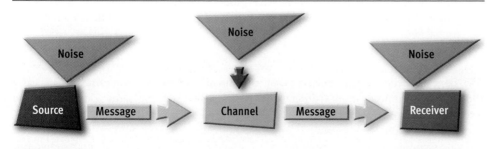

Source: Adapted from Claude E. Shannon and Warren Weaver, *The Mathematical Theory of Communication.* Copyright 1949, 1998 by the Board of Trustees of the University of Illinois. Used with permission of the University of Illinois Press.

encoding
A process of translating ideas, feelings, and thoughts into a code.

decoding
A process of interpreting ideas, feelings, and thoughts that have been translated into a code.

receiver
Person who decodes a message and attempts to make sense out of what the source has encoded.

message
Written, spoken, and unspoken elements of communication to which people assign meaning.

channel
Pathway through which messages are sent.

noise
Information, either literal or psychological, that interferes with the accurate encoding or decoding of the message.

Translating ideas, feelings, and thoughts into a code is called **encoding.** Vocalizing a word, gesturing, and establishing eye contact are signals that we use to encode our thoughts into a message that can be decoded by someone. **Decoding,** the opposite process of encoding, occurs when the words or unspoken signals are interpreted by the receiver.

Receiver

The **receiver** is the person who decodes the signal and attempts to make sense out of what the source encoded. Think of a TV station as a source broadcasting to a receiver that picks up the station's signal. In human communication, however, there is something in between the source and the receiver: We filter messages through past experiences, attitudes, beliefs, values, prejudices, and biases.

Message

Messages are the written, spoken, and unspoken elements of communication to which we assign meaning. You can send a message intentionally (talking to a friend before class) or unintentionally (falling asleep during class); verbally ("Hi. What's up?"), nonverbally, (a smile and a handshake), or in written form (this book).

Channel

A message is communicated from sender to receiver via some pathway called a **channel.** With today's technological advances, we receive messages from a variety of channels. Through the Internet or a fax transmission, the communication channel may be a telephone line. Cellular telephones use a wireless channel to help you talk to colleagues, friends, and loved ones. Ultimately, communication channels correspond to your senses. When you call your mother on the telephone, the message is conveyed via an electronic channel that activates auditory cues. When you talk with your mother face-to-face, the channels are many. You see her: the visual channel. You hear her: the auditory channel. You may smell her perfume: the olfactory channel. You may hug her: the tactile channel.

Noise

Noise is interference. Noise keeps a message from being understood and achieving the intended effect. Without noise, all of our messages would be communicated with considerable accuracy. But noise is always present. It can be literal—the obnoxious roar of a gas-powered lawn mower—or it can be psychological, such as competing thoughts, worries, and feelings that capture our attention. Instead of concentrating on your teacher's lecture, you may start thinking about the chores you need to finish before the end of the day. Whichever kind it is, noise gets in the way of the message and may even distort it. Communicating accurate messages involves minimizing both external and psychological noise.

It may appear that scholars have neatly identified the components of communication, such as source, message, channel, receiver, and noise, and can prescribe precisely what is needed to make communication effective. Although the communication-as-action approach is simple and straightforward, it has a key flaw: Human communication rarely, if ever, is as simple and efficient as "what we put in is what we get out." Others cannot automatically know what you mean just because you think you know what you mean. Although by Lasswell's time communication scholars had already begun identifying an array of key elements in the communication process, the action approach overlooked their complexity.

⋯⟩ Communication as Interaction: Message Exchange

The next big leap in our understanding of human communication came in the early 1950s. The communication-as-interaction perspective used the same elements as the action models but added two new ones: feedback and context.

Think of a ping-pong game. Like ping-pong balls, messages bounce back and forth. We talk; someone listens and responds; we respond to this response. This perspective can be summarized using a physical principle: For every action there is a reaction.

ReCAP ←···

Components of the Human Communication Process

TERM	DEFINITION
Source	Originator of an idea or emotion
Receiver	Person or group toward whom the source directs messages
Message	Written, spoken, and unspoken elements of communication to which we assign meaning
Channel	Pathway through which messages pass between source and receiver
Noise	Anything, either literal or psychological, that interferes with the clear encoding or decoding of a message
Encoding	Translation of ideas, feelings, and thoughts into a code
Decoding	Interpretation of ideas, feelings, and thoughts that have been translated into a code
Context	Physical and psychological communication environment
Feedback	Verbal and nonverbal responses to message

Feedback is the response to the message. Without feedback, communication is less likely to be effective. When you order your pepperoni pizza and the server says in response, "That's a pepperoni pizza, right?" the server has provided feedback to ensure that he or she encoded the message correctly.

Feedback is really a response message. Like other messages, it can be intentional (applause at the conclusion of a symphony) or unintentional (a yawn as you listen to your uncle tell his story about bears again); verbal ("That's two burgers and fries, right?") or nonverbal (blushing after being asked for a date).

A second component recognized by the interaction perspective is **context**—the physical, historical, and psychological communication environment. All communication takes place in some context. As the cliché goes, "Everyone has to be somewhere." A conversation with your good friend on the beach would be likely to differ from one the two of you might have in a funeral home. Context encompasses not only the physical environment but also the number of people present, their past relationship with the communicators, the communication goal, and the culture in which the communicators are steeped. The psychological context includes the impact of what is going on in the minds of the communicators; the speaker's and listener's personalities and styles of interacting with others influence how messages are understood.

This perspective, as shown in Figure 1.2 on page 14, is more realistic, but it still has limitations. Although it emphasizes feedback and context, it does not quite capture the complexity of the communication process if the communication takes place *simultaneously*. The interaction model of communication still views communication as a linear, step-by-step process. But in many communication situations, both the source and the receiver send and receive messages at the same time.

feedback
Response to a message.

context
Physical and psychological communication environment.

···→ Communication as Transaction: Message Creation

The communication-as-transaction perspective, which evolved in the 1960s, acknowledges that when we communicate with another, we are constantly reacting to what our partner

FIGURE 1.2   A Model for Communication as Interaction

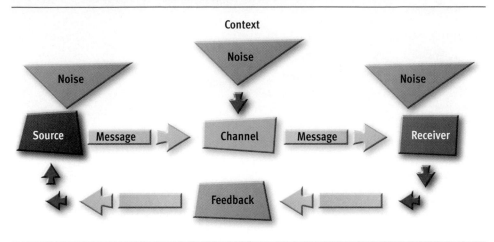

Interaction models of communication include feedback as a response to a message sent by the communication source.

is saying and expressing. Most scholars today view it as the most realistic model for communication. Although it uses such components as action and interaction to describe communication, in this model all of the interaction is simultaneous. As Figure 1.3 indicates, we send and receive messages concurrently. Even as we talk, we are also interpreting our partner's nonverbal and verbal responses. Transactive communication also occurs within a context, and noise can interfere with the quality and accuracy of the meaning of messages.

As we send messages, we monitor the degree to which the other person understands each message. We mutually define the symbols we use. If one partner misunderstands a message, both can work to clarify the meaning. For example, if I ask you to hand me the book off my desk and you hand me a pad of paper, we have failed to create a shared meaning. I might then say, "No, not the pad of paper, the red book next to the phone";

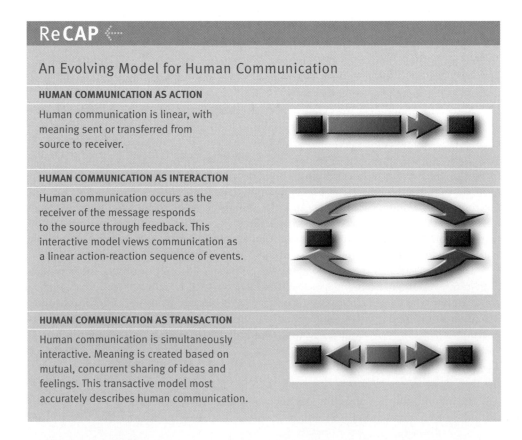

ReCAP

An Evolving Model for Human Communication

HUMAN COMMUNICATION AS ACTION

Human communication is linear, with meaning sent or transferred from source to receiver.

HUMAN COMMUNICATION AS INTERACTION

Human communication occurs as the receiver of the message responds to the source through feedback. This interactive model views communication as a linear action-reaction sequence of events.

HUMAN COMMUNICATION AS TRANSACTION

Human communication is simultaneously interactive. Meaning is created based on mutual, concurrent sharing of ideas and feelings. This transactive model most accurately describes human communication.

FIGURE 1.3 A Model for Communication as Transaction

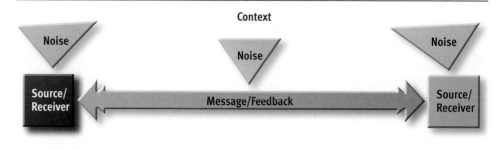

The source and receiver of a message experience communication simultaneously.

you then would hand me the book. Your action would require me to explain and be more specific. We would not simply transfer or exchange meaning; we would create it during a communication transaction.

One research team says that communication is "the coordinated management of meaning" through episodes, during which the message of one person influences the message of another.[24] Technically, only the sender and receiver of those messages can determine where one episode ends and another begins. We make sense out of our world in ways that are unique to each of us.

COMMUNICATION CHARACTERISTICS

Now that we have defined communication, noted its importance, and seen how our understanding of it evolved over the last half of the 20th century, we turn our attention to describing how it works by examining the characteristics of communication. The following characteristics are evident when communication occurs: Communication is inescapable, irreversible, and complicated; it emphasizes content and relationships; and it is governed by rules.

⋯⟩ Communication Is Inescapable

The opportunity to communicate is ubiquitous—it is everywhere. Even before we are born, we respond to movement and sound. With our first cry, we begin the process of announcing to others that we are here. And once we make contact with other humans, we communicate and continue to do so until death. Even though many of our messages are not verbalized, we nonetheless intentionally, and sometimes unintentionally, send them to others. As we noted earlier, some communication scholars question whether it is possible to communicate with someone unintentionally. What experts do agree on is this: Communication with others plays an ever-present role in our life. We spend most of our waking hours in thought or interpreting messages from others.[25] Even as you silently stand in line at a supermarket checkout line, your lack of eye contact with others waiting in line suggests you're not interested in striking up a conversation. Your unspoken messages may provide cues to which others respond. Even when you don't intend to express a particular idea or feeling, others may try to make sense out of what you are doing—or not doing. Remember: People judge you by your behaviour, not your intent.

⋯⟩ Communication Is Irreversible

"Disregard that last statement made by the witness," instructs the judge. Yet the clever lawyer knows that once her client has told the jury that her husband gave her a black eye during an argument, the client cannot really "take back" the message. In our personal conversations we may try to modify the meaning of a spoken message by saying something like, "Oh, I really didn't mean it." But in most cases, the damage has been done. Once created, communication has the physical property of matter; it can't be uncreated. As the

FIGURE 1.4   A Helical Model of Communication

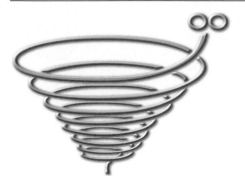

Interpersonal communication is irreversible. This helical model shows that communication never loops back on itself. It begins at the bottom and expands infinitely as the communication partners contribute their thoughts and experiences to the exchange.

Source: Copyright © F.E.X. Dance in *Human Communication Theory* (Holt, Rinehart and Winston, 1967), 294. Reprinted with permission.

helical model in Figure 1.4 suggests, once communication begins, it never loops back on itself. Instead, it continues to be shaped by the events, experiences, and thoughts of the communication partners. A Russian proverb nicely summarizes the point: "Once a word goes out of your mouth, you can never swallow it again."

⋯⟩ Communication Is Complicated

Pick up any newspaper this morning, and you will see that there is some conflict brewing or erupting in some part of the world. Perhaps there is conflict and disagreement in your own home or in a relationship with someone you care about. Communicating with others is not simple. If it were, we would know how to reduce dramatically the number of misunderstandings and conflicts in our world. We would also be able to offer you a list of simple techniques and strategies for blissful management of your communication hassles. You won't find that list in this book or any other credible book. Human communication is complicated because of the number of variables and unknown factors involved when people interact. To illustrate the complexity of the process, communication scholar Dean Barnlund has suggested that whenever we communicate with another person, there are really at least six "people" involved: (1) who you think you are; (2) who you think the other person is; (3) who you think the other person thinks you are; (4) who the other person thinks he or she is; (5) who the other person thinks you are; and (6) who the other person thinks you think he or she is.[26] Whew! And when you add more people to the conversation, it becomes even more complicated.

Messages are clearly not always interpreted as we intend them. Osmo Wiio, a Scandinavian communication scholar, points out the challenges of communicating with others when he suggests the following maxims:

1. If communication can fail, it will.
2. If a message can be understood in different ways, it will be understood in just that way that does the most harm.
3. There is always somebody who knows better than you what you meant by your message.
4. The more communication there is, the more difficult it is for communication to succeed.[27]

Although we are not as pessimistic as Professor Wiio, we do suggest that the task of understanding each other is challenging.

⋯⟩ Communication Emphasizes Content and Relationships

What you say—your words—and how you say it—your tone of voice, amount of eye contact, facial expression, and posture—can reveal much about the true meaning of your message. If one of your roommates frowns and abruptly bellows, "HEY! PLEASE CLEAN THIS ROOM NOW!" and another roommate uses the same verbal message but smilingly and

---

ETHICAL PROBE

Because communication is irreversible, is it ethical to say something that you know may be misleading but then discount your statement by "taking it back"? Does "taking it back" or apologizing for something you've said absolve you of any error in judgment in making statements that may be offensive to others?

ETHICAL PROBE

In the past few weeks, Matt and Arlette seem to be having more conflict and stress in their relationship than they've had earlier. Arlette would like to learn some strategies to help Matt treat her with more respect. Is it ethical for Arlette to seek ways to change Matt's behaviour? Is it ethical to be motivated to study communication in order to change others?

calmly suggests, "Hey. Please clean this room now," both are communicating a message seeking the same outcome. But the two messages have different relationship cues. The first shouted message suggests that your roommate may be grumpy and frustrated that the room still has echoes of last night's pizza party, while roommate number two's more calmly expressed request suggests he or she may be less frustrated and simply wants the room tidied up a bit.

The **content** of communication messages focuses on the new information, ideas, or suggested actions that the speaker wishes to share. The **relationship** aspect of a communication message is usually more implied; it offers cues about the emotions, attitudes, and amount of power and control the speaker feels toward the other.[28]

Another way of distinguishing between the content and relationship dimensions of communication is to consider that the content of the messages refers to *what* is said. The relationship cues are provided in *how* it is communicated. For example, when you read a transcript of what someone says, compared to actually hearing the message, you can get a different meaning. The tone of voice, posture, and facial expression of a communicator add cues about intended meaning. When studying communication, it is important to understand all aspects of your communication style if you are to communicate effectively.

THE FAR SIDE® By GARY LARSON

"The wench, you idiot! Bring me the *wench!*"

Communication Is Governed by Rules

When you play Monopoly, you know that there are explicit rules about how to get out of jail, buy Boardwalk, or pass "Go" and get $200. The rules are written down. When you play a game with others, there may even be some unwritten rules, such as "When you play Monopoly with Grandpa, always let him buy Boardwalk. He gets grumpy as a bear before breakfast if he doesn't get to buy it." There are also rules that govern how we communicate with others. Most of the rules are imbedded in our culture or discussed verbally rather than written in a rulebook.

According to communication researcher Susan Shimanoff, a **rule** is a "followable prescription that indicates what behaviour is obligated, preferred, or prohibited in certain contexts."[29] These rules, which help define appropriate and inappropriate communication in any given situation, may be explicit or implicit. For this class, explicit rules are probably spelled out in your syllabus. But your instructor has other rules that are more implicit. They are not written or verbalized because you learned them long ago: Only one person speaks at a time; you raise your hand to be called on; you do not pass notes.

The rules of both formal and informal communication often include a form of greeting.

content
The part of a message that focuses on the new information, ideas, or suggested actions that a communicator wishes to share; communicates what is said.

relationship
The aspect of a communication message that offers cues about the emotions, attitudes, and amount of power and control the speaker directs toward others; communicates how something is said.

rule
A followable prescription that indicates what behaviour is expected or preferred as well as prohibited in a specific situation.

Communication rules are developed by those involved in the interaction and by the culture in which the individuals are communicating. Most people learn communication rules from experience, by observing and interacting with others.

COMMUNICATION PRINCIPLES FOR A LIFETIME

As we saw on page 4, underlying our description of human communication are five principles that provide the foundation for all effective communication. These fundamental principles underpin all effective and appropriate human interaction, whether communicating with others one-on-one, in groups or teams, or to an audience by presenting a public speech. Throughout the book we will emphasize how these principles are woven into the fabric of each communication context. We will expand on the discussion here with a brief introduction and then will provide a more comprehensive discussion in the following five chapters to describe and illustrate these principles' scope and power. The five communication principles for a lifetime are:

- Principle One: Be aware of your communication with yourself and others.
- Principle Two: Effectively use and interpret verbal messages.
- Principle Three: Effectively use and interpret nonverbal messages.
- Principle Four: Listen and respond thoughtfully to others.
- Principle Five: Appropriately adapt messages to others.

These five principles operate together rather than independently to form the basis of the fundamental processes that enhance communication effectiveness. The model in Figure 1.5 illustrates how these principles interrelate. Moving around the model clockwise, the first principle, being aware of your communication with yourself and others, is followed by the two principles that focus on communication messages, verbal messages (principle 2) and nonverbal messages (principle 3). The fourth principle, listening and responding, is followed by appropriately adapting messages to others (principle 5). Together, these five principles can be used to help explain why communication can be either effective or ineffective. A violation of any one principle can result in inappropriate or poor communication.

To help you see relationships among the five communication principles for a lifetime and the various skills and content we will present in Chapters 7 through 13, we will place in the margin a small version of the model presented in Figure 1.5. We will also label which principle or principles we are discussing. We present this principles pentagon below as we introduce the principles to you.

FIGURE 1.5 Communication Principles for a Lifetime

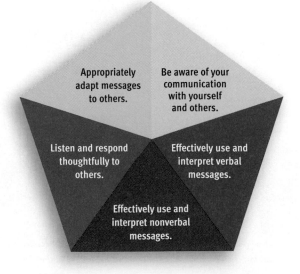

Throughout this book we will remind you of how these principles can be used to organize the theory, concepts, and skills we offer as fundamental to human communication. Chapters 2 through 6 will each be devoted to a single principle. Chapters 7 through 13 will apply these principles to the most prevalent communication situations we experience each day—communicating with others interpersonally, in groups and teams, and when giving a talk or presentation.

Principle One: Be Aware of Your Communication with Yourself and Others

The first foundation principle is to be aware of your communication with yourself and others. Effective communicators are conscious or "present" when communicating. Ineffective communicators mindlessly or thoughtlessly say and do things that they may later regret. Being aware of your communication includes being conscious not only of the present moment, but also of who you are, your self-concept, your self-worth, and your perception of yourself and others. Being aware of your typical communication style is also part of this foundation principle. For example, some people realize that they have a communication style of being emotional when interacting with others. Others may be shy.

The process of self-awareness also includes being conscious of your intrapersonal communication messages. By **intrapersonal communication,** we mean the communication that occurs within yourself, including your thoughts, your emotions, and your perceptions of yourself and others. Talking to yourself is an example of intrapersonal communication. Although our intrapersonal communication is often the focus of psychologists, our intrapersonal messages also form the basis of our communication with others.[30]

intrapersonal communication
Communication that occurs within yourself, including your thoughts and emotions.

Competent communicators are aware of the choices they make when they communicate both intrapersonally and with others; incompetent communicators react in thoughtless, quick, knee-jerk responses. Without mindfully censoring themselves, they may blurt out obscene, offensive, or profane words. Ineffective communicators operate in an unthinking "default" mode. Being aware of our communication is a foundation principle because all of the choices we make when communicating rest on our ability to make conscious choices when we respond to others.

Earlier in this chapter we noted that human communication is the process of making sense out of the world and sharing that sense with others. Being aware of who we are and how we perceive or "make sense" out of what we observe is a fundamental principle that helps explain both communication effectiveness and ineffectiveness. In the next chapter we develop this principle and foreshadow how it relates to a variety of communication situations.

Principle Two: Effectively Use and Interpret Verbal Messages

The second principle we introduce here and elaborate on in Chapter 3 is to use and interpret verbal messages effectively. Verbal messages use words that form a language. A **language** consists of symbols and a system of rules that make it possible for people to understand one another when using symbols. A **symbol** is a word, figure, sound, or nonverbal expression that represents a thought, concept, object, or idea. The words you are reading on this page are symbols. The word is not the thing it represents; it stands for the thing or idea it symbolizes. Your reading skill permits you to make sense out of these symbols. The word "tree," for example, may trigger a thought of the tree you may be reading under now, a tree in your own yard or a nearby park, or a great maple you saw on your family vacation in Algonquin Park. Effective communicators use appropriate symbols to create accurate meaning. Author Daniel Quinn once commented, "No story is devoid of meaning, if you know how to look for it. This is as true of nursery rhymes and daydreams as it is of epic poems."[31] Meaning is created when people have a common or shared understanding.

language
The system of symbols (words or vocabulary) structured by rules (grammar) that makes it possible for people to understand one another.

symbol
A word, figure, sound, or expression that represents a thought, concept, object, or idea.

The effective communicator both encodes and decodes messages accurately; appropriate symbols are selected to form a message, as well as interpreted to understand the messages of others. The process of using and interpreting symbols is the essence of how we make sense out of the world and share that sense with others.

Words have power. The words we use to describe ourselves and our world have considerable influence on how we perceive what we experience. Any good advertising copywriter knows how to use words to create a need or desire for a product. Political consultants tell politicians how to craft sound bites that will create just the right audience response. As children we may have chanted, "Sticks and stones may break my bones but words can never hurt me," but words *can* hurt us. Words have the ability to offend and create stress. For example, derogatory words that make a negative comment about our gender or race can do considerable harm. Throughout this book we will present strategies and suggestions for selecting the best word or symbol to enhance your listeners' understanding.

Nonverbal

⋯⟩ Principle Three: Effectively Use and Interpret Nonverbal Messages

Messages are also nonverbal. Nonverbal communication is communication other than written or spoken language that creates meaning for someone. Unspoken messages can communicate powerful ideas or express emotions with greater impact than mere words alone. An optimistic hitchhiker's extended thumb or an irate driver's extended finger is a nonverbal symbol with clear and intentional meaning. But not all nonverbal symbols are clearly interpreted or even consciously expressed. You may not be aware of your frown when someone asks if he or she may sit next to you in a vacant seat in a restaurant. Or your son may excitedly be telling you about his field trip to the fire station while you stare into the pages of your newspaper. You have no intention of telling your son he is not important, but your lack of nonverbal responsiveness speaks volumes.

One of the most important reasons our unspoken messages are significant is because they are the primary way we communicate feelings and attitudes toward others. There may be a person whom you like or love very much, yet you may spend a very small percentage of your time with this person verbalizing your affection and friendship. The other person can discern your interest and admiration based on your nonverbal expressions, your time spent with him or her, your eye contact with him or her. Your facial expression and tone of voice also communicate the pleasure of his or her company. You may know someone who doesn't like you. This less-than-friendly person may never have to utter explicit words to say, "I don't like you." But you know you're not on friendly terms based upon nonverbal cues: A scowl, an uninterested tone of voice, and a lack of eye contact signal that you're not held in high esteem. Our nonverbal messages communicate how we feel toward others.

When there is a contradiction between what you say and what you do, your nonverbal message is more believable than your verbal message. When asked how your meal is, you may tell your server that the meal is "great" but your nonverbal message—facial expression and tone of voice—clearly communicates your unhappiness with your cuisine. As we noted when we discussed the concept of content and relationship messages, our nonverbal cues often tell people how to interpret what we are saying.

Effective communicators develop skill in interpreting nonverbal messages of others. They also monitor their own messages to avoid unintentional contradictory verbal and nonverbal messages. It's sometimes hard to interpret nonverbal messages because they don't neatly have a definitive beginning and ending point—the flow of information is continuous. It may not be clear where one gesture stops and another begins. Cultural differences, and the fact that so many different nonverbal messages (such as eye contact, facial expression, gestures, posture) can be occurring at the same time, make it tricky to "read" someone's nonverbal message accurately. We amplify our discussion of the power of nonverbal messages in Chapter 4.

Listen and Respond

⋯⟩ Principle Four: Listen and Respond Thoughtfully to Others

So far, our list of principles may appear to place much of the burden for communication success on the person sending the message. But effective communication with others also places considerable responsibility on the listener. Because we explained earlier in the chapter that communication is a transactional process—both senders and receivers are mutually and usually simultaneously expressing and responding to symbols—listening to words with sensitivity and "listening" between the lines to nonverbal messages join our list as this fundamental principle.

Listening can be hard because it looks easy. You spend more time listening than performing any other communication activity—probably more than any other thing you do except sleep.[32] Despite spending the greatest portion of our communication time listening, there is evidence that many if not most of us do not always listen effectively. What's tricky about listening? Both psychological or internal noise (our own thoughts, needs, and emotions) and external distractions (noise around us or the surroundings in which we listen) can create barriers to effective listening. The fact that it is perceived to be a passive rather than an active task makes listening and accurately interpreting information a challenge. Effective listening is *not* a passive task at all; the effective and sensitive listener works hard to stay on task and focus mindfully on a sender's message.

At the heart of this principle is developing sensitivity to others. By sensitivity we are not talking about the touchy-feely-emotional-what-I-hear-you-saying approach to interpersonal relationships. We are, however, suggesting that you develop an orientation or sensitivity to others when you listen and respond. Being **other oriented** suggests that you consider the needs, motives, desires, and goals of your communication partners while still maintaining your own integrity. The choices you make in both forming the message and selecting when to share it should consider your partner's thoughts and feelings.

Most of us are egocentric—self-focused. We are born with an innate desire to meet our own needs. As we grow and mature, we develop a consciousness of more than just meeting our own needs. Scholars of evolution might argue that it is good that we are self-focused; looking out for number one is what perpetuates the human race.

Yet when the focus is *exclusively* on ourselves, it inhibits effective communication. Do you know anyone who is self-absorbed? Most of us find such a person tedious and uncomfortable to be around. People who are skilled communicators both listen and respond with sensitivity; they are other oriented.

---> Principle Five: Appropriately Adapt Messages to Others

Adapt

It is not enough to be sensitive and accurately understand others; you must use the information you gather to modify the messages you construct. It is important to **adapt** your response appropriately to your listeners. When you adapt a message, you make choices about how best to formulate a message and respond to others to achieve your communication goals. Adapting involves appropriately editing and shaping your responses so that your messages are accurately understood by others and so that you achieve your goal without coercing or using untruthful information or other unethical methods. To adapt a message is to make choices about all aspects of message content and delivery. Just as a chameleon changes its colour to blend in with its surroundings, a good communicator adapts his or her

adapt
To adjust both what is communicated and how a message is communicated; to make choices about how best to formulate a message and respond to others to achieve your communication goals.

<--> COMMUNICATION and DIVERSITY

Assessing Your Communication with Strangers

Your comfort level in communicating with others who are different from you and adapting to those differences is related to your confidence in approaching and interacting with people from different cultures. Respond to each of the following statements by indicating the degree to which it is true of your communication with strangers: Always False (answer 1), Usually False (answer 2), Sometimes True and Sometimes False (answer 3), Usually True (answer 4), or Always True (answer 5).

_____ 1. I accept strangers as they are.

_____ 2. I express my feelings when I communicate with strangers.

_____ 3. I avoid negative stereotyping when I communicate with strangers.

_____ 4. I find similarities between myself and strangers when we communicate.

_____ 5. I accommodate my behaviour to strangers when we communicate.

To find your score, add the numbers you wrote next to each statement. Scores range from 5 to 25. The higher your score, the greater your potential for developing a strong relationship with someone from a different background.

Source: William B. Gudykunst, *Bridging Differences: Effective Intergroup Communication* (Newbury Park: Sage, 1998), 143. Reprinted by permission of Sage Publications, Inc.

style of communication to reflect the needs of others. Knowledge of cultural differences promotes the ability to adapt successfully, thus enhancing communication effectiveness.

Regardless of whether you are giving a presentation, talking with a friend, or participating in a small-group meeting, the effective communicator considers who the listeners are when deciding what to say and how best to say it. One of the elements of a message that you adapt when communicating with others is the structure or organization of what you say. Informal, interpersonal conversations typically do not follow a rigid, outlined structure. Our conversation freely bounces from one topic to another. Formal presentations delivered in North America, however, are usually expected to have a more explicit structure—an introduction, a body, and a conclusion. The major ideas of a formal presentation are expected to be clearly identified. North American audiences also seem to prefer a presentation that could be easily outlined. Other cultures, such as in the Middle East, expect a greater use of stories, examples, and illustrations, rather than a clearly structured, outlined presentation. Knowing your audiences' expectations can help you adapt your message so that it will be listened to and understood.

You also adapt the general style or formality of your message to the receiver. If you are speaking to your lifelong best friend, your style is less formal than if speaking to the president of your university. The language you use and jokes you tell when around your best chums will undoubtedly be different than when you are invited to attend a meeting with your boss or with faculty members from your school. Our point is that effective communicators not only listen and respond with sensitivity, but they also use the information they gather to shape the message and delivery of their responses to others. In Chapter 6 we will discuss this principle in greater detail by discussing the diverse nature of potential listeners and how to adapt to them. Adapting to differences in culture and gender, for example, may mean the difference between a message that is well received and one that creates hostility.

COMMUNICATING WITH OTHERS: THREE SITUATIONS

The five communication principles that we unveiled in this chapter operate whenever people communicate, regardless of the number of people present or the content of the messages discussed. The three classic situations to which communication researchers apply these principles are interpersonal communication, group communication, and presentational communication contexts.

Each of the next five chapters is devoted to one of the five principles we've identified and then relates these principles to the three most typical unmediated communication situations you will experience. By unmediated, we mean those communication encounters that do not involve some kind of medium such as Internet, TV, fax, or another type of technology (which are all mediated forms of communication). Most of the research conclusions about interpersonal, group, and presentational situations are based upon communication that takes place live and in person. So we'll spend most of our discussion focusing on how communication is expressed and interpreted when people are present in face-to-face situations. There is a growing collection of research findings, however, that is helping us understand how the Internet and other technological tools are affecting our communication. When appropriate, we'll offer some ideas and suggestions for interacting with others via mediated settings. But, for the most part, our discussion will concentrate on how we interact with others when we are physically present.

We now turn our attention to introducing these three applications of communication: interpersonal, group, and presentational communication.

⤳ Interpersonal Communication

interpersonal communication
Communication that occurs simultaneously with another person in an attempt to mutually influence each other, usually for the purpose of managing relationships.

Many communication scholars used to consider any two-person interaction interpersonal communication. Today, however, **interpersonal communication** is usually defined as a special form of human communication that occurs when we interact simultaneously with another person and attempt to influence each other mutually, usually for the purpose of managing relationships.[33]

Interpersonal communication is also defined not just by the number of people who communicate, but also by the quality of the communication. Interpersonal communication occurs not just when we interact with someone, but also when we treat the other person as a unique human being. **Impersonal communication** occurs when we treat people as objects, or when we respond to their roles rather than to who they are as unique people. Asking a server for a glass of water at a restaurant is impersonal rather than true interpersonal communication. If you strike up a conversation with the server—say you discover it's his or her birthday, or you discover that you both know the same people—your conversation moves from impersonal to interpersonal. We're not suggesting that impersonal communication is unimportant. Competent communicators are able to interact with others in a variety of situations.

Another attribute of interpersonal communication is that the communication is simultaneous. Both people are communicating at the same time, and there is mutual influence—both persons are reacting or involved in the process. Interpersonal communication is not a one-sided monologue; it's a dialogue in the sense that all communicators are influenced and meaning is created simultaneously.[34] Interpersonal communication reflects the characteristics of the transactional model of communication that we discussed earlier.

A final attribute, and among the most important, is that interpersonal communication is the fundamental means we use to manage our relationships. A relationship is an ongoing connection we make with others through interpersonal communication. To relate to someone is to give and take, listen and respond, act and react. When we talk about a good or positive relationship with someone, we often mean that we are together or in sync. In an effective relationship, all individuals involved feel that their verbal and nonverbal messages are understood and that there is a relational harmony based on a common understanding between the communicators. We will apply the five principles of human communication to interpersonal communication in Chapters 7 and 8.

⇢ Group Communication

Each of us belongs to a gang of some type; it's just that some gangs are more socially acceptable than others. Comparisons between a rambunctious street gang and the local PTA may seem a stretch. Even though these two groups have radically different objectives, both share similarities of function and form that make them a **group:** They have goals, their members feel they belong to the group, and the group members influence others in the group.

We are social, collaborative creatures. We do most of our work and play in groups or on or with teams. And today's globe-shrinking technology makes it possible for us to be linked with others in virtual groups and teams even when the other people are not physically present. We define **small-group communication** as the verbal and nonverbal message transaction among three to about fifteen people who share a common purpose or goal, who feel a sense of belonging to the group, and who exert influence on others.[35]

A group must have at least three people; two people are usually referred to as a **dyad.** What's the upper limit on the number of people for meaningful group discussion? Some scholars say 15, others say more. The bigger the group, the less influence each person has on the group and the greater the chance that subgroups or splinter factions will emerge.

Our definition of group communication includes the notion that for a group to be a group, it needs a common goal—something that members all would agree is the reason for their existence. Group members also have a sense of belonging to the group. A collection of travellers waiting for the subway may have a common goal of catching the train, but they probably don't see themselves as belonging to a group with a single goal of going to the same place. Members of a small group need to have a sense of identity with the group; they should sense that it is their group.

Here's another attribute of a small group: Group members exert influence on one another. Each person potentially influences the actions and responses of others. Even if a group member sits like a lump and says nothing, there is influence from the nonverbal messages communicated. Each group member, by virtue of being a member of the group, has the potential to exert leadership on the group. To lead is to influence.

impersonal communication
Communication that treats people as objects, or that responds only to their roles, rather than who they are as unique people.

group
A collection of three to fifteen people who have a common goal, feel a sense of belonging to the group, and influence others.

small-group communication
The transactive process of creating meaning among three to fifteen people who share a common purpose, feel a sense of belonging to the group, and exert influence on one another.

dyad
A two-person interaction.

team
A coordinated small group of people organized to work together to achieve a common goal.

What's the difference between a group and a team? Although some people use the two terms interchangeably, we see a distinction. A **team** is a coordinated group of individuals organized to work together to achieve a specific, common goal. To us, a team is more highly structured and organized than a group. Teams have evolved to have more clearly defined roles, duties, and responsibilities for team members. Think of a sports team. Team members have assigned roles, well-thought-out assignments. Team members don't just show up and mill around and do what comes their way. They are focused. Teams also have clearly defined rules and explicit expectations for team operations. Their goals are well defined and measurable. And they coordinate their work efforts as they collaborate to achieve their well-articulated goals. We will discuss the five communication principles for a lifetime as applied to groups and teams more thoroughly in Chapters 9 and 10.

⇢ Presentational Communication

presentational communication
A context of communication that occurs when a speaker addresses a large audience in person.

For many people, speaking in public is a major source of anxiety. **Presentational communication** occurs when a speaker addresses a gathering of other people to inform, persuade, or entertain. In this book we will focus on applying the principles of communication for purposes of informing and persuading listeners.

Of the three applications of the principles we present in this book, this application has the distinction of being the one that has been formally studied the longest. In 333 BC, Aristotle wrote his famous work *Rhetoric,* the first fully developed treatment of the study of speech to convince an audience. He defined **rhetoric** as the process of discovering the available means of persuasion in a given situation. Today many communication departments have several courses that focus exclusively on how to persuade others, design and deliver both informative and persuasive messages, and evaluate the messages of others. Although we have certainly advanced in our understanding of informing and persuading others in the past two millennia, much of what Aristotle taught has withstood the tests of both time and scholarly research.

rhetoric
The process of using symbols to influence or persuade others.

Our focus in Chapters 11, 12, and 13 is to present the basic strategies of how to design and deliver a speech to others. As with interpersonal and group communication, we will discuss presentational communication through the perspective of the five principles that anchor our study. Effective presentational speakers are aware of their communication and how they interact with their audience. They also effectively use, interpret, and understand verbal and nonverbal messages; respond to their audience; and adapt their message to their listeners.

There is a great wealth of information and strategies about each of these three applications of communication. Most communication departments offer separate courses on these three areas. Our challenge is to present fundamental principles that illuminate all applications of human communication. Being aware of how you interact with others, monitoring your verbal and nonverbal messages, listening and responding thoughtfully, and adapting your messages to others will serve you well whether you are talking with a friend, participating in a meeting, or giving a speech. In the chapters ahead we unpack the five principles as they apply to three typical communication situations, with the principal goal of helping you better understand your communication and improve your ability to communicate with others for the rest of your life.

SUMMARY

Communication is essential for life. At its most basic level, communication is the process of acting on information. Human communication is the process of making sense out of the world and sharing that sense with others. It is important to learn about communication because it can help you obtain a good job and enhance the quality of your relationships, as well as improve your physical and emotional health. Early models viewed human communication as a simple message-transfer process. Later models evolved to view communication as interaction and then as simultaneous transaction. Key components of communication include source, receiver, message, channel, noise, context, and feedback.

Communication has five characteristics: It is inescapable; it is irreversible; it is complicated; it emphasizes content and relationships; and it is governed by rules.

Five principles are fundamental to the communication process. First, be aware of your communication with yourself and others. Being mindful of your communication is important to help you improve your communication. Second, effectively use and interpret verbal messages. Words are powerful and influence our thoughts, our actions, and our relationships with others. Third, effectively use and interpret nonverbal messages. Unspoken cues provide important information about our emotions, feelings, and attitudes. Fourth, listen and respond thoughtfully to others. Being able to interpret accurately the messages of others enhances comprehension and relational empathy. Fifth, appropriately adapt messages to others. In some way we are each estranged from one another. We are different from others. It is important to adapt messages to others to enhance both understanding and empathy.

These five principles are applicable to the most common communication situations: interpersonal, group, and presentational communication. Interpersonal communication is a special form of communication that occurs when we interact simultaneously with another person and mutually influence each other, usually for the purpose of managing relationships. Small-group communication is interaction among a small group of people who share a common purpose or goal, who feel a sense of belonging to the group, and who exert influence on the others in the group. Presentational communication occurs when a speaker addresses an audience for the purpose of informing, persuading, or entertaining.

Discussion and Review ⚜

1. Define the term *communication*. Compare and contrast this definition with the text's definition of *human communication*.

2. Why is it important to study communication?

3. Compare and contrast communication as action, interaction, and transaction.

4. What are characteristics of communication?

5. Identify the five fundamental principles of communication.

6. Apply the five principles of communication to interpersonal, group, and presentational speaking situations.

Developing Your Skills: Putting Principles into Practice ⚜

1. Working alone or with a team of your classmates, develop one or more original models of communication. Include all of the elements that describe how communication works. You could develop a model for each of the three communication situations that we presented in this chapter (interpersonal, group, presentational speaking). Your model could be a drawing or you could use objects (such as Tinkertoys or other building toys) to illustrate the communication process. Explain your model to the class.

2. In this chapter we noted that communication is complicated. There are really "six people" involved in a conversation that seemingly involves just two people. Choose a partner and try to verbalize your impressions about the "six people" involved in your exchanges with that person.

3. To help get better acquainted, try this ice-breaker activity in a small group. Tell three things about yourself, one of which is not true. Other group members should guess which one of the three things you have disclosed is false. The purpose of this activity is not to teach you how to lie or be unethical, but to assess the power and sometimes inaccuracy of the impressions we make on others. After all group members have made their guesses, provide the correct information. Discuss how you form first impressions and the role these impressions play in your communication with others.

4. In small groups, take turns introducing yourself to other class members. Consider the following ideas as ways to tell other classmates about yourself.

   - What does your name mean to you?
   - Describe what you do best and what you wish you did better.
   - Draw or symbolize your "lifeline." Show the high points and low points of your life, perhaps using simple drawings of symbols to illustrate your life hopes, joys, concerns, and goals.
   - If you could be someone other than yourself, who would you be? Why?

   After you have each introduced yourselves, discuss the interaction you've had according to the characteristics of communication included in the chapter. For example, how was your discussion based upon rules?

Marc Chagall, "The Painter," 1976. © 2003 Artists Rights Society (ARS), New York/ADAGP, Paris. © Scala/Art Resource/NY.

A person who buries his head in the sand offers an engaging target.

— MABEL A. KEENAN

2 Self-Awareness and Communication

AFTER STUDYING THIS CHAPTER, YOU SHOULD BE ABLE TO

1. Discuss the importance of self-awareness in the process of improving our communication skills.

2. Define attitudes, beliefs, and values as they relate to self-concept development.

3. Provide and briefly describe the three types of selves, according to James's research.

4. Describe the four factors that affect the development of self-concept.

5. Explain the difference among the following terms: self-concept, self-image, self-esteem, self-worth.

6. Describe how gender, social comparisons, self-expectations, and self-fulfilling prophecies affect self-esteem.

7. Provide examples of positive self-talk, visualization, and reframing that demonstrate the connection between these techniques and the enhancement of self-esteem.

8. Define perception and explain its three stages.

9. Discuss three ways to enhance your perceptual accuracy.

Here's a suggestion for you: Design your own personal Web page—a Web page devoted entirely to the purpose of communicating you to readers. For some of you, this isn't much of a challenge because you have already created your own Web pages, perhaps as part of a course you took at your college or university. For many others, the thought of creating a Web page that communicates who you are to multitudes of nameless, faceless people is quite a new and possibly daunting idea. What if you were to create an insertyourname.com on the Web for all to see? Would you include pictures of yourself or only text? If you use pictures, would they be of just you or you with your friends and family? What information would you offer about yourself? Would you focus on physical attributes, personality dimensions, intellectual ability? How personal or superficial would you be with the information you choose to reveal to basic strangers? What information would you leave out, either because you're not proud of those aspects of yourself, you don't think anyone would be interested in that, or you have privacy concerns?

Your ability to respond to this suggestion begins with a central, important element: awareness. Stephen Covey, author of the best-selling book *The Seven Habits of Highly Effective People,* describes self-awareness as that which "allows us to stand apart and examine even the way we 'see' ourselves—our self-paradigm, the most fundamental paradigm of effectiveness. It affects not only our attitudes and behaviours, but also how we see other people."[1]

Have you ever been standing in a line at the grocery store checkout and felt something brush past your legs? You look down and realize that a small child has crossed your path, no doubt on the way to the candy display. The child has no real understanding of what has occurred—the fact that she or he has inadvertently touched a stranger while attempting to satisfy a goal. The child isn't really aware of what is happening, but you, as an adult, are aware. We don't really know at what point humans move from being unaware to aware of themselves, their surroundings, and the presence of other people in the world. Moments of self-awareness arrive at different times for different people, and self-awareness is a never-ending process. You don't reach a point where you've maxed out your self-awareness. This fascinating experiment of coming to realize and understand your own existence continues throughout life.

Social psychologists have categorized self-awareness into three types or dimensions.[2] The first is **subjective self-awareness,** an ability that humans and animals have to differentiate themselves from their social and physical environment. We see ourselves as being different and apart from the physical world and from other beings in it. A second category is termed **objective self-awareness,** which humans and only a few animals (primates) possess. This involves the ability to be the object of one's own attention, to be aware of one's state of mind, to realize that one is thinking and remembering. The final awareness state is termed **symbolic self-awareness,** a unique human ability to develop a representation of oneself and communicate that representation to others through language. This last form of awareness holds the most interest for those of us who study communication.

One framework, attributed to Abraham Maslow, helps explain the process of becoming self-aware; it has also been applied successfully to communication skill attainment. The framework suggests that people operate at one of four levels:

1. *Unconscious incompetence:* We are unaware of our own incompetence. We don't know what we don't know.
2. *Conscious incompetence:* At this level, we become aware or conscious that we are not competent; we know what we don't know.
3. *Conscious competence:* We are aware that we know or can do something, but it has not yet become an integrated skill or habit.
4. *Unconscious competence:* At this level, skills become second nature. You know or can do something but don't have to concentrate to be able to act upon that knowledge or draw upon that skill.

To better understand how this framework operates, let's use conversation skills as an example. Janie is a poor communicator but doesn't realize it, so she is at level 1 when it comes to interacting with other people. Either Janie hasn't thought about developing interaction skills or she actually believes herself to be a good conversationalist. Then Janie

---

subjective self-awareness
An ability to differentiate the self from the social and physical environment.

objective self-awareness
An ability to be the object of one's own attention, to be aware of state of mind, and to realize that one is thinking and remembering.

symbolic self-awareness
A unique human ability to develop and communicate a representation of oneself to others.

starts becoming more self-aware and realizes that her style of talking with people isn't winning her any friends. She's unsure about how to fix this problem, but is conscious that she has some deficits in this area (level 2). She sets out to improve her communication skills by taking a class, purposefully working on how she talks with people, and soliciting honest feedback from people with whom she interacts. Janie develops an improved interaction style and is now at the level of conscious competence. Once these skills are fully integrated into Janie's behaviour with people, such that she doesn't have to strive to communicate effectively, she will have reached level 4, unconscious competence. Progress through these levels is possible for any given skill. It is also possible to be at one level for one skill and another level for another skill. For example, you may be skilled at meeting new people, but less skilled at managing conflict.

There are moments of heightened self-awareness and significant personal growth. Taking a communication course like the one you're enrolled in can spark such a moment. In this course, you will be challenged to think long and hard about your answers to the "Who am I?" question. You'll be encouraged to survey what you believe about yourself, as a result of your years of human experience, and to think about the role such aspects as your gender, race or ethnicity, nationality, sexual orientation, and social class play in your view of self. You'll be challenged to consider how you communicate with others, how you are shaped and affected by those with whom you interact, and how you can use your powers of communication in the world. But the key beginning point is awareness. When you attempt to communicate who you are to others, you must first be aware of yourself.

In Figure 2.1, we present the model introduced to you in Chapter 1—our "communication principles for a lifetime" model. You will no doubt become quite familiar with this model and its five principles as you work through this text. As we said in Chapter 1, these integrative principles provide the foundation for effective communication in various contexts that you encounter throughout your life. In this chapter, we explore the first principle: *Be aware of your communication with yourself and others.* The process of awareness involves being conscious not only of the present moment, but also of who you are (your self-concept), your value in this life (your self-esteem), and your perception of yourself and others.

SELF-CONCEPT: WHO ARE YOU?

Aware

If someone were to say to you, "Who are you?" how would you respond? You might start with basic demographics, such as your age and where you're from; perhaps you would

FIGURE 2.1 Communication Principles for a Lifetime

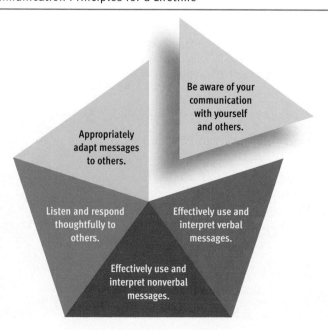

describe yourself in relation to groups and organizations to which you belong. Or you might talk about yourself according to various roles you assume, such as "I'm a student" or "I'm so-and-so's daughter (or son)." Whatever answer you give will be incomplete, because you can't really convey the totality of who you are to others. But it's an interesting place to begin, considering just how you would answer the "Who am I?" question.

Psychologist Karen Horney defines **self** as "that central inner force, common to all human beings and yet unique in each, which is the deep source of growth."[3] Your "Who am I?" responses are also part of your **self-concept,** your identity, your subjective description of who you think you are, how you see *you as a person*.[4] Some people use the term **self-image** synonymously with self-concept, but we want to avoid confusion over these terms. We subscribe to a more narrow meaning for the term self-image, in that self-image is your view of yourself *in a particular situation*.[5] That view changes from situation to situation. For example, you may be extroverted in chemistry class but not at a party where you don't know too many people. You may become very nervous when giving a public speech but are quite comfortable communicating with people one-on-one. You have several self-images, because they change as the situation changes. These different self-images are part of the larger component we call self-concept. The self-concept is the way we *consistently* describe ourselves to others; it is deeply rooted and slow to change. It is important to review the Johari Window in Chapter 7 to help you discover answers to the question, "Who are you?"

⋯⟩ Self-Concept Components

Who you are is also reflected in the attitudes, beliefs, and values that you hold. An **attitude** is a learned predisposition to respond to a person, object, or idea in a favourable or unfavourable way. Attitudes reflect what you like and what you don't like. If you like sports, spaghetti, and history, you hold positive attitudes toward these things. You were not born with a fondness for sports; you learned to like them just as some people learn to enjoy the taste of exotic foods.

Beliefs are the way in which you structure your understanding of reality—what is true and what is false. Most of your beliefs are based on previous experience. You trust that the sun will rise in the morning and that you will get burned if you put your hand on a hot stove.

Values are enduring concepts of good and bad, right and wrong. Your values can be difficult to identify because they are so central to who you are. But knowing what you value in your life is part of this principle of self-awareness that we focus on in this chapter. When you go to the supermarket, you may spend a few minutes deciding on whether to buy chocolate or vanilla ice cream, but you probably do not spend much time deciding whether you will steal the ice cream or pay for it. Your value of honesty over dishonesty is the guiding principle in this example. Other values include such things as your sense of loyalty, patriotism, justice and fairness, and love and caring for others. Our values are instilled in us by our earliest connections with others; for almost all of us, our parents are the first influences on

self
The sum total of who a person is; a person's central inner force.

self-concept
A person's subjective description of who he or she is.

self-image
A person's view of self in a particular situation or circumstance.

attitude
Learned predisposition to respond to a person, object, or idea in a favourable or unfavourable way.

belief
The way in which you structure your understanding of reality—what is true and what is false.

value
Enduring concept of good and bad, right and wrong.

ReCAP ⇠┈┈

Self-Concept Components

TERM	DEFINITION	DIMENSIONS	EXAMPLE
Attitude	Learned predisposition to respond favourably or unfavourably toward something	Likes–Dislikes	You like ice cream, scented candles, and tennis.
Belief	The way in which we structure reality	True–False	You believe your parents love you.
Value	Enduring concept of what is right and wrong	Good–Bad	You value honesty and truth.

our development of values. Of the three elements, attitudes are the most superficial and likely to change; values are more at the core of a person and least likely to change. We consider attitudes, beliefs, and values again in our discussion of persuasion in Chapter 13.

┈┈⟩ One or Many Selves?

Shakespeare's famous line, "To thine own self be true," suggests that you have a single self to which you can be true. But do you have just one self? Or is there a more "real you" buried somewhere within? "I'm just not myself this morning," sighs Sandy, as she drags herself out the front door to head for her office. If she is not herself, then *who is she*? Most scholars conclude that we have a core set of behaviours, attitudes, beliefs, and values that constitute our self—the sum total of who we are. But our *concept* of self can and does change, depending on circumstances and influences.

Perhaps the most enduring and widely accepted framework for describing who you are was developed by the philosopher William James. He identified three components of the self: the material self, the social self, and the spiritual self.[6]

The Material Self

Perhaps you've heard the statement, "You are what you eat." The **material self** goes a step further by suggesting, "You are what you have." The material self is a total of all of the tangible things you own: your body, your possessions, your home.

One element of the material self receives considerable attention in our culture: the body. Do you like the way you look? Most of us would like to change something about our appearance. Research has determined that both men and women in Canada experience negative feelings about their bodies. As a society, we are obsessed with being attractive and having a perfect body. Popular television shows such as *Extreme Makeover*, *Hard Bodies*, and *The Bold and the Beautiful* focus on youthful perfection. To conform to society's ideals, men appear to focus on strength and muscle while women tend to focus on an unrealistic ideal— an impossibly lean body! Women's dissatisfaction with their bodies has markedly increased over the past 25 years.[7] However, research also shows that men are not immune from body dissatisfaction, in that they compare their own physicality with ideal male bodies displayed in the media and are concerned about what others want and expect them to look like.[8] When there is a discrepancy between our desired material self and our self-concept, we may respond to eliminate the discrepancy. We may try to lose weight, get a nose job, or acquire more hair. The multibillion-dollar diet industry is just one of many that profit from our collective desire to change our appearance. The National Population Health Survey (NPHS), which collects information about the health of Canadians every two years, has noted that close to one in ten Canadians was underweight in 1999. These individuals were most likely under 25 years of age and many in this subgroup were female and single.[9] According to some researchers, health risks associated with being moderately underweight are comparable to the health risks of being quite overweight.

material self
Your concept of self as reflected in all the tangible things you own.

We also attempt to keep up with the proverbial Joneses by wanting more expensive clothes, cars, and homes. By extension, what we own becomes who we are. The bigger, better, more "high-tech," and more luxurious our possessions, we may subconsciously conclude, the better *we* are.

The Social Self

social self
Your concept of self as developed through your personal, social interactions with others.

Your **social self** is that part of you that interacts with others. William James believed that you have as many social selves as you have people who recognize you and that you change the way you are depending on the friend, family member, colleague, or acquaintance with whom you are interacting. For example, when you talk to your best friend, you are willing to "let your hair down" and reveal more thoughts and feelings than you might in a conversation with your communication professor, your parents, or your boss. Each relationship that you have with another person is unique because you bring to it a unique social self. This means that you are multifaceted, not false with people, because you have different selves in relation to different people.

The Spiritual Self

spiritual self
Your concept of self, based upon your thoughts and introspections about your values and moral standards.

Your **spiritual self** consists of all your internal thoughts and introspections about your values and moral standards. It is not dependent on what you own or with whom you talk; it is the essence of who you *think* you are and of your *feelings* about yourself. It is a mixture of your spiritual beliefs and your sense of who you are in relationship to other forces in the universe. It is your attempt to understand your inner essence, whether you view that essence as consciousness, spirit, or soul. Your spiritual self is the part of you that attempts to answer the question, "Why am I here?"

⇢•⇠ COMMUNICATION and TECHNOLOGY

Exploring Self-Identity through Computer-Mediated Communication

Technology, particularly through the advances of computers and the Internet, allows us to explore our identities in ways not possible to previous generations. Perhaps long-distance pen pals experienced something similar, in that they could choose which aspects of themselves to highlight in letters to someone they would never meet. But the ease with which the Internet enables us to experiment with expressions of our self-concepts to others online makes this a fascinating area of study.

One person who has conducted extensive research into online communication is Annette Markham, author of *Life Online: Researching Real Experience in Virtual Space*. Markham examines ways that online users communicate their sense of self in CMC (shorthand for computer-mediated communication) versus RL (real life).[10] In one online interview, Markham asked a user to compare his CMC and RL selves. His response was that he was "more confident online, because I'm a better editor than writer/speaker. I do well when I can backspace." Markham agreed with the user regarding the luxury of being able to edit one's online communication, saying that she liked the backspace key for its "ability to correct everything you say and therefore are." Markham recounts one particularly

interesting exchange with a user named Sherie, who felt much more confident and expressive online. Sherie explained:

> i choose to exist as myself in language online. i don't try to come up with other personae, so it feels more like being me than i sometimes feel offline. offline one often finds oneself in certain social roles that one must maintain; student, teacher, family member, etc. . . . i don't like my appearance all that much, and so i don't like myself in flesh all that much. i think myself in language is more communicative of who i am. eloquence makes me beautiful online.

Who is to say which is more real for an avid computer user—the online self or the offline self? As we delve more and more into what computers can do for us, and what they do *to* us, we will no doubt continue to question the real versus virtual self. Perhaps these selves aren't distinct; perhaps the online persona is merely an extension or facet of the real person. Should it be cause for concern when people feel positive self-esteem only when they are online? Or should we be glad that people have an outlet that allows them to feel good about themselves?

ReCAP

William James's Dimensions of Self

DIMENSION	DEFINITION	EXAMPLES
Material Self	The physical elements that reflect who you are	Body, clothes, car, home
Social Self	A variety of selves that change in situations and roles, reflected in your interactions with others	Your informal self interacting with friends; your formal self interacting with your professors
Spiritual Self	Introspections about values, morals, and beliefs	Belief or disbelief in God; regard for life in all its forms

How the Self-Concept Develops

Some psychologists and sociologists have advanced theories that suggest we learn who we are through four basic means: (1) our communication with other individuals, (2) our association with groups, (3) roles we assume, and (4) our self-labels.

Communication with Others

A valued colleague of ours often says, when he teaches communication courses, that every time you lose a relationship you lose an opportunity to see yourself. What he means is that we don't come to know and understand ourselves in a vacuum. We learn who we are by communicating with others, receiving their feedback, making sense out of it, and internalizing or rejecting all or part of it, such that we are altered by the experience. For example, probably someone in your life has told you that you have a good sense of humour. But think about it for a moment: How would you know if you're funny if it were not for others laughing at humorous things you say or do? Sure, you can crack yourself up, but the real test of a sense of humour is how it manifests itself with others.

In 1902, scholar Charles Horton Cooley first advanced the notion that we form our self-concepts by seeing ourselves in a figurative looking glass: We learn who we are by interacting with others, much as we look into a mirror and see our reflection.[11] Like Cooley, George Herbert Mead, author of *Mind, Self, and Society,* also believed that our sense of who we are is a consequence of our relationships with others.[12] So when we form new relationships and sustain the old ones, we gain opportunities to know ourselves better.

Self-concept development begins at birth. Names and nicknames reveal how we are viewed by important others; thus they are some of our earliest indicators of identity. During the early years of our lives, our parents and siblings are the key individuals who reflect who we are. Sometimes it seems as if, as much as we try or might like to, we cannot escape those early messages we received from our families—messages that shaped our view of self more than any other influence. As we become less dependent on family members, friends become highly influential in shaping our attitudes, beliefs, and values. Your earliest peer groups have had a profound effect on who you have become. Friends, teachers, and co-workers provide feedback on how well we perform certain tasks. This, in turn, helps us shape our sense of identity as adults. The media also have an effect on our view of self, although this indirect effect has less impact than the people in our lives.

Association with Groups

I'm a Canadian. I'm a soccer player. I'm a rabbi. I'm a real estate agent. I'm a member of the Liberal Party. Each of these self-descriptive statements answers the "Who am I?" question by providing identification with a group or organization. Our awareness

The self-concept we develop through communication with our family stays with us throughout our life.

of who we are is often linked to whom we associate with. How many of these kinds of group-associated terms could you use to describe yourself? Religious groups, political groups, ethnic groups, social groups, study groups, and occupational and professional groups play important roles in shaping your self-concept. Some of these groups we are born into; others we choose on our own. Either way, group associations are significant parts of our identities.

As we alluded to earlier, peer pressure is a powerful force in shaping attitudes and behaviour, and adolescents are particularly susceptible to it. But adolescents are not alone in allowing the attitudes, beliefs, and values of others to shape their expectations and behaviours. Most adults, to varying degrees, ask themselves, "What will the neighbours think? What will my family think?" when they are making choices.

Assumed Roles

A large part of most people's answers to the "Who am I?" question reflects roles they assume in their lives. Mother, aunt, brother, uncle, manager, salesperson, teacher, spouse, and student are labels that imply certain expectations for behaviour, and they are important in shaping self-concept.

Gender asserts a powerful influence on the self-concept from birth on. As soon as parents know the sex of their child, many begin associating their children into a gender group by adhering to cultural rules. They give children sex-stereotypical toys, such as catcher's mitts, train sets, or guns for boys, and dolls, tea sets, and "dress-up" kits for girls. These cultural conventions and expectations play a major role in shaping our self-concept and our behaviour.[13] Research indicates that up until the age of three, children are not acutely aware of sex roles. Between the ages of three and five, however, masculine and feminine roles begin to emerge (as encouraged by parents), and they are usually solidified between the ages of five and seven.[14] Research shows that by the time we reach adulthood, our self-concepts are quite distinguishable by gender, with men describing themselves more in terms of giftedness, power, and invulnerability, and women viewing themselves in terms of likeability and morality.[15]

Self-Labels

Although our self-concept is deeply affected by others, we are not blank slates for them to write on. The labels we use to describe our own attitudes, beliefs, values, and actions also play a role in shaping our self-concept. From where do we acquire our labels? We interpret what we experience; we are self-reflexive. **Self-reflexiveness** is the human ability to think about what we're doing while we're doing it. We talk to ourselves about ourselves. We are both participants and observers in all that we do. This dual role encourages us to use labels to describe who we are.

self-reflexiveness
The human ability to think about what you are doing while you are doing it.

ReCAP ⤶····

How the Self-Concept Develops

Communication with Others	The self-concept develops as we communicate with others, receive their feedback, make sense out of it, and internalize or reject all or part of it.
Association with Groups	We develop our self-concept partly because of and through our identification with groups or organizations.
Assumed Roles	The self-concept is affected by roles we assume, such as son or daughter, employee, parent, spouse, student.
Self-Labels	The terms we use to describe our attitudes, beliefs, values, and actions play a role in shaping the self-concept.

When you were younger, perhaps you dreamed of becoming a rocker or a movie star. People along the way may have told you that you were a great musician or a terrific actor, but as you matured, you probably began observing yourself more critically. You struck out with a couple of bands; you didn't get the starring role in a local stage production. So you self-reflexively decided that you were not, deep down, a rocker or an actor, even though others may have labelled you as "talented." Sometimes, through this self-observation, we discover strengths that encourage us to assume new labels.

Self-Esteem: What Is Your Value?

It may sound crass to consider the *value* of a person, but we do this every day. Our assessment of our value as persons is termed **self-esteem.** Closely related to your self-concept or your *description* of who you are is your self-esteem, your *evaluation* of who you are. The term **self-worth** is often used interchangeably with self-esteem. As Gloria Steinem describes it, in her book *Revolution from Within: A Book of Self-Esteem,* "It's a feeling of 'clicking in' when that self is recognized, valued, discovered, esteemed—as if we literally plug into an inner energy that is ours alone, yet connects us to everything else."[16]

Although the self-concept pertains to one's enduring identity, self-esteem pertains more to one's daily state of mind or view of self. Self-esteem can fluctuate because of relatively minor events, such as getting a lower grade on a paper than you expected, or major upheavals, such as the breakup of an important relationship. Self-esteem can rise or fall within the course of a day; sometimes just a look from someone (or the opposite, going unnoticed) can send you into a tailspin, such that you feel your value as a person is diminished. Or self-esteem can be more periodic, meaning that you may have a series of months or even years on which you look back and think, "Yeah; I was in a bad way back then; I felt pretty lousy about myself those days. Glad that period is over."

Factors Affecting Self-Esteem

Researchers have identified four factors that provide clues about the fluctuating nature of self-esteem.

Gender

In Chapter 6 we provide a more extensive discussion of the role of sex and gender in the communication process. But research reveals that sex and gender have an impact on self-esteem. Before exploring that impact, let's first clarify our use of the terms **sex** and **gender,** because many people use them interchangeably, and that can lead to confusion. One meaning for the term *sex* is the biological/physiological characteristics that make us male or female. In another usage, *sex* can refer to sexual activity between persons. The term used most often in this text is *gender.* In its most specific sense, gender refers to psychological and emotional characteristics of individuals that cause them to be masculine, feminine, or androgynous (a combination of both feminine and masculine traits). Defined broadly, the term *gender* is a cultural construction that contains psychological characteristics but also includes your sex (being female or male), your attitudes about appropriate roles and behaviour for the sexes in society, and your sexual orientation (to whom you are sexually attracted).[17] Because the term *gender* is more broad and all-inclusive, it's our preferred term in this text.

Research that has primarily focused on the development of self-esteem in childhood and adolescence documents ways that boys' self-esteem develops differently from girls'. In a patriarchal (or male-dominated) culture, such as Canadian culture, women and girls suffer loss of self-esteem to a much greater degree than men and boys.[18] According to Statistics Canada, both male and female self-esteem levels were identified among those 12 years of age and older. There were 91 028 females who reported having low self-esteem compared to 47 069 males. In other words, almost twice as many females reported having low self-esteem compared to males.[19]

self-esteem (self-worth)
Your evaluation of your worth or value as reflected in your perception of such things as your skills, abilities, talents, and appearance.

sex
A biological designation of being female or male.

gender
A cultural construction that includes biological sex (male or female), psychological characteristics (femininity, masculinity, androgyny), attitudes about the sexes, and sexual orientation.

Supportive relationships with friends can help young women overcome feelings of low self-esteem.

COMMUNICATION and DIVERSITY

Self-Esteem and the Sexes

We talk at several points in this book about the most basic form of human diversity: gender. Gender is a simple division by two, but the implications of that division are not so simple. For decades, research has documented significant differences in the self-esteem of the sexes, with women experiencing lower levels of self-esteem than men.

Many factors play into this gender differential, including cultural roles and rules for the sexes; family influences on gender identity; and ways that individuals are socialized through their contact with peers, schools, and media. Research suggests that in North American culture, high self-esteem in men tends to be associated with how well they fulfil qualities ascribed to their gender, such as independence and competitiveness.[20] For many women, high self-esteem is related to a sense of being attuned to and connected with others. In a culture that values independence more than connectedness, and competitiveness more than collaboration, it's understandable that women often suffer lower self-esteem when compared to men.

In an interesting study examining perceptions of shyness and self-esteem of children in grades five and six, researchers from the University of Guelph's psychology department found that children, particularly girls, feel shyness more intensely than adults are able to judge. The study found that approximately one-third of children who rated themselves as shy had lower self-esteem than children whose shyness was recognized. Researchers found that addressing shyness early can help people avoid such health difficulties as social anxiety disorder, depression, and low self-esteem.[21]

The gender difference in self-esteem levels seems to pertain to such factors as boys feeling better able to do things than girls. A related factor is the differential reinforcement boys receive from athletics, which helps them cope with changes in their bodies better than girls. But this trend has begun to change, as we witness rising participation in and appreciation for women's athletics.[22] More professional teams for women—as well as college, university, and school teams—are being established and gaining momentum, as we continue to recognize the impact of athletic accomplishment on people's self-esteem.

Social Comparisons

social comparison
Process of comparing yourself to others to measure your worth in relationship to others who are similar to you.

One way we become more aware of ourselves and derive our sense of self-worth is by measuring ourselves against others, a process called **social comparison.** I'm good at playing basketball (because I'm part of a winning team); I can't cook (because others cook better than I do); I'm good at meeting people (because most people seem to be uncomfortable interacting with new people); I'm not handy (but my dad can fix anything). Each of these statements implies a judgment about how well or badly you can perform certain tasks, with implied references to how well others perform the same tasks. A belief that you cannot fix a leaky faucet or cook like a chef may not in itself lower your self-esteem. But if there are *several* things you can't do, or *many* important tasks that you cannot seem to master, these shortcomings may begin to colour your overall sense of worth. If it seems like you're a "jack of all trades, master of none," and everyone else is a "master," your self-esteem may suffer as a result.

It can be self-defeating to take social comparisons too far, to cause your self-esteem to suffer because you compare yourself unfairly or unrealistically to others. The wiser approach is to compare yourself to your friends and neighbours, people you know and who are similar to you in many ways, rather than to people who are obviously not like you. Expecting to be as wealthy as Microsoft Chair Bill Gates is unrealistic for most of us, so it's unwise to compare your income to his. You might, however, compare how much you make at your job with the incomes of others who have similar positions or abilities comparable to yours. Our sense of self-worth is derived in part from the conclusions we draw from realistic, fair comparisons.

Self-Expectations

self-expectations
Goals you set for yourself; how you believe you ought to behave and what you ought to accomplish.

Another factor that affects your self-esteem is an estimation of how well you accomplish your goals. **Self-expectations** are those goals we set for ourselves, such as losing weight, developing a "buff" body, making better grades, achieving an important office in an organization, graduating by a certain time, being married by a certain age. Self-esteem is affected when you evaluate how well you measure up to your own expectations. For instance, if you expect to receive all A's this semester and you don't achieve that, it's likely that your self-esteem will be affected negatively. You may have to readjust your goals and expectations, or just become more determined to achieve the straight-A's goal next semester.

Some people place enormous expectations on themselves, probably because their parents had enormous expectations of them when they were growing up. We wish people who are stressed out all the time could give themselves a break, because they place such unrealistic, high demands on themselves. The popular achievement gurus will tell you that setting high goals is a good thing, that you will not accomplish much if you set mediocre, easily attainable goals. But we are suspect of that advice; we see many people with low self-esteem because they place such pressurizing, unrealistic demands on themselves. When they can't live up to those demands, they feel guilty and begin to see themselves as failures. A downward trend involving expectation, failure, guilt, and low self-esteem is hard to reverse.

Self-Fulfilling Prophecy

A concept related to the creation of self-expectations is **self-fulfilling prophecy,** the idea that what you believe about yourself often comes true because you expect it to come true. If you think you'll fail a math quiz because you have labelled yourself inept at math, then you must overcome not only your math deficiency but also your low expectations of yourself. If you hold the self-perception that you're pretty good at conversation, then you're likely to act on that assumption when you approach a conversation with someone. Your conversations, true to form, go well, thus reinforcing your belief in yourself as a good conversationalist.

self-fulfilling prophecy
Notion that predictions about your future actions are likely to come true because you believe that they will come true.

Your level of self-esteem also affects the kinds of prophecies you make about yourself and colours your interpretation of events.[23] Persons with high self-esteem tend to anticipate or prophesy successes for themselves, which are then reinforced when those successe are experienced. Conversely, persons with low self-esteem tend to interpret their successes as flukes; they attribute an achievement to luck rather than their own efforts. Successes can enhance your self-esteem, but if you are in a downward spiral of low self-esteem, you may not recognize your own achievements to let them have a positive effect on your self-esteem.

ReCAP ⬅

Factors Affecting Self-Esteem

Gender Differences	In male-dominated cultures, females suffer self-esteem loss to a much greater degree than men and boys, primarily related to males feeling better able to do things than females.
Social Comparisons	Judgments about how well or poorly you can perform certain tasks compared to others can be self-defeating and can cause self-esteem to suffer.
Self-Expectations	Your estimation of how well you perform in comparison to your own goals or self-expectations has a profound impact on self-esteem.
Self-Fulfilling Prophecies	What you believe about yourself often comes true because you expect it to come true.

COMMUNICATION AND THE ENHANCEMENT OF SELF-ESTEEM

We know the damage low self-esteem can do to a person—her or his ability to develop and maintain satisfying relationships, to experience career successes and advancement, and to create a generally happy and contented life. But in recent years, teachers, psychologists, self-help gurus, clergy members, social workers, and even politicians have suggested that many of our societal problems stem from our collective feelings of low self-esteem. Our feelings of low self-worth may contribute to our choosing the wrong partners; becoming addicted to drugs, alcohol, sex, or gambling; experiencing problems with eating and other vital activities; and opting, in too many cases, for death over life. So we owe it to society, as well as to ourselves, to develop and work to maintain a healthy sense of self-esteem, as an integral part of the process of becoming more self-aware.

While no simple list of tricks can easily transform low self-esteem into feelings of being valued and appreciated, you can make improvements in how you think about yourself. One thing is clear from research about self-esteem: Communication is essential in the process of building and maintaining self-esteem.[24]

⤳ Engage in Positive Self-Talk

Intrapersonal communication refers to how you take in information or stimuli in your environment and make sense out of them.[25] It also involves communication within yourself—**self-talk** or what some scholars term "inner speech."[26] Your self-concept and your level of self-esteem influence the way you talk to yourself about your abilities and skills. The reverse is also true, in that your inner dialogue has an impact on both your self-concept and your level of self-esteem. One of your textbook authors recalls a snow-skiing experience. After several unsuccessful tries to manage an archaic ski lift contraption (not your simple chair lift), she was determined to reach the top of the slope (just so she could fall down it). She remembers actively talking to herself throughout the climb to the top, willing herself not to fall off the lift, and feeling exhilarated upon achieving even this small piece of the process. The "You can do this" self-talk helped her keep focus on the task at hand, as well as served as positive reinforcement to the self-concept.

Although becoming your own cheerleader may not enable you to climb metaphorical mountains quite so easily, there is evidence that self-talk, both positive and negative, is related to the building and maintaining of one's self-concept.[27] Realistic, positive self-talk can have a reassuring effect upon your level of self-worth and therefore your interactions with others. Conversely, repeating negative messages about your lack of skill and ability can keep you from trying and achieving.

Positive self-talk is important in all forms of communication. When you interpersonally communicate with someone, you probably have some form of inner dialogue taking place as you process what the other person is saying and doing and how you want to respond. In group meetings, self-talk enables group members to process the interaction. If the communication is excited or even heated, positive self-talk can motivate you to engage in the interaction, possibly offering disagreement with members' ideas. Another example of a situation that calls for positive self-talk is one that is challenging to most people—the presentational speaking context.

Most speakers experience feelings that range from mild activation (feeling "jazzed" or "up" for the event) to debilitating, blinding fear—but don't worry, there are only a very few people at the upper end of the anxiety scale. When you make a presentation, you definitely need positive self-talk. You can create a negative self-fulfilling prophecy by telling yourself, "I can't do this; I won't be able to get through it. This speech is going to be lousy, and I'm going to fall flat on my face. My topic is lame; the audience will be bored and think I'm pathetic." Over years of teaching presentational speaking, we know that some students tell themselves just those kinds of negative messages.

But others have learned the power of getting "psyched" for presentations, just as an athlete would get psyched for a game or a performer for a show. These people harness the power of positive self-talk to get themselves "pumped" for a good outcome. When they

intrapersonal communication
How you take in information or stimuli in the environment and make sense out of them; also thoughts and ideas that you say to yourself.

self-talk
Inner speech; communication with the self.

On the WEB ⋯⋯●

Because many people fear public speaking, organizations such as First Canadian Toastmasters exist. This organization recognizes the need to improve public speaking and communication skills and thus offers suggestions and provides networking opportunities to accomplish this goal. For more information, visit them at **www.speakability.org/clubs/ first.htm.**

LUANN reprinted by permission of United Feature Syndicate, Inc.

hear negative messages creeping into their heads and creating self-doubt, they quash those messages before they have a chance to take hold. For any situation—from a mild challenge up to the most pressurizing circumstance you can envision—if you hear yourself start to say in your head, "I'm not sure I can do this" or "This isn't going to go well," stop right there and rephrase those statements. It may be unrealistic to completely turn the statement around, as in saying "This will be easy; piece of cake," because you might not believe it. But simply tone down the negativity and say, "I can get through this; I'll be just fine. I CAN do this; I'll survive." Although positive self-talk is not a substitute for preparation and effort, it can keep you on track by helping you focus and, ultimately, achieve your goal.

⤳ Visualize

Visualization takes the notion of self-talk one step further. Besides just telling yourself that you can achieve your goal, you can actually try to "see" yourself conversing effectively with others, performing well on a project, or exhibiting some other desirable behaviour. Because Canada is such a visual culture, most of us have no trouble visualizing elaborate scenarios in our heads.

Research suggests that an apprehensive public speaker can manage her or his fears by visualizing positive results.[28] In fact, visualization reduces anxiety as well as negative self-talk or the number of debilitating thoughts that enter a speaker's consciousness.[29] If you are one of the many people who fears making presentations, try visualizing yourself walking to the front of the room, taking out your well-prepared notes, delivering a well-rehearsed and interesting presentation, and returning to your seat to the sound of applause from your audience. This visualization of positive results enhances confidence and speaking skill. The same technique can be used to boost your sense of self-worth about other tasks or skills. If you're nervous about a date, for example, visualize each step of the date (as realistically as you can). Think through what you might talk about on the date and how the night will progress. This mental rehearsal will help reduce your anxiety. In addition, visualizing yourself interacting or performing well can help you change long-standing feelings of inadequacy.

⤳ Reframe

The process of redefining events and experiences, of looking at something from a different point of view, is termed **reframing.** When a movie director gets different "takes" or shots of the same scene, she or he is striving to get the best work possible. The director alters small details, like camera angles or actor movements, to get yet another look or vision for a scene. Just like that movie director, you can reframe your "take" on events or circumstances that cause you to lose self-esteem.

visualization
Technique of imagining that you are performing a particular task in a certain way; a method of enhancing self-esteem.

reframing
Process of redefining events and experiences from a different point of view.

Here's an example: If you get a report from your supervisor that says you should improve one area of your performance, instead of engaging in self-talk that says you're terrible at your job, reframe the event within a larger context. Tell yourself that one negative comment does not mean you are completely a bad employee.

Of course, you shouldn't leave negative experiences unexamined, because you can learn and profit from your mistakes. But it is important to remember that our worth as human beings is not contingent on a single *anything*—a single grade, a single failed relationship, a single response from a prospective employer, or a single play in a football game. Looking at the big picture—what effect this one event will have on your whole life, on society, on history—places negative experiences we all have in realistic contexts.

Develop Honest Relationships

The suggestion that you develop honest relationships sounds like some advice out of the latest pop-psychology, self-help book, but it is actually harder to accomplish than it sounds. Think about it: How many people are in your life who really give you the straight scoop about yourself? How many people are so solid in their relationship with you that they can tell you the things that are the hardest to hear, things that no one else would dare tell you? For most of us, we can count the number of those people on one hand. That doesn't mean we aren't honest with the many friends and acquaintances we have in our lives, but for most of us, only a select few we really trust enough to deal with the tough stuff.

Having at least one other person who will give you honest feedback and help you objectively reflect on your virtues and vices can be extremely beneficial in fostering healthy, positive self-esteem. As we noted earlier, other people play a major role in shaping our self-concept and self-esteem. You don't want to find yourself at a point where you're oblivious to the feedback of others. That kind of posture can take you out of reality and make you rigid, unable to adjust to life's changing circumstances. Most people who reject or overlook significant others' feedback end up isolated and with low self-esteem.

Surround Yourself with Positive People

Related to the development of honest relationships is a suggestion about the people you choose to associate with the most in your life. If you want to improve your self-esteem and to develop a more positive outlook, it's better to surround yourself with people who tend to have higher levels of self-esteem than people who will bring you down. Granted, sometimes you don't have a choice; you get assigned a roommate in college, you end up with an instructor's choice of lab or study partner, and you rarely get to choose the people you work with. So we don't mean that you disassociate yourself from people who have low self-esteem, because that's unrealistic. Plus, we all suffer from bouts of low self-esteem at some time or another. People with low self-esteem need to be around uplifting people—those whose positive self-regard will rub off on them. What we mean is that it is hard enough to actively work on your self-esteem without constantly being around people with negative attitudes. Engaging in "pity parties" can lead to wallowing in poor self-esteem, which makes it doubly hard to alter that downward course. If you don't have a choice and must be around someone with low self-esteem, you can try to immunize yourself against their negativity—possibly by attempting to change a negative subject of conversation into a positive one or by ignoring or minimizing the other person's communication with you.

As an example, we know an elderly woman, Hazel, who was in good enough health to be able to help the Meals on Wheels organization deliver food to shut-ins in her town. Hazel often talked about how sour many of the shut-ins on her route were, how their attitudes had "gone south" because of poor health, limited options, and fading hope. She felt that her main purpose wasn't to deliver a hot meal but to extend the gift of her positive outlook. She often told us about how many complaints she heard in the course of one day, but she was determined to stay optimistic and to offer hope to those she visited. One time Hazel described what she viewed as a personal triumph. The most sour person on her route—a woman with very low self-esteem and a cranky disposition, one who never did anything but gripe to Hazel when she visited—began to "thaw." One day when Hazel delivered her meal, the woman actually greeted her at the front door and seemed genuinely glad to see Hazel. She complained less often as she slowly began to enjoy the warm glow of Hazel's sunny disposition and empathic responses. Hazel felt that the woman's self-esteem had begun to improve, that her outlook on life had begun to change.

So this is what we mean by surrounding yourself with positive people whenever you feel a loss of self-esteem. Misery may love company, but misery gets old quickly and can degenerate into permanent low self-esteem, sometimes without your realizing it's happening.

⇢ Lose Your Baggage

Not making the team. Getting passed over for a key promotion at work. Seeing a long-term relationship end. Feeling like a failure. We've all had experiences in our pasts that we would like to undo or get a second chance at, so that we could do it differently or so that we would *be* different. We all carry around experiential or psychological baggage, but the key question is: How much space does that baggage take up within your self-concept? Phrased another way, how negatively is your self-esteem affected by your baggage?

Individuals with low self-esteem tend to lock on to events and experiences that happened years ago and tenaciously refuse to let go of or move past them. Looking back at what we can't change only reinforces a sense of helplessness. Constantly replaying negative experiences only serves to make our sense of worth more difficult to repair. As Stephen Covey explains, with regard to his Highly Effective Habit #2, "Begin with the End in Mind," self-awareness leads us to an exploration of our values. The way we are living, our "script" as Covey terms it, may not be in harmony with our values, but we have the power to change. Covey suggests "I can live out of my imagination instead of my memory. I can tie myself to my limitless potential instead of my limiting past. I can become my own first creator."[30]

On the WEB ·····•

Some people are outgoing, others are shy. Extroverted, introverted—it takes all kinds. But shy people often struggle with self-esteem issues because it seems as though everyone around them can carry on conversations or give speeches with no problem. It's hard when you feel you have a lot to say but not the means or the confidence to say it. You probably won't be surprised to find that there are several Web sites devoted to just these kinds of problems. Two sites we visited offer particularly helpful insight into the problems of shyness and lack of self-confidence, so we recommend them: **treasurecoasthealth.com/ treasurecoasthealth.php/ Health/Mental_Health/ Self-Help/Self-Esteem** and **www.psychlinks.ca/Pages/ assertive.htm.**

Re**CAP** ⇠·····

Strategies for Enhancing Self-Esteem

Engage in Positive Self-Talk	If you want positive results, talk positively to yourself. If you are self-critical and negative, you may set yourself up for failure. Rephrase doubts and negative thoughts into positive, uplifting encouragement.
Visualize	In anticipation of a significant event, picture how you want the event to go, as sort of a mental rehearsal. If you feel anxious or nervous, visualize success instead of failure.
Reframe	Try to look at experiences and events, especially those that can cause you self-esteem loss, from a different point of view. Keep the larger picture in mind, rather than focusing on one isolated, negative incident.
Develop Honest Relationships	Cultivate friends in whom you can confide and who will give you honest feedback for improving your skills and abilities. Accept that feedback in the spirit of enhancing your self-esteem and making yourself a wiser, better person.
Surround Yourself with Positive People	Associating with persons with high self-esteem can help you enhance your own self-esteem and develop a more positive outlook.
Lose Your Baggage	Dump your psychological and experiential baggage from the past; work to move beyond the negatives of your past, so that you focus on the present and relieve your self-esteem of the burden of things you cannot change.

If you were overweight as a child, you may have a difficult time accepting that who you are today does not hinge upon the kilograms you carried years ago. A traumatic or defining experience in the past has a serious impact on your self-concept; it will probably always remain a part of you. But it doesn't have to affect your current level of self-esteem. Becoming aware of changes that have occurred in your life can assist you in developing a more realistic assessment of your value. It's important to take mental inventory of experiences in your past, and then decide to let go of and move past those experiences that cause your present-day self-esteem to suffer.

THE PERCEPTION PROCESS

This chapter focuses on the principle of awareness—developing greater understanding and skill by becoming more cognizant of yourself, others, and communication. In the first part of this chapter, we discussed self-concept (how we perceive ourselves) and self-esteem (how we value ourselves). We continue now by exploring how we perceive ourselves and our communication with others, as well as the many ways in which we perceive other people and their communication. But just what is perception?

perception
The arousal of any of your senses.

On the most basic level, **perception** is the arousal of any of our senses. A sound travels through the air, vibrates in the eardrum, activates the nerves, and sends a signal to the brain. A similar sequence of events takes place when we see, smell, feel, or taste something. So perception begins by the simple process of internally attending to stimuli from our environment. The process of perception also includes structuring and making sense out of information provided by the senses. You come out of a building and see wet pavement and puddles of water, hear thunder, smell a fresh odour in the air, and feel a few drops of water on your head. You integrate all those bits of information and conclude that it is raining and has been for a while.

When we perceive people, however, the analysis goes beyond the simple processing of sensory information. We try to decide what people are like, making judgments about their personalities, and we give meaning to their actions by drawing inferences from what we observe.[31] When you meet someone new, you notice certain basic attributes, such as the person's sex, general aspects of physical appearance, the sound of her or his voice, whether he or she smiles, uses a friendly tone of voice, has an accent and so forth. You also attend to specific details that the person communicates, verbally and nonverbally. Once you've chosen these stimuli to pay attention to, you then categorize the information into some sort of structure that works for you. Finally, you attempt to make sense out of your structured perceptions; you assign meaning to what you have perceived. Let's examine each of these three stages in the perception process.

⤳ Stage One: Attention and Selection

You are watching a group of parents at a playground with their children. The kids are playing, running around, laughing, and squealing, as children will do. You view the activity, hear the noise, feel the heat of the day on your skin, and perhaps smell hot dogs cooking on a grill. They smell so good you can almost taste them. After a moment, one of the parents who was sitting and chatting with other parents jumps up and runs over to comfort his or her child who has fallen down and is crying. You were watching the action but didn't see the particular incident and didn't register the child's cry amid all the noise. But the child's parent did. How did this happen?

attention
What you attend to or notice in your environment.

selection
What you choose to focus on within a range of stimuli in your environment.

The ability of parents to discern their own child's voice from a chorus of voices is one of those mysteries of human nature, but it also exemplifies the first stage of perception. Our human senses simply cannot process all of the stimuli that are available at any given moment, so we select which sensations make it through to the level of awareness and ignore or filter out the rest. The activities of **attention** and **selection** constitute the first stage within the perception process. Have you ever listened to music in the dark, so you could eliminate visual sensations and focus only on what you're hearing? Have you ever watched TV with the sound turned off, just so you could enjoy the visual images without the "static" of sound? This is a particularly helpful strategy during televised sporting events, when the announcers continue talking over every bit of the action. (We believe this to be the original motivation for the development of the remote control's mute button.) What we're doing in these instances is selecting what we will attend to and what we will not.

Here's another example: Imagine a grocery store and a parent pushing a cart with a small child sitting in it. The child wants something, so she or he says, "Mommy, I want this." When there's no reaction from the mother, the child repeats the statement, "Mommy, I want this." If there's still no response, the child will likely say the statement over and over again, increasing the volume and stressing different words each time, as in "Mommy, I WANT this." What's amazing to the casual observer is the way the parent can tune out the child's request. Sometimes, the child will repeat the phrase so many times that you want to intervene and say, "Hey, your kid's talking to you; get that thing for him (her)." But the parent has heard the child's voice many times before, so in this instance it was easy to choose not to attend to that particular stimulus.

This selectivity can also cause us to fail to perceive information that is important.[32] Jack and Jill are having an argument; Jack is so absorbed in making his points that he fails to see that Jill is crying. By selecting certain stimuli, we sometimes miss other clues that might be important, that might help us better understand what is happening and how to respond.

Stage Two: Organization

After we select stimuli to attend to and process, we start to convert the information into convenient, understandable, and efficient patterns that allow us to make sense of what we have observed. This activity, termed **organization,** makes it easier for us to process complex information because it allows us to impose the familiar onto the unfamiliar, and because we can easily store and recall simple patterns.

Look at the three items in Figure 2.2. What does each of them mean to you? If you are like most people, you will perceive item A as a horseshoe, item B as the word *communication,* and item C as a circle. Strictly speaking, none of those perceptions is correct. For item A, you see a pattern of dots that you label a horseshoe because a horseshoe is a concept you know and to which you attach various meanings. The item really isn't a horseshoe; it could be an inverted U. It's actually a set of dots. But rather than processing a set of dots, it's much easier to organize the dots in a way that refers to something familiar. For similar reasons, we organize patterns of stars in the sky into various constellations with shapes, like the Big and Little Dippers.

In Figure 2.2, items B and C reveal our inclination to superimpose structure and consistency on what we observe. This tendency leads us to create a familiar word from the meaningless assemblage of letters in item B and to label the figure in item C a circle, even though a circle is a continuous line without any gaps. The process of filling in missing information is called **closure,** and it applies to our perceptions of people as well. When we have an incomplete picture of another human being, we impose a pattern or structure, classify the person on the basis of the information we do have, and fill in the gaps.

Perhaps you've sat in an airport or busy shopping mall watching people and tried to guess what they did for a living, what their personalities were like, or what their backgrounds were. Maybe you saw people you guessed were wealthy, hotheads, teachers, losers, athletes, loners, or skater boys. As you looked at people's clothing and the manner

organization
Converting information into convenient, understandable, and efficient patterns that allow us to make sense of what we have observed.

closure
Perceptual process of filling in missing information.

FIGURE 2.2   What Do You See?

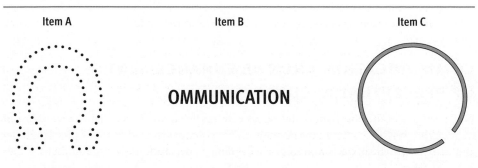

Item A   Item B   Item C

OMMUNICATION

ReCAP

The Perception Process

TERM	EXPLANATION	EXAMPLES
Perception	The arousal of any of our senses	Tasting spicy food; hearing the sound of laughter; smelling smoke
Attention and Selection	The first stage in the perception process, in which we notice and choose sensations for our awareness	Watching TV in your room while hearing giggling and laughter from another part of the house
Organization	The second stage in the perception process, in which we structure stimuli into convenient and efficient patterns	Realizing that the laughter is coming from your younger sister who's on the phone
Interpretation	The final stage in the perception process, in which we assign meaning to what we have observed	Deciding that your sister is talking on the phone to her boyfriend, because she only laughs like that when she talks to him

in which they walked or behaved, you made inferences about them. You superimposed some structure by using a general label and filling in the gaps in your information. This activity can get you into trouble, of course, but we'll save that discussion until the end of the chapter, when we focus on the problem of stereotyping.

Stage Three: Interpretation

Once we have organized stimuli, we are ready to assign meaning, a process termed **interpretation.** We attach meaning to all that we observe. In some cases, the meanings are fairly standardized, as they are for language, for example. But others are much more personalized. If you shake someone's hand and it feels like a wet, cold fish, what is your reaction and interpretation? If you notice someone you don't know staring at you from across a room, what thoughts go through your head? If a toddler is crying in a room full of people and a woman comes over and picks the child up, what do you assume about the woman? These examples all illustrate how we impose meaning on what we observe to complete the perceptual process.

Of course, our interpretations can be inaccurate or off-base; we may simply perceive a situation one way, when in fact something entirely different is occurring. For example, the final scene in the movie *Swingers* is hilarious because it illustrates the faulty nature of human interpretation. Two of the major "swinging" male characters are sitting in a booth at a diner. One of them thinks that a woman several booths away is making eyes at him. She appears to be making flirtatious facial expressions and mouthing something which he interprets as a come-on. He's just about to make his move when he realizes that the woman is looking across her table at a baby in a portable carrier, positioned in the opposite side of the booth, and she's cooing and making faces at the child.

COMMUNICATION AND THE ENHANCEMENT OF PERCEPTUAL ACCURACY

Our perceptions of others affect the way we communicate, just as others' perceptions of us affect the way they communicate with us. We continually modify the topics, language, and manner in which we communicate according to perceptions—ours and theirs.

Patrick sees Maria at a party and thinks she is attractive; Maria is nicely dressed and seems to be enjoying herself, laughing occasionally at a story someone is telling. Patrick thinks, "This might be someone I want to get to know," so he works his way over to join the conversation of Maria and the group she's sitting with. Maria notices Patrick coming over, because she checked him out too. However, not too long after joining the group, Patrick attempts to tell a humorous story, hoping to get a positive reaction from Maria. Instead, he gets a cold stare from her, as though she didn't understand or appreciate his attempt at humour. Maria walks away from the conversation thinking that Patrick is rude while Patrick thinks that Maria is not as attractive as he first thought. In this example, the man and woman both formed perceptions based on minimal information. They then experienced each other in the form of a brief conversation, and that bit of communication significantly altered their original perceptions. This process happens often in daily life.

The goal in the perception process is to form the most accurate perceptions you can, because then you have better, more reliable information upon which to act. So how do we improve our ability to form accurate perceptions? We offer three suggestions.

⟩ Increase Your Awareness

We've made this topic—awareness—our first of five communication principles for a lifetime and did so for a reason. Developing your skills in perceiving and then decoding others' verbal and nonverbal communication, as we discuss in the next two chapters, is critical as you strengthen existing relationships and establish new ones.

Exercise your senses, especially your sense of hearing. Work at really listening to people—fully listening, without interrupting them to put in your two cents' worth. Try to be more verbally and nonverbally aware, meaning that you monitor how you communicate with others and how people respond to you. If you don't like the responses you're getting from people, it may be time for a change in *your* behaviour, not theirs. You also want to monitor the verbal and nonverbal cues others exhibit. Pay attention to contextual cues, such as where an interaction is taking place, the time of day, the perceived moods of those interacting, and any physical or psychological barriers that impede the communication exchange. Learn from your mistakes, rather than repeat them.

The last thing anyone wants to be is a "communication clod," the kind of person who never notices things unless they're on fire. Communication clods seem to be in their own worlds, rarely acknowledging that others exist, rarely pausing to perceive what's going on in the world around them. We suspect that all of us have known people like this. And we are all capable of clodlike behaviour from time to time, but you just don't want "communication clod" to be what comes to mind when people think of you.

⋯⟩ Avoid Stereotypes

"She's a snob." "He's a nerd." "They're a bunch of dumb jocks." All of these statements reflect **stereotypes,** or generalizations we apply to persons because we perceive them to have attributes common to a particular group.[33] Social psychologist Douglas Kenrick and his colleagues suggest: "Stereotyping is a cognitively inexpensive way of understanding others: By presuming that people are like other members of their groups, we avoid the effortful process of learning about them as individuals."[34]

What comes to mind when you hear the term *Canuck*? (Maybe you think of those Crazy Canucks, downhill ski team of the 1980s.) Do you associate with the term such qualities as being party animals, laid back, overly friendly, snowshoe wearing, or igloo dwellers? If you perceive someone to have these qualities and you consider that person a Canuck, then you have just invoked a stereotype.

First, let's examine the positive or functional aspects of stereotypes. They emerge from our human nature to simplify and categorize stimuli in our environment, which we described as components of the perception process. Further, they serve as a baseline of information. If you know nothing else about a person other than she or he is a "easterner," for instance, then you can think about commonly held characteristics of other persons you've met from the eastern part of Canada and go from there. But, obviously there's a serious downside.

stereotype
Generalization applied to persons because you perceive them to have attributes common to a particular group.

These people are attending a Star Trek convention in Vulcan, Alberta. Do you make any assumptions about them based on their outfits and behaviour?

On the WEB ·····•

The Public Service Commission of Canada recognizes that stereotypes are everywhere and that everyone has them. According to its site, "Stereotyping plays a profound role in our everyday lives. Understanding how we create and use our stereotypes improves our capacity to deal effectively with people whose views or behaviour is different [from] our own." This site describes stereotyping and problems associated with it and offers constructive advice on overcoming problems related to stereotypical behaviour. Here is the address: **www .psc-cfp.gc.ca/publications/ monogra/mono3_e.htm**

Have you ever taken a class and, from day one, felt that the teacher pegged you a certain way? The teacher perceived you to be a slacker or uninterested in the course topic, on the negative side, or a straight-A student or future PhD in the topic of the class, on the positive side. The bottom line is that no one likes to be treated as a stereotype because it's limiting and impersonal. It can also be pressurizing if you feel that you have to try to live up to a stereotype, such as "All Asian students are exceptionally bright." Stereotypes are often degrading, as in age-old references to "dumb blondes," "bad women drivers," and "dirty old men." Many of the worst stereotypes are related to gender, race or ethnicity, age, and physical appearance.

A group of scholars has been studying stereotypes for a couple of decades; their most recent research explores the ways we try to inhibit stereotypical thoughts before they have a chance to affect our behaviour.[35] For example, if you grew up hearing family members invoke stereotypes about different racial groups, you may decide as an adult that you will not follow suit—that inflicting racial stereotypes is inappropriate. However, because it's part of your upbringing and ingrained in you, your first thoughts may be stereotypical when you encounter someone from a racial group other than your own. You have to assert mental control to suppress the stereotypical thoughts. But these researchers found that this suppression actually has the opposite effect than desired, in that stereotypical thoughts are highly likely to subsequently reappear with even stronger intensity, what the researchers term a "rebound effect."[36] So it may be better never to let stereotypes form into expectations, rather than trying to rid ourselves of harmful stereotypical thinking after the fact.

In Chapter 3, we explore language that reveals stereotypical thoughts. In Chapter 6, when we discuss the skill of adapting our communication to our listeners, we revisit the topic of stereotypes. For now, just remember that there's nothing inherently wrong with a stereotype, as a baseline of information. But the rigid way we enforce a stereotype, the expectations we form based on the stereotype, and our ensuing communication toward the stereotyped person are problematic.

···⋗ Check Your Perceptions

You can check out the accuracy of your perceptions and attributions indirectly and directly, so that you increase your ability to perceive things and people and respond to them effectively. **Indirect perception checking** involves an intensification of your own perceptual powers. You passively seek additional information to either confirm or refute your interpretations of someone's behaviour. If you suspect that your relational

indirect perception checking
Passively seeking additional information to confirm or refute your interpretations of someone's behaviour.

ETHICAL PROBE

Although we advocate perception checking, it can also be turned into a manipulative activity. Imagine that one co-worker perceives another co-worker to be acting unprofessionally. (Remember that we said unprofessionally, not illegally or unethically.) Should the observer conduct a perception check with the co-worker's boss about the observed worker's behaviour? What if doing so could get that person into trouble or cause her or him professional problems?

partner wants to break up, for instance, you are likely to look for cues in his or her tone of voice, eye contact, and body movements to confirm your suspicion. You will probably also listen more intently and pay attention to the language your partner chooses to use. The information you gain is "checked" against your original perceptions.

Direct perception checking involves asking straight out whether your interpretations of a perception are correct. You can accomplish this in two ways: asking people directly for their interpretations of their own actions or asking other observers for their "take" on a situation (going to a third or outside party). Asking people directly is often more difficult than asking a third party for an interpretation. For one thing, we don't like to admit uncertainty or suspicions to others; we might not trust that they will respond honestly. And if our interpretations are wrong, we might suffer embarrassment or anger. But asking someone to confirm a perception shows that you are committed to understanding his or her behaviour. If your friend's voice sounds weary and her posture is sagging, you may assume that she is depressed or upset. If you ask, "I get the feeling from your tone of voice and the way you're acting that you are kind of down and depressed; what's wrong?" your friend can then either provide another interpretation: "I'm just tired; I had a busy week"; or expand on your interpretation: "Yeah, things haven't been going very well. . . ." Your observation might also be a revelation: "Really? I didn't realize I was acting that way. I guess I am a little down."

We have found over our years as professors that perception checking with our colleagues, as well as family members and trusted friends, is an invaluable tool, particularly when emotions are involved. It's wise to bounce situations off other people, to get their input as to what happened, why it happened, how they would feel about it if it happened to them, and what you might do about it. This is especially advisable in work settings, when the wisdom of someone else's perceptions can save you professional embarrassment or prevent you from losing your job because of an emotional or rash reaction. So we highly advocate seeking out the wise counsel of trusted colleagues. The "Can I run something by you?" strategy gives you a broader perspective and a basis of comparison.

direct perception checking
Asking other persons or the person you are observing whether your interpretations of a perception are correct.

SUMMARY ⁙

This chapter is devoted to the first communication principle for a lifetime: *Be aware of your communication.* Self-awareness is a process that continues throughout life, as we perceive and come to understand our own existence in the social world. The way we view ourselves is termed self-concept, which includes our attitudes, beliefs, and values. William James viewed the self as containing three components: The material self includes our bodies and those tangible possessions that give us identity. The social self is the part that engages in interaction with others. The spiritual self consists of thoughts and assumptions about values, moral standards, and beliefs about forces that influence our lives.

The self-concept develops through our interactions with other people and the groups with which we associate. Our roles as sister, brother, student, or parent are important in our view of self; the roles we assume provide labels for who we are.

Self-concept, or who you think you are, and self-esteem, your evaluation of your self-worth, affect how you interact with others. Your gender has an effect on your self-esteem. When you compare yourself to others, especially others who are different from you, your self-esteem can be affected—positively and negatively. Your view of your own worth is also affected by those expectations or goals you set for yourself and how closely you come to achieving them. You may set a goal for yourself that ends up creating a self-fulfilling prophecy. You may believe something about yourself and act in a way that reinforces that belief, and the cycle continues.

It is difficult to alter your self-esteem, but various techniques can prove helpful: engaging in positive self-talk, visualizing success instead of failure, avoiding inappropriate comparisons with others, reframing events and relationships from a different perspective, developing honest relationships with others, surrounding yourself with uplifting people, and letting go of the past by losing old baggage.

We also learned in this chapter that perception is the process of taking in stimuli through our senses, and it involves three components: attention and selection, organization, and interpretation. Our perceptions of others affect how we communicate, and how others perceive us affects how they communicate with us. If you want to increase your powers of perception, so that you develop greater sensitivity and awareness, you first need to pay greater attention to things and people around you. Observe with more detail over time, so that you take in more data. Second, when you're in the organizing stage of perception, avoid imposing stereotypes or rigid categories onto people, such that you expect certain behaviour and may exert pressure on individuals to behave as expected. Finally, conduct indirect and direct perception checks to determine the accuracy of your "take" on people and situations.

Discussion and Review ⁙

1. Why is self-awareness critical to the development of communication skill? How can you tell the self-aware communicators from those who are not self-aware?

2. What makes up the material self? The social self? The spiritual self?

3. What is the difference between your self-concept and your self-image? What is the difference between your self-concept and your self-esteem?

4. Do you believe that your gender is related to your self-esteem? Why or why not?

5. Have you known or do you know someone who has experienced a self-fulfilling prophecy? How did this affect your or the person's communication and general behaviour?

6. If you were to suffer lowered self-esteem because of an event, circumstance, or person's actions, what techniques (from the ones provided in this chapter) do you think would help you regain esteem?

7. Imagine that you're attending a sporting event. Describe how the three stages of perception would affect the way you process the action.

8. Think of occasions when you've directly checked your perceptions with others. Did the perception checks change your perspective?

Developing Your Skills: Putting Principles into Practice ⁙

1. On a clean sheet of paper, write down major things you know to be true of yourself. For example, you can start with your values and write down, "I am an honest person." Include positive and negative attributes that you're aware of in your personality. After you've generated as many items as possible, review the list and see whether it encapsulates your self-concept.

2. What experiences have you had where you needed the power of positive self-talk and visualization to get you through the experience? Probably everyone has had a nerve-racking first date experience. What kind of self-talk is helpful versus hurtful in such a situation? How can visualization help increase your self-confidence in a pressurizing situation such as a first date?

3. In a small group of classmates, venture outside the building where your class meets and conduct a perceptual experiment. Watch people passing by on their way

to classes or as they leave campus. Decide as a group to focus on certain individuals and then discuss your differing perceptions of them. How do you each perceive the physical appearances of people you see? What clues do their nonverbal behaviours give about their personalities? Do you invoke any stereotypes as you perceive different people?

4. Using the following list of groups of people, generate statements that reveal common stereotypes. Try to generate stereotypes that reflect positive as well as negative perceptions. We provide a couple of examples, just to get you started. Then focus on the damage that preconceived stereotypes can do to someone's self-esteem. Also think about how your communication might be altered with persons of these groups, if you bought into the stereotype.

Group	Positive Stereotype	Negative Stereotype
elderly	Old people are wise.	Old people can't fend for themselves.
women	Women are naturally more loving and nurturing than men.	Women are terrible drivers.
men		
"blondes"		
overweight people		
people of Irish descent		
athletes		
Maritimers		
politicians		
environmentalists		
tax accountants		
librarians		
professors		

Adolf Fenyes, "Brother and Sister." National Gallery, Budapest/ET Archive, London/SuperStock.

The difference between the right word and the almost right word is the difference between lightning and the lightning bug.

— MARK TWAIN

3 Understanding Verbal Messages

CHAPTER OUTLINE

AFTER STUDYING THIS CHAPTER, YOU SHOULD BE ABLE TO

1. Identify elements of Canada's linguistic diversity.

2. Describe the relationship between words (symbols) and meaning.

3. Explain the difference between denotative and connotative meanings people develop for words.

4. Explain the difference between concrete and abstract meanings of words.

5. Define culture-bound words and context-bound words.

6. Identify four primary ways in which words have power.

7. Describe the major ways in which biased language reveals attitudes about race, ethnicity, nationality, and religion.

8. Provide examples of language that reflect bias related to gender and sexual orientation.

9. Explain how biased language reveals attitudes about age, class, and ability.

10. Explain the difference between supportive and defensive ways to relate to others.

Consider this: What you say is who you are. That may sound like a strong statement, but think of it like this: The words you use reveal who you are. What do you think about people who say the following?

"My ball and chain at home just sits around all day complaining and watching
   Jerry Springer."
"I really hate corporate CEOs; they're all a bunch of crooks."
"Old people make the worst drivers. They shouldn't be on the road."
"She's really weird; she's always got her head in a book like she's scared of people."
"The handicapped get all the best parking spots. Why are there so many empty spaces
   marked for handicapped people?"

You might have negative reactions to the people making these statements, or you might not be offended at all. But no matter your reaction, what people say reveals a great deal about who they are.

Let's review for a moment. Figure 3.1 depicts our five core principles of communication. In Chapter 2, the first of our presentations of five principles for a lifetime, we explored ways to become more aware of yourself and your perceptions of things and people with whom you come into contact. An important step in this process of coming to know and understand yourself better is an honest, insightful examination of how you talk. How do you come across when meeting someone new? When conversing with your best friends? What kind of communicator do your closest friends and family members think you are? How would they describe the way you talk?

Former Canadian prime minister Pierre Elliott Trudeau.

Granted, you communicate with more than your words. Your background, culture, values, experiences, and the way you express yourself nonverbally reveal who you are as well. We focus on nonverbal communication in the next chapter. But now, as we explore the power of words, we challenge you to think about the incredible tool you have at your disposal: verbal communication. Take an inventory of your use of language as you read this chapter. Do you use language that accurately and effectively represents to other people who you are? Do some areas need improvement? Because of the tremendous potential of verbal communication—its power to reveal the self, to make and break relationships and careers, and to shape cultures—we've chosen to make this one of our five key principles for a lifetime.

FIGURE 3.1 Communication Principles for a Lifetime

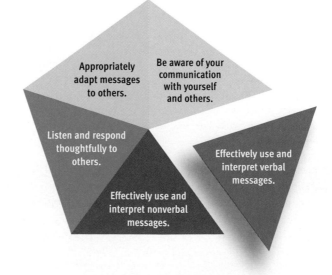

WHY FOCUS ON LANGUAGE?

On occasion, we do stop to consider the effects of our language on others—usually when we're attempting to persuade or we've said something that has injured or angered someone else. We've all been in situations where we wish we could get a second chance so that we could say something differently from the first time. But it's important to keep in mind that every time we speak, every time we use language, we are revealing our thoughts, our very selves to others—no matter how inane, superficial, or emotion-laden the conversation.

One of our main messages in this chapter is this: *Words are powerful*. They affect your emotions, thoughts, actions, and relationships; they play a significant role in the furtherance of culture. If you better understand the nature and power of language, if you attend to your use of language and work to use words with forethought and skill, you can exert great influence and enhance your relationships.

Our second main theme in this chapter is this: *You choose language*. You do not use language involuntarily, in the way that your knee might jerk when rapped with a doctor's mallet as an involuntary reflex to a stimulus. You choose the language you use—even if you make that choice in the split second it takes your brain to select a symbol (word) to communicate your thought or impulse. At times we go into "default mode," choosing language we've chosen before. We are prone to patterns in our language because as humans, we prefer regularity. We also choose particular words because we like them, they've worked well for us in the past, or we grew up with those words and have used them for many years. But pattern and history can breed too much comfort, preventing you from asking yourself, "Is this the best way to say this? Should I say this another way?" You have an incredible wealth of words from which to choose, and the power to make choices that allow you to communicate who you are to others in the most effective way possible.

Our goal in this chapter is to help you improve your ability to choose and use verbal communication effectively, as well as interpret the verbal communication of others. To accomplish that goal we explore the nature of language, the power of words, and ways to expose subtle and not-so-subtle bias in language—bias that can inhibit your ability to communicate yourself to others in a manner you desire. Finally, we examine the role of verbal communication in establishing supportive relationships with others.

⋯⟩ Canada's Linguistic Diversity

When discussing the complexities of language, it is important to be aware of Canada's multilingual environment. There is wide language diversity in Canada due to English, French, and Aboriginal heritages and immigration of people who speak other languages. According to Statistics Canada, our country's increasingly ethnocultural profile varies from province to province, city to city, and community to community. Immigration has shaped our multi-ethnic and multicultural environment, and Canada encourages multilingualism and supports preservation of the "ancestral tongue" within the home and the community. While researching Canada's linguistic diversity, one of your authors discovered many examples of support for multilingualism. For example, Statistics Canada is committed to serving clients in the official language of their choice.

Statistics Canada provides an overview of languages spoken both at home and in the community. Although English and French (Canada's two official languages) are most common, many other languages are spoken in Canada by Aboriginal people and by immigrants and their families. In Canada, the languages most often spoken at home are English (67.5%) and French (22.0%), leaving 10.5% speaking other, nonofficial languages. Canada's top 10 nonofficial languages are listed in Table 3.1 on page 54.

Many new immigrants migrate to urban centres (metropolitan areas). Toronto and Vancouver have the largest percentages of people who speak neither official language in the home—Toronto with 24.7% and Vancouver with 23.8%. Ottawa-Hull and London have the lowest percentages—Ottawa-Hull with 8.7% and London with 7.5%. According to Statistics Canada, since the late 1980s Canada has had a proportionally higher annual intake of immigrants than either the United States or Australia.

On the WEB ·····•

So you decide that your vocabulary needs a bit of expansion. Where do you turn? The dictionary you got as a high school graduation present? Reruns of South Park? Try a Web site that will expand your capacity for English through its creative plays on words, visual puzzles, and innovative approaches to crosswords and word searches: **www.puzzability.com.**

TABLE 3.1 Canada's Top 10 Languages Spoken in the Home, Excluding English and French, and Aboriginal Languages

Home Language	Number	Home Language	Number
1. Chinese	392 950	7. Arabic	209 240
2. Italian	371 200	8. Portuguese	187 475
3. Cantonese	345 730	9. Tagalog (Filipino)	185 420
4. Punjabi	280 535	10. Polish	163 745
5. Spanish	258 465	Aboriginal languages*	181 350
6. German	220 685		

*There are 50 Aboriginal languages.

Source: Adapted from Statistics Canada Web site, www12.statcan.ca/english/census01/teacher's_kit/activity8_table2.cfm2001.

It is important to note that the 2001 census also revealed that some people speak different languages at home than the one they first learned as a child. This is especially true for children of immigrants. A language shift occurs when these children become integrated into Canadian society and adopt English or French as their home language.

It is safe to say that many factors affect language patterns: immigration, migration, marriage, and the size of the language group. Canada's rich, multicultural and multilingual environment enriches the Canadian context while it also creates a greater need to focus on the complexities of communication.

THE NATURE OF LANGUAGE

language
System of symbols (words or vocabulary) structured by rules (grammar) and patterns (syntax) common to a community of people.

A **language** is a system of symbols (words or vocabulary) structured by grammar (rules and standards) and syntax (patterns in the arrangement of words) common to a community of people. Australian communication scholar Dale Spender explains that language is "our means of ordering, classifying, and manipulating the world. It is through language that we become members of a human community, that the world becomes comprehensive and meaningful, that we bring into existence the world in which we live."[1] That last phrase is particularly important, because it suggests that the very words we use help create our world.

Words dictate and limit the nature of our reality. To extend the theory further, one could argue that the quality of one's language reflects the quality of one's thought. Said more simply, your verbal communication reveals how you think and what you think about. This is only one explanation for how language and thought operate in human beings, but it is a provocative notion to consider that language has such a powerful influence on our everyday thinking processes.

···⟩ People Use Words as Symbols

symbol
A word, sound, or visual device that represents a thought, concept, or object.

As we noted in Chapter 1, words are **symbols** that represent something else. Just as a flag is a symbol of a country, words are symbols that trigger images, sounds, concepts, emotions, and experiences. For instance, what comes to mind when you see or hear the word *poverty*? The word may conjure up in your mind's eye a homeless person begging for change on the street corner or televised images of starving children in developing countries. Or perhaps you envisioned your own lighter-than-you'd-like wallet.

···⟩ People Attach Meanings to Words

meaning
How a person interprets or makes sense of a symbol.

Now imagine that you're in a conversation with someone and you use the word *poverty*, in an effort to convey to the other person the concept or image in your mind. You know what you're thinking when you say the word; the challenge is for the other person to understand your thoughts behind your choice of word. In communication terms, this is the process of creating **meaning.** The meaning of a word is how a person interprets or makes sense of

<::::> **COMMUNICATION and DIVERSITY**

Words across the Country

One of the many forms of cultural diversity emerges between members of co-cultures, or groups within a larger culture. Persons with disabilities, the elderly, Asian Americans, and gays and lesbians are examples of co-cultural groups within the larger Canadian culture. Another form of diversity that is less often researched and discussed consists of regional differences. Canada is a huge country, with many variations of persons living in it. Bypassing, or differences in meanings or usages of certain words, among persons from various regions of the country is quite interesting to explore.

One of your authors lived in Newfoundland for three years and realized very quickly that Newfoundlanders have their own dialect, which doesn't sound like the English of their "mainland" counterparts. She remembers that at times proper English was spoken and on other occasions some letters were dropped or added and words were linked to form long phrases. This dialect seems to change from town to town and city to city. Whether in Placentia Bay, Gander, or Cornerbrook, two habits appear to be common: adding "b'y" after most phrases and speaking very quickly. For example, Tony Watson, an environmental specialist from Saskatoon, arrived in Gander to do business with Ron Jones

of Green Thumb Lawn Doctor. When Tony called Ron to tell him of his arrival, Ron said, "How's ya giten on b'y? Stay where ya to till I come where ya at." Tony, being from Saskatoon, didn't understand these common Newfoundland phrases and was not sure how to respond. Ron had simply greeted Tony, asked him where he was staying, and told Tony that he would come to meet him. The miscommunication had to do with simple differences in terms and their meanings and in accepted norms common to various communities within Canada.[2]

A good resource for those of you who would like to explore further examples of Newfoundland English can be found in the book entitled, *The Dictionary of Newfoundland English*, edited by G.M. Story, W.J. Kirwan and J. Widdowson, University of Toronto Press, 1982.

Because we are such a mobile society now, you will no doubt encounter language differences as you move about the country or as you meet people from other areas who have moved to where you live. It's important to be aware of the potential for language differences right here in our own country, even if English and French are Canada's official languages.

---

a symbol. Meanings don't reside in the words themselves but in the ways in which communicators use the words. You attach a meaning to the word *poverty*, the symbol you choose in conversation; your listener creates meaning for the word when he or she attempts to interpret what you've said. Words aren't the culprits in communication problems; the meanings people create for words lead to successful or problematic communication.

Sometimes the speaker's and the receiver's meanings do not correspond because the same words mean different things to different people; the term for this phenomenon is **bypassing.** For example, have you ever found yourself at odds with someone because you held a different sense of what it meant to arrive "early" or "late" to an event? For some, getting there "early" means at least a half an hour before the event begins; for some, "early" means right on time. Being "late" can mean different things to different people as well. Some heated arguments can be boiled down to a simple misconnection in meaning.

bypassing
The same words mean different things to different people.

···> ## People Create Denotative and Connotative Meanings for Words

As we have said, language is a vehicle through which we share with others our sense of the world and who we are. Through language we transfer our experience into symbols and then use the symbols to share that experience. But as we learned in Chapter 1, the process of symbol sharing through language is not just a simple process of uttering a word and having its meaning clearly understood by another. Messages convey both content and feelings. So people create meanings for language on two levels: the denotative and the connotative.

The **denotative** level conveys content. Denotation is the restrictive or literal meaning of a word. For example, here is one dictionary definition for the word *school:*

denotative meaning
Restrictive or literal meaning of a word.

A place or institution, with its buildings, etc., for teaching and learning.[3]

This definition is a literal or denotative definition of the word *school;* it describes what the word means in Canada's culture.

Frank and Ernest

COMMUNICATION
WORKSHOP

SOMETIME TONIGHT
IN A ROOM UPSTAIRS

E-mail FandEBobT@aol.com
THAVES 2·14
© 1995 by NEA, Inc.

© 1998 Thaves/Reprinted with permission. Newspaper dist. by NEA, Inc.

connotative meaning
Personal and subjective meaning
of a word.

By contrast, the **connotative** level of language conveys feelings; people create personal and subjective meanings for words. Using the example above, the word *school* might mean to you a wonderful, exciting place where you meet your friends, have a good time, and occasionally take tests and perform other tasks that keep you from enjoying everything else. To others, though, "school" could be a restrictive, burdensome obligation that stands in the way of making money and getting on with life. Clearly, the connotative meaning of a word is more individual. Although the denotative or objective meaning of the word *school* can be found in your dictionary and Canadian encyclopedias, your subjective response to the word is probably not contained there.

⟶ People Convey Concrete and Abstract Meanings through Words

concrete meaning
Related to being able to experience a
referent with one of the senses.

abstract meaning
Meaning resulting from an inability to
experience a referent with one of
the senses.

Meanings for words can be placed along a continuum from concrete to abstract. A word's meaning is **concrete** if we can experience what the word refers to (the referent) with one of our senses; if we can see it, touch it, smell it, taste it, or hear it, then it's concrete. If we cannot do these things with the referent, then the word's meaning is **abstract.** In general, the more concrete the language, the easier it is for others to understand. The more abstract a word, the more difficult it is to understand or agree on a meaning. For example, the word *patriotism* is abstract because we cannot hear or taste patriotism. But a word that suggests a demonstration of patriotism, such as voting, is more concrete because we can physically perform the act of voting. It's wise to minimize the use of abstract words when you're trying to clarify a message. Concrete terms help make a message more clear.

⟶ Meanings Are Culture Bound

culture
A learned system of knowledge,
behaviour, attitudes, beliefs, values,
rules, and norms that is shared by a
group of people and shaped from one
generation to the next.

Culture consists of the rules, norms, and values of a group of people that have been learned and shaped from one generation to the next. The meaning of a word, just like the meaning of any symbol, can change from culture to culture. To a European, for example, a *Canuck* is someone from Canada, a player on the 1980s international downhill ski team known as the "Crazy Canucks," or a member of the Vancouver-based National Hockey League team.

⟶ Meanings Are Context Bound

A lot of people quoted in the media can be heard to say later, when questioned or interviewed, "My comments were taken out of context." We now have a term for a short statement that summarizes the essence of a longer message—the "sound bite." When you lift only a small piece of the greater text of what people have said, you take their words out of context. This practice can confuse and misrepresent a speaker's original message. Your English or speech communication teacher has undoubtedly cautioned you that taking something out of context changes its meaning. The meanings people attach to symbols are affected by situations. The statement, "That car is really bad," could mean that the car is a piece of junk or, in contemporary slang, a really great car. We need to know the context in order to decipher the communicator's specific meaning.

> ## Re**CAP** ⬅····
>
> ### The Nature of Language
>
> - People use words as *symbols:* Symbols represent something else.
> - People create *meanings* for words: Meaning is how a person interprets or makes sense of a symbol.
> - People create *denotative* and *connotative* meanings for words: The denotative meaning is a restrictive or literal meaning; the connotation is a personal and subjective meaning.
> - People convey *concrete* and *abstract* meanings through words: A word's meaning is concrete if we can experience it with one of our senses; if not, then the meaning is abstract.
> - Meanings are *culture* bound: The meaning of a word can change from culture to culture.
> - Meanings are *context* bound: The situation or context for communication aids people as they attach meanings to symbols.

THE POWER OF WORDS

No doubt we've all heard the old schoolyard chant, "Sticks and stones may break my bones, but words can never hurt me." We don't know who first came up with that statement, but we imagine it to be someone who had never experienced the sting of name-calling, the harmful effects of being labelled a "slow reader," or the legacy an unfortunate family nickname can bring. Words *do* hurt. They have the power to evoke a wide range of emotions in listeners. But words can also heal and inspire and transform the human spirit. Let's explore a few of the powerful attributes of words.

⸱⸱⸱⟩ The Power to Create and Label Experience

How many diseases or medical conditions can you think of that are named after the person who discovered the condition? Some that come to mind include Alzheimer's, Parkinson's, and Tourette's Syndrome. While you might not want your name associated with a disease, the point is that the name for a phenomenon labels the experience, thus making it more real. It also etches it into history. As the English language continues to evolve, so does the need to name and describe new phenomena. For example, the term *sexual harassment* did not emerge until the 1970s; it was generated by feminists who wanted a term to correspond to a very real behaviour many people experienced in the workplace.[4] Words give us tools to create and understand our world by naming and labelling what we experience.

Words also give us symbolic vehicles to communicate our creations and discoveries to others. As another example, when you label something "good" or "bad," you use language to create your own vision of how you experience the world. If you tell a friend that the movie you saw last night was vulgar and obscene, you not only provide your friend with a film critique but also communicate your sense of what is appropriate and inappropriate.

One theorist believes that you also create your moods and emotional states with the words you use to label your feelings.[5] If you get tired from a job, you might say that you feel angry and helpless or liberated and relieved. The first response might lead to depression and the second to happiness. One fascinating study conducted over a 35-year period found that people who described the world in pessimistic terms when they were younger were in poorer health during middle age than those who had been optimistic.[6] Your words and corresponding outlook have the power to affect your mental, emotional, and physical health.

⸱⸱⸱⟩ The Power to Affect Thoughts and Actions

A line from a Shakespearean tragedy reads, "That which we call a rose by any other name would smell as sweet." Would it really? If the name for this fragrant flower were "aardvark," would it still be the flower of people in love? Can you imagine getting a delivery of a dozen long-stemmed red aardvarks?

Some of you may remember a weight-loss product called Ayds. Ayds were small, brown, chewy squares that helped reduce the appetite (or so the manufacturers claimed). You can only guess why this product disappeared in the 1980s; if it is still on the market it has certainly been renamed. Given what we now know about the threat of the deadly disease AIDS, who in their right mind today would willingly ingest a product with a same-sounding name? Advertisers have long known that the way a product is labelled greatly affects the likelihood of someone buying it. So words affect the way we think about things and react to them.

Words not only have the power to affect how we think about and respond to something, but they also affect policy and procedures. Since September 11, 2001, heightened security measures have resulted in new policies and procedures being put into place. Particular sensitivity to the power of words is demonstrated in the following event that took place on a Canadian airline. A man of Arabic descent was travelling with Air Canada. When this passenger was asked to move his bag, he asked for an "exception." The flight attendant heard "explosion" and the man ended up spending nearly a month in jail![7]

⟶ The Power to Shape and Reflect Culture

If an impartial investigator from another culture were to study a transcript of all of your spoken utterances last week, what would she or he learn about you and the culture in which you live? If you frequently used words like *CD* and *inline skates,* the investigator would know that these things are important to you. But he or she might not know what you mean if these things are not also part of her or his culture.

The language you choose to use shapes your culture, and your culture shapes your language. You have grown up within a culture; you've learned the language of that culture. And the way you use the language, the words and meanings you choose as well as interpret from others' communication, have the effect of shaping your culture. For example, author Devorah Lieberman recounts a story of one of her students who was a professional

---

⟶•⟵ COMMUNICATION and TECHNOLOGY

Minding Your Manners, Even on the Net

If you have access to a computer, it's highly likely that you have used e-mail. It has become the communication channel of choice for many people, but there are some important differences between e-mail and other forms of communication.

Columnist Jim Barlow discusses e-mail etiquette beyond simply knowing some basic rules—such as using all caps means you're shouting or being emphatic.[8] He stresses that, just as with other more personal forms of communication, we should take the time to think before we hit the reply button in response to an e-mail message. Because of the distance and impersonality of e-mail, many people communicate electronically in ways they wouldn't dare in person. A couple of Barlow's suggestions relate to appropriate language; the first is to remember your manners:

I've noticed over the years that people are often incredibly rude in e-mail. Ask yourself, would you say that in person? If the answer is no, then why are you sending it via e-mail? Over the years when I've gotten a nasty e-mail, I've sometimes called the person and pleasantly asked if he or she realized just how insulting that message sounded after it was read aloud. A couple of times my correspondent said indeed, that was why it was sent. But for the most part, there was simply an embarrassed silence.

Barlow also discusses bandwidth, meaning the number of cues a form of communication contains that helps listeners discern meaning. Face-to-face conversation has the greatest bandwidth, e-mail has the least. Barlow contends that the greater the bandwidth, the better the understanding. So he suggests that complicated subjects are best discussed in person, with a full range of verbal and nonverbal cues. Telephonic communication is second best for complicated topics, and e-mail has the greatest potential for misunderstanding.

We sometimes forget—because of the lure, ease, and dazzle of technology—to select the channel of communication that will best serve our purposes. E-mail may be a highly expedient means of communicating, but it may not be the best of all possible choices.

translator of Japanese and English.[9] On one occasion when she was translating for a North American speaker to a Japanese audience, the speaker began with "humorous" anecdotes about his experiences in Japan. The translator's version of these anecdotes was, "The speaker is telling phrases that are considered funny in English but not in Japanese. I will tell you when he is finished so that you can laugh."

Co-cultures (cultural groups within a larger culture) also develop unique languages of their own as a way of forging connections and enhancing solidarity. For example, some gays and lesbians have reclaimed the once derogatory term "queer" and altered its meaning so that it's now a term of pride. Perhaps you have seen or heard of the cable television show *Queer as Folk*. Gang languages and symbols are prevalent as a means of establishing an identity unique from other groups. This principle can even extend to just two people in a romantic relationship who develop nicknames or other forms of language as secret codes. They don't dare use that language in the company of others; the privacy of the language and their shared experiences create a sort of microculture—a culture of two.

⋯⟩ The Power to Make and Break Relationships

Probably all of us have had the experience of saying something foolish, ridiculous, or embarrassing to another person. It seems that one of life's cruel ironies is the potential for human beings to say things they later regret. But if you've ever said something so inappropriate that it cost you a relationship—either one that didn't get off the ground or that ended because of what you said—then you know firsthand the power of words to make and break relationships. For example, people in love sometimes overstate things when they get emotional. That's understandable. But it's wise to try to avoid word barriers, such as **polarization**—the tendency to describe things in extremes or opposites without any middle ground. You might hear one romantic partner say to the other, "You either love me or you don't." These kinds of pronouncements can make people feel controlled, as though there are only two options and no compromise position.

polarization
The tendency to describe things in extremes, as though no middle ground exists.

CONFRONTING BIAS IN LANGUAGE

We don't want to sound like the "language police" here—that is, we don't want to dictate to you how you ought to talk. But we have found that even well-meaning, knowledgeable people can communicate bias through the language they choose to use. Oftentimes insensitive or stereotypical language usage arises out of ignorance or a lack of education. Words that reflect bias toward members of other cultures or groups can create barriers for listeners. In addition, such language ignores the fact that the world is constantly changing.

Re**CAP** ⟵⋯

The Power of Words

Words . . .

- Create and Label Experience: A personal connection that forms over the Internet can be called a "cyber-ship"—a combination of the terms "cyberspace" and "relationship."

- Affect Thoughts and Actions: Product names are critical to audience response and sales success. The critically acclaimed film *The Shawshank Redemption* was a box office failure, which some attributed to the film's obtuse title.

- Shape and Reflect Culture: Cultures change; language both creates and reflects the changing nature of culture.

- Make and Break Relationships: Verbal communication creates opportunities for us to know and be known by others. It is a primary tool for establishing relationships and deepening them; it can also be the reason a relationship ends.

ETHICAL PROBE

Language is a readily identifiable symbol of culture and group identity. According to Mary Jane Morris, "language connects people with their past and rounds their social, emotional and spiritual vitality." In an article entitled "Canada's Aboriginal Languages," Morris explains that societal factors such as dominant languages and modernization may contribute to the decline of minority language. She states, "In the case of Aboriginal languages, historical events such as the prohibition of indigenous language use in residential schools have also contributed to this process."[10] Its oral tradition may also have promoted a difficult survival. Of those Canadians claiming to have Aboriginal identity in 1996 (800 000), only 26% said an Aboriginal language was their mother tongue.[11]

The Royal Commission on Aboriginal Peoples (RCAP) has taken steps to save Aboriginal languages by promoting the use of these languages within the confines of Aboriginal communities via formal education and extended research. RCAP states "that everyday language use in the home and in the community is critical for intergenerational transmission and for acquiring Aboriginal languages as a mother tongue."[12]

Do you believe that your mother tongue should be supported in the same manner within your community and in society in general? Can we as Canadians practise different languages within the community and still have a sense of integration?

Also, this is not a lesson in "how to be P.C." The term *political correctness* with regard to language is an unfortunate contemporary label for something communication instructors have taught for decades—the use of language that doesn't exclude or offend listeners. In the following pages, we explore a few categories of language that illustrate the constant evolution of verbal communication and represent areas in which we can all heighten our sensitivity.

⤑ Biased Language: Race, Ethnicity, Nationality, and Religion

Think about whether you have ever said or overheard someone say the following:

"I got a great deal on a car; the sticker price was a lot higher, but I jewed the dealer way down."
"You can't have that back, you Indian giver!"
"She's a real Bible banger."
"He doesn't have a Chinaman's chance to make the team."
"That divorce settlement gypped me out of what's rightfully mine!"

That last statement tends to puzzle people more than the others. It includes the term *gypped,* which is derived from the word for the nomadic cultural group known throughout the world as gypsies. The stereotype relates to being suckered or cheated out of what a person is due.

What would your impression be of a person who made one of these statements? The language used in each of these examples demonstrates an insensitivity to members of other cultures and groups. Such language reflects a word barrier known as **allness,** which occurs when words reflect unqualified, often untrue generalizations that deny individual differences or variations. It's important to continue to educate yourself and monitor your speech so that you are not, even unconsciously, using phrases that depict a group of people in a negative, stereotypical fashion.

Given the power of words, the terms we use in reference to ethnic groups have a direct reflection upon perceptions of culture and identity. If you use the wrong word, you may be labelled "politically incorrect" or worse, a "bigot."

A sensitive communicator keeps abreast of linguistic changes and adopts the designations currently preferred by members of the ethnic groups themselves. Sometimes students ask why this is so, out of both a resistance to change and a general wish that language (and other things in life) were simpler. Consider this: What if you really liked your

allness
Language that reflects unqualified, often untrue generalizations that deny individual differences or variations.

first name but didn't like a shortened or nickname version of it? And what if someone you work with never got your name right, if she or he constantly used that more familiar or "playful" version of your name? You'd probably get irritated and try to correct the person. The principle is the same with ethnic and cultural designations. It's wise to allow members of a certain group to designate their own terms, than to attempt to learn and inappropriately use those terms. Don't be afraid to ask directly, but sensitively, what term or terms are appropriate. For example, celebrity Whoopi Goldberg was asked by an interviewer whether she preferred to be called black or African American. Her reply was, "Just call me Whoopi—that's what I prefer."

⤳ Biased Language: Gender and Sexual Orientation

Language that reveals bias in favour of one sex and against another, termed **sexist** or **exclusive language,** is more prevalent than you'd think. Decades of effort, spurred by the women's liberation movement in the 1960s, have illuminated the consciousness of Canadian culture on the topic of exclusive language. But many people do not alter their language to reflect and include both sexes. In addition, insensitivity or intolerance toward persons who are gay, lesbian, or bisexual is often reflected in what is termed **heterosexist** or **homophobic language.** A person who uses heterosexist language speaks from an assumption that the world is heterosexual, as if same-sex or both-sex attractions simply do not exist. Homophobic language more overtly denigrates persons of nonheterosexual orientations. We briefly consider sexist and heterosexist forms of biased language below.

Language and the Sexes

Even though women now constitute more than 50.5% of Canada's population, to listen to the language of some people, you'd think it was still a "man's world." Sexist language can reflect stereotypical attitudes or describe roles in exclusively male or female terms. Research indicates that exclusive language usage does the following: (1) maintains sex-biased perceptions, (2) shapes people's attitudes about careers that are appropriate for one sex but not the other, (3) causes some women to believe that certain jobs and roles aren't attainable, and (4) contributes to the belief that men deserve more status in society than women do.[13] Even dictionaries fall into patterns of describing women and men with discriminatory language.[14] Included in the *Oxford English Dictionary* definition for woman were: (1) an adult female being, (2) female servant, (3) a lady-love or mistress, and (4) a wife. Men were described in more positive and distinguished terms: (1) a human being, (2) the human creation regarded abstractly, (3) an adult male endowed with many qualities, and (4) a person of importance of position.

THE FAR SIDE® By GARY LARSON

sexist (exclusive) language
Language that reveals bias in favour of one sex and against another.

heterosexist language
Language that reveals an assumption that the world is heterosexual, as if homosexuality or bisexuality did not exist.

homophobic language
Language that overtly denigrates persons of nonheterosexual orientations, usually arising out of a fear of being labelled gay or lesbian.

On the WEB ·····●

Check out this informative Web site: **www.rabble.ca.**

  Rabble.ca is an online magazine where proactive journalists, writers, artists, and activists across Canada provide original news stories, in-depth features, provocative interviews, and commentaries. Here you will discover a wealth of information via an activist advice column, an innovative debates series, and searchable archives. Rabble.ca also seeks to build on the strengths of existing diverse movements that focus on equality and social justice. Much information can be found regarding people's differences in the Canadian context. You can even share your personal views via a link called "Babble." This is an excellent site to explore issues that affect Canadians.

generic language
General terms that stand for all persons or things within a given category.

The most common form of sexism in language is the use of a masculine term as though it were **generic,** or a term to describe all people. There are two primary ways that masculine-as-generic language typically appears in written and oral communication: (1) pronoun usage and (2) man-linked terminology.

Consistent evidence from research on sexist language shows that people—particularly in Canadian and American culture—simply do not tend to think in neuter. We think in male or female, which is another example of the polarization aspect of language discussed earlier. We don't tend to think of living entities as *it*s, and we rarely use that pronoun to refer to them. When most people read or hear the word *he,* they think of the masculine, not some image of a sexless person.[15] Using generic masculine language, in essence, turns all persons into male persons.

Sexist language can be so deeply embedded in some persons' experience that it is used habitually, without much thought. For example, a student was giving a speech on how to project a winning, confident style on a job interview. The student said, "When you greet the boss for the first time, be sure to look him straight in the eye, give him a firm handshake, and let him know you're interested in the job." This language would be perfectly acceptable if the speaker were only describing a specific situation in which the job candidate was to meet a male boss. But his exclusive language choice only allowed for the possibility of a male boss, not a female boss, unless he meant the term *he* to stand for all persons—male and female bosses, in this case. What if the speaker had used only female pronouns, as in "look her straight in the eye, give her a firm handshake, and let her know you're interested in the job"? No doubt the exclusive female language would have drawn undue attention and perhaps distracted listeners. It is a common occurrence for male language to be substituted as terms for all persons, but less common for female language to serve as generics.

We don't know what you were taught in high school or in other postsecondary classes about generic language. Nevertheless, publishing standards today require the use of nonsexist language, which allows no masculine terms to stand for all persons. If you notice, we use inclusive language in this text—because it reflects our value system and because our publisher requires it.

The solution to this problem is not to replace all cases of *he* with *she*, which would be an equally sexist practice. The point is to use terms that include both sexes so that your language reflects the contemporary world in which we live. If you want to refer to one person—any person of either sex—the most clear, grammatical, nonsexist way to do that is to use either *she or he, he/she,* or *s/he.*[16] Other options include (1) omitting a pronoun altogether, either rewording a message or substituting an article (*a, an,* or *the)* for the pronoun; (2) using *you* or variations of the indefinite pronoun *one;* or (3) using the plural pronoun *they* (most persons' term of choice).[17]

As was the case for pronouns, research shows that masculine mental images arise when the term *man* is used, again rendering women invisible and reinforcing the male-as-standard problem.[18] Words such as fire*man*, police*man*, and *man*kind belittle the fact that

The gender-neutral term firefighter *describes both of these people, whereas the sexist term* fireman *excludes the person on the right.*

women are part of the workforce and the human race. Contrast these with *firefighter, police officer,* and *humankind,* which are gender neutral and allow for the inclusion of both men and women. Some progress in this area has been made to reflect changed attitudes toward women in the professional arena. Compare some terms used in the past to describe workers to terms we now use (see Table 3.2).

Consciously remembering to use nonsexist, inclusive language brings several benefits.[19] First, inclusive language reflects inclusive attitudes. Your attitudes are reflected in your speech and your speech affects your attitudes. Monitoring your verbal communication for sexist remarks can help you monitor your attitudes about sexist assumptions you may hold. Second, using gender-inclusive language helps you become more other oriented, which will have a positive impact on your relationships. Consciously ridding your language of sexist remarks reflects your sensitivity to others. Third, inclusive language makes your speech more contemporary and unambiguous. If you use *he,* for example, how is a listener to know whether you are referring to a male person or any person in general? And finally, inclusive language strengthens your style and demonstrates sensitivity that can empower others. By eliminating sexist bias from your speech, you affirm the value of all individuals with whom you interact.

Language and Sexual Orientation

We realize that this is one of the more difficult areas to discuss, mainly because people tend to hold strong opinions about sexual orientation. But no matter your views about sexuality, the underlying lesson here is to use sensitive, appropriate communication with whomever you encounter. Whether you approve or disapprove of someone's orientation and lifestyle should not affect your goal of being an effective communicator.

Just as you have learned to avoid racially charged terms that degrade and draw attention to someone's ethnicity, it's important to learn to avoid language that denigrates a person's sexual orientation and draws undue attention to this element of cultural diversity. One of your textbook authors was quite taken aback a few years ago when she received a paper from a first-year student in which the derogatory term *fag* frequently appeared. You've no doubt heard this term, probably bantered about in high school, but its use can be a signal of homophobia—the fear of being labelled or viewed as gay or lesbian. Heterosexist language is more subtle; it often emerges through omission, meaning what is *not* said, rather than commission, or what *is* said. For example, have you ever heard an instructor in one of your classes give a dating example using two persons of the same sex? Most examples about relationships that you read or hear in courses such as interpersonal communication or introduction to psychology reflect heterosexual romantic relationships. As another example, how often do you hear or use the term *partner* instead of *husband* or *wife*? The first term, *partner,* is inclusive of all forms of coupling, while the latter terms refer only to heterosexual marriage. These tendencies can communicate a heterosexual bias and suggest that other sexual orientations are inappropriate or nonexistent. Again, no matter your particular stance on the issue of sexual orientation, the goal is to use sensitive, inclusive language so that you are perceived as a contemporary, effective communicator.

TABLE 3.2

Terms from the Past	Terms Used Today
stewardess	flight attendant
chairman	chair
fireman	firefighter
salesman	salesperson or clerk
mailman	letter carrier
female doctor or lady doctor	physician
girls at work or girl Friday	women at the office
Miss/Mrs.	Ms.
mankind	people, humans, or humankind

⋯⟶ Biased Language: Age, Class, and Ability

"Just turn the car, grandpa!" Ever heard a driver say this in irritation, or said it yourself? Ever call an elderly person a "geezer" or an "old-timer"? Just as some people contend that Canadians are concerned with gender and ethnocultural diversity, many believe that Canadians are youth obsessed. We live in a culture that glorifies youth and tends to put its elders "out to pasture." Age discrimination is a very real problem in the workforce, such that laws have been enacted to guard against someone being denied professional opportunities because of age. Likewise, some young people are stereotypically communicated to as though their youth exempted them from intelligence or responsible action. We recommend that you inventory your language for any terms that either show disrespect for elders or are patronizing or condescending to younger persons.

Another area within language that has received research attention of late surrounds socioeconomic class. Class distinctions typically come in the form of derogatory references to "blue-collar workers," "manual labourers," or "welfare recipients." Watch references that reveal a condescending or disrespectful attitude toward someone's education (or lack of it) and socioeconomic status.

Finally, an area of bias in language that entered most persons' consciousness by the turn of the 21st century relates to ability. Some years ago, Helen Keller was described as "deaf, dumb, and blind." Nowadays, the appropriate term for her inability to vocally communicate would be "mute." Be careful that your language doesn't make fun of or draw attention to someone's physical, mental, or learning disability, such as calling someone a "cripple," "retard," or "slow reader." Also, scholars who research communication and disability recommend that you use the reference "persons with disabilities" rather than "disabled persons." The former language usage makes the person primary and the disability secondary. The importance is on a person, who just happens to have some form of disability. The latter usage emphasizes the disability over the human-ness of the person.[20]

Re**CAP** ⟵⋯

Confronting Bias in Language

Inventory your language for subtle and not-so-subtle indications of bias according to

- *Race, Ethnicity, and Nationality:* Avoid language that denigrates members of a racial or ethnocultural group; be careful not to overemphasize or "mark" a person by using adjectives referring to national origin, as in "that Oriental student in my class."
- *Religion:* Watch stereotypical language pertaining to religious affiliation, such as derogatory references to Jews, Muslims, or fundamentalist Christians, for example.
- *Gender:* Include both sexes in your language, especially in your use of pronouns; avoid masculine generic pronouns and man-linked terms that exclude women.
- *Sexual Orientation:* Be alert to the potential for your language to reveal heterosexism—the assumption that everyone is heterosexual or that heterosexuality is the only existing orientation. Eliminate homophobic language that degrades and stereotypes gays, lesbians, and bisexuals.
- *Age:* Avoid calling too much attention to a person's age in your verbal communication. Be especially vigilant not to label or stereotype the elderly, or to condescend to or glorify youth.
- *Class:* Monitor references to socioeconomic differences, such as distinctions between blue- and white-collar workers.
- *Ability:* Avoid verbal communication that draws attention to a person's physical, mental, or learning ability.

USING WORDS TO ESTABLISH
SUPPORTIVE RELATIONSHIPS

As we said early on in this chapter, one reason verbal communication is important is its impact on other people. Language is our primary tool for communicating who we are to others—for knowing them and being known by them. Relationships of all sorts bring life's greatest satisfactions, so the motivation for assessing and improving our verbal communication with others is obvious.

In our introductory communication classes, we often discuss with students **trigger words**—those forms of language that arouse certain emotions in us. One student, Travis, was immediately able to identify a word his wife used during arguments that really sparked his frustration and anger more than anything else. When Travis would make a point that would frustrate his wife—one for which she had no comeback—she would look at him, toss her hand in the air, and say, "Whatever." Perhaps this word triggers you too, because it punctuates a conversation; it acts as a dismissal of the other person and her or his point. Do you know what words trigger your emotions? These words or phrases can incite positive feelings as well as negative, but they acutely illustrate the power of words in the context of relationships. Certain uses of language can make us feel accepted and appreciated, or disrespected and hostile.

For more than four decades, communication scholar Jack Gibb's research has been used as a framework for both describing and prescribing verbal behaviours that contribute to feelings of either **supportiveness** or **defensiveness**.[21] Gibb spent several years listening to and observing groups of individuals in meetings and conversations, noting that some exchanges seemed to create a supportive climate whereas others created a defensive one. Words and actions, he concluded, are tools we use to let someone know whether we support them or not. When someone gets defensive, communication is seriously impeded. Think about times when your words made someone defensive and how hard you had to work (if you attempted it at all) to get the person to let the defences down. In this section, we suggest ways to use verbal communication to create a supportive climate rather than an antagonistic one.

⇢ Describe Your Own Feelings Rather Than Evaluate Others

Most of us don't like to be judged or evaluated; not only do we fear negative responses from others, we fear the potential that we will become defensive and say things we'll later regret. Criticizing and name-calling obviously can create relational problems, but so can our attempts to diagnose others' problems or weaknesses. As Winston Churchill declared, "I am always ready to learn, although I do not always like being taught."

One way to avoid evaluating others is to attempt to decrease your use of an accusatory *you*. Statements such as, "You always say you'll call but you never do" or "You need to pick up the dirty clothes in your room" attack a person's sense of self-worth and usually result in a defensive reaction. Instead, use the word *I* to describe your own feelings and thoughts about a situation or event: "I find it hard to believe you when you say you'll call" or "I don't enjoy the extra work of picking up your dirty clothes." When you describe your own feelings instead of berating the receiver of the message, you take ownership of the problem. This approach leads to greater openness and trust because your listener is less likely to feel rejected or as if you are trying to control him or her.

Related to this point about description versus evaluation is the suggestion that you separate behaviours from persons in order to create a supportive climate. We probably all know people whose behaviours seem self-destructive, and we all probably do something from time to time that isn't in our own best interest. Maybe in reaction to getting dumped in a relationship that means a great deal to you, you call that person's answering machine 20 times, just to hear the voice recording. Maybe you indulge in self-defeating behaviours like drinking too much, overeating (or the opposite, starving yourself), or driving around late at night with the music blasting, feeling sorry for yourself. In these critical moments, does someone respond to you, as a person, or to your behaviour? A supportive response focuses on the behaviour, not the person. A supportive response sounds

trigger word
A form of language that arouses strong emotions in listeners.

supportive communication
Language that creates a climate of trust, caring, and acceptance.

defensive communication
Language that creates a climate of hostility and mistrust.

something like this: "Here's what I see you doing; I'm still your friend and I care about you, but this behaviour isn't healthy. How can I help you?" Responses that engender defensiveness might sound something like "You're really out of control," "You've become someone I don't recognize," and "Stop acting like this or I won't be able to be around you or be your friend." The supportive response doesn't characterize the person as the embodiment of his or her destructive behaviour; it focuses only on the behaviour, because that what's happening at the moment. In religious circles, the advice goes: "Hate the sin, love the sinner."

Solve Problems Rather Than Control Others

When you were younger, your parents gave you rules to keep you safe. Even though you may have resented their control, you needed to know what was hot, when not to cross the street, and how dangerous it is to stick your finger in a light socket. Now that you are an adult, when people treat you like a child, it often means they are trying to control your behaviour, to take away your options. In truth, we have little or no control over others.

Most of us don't like to be controlled by others. Someone who presumes to tell us what's good for us instead of helping us puzzle through issues and problems to arrive at our own solutions or higher understanding is likely to engender defensiveness. Open-ended questions, such as "What seems to be the problem?" or "How can we deal with this issue?" create a more supportive climate than critical comments, such as "Here's where you are wrong" and "You know what your problem is?" or commands such as "Don't do that!"

Be Genuine Rather Than Manipulative

To be genuine means that you honestly seek to be yourself rather than someone you are not. It also means taking a sincere interest in others, considering the uniqueness of each individual and situation, and avoiding generalizations or strategies that focus on your own needs and desires. A manipulative person has hidden agendas and her or his own concerns and interests most at heart. A genuine person has the other person's interests at heart and uses language to facilitate an open and honest discussion of issues and problems.

Empathize Rather Than Remain Detached from Others

empathy
Feeling what another person is feeling.

Empathy, one of the hallmarks of supportive relationships, is the ability to understand and actually feel or approximate the feelings of others and then to predict the emotional responses they will have to different situations. You work to put yourself in the shoes of the other person, to experience as closely as you can what she or he is experiencing. The opposite of empathy is neutrality. To be neutral is to be indifferent or apathetic toward others. Even when you express anger or irritation toward another, you are investing some energy in the relationship.

Remaining detached from someone when empathy is obviously called for can generate great defensiveness and damage a relationship. Here's an example: You're upset about an argument you just had with someone you're dating, so you seek the support and listening ear of a good friend. But that friend is in "party mode" or in such a good mood that he or she chooses not to concentrate and listen to what's going on with you. Rather than engage in your situation, your friend remains detached and blows off your concerns. In situations like this, most of us become defensive and frustrated. Empathy takes work, but it is a building block of a supportive relationship.

Be Flexible Rather Than Rigid toward Others

Some people are just *always* right, aren't they? (These people spend a lot of time alone, too.) Most people don't like someone who always seems certain that she or he is right. A "you're wrong, I'm right" attitude creates a defensive climate. This does not mean that you should have no opinions and go through life passively agreeing to everything. And it doesn't mean that there isn't a clear-cut right and wrong in a given situation. But instead of making rigid pronouncements, at times you may want to qualify your language by using

At times, everyone needs an empathic word from a friend.

phrases such as "I may be wrong, but it seems to me ..." or "Here's something you might want to consider." Conditional language gives your opinions a softer edge that allows room for others to express a point of view; it opens the door for alternatives. Declarations tend to shut the door. Again, there are times when equivocation is not an appropriate or advisable way to communicate. But in those cases when you want to induce supportiveness and reduce the potential for defensiveness, conditional, flexible language works best.

⇢ Present Yourself as Equal Rather Than Superior

You can antagonize others by letting them know that you view yourself as better or brighter than they are. You may be gifted and extraordinarily intelligent, but it's not necessary to announce or publicize it. And although some people have the responsibility and authority to manage others, "pulling rank" does not usually produce a supportive climate. With phrases such as "Let's work on this together" or "We each have a valid perspective," you can avoid erecting walls of resentment and defensiveness. "We" language can be preferable to "you" language; it builds a sense of camaraderie and shared experience rather than setting yourself apart from listeners.

Also, avoid using "high-falutin'" (or unnecessarily complicated) words just to impress others or to project some image. Sometimes referred to as "bafflegab," this language can come in the form of words, phrases, or verbal shorthand that no one understands but you. Persons with particular expertise may use abbreviated terms or acronyms, which are words derived from the first letters of several words in a string. Technology is notorious for its use of language that doesn't easily translate outside technical circles; for example, "bytes," "body text," "hyperlink," and "macro." If both speaker and listener for those words are computer technicians, then it's a perfectly acceptable way to communicate. The problem comes when you use jargon no one understands, perhaps for the purpose of creating drama, excluding someone from the conversation, or posturing yourself. It's better to use informal language appropriate to the situation and your listeners than to attempt to talk over the heads of everyone in the room.

You can also create defensiveness by using language that is too simplistic for your listeners. Granted, when you communicate with someone from another culture or even from another cultural group within Canada's multicultural environment, you may need to alter your message to get your meaning across. But this means that your verbal communication should be explicit, not condescending. For example, some people use oversimplified words when communicating with elderly persons. It's inappropriate to assume that aging equates to a diminished capacity to understand. Try to use language to present yourself on equal ground with your listeners and establish a supportive, open climate for communication.

On the WEB ·····•

If you encounter someone whose language is such "bafflegab" that a common dictionary won't help you decipher meanings, try the Creative Word Generator Web site. This site offers seldom-used words and their definitions, so that you won't be stumped again by someone who is "ultracrepidarian" (acting or speaking outside one's experience, knowledge, or ability). The address is **www.celerity.co.uk** (once at the site, try the link **/words/**).

ReCAP ⇠

Using Words to Create a Supportive Climate

- Describe your own feelings instead of evaluating the points of view or behaviour of others.
- Keep the focus on problem solving, not on control of others.
- Be genuine rather than manipulative in your approach.
- Show that you understand others' points of view instead of ignoring their feelings.
- Use conditional language and demonstrate flexibility rather than rigidity in your communication with others.
- Present yourself as an equal rather than as a superior. Make it clear that you do not have all the answers rather than be perceived as a know-it-all. Don't attempt to talk over or under the heads of listeners, because that can breed defensiveness.

SUMMARY ⬇

Canada's linguistic diversity highlights the need to recognize and understand the complexities of language and how it contributes to the communication process. In this chapter, we explored the importance of effective verbal communication with others. The words we choose have great power to communicate who we are and to influence the relationships we establish. People use words as symbols for objects, events, and ideas, and they create meanings for those symbols. We interpret their meanings through the culture and context to which they belong. Communication is complex because people develop both denotative (literal) meanings and connotative (subjective) meanings for words and because words range from concrete to abstract.

The power of words stems from their ability to create images and to help us label and understand our experience.

Words influence our thoughts, feelings, and actions, as they both shape culture and are shaped by culture. Language also has the power to make and break relationships with others.

Biased language that is insensitive and exclusive of others creates noise that interferes with the meaning of a message; it also can project a discriminatory image of the user of such language and impede the development of satisfying relationships. The most common forms of biased language surround a person's race, ethnicity, nationality, religion, gender, sexual orientation, age, class, and ability.

The words you use can enhance or detract from the quality of relationships you establish with others. In contrast to defensive communication, supportive communication is descriptive rather than evaluative, problem oriented rather than control oriented, genuine rather than contrived or manipulative, empathic rather than neutral, flexible rather than rigid, and equal rather than superior.

Discussion and Review ⬇

1. Why should we focus on language?

2. How does Canada's linguistic diversity and rich multicultural environment affect how one should communicate with others?

3. Explain the nature of words, as symbols to which people attach meanings. How can meanings vary across persons?

4. Describe what is meant by denotative and connotative meanings for words.

5. Describe what is meant by concrete and abstract meanings for words.

6. What does it mean when we say that language is culture bound and context bound? How does one's culture shape language? How does one's language shape culture?

7. Identify four ways that words have power.

8. Provide some examples of biased language according to race, ethnicity, nationality, and religion.

9. Provide some examples of biased language according to gender, sexual orientation, age, class, and ability.

10. What is the role of verbal communication in the establishment of supportive relationships? Identify some ways that one can create a supportive communication climate with others.

Developing Your Skills: Putting Principles into Practice ⬇

1. Here we review the differences between denotative and connotative meanings of words and provide an example using the word teacher.

Level	Definition	Examples
Denotative	Literal, restrictive definition of a word	Teacher: the person primarily responsible for providing your education
Connotative	Personal, subjective reaction to a word	Teacher: the warm, supportive person who fostered a climate in which you could learn OR the cold taskmaster who drilled lessons into you and made you feel inferior

For each of the following terms, provide a denotative or dictionary-type definition; then generate connotative meanings of your own.

work   love   professionalism
parent   commitment   loyalty

2. We know that words have the power to influence our thoughts and actions. With a group of classmates, have each member reveal a nickname—given to them by either a family member or friends. Discuss whether group members hold positive meanings or negative meanings for the nicknames and how each person's development was affected by his or her nickname.

3. This activity illustrates how people reveal their biases through their use of language. Use the words below to generate a list of stereotypical language that is often associated with that group. For example, for the word "New Democratic Party," one might think of positive and negative terms like "pro-labour," "social spending," and "progressive."

conservatives   the military
foreigners   churchgoers
homeless persons   politicians

4. With a group of classmates, generate and write down a list of trigger words—terms that set off emotional reactions. Consider those words that evoke positive emotions, such as happiness and surprise. Then explore words that prompt anger, fear, sadness, and disgust. Discuss how it came to be that certain words trigger your emotions; look for common experiences across group members.

5. In this chapter you've learned that the words you use can enhance or detract from the quality of relationships you establish with others. Conduct role plays with classmates, using the six ways we discussed for establishing supportive communication climates with others: (1) being descriptive rather than evaluative, (2) being problem oriented rather than control oriented, (3) communicating in a genuine rather than a contrived or manipulative manner, (4) showing empathy rather than neutrality, (5) being flexible rather than rigid, and (6) representing yourself as equal rather than superior to others. These role plays work best when you first act out the wrong way to behave or an example of ineffective communication that leads to defensiveness. Then repeat the role play, using the same or different players, altering the conversation so that a supportive climate is established.

Henri Matisse, "Conversation," 1908/09–1912. Oil on canvas, 177 x 217 cm. © 2003 Succession H. Matisse, Paris/Artists Rights Society (ARS), New York. © Art Resource/NY.

We respond to gestures with an extreme alertness and,
one might say, in accordance with an elaborate and secret
code that is written nowhere, known by none, and
understood by all.

— EDWARD SAPIR

4 Understanding Nonverbal Messages

AFTER STUDYING THIS CHAPTER, YOU SHOULD BE ABLE TO

1. Provide four reasons for studying nonverbal communication.

2. Describe the ways in which nonverbal communication serves various functions with verbal communication.

3. Discuss six elements that reveal the nature of nonverbal communication.

4. Be able to identify and explain the seven groupings of nonverbal communication codes.

5. Summarize major research findings for the codes of nonverbal communication.

6. Explain Mehrabian's three-part framework for interpreting nonverbal cues.

"I knew that was you coming down the hall; I know the sound of your footsteps."
"Don't roll your eyes at me, young lady. I'm your mother and I deserve some respect."
"I don't think you could carry on a conversation without using your hands."
"You're crowding me, man; I need my space."
"I can hear that tone in your voice again—that disapproving, guilt-tripping tone."

What do these statements have in common? They all have to do with a form of human communication that exists without words—what we term nonverbal communication. **Nonverbal communication** is communication other than written or spoken language that creates meaning for someone. There is one exception related to this definition: To hearing persons, sign language appears to be nonverbal communication. However, to persons who are deaf, sign language is verbal communication, with certain movements, signs, and facial expressions conveying words, phrases, and emphasis.

nonverbal communication
Behaviour other than written or spoken language that creates meaning for someone.

We know you're becoming familiar with our five-sided model of communication principles for a lifetime, but let's do a quick recap (see Figure 4.1). In Chapter 2 we explored ways to become more aware of yourself and your perceptions of things and people with whom you come into contact. An important step in this process of coming to know and understand yourself better is an honest, insightful examination of how you talk. In Chapter 3 we challenged you to consider the power of words, to take inventory of your use of language, and to think about ways to improve your verbal communication so that you extend yourself to others and respond to them in an appropriate, effective manner. Now we get to what most people consider an even greater challenge—understanding and evaluating your nonverbal communication and improving your ability to interpret the nonverbal behaviour of others. Nonverbal communication is of great importance; a person who uses and reads others' nonverbal communication with sensitivity and skill is very impressive and highly memorable to other people. Because of the power of nonverbal communication to complement verbal communication, to further reveal the self—particularly in those situations when talking is inappropriate, impossible, or inadequate—and to affect how you connect with others as you initiate and build relationships, we've chosen to make this the third of our five key principles for a lifetime.

We have two primary goals in this chapter. The first is to help you become more aware of your own nonverbal behaviour, understanding how and why you behave as you do. Because much nonverbal communication behaviour is subconscious, most people have

FIGURE 4.1 Communication Principles for a Lifetime

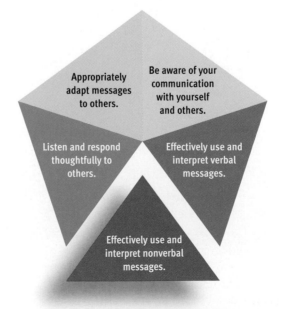

limited awareness or understanding of it. Once you become more aware of this important form of communication, you will increase your ability to use nonverbal skills to interact more effectively with others. The second goal is to enhance your nonverbal receiving skills, or your ability to detect and interpret the nonverbal communication of others more accurately.

WHY FOCUS ON NONVERBAL COMMUNICATION?

Have you ever watched someone interact with someone else and thought, "That person just doesn't have a clue?" We've all seen or

Which communicates emotions more effectively: body movements; the volume, pitch, and intensity of the voice; or the meaning of the actual words spoken?

met people who seem as if they don't pick up on communication clues of others. For example, have you ever tried to end a conversation because you were late or needed to be somewhere else and the person you were talking to just wouldn't let you out of the conversation? The person didn't seem to notice you looking at your watch, angling your body away, taking a few steps back, and making minimal vocal responses to what was being said. Now, we all have times when we can't "catch a clue," even if we consider ourselves to be fairly sensitive, perceptive people. Certain people, places, moods, or topics of conversation may impede our ability to give and receive nonverbal communication effectively. But we don't want to be clueless. We want to be able to exhibit effective nonverbal communication and to more sensitively and accurately read and interpret the clues others give us.

However, there's something very important to keep in mind as we proceed: No one can become a perfect interpreter of the nonverbal communication of others. It's unwise and inappropriate to assume that you can become an infallible judge of others' nonverbal cues, because human beings are unique, complicated, and ever-changing creatures. Although we encourage you to deepen your understanding of nonverbal communication, sharpen your powers of observation, and develop greater skill in interpreting the meanings behind others' nonverbal actions, we also suggest that you remain keenly aware of the idiosyncratic and complex nature of nonverbal communication. We hope that you catch more clues as a result of studying this topic, but avoid making the mistake of believing that your interpretations of nonverbal messages are always correct. To begin to explore this topic, let's look at four reasons for studying nonverbal communication.

⋯⋗ Nonverbal Messages Communicate Feelings and Attitudes

What do you look like when you're happy and excited about something? When you're mad? When you're really worried about something? When you're surprised or disappointed? Seeing videos or pictures of yourself in different moods can be quite revealing, because your face, body, and voice communicate volumes about what's going on inside of you.

Nonverbal communication is a primary tool for conveying our feelings and attitudes and for detecting the emotional states of others. In the study of nonverbal communication, Albert Mehrabian is an expert. He concluded from his research that the most significant source of emotional information is the face, which can channel as much as 55% of our meaning. Vocal cues such as volume, pitch, and intensity convey another 38% of our emotional meaning. In all, we communicate approximately 93% of the emotional meaning of our messages nonverbally; as little as 7% of the emotional meaning is communicated through explicit verbal channels.[1] Although these percentages do not apply to every communication situation, Mehrabian's research illustrates the potential power of nonverbal cues to communicate emotion and attitude.

⋯⋗ Nonverbal Messages Are More Believable Than Verbal

"Hey—are you mad or something?" asks Jonas.

(Big sigh.) "Oh, no. I'm not mad," responds Danita (in a subdued tone of voice and without making eye contact).

"You sure? Because you're acting funny, like you're ticked off." (One more try and then Jonas will likely give up.)

"I SAID I'M NOT MAD, OKAY? WILL YOU LEAVE IT ALONE PLEASE?"

For all Danita's protestations, the real story is—she's mad. "Actions speak louder than words." This cliché became a cliché because nonverbal communication is more believable than verbal communication. Verbal communication is a conscious activity; it involves the translation of thoughts and impulses into symbols, as you learned in Chapter 3. Some nonverbal communication is conscious, but a great deal of it is generated subconsciously as we act and react to stimuli in our environment. It's easier to control your words than to control a quiver in your voice when you're angry, the heat and flush in your face when you talk to someone you're attracted to, or shaky knees when you're nervous.

When a person's verbal and nonverbal communication contradict, as in Danita's case above, which should an astute observer believe? The nonverbal actions carry the truer message most of the time. When we can't catch a clue, it's most likely because we're wrapped up in ourselves or because we attend more to a person's verbal messages than nonverbal messages.

···⟩ Nonverbal Messages Are Critical to Successful Relationships

One researcher suggests that as much as 65% of the way we convey meaning in our messages is through nonverbal channels.[2] Of course, the meaning others interpret from your behaviour may not be the one you intended. But we begin making judgments about people just a fraction of a second after meeting them, based on nonverbal information. You may decide whether a date is going to be pleasant or dull during the first 30 seconds of meeting your partner, before your partner has had time to utter more than "Hello."[3]

As another example, consider the handshake—a simple ritualistic greeting between persons, which many cultures enact. Have you ever considered the power of a handshake to communicate? If you get a weak, half-handed, limp handshake from someone, what are you likely to conclude about that person? Recent research focused on just that, judgments we make about someone's personality based on a simple greeting ritual. William Chaplin and his colleagues first determined characteristics of handshakes that contribute to what they term a handshake index.[4] Such attributes as strength, vigour, completeness of grip, and duration were examined. The high index or most positive handshake was strong (but not so strong as to cut off the blood supply), vigorous (meaning it had an appropriate amount of energy exuded), adequate in duration (not too brief or too long), and complete in its grip (meaning that full hands were gripped, with palms touching). Next they studied subjects' judgments of persons with a high handshake index versus a low handshake index. These researchers found that the higher a person's handshake index, the more that person was believed to be extroverted, open to experience, and less shy. In addition to these traits, women with high handshake indexes were also perceived to be highly agreeable, in comparison to women with weak or poor handshakes. Subjects in the study also formed more favourable first impressions of those persons with high handshake indexes than those with low indexes. A simple symbolic, culturally rooted gesture can have a definite and long-lasting impact on how others perceive you.

Nonverbal cues are important not only in the early stages of relationships, but also as we maintain, deepen, and sometimes terminate those relationships. In fact, the more intimate the relationship, the more we use and understand the nonverbal cues of our partners. Long-married couples spend less time verbalizing their feelings and emotions to each other than they did when they were first dating; each learns to interpret the other's subtle nonverbal cues. If a spouse is silent during dinner, the other spouse may know that the day was a tough one and to give the person a lot of space. In fact, all of us are more likely to use nonverbal cues to convey negative messages than to announce our explicit dislike of something or someone.[5] We also use nonverbal cues to signal changes in the level of satisfaction with a relationship. When we want to cool things off, we may start using a less vibrant tone of voice and cut back on eye contact and physical contact with our partner.

Nonverbal Messages Serve Various Functions for Verbal Messages

Although we rely heavily on nonverbal messages alone, they can serve multiple functions for spoken messages in our relationships. First, nonverbal cues can *substitute* for verbal messages. An extended thumb signals that a hitchhiker would like a ride, a water skier wants more speed, or a pilot is ready for takeoff. When someone asks, "Where's the elevator?" we can point instead of voicing a response. In these instances, we substitute nonverbal cues for verbal messages.

Nonverbal cues delivered simultaneously with verbal messages *complement,* clarify, or extend the meaning of the verbal, allowing for fuller information and a more accurate interpretation. When someone waves, makes eye contact, and says "hello," the gesture and eye contact serve as nonverbal complements to the verbal greeting. Complementary cues also help colour our expressed emotions and attitudes. The length of a hug while you tell your daughter you're proud of her provides additional information about the intensity of your pride. A long, heavy sigh may reveal how tired or bored you are.

Sometimes, however, our nonverbal cues *contradict* rather than complement our verbal cues. Remember Danita, who said she wasn't mad the whole time she was acting and sounding mad? In an instance like this, the nonverbal cues contradict the verbal ones. The nonverbal message is almost always the one we should believe.

We also use nonverbal cues to *repeat* our words. "I'm new on campus; where's the Centre for the Arts?" asks a student. "Go to the right of that two-storey, red brick building, and it's just on the other side" says a security guard, who then points to the building. The guard's pointing gesture repeats the verbal instruction and clarifies the message.

We also use nonverbal cues to *regulate* our participation in conversation. In most informal meetings, it's not appropriate or necessary to signal your desire to speak by raising your hand. Yet somehow you're able to signal to others when you'd like to speak and when you'd rather not. You use eye contact, raised eyebrows, an open mouth, an audible intake of breath, a change in posture or seating position, or a single raised index finger to signal

ReCAP

Why Focus on Nonverbal Communication?

- Nonverbal communication is our primary means of communicating feelings and attitudes toward others.
- Nonverbal messages are usually more believable than verbal messages.
- Nonverbal communication is critical in relationship initiation, development, and termination.
- Nonverbal messages can substitute for, complement, contradict, repeat, regulate, and accent verbal messages.

that you would like to make a point. If your colleagues don't see these signals, especially the eye contact, they may assume you're not interested in engaging in conversation.[6]

Finally, we use nonverbal behaviour to *accent* or reinforce a verbal message. "We simply must do something about this problem," bellows the mayor, "or else we will all bear the blame." When the mayor said the word "must," she pounded the podium and increased her volume for emphasis. When she said "all bear the blame," she used a circling gesture with her arms, as if to convey a shared responsibility among those in the room. These vocalizations and gestures serve to accent or add intensity to the verbal message.

THE NATURE OF NONVERBAL COMMUNICATION

While the benefits of studying and improving our facility with nonverbal communication are clear, deciphering unspoken messages is a tricky activity. Dictionaries help us interpret words, but no handy reference book exists to help decode nonverbal cues. Below are some of the challenges inherent in the interpretation of nonverbal communication.

The Culture-Bound Nature of Nonverbal Communication

Some evidence suggests that humans from every culture smile when they are happy and frown when they are unhappy.[7] They also all tend to raise or flash their eyebrows when meeting or greeting others, and young children in many cultures wave to signal they want their parents, raise their arms to be picked up, and suck their thumbs for comfort.[8] This evidence suggests that there is some underlying commonality or shared experience in human emotion. Yet each culture tends to develop unique rules for displaying and interpreting the expression of emotion.

It's important to realize that nonverbal behaviour is culture bound. No common cross-cultural dictionary of nonverbal meaning exists. You will make critical errors in communicating nonverbally, as well as in attempting to interpret the nonverbal behaviour of others, if you don't situate nonverbal actions within a cultural context. As intercultural communication scholars Richard Porter and Larry Samovar explain, "Because most nonverbal communication is culturally based, what it symbolizes often is a case of what a culture has transmitted to its members."[9] They also offer this important advice: Be aware that one culture's friendly or polite action may be another culture's obscene gesture.

When Canadian diplomats travelled to the former Soviet Union, they had to be fully briefed on Soviet customs. If they weren't briefed, they might have misinterpreted a Soviet leader's response to applause—a hand-clasped, shaking gesture to the side of the head—as indicating, "We've won the Cold War," instead of being the Canadian equivalent of applauding along with an audience or waving to acknowledge a crowd. Or consider the story of one of our former students—a man of 25 or so—who described his awkwardness when walking down the streets of a city in Turkey, holding the hand of the Turkish father of his girlfriend while she held the father's other hand. The student's girlfriend made him aware of the custom and warned him not to react negatively or try to loosen his hand from the father's, which would have been a serious cultural offence. His Canadian cultural background made this an uncomfortable experience, but he adapted out of respect.

Most nonverbal communication is culture bound. But one of the most universal nonverbal cues among human beings is the smile.

The Rule-Governed Nature of Nonverbal Communication

You have many rules operating with regard to nonverbal communication. You may be unaware that you function according to these rules, but when your rules are violated, you definitely know it. For example, have you ever been in a conversation with someone who seemed as though he or she just couldn't talk to you without touching you? Maybe it's just a series of simple touches on the forearm or shoulder, but it's not what you expect in casual conversation. For some reason, the other person's rule about appropriate touch is likely to be different from yours. Or perhaps you've been annoyed when people talk at the movie theatre, as if they were sitting at home in their own living rooms instead of out in public. Maybe you have a rule that says people lower their voices and whisper at movie theatres, if they must talk at all; other people may not hold that same rule.

One of the most prolific nonverbal communication researchers is Judee Burgoon, who developed a fascinating model for how nonverbal communication functions, termed the **expectancy violations model.**[10] The model suggests that we develop expectations for appropriate nonverbal behaviour in ourselves and others, based on our cultural background, personal experiences, and knowledge of those with whom we interact. When those expectations (or rules) are violated, we experience heightened arousal (we become more interested or engaged in what's happening), and the nature of our interpersonal relationship with the other person becomes a critical factor as we attempt to interpret and respond to the situation. Because the expectancy violations model was first developed with regard for personal space, let's consider an example that deals with this form of nonverbal communication.

A hilarious *Seinfeld* episode depicted a person nicknamed the "close talker," because he got too close for most people's comfort when he talked to them. Most people within a given culture adhere to a widely agreed-upon rule or expectation as to appropriate conversational distances. But then there are those people who don't seem to catch the cultural clue—those who get too close to our face in casual conversation. Burgoon's model says that we register such nonverbal violation and react in order to adjust to the circumstances. If the violating person is what Burgoon terms a "rewarding" communicator, meaning that the person has high credibility, status, and attractiveness (physically or in personality), we may view the behaviour as less of a rule violation and simply adjust our expectations. We may even reciprocate the behaviour. However, if the violator is not a rewarding communicator, we will use reactive nonverbal behaviours in an effort to compensate for or correct the situation. So if an attractive, credible, and high-status person talks too closely to you, you may adapt to the situation and not think negatively of the person. If the person has less attractiveness, credibility, and status, you may back up from the person, move away or to the side so as to increase the conversational distance, break eye contact, and so forth.

Our tendency in a rules violation situation is to attempt to adapt or correct the violation by nonverbal means before resorting to verbal communication. You're more likely to back up from the "close talker" than to say to her or him, "Please back up; you're violating my personal space." We all violate nonverbal rules from time to time; it is at those moments when we become acutely aware that rules or expectations of appropriateness have a powerful influence on nonverbal communication.

⋯⟩ The Ambiguous Nature of Nonverbal Communication

Most words are given meaning by people within a culture who speak the same language. But the exact meaning of a nonverbal message is known only to the person displaying it; the person may not intend for the behaviour to have any meaning at all. Some people have difficulty expressing their emotions nonverbally. They may have frozen facial expressions or monotone voices. They may be teasing you, but their deadpan expressions lead you to believe that their negative comments are heartfelt. Often it's a challenge to draw meaningful conclusions about other persons' behaviour, even if we know them quite well. One strategy that helps us interpret others' nonverbal cues is called **perception checking,** a strategy we mentioned in Chapter 2 in our discussion of self-awareness. Observe in detail the nonverbal cues, make your own interpretation, and then do one of two things (or both): (1) Ask the people you're observing how they feel or what's going on and (2) run your interpretation by another observer, to get a second opinion or more input before you draw a conclusion. Remember our earlier warning about not assuming that your interpretation is necessarily the right one; perception checking can enhance the likelihood of your interpretation being more accurate.

⋯⟩ The Continuous Nature of Nonverbal Communication

Words are discrete entities; they have a beginning and an end. You can point to the first word in this sentence and underline the last one. Our nonverbal behaviours are not as

---

ETHICAL PROBE

If you took a job with an organization in a foreign country, you would move and take your culturally rooted nonverbal behaviour with you. For example, when meeting new people, you would most likely make direct eye contact and extend your hand for a handshake, just as you are used to doing in Canada. But what if this isn't the custom in the new country? Should you change some of your nonverbal behaviour when you choose to live in another culture, or should you retain the nonverbal customs of your culture of origin? As another example, a behaviour that is perfectly acceptable in the Canadian workplace could be construed as sexual harassment in a foreign workplace. Would your actions constitute an ethical breach, or should your international hosts cut you some slack because you come from a different culture?

expectancy violations model
A model that suggests that we develop rules or expectations for appropriate nonverbal behaviour and react when those expectations are violated.

perception checking
Skill of asking other observers or the person being observed whether your interpretation of his or her nonverbal behaviour is accurate.

easily dissected. Like the sweep of a second hand on a watch, nonverbal behaviours are continuous. Because gestures, facial expressions, and eye contact can flow from one situation to the next with seamless ease, interpreting nonverbal cues is challenging.

···⟩ The Nonlinguistic Nature of Nonverbal Communication

Even though writers in the 1960s and 1970s tried to make us think otherwise, there is no "language of the body." Julius Fast, author of the 1970 book *Body Language,* believed that nonverbal communication was a language with pattern and grammar, just like verbal communication.[11] He suggested that if you were savvy and observant enough, you could quickly and easily interpret certain nonverbal behaviours to mean certain things—in any case, at any time. For example, Fast contended that if a woman sat cross-legged and pumped her foot up and down while talking to a man, that was a clear-cut sign of her romantic interest in him. If someone didn't make eye contact, she or he was automatically dishonest and untrustworthy. If people crossed their arms in front of them, that indicated hostility.

The problem with this approach is that it didn't take into account the complexities of individual, contextual, and cultural differences. Pumping the foot might be an indication of nervousness, not attraction. Some people are shy; others come from a culture in which making direct eye contact is considered rude. Crossed arms may be a comfortable position, or they may signal that one is cold (temperature-wise). It's important to remember that nonverbal communication doesn't conform to the patterns of a language.

···⟩ The Multichannelled Nature of Nonverbal Communication

Have you ever tried to watch two or more TV programs at once? Some televisions let you see as many as eight programs simultaneously so that you can keep up with three ball games, two soap operas, the latest news, and your favourite sitcom. Like a multichannel TV, nonverbal cues register on our senses from a variety of sources simultaneously. Just as you can watch only one channel at a time on your multichannel television, you actually attend to only one nonverbal cue at a time, although you can move among them very rapidly. Even though you can only process one nonverbal cue at a time, before you try to interpret the meaning of someone's behaviour, look for clusters of corroborating nonverbal cues, in conjunction with verbal behaviour, to get the most complete picture possible.

CODES OF NONVERBAL COMMUNICATION

Because human nonverbal behaviour is so diverse and vast, the need arises for classifications. Many individuals have long been fascinated with nonverbal communication, but

---

Re**CAP** ⟨···

The Nature of Nonverbal Communication

- *Nonverbal Communication Is Culture Bound:* Nonverbal behaviours vary widely across cultural and co-cultural groups. Interpret nonverbal cues within a cultural context.

- *Nonverbal Communication Is Rule Governed:* We develop rules or expectations for appropriate nonverbal behaviour in ourselves and others.

- *Nonverbal Communication Is Ambiguous:* Nonverbal behaviour is difficult to accurately interpret because the meanings for different actions vary from person to person.

- *Nonverbal Communication Is Continuous:* Unlike the stop–start nature of verbal communication, nonverbal messages flow from one situation to the next.

- *Nonverbal Communication Is Nonlinguistic:* Nonverbal communication does not have the regularities of vocabulary, grammar, and pattern that language has.

- *Nonverbal Communication Is Multichannelled:* Nonverbal cues register on our senses from a variety of sources simultaneously, but we can actually attend to only one nonverbal cue at a time.

perhaps the minds making the greatest contributions belong to Paul Ekman and Wallace Friesen, sometimes referred to as the "great classifiers" of nonverbal behaviour. The primary categories or codes of nonverbal information researchers have studied include appearance; body movement, gestures, and posture; eye contact; facial expressions; touch; the voice; and use of the physical environment, space, and territory. Although we concentrate on these codes as they are exhibited in mainstream Western culture, recognize that these behaviours are evidenced differently in other cultures. We introduce and explain each code, then provide a few research findings to illustrate how we can apply knowledge of nonverbal communication to our understanding of human behaviour.

Appearance

Many cultures around the world place a high value on appearance—body size and shape, skin colour and texture, hairstyle, and clothing. We realize that we're writing from a North American perspective, but it seems as though North Americans place an undue emphasis on looks. We put such pressure on ourselves and others to be physically attractive that lowered self-esteem may result if we realize we cannot match up with some perceived "ideal."[13] Americans elevate onto a pedestal persons who are perceived to be highly physically attractive, whether or not they actually deserve this kind of accolade. We also attach all sorts of desirable qualities to highly attractive people. Research shows that we tend to think physically attractive people are more credible, happy, popular, socially skilled, prosperous, employable, persuasive, honest, poised, strong, kind, outgoing, and sexually warm.[14]

Clothing functions primarily to keep us warm and within society's bounds of decency. Another important function is to convey a sense of one's culture. For example, clothing such as baseball caps, baggy pants, and specialized T-shirts, as well as other appearance aspects, termed **artifacts** (jewellery, tattoos, piercings, makeup, cologne, eyeglasses, and so on), are displays of culture. This is particularly detectable when you travel abroad or entertain visitors from foreign lands in your home country. The brightly coloured gowns and matching headpieces worn by some African women, the beautiful saris (draped dresses) many Indian women wear, and veils over the faces of Muslim women are but a few examples of how clothing reveals one's culture.

Although we don't believe that "clothes make the man," clothing and artifacts do affect how we feel about ourselves and how we are perceived by others.[15] Studies have attempted to identify a "power" look. Advertisers are constantly giving us prescriptions for ways to be attractive and stylish, but the fact is that there is no formula for dressing for success.[16] Styles and expectations about appearances change. We have only to look at the clothing norms of the 1950s, 1960s, or 1970s (if you dare) to note how they are different from those of today. Other interesting applications of what we know about appearance include the development of "casual Friday" in the corporate world, the connection between black uniforms and aggression in sports, and the growing trend in public schools to require school uniforms.[17]

Body Movement, Gestures, and Posture

Have you ever travelled in a country in which you couldn't speak the language? Or have you tried to have a conversation locally with a person who didn't speak English or who was deaf and didn't read lips? What does a person do in these situations? Chances are, the person will risk looking extremely foolish by using overexaggerated gestures or slowly and deliberately shouting words the listener cannot understand. These responses are nonverbal attempts to compensate for a lack of verbal understanding. Even when we do speak the same language as others, we often use gestures to help us make our point.

Kinesics is a general term for human movements, gestures, and posture. Technically, movements of the face and eyes are contained within this category, but because one's face and eyes can produce such a wealth of information, we discuss them as separate codes. We have long recognized that our kinesics provide valuable information to others. In Chapter 12 we explore ways that the movements, gestures, and posture of a public speaker reveal volumes of information to an audience.

Various scholars and researchers have proposed models for analyzing and coding kinesics, just as we do for spoken or written language.[18] In one of their most comprehensive

artifact
Clothing or another element of appearance (e.g., jewellery, tattoos, piercings, makeup, cologne).

kinesics
The study of human movement, gesture, and posture.

contributions to nonverbal research, Paul Ekman and Wallace Friesen classified movement and gestures according to their function. They identified five kinesic categories: emblems, illustrators, affect displays, regulators, and adaptors.[19]

Emblems

emblem
A nonverbal cue that has a specific, generally understood meaning in a given culture and may substitute for a word or phrase.

Nonverbal cues that have specific, widely understood meanings in a given culture and may actually substitute for a word or phrase are called **emblems.** When you're busy typing a report that is due tomorrow and your roommate barges in to talk about weekend plans, you turn from your computer and hold up an open palm to indicate your desire for uninterrupted quiet. A librarian wants people to stop talking in the stacks, so he or she puts an index finger up to pursed lips. But remember that emblems emerge or are negotiated within cultures. Something as seemingly universal as a smile can be seen by people in some cultures as a sign of aggression, just as an animal would bare its teeth.

Illustrators

illustrator
A nonverbal behaviour that accompanies a verbal message and either complements, contradicts, or accents it.

We frequently accompany a verbal message with nonverbal behaviours or **illustrators** that either contradict, accent, or complement the message.[20] Yawning while proclaiming that you're not tired is an example of a nonverbal illustrator that contradicts the verbal message. Slamming a book closed while announcing, "I don't want to read this any more" is a nonverbal accent to a verbal message. Frequent complementary illustrators are used when one person gives another directions to a location. You probably even use them when you talk on the phone, although probably not as many as you use in face-to-face conversation.[21]

Affect Displays

affect display
A nonverbal behaviour that communicates emotions.

Nonverbal cues that communicate emotion are called **affect displays.** As early as 1872, when Charles Darwin systematically studied the expression of emotion in both humans and animals, humans realized that nonverbal cues are the primary ways we communicate emotion.[22] For most of us, our facial expressions, posture, and gestures reveal our emotions.[23] Your face tends to express which *kind* of emotion you are feeling, while your body reveals the intensity or how *much* of the emotion you are feeling. If you're happy, for example, your face may telegraph your joy to others. The movement of your hands, the openness of your posture, and the speed with which you move tell others just how happy you are. Likewise, if you're depressed, your face reveals your sadness or dejection, unless you're very practised at masking your emotions. Your slumped shoulders and lowered head indicate the intensity of your despair.

Regulators

regulator
A nonverbal message that helps to control the interaction or level of communication between people.

Regulators control the interaction or flow of communication between ourselves and other persons. When we're eager to respond to a message, we're likely to make eye contact, raise our eyebrows, open our mouth, take in a breath, and lean forward slightly. When we do not want to be part of the conversation, we do the opposite: We avert our eyes, close our mouth, cross our arms, and lean back in our seats or away from the verbal action.

Adaptors

adaptor
A nonverbal behaviour that helps satisfy a personal need and helps a person to adapt or respond to the immediate situation.

As teachers, it's interesting to watch a group of students take an exam. Students who are nervous about the exam or who have general test anxiety exhibit their nervousness in many different ways. They shift frequently in their seats, tap their pencil or pen on the desktop (often unconsciously), or run their hands through their hair over and over again. Then there's the thigh shaker. Some students can make their legs quiver up and down at a high speed, and they don't usually realize they're doing it. All of these behaviours are examples of **adaptors**—nonverbal behaviours that help us to satisfy a personal need and adapt to the immediate situation.

What are some of the more interesting applications of the research on kinesics? How about flirting? Even if you're married or in some other form of committed relationship, you probably find it interesting to think about how people flirt or show attraction and interest in one another. Research has explored verbal and nonverbal indications of attraction.[24] One study found 52 gestures and nonverbal behaviours that women use to signal their interest in men. Among the top nonverbal flirting cues were smiling, surveying a crowded room with the eyes, and moving closer to the object of one's affection.[25] However, there's a downside to this line of research: Other studies have found that men often misinterpret women's friendly behaviour as signs of sexual attraction and interest.[26] One study found that the likelihood for this kind of misinterpretation greatly increased as alcohol consumption increased.[27]

Another body of research along these lines has examined **quasi-courtship behaviour,** those nonverbal actions we consciously and unconsciously exhibit when we are attracted to someone.[28] The first stage of quasi-courtship behaviour is *courtship readiness.* When we are attracted to someone, we may alter our normal pattern of eye contact, suck in our stomach, tense our muscles, and stand up straight. The second stage includes *preening* behaviours, which include combing our hair, applying makeup, straightening our tie, pulling up our socks, and double-checking our appearance in the mirror. Research shows that women tend to preen more than men.[29] In stage three, we demonstrate *positional cues,* using our posture and body orientation to be seen and noticed by another person, as well as to position ourselves to prevent invasion by a third party. We intensify these cues in the fourth stage, termed *appeals to invitation,* using close proximity, exposed skin, open body positions, and direct eye contact to signal our availability and interest.

quasi-courtship behaviour
Nonverbal actions consciously and unconsciously exhibited when we are attracted to someone.

⤏ Eye Contact

Do you agree that the eyes truly are the "windows to the soul"? What can people tell about you by looking into your eyes? Are you comfortable making eye contact with most people or only with people you know well? Eye contact is extremely important in North American culture, as well as many other cultures around the world. North Americans, in particular, make all kinds of judgments about others—particularly their trustworthiness and sincerity—from the way they make or avoid eye contact. It's an interesting exercise to inventory your own eye behaviour, thinking about when you're apt to look at someone and when you're apt to avert your gaze.

You are most likely to look at a conversational partner when you are physically distant from her or him, discuss impersonal topics, have nothing else to look at, are interested in your partner's reactions, are romantically interested in your partner, try to dominate or influence your partner, come from a culture that emphasizes visual contact in interaction, are an extrovert, are listening rather than talking, and are female. You are less likely to look at your partner when you are physically close; discuss intimate topics; have other relevant objects, people, or backgrounds to look at; are not interested in your partner's reactions;

ReCAP ⤛┈┈

Categories of Movements and Gestures

CATEGORY	DEFINITION	EXAMPLE
Emblems	Behaviours that have specific, generally understood meanings	A hitchhiker's raised thumb
Illustrators	Cues that accompany verbal messages and provide meaning	A speaker's pounding on the podium to emphasize a point
Affect Displays	Expressions of emotion	Hugging to express love
Regulators	Cues that control and manage the flow of communication	Making eye contact when you wish to speak
Adaptors	Behaviours that help you adjust to your environment	Chewing your fingernails, indicating nervousness

are talking rather than listening; are not interested in or dislike your partner; come from a culture that does not value visual contact during interaction; are an introvert; are embarrassed, ashamed, sorrowful, sad, submissive, or trying to hide something; and are male.[30]

Research shows that eye contact plays a significant role in the judgment of a public speaker's credibility, as we discuss more thoroughly in Chapter 12.[31] Patrick Gossage, a former press secretary and speech writer for Pierre Trudeau, coaches people on communicating more effectively through his Toronto-based company, Media Profile. Gossage's theory was developed in part by watching speeches made by people such as Pierre Trudeau and Henry Kissinger. They used techniques such as modulation of tone and pace, incorporating pauses and making eye contact. When speaking about good communication Gossage states, "you engage the audience with your body and your eyes and your whole person."[32]

Studies on eye behaviour continue to contribute to our understanding of deception, meaning how people behave when they lie or mislead others.[33] Eye behaviours most often associated with deception include rapid eye blinking, diminished eye contact, and rapid eye movement.

Facial Expressions

No matter whether or not you like actor/comedian Jim Carrey, you've got to admit that the guy's face is made of rubber. He seems to be able to display a broader range of emotions and reactions on his face than the average person, even if many of these facial contortions are more exaggerated than the average person would desire to use. Ekman and Friesen, prominent scholars we mentioned previously, suggest that the human face is capable of producing 250 000 different facial expressions.[34] Jim Carrey can probably make all of them.

The face is the exhibit gallery for our emotional displays. You buy a new expensive gadget and show it to your romantic partner or a friend. As an interviewer reads your resumé, you sit in silence across the desk. In both of these situations, you scan the other person's face, eagerly awaiting some reaction. To interpret someone's facial expressions accurately, you need to focus on what the other person may be thinking or feeling. It helps if you know the person well, can see her or his whole face, have plenty of time to observe, and understand the situation that prompted the reaction.[35]

How accurately do we interpret emotions expressed on the face? Researchers who have attempted to measure subjects' skill in identifying the emotional expressions of others have found it a tricky business.[36] According to Ekman and Friesen, the human face universally exhibits six primary emotions: happiness, sadness, surprise, fear, anger, and disgust or contempt. But these researchers suggest that, even though our faces provide a great deal of information about emotions, we quickly learn to control our facial expressions.[37] One fascinating study examined children's facial expressions when they received either wonderful, new toys or broken, disappointing toys.[38] With the disappointing toys, the children flashed disappointment on their faces, but then very quickly masked their disappointment and changed their facial expressions to reveal a more positive, socially appropriate reaction. Even very young children learn to control the way an emotion registers on their face. Another study found that abused children, sensitive to violence at home, are hypersensitive to anger in facial expressions. They are more likely to interpret sad or fearful facial expressions as angry.[39]

As adults, we come to realize that there are times when it is inappropriate and unwise to reveal our emotions fully, such as crying in front of superiors when we've been passed over for promotion or becoming visibly angry when a project doesn't come our way. But there are times when this learned masking of emotion—the development of a "poker face"—can endanger your relationships. Consider aloof, distant parents who can't separate themselves from their work to enjoy the company of their own children, or romantic partners who complain that they can't tell how their partners feel about them because emotional displays have been squelched and masked. The best approach is a balance of control and spontaneity. You want to stay real and human, to be able to reveal to others what you feel, but there are times when doing so can be inappropriate or damaging.

COMMUNICATION and TECHNOLOGY

Conveying Emotions Electronically

Without the usual nonverbal mechanisms in face-to-face communication that allow us to reveal our emotions to others, how do we let others at a distance know what we're feeling? E-mail has all but replaced the fine art of letter writing, but people who used to or still write letters typically insert a parenthetical phrase or symbol to convey the nonverbal message behind the verbal. The most common usage is the happy face or "smiley" that can be easily written into the text of a letter. But how is this accomplished when e-mail is your primary communication channel with someone?

If you use e-mail, perhaps you've learned a few nonverbal methods for communicating emotion. One form is to put certain words in all caps, a technique known as "shouting," which typically reveals emphasis, frustration, or even anger. You may have also seen the clever use of punctuation and other symbols that the common keyboard can make to form a visual image. These sideways images, termed "emoticons," are forms of nonverbal communication that help convey the meaning or emotion behind a message. The most common emoticon is the happy face, made by combining a colon, dash, and right parentheses mark, as in :-). Here are others located from various sources.[40]

:-(	Depressed or upset by a remark
:-l	Indifferent
:-|	Straight face
:-o	Surprise
;-)	Winking at a suggestive or flirtatious remark
:-/	Skeptical
:-P	Sticking your tongue out
:-D	Laughing
:-@	Screaming
:D	Drunk
8-)	Wearing sunglasses
::-)	Wearing regular glasses
(-:	Left-handed

Touch

Touch is the most powerful form of nonverbal communication; it is also the most misunderstood and carries the potential for the most problems if ill used. Consider some moments involving accidental touch. Standing elbow to elbow in an elevator or sitting next to a large individual in a crowded airplane, you may find yourself in physical contact with total strangers. As you stiffen your body and avert your eyes, a baffling sense of shame and discomfort floods over you. Why do we react this way to accidental touching? Normally, we touch to express intimacy. When intimacy is not our intended message, we instinctively react to modify the impression our touch has created.

Countless studies on touch, termed **haptics** in research, have shown that intimate human contact is vital to our personal development and well-being.[41] Infants and children need it to confirm that they are valued and loved. Advocates of breast-feeding argue that this form of intimate touching strengthens the bond between mother and child.[42]

haptics
The study of human touch.

Think about your role models and the lessons you learned about touch while growing up. If you grew up in a two-parent family, did your parents display affection in front of the children? If not, you may have grown up believing that affectionate touch between intimates is not something done within view of anyone. As an adult, you may be uncomfortable with

touch ethic
A person's own guidelines or
standards as to appropriate and
inappropriate touch.

public displays of affection. If you grew up with parents and extended family members who were affectionate with each other and their children, then, as an adult, your **touch ethic**—what you consider appropriate touching—is influenced by that experience. We don't mean to insinuate that a touch ethic that accepts public affection is somehow more psychologically healthy than one in which touching is relegated to private moments. But what if you date or partner with someone whose experiences while growing up led to a touch ethic very different from yours? You may be headed for some conflict and we hope some compromise.

The amount of touch we need, initiate, tolerate, and receive depends on many factors. As we've indicated, the amount and kind of touching you receive in your family is the biggest influence. Your cultural background has a significant effect as well. Certain cultures are high-contact—meaning that touching is quite commonplace—such as in some European and Middle Eastern countries where men kiss each other on the cheek as a greeting. Other cultures are low-contact, like some Asian cultures in which demonstrations of affection are rare and considered inappropriate.[43]

Research on haptics has explored such topics as how touch may be involved in behaviour deemed sexually harassing.[44] Other research continues to focus on gender differences and touch. For years, studies showed that women touched members of both sexes more often and received more touches than men, leading to the conclusion that touch was more a female-appropriate than male-inappropriate behaviour. Recent studies suggest that sex differences have diminished in terms of the frequency of touch, but men and women still tend to differ in the meanings they assign to touch.[45] For example, some touches extended from women to men, intended as indications of friendship, are often interpreted by men as signals of romantic or sexual interest.

····⟩ The Voice

Like your face, your voice is a major vehicle for communicating your thoughts and emotions. The pitch, rate, and volume at which you speak, and your use of silence—elements termed **paralanguage** or **vocalics**—all provide important clues. Imagine that your spouse, romantic partner, or best friend purchased and modelled a new outfit, asking you what you think. If you really hated the person's new outfit, would you say enthusiastically, "That looks GREAT!"—which could either be an untruth designed to

paralanguage (vocalics)
Nonverbal aspects of voice (e.g.,
pitch, rate, volume, use of silence).

····⟩•⟨···· **COMMUNICATION and TECHNOLOGY**

Listening and Silence in Cyberspace

In her fascinating book, *Life Online: Researching Real Experience in Virtual Space*, Annette Markham discusses silence in cyberspace.[46] She describes the experience of interviewing online users for information for her book, and how she had to learn to be patient and to tolerate silence in order to give the other person time to respond.

I had to learn to slow down to give participants enough time to respond fully to the questions. When I was interviewing Beth, I would ask a question and wait for what seemed like a long time for her to respond. Sometimes, if I didn't see writing on the screen shortly . . . I would wonder if she had received the message. Then I would wonder if she was still there. Then, to make sure she was there, I would send the same message again, or another message asking if she got the first one. I'm sure it drove Beth crazy. In

effect, I interrupted almost every story she tried to tell. I couldn't help myself. I felt compelled to fill the blank, black void with more green writing. I couldn't stand what I thought to be silence. To solve this problem, I forced myself to focus on other things. Most interviewers learn to wait patiently in face-to-face contexts, but here it took concentrated effort to not type. Sometimes I resorted to sitting on my hands.

In a world of "instant everything" and immediate communication channels like e-mail and faxes, it's interesting to consider how some everyday experiences, like silence, are being redefined. If you chat with people in an electronic newsgroup format, how do you handle response time lags that some technology causes? Is the amount of time it takes for us to register silence in a face-to-face conversation similar to the amount of time in an electronic format?

<···> **COMMUNICATION** and **DIVERSITY**

Cultural Meanings

In "Culture Shock—Exploring Cross-Cultural Diversity," Mumtax Mahal stresses the importance of understanding cultural differences when trying to sell a new product in the marketplace.[47] He believes that language, communication styles, colours, numbers, symbols, tradition, and individualistic versus collectivist environments are factors to be taken into consideration. Within communication styles, he suggests that Canadians, Americans, and most Europeans are very low-context people—they state what they are thinking with little need for nonverbal cues or nuances. Asians and Latin Americans are high-context people and use body language, status, relationships, and silence to communicate meaning.

The Asia Connects Youth Conference, held in Winnipeg in 1998, intended to bring together Canadian and Asian youth to identify and appreciate similarities and differences between both cultures. Emphasis was placed on various aspects of these two cultures, including cross-cultural communication. Included in these discussions was the use of "silence" in the communication process. Canadians were perceived as not being comfortable with silence, tending to fill spaces with "small talk." In contrast, in some Asian countries silence is an acceptable form of communication, used to seek understanding, perceiving others in silence, without words. For more information, visit **www.tgmag.ca/ap/report/reporta_e.html.**

prevent hurt feelings or an expression of sarcasm? Or would you say, "That looks nice" in a half-hearted way? Or would you go into some long, careful explanation of why you thought the outfit was okay, but just not your favourite thing? Your ability to convey these different reactions is accomplished by the human voice.

The voice reveals our thoughts, emotions, and the nature of our relationships with others, but it also provides information about our self-confidence and knowledge. Most of us would conclude, as has research, that a speaker who mumbles, speaks very slowly and softly, continually mispronounces words, and uses "uhs" and "ums" is less credible and persuasive than one who speaks clearly, rapidly, fluently, and with appropriate volume.[48]

In addition to providing information about thoughts, emotions, self-confidence, and knowledge, vocal cues serve a regulatory function in conversation, signalling when we want to talk and when we don't. When we're finished talking, we tend to lower the volume and pitch of our final words. When we want to talk, we may start by interjecting sounds such as "I . . . I . . . I . . . " or "Ah . . . Um . . . " to interrupt the speaker and grab the verbal ball. We also may use more cues like "Sure," "I understand," "Uh-huh," or "Okay" to signal that we understand another's message and now we want to talk or end the conversation. These vocalizations, termed **back-channel cues,** are particularly useful in telephone conversations when no other nonverbal cues can help signal that we would like to get off the phone.

Sometimes it's not what we say or even how we say it that communicates our feelings. Pausing and being silent communicate volumes.[49] You may be at a loss for words or need time to think about what you want to contribute to a conversation, so pausing or being silent may be better than fumbling about for the right way to express yourself. When someone tells a lie, he or she may need a few moments to think up what to say. Nonverbal researchers have studied **response latencies,** or how long it takes someone to formulate a response to a statement or question in conversation, to better understand vocal cues that may indicate deception.[50] You may be silent because you want to distance yourself from those around you or indicate that you don't want to engage in conversation. Silence can be a sign of respect, but it can also be an indication of anger, as in giving someone "the silent treatment," or discomfort, as in "an awkward silence." At other times you may feel so comfortable with someone that words aren't necessary; psychologist Sidney Baker calls these moments "positive silence."[51]

back-channel cue
A vocal cue that signals when we want to talk and when we don't.

response latency
How long it takes someone to formulate a response to a statement or question in conversation.

···> Environment, Space, and Territory

Close your eyes and picture your bedroom as it is right now—whether it's a dorm room that you share with someone, the room you've lived in for many years in your parents' house, or a bedroom shared with a spouse or partner. Try to get a clear, detailed mental image of how that room looks right now. Then think about this: If a total stranger were to walk into your bedroom right now, what would she or he think about you? What impressions about you would be conveyed by the physical setup of that room? Does the room reveal how you relate to space? Does it show its owner's need for privacy? Are there hints as to who owns the space, meaning do you have any territorial clues in the room? Is the closet door in that room open or closed? What would the status of your closet reveal about you if a stranger looked in?

These questions all have to do with your interaction with the physical environment and the space around you. You may be unused to looking at the environment as a form of nonverbal communication, but the mini-world you create for yourself reveals a good deal about you. Also, your preferences for space, the level of ownership you attach to that space, and your behaviour as you delineate and protect that space are fascinating nonverbal elements that researchers continue to study.

The Physical Environment

What's so great about a corner office with wall-to-wall windows? It's one of many indications in Canadian culture of high status. As one scholar put it, "People cannot be understood outside of their environmental context."[52] In Chapter 3 we learned several principles governing the use of verbal language, one being that language is context bound or that people derive meaning of words in context. Likewise, nonverbal actions are only meaningfully interpreted when context is taken into account.[53] The environment is important to the study of nonverbal behaviour in two ways: (1) The choices you make about the environment in which you live and operate reveal a good deal about who you are, and (2) your nonverbal behaviour is altered by the changing environments with which you come into contact.

First, the physical environments in which we function can be seen as extensions of our personalities. You may not be able to manipulate all elements of your environment, such as the physical limitations of room size, but to whatever extent you are allowed, you will make your "signature" on your physical environs. Humans like to structure and adorn the settings in which they work, study, and reside to make them unique and personal. Rarely will you find an office, even a cubicle, that contains absolutely no personal artifacts.

Second, your behaviour and perceptions are altered because of the physical environments in which you find yourself.[54] Your body may be more rigid, gestures more restrained, clothing more formal, and talking minimal and at a whisper when you're in a church. (Obviously, this depends on the church.) In contrast, at a concert of a favourite musician, you move freely, wear comfortable clothing, and scream and applaud wildly.

The knowledge that humans react according to their interface with a physical environment has been put to some interesting uses. For example, designers of fast-food restaurants often use vibrant colours, uncomfortable seating, and brightly lit eating areas to discourage patrons from lingering. The point in the fast-food business is high volume, which means high turnover. So these environments are constructed so that you will be attracted to come in, eat, and leave quickly to make room for another customer. In contrast, some restaurants want to create an intimate and warm environment, one that makes customers want to linger and enjoy a long meal (with a pricey tab).[55]

Space

Imagine that you are sitting alone at a long, rectangular table in your campus library. As you sit dutifully with your head in a textbook, you are startled when a complete stranger sits directly across from you at the table. Since there are several empty chairs at the other end of the table, you may feel uncomfortable that this unknown individual has invaded *your* area.

Every culture has well-established ways of regulating spatial relations. Normally, we don't think much about the rules or norms we follow regarding space, until those rules are violated. Violations can be alarming, possibly even threatening. How physically close we are willing to get to others relates to how well we know them, to considerations of power and status, and to our cultural background.

FIGURE 4.2   Edwin T. Hall's Four Zones of Space

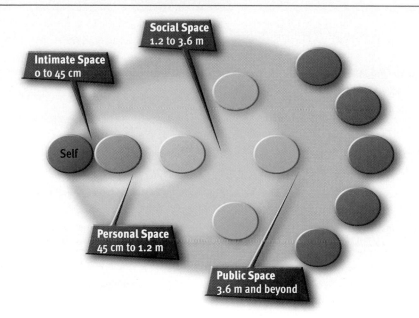

One of the pioneers in helping us understand personal space was Edward T. Hall. In his study of **proxemics,** Hall identified four spatial zones that we unconsciously define for ourselves, shown in Figure 4.2.[56] When we're between zero and 45 centimetres from someone, we're occupying an *intimate space* in which the most personal communication occurs. It is open only to those with whom we are well acquainted, unless we're forced to stand in an elevator or some other crowded space.

The second zone, ranging from 45 centimetres to 1.2 metres, is called *personal space.* Most of our conversations with family and friends occur in this zone. If someone we don't know well invades this space on purpose, we may feel uncomfortable. Zone three, *social space,* ranges from 1.2 to 3.6 metres. Most formal group interactions, as well as many of our professional relationships, take place in this zone. *Public space,* the fourth zone, begins at 3.6 metres. Interpersonal communication does not usually occur in this zone; many presentational speakers position themselves at least 3.6 metres away from their audiences.

The specific space that you and others choose depends upon several variables, most specifically your cultural background. But the more you like people, the closer you will stand to them. Higher-status and larger persons are afforded more space than lower-status and smaller persons.[57] We also tend to stand closer to others in a large room than we do in a small room. In general, women tend to stand closer to others than men do.[58]

proxemics
Study of how close or far away from people and objects we position ourselves.

Territory

The study of how people use space and objects to communicate occupancy or ownership of space is termed **territoriality.**[59] You assumed ownership of that table in the library and

territoriality
Study of how humans use space and objects to communicate occupancy or ownership of space.

ReCAP

Edward T. Hall's Classification of Spatial Zones

CATEGORY	DEFINITION	EXAMPLE
Zone One	Intimate Space	Zero to 45 centimetres
Zone Two	Personal Space	45 centimetres to 1.2 metres
Zone Three	Social Space	1.2 to 3.6 metres
Zone Four	Public Space	3.6 metres and beyond

ReCAP ⬅······

Codes of Nonverbal Communication

Appearance	Influences perceptions of credibility and attraction
Body Movement, Gestures, and Posture	Communicate information, status, warmth, credibility, interest in others, attitudes, and liking
Eye Contact	Conveys trustworthiness, sincerity, honesty, and interest
Facial Expressions	Reveal thoughts and express emotions and attitudes
Touch	Communicates intimacy, affection, and rejection
The Voice	Communicates emotion through pitch, rate, and volume; clarifies the meaning of messages
Environment	Communicates information about the person who owns an environment; provides context that alters behaviour
Space	Provides information about status, power, and intimacy
Territory	Provides cues as to use, ownership, and occupancy of space

territorial marker
A thing or action that signifies an area has been claimed.

the right to determine who sat with you. You may have reacted negatively not only because your sense of personal space was invaded but also because the intrusive stranger broke a cultural rule governing territoriality.

You announce your ownership of space with **territorial markers**—things and actions that signify an area has been claimed. When you arrive at class, for example, you may put your book bag on a chair while you get up and sharpen a pencil or run across the hall to the "facilities." That book bag signifies temporary ownership of your seat. If you returned to find that someone had moved your stuff and was sitting in your seat, you would probably become indignant. The most common form of territorial marker is a lock. We lock our doors and windows, cars, offices, briefcases, luggage, televisions (in the form of V-chips), and computers so as to keep out intruders.

We also use markers to indicate where our space stops and someone else's starts. "Good fences make good neighbours," wrote the poet Robert Frost. When someone sits too close, we may try to erect a physical barrier, such as a stack of books or a napkin holder, or we might use our body as a shield by turning away. If we can't erect a physical barrier, we may erect a symbolic barrier to convey ownership, through the use of such things as partitions, objects, lighting, or elevation.[60] If an intruder doesn't get the hint that "this land is our land," we may ultimately resort to words to announce that the space is occupied.

One interesting line of research explores workplace verbal and nonverbal behaviours that contribute to a "hostile climate" of sexual harassment.[61] In relation to the environment, space, and territoriality, a workplace might contain art (posters, flyers on bulletin boards) that depicts sexual images, a boss might come too far into the personal space of an employee, or a co-worker might commit a territorial breach by "snooping" in someone's office for evidence of personal relationships, such as photos.

HOW TO INTERPRET NONVERBAL CUES MORE ACCURATELY

How do we make sense out of all of the nonverbal cues we receive from others? Time and patience improve your receiving ability. If you earnestly want to accurately interpret and sensitively respond to someone's nonverbal communication, it takes time and diligent effort to develop this skill. You have already learned a good deal about nonverbal communication from reading this chapter, studying this topic in class, and living as many years as you have lived. But enhancing this skill requires, first, an awareness of the importance of nonverbal elements in the communication process. Many people make interpretive mistakes because they overemphasize the words people say. Verbal communication is important; but remember that the greater portion of someone's total message is conveyed nonverbally. A second requirement is the willingness and emotional maturity to make your own behaviour secondary to that of someone else. In other words, if you're wrapped up in yourself or so emotionally out of control that you can only think about and deal with how you're feeling, what you're thinking, and what you want at a given moment, you can't possibly hope to take in others' nonverbal cues, accurately interpret them, and respond appropriately. As we discussed in Chapter 2, an awareness of oneself as a communicator expands with each interaction with another person.

It's also important to remember to take into account the cultural backgrounds of persons you observe. Be careful not to automatically attach your own cultural frame of reference when you decipher nonverbal cues. As we've stated, the context within which nonverbal cues are communicated plays an important role. It's wise to be aware of your surroundings and other situational factors when interpreting meaning from nonverbal actions. Be prepared to fail. We all struggle to make sense out of others' actions; no one has this skill down pat. Use your interpretive failures as lessons learned for the next encounter.

Albert Mehrabian, an expert in the area of nonverbal communication, provides a helpful framework for interpreting nonverbal communication. He found that we synthesize and interpret nonverbal cues along three primary dimensions: immediacy, arousal, and dominance.[62]

What nonverbal cues tell you that these people genuinely like each other? Are there any cues that contradict that impression?

 Immediacy

Why do we like some people and dislike others? Sometimes we can't put a finger on the precise reason. Mehrabian contends that **immediacy**—nonverbal behaviour that communicates liking and engenders feelings of pleasure—is a probable explanation. The principle underlying immediacy is simple: We like and respond positively to people who tend to display immediacy cues and avoid or respond negatively to those who don't. In brief, immediacy cues that show liking and interest include the following:[63]

immediacy
Feelings of liking, pleasure, and closeness communicated by such nonverbal cues as eye contact, forward lean, touch, and open body orientation.

- Proximity: Close, forward lean
- Body orientation: Direct, but could be side-by-side
- Eye contact: Eye contact and mutual eye contact
- Facial expression: Smiling
- Gestures: Head nods, movement
- Posture: Open and relaxed, arms oriented toward others
- Touch: Cultural- and context-appropriate touch
- Voice: Higher pitch, upward pitch

So how do you apply this information to help you improve your nonverbal receiving skills? Let's say that you go to a party and become attracted to someone there. You're introduced to the person and engage in a get-to-know-you kind of conversation. Your best bet is to attend to the person's nonverbal cues to determine whether the person likes you or not. Although you can't know for sure that someone's nonverbal behaviour translates into liking, immediacy cues can provide some information. Watch for a direct body orientation, as opposed to someone who tends to turn away from you and orient herself or himself toward the rest of the room. Watch for eye contact, smiling and other pleasant facial expressions, a rising intonation in the voice, and a forward lean toward you, rather than a backward lean, which can signal disinterest.

Arousal

When the term **arousal** is used in nonverbal research, it doesn't necessarily mean sexual arousal. According to nonverbal scholar Peter Andersen, the term relates to "the degree to

arousal
Feelings of interest and excitement communicated by such nonverbal cues as vocal expression, facial expressions, and gestures.

which a person is stimulated or activated."[64] Arousal prepares the body for action, with such physiological indications as increased heart rate, blood pressure, and brain temperature. Arousal, in this sense, can occur when you drive fast or experience athletic exhilaration. Externally, the face, voice, and movement are primary indicators of arousal. If you detect arousal cues in someone, such as increased eye contact, closer conversational distances, increased touch, animated vocalics, more direct body orientation, and more smiling and active facial expressions, you can conclude with some degree of certainty that the other person is responsive to and interested in you or what you have to say. If the person acts passive or bored, as evidenced by non- or low-arousal cues, you can safely conclude that he or she is uninterested.

Imagine you're at that same party and you decide to become a people-watcher for a moment. Check out which people look interested in the persons they're talking to and which ones look bored or as if they'd rather be somewhere else, anywhere else. You can tell how people feel about each other—not with absolute accuracy, but with a high degree of certainty—just by looking for things like body orientation (whether they are facing each other directly or not), synchronized movement (meaning that when one shifts in position, the other shifts, as in a rhythmic response), smiling, laughter, and other arousal cues.

⋯⟩ Dominance

dominance

Feelings of power, status, and control communicated by such nonverbal cues as relaxed posture, greater personal space, and protected personal space.

The third dimension of Mehrabian's framework communicates the balance of power in a relationship. **Dominance** cues communicate status, position, and importance. When interacting with a person of lower status, a higher-status person tends to have a relaxed body posture, less direct body orientation to the lower-status person, and less smiling and facial animation.[65] When you talk to professors, they may lean back in the chair, put their feet on the desk, and fold their hands behind their head during the conversation. But unless your professors are colleagues or friends, you will maintain a relatively formal posture during your interaction in their offices.

The use of space is another dominance cue. High-status individuals usually have more space around them; they have bigger offices and more "barriers" (human and nonhuman) protecting them. A receptionist in an office is usually easily accessible, but to reach the CEO of the company you probably have to navigate through several corridors and past several secretaries and administrative assistants who are "guarding" the door.

Other power cues include the use of clothing, furniture, and locations. You may wear jeans and a T-shirt to class; the president of the university probably wears a business suit. You study at a table in the library; the college dean has a large private desk. Your dorm may be surrounded by other dorms; the president's residence may be a large house surrounded

ReCAP ⋯⟩

Dimensions for Interpreting Nonverbal Behaviour

DIMENSION	DEFINITION	NONVERBAL CUES
Immediacy	Cues that communicate liking and pleasure	Eye contact, touch, forward lean, direct body orientation, close distances, smiling
Arousal	Cues that communicate active interest and emotional involvement	Eye contact, varied vocal cues, touch, animated facial expressions, direct body orientation, movement, close distances
Dominance	Cues that communicate status	Larger and protected space, eye contact, initiated touch, relaxed posture, status symbols

by a lush, landscaped garden in a prestigious neighbourhood. You struggle to find a parking place within a half-a-globe from your classroom buildings; high-ranking campus administrators usually have reserved, plum parking spots (sometimes with their names on them).

When you attempt to interpret someone's nonverbal communication, realize that there is a good deal of room for error. Humans are complex, and they don't always send clear signals. But the more you learn about nonverbal communication, the more you become aware of your own communication and the communication of others, the greater your chances of accurately perceiving and interpreting someone's nonverbal message.

SUMMARY

Successful communicators effectively use and interpret nonverbal messages. Nonverbal communication is central to our ability to function competently in relationships, because we convey our feelings and attitudes and detect the emotional states of others primarily through nonverbal channels. In most cases, when verbal and nonverbal messages contradict, we should believe the nonverbal because it tends to carry the truer meaning of the message. (Again, leave open the option that you may be wrong.) Nonverbal cues are important not only in the early stages of relationships, but also as we maintain and deepen and sometimes terminate those relationships. Nonverbal messages function with verbal messages, in that they can substitute for, complement, contradict, repeat, regulate, and accent our words.

Accurately interpreting nonverbal cues is a challenge because of the nature of nonverbal communication. First, nonverbal communication is culture bound, meaning that we must account for the cultural context within which behaviour occurs before making an interpretation as to what that behaviour means. Second, nonverbal communication is rule-governed, in that we form rules or expectations as to appropriate behaviour. Third, nonverbal communication is ambiguous; the exact meanings of nonverbal messages are truly known only to the person displaying them. Fourth, nonverbal communication is continuous; it flows in a steady stream without a definite starting and stopping point. Fifth, unlike verbal communication, nonverbal communication is not a language with a set pattern and rules of usage. Its nonlinguistic nature makes for more complicated interpretation. Finally, nonverbal communication is multichannelled,

meaning that cues register on our senses from a variety of sources simultaneously.

Nonverbal cues have been categorized into separate codes. Personal appearance is a powerful communicator, especially in North American culture where we make all sorts of personality judgments based on someone's looks. Kinesics, which include body movement, posture, and gestures, communicate both content and relational information when we use them as emblems, illustrators, affect displays, regulators, and adaptors. Eye contact is an important code for conveying liking and regulating interaction. Facial expressions and vocal cues provide a wealth of information about our thoughts, emotions, and attitudes. Touch is the most powerful nonverbal cue; it communicates the level of intimacy in a relationship, as well as liking and status. Finally, the way we react to and manipulate environments, as well as our use of space and territory, communicate a variety of messages related to power and status.

It is a challenge to assess our own nonverbal communication and to read and interpret others' nonverbal messages, but a general framework developed by Mehrabian can assist us in the process. Three primary dimensions for interpreting nonverbal messages have been identified in research: Immediacy cues provide information about liking and disliking; arousal cues tip off others as to our interest and level of engagement with them; and position, power, and status are often communicated through dominance cues. Humans are complex, so the interpretation of nonverbal cues is never simple. However, the more we learn about this form of behaviour and become aware of our own and others' nonverbal communication, the more sensitively and effectively we will interact with others.

Discussion and Review

1. Why focus on nonverbal messages? Why are nonverbal cues important?

2. Identify six elements that describe the nature of nonverbal communication. Then think about persons who seem to be "clueless," meaning that they do not readily attend to or accurately interpret others' nonverbal behaviour. What makes some people savvy readers of nonverbal cues while others remain clueless?

3. How is nonverbal communication affected by culture? Provide examples of ways that a lack of cultural understanding can cause problems.

4. Why do you think that Canada places such importance on appearance and attractiveness? Is this emphasis helpful, harmful, or a bit of both?

5. Explain how eye contact, facial expressions, and various vocal cues reveal our thoughts, emotions, and attitudes.

6. What is your "touch ethic"? What experiences growing up contributed to your standards for appropriate and inappropriate touch?

7. How you manipulate the environments within your control and use space and territory reveal a great deal about you. What would someone learn about you if she or he observed you in your home environment? What kind of interpretations would the observer make from watching you use and control space?

8. Explain the three-part system Mehrabian developed that enables us to interpret nonverbal cues more accurately.

Developing Your Skills: Putting Principles into Practice ⋮

1. Take a mini-field trip with some classmates to a fast-food restaurant. Assign some members the task of observing nonverbal cues related to the environment, noting colours, furniture and other fixtures, lighting, and temperature. Others should take note of the employees' appearance, paying special attention to clothing and signs of status and individuality. Finally, have some members watch for gestures that develop into emblems, such as signals as to how many burgers a customer wants. Co-workers often develop nonverbal "shorthand" that facilitates efficient communication.

2. How are "normal" nonverbal cues altered when a person attempts to be deceptive? Using the categories of kinesics, facial expressions, eye contact, and proxemics, generate examples of how nonverbal behaviours are affected by deception. For example, how is eye contact affected? Do the best liars avert their gaze, or do they learn to lie while looking right in someone's eyes?

3. For the following six emotions, generate examples of body movements that reveal that emotion. Then generate alternative meanings for the movement. For example, we've said that crossed arms might reveal anger but also that someone is closed off or not open to discussing something. We've provided a sample using the emotion of embarrassment.

Emotion	Body Movements	Alternative Meanings
Embarrassment	Covering the face with one's hands	Could also indicate deception
Happiness		
Anger		
Surprise		
Fear		
Disgust		
Sadness		

4. We've explored the nonverbal codes of space and territory and have a better understanding of the range of human reactions to space invasions. Read each of these situations, decide whether a proxemic or territorial violation has occurred, and then generate two tactics you would use in response to each situation. Try not to think of things a person might do, but of what you would realistically do in the situation.

   a. You are at a bar or club, sitting alone, possibly waiting to order or for a friend to join you. A stranger sits down beside you and starts a conversation.

   b. You are a business executive. You enter your office after lunch and find your secretary sitting at your desk.

   c. You are taking a racquetball class, and it is your turn on the glass (observable) court. A group of people gather to watch your lesson.

   d. You are interviewing for a part-time job. The interviewer moves from behind the desk toward you and touches you on the knee.

   e. You want to wear your favourite sweater but can't find it. You discover it wadded up in the bottom of the laundry hamper, reeking of smoke, and realize that your roommate or a family member wore it without your permission.

5. Conduct a series of role plays that illustrate Mehrabian's system for interpreting nonverbal behaviour. Using a hypothetical situation, such as two students sitting in a classroom listening to a biology lecture, have one student role-play high immediacy and one role-play low immediacy, using nonverbal cues only. Do the same for arousal and dominance.

Martha Walter, "Slavs against the White Wall," 1921. Oil on canvas. © David David Gallery, Philadelphia/SuperStock

Listening, not imitation, may be the sincerest form of flattery.

— JOYCE BROTHERS

5 Listening and Responding

AFTER STUDYING THIS CHAPTER, YOU SHOULD BE ABLE TO

1. Explain the principle of listening and responding thoughtfully to others.

2. Identify the elements of the listening process.

3. Identify and describe barriers that keep people from listening well.

4. Identify skills that can improve communication sensitivity.

5. Identify and use appropriate responding skills and understand strategies for improving them.

It shows up on every list of what effective communicators do: They listen. You spend more time listening to others than almost anything else you do. Canadians spend 70% of their "awake time" communicating. Of that time, 10% is spent writing, 15% is spent reading, 30% is spent speaking, and 45% is spent listening.[1] One of the hallmarks of being an effective leader is to be a good listener.[2] To be sensitive is to be aware of others and to be concerned about others. Increasing your skill in listening to others is one of the most productive ways to increase your communication sensitivity. As shown in Figure 5.1, if you're typical, you spend the least amount of your communication time writing, yet that is where you receive more training than any other communication skill. Most people have not had formal training in listening or responding. In this chapter we focus on the principle of increasing your sensitivity to others by listening. Becoming sensitive to others includes more than just understanding and interpreting the words, thoughts, and ideas of another—sensitivity also involves understanding the emotions of words and unspoken messages of others.

In addition to listening, as shown in our now familiar model of the communication principles for a lifetime in Figure 5.2, we also discuss strategies for responding thoughtfully to others. Effective communicators do more than absorb a message; they provide an appropriate response to the speaker. We'll address both listening and responding to others in this chapter.

Listening and responding to others is an important principle of communication, not only because you spend more time listening than any other communication activity, but also because of its importance in establishing and maintaining relationships with others. In interpersonal communication situations, your ability to listen and respond is at the heart of your ability to maintain a conversation with someone. A satisfying conversation occurs when all participants feel a comfortable level of give and take in listening and responding to others. The essence of being a good conversationalist is being a good listener. Rather than focusing only on what to say, a person skilled in the art of conversation listens and picks up on interests and themes of others.

Being a good listener is also an essential skill when communicating with others in small groups. Whether you are the appointed or emerging leader of a group or are a stalwart group or team member, your ability to listen and connect to others will affect your value to other group members. Group members afflicted with bafflegab, those who verbally dominate group meetings, are not typically held in high esteem. Groups need people who can listen and connect conversational threads that often become tangled or dropped in group dialogue.

It may be less clear how being an effective listener can enhance a presentational speaker's ability to connect with an audience. Effective speakers, however, are those who

FIGURE 5.1 What You Do with Your Communication Time

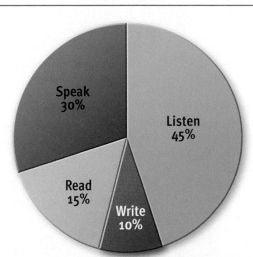

FIGURE 5.2 Fundamental Principles of Human Communication

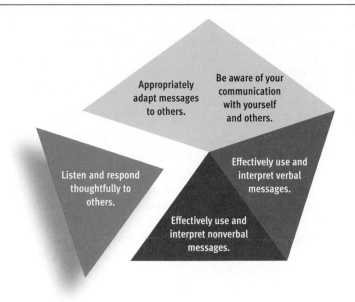

can relate to their listeners; good speakers know how to establish a relationship with the audience by listening to audience members one on one before a talk or lecture. Good speakers are also audience-centred. They consider the needs of their listeners first. They understand what will hold listeners' attention.

HOW WE LISTEN

Do you know someone who is interpersonally inert? Interpersonally inert people are those who just don't "get it." You can drop hints that it's late and you'd rather they head home instead of playing another hand of cards, but they don't pick up on your verbal and nonverbal cues. They may *hear* you, but they certainly aren't listening; they are not making sense out of your symbols. **Hearing** is the physiological process of decoding sounds. You hear when the sound vibrations reach your eardrum and buzz the middle ear bones: the hammer, anvil, and stirrup. Eventually, the sound vibrations are translated into electrical impulses that reach your brain. In order to listen to something, you must first select that sound from competing sounds. **Listening** is the process we use to make sense out of what we hear. Stated succinctly, listening is a complex process of receiving, constructing meaning from, and responding to verbal and nonverbal messages.[3] Listening involves five activities: (1) selecting, (2) attending, (3) understanding, (4) remembering, and—to confirm that listening has occurred—(5) responding.

···⟩ Selecting

To **select** a sound is to focus on one sound bite as you sort through the myriad noises competing for your attention. Even now, as you are reading this book, there are probably

hearing
The physiological process of decoding sounds.

listening
A complex process of receiving, constructing meaning from, and responding to verbal and nonverbal messages, which involves five steps: selecting, attending, understanding, remembering, and responding.

selecting
The process of sorting through various sounds competing for your attention.

Once we select the sounds we want to listen to, we need to attend to, or focus on, those sounds for communication to take place.

attending
The process of focusing on a particular sound or message.

understanding
The process of assigning meaning to messages.

remembering
The process of recalling information that has been communicated.

countless sounds within earshot. Stop reading for a moment. What sounds surround you? Do you hear music? Is a TV on? Maybe there is the tick of a clock, a whir of a computer, or a whoosh of a furnace or an air conditioner. To listen—to be sensitive to another person—you must first select the sound or nonverbal behaviour that symbolizes meaning. The interpersonally inert person does not pick up on the clues because he or she is oblivious to the information. To listen, you must select which of the sounds or behaviours will receive your attention.

Attending

After selecting a sound, you attend to it. To **attend** is to focus on a particular sound or message. When you change channels on your TV, you first select the channel and then you attend to or focus on the program you've selected. Attention can be brief. You may attend to the program or commercial for a moment and then move on or return to other thoughts or other sounds. Just as you tune in to TV programs that reflect your taste in information while you channel surf, you attend to messages of others that satisfy your needs or whims.

What holds our attention? In general, conflict, humour, new ideas, and real or concrete things command your attention more easily than abstract theories or other topics that don't relate to you. Most people focus on their own needs. You are also more likely to tune someone in when you are specifically invited to listen and respond, than when someone speaks or behaves in ways that aren't other oriented and don't take your needs into consideration. You become bored when your needs aren't met.

Understanding

To **understand** is to assign meaning to messages—to make sense out of what you hear. You can select and attend to sounds and nonverbal cues but not interpret what you see and hear. Seeing and hearing are physiological processes. Understanding occurs when we relate what we see and hear to our experiences or knowledge. There are several theories about how you assign meaning to words you hear, but there is no single theory that best explains how the process works. We know that you are more likely to understand messages if you can relate what you are hearing and seeing to something you already know.

The more similar you are to others, the greater the likelihood that you will accurately understand them. People from different cultures who have substantially different religions, family lifestyles, values, or attitudes often have difficulty understanding each other, particularly in the early phases of a relationship.

You understand best that which you also experience; the more senses that are involved, the greater the chance of holding your attention and increasing your accuracy of interpretation. Perhaps you have heard the Montessori school philosophy: I hear, I forget; I see, I remember; I experience, I understand. Hearing alone does not provide us with understanding. It's been estimated that we hear more than one billion words each year, but we understand a mere fraction of that number.

Remembering

Remembering information is included in the listening process because it's the primary way we determine whether a message was understood. To **remember** is to recall information. Some scholars speculate that you store every detail you have ever heard or witnessed; your mind operates like a computer's hard drive, recording each life experience. But you cannot retrieve or remember all of the bits of information. Sometimes, even though you were present, you have no recollection of what occurred in a particular situation. You can't consciously remember everything; your eye is not a camera; your ear is not a microphone; your mind is not a hard drive.

The first communication principle we presented in this book is to become self-aware. When we are not self-aware of our actions, thoughts, or what we are perceiving—when

COMMUNICATION and DIVERSITY

Gender and Listening

Do men and women listen differently? One researcher says it's not so much that they listen differently as that they attend to information in different ways.[4] When men listen, they may be looking for a new structure or organizational pattern or to separate pieces of information they hear. The male attention style is to shape, form, observe, inquire, and direct effort toward a goal. Men's attention style also is reported to be more emotionally controlled than women's attention style. Women's attention style is more emotionally involved and tends to be more empathic and subjective. Women are more likely to search for relationships among parts of a pattern and to rely on more intuitive perceptions or feelings. These differences in attention styles and the way men and women process information can potentially affect listening, even though we do not have clear-cut research that links attention style to listening skills.

Research suggests that men tend to listen to solve a problem—to get to the bottom line when listening. Women are more likely to listen to seek new information to enhance understanding. Women also listen to establish personal relationships. It is not accurate to suggest that men listen better than women or vice versa. Emerging patterns in the research suggest there are listening differences. Perhaps men need to listen a bit more like women, and women need to listen more like men. In any case, gender-based differences in attention style and information processing may explain some of the relational problems that husbands and wives, lovers, siblings, and men and women friends and colleagues experience.[5] We caution you, however, in assuming that communicating with a member of the opposite sex is like interacting with someone from a different planet. Avoid making sweeping generalizations about the way others speak and listen.

Research suggests that women and men can be equally good listeners; but in addition to differences in how we focus on messages, we often listen for different reasons. Communication researcher Melanie Booth-Butterfield found that the sexes actually learn to listen for different reasons.[6] Because men tend to view communication as serving the primary purpose of information exchange, they tend to listen to receive facts. They listen more for the "big picture" or major ideas than for details. They also listen so that they can give advice and solve problems, rather than listening to reflect understanding of the other person. Women tend to attend to the details of what is being said, as well as to the speaker's nonverbal behaviours (such as tone of voice, gestures, and facial expressions accompanying certain words). And they tend to listen primarily to detect the mood of the other person and to offer support.[7] Obviously, this difference in approaches to listening can cause serious problems when a man and a woman attempt to converse.

So how can you use this information? It's not that women cannot listen for information and men cannot listen in support of others; it's more in how we prefer to listen, how we are taught and reinforced to listen. So we may have to reteach ourselves or unlearn some listening habits. If the situation suggests that listening to gain information is warranted, men and women are equally capable of accomplishing that task. Women may have a harder time merely listening for facts, rather than reading into the conversation more than those facts or attempting to "take the emotional temperature" of the other person. What if, however, the information someone is relating doesn't seem to be the main reason for the conversation? What if you perceive that the person just needs you to listen—not to solve the problem or offer advice or disagree to show him or her the error in his or her thinking? In this circumstance, you should work to adapt your approach and offer support as a listener by listening with your ears and your eyes. The skill comes in detecting accurately what the situation requires (the principle of self-awareness) and then adapting your behaviour so that you engage in the situation appropriately and communicate effectively.

we are mindless—our ability to remember what occurs plummets. We increase our ability to remember what we hear by being not only physically present, but mentally present.

Our brains have both short-term and long-term memory storage. Short-term memory is where you store almost all the information you hear. You look up a phone number in the telephone book, mumble the number to yourself, then dial the number, only to discover that the line is busy. Three minutes later you have to look up the number again because it did not get stored in your long-term memory. Our short-term storage area is limited. Just as airports have relatively few short-term parking spaces, but many spaces for long-term parking, our brains can accommodate a few things of fleeting significance, but not vast amounts of information. Most of us forget hundreds of bits of insignificant information that pass though our cortical centres each day.

You tend to remember what is important to you, or something you try to remember or have practised to remember (like the information in this book for your next communication test). You tend to remember dramatic information (such as where you were when you heard about the SARS outbreak) or vital information (such as your phone number or your mother's birthday).

⇢ Responding

As we learned in Chapter 1, communication is a transactive process—not a one-way, linear approach. Communication involves responding to others as well as simply articulating messages. You **respond** to people to let them know you understand their message. Your lack of response may signal that you didn't understand the message. As we learned in the previous chapter, our predominant response is unspoken; direct eye contact and head nods let our partner know we're tuned in. An unmoving, glassy-eyed, frozen stupor may tell our communication partner that we are physically present, yet mentally a thousand kilometres away.

LISTENING BARRIERS

Although we spend almost half of our communication time listening, some say we don't use that time well. Most people remember a day later only about half of what was said. It gets worse. An additional day later, our listening comprehension drops by another 50%. The result: Most of us remember about 25% of what we hear two days after hearing a lecture or speech.

Our listening deteriorates not only when we listen to speeches or lectures, but also when we interact interpersonally. Even in the most intimate relationships (or perhaps we should say especially in the most intimate relationships), we tune out what others are saying. One study reported that we sometimes pay more attention to strangers than to our close friends or spouses. Married couples tend to interrupt each other more often than nonmarried couples and are usually less polite to each other than are strangers involved in a simple decision-making task.[8]

What keeps us from listening well? The most critical elements viewed from the perspective of the model of communication we introduced in Chapter 1 include three things: (1) self-barriers—personal habits that work against listening well; (2) information processing—the way we mentally manage information; and (3) context—the surroundings in which we listen.

⇢ Self-Barriers

Some people find that yoga or quiet meditation can help them control the internal barriers that prevent them from listening effectively.

"We have met the enemy and he is us" is the oft-quoted line from the comic strip *Pogo*. Evidence suggests we are our own worst enemy when it comes to listening to others—whether it's listening to enjoy, learn, evaluate, or empathize. We mentally comment on the words and sights that we see and hear. Our internal thoughts are like a play-by-play sports commentator describing the action of a sports contest. If our internal narration is focused on the message, then it may be useful. But we often attend to our own internal dialogues and diatribes instead of others' messages; when we do that, our listening effectiveness plummets.

Inattentive listening is like channel surfing when we watch TV—pushing the remote control button to switch from channel to channel, avoiding commercials, and focusing for brief periods on attention-grabbing program "bites." When we listen to others, we may tune in to the message for a moment, decide that it is boring or useless, and then focus on a personal thought. These personal competitions for listening to others stem from several habits and tendencies.

Self-Focus

That personal play-by-play commentary we may be carrying on in our minds is typically about us. "How long will I have to be here for this lecture?" "Wonder what's for dinner tonight?" "I've got to get that report finished." "She's still talking—will we be out of here in ten minutes?" "Do I have a school meeting tonight or is that tomorrow night?" Focusing on an internal message often keeps us from selecting and attending to the other person's message. If there is a competition between listening to what someone else may be droning on about and focusing on our own needs and agenda, our personal needs often bubble to the top of the list of priorities. Another symptom of self-focus is our tendency to think about what we are going to say while we look like we are listening to someone else.

What's the antidote for the self-focus we typically have when listening to others? The first and one of the most important actions is drawing on the first principle of communication we introduced in Chapter 1 and developed in Chapter 2: Become aware of your actions. Diagnosing the problem is the first step in managing the problem. Become consciously competent. Note consciously when you find yourself drifting off, thinking about your agenda or running commentary on what you see and hear, rather than concentrating on the speaker.

A second suggestion: Concentrate. When you become aware that your internal messages are distracting you from listening well, double your efforts to stay on task. If your internal "announcer" is telling you the message is boring, useless, or stupid, make sure you don't automatically tune out. Yes, some messages are boring, useless, and stupid. But the habit of quickly dismissing ideas and messages without effort will keep you from being nominated for the Listening Hall of Fame.

You can also improve your concentration by relating the speaker's topic to your own interests. Dig for information you can use. Search for connections between what you already know and information that is unfamiliar to you.

Here's another suggestion: Be actively involved in the communication process by taking notes and, when appropriate, providing feedback to the speaker; this strategy can also help you stay on track. Also, if the speaker is using words and phrases you don't understand, write down the words you don't understand so you can look them up later. The key to concentration is finding ways to be active rather than passive when words bombard your ears. Don't just sit there and "take it"; if you find your concentration waning, you'll more than likely "leave it."

Emotional Noise

Emotions are powerful. Your current body posture, facial expression, and even your blood pressure are affected by your emotional state. What we see and hear affects our emotions. **Emotional noise** occurs when our emotional arousal interferes with communication effectiveness. Certain words or phrases can arouse emotions very quickly; and, of course, the same word may arouse different emotions in different people. You respond emotionally because of your cultural background, religious convictions, or political philosophy. Words that reflect negatively on your nationality, ethnic origin, or religion can trigger strong emotional reactions. Cursing and obscene language may also reduce your listening efficiency. If you grew up in a home in which R-rated language was never used, then four-letter words may distract you.

emotional noise
A form of communication noise caused by emotional arousal.

Sometimes it's not just a word but a concept or idea that causes an emotional eruption. Third-trimester abortion and public school prayer, for example, are sure-fire ways to get radio talk show hosts' audiences involved in lively discussion. Whether you love him or hate him, TV talk show host Jerry Springer is a master at pushing emotional hot buttons for his talk show guests; and when emotions become heated, thoughtful listening is rare.

The emotional state of the speaker may also affect your ability to understand and evaluate what you hear. One researcher found that if you are listening to someone who is emotionally distraught, you will be more likely to focus on his or her emotions than on the content of the message.[9] Another researcher advises that when you are communicating with someone who is emotionally excited, you should remain calm and focused, and try simply to communicate your interest in the other person.[10]

What are other strategies to keep your emotions from getting the best of you? It's not always easy, but research suggests there are ways of not letting your emotions run amok. Daniel Goleman offers several research-based strategies in his best-selling book *Emotional Intelligence*.[11] To be emotionally intelligent is to have the ability to understand, manage, and appropriately express emotions. For example, one simple yet powerful strategy to manage emotions when you find you may be ready to lose it is to take a deep breath. Yes, just breathe. Taking a deep, slow breath is a way of regaining control by calming us down. It helps makes us more conscious of our anger or frustration, much like the old technique of counting to ten. Another strategy for managing emotions is to use the power of self-talk, a concept we discussed in Chapter 2. Tell yourself you won't get angry. Early detection of

Mother Teresa understood the value of open listening without prejudging a person.

the emotions bubbling inside you can help you assess and then manage emotions before your nonrational, emotional impulses take control. As we've noted, we're not suggesting it's inappropriate to experience emotions; however, unchecked, intense emotional outbursts do not enhance your ability to listen, comprehend, or empathize with others.

Sometimes, of course, expressing your frustration is appropriate. We're not suggesting you go through life unrealistically serene or that you avoid experiencing emotions. Only the dead and mentally incompetent could follow the prescription of never becoming emotional. We do suggest that you become aware of the effect that emotions have upon your listening ability; this is a constructive first step to avoid being ruled by unchecked emotions. The principle of self-awareness gives you *choice* and control, rather than simply letting emotions go unchecked. Your listening challenge is to avoid emotional sidetracks and keep your attention focused on the message. When emotionally charged words or actions kick your internal dialogue into high gear, make an effort to quiet it down and steer back to the subject at hand. Becoming consciously aware of our emotions and then talking to ourselves about our feelings is a way of not letting emotions get out of hand.

Criticism

We usually associate the word "criticism" with negative judgments and attitudes. Although critiquing a message can provide positive as well as negative insights, most of us don't like to be criticized. Mother Teresa once said, "If you judge people, you have no time to love them."[12] Being inappropriately critical of the speaker may distract us from focusing on the message.

A person's appearance and speech characteristics can affect your ability to listen to him or her. Many a speaker's droning monotone, lack of eye contact, and distracting mannerisms have contributed to his or her ideas not being well received—even if the ideas are potentially life-changing for the listener. The goal of a sensitive communicator is to be conscious of when the delivery or other distracting features of the message or messenger are interfering with your ability simply to listen. In fact, now that you are studying principles of communication, you may find that this problem looms even larger, because you now pay more attention to nonverbal cues.

It would be unrealistic to suggest that you refrain from criticizing speakers and their messages. It is realistic, however, to monitor your internal critiques of speakers to make sure you are aware of your biases. Good listeners say to themselves, "While this speaker may be distracting, I am simply not going to let the appearance or mannerisms keep my attention from the message." For example, Stephen Hawking is a prize-winning physicist at Cambridge University in England; because of a disability, he is able to speak only with the aid of computer-synthesized sounds. He is unquestionably brilliant. If you let his speaking delivery overpower you, you'd miss his marvellous message. Avoid using your mental energy to criticize a speaker unnecessarily; the longer your mental critique, the less you'll remember.

Information-Processing Barriers

In addition to self-barriers that contribute to our loss of focus on messages, sometimes the way in which we use the information that comes to our eyes, minds, and hearts creates listening problems. The way in which we process the information we hear may keep us from being a good listener. Four information-processing listening barriers include (1) our information-processing rate, (2) information overload, (3) receiver apprehension, and (4) shifting attention.

Processing Rate

An extension of the self-barriers of self-focus, emotions, and criticism is the manner in which we process information. One of the barriers that has long been documented is the difference between our ability to process information and the rate at which information comes to us. The barrier boils down to this: You can think faster than people speak. Most people speak 125 words per minute, give or take a few words. You have the tremendous ability, however, to process four to ten times that amount of information. Some people can listen to 600 to 800 words a minute and still make sense out of what the speaker is saying;

another estimate puts the processing rate up to 1200 words per minute. Yet another estimate claims that we think not just in words but also in images and sounds: We can process 2000 bits of information a minute for short periods of time. This difference between your capacity to make sense out of words at the speed at which they register in your cortical centres can cause trouble. You have extra time on your hands to tune in to your own thoughts, rather than to focus on the speaker.[13]

You can use your information-processing rate to your advantage if you use the extra time to summarize mentally what a speaker is saying. By periodically sprinkling in mental summaries during a conversation, you can dramatically increase your listening ability and make the speech-rate/thought-rate difference work to your advantage.

Information Overload

Information abounds. We are constantly bombarded with sights and sound bites, and experts suggest that the amount of information competing for our attention is going to increase in the future. Incoming messages and information on computers, fax machines, e-mail, car phones, beepers, and other technological devices can interrupt conversations and distract us from listening to others.

The amount of information coming at us on any given day also wears us out. The one word to describe many a poor listener is "weary." We spend 45% of our communication time listening, and the pace at which the information zips toward us exhausts us. The billion words that we hear contribute to our fatigue.

Again we recommend self-awareness. Be on the alert for drifting attention due to information overload. And when the encroaching information dulls our attentiveness to messages, either take a break or consider communication triage (determine what's urgent and what's not urgent) to sort through the information that is most important.

Receiver Apprehension

Just as some people are fearful of presenting a speech or speaking up during a meeting, research suggests that some people are fearful of receiving information. **Receiver apprehension** is being fearful of misunderstanding or misinterpreting the messages spoken by others or not being able to adjust psychologically to messages expressed by others.[14] Some people may just be fearful of receiving new information and being able to understand it. Or it may just be a characteristic or pattern in the way some people respond psychologically to information; they may not be able to make sense out of some of what they hear, which causes them to be anxious or fearful of listening to others.[15] If you are fearful of receiving information, you'll remember less information.

What are the implications of these research studies for you? If you know that you are one of those people who is fearful of listening to new information, you'll have to work harder to understand the information presented. Using a tape recorder to record a lecture may help you feel more comfortable and less anxious about trying to remember every point. Becoming actively involved in the listening experience by taking notes or mentally repeating information to yourself may also help.

receiver apprehension
Fear of misunderstanding or misinterpreting the messages spoken by others, or not being able to adjust psychologically to messages expressed by others.

Shifting Attention

Can you multi-task? Some people can easily do two things at once, and some people can't. Emerging research evidence suggests that men are more likely to have difficulty attending to multiple messages: When they are focused on a message, they may have more difficulty than women in carrying on a conversation with another person.[16] Men have a tendency to lock on to a message, while women seem more adept at shifting between two or more simultaneous messages. When many men watch a TV program, they seem lost in thought—oblivious to other voices around them. Women, on the other hand, are more likely to be carrying on a conversation with one person and also focusing on a message they may hear nearby. No, this difference doesn't mean that women are more likely to eavesdrop intentionally; it means that some women have greater potential to listen to two things at once. What are the implications? It may be especially important for women to stop and focus on the message of others, rather than on either internal or external competing messages.

And men may need to be sensitive to others who may want to speak to them, rather than become fixated on their own internal message or a singular external message such as watching sports, news, opera, or a movie on TV.

⤳ Context Barriers

Not only are there listening barriers related to how you process information or self-barriers that occur when your emotions and thoughts crowd out a message, but the communication context or situation is sometimes fraught with obstacles that may distract you from your listening task. Specifically, the time and place where you listen, as well as outside noise, can distract you from selecting, attending, understanding, remembering, and responding to messages.

Barriers of Time and Place

Besides our own inadequacies and the way in which we process information, the communication situation can hinder effective listening. The time of day can interfere with your listening acuity. Are you a morning person or an evening person? Morning people are cheerfully and chirpily at their mental peak before lunch. Evening people prefer to tackle major projects after dark; they are at their worst when they arise in the morning. Use the skill development activity on page 115 to plot your ideal work time, the period when you are at your sharpest.

ReCAP ⟵

Managing Listening Barriers

LISTENING BARRIERS	WHAT TO DO
Self-Barriers	
Self-Focus	• Consciously become aware of the self-focus and shift attention back to the speaker. • Concentrate: Find ways of becoming actively involved in the message, such as taking meaningful notes.
Emotional Noise	• Act calm to remain calm. • Use self-talk to stay focused on the message. • Take a deep breath if you start to lose control.
Criticism	• Focus on the message, not the messenger.
Information-Processing Barriers	
Processing Rate	• Use the difference between speech rate and thought rate to mentally summarize the message.
Information Overload	• Realize when you or your partner is tired or distracted and not ready to listen. • Assess what is urgent and not urgent when listening.
Receiver Apprehension	• If you are fearful or anxious about listening to new information, use a backup strategy such as a tape recorder to help you capture the message; review the tape later. Seek ways to become actively involved when listening, such as taking notes or making mental summaries of the information you hear.
Shifting Attention	• Men are more likely to focus on a single message; women typically shift their attention between two or more messages.
Context Barriers	
Barriers of Time and Place	• Note when your best and worst listening times are; if possible, shift difficult listening situations to when you're at your best.
Noise	• When appropriate, modify the listening environment by eliminating distracting, competing noise.

If you know you are sharper in the morning, whenever possible schedule your key listening times then. Evening listeners should try to shift heavy listening to the evening hours. Of course, that's not always practical. If you can't change the time of listening, you can then increase your awareness of when you will need to listen with greater concentration.

Don't assume that because you are ready to talk, the other person is ready to listen. If your message is particularly sensitive or important, you may want to ask your listening partner, "Is this a good time to talk?" Even if he or she says yes, look for eye contact and a responsive facial expression to make sure the positive response is genuine.

Noise

You have undoubtedly noticed one obvious barrier to listening well: It is hard to concentrate on a friend's comments while the TV is blaring or when you are sitting in a noisy restaurant. Or have you tried to enjoy a concert or movie while the family in front of you use the outing to provide their own narration of the action or catch up on family business? No matter how interesting or important a message is to you, if you can't hear or if other messages are noisily competing for your attention, your listening efficiency will suffer.

Noise can be in the form of sights or sounds. The best environment for listening for most people is one that offers as few audio and visual distractions as possible. When you want to talk to someone, pick a quiet time and place, especially if you know you will be discussing a potentially conflict-producing subject. In the context of a family, it may be a challenge to find a quiet time to talk. With one family member going to play ball, another going shopping, and a third coming home from an exhausting day and just wanting to relax, it is difficult to find moments when all are available for conversation.

Perhaps a good title for a listening text would be *How to Turn Off the TV.* It is difficult to listen with the ever-present background chatter of cartoons, comedies, music videos, news, and dramatic monologue in the background. Listening takes all the powers of concentration that you can muster. A good listener seeks a quiet time and place to maximize listening comprehension. Closing a door or window, turning off a radio, and even asking inappropriate, offending talkers to converse more quietly or not at all are action steps that you may need to pursue to manage the listening noise barrier.

LISTENING SKILLS

At the heart of listening is developing sensitivity to focus on the messages of others, rather than your own thoughts. Improving your listening involves a set of skills that can increase your sensitivity toward others. At first glance, these skills may look deceptively simple—as simple as the advice given to most elementary students about crossing the street: (1) stop, (2) look, and (3) listen. Despite the appearance of simplicity, decades of research and insight about how to avoid being labelled "interpersonally inert" can be summarized around these three skills. Let's consider each separately.

⋯⟩ Stop: Turn off Competing Messages

Many of the barriers to improved listening skill relate to the focus we often place on ourselves and our own messages, rather than focusing on others. As we noted earlier, while you are "listening," you may also be "talking" to yourself—providing a commentary about the messages you hear. These internal, self-generated messages may distract you from giving your undivided attention to what others are saying. In order to select and attend to the messages of others, we need to become aware of our internal dialogue and stop our own running commentary about issues and ideas that are self-focused rather than other-focused.

Try a process called **decentring.** Decentring involves stepping away from your own thoughts and attempting to experience the thoughts of another. In essence, you're asking yourself this question: "If I were the other person, what would I be thinking?" To decentre is to practise the first principle of communication—self-awareness—to be aware that your own thoughts are keeping you from focusing on another's message, so that you can focus on another person.[17] Of course, we are not suggesting that your own ideas and internal dialogue

decentring
Stepping away from your own thoughts and attempting to experience the thoughts of another.

should be forever repressed; that would be both impossible and inappropriate. We are suggesting, however, that to connect to another, you must place the focus on the other person rather than on yourself. To decentre requires conscious effort. Decentring is a mental or cognitive process that involves trying to guess what someone else may be thinking. In attempting to decentre, consider this question, "If I were my communication partner, what would I be thinking?"

The essence of the "stop" step is to become aware (our first communication principle for a lifetime that we discussed in Chapter 2) of whether you are listening or not listening to someone. You are either on task (focusing on another) or off task (oblivious to another and focusing on your own thoughts and emotions). The goal, of course, is to be on task—listening to others.

⤑ Look: Listen with Your Eyes

As we learned in Chapter 4, nonverbal messages are powerful, especially in communicating feelings, attitudes, and emotions. Up to 93% of emotional information may be expressed by nonverbal cues.[18] A person's facial expression, presence or lack of eye contact, posture, and use of gestures speak volumes, even when no word is uttered. When words are spoken, the added meaning that comes from vocal cues provides yet another dimension to the emotion and nature of the relationship. When there is a contradiction between the verbal and the nonverbal message, we will almost always believe the unspoken message; nonverbal cues are more difficult to fake.

Sensitive listeners are aware of nonverbal as well as verbal messages; they listen with their eyes as well as their ears. A person's body movement and posture, for example, communicate the intensity of his or her feelings, while the facial expression and vocal cues provide clues as to the specific emotion being expressed. A competent listener notices these cues, and an incompetent listener attempts to decode a message based only on what is said rather than "listening between the lines."

Besides looking at someone to discern his or her emotions and relational cues, it is important to establish eye contact, which signals that you are focusing your attention on your partner. Even though mutual eye contact typically lasts only one to seven seconds, when we carry on an interpersonal conversation, it is important to establish and re-establish eye contact to signal that you are on task and listening. We usually have more eye contact with someone when we are listening than talking.[19] Looking over your partner's head, peeking at your watch, or gazing into space will likely tell him or her you're not tuned in. Even though there are cultural variations in the advice to establish eye contact (for example, some children in Asian-Canadian homes have been taught to avoid eye contact with high-status people), generally, for most North Americans, eye contact signals that the communication channel is open and the communication is welcome.

Not only is eye contact important, but other nonverbal cues signal whether you are on task and responsive to the messages of others. If you look as if you are listening, you will be more likely to listen. Maintaining eye contact, remaining focused, not fidgeting with your hands and feet, and even leaning forward slightly are nonverbal cues that communicate to someone that you are listening. Appropriate head nods and verbal responses also signal that you are attending to your partner's message.[20]

ETHICAL PROBE

You find yourself listening to a friend who is very troubled by something. As you listen, you hear the friend contradict herself, and you know that you could offer some insight that would help solve your friend's problem. You also wonder whether the friend is ready to hear your solution; perhaps an empathetic response would be more appropriate. But is it your ethical obligation in a case like this, when you have information that you're certain will be useful, to relate the information, no matter the emotional state of your friend? If you don't offer the information, will your friend be upset later to find that you didn't offer a solution?

⋯⟩ Listen: Understand Both Details and Major Ideas

How do you improve your listening skill? First, stop the internal dialogue that may distract your attention from your partner. Look for nonverbal clues about emotions and the nature of the relationship. Here are several additional strategies that can improve your listening skill.

1. *Identify your listening goal.* You listen to other people for a variety of reasons. Knowing your listening goal can increase your self-awareness of the listening process and increase your skill. If you're primarily listening to Aunt Deonna talk about her recent trip to the Northwest Territories, you need not worry about taking extensive notes and trying to remember all of the details of her trip. But when your communication professor tells a story to illustrate a communication theory, you should be more attuned to the point he or she is making; the implications of the anecdote may be on a test. There are also times when you need to be on your guard to evaluate the message of a politician or salesperson. What are the primary listening goals? There are four: to enjoy, to learn, to evaluate, and to empathize.

   * *Listening to Enjoy:* Sometimes we listen just because it's fun. You might listen to music, watch TV, go to a movie, or just visit with a friend. Because you know you won't be tested on Jay Leno's *Tonight Show* comedy monologue, you can kick back, relax, and just enjoy the humour; you don't have to worry about passing a test to remember each punchline.

   * *Listening to Learn:* Nothing snaps a class to attention more quickly than a professor's proclamation that "This next point will be covered on the test." Another key reason we listen is to learn. At some colleges and universities, tuition, room, and board cost $1000 a week! Regardless of the cost of your university tuition, you spend time, money, and energy listening to learn. You don't have to be a student to listen to learn. Phone calls from family and friends contain information that we want to remember. In interpersonal situations, you listen for such everyday information as who will pick up the kids after school and what to buy at the grocery store for tonight's dinner. If you are aware that your listening goal is to learn and remember information, you can throttle up your powers of concentration and pay more attention to understanding and remembering the message.

   * *Listening to Evaluate:* When you listen to evaluate, you try to determine whether the information you hear is valid, reliable, believable, or useful. One problem you may have when you listen to evaluate is that you may become so preoccupied with your criticism that you may not completely understand the message. Often the very process of evaluating and making judgments and decisions about information interferes with the capacity to understand and recall. To compensate for this tendency, first make sure that you understand what a person is saying before making a judgment about the value of the information. When listening to evaluate, you use critical-listening skills such as separating facts from inferences, identifying fallacies in reasoning, and analyzing evidence. We discuss these important skills throughout this book. In Chapter 13, for example, we describe how to spot invalid, illogical approaches to reasoning and structuring arguments. We also identify how to evaluate the facts, statistics, opinions, and examples other people offer as evidence to support their conclusions.

   * *Listening to Empathize:* The word *empathy,* which we introduced in Chapter 1 and will discuss in more detail later in this chapter, comes from a Greek word for "passion" and a translation of the German word *Einfühling,* meaning "to feel with." To empathize with someone is to try to feel what he or she is feeling, rather than just to think about or acknowledge the feelings. In effect, you act as a sounding board for the other person. Empathic listening serves an important therapeutic function. Just having an empathic listener may help someone out. No, we are not empowering you to be a therapist, but we are suggesting that simply listening and feeling with someone can help your communication partner sort things out. Empathic listeners don't judge or offer advice. They listen because the process of sharing and listening is soothing and can often restore a person's perspective. Being aware that your listening goal is to empathize, rather than to remember or to evaluate what you are listening to, is the first step to being a skilled empathic listener.

2. *Mentally summarize the details of the message.* This suggestion may seem to contradict the suggestion to avoid focusing *only* on facts, but it is important to have a grasp of the details your partner presents. To listen is to do more than focus on facts. Studies suggest that poor listeners are more likely to focus on *only* facts and data, rather than the overall point of the message.[21] To listen is to connect the details of the message with the major points. You can process words quicker than a person speaks, so you can use the extra time to your advantage by periodically summarizing the names, dates, and facts embedded in the message. If the speaker is disorganized and rambling, use your tremendous mental ability to organize the speaker's information into categories, or try to place events in chronological order. If you miss the details, you will likely miss the main point.

3. *Link message details with the major idea of the message.* Facts and data make the most sense when we can use them to support an idea or point. Mentally weave your summaries of the details into a focused major point or series of major ideas. So as you summarize, link the facts you have organized in your mind with key ideas and principles. Use facts to enhance your critical thinking as you analyze, synthesize, evaluate, and finally summarize the key points or ideas your partner makes.

4. *Practise by listening to difficult or challenging material.* You can also sharpen your listening skill by consciously developing your abilities to stop, look, and listen. You learn any skill with practice. Listening experts suggest that our listening skills deteriorate if we listen only to easy and entertaining material. Make an effort to listen to news or documentary programs. As you listen to material in a lecture that may seem chock full of content, make a conscious effort to stay focused, concentrate, and summarize facts and major ideas.

   While listening to someone give you directions to Seneca Hall, one of the oldest buildings on campus, you would listen differently than if your sister were telling you about her fears that her marriage was on the rocks. In the case of your sister, your job is to listen patiently and provide emotional support. In trying to get to Seneca Hall, you would be focusing on the specific details and making either mental or written notes.

5. *Transform listening barriers into listening goals.* If you can transform the listening barriers we presented earlier, you will be well on your way to improving your listening skill. Make it a deliberate goal not to be self-focused, let emotional noise distract you, or criticize a message before you've understood it. Watch out for information overload. And, when possible, take steps to minimize external noise and provide an ideal listening environment.

RESPONDING SKILLS

To respond is to provide feedback to another about his or her behaviour or communication. Your response can be verbal or nonverbal, intentional or unintentional.

ReCAP

How to Listen Well

WHAT TO DO	HOW TO DO IT
STOP	• Focus on your partner, not your own thoughts. • Cease what you are doing; give your undivided attention to your partner.
LOOK	• Observe the nonverbal messages of your listening partner. • Make sure your nonverbal message communicates your interest in your partner.
LISTEN	• Listen for both details and major ideas, while being aware of your listening goal. • Mentally summarize key ideas.

Your thoughtful response serves several purposes. First, it tells a speaker how well his or her message has been understood. Second, your response lets a speaker know how the message affects you. It indicates whether you agree or disagree. Third, it provides feedback to correct statements or assumptions that you find vague, confusing, or wrong. It helps an individual keep the communication on target and purposeful. Finally, your response signals to the speaker that you are still "with" him or her. Your verbal or nonverbal response lets the speaker know you are still ready to receive messages. To respond appropriately and effectively, consider the following strategies.

Be Descriptive

"I see that from a different point of view" sounds better than "You're wrong, I'm right." Effective feedback describes rather than evaluates what you hear. Although one type of listening is to evaluate and make critical judgments of messages, evaluate once you're sure you understand the speaker. We're not suggesting it's easy to listen from a nonevaluative perspective, or that you should refrain from ever evaluating messages and providing praise or negative comments. Remember: Feedback that first acts like a mirror to help the speaker understand what he or she has said is more useful than immediately providing a barrage of critical comments. Describing your own reactions to what your partner has said rather than pronouncing a quick judgment on his or her message is also more likely to keep communication flowing. If your partner thinks your prime purpose in listening is to take potshots at the message or messenger, the communication climate will cool quickly.

Be Timely

Feedback is usually most effective at the earliest opportunity after the behaviour or message is presented, especially if the purpose is to teach. Waiting to provide a response after much time has elapsed invites confusion.

Now let us contradict our advice. Sometimes, especially if a person is already sensitive and upset about something, delaying feedback can be wise. Use your critical-thinking skills to analyze when feedback will do the most good. Rather than automatically offering immediate correction, use the just-in-time (JIT) approach. Provide feedback just before the person might make another mistake, just in time for the feedback to have the most benefit.

Be Brief

Less information can be more. Cutting down on the amount of your feedback can highlight the importance of what you do share. Don't overwhelm your listener with details that obscure the key point of your feedback. Brief is usually best.

Be Useful

Perhaps you've heard this advice: "Never try to teach a pig to sing. It wastes your time, it does not sound pretty, and it annoys the pig." When you provide feedback to someone, be certain that it is useful and relevant. Ask yourself, "If I were this person, how would I respond to this information? Is it information I could act on?" Immersing your partner in information that is irrelevant or that may be damaging to the relationship may make you feel better, but it may not enhance the quality of your relationship or improve understanding.

Be Active

The underlying premise of this chapter is: Effective communicators are sensitive to others. They listen and thoughtfully respond to confirm their understanding of the content and, when appropriate, the feelings of the communicator. A sensitive communicator is actively rather than passively involved in the message, whether the message is a friend's story about a flat tire, a professor's lecture, or your mother's request that you come home for the holidays.[22]

Passive listeners sit with a blank stare or a frozen facial expression. Often they have not "stopped" their own thoughts and may be a thousand kilometres away, even though physically present. Active listeners, in contrast, respond mentally, verbally, and nonverbally to a speaker's message.

Boyd likes to bring empathy to the task at hand.

So what precisely do you do to become an active listener? Active listeners offer nonverbal feedback to signal that they are still listening. Remember, you don't get any credit for being a good listener if you don't look like you're listening. Appropriate facial expressions, head nods, and an attentive posture indicate you're "there." Besides unspoken cues, appropriate verbal responses such as asking good questions, or saying, "Oh yes, I understand" are clues to your listening partner that you're focused on him or her. The best active listeners are those who can respond with empathy to what their partner is saying.

RESPONDING WITH EMPATHY

Empathy, as we noted earlier in the chapter, is the process of feeling what another person is feeling. To empathize is more than just to acknowledge that another person feels a particular emotion—empathy is making an effort to feel the emotion yourself. Responding with empathy is especially important if you are listening to provide support and encouragement to someone. Empathy is not a single skill but several related skills that help you predict how others will respond.[23]

Central to being empathic is being emotionally intelligent. As we noted earlier in this chapter, emotional intelligence, according to psychologist and journalist Daniel Goleman, who helped popularize the concept, is the ability to understand and express emotion, interpret emotions in yourself and others, and regulate or manage emotions.[24] Goleman suggests that people who are emotionally intelligent—sensitive to others, empathic, and other oriented—have better relationships with others. Goleman summarizes the importance of emotions in developing empathy by quoting Antoine de Saint Exupéry: "It is with the heart that one sees rightly; what is essential is invisible to the eye."[25]

At the heart of empathic listening is the ability not only to know when to speak but also to know when to be silent. Henri Nouwen eloquently expressed both the challenge and rewards of empathic listening when he wrote the following:

> To listen is very hard, because it asks of us so much interior stability that we no longer need to prove ourselves by speeches, arguments, statements, or declarations. True listeners no longer have an inner need to make their presence known. They are free to receive, to welcome, to accept.
>
> Listening is much more than allowing another to talk while waiting for a chance to respond. Listening is paying full attention to others and welcoming them into our very beings. The beauty of listening is that those who are listened to start feeling accepted, start taking their words more seriously and discovering their true selves. Listening is a form of spiritual hospitality by which you invite strangers to become friends, to get to know their inner selves more fully, and even to dare to be silent with you.[26]

Some people are simply better at being empathic than others. Just as you inherit physical qualities from your parents, there is also evidence that you inherit communication traits as well.[27] This does not mean that if you or others are not naturally empathic, you don't have to work to cultivate these skills; on the contrary, it means you may have to work a bit harder to enhance your empathic responding skills. To assess your empathic skill, take the "Test Your Empathy Ability" quiz at the end of this chapter.

Research suggests that some of us have a people-oriented listening style.[28] People-oriented listeners are better at empathizing with others. We are not suggesting that ferreting out someone's emotions is the goal of every listening encounter. That would be tedious for both you and your listening partners. But when you do want to listen and respond empathically, you must shift the focus to your partner and try to understand the message from his or her perspective. Here are four strategies to help you respond empathically when you listen.

⟶ Understand Your Partner's Feelings

If your goal is to empathize or "feel with" your partner, you might begin by imagining how you would feel under the same circumstances. If your roommate comes home from a hassle-filled day at work or school, try to imagine what you might be thinking or feeling if you had had a stressful day. If a friend calls to tell you his mother died, consider how you would feel if the situation were reversed. Even if you've not yet experienced the loss of your mother, you can identify with what it would be like to suffer such a loss. Of course, your reaction to life events is unlikely to be exactly like someone else's response. Empathy is not telepathically trying to become your communication partner.[29] But you do attempt to decentre—consider what someone may be thinking—by first projecting how you might feel, followed by appropriate questions and paraphrases to confirm the accuracy of your assumptions. Considering how others might feel has been called the Platinum Rule—even more valuable than the Golden Rule ("Do unto others as you would have others do unto you"). The Platinum Rule invites you to treat others as *they* would like to be treated—not just as *you* would like to be treated.

Ask Appropriate Questions

As you listen for information and attempt to understand how another person is feeling, you may need to ask questions to help clarify your conclusions. Most of your questions will serve one of four purposes: (1) to obtain additional information ("How long have you been living in Newfoundland?"); (2) to check out how the person feels ("Are you frustrated because you didn't get your project finished?"); (3) to ask for clarification of a word or phrase ("What do you mean when you say you wanted to telecommute?"); and (4) to verify that you have reached an accurate conclusion about your partner's intent or feeling ("So are you saying you'd rather work at home than at the office?").

Here's another suggestion for sorting out details and trying to get to the emotional heart of a dialogue: Ask questions to help you (and your partner) identify the sequence of events. "What happened first?" and "Then what did he do?" can help both you and your partner clarify a confusing event.

Your ability to ask appropriate questions will demonstrate your supportiveness of your partner, as well as signal that you are interested in what he or she is sharing. Of course, if you are trying to understand another's feelings, you can just ask how he or she is feeling in a straightforward way. Don't ask questions just for the sake of asking questions. Also, monitor the way in which you ask your questions. Your own verbal and nonverbal responses will contribute to the emotional climate of your interaction.

Paraphrase the Content

After you have listened and asked questions, check whether your interpretations are accurate by paraphrasing the content you have heard. **Paraphrasing** is restating in your own words what you think a person is saying. Paraphrasing is different from repeating something exactly as it was spoken; that would be parroting, not paraphrasing. Your paraphrase can summarize the essential events, uncover a detail that was quickly glossed over, or highlight a key point. Typical lead-ins to a paraphrase include statements such as

paraphrasing
Restating in your own words what you think someone is saying.

"So here is what seemed to have happened. . . ."
"Here's what I understand you to mean. . . ."
"So the point you seem to be making is. . . ."
"You seem to be saying. . . ."
"Are you saying. . . ?"

Here's an example of a conversation punctuated by appropriate paraphrases to enhance the accuracy of the message receiver:

Alice: I'm swamped. My boss asked me to take on two extra projects this week. And I already have the Henrikson merger and Affolter project. I promised I'd arrange to have the lawn mower fixed and pay the bills. I also don't see how I can take the dog to the vet, pick up the kids after school, and get Keshia to the orthodontist at 7 A.M. I'm up to my neck in work. Can you help?

Matt: So you'd like me to take care of the stuff around the house so you can focus on office assignments.

COMMUNICATION and DIVERSITY

East and West Listening Styles

North American communication very often centres on the sender, and until recently the linear, one-way model from sender to receiver was the prevailing model of communication. Much emphasis has been placed on how senders can formulate better messages, improve source credibility, polish their delivery skills, and so forth. In contrast, the emphasis in East Asia has always been on listening and interpretation.

Communication researcher C. Y. Cheng has identified infinite interpretation as one of the main principles of Chinese communication.[30] The process presumes that the emphasis is on the receiver and listening rather than on the sender and speaking. According to T. S. Lebra, "anticipatory communication" is common in Japan—instead of the speaker's having to tell or ask for what he or she wants specifically, others guess and accommodate his or her needs, sparing him or her embarrassment in case the verbally expressed request cannot be met.[31] In such cases, the burden of communication falls not on the message sender but on the message receiver. A person who "hears one and understands ten" is regarded as an intelligent communicator. To catch on quickly and to adjust to another's position before his or her position is clearly revealed is regarded as an important communication skill. One of the common puzzles expressed by foreign students from East Asia is why they are constantly being asked what they want when they are visiting in Canadian homes. In their own countries, the host or hostess is supposed to know what is needed and serve accordingly. The difference occurs because in North America it is important to provide individual freedom of choice; in East Asia, it is important to practise anticipatory communication and to accommodate accordingly.

With the emphasis on indirect communication, the receiver's sensitivity and ability to capture the under-the-surface meaning and to understand implicit meaning becomes critical. In North America, an effort has been made to improve the effectiveness of senders through such formal training as debate and public speaking, whereas in East Asia, the effort has been on improving the receiver's sensitivity. The highest sensitivity is reached when one empties the mind of one's preconceptions and makes it as clear as a mirror.[32]

Both communication scholars and practitioners recognize that listening is necessary not only for the instrumental aspect of communication (comprehension) but, more importantly, for the affective aspect (satisfaction of being listened to).

Source: J. O. Yum, "The Impact of Confucianism on Interpersonal Relationships and Communication Patterns in East Asia," in L. A. Samovar and R. E. Porter, eds., *Intercultural Communication: A Reader* (Belmont, CA: Wadsworth Publishing Company, 2000), 86.

Alice: Well, some of them, yes. Could you take on a couple of things I said I'd do?

Matt: You'd like me to help around here more?

Alice: Yes, could you?

Matt: Okay. I'll take care of the kids and run several of the time-consuming errands.

We are not suggesting that you paraphrase when it's not needed or appropriate, only when you need to confirm your understanding of a murky message or to help the speaker sort out a jumbled or confusing situation. When a listener paraphrases the content and feelings of a speaker, the speaker is not only more likely to ensure the message is understood, but also will be more likely to trust and value the listener.

⋯⟩ Paraphrase Emotions

The bottom line in empathic responding is to make certain that you understand how someone is feeling—not their health, but their emotional state.

"So you feel. . . ."
"So now you feel. . . ."
"Emotionally, you are feeling. . . ."

These are typical lead-in phrases when paraphrasing feelings.

We have discussed empathic responses and the active listening process from a tidy step-by-step typical textbook approach. Realize that in practice, it won't be so neat and tidy. You may have to back up and clarify content, ask more questions, and rethink how you would feel before you summarize how someone feels. Or you may be able to summarize feelings without asking questions or summarizing the content of the message. A

Can Computers Listen Empathically?

Is it possible for a computer to listen and respond sensitively to others? Although there is software that permits you to speak words that your personal computer will then print, computers do not yet have the sophistication to listen and respond with the same sensitivity as people. But computer programmers are working on it. Stanford University professors Clifford Nass and Byron Reeves have been working since 1986 to help PCs interact with people in human ways.[33] They have summarized research regarding how people respond to other people and have been trying to translate these research conclusions into strategies that can be used by a computer to interact with others in real-time dialogues. Professors Nass and Reeves have identified four major personality types—dominant, submissive, friendly, and unfriendly—and have programmed computers to respond to the computer user. The researchers are trying to match more than personality. As Professor Nass explains, "Personality is one aspect. Gender, politeness, cooperation, and even humor are other factors. We decide what the agent [computer user] is going to do, then develop a backstory—each character's likes and life history. This guides the scripting, voice type, animation, and interaction style."[34] The researchers are also working on integrating computer-generated speech into the program. Although computers may not yet listen with the sensitivity and empathy of your best friend, researchers are working on software that can emulate human interaction and responses. So, for now, realize that the opportunity to listen to others is something that can't be delegated to a virtual friend.

sensitive communicator doesn't try to let his or her technique show. Overusing paraphrasing skills can slow down a conversation and make the other person uncomfortable or irritated. But if used with wisdom, paraphrasing can help both you and your partner clarify messages accuracy.

Reflecting on the content or feeling through paraphrasing can be especially useful in the following situations:

Before you take an important action
Before you argue or criticize
When your partner has strong feelings
When your partner just wants to talk
When your partner is speaking "in code" or using unclear abbreviations
When your partner wants to understand your feelings and thoughts
When you are talking to yourself (you can question and check your own emotional temperature)
When you encounter new ideas[35]

When you ask questions and paraphrase content and feelings, keep the following additional guidelines in mind:

Use your own words—don't just repeat exactly what the other person says.
Don't add to the information presented when paraphrasing.
Be brief.
Be specific.
Be accurate.

Don't use reflecting skills if you aren't able to be open and accepting; if you are using paraphrasing skills and simply try to colour your paraphrased comments to achieve your own agenda, you aren't being ethical.

Don't be discouraged if your initial attempts to use these skills seem awkward and uncomfortable. Any new set of skills takes time to learn and use well. The instructions and samples you have seen here should serve as guides, rather than as hard-and-fast prescriptions to follow every time. Being an empathic listener can be rewarding in both your personal and professional lives.[36]

On the WEB ·····•

Several Web sites provide a wealth of information about how to improve your listening skills. Several sites offer specific strategies for improving your paraphrasing skills. The following Web addresses give you additional tips, strategies, and information to help you listen better:
• **www.listen.org**
• **www.educationplanet.com/ search/Language-Arts/ Languages/Listening_Skills**
• **www.positive-way.com**

ReCAP ←┈┈

How to Respond with Empathy

RESPONDING WITH EMPATHY	ACTION
Understand Your Partner's Feelings	Ask yourself how you would feel if you had experienced a similar situation or recall how you did feel under similar circumstances. Or recall how your partner felt under similar circumstances.
Ask Questions	Seek additional information to better understand your partner's message.
Reflect Content by Paraphrasing	Summarize the essence of the information, as you understand it, for your partner.
Reflect Feelings by Paraphrasing	When appropriate, try to summarize what you think your partner may be feeling.

SUMMARY

An important principle of communication is to listen and respond thoughtfully to others. Listening is the process of receiving, constructing meaning from, and responding to verbal and nonverbal messages. It includes the processes of selecting, attending, understanding, remembering, and responding to others.

Most people struggle with the skill of listening. Barriers to effective listening include focusing on our personal agendas, being distracted by emotional noise, criticizing the speaker, daydreaming, shifting attention, and being distracted by information overload and external noise.

To become a better listener, consider three simple processes: Stop, look, and listen. To stop means to be mindful of the message and avoid focusing on your own distracting "talk," which may keep you from focusing on the messages of others. To look is to listen with your eyes—to focus on the nonverbal information that provides a wealth

of cues about emotional meaning. To listen involves the skill of capturing the details of a message while also connecting those details to a major idea.

The other half of listening is responding to others accurately and appropriately. To respond thoughtfully means to stop and consider the needs of the other person. Check the accuracy of your listening skill by reflecting your understanding of what your partner has said. Responding skills are especially important if the goal is to empathize with and support others. Responding skills include understanding the feelings of others, asking appropriate questions, and paraphrasing the message's content and the speaker's feelings. Responding effectively does not mean being a parrot and repeating a message exactly as it was spoken. Paraphrasing means summarizing the gist of the message. The most effective responses to others are carefully timed, provide usable information, avoid cluttering details, and are descriptive rather than evaluative.

Discussion and Review

1. What is the difference between listening and hearing?

2. What are some of the key barriers that keep people from listening effectively?

3. Name the four goals of listening.

4. What are similarities and differences among listening to learn, to evaluate, to enjoy, and to empathize?

5. List the essential skills to improve your listening, and discuss which strategies will help you improve your listening skills.

6. What are suggestions for improving your ability to empathize with others?

7. What are suggestions for effectively paraphrasing or reflecting messages back to others?

8. How do you appropriately and thoughtfully respond to others?

Developing Your Skills: Putting Principles into Practice

1. Test Your Empathy Ability
   Take this short test to assess your empathy. Respond to each statement by indicating the degree to which the

statement is true regarding the way you typically communicate with others. When you think of how you communicate, is the statement always false (answer 1), usually false (answer 2), sometimes false and sometimes true (answer 3), usually true (answer 4), or always true (answer 5)?

_____ 1. I try to understand others' experiences from their perspectives.

_____ 2. I follow the Golden Rule ("Do unto others as you would have them do unto you") when communicating with others.

_____ 3. I can "tune in" to emotions others are experiencing when we communicate.

_____ 4. When trying to understand how others feel, I imagine how I would feel in their situation.

_____ 5. I am able to tell what others are feeling without being told.

_____ 6. Others experience the same feelings I do in any given situation.

_____ 7. When others are having problems, I can imagine how they feel.

_____ 8. I find it hard to understand the emotions others experience.

_____ 9. I try to see others as they want me to.

_____ 10. I never seem to know what others are thinking when we communicate.

To find your score, first reverse the responses for the even-numbered items (if you wrote 1, make it 5; if you wrote 2, make it 4; if you wrote 3, leave it as 3; if you wrote 4, make it 2; if you wrote 5, make it 1). Next add the numbers next to each statement. Scores range from 10 to 50. The higher your score, the more you are able to empathize.

Source: William Gudykunst, _Bridging Differences,_ 2nd Ed. (Thousand Oaks, CA: Sage Publications, 1998). Reprinted by permission of Sage Publications, Inc.

2. Assessing Receiver Apprehension

Take the following test to assess your level of receiver apprehension. Scores range from 50 to 10. The higher your score, the more you're likely to experience some anxiety when you listen to others and the harder you'll have to work at developing strategies to improve your listening comprehension.

Receiver Anxiety Scale

Respond to each of these questions about how much this _describes you,_ using a five-point scale.
5 = Strongly Agree; 4 = Agree; 3 = Uncertain or Sometimes; 2 = Disagree; 1 = Strongly Disagree

_____ 1. When I am listening, I feel nervous about missing information.

_____ 2. I worry about being able to keep up with the material presented in lecture classes.

_____ 3. Sometimes I miss information in class because I am writing down the notes.

_____ 4. I feel tense and anxious when listening to important information.

_____ 5. I am concerned that I won't be able to remember information I've heard in lectures or discussions.

_____ 6. Although I try to concentrate, my thoughts sometimes become confused when I'm listening.

_____ 7. I worry that my listening skill isn't very good.

_____ 8. I regularly can't remember things that I have just been told.

_____ 9. I feel anxious and nervous when I am listening in class.

_____ 10. I prefer reading class material rather than listening to it, so I don't have to be stressed about catching all the information the first time.

Source: L. Wheeless, "An Investigation of Receiver Apprehension and Social Context Dimensions of Communication Apprehension," _The Speech Teacher_ 24 (1975): 261–268.

3. On pages 100–105 we noted several barriers to listening. Rank order these barriers, with 1 being the most problematic. After you have identified your top three or four barriers, identify at least one specific strategy for overcoming your problematic listening behaviour.

4. Charting Your Listening Cycle
Are you a morning person or an evening person? Use the chart in Figure 5.3 to plot your listening energy cycle. Draw a line starting at 6:00 A.M., showing the highs and lows of your potential listening effectiveness. For example, if you are usually still asleep at 6:00 A.M., your line will be at 0 and start upward when you awake. If you are a morning person, your line will peak in the morning. Or perhaps your line will indicate that you listen best in the evening.

After you have charted your typical daily listening cycle, gather in small groups with your classmates to compare listening cycles. Identify listening strategies that can help you capitalize on your listening "up" periods. Also, based upon information you learned from this chapter and your own experiences, identify ways to enhance your listening when you traditionally have low listening energy.

FIGURE 5.3 Your Listening Energy Cycle

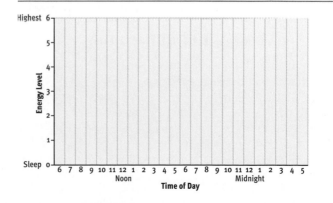

Christian Pierre, "Share the World." © SuperStock

You see in this one location all the faces, all the races,
and the colours, and religions that make up this planet.
This is Canada today. And it is our mission to the world
to show how it is possible to live together in diversity
and in harmony.

— JEAN CHRÉTIEN

6

Adapting to Others: Bridging Culture and Gender Differences

CHAPTER OUTLINE

AFTER STUDYING THIS CHAPTER, YOU SHOULD BE ABLE TO

1. Define culture.

2. Describe Canada's ethnocultural environment.

3. Describe, compare, and contrast high-context and low-context cultures.

4. Describe four cultural values.

5. Identify differences and similarities between male and female communication patterns.

6. Describe the importance of gender within the larger concept of culture.

7. Understand how gender relates to content and relational approaches to communication.

8. Illustrate four barriers that inhibit communication between people.

9. Describe six strategies that will help bridge differences between people, as well as help people adapt to differences.

Given the inherent differences between and among people, we introduce our final communication principle: Effective communicators appropriately adapt their messages to others. We introduce this principle last because we often develop it after we have learned the other communication principles. Figure 6.1 presents our now-familiar model, which features this final principle of appropriately adapting to others. Being able to adapt to others suggests that you already have a sense of who you are and a consciousness of the presence of others—self-awareness and other-awareness, the components of the first principle we presented. As infants, we learn to use verbal and nonverbal messages, even though it may take several years to develop sophistication in using language and nonverbal symbols. Hearing and listening also develop early in our lives. Studies in developmental communication suggest that the ability to appropriately adapt our behaviour to others evolves after we have become aware that there is a "me," after we have learned to use verbal and nonverbal symbols to communicate, and after our ability to hear and listen to others is present. To adapt to others requires a relatively sophisticated understanding of the communication process.

One of life's unprofound principles with profound implications for human communication is this: *We each have different backgrounds and experiences.* As we learned in Chapter 2, we each see, hear, and experience the world differently. To some degree, we are each estranged from others.

In a world of ever-increasing tensions and conflict due to differences in culture, religious beliefs, and political ideologies and considering Canada's multicultural environment, being able to understand and appropriately adapt to others is of vital importance. When differences are heightened by attitudes of superiority and beliefs of being divinely ordained to dominate others, violence is the typical result.

Our suggestion that it is appropriate and important to adapt messages to others does not mean you only do or say what others expect. We are not suggesting that you become a spineless jellyfish and shape your comments and actions primarily to please others. Such placating behaviour is neither wise, effective, nor ethical. Effective communicators have, however, learned to be sensitive to others and to use messages and actions that enhance the probability that the message communicated by the sender will be the message interpreted by the receiver. Adapting your communication to others also does not mean that your intention is to manipulate the conversation and the person so that you can accomplish only your goals. A successful conversation means that both (or all) parties' goals are met. So we do not advocate a form of adapted communication that is false or manipulative. Whether you are speaking to others in interpersonal, group, or presentational speaking situations, adapting your message to others makes intuitive common sense. Even so, being sensitive to others and adapting behaviours to others are often not so common.

FIGURE 6.1 What You Do with Your Communication Time

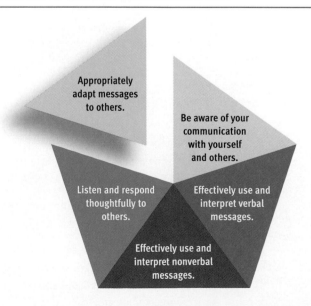

The greater our differences in background, experience, religion, and culture, the more difficult it is for us to interpret verbal and nonverbal symbols and to listen accurately to the messages of others, and the more challenging it is for us to adapt messages to others. When we meet someone for the first time, we often explore people, places, and backgrounds that we have in common. It is usually easier to develop a relationship with someone who is similar rather than dissimilar to us.

The goal of this chapter is to identify culture and gender differences that may inhibit communication with others and to suggest adaptive strategies that can improve the quality and effectiveness of our communication with others. Throughout the first five chapters, we have noted in our discussions (and in the special boxed feature Communication and Diversity) that culture and gender differences affect our communication with others. In this chapter we examine in more detail the influence that these differences have on our lives and suggest some communication strategies for bridging these differences in our relationships with others.

As we focus on culture and gender differences and how to adapt to them, we will focus on the nature of culture and gender, identify barriers that stem from culture and gender differences, and suggest strategies that can help you better understand, appreciate, and adapt to people who are not just like you. Our premise: In order to live comfortably in the 21st century, we must learn ways to appreciate and understand culture and gender differences, rather than ignore them, suffer because of them, or wish they would disappear. But simply understanding that there are differences is not enough to improve communication; it is important to learn how to use effective communication skills to adapt to those differences.

Even though the focus of this chapter is on culture and gender differences, realize that these are only two of many ways of categorizing differences that divide one person from another. Differences in age (sometimes called the generation gap), socioeconomic status, sexual orientation, and even a person's height, weight, or clothing choices are differences that have created tension between people in the past and probably will in the future. The principle of adapting to others is applicable to virtually all communication situations. The ideas and strategies we suggest at the end of this chapter about bridging differences in culture or gender apply to other differences that create conflict and tension. The simple fact is, we are each different from one another; the challenge is not to let our differences create a chasm so large that we can't find ways to ethically adapt our communication to create shared meaning.

CULTURE AND COMMUNICATION

Overheard from a student before class:

> I've had it with all this cultural diversity and gender stuff. It seems like every textbook in every class is obsessed with it. My music appreciation class is trying to force the music of other cultures down my throat. What's wrong with Bach, Beethoven, and Brahms? In English lit, all we're reading is stuff by people from different countries. And it seems my history prof talks only about obscure people I've never heard of before. I'm tired of all this politically correct nonsense. I mean, we're all Canadians, aren't we? We're not going off to live in Africa, China, or India. Why don't they just teach us what we need to know and cut all this diversity garbage?

Have you heard this kind of sentiment expressed before? Perhaps you've encountered this kind of "diversity backlash" among some of your classmates, or you may harbour this attitude yourself. It may seem unsettling to some that our curricula and textbooks are focusing on issues of culture and gender differences. But these changes are not motivated by an irrational desire to be politically correct. They are taking place because Canada is changing. The 2001 census analysis series developed by Statistics Canada documents Canada's ethnocultural portrait as indicated in the Communication and Diversity box. With Canada's growing diversity comes a heightened awareness that learning about cultural

ETHICAL PROBE ⋮⋰

Professor Smothers strongly believes that each student at the university should be required to take a course in multicultural studies. Is it ethical to require students to take courses in cultural or gender studies as part of their degree requirements? Or should such courses be elective options for students?

Canada's multicultural portrait is continually changing, growing, and enriching our nation.

COMMUNICATION and DIVERSITY

Canada's Ethnocultural Portrait

Immigrants have come to Canada from countries all over the world.

1. Data from the 2001 census show that the proportion of Canada's population born outside the country has reached its highest level in 70 years. Between 1991 and 2000, 2.2 million immigrants were admitted to Canada, the highest number for any decade in the past century.

2. As of May 15, 2001, 5.4 million people, or 18.4% of the total population, were born outside the country.

3. For the past 60 years, the United Kingdom, Italy, Germany, the Netherlands, and the United States were the primary sources of immigrants to Canada. Today, the majority of immigrants come from Asian countries.

4. In 2001, 61% of the immigrants who arrived in Canada during the 1990s used a nonofficial language (that is, neither French nor English) as their primary home language.

5. In 2001, 13.4% of Canadians (or 4 million) identified themselves as visible minorities.

6. Proportions of Canadian-born visible minorities vary widely from group to group. About 65% of Japanese were born in Canada, followed by 45% of blacks, 29% of South Asians, 25% of Chinese, 21% of Arabs and West Asians, 20% of Latin Americans, and 17% of Koreans.

7. Combined, the three largest visible minority groups in 2001—Chinese, South Asians, and blacks—accounted for two-thirds of the visible minority population. They were followed by Filipinos, Arabs and West Asians, Latin Americans, Southeast Asians, Koreans, and Japanese.

8. Chinese is the largest proportion of the visible minority population, accounting for 3.5% of the total national population and 26% of the visible minority population.

9. In 2001, more than 200 different ethnic origins were reported in Canada.

10. The list of origins includes cultural groups associated with Canada's first people—North American Indian, Métis, and Inuit—and groups associated with the founding of Canada, such as French, English, Scottish, and Irish. It also reflects the history of immigration to Canada in the past 100 years by including such groups as German, Italian, Chinese, Ukrainian, Dutch, Polish, and so on.

11. The changing sources of immigrants to Canada has resulted in emerging new ethnic origins from groups such as Kosovars from the former Yugoslavia; Azerbaijani and Georgians from Central Asia; Pashtun from Afghanistan; Yemeni and Saudi Arabians from the Middle East; Khmer from Southeast Asia; Nepali and Kashmiri from South Asia; Congolese, Yoruba, and Ashanti from Africa; and Bolivians, Maya, and Carib Indians from Central and South America.

Figure 6.2 shows that immigrants have settled in certain provinces over others. When visiting these provinces, take time to notice the richness that immigrant groups have contributed to the local culture.

Source: Statistics Canada, 2001 Census Results Teacher's Kit, Activity 10, Immigration and Citizenship.

FIGURE 6.2 Immigrants as a Percentage of Total Provincial Population, 2001

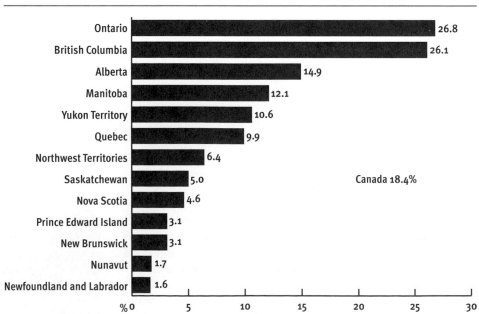

Source: Adapted from Statistics Canada Web site, www12.statcan.ca/english/census01/Teacher%27s_kit_ten.pdg_page62001.

as well as gender differences can affect every aspect of our lives in positive ways. You may not plan to travel the world, but the world is travelling to you. Your employers, teachers, religious leaders, best friends, or romantic partners may have grown up with cultural traditions different from your own. Our textbooks and courses are *reflecting* the change, not *initiating* it.

One statistician notes that if the world were a village of 1000 people, the village would have 590 Asians, 123 Africans, 96 Europeans, 84 Latin Americans, 55 members of the former Soviet Union, and 53 North Americans.[1] Clearly, a global economy and the ease with which technology permits us to communicate with others around the world increase the likelihood that you will establish relationships with people who are different from you and your own cultural traditions. You need not travel abroad to encounter cultural differences; the world is here.

Culture is a learned system of knowledge, behaviour, attitudes, beliefs, values, and norms that is shared by a group of people.[2] Communication and culture, says anthropologist Edward T. Hall, are inseparable—you can't talk about one without the other.[3] In the broadest sense, culture includes how people think, what they do, and how they use things to sustain their lives. Researcher Geert Hofstede says culture is the "mental software" that helps us understand our world.[4] Like the software and operating system in a personal computer, our culture provides the basis by which we interpret the "data" and information that enter our life.

Cultures are not static; they change as new information and new technologies penetrate their stores of knowledge. We no longer believe that bathing is unhealthy or that we should use leeches as the primary medical procedure to make us healthy. Through research, we have replaced both of these cultural assumptions with the values of personal hygiene and modern, sophisticated methods of medical care.

Some groups of individuals can best be described as a **co-culture**—a cultural group within a larger culture. A person's gender is one of the co-cultures that researchers have used to analyze and investigate the influence of communication on our relationships with others. We discuss the impact of gender on our communication in more detail later in the chapter. Gays and lesbians constitute another example of an important co-culture in our society.

Intercultural communication occurs when individuals or groups from different cultures communicate. The transactional process of listening and responding to people from different cultural backgrounds can be challenging. As we stressed earlier, the greater the difference in culture between two people, the greater the potential for misunderstanding and mistrust. That's why it is important to understand the nature of culture and how cultural differences influence our communication with others. Such understanding helps us develop strategies to make connections and adapt to others with different "mental software."

Misunderstandings and miscommunication occur between people from different cultures because of different rules for interpreting messages and different cultural expectations, which play a major role in shaping our communication. The greater the differences between the cultures, the more likely it is that people from those cultures will use different verbal and nonverbal messages.

When you encounter a culture that has little in common with your own, you may experience **culture shock,** a sense of confusion, anxiety, stress, and loss. If you are visiting

culture
A learned system of knowledge, behaviour, attitudes, beliefs, values, and norms that is shared by a group of people and shaped from one generation to the next.

co-culture
A culture that exists within a larger cultural context (e.g., gay and lesbian cultures, Mennonite culture).

intercultural communication
Communication between or among people who have different cultural traditions.

culture shock
Feelings of stress and anxiety a person experiences when encountering a culture different from his or her own.

Members of high-context cultures are skilled in using nonverbal cues to communicate. Members of low-context cultures rely more on actual words to send and receive messages.

world view
Perception shared by a culture or group of people about key beliefs and issues, such as death, God, and the meaning of life, which influences interaction with others; the lens through which people in a given culture perceive the world around them.

cultural context
Information not explicitly communicated through language, such as environmental or nonverbal cues.

high-context culture
Culture that derives much information from nonverbal and environmental cues and less information from the words of a message.

low-context culture
Culture that derives much information from the words of a message and less information from nonverbal and environmental cues.

or actually living in the new culture, your uncertainty and stress may take time to subside as you learn the values and message systems that characterize the culture. But if you are trying to communicate with someone from a background quite different from yours—even on your home turf—it is important to consider the role of culture as you interact.

Our culture and life experiences determine our **world view**—the general cultural perspective that determines how we perceive and respond to what happens to us. According to intercultural communication scholar Carley Dodd, "A culture's worldview involves finding out how the culture perceives the role of various forces in explaining why events occur as they do in a social setting."[5] These beliefs shape our thoughts, language, and actions. Your world view permeates all aspects of how you interact with society; it's like a lens through which you observe the world. If, as we noted in Chapter 1, communication is how we make sense out of the world and share that sense with others, our world view is one of the primary filters that influences how we make sense out of the world. Two frameworks for describing how culture influences our world view include cultural context and cultural values.

⤍ Cultural Contexts

People from different cultures respond to their surroundings or **cultural context** cues in different ways to influence the meaning of messages. Cultural context cues consist of the verbal and nonverbal messages that we use to create meaning when interacting with others. For example, when you interview for a job, you may be scanning the face of your interviewer and looking for nonverbal messages to provide cues about the impression you are making on the interviewer. These contextual cues (in this case, the nonverbal messages) give meaning to help you interpret the message of your interviewer. Edward T. Hall helped us understand the importance of cultural context when he categorized cultures as either high- or low-context.[6]

High-Context Culture

In **high-context cultures,** nonverbal cues are extremely important in interpreting messages. Communicators rely heavily on the context of more subtle information such as facial expression, vocal cues, and even silence to interpret messages; hence, the term *high-context cultures,* to indicate the emphasis placed upon the context. Asian, Arab, and Southern European peoples are more likely to draw upon the context for message interpretation.

Low-Context Culture

Low-context cultures rely more explicitly on language and the meaning of words and use fewer contextual cues to send and interpret information. Individuals from low-context cultures, such as North Americans or people from Germany or Scandinavia, may perceive that persons from high-context cultures are less attractive, knowledgeable, and trustworthy, because they violate unspoken rules of appearance, conduct, and communication. Individuals from low-context cultures often are less skilled in interpreting unspoken contextual messages.[7] Figure 6.3 describes differences between high- and low-context cultures.

⤍ Cultural Values

Ancient Egyptians worshiped cats. The Druids of England valued the experience of tapping into spiritual powers in the shadow of the mysterious rock circle of Stonehenge at the summer solstice. Some would say contemporary North Americans place a high value on accumulating material possessions and making pilgrimages to sports arenas on weekends. Making generalizations about what a culture values can provide important clues about how to respond to communication messages, establish relationships, and avoid making

FIGURE 6.3 High/Low Contexts: Where Different Cultures Fall on the Scale

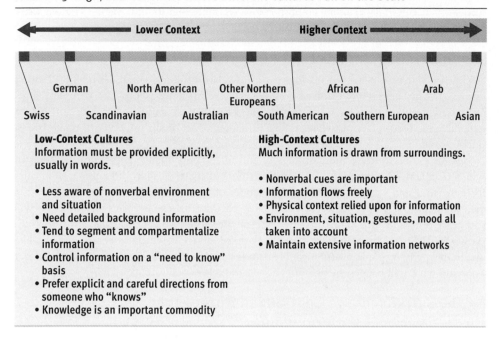

Lower Context ◄───── **Higher Context** ─────►

German   North American   Other Northern   African   Arab
                                         Europeans

Swiss   Scandinavian   Australian   South American   Southern European   Asian

Low-Context Cultures
Information must be provided explicitly, usually in words.

- Less aware of nonverbal environment and situation
- Need detailed background information
- Tend to segment and compartmentalize information
- Control information on a "need to know" basis
- Prefer explicit and careful directions from someone who "knows"
- Knowledge is an important commodity

High-Context Cultures
Much information is drawn from surroundings.

- Nonverbal cues are important
- Information flows freely
- Physical context relied upon for information
- Environment, situation, gestures, mood all taken into account
- Maintain extensive information networks

embarrassing errors when interacting with people from a given culture. Identifying what a given group of people values or appreciates can provide insight into the behaviour of an individual raised within that culture. Although there are considerable differences among the world's **cultural values**—clearly, not all cultures value the same things—Geert Hofstede has identified four categories for measuring values that are important in almost every culture.[8] Even though his research data were collected more than 30 years ago and only sampled employees (predominantly males) who worked at IBM—a large international company with branch offices in many countries—his research remains one of the most comprehensive studies to help us understand how to describe what people from a culture may value. According to Hofstede's research, each culture places relative value on (1) masculine and feminine perspectives, (2) avoidance or tolerance of uncertainty, (3) distribution of power, and (4) individualism or collectivism. Hofstede's research conclusions for several countries are included in Table 6.1 on page 125. These research conclusions are based on several tests that he developed and administered to more than 100 000 people.

> **cultural values**
> That which a given group of people values or appreciates.

⋯⟩ Masculine and Feminine Cultural Values

Some cultures emphasize traditional male values—such as getting things done and being more assertive; other cultures place greater emphasis on traditional female values—building relationships and seeking peace and harmony with others. People from **masculine cultures** also tend to value more traditional roles for men and women. These values are not only about biological sex differences; they are general approaches to interacting with other people. Later in this chapter, we will discuss how gender contributes to the development of a culture, but you first need to realize that whole cultures can be typified by whether they identify with or emphasize masculine or feminine values. People (both men and women) from masculine cultures value achievement, heroism, material wealth, and making things happen. Men and women from **feminine cultures** tend to value such things as caring for the less fortunate, being sensitive toward others, and enhancing the overall quality of life.[9] It is important to note that some would object to a rigid differentiation of female versus male values and cultures. This is simply one of many perspectives used to understand cultural differences.

> **masculine cultural values**
> Emphasize achievement, assertiveness, heroism, material wealth, and traditional male and female roles.

> **feminine cultural values**
> Emphasize being sensitive toward others and fostering harmonious personal relationships with others.

We caution you to avoid making sweeping generalizations about any culture. Just as there are differences between and among cultures, there are differences within a cultural group. For centuries, most countries in Asia and South America have had masculine

collectivistic culture
A cultural perspective that places a high value on collaboration, team-work, and group achievement.

individualistic culture
A cultural perspective that values individual achievement and personal accomplishments.

Members of a collectivistic culture may find team sports to be more satisfying than individual sports.

cultures. Men and their conquests are featured in history books and all aspects of society more than women. But today's cultural anthropologists see some shift in these values. There is some movement toward the middle, with greater equality between masculine and feminine roles.

⋯⃗ Uncertainty and Certainty Cultural Values

"Why don't they tell me what's going on?" exclaims an exasperated student. "I don't know what my grades are. I don't know what my exam score is. I'm in a complete fog." Many people like to know "what's going on." They like to avoid uncertainty and have a general sense for predicting what's going to happen. Too much uncertainty makes them uncomfortable.

Some people tolerate more ambiguity and uncertainty than others. Those cultures in which people need certainty to feel secure are more likely to develop and enforce rigid rules for behaviour and establish more elaborate codes of conduct. People from cultures with a greater tolerance for uncertainty have more relaxed, informal expectations for others. "It will sort itself out" and "Go with the flow" are phrases that characterize their attitudes.[10] As shown in Table 6.1, people from Greece, Portugal, and Guatemala generally do not like uncertainty, while people from Singapore, Jamaica, and Denmark are more comfortable not knowing what will happen next.

⋯⃗ Decentralized and Centralized Approaches to Power and Cultural Values

Some cultures are more comfortable with a broad distribution of power. People from such cultures prefer a decentralized approach to power. Leadership is not vested in just one person. Decisions in a culture that values decentralized power distribution are more likely to be made by consensus rather than by decree. Research suggests that people from Austria, Israel, Denmark, New Zealand, and Ireland typically prefer minimized power differences between others; they strive for more equal distribution of authority and control.[11]

Those cultures that place a high value on centralized power are more comfortable with a militaristic approach to power; centralized power cultures prefer a strongly organized, centrally controlled form of government, as well as managerial styles that feature clear lines of who reports to whom. Hierarchical bureaucracies are common, and the general assumption is that some people will have more power, control, and influence than others. Research by Geert Hofstede suggests that people from Malaysia, Guatemala, Panama, and the Philippines are all high on the centralized power scale.[12]

⋯⃗ Individualistic and Collectivistic Cultural Values

Which of the following two sayings best characterizes your culture: "All for one and one for all" or "I did it my way"? If you chose the first one, your culture is more likely to value group or team collaboration—what researchers call a **collectivistic culture.** Collectivistic cultures champion what people do together and reward group achievement. The "I did it my way" phrase emphasizes the importance of the individual over the group. A culture that celebrates individual achievement in entertainment, where shows such as *Canadian Idol* typically get high TV ratings, and in which individual recognition is important is one that emphasizes **individualistic** cultural values.

Traditionally, North Americans place a high value on individual achievements. People from Asian cultures are more likely to value collective or group achievement.

In a collectivistic culture, conversely, people strive to accomplish goals for the benefit of the group rather than the individual. Here's a description of a Kenyan culture's emphasis on group or team collaboration:

> . . . nobody is an isolated individual. Rather, his [or her] uniqueness is a secondary fact. . . . In this new system, group activities are dominant, responsibility is shared and accountability is collective. . . Because of the emphasis on collectivity, harmony and cooperation among the group tend to be emphasized more than individual function and responsibility.[13]

Individualistic cultures tend to be more loosely knit socially; individuals feel responsibility for taking care of themselves and their immediate families.[14] Individuals in collectivistic

TABLE 6.1 Examples of Countries That Illustrate Four Cultural Values

Cultural Value	Examples of Countries That Scored Higher on This Cultural Value	Examples of Countries That Scored Lower on This Cultural Value
Masculinity: People from countries with higher masculinity scores prefer high achievement, men in more assertive roles, and more clearly differentiated sex roles than people from countries with lower scores on this cultural dimension.	Japan, Australia, Venezuela, Italy, Switzerland, Mexico, Ireland, Jamaica, Great Britain	Sweden, Norway, the Netherlands, Denmark, Yugoslavia, Costa Rica, Finland, Chile, Portugal, Thailand
Uncertainty Avoidance: People from countries with higher uncertainty avoidance scores generally prefer to avoid uncertainty; they like to know what will happen next. People from countries with lower scores are more comfortable with uncertainty.	Greece, Portugal, Guatemala, Uruguay, Belgium, Japan, Yugoslavia, Peru, France	Singapore, Jamaica, Denmark, Sweden, Hong Kong, Ireland, Great Britain, Malaysia, India, Philippines, United States
Power Distribution: People from countries with higher power distribution scores generally prefer greater power differences between people; they are generally more accepting of someone having authority and power than are those from countries with lower scores on this cultural dimension.	Malaysia, Guatemala, Panama, Philippines, Mexico, Venezuela, Arab countries, Ecuador, Indonesia, India	Austria, Israel, Denmark, New Zealand, Ireland, Sweden, Norway, Finland, Switzerland, Great Britain
Individualism: People from countries with higher individualism scores generally prefer individual accomplishment, rather than collective or collaborative achievement.	Canada, Australia, Great Britain, United States, the Netherlands, New Zealand, Italy, Belgium, Denmark, Sweden, France	Guatemala, Ecuador, Panama, Venezuela, Columbia, Indonesia, Pakistan, Costa Rica, Peru, Taiwan, South Korea

Source: Adapted from Geert Hofstede, *Cultures and Organizations: Software of the Mind* (London: McGraw-Hill, 1991). © Geert Hofstede.

cultures expect more loyalty and support from others, and demonstrate more loyalty to the community. Because collectivistic cultures place more value on "we" than "I," teamwork approaches usually succeed better in their workplaces. Canadian businesses have tried to adopt some of Japan's successful team strategies for achieving high productivity. However, while teamwork training has been successful, Canadian workers still need constant reminders to collaborate and work collectively.

GENDER AND COMMUNICATION

Perhaps the most prevalent form of human diversity is gender—the division of human beings into female and male. As we pointed out

ReCAP ←⋯

Cultural Values

Masculine and Feminine	• Masculine cultures value achievement, assertiveness, heroism, material wealth, and more traditional sex roles.
	• Feminine cultures value relationships, caring for the less fortunate, overall quality of life, and less traditional distinctions between sex roles.
Uncertainty and Certainty	• Cultures that value certainty do not like ambiguity and value feeling secure.
	• Cultures that value uncertainty are comfortable with ambiguity and less information.
Decentralized and Centralized Power	• Centralized power cultures value having power in the hands of a smaller number of people.
	• Decentralized power cultures favour more equality and a more even distribution of power in government and organizations.
Individualistic and Collectivistic	• Individualistic cultures value accomplishments of individual achievement.
	• Collectivistic cultures value group and team collaboration.

in Chapter 2, a person's sex is determined by biology; gender is the culturally constructed and psychologically based perception of the self as feminine, masculine, or androgynous (a combination of both feminine and masculine traits). Gender is learned and socially reinforced by others, as well as by life experience and genetics. Some scholars prefer to study gender as a subset of culture (a co-culture), as a form of cultural diversity on the level of such other aspects as race, ethnicity, and religion. We view gender as one of many basic elements of culture; but because it so pervades our everyday existence, we choose to treat it more fully in this chapter as we continue our focus on adapting to others—especially others who are different from you.

At one time or another, you have probably thought, "Why doesn't she (or he) act like persons of *my* sex?" Have you ever heard yourself or someone else say, "You men are all alike," or "If women would just be more reasonable, like men are, life would be simpler"? You may also have heard (or said) *"Vive la différence"*—a French expression that celebrates the fact that men and women are different. Why? Because that difference makes us fascinating and mysterious, and it keeps the world from being awfully dull. No matter your stance, your day-to-day interaction with members of both sexes is a fact of life (unless you're a hermit). Women and men work, live, and play together, so it's important to explore the effects of gender on communication in order to improve our ability to relate to one another.

In fact, the likelihood that all of us will come into more frequent contact with members of both sexes working outside the home is increasing. According to Statistics Canada, in 2002 the civilian workforce was 54% male and 46% female.[15] Many more women are working outside of the home than ever before, and projections indicate that this trend will continue.

Gender differences add to the complexity of the communication process.

⋯⟩ The Importance of Gender in Culture

In the predominant culture of Canada, being male or female is an important thing to know about a person. Think about it: What's the first question a new parent is asked? "Ten fingers and ten toes?" "Hairy or bald-headed?" "Blue eyes or brown?" The first question almost always asked is, "Is it a boy or girl? Pink or blue?" We place a great deal of importance on the sex of a person in this culture, as do many other cultures around the world. Some critics contend that we're too concerned with gender, with emphasizing differences between women and men and conditioning boys to be masculine and girls to be feminine. Some men and women in our culture are chastised or ostracized because they don't conform to society's expectations for their sex.

Fascinating research reveals that sex-based expectations and conditioning start practically from birth. Girls and boys are talked to and responded to differently by adults, beginning with their parents.[16] Female babies are held more gingerly; as they become toddlers, they receive more attention from parents when they fall and are kept in closer proximity than male children. Boys are encouraged to be rough and tumble, to "shake it off" when they fall, and to explore greater distances than girls. Girls are often allowed to reveal their emotions more readily than boys, while many boys may be taught to control or hide their emotions. When carried into adulthood, these early sex-based lessons may cause serious harm to our bodies, professional advancement, and relationships. For example, women who want to succeed in their careers often learn the hard way that revealing their emotions isn't considered professional. Many men find that years of suppressing emotion can lead to health problems and estrangement from family members.

An important question for us to consider is this: Just how different are you and members of your sex from members of the opposite sex? Do you think that women are from one planet and men another? Do you think that men constitute one cultural group and women another? Or do you think the media and other moneymaking enterprises oversell sex differences in an effort to create conflict and drama to generate high ratings and profits?

John Gray, author of the book *Men Are from Mars, Women Are from Venus,* would have us believe that the sexes are so different that we actually approach life from two distinct "planets" or spheres of perspective.[17] Although several of Gray's conclusions have been challenged by communication scholars because many of his points are not supported by research, there are some research-documented differences between the ways men and women communicate.[18] Deborah Tannen, author of several books on the behaviour of the sexes, views men and women as distinctly different cultural groups.[19] She suggests that female–male communication is cross-cultural communication, with all the challenges inherent in exchanging messages with persons of very different backgrounds and value systems. Perhaps these viewpoints are a bit extreme, and the sexes are actually more alike than different.

There are, however, some interesting differences based on research—not popular opinion or media hype—that are worthy of mention. Here's what we suggest:

- First, work to understand the differences we discuss.
- Second, make an insightful examination of your own behaviour in light of what is described as pertaining to your sex and then determine how you conform to and differ from the description.
- Finally, attempt to adapt your behaviour appropriately.

We don't mean that you have to communicate as you think members of your sex would or should communicate, but be mindful of how you interact with others to enhance the quality of your relationships with them. There may be times when you can communicate in a non-sex-specific manner appropriate to the situation. If you can accomplish these things, you will have made real progress toward enhancing your communication understanding and skill.

⌁ Why Women and Men Communicate Versus How

In an earlier section of this chapter, we explored ways in which aspects of cultures may be typified by their emphasis on masculine or feminine values. Some of the values associated with masculinity include being assertive and getting things done. Classic sociological research has termed such qualities an **instrumental orientation,** a term that implies action and a "me against the world" view of the self.[20] Feminine cultural values emphasize connecting with others and fostering harmonious relationships, what has been termed an **expressive orientation.**

Translating these orientations into actual communication behaviour is revealing. Research using multiple methods and originating in various disciplines consistently shows

instrumental orientation
A masculine approach that involves assertiveness and action, in a "me against the world" view of self and reality.

expressive orientation
A feminine approach that emphasizes connecting with others and fostering harmonious relationships and community.

content dimension
The what of a communication message; the verbal message.

relational dimension
The nonverbal elements of a message, such as tone of voice and facial expressions, that convey how the message should be interpreted and provide clues about the state of the relationship between the interactants.

that differences in men's and women's communication have more to do with *why* we communicate than *how.* Men tend to talk to accomplish something or achieve a task. Women often use conversation to establish and maintain relationships.

In Chapter 1, we discussed some basic characteristics of communication, the first being that communication is inescapable. We expanded on that characteristic by describing how every message has a content dimension and a relational dimension. The **content dimension** contains what is said or the verbal message. The **relational dimension** involves how the verbal message is said, including tone of voice, facial expressions, and other nonverbal behaviours. The content is the *what,* the relational is the *how;* the latter aspect tells you how to interpret the former. You also receive clues about the state of the relationship between the two interactants from the relational dimension. How are these characteristics of communication affected by gender?

Research reveals that men tend to approach communication from a content orientation, meaning that they view communication as functioning primarily for information exchange. You talk when you have something to say. This is also consistent with the tendency for men to base their relationships, especially their male friendships, on sharing activities rather than talking. Women, as research suggests, tend to approach communication for the purpose of relating or connecting to others, of extending themselves to other persons to know them and be known by them. What you talk about is less important than the fact that you're talking, because talking implies a relationship. A short way of summarizing this difference: *Men often communicate to report; women often communicate to establish rapport.*[21] So the point of difference isn't in the way the sexes actually communicate but in the motivations or reasons for communicating. The *how* may not be that different; the *why* may be very different.[22] Our instrumental and expressive orientations to the world translate into our communication behaviour.

⟶•⟵ COMMUNICATION and TECHNOLOGY

As you are no doubt aware, many people today are "virtually" meeting and initiating relationships over the Internet. Given the increasing frequency with which this happens, do you think that the absence of in-person contact changes our approach to conversation? For example, are men just as likely to approach an online chat for the purpose of exchanging information as they are in a face-to-face conversation? Are women likely to approach the chat for the purpose of establishing a connection or relationship? It's interesting to consider how online conversations either diminish or reaffirm some of the sex-based behaviours that research has documented from face-to-face encounters.

ReCAP ⟵···

Gender-Based Approaches to Communication

MASCULINE	FEMININE
More instrumental: Characterized by assertiveness and getting things done	More expressive: Characterized by an emphasis on connecting with others and fostering harmonious relationships
More emphasis on the content of communication messages: Focuses more on the information being exchanged (the what) rather than relational elements (the how) in the message.	More emphasis on the relational elements of communication messages: Focuses more on the quality of the relationship between communicators than on information exchanged. Attending more to nonverbal elements, how something is said rather than what is said.

So here's one point where adaptation is a premium skill. Can you see that by understanding both approaches to communication—content and relational (or instrumental and expressive)—and by developing the ability to accomplish both, you broaden what you can do? Just because you're female doesn't mean that you have to take an expressive approach to every interaction; just because you're male doesn't mean that conversations are always about information exchange. In a conversation with a member of the opposite sex, try to assess the person's communication motivation. Analyze what the other person must view as the purpose for the conversation, and adjust your response accordingly. Sometimes it's wise simply to ask the person what he or she wants.

BARRIERS TO BRIDGING DIFFERENCES AND ADAPTING TO OTHERS

Now that we've seen how people are different from one another, let's identify those barriers that increase the differences that exist between people. Differences, whether culture or gender based, often breed misunderstanding. And misunderstanding can lead to feelings of distrust, suspicion, and even hostility. The phrase "battle of the sexes" suggests that men and women perceive and respond to the world differently, which may result in disagreement and evolve into literal battles. According to a 1993 study of violence against women funded by Statistics Canada, approximately 25% of all Canadian women have experienced physical or sexual violence inflicted by a male partner.[23] Canadian victim surveys revealed that serious repeated wife assault occurs in approximately 6.8% of all marriages.[24]

The front pages of our major newspapers continue to chronicle the prevalence of terrorism, war, and conflict around the globe, which are due, in part, to different cultural perspectives. Our hopes for harmony in our own country can also erode when we learn of hate crimes committed against members of co-cultural groups within the Canadian context. During the first decade of the new millennium, our hopes for peace and prosperity among all of the world's peoples are often dashed when we read of violent clashes between people of different religions, races, sexual orientation, and ethnicities.

Is it possible to develop effective relationships with people who are different from ourselves? The answer is, "Of course." Although almost every relationship experiences some degree of conflict, most of the world's people do not witness annihilating destruction each day. Bridging culture and gender differences is possible.

The first step to bridging differences between people is to identify what hinders effective communication. Sometimes communication falters because of different meanings created by different languages or interpretations of nonverbal messages. And sometimes communication falters because of our inability to stop focusing exclusively on our own goals; we fail to consider the needs of our communication partners. To develop effective strategies to adapt to others who are different from ourselves, we'll examine some of the barriers that often separate us from one another.

⤑ Assuming Superiority

Canadians across the country shook their heads in absolute horror and disbelief as they watched TV images of the twin towers of the World Trade Center crumbling in a shroud of smoke and ash and the Pentagon erupting in flames. These indelible images of September 11, 2001, are seared in our consciousness. Collectively we asked, "Why?" There are no easy answers. Part of the answer, however, may lie in the belief of self-righteous superiority held by those who seek to destroy cultural and religious traditions that are different from their own. Of course, terrorism and violence are not new; early historical records document that differences, especially religious differences, have for centuries created conditions that have resulted in unspeakable human atrocities. One of the most powerful barriers to adapting to others is the belief that our own culture or gender is better than others.

Ethnocentrism is the attitude that our own cultural approaches are superior to those of other cultures. Extreme ethnocentrism is the opposite of being other oriented. When fans from rival teams at a Friday-night hockey game both scream, "We're number one!"

ethnocentrism
The belief that your cultural traditions and assumptions are superior to others.

they may find it difficult to establish quality communication with each other. Competition is, of course, expected in sports; but when the mindset of unquestioned superiority exists only because of cultural or religious identification, the resulting mistrust and suspicion are breeding grounds for conflict in any relationship. Ethnocentrism and cultural snobbery make up one of the quickest ways to create a barrier that inhibits rather than enhances communication. It would probably be impossible to eliminate completely the feeling that we are more comfortable with our own culture and people who are like us. In fact, some degree of ethnocentrism can play a useful role in perpetuating our own cultural traditions; we form communities and groups based upon having common traditions, beliefs, and values. A problem occurs, however, if we become so extremely biased in favour of our own cultural traditions that we fail to recognize that people from other cultural traditions are just as comfortable with their approach to life as we are with ours. And when we mindlessly attack someone else's cultural traditions (which may be a prelude to physical aggression), we begin to erect communication barriers.

"My dad is smarter than your dad." "Boys are smarter than girls." "Canadian citizens are more industrious than workers in other countries." What may start out as a child's chant may continue to be part of a cultural consciousness that leads to perceptions of cultural and gender superiority. Cultural anthropologists caution against assuming that one culture is superior to another; as we just noted, this creates a barrier. If you have ever talked with someone who had an overinflated ego, you know what a hindrance such a self-promoting attitude can be to communication. If a group or nation harbours that sense of unchallenged superiority and feeling of ordained righteousness, it will be difficult to establish quality communication relationships with that group.

A person who assumes superiority may also assume greater power and control over others. Conflicts are often about power—who has it and who wants more of it. Differences in power, therefore, are breeding grounds for mistrust and conflict. The 19th-century British scholar Lord Acton said that absolute power corrupts absolutely; although this may not always be the case, an ethnocentric mindset that assumes superiority may add to the perception of assumed power over others. Although it's true that there are cultural differences in how much acceptance a cultural group has toward power (whether power is centralized or decentralized), world history documents that those who are excessively pushed and pulled and pummelled eventually revolt and seek greater equity of power.

Although the communication process may be difficult between members of different cultures, both parties need to work to understand each other.

---》 Assuming Similarity

Just as it is inaccurate to assume that all people who belong to another social group, gender, or class are worlds apart from you, it is also erroneous to assume that others act and think as you do. Even if they appear to be like you, all people are not alike. Focusing on superficial factors such as appearance, clothing, and even a person's occupation can lead to false impressions. Instead, we must take the time to explore the person's background and cultural values before we can determine what we really have in common.

On meeting a new acquaintance, we usually explore what we may have in common. "Do you know so and so?" "Oh, you're from Vancouver. Do you know Mamie Smith from Parksville?" The search for similarities helps us develop a common framework for communication. But even when we find a few similarities, we would be in error if we made too many assumptions about our new friend's attitudes and perceptions. Because of our human tendency to develop categories and use words to label our experiences, we may lump people into a common category and assume similarity where none exists. As we discussed in Chapter 2, each of us perceives the world through his or her own frame of reference. As one ancient Greek sage put it, "Every tale can be told in a different way." We not only see the world differently, but we express those differences in the way we talk, think, and interact with others. If we fail to be mindful that each of us is unique, we may take communication shortcuts, use unfamiliar words, and assume our communication will be more effective than it is.

Stereotyping and Prejudice

Closely related to ethnocentrism and feelings of cultural and gender superiority is the barrier of making a rigid judgment against a class or type of people.

All Canadians drink beer.
All Russians like vodka.
All men like to watch wrestling.
All Asians are good at math.
All women like to go shopping.

These statements are stereotypes. They are all inaccurate. To **stereotype** someone is to push him or her into an inflexible, all-encompassing category. The term *stereotype* comes from a printing term in which the typesetter uses the same type to print the text again and again. When we stereotype, we "print" the same judgment over and over again, failing to consider the uniqueness of individuals, groups, or events. Such a "hardening of the categories" becomes a barrier to effective communication and inhibits our ability to adapt to others. Two anthropologists suggest that every person is, in some respects, (1) like all other people, (2) like some other people, and (3) like no other people.[25] Our challenge when meeting others is to sort out how they are alike and how they are unique. Stereotypes and prejudices result from rigid, inflexible thinking. Mark Twain once said, "It is discouraging to try and penetrate a mind such as yours. You ought to get out and dance on it. That would take some of the rigidity out of it." Learning how to break rigid stereotypes is an important part of the process of learning how to adapt to others.

A related barrier, **prejudice,** is a judgment we make based on the assumption that we already know all of the information we need to know about a person. To prejudge someone as inept, inferior, or incompetent based upon that person's ethnicity, race, sexual orientation, gender, or some other factor is a corrosive force that can raise significant barriers to effective communication. Some prejudices are widespread. Although there are more females than males in the world, one study found that even when a male and a female held the same type of job, the male's job was considered more prestigious than the female's.[26] Even though it is illegal in Canada to discriminate because of a person's gender, race, or age in offering employment or promotions, women and members of minority groups may still be discriminated against. In the workplace, stereotyping and prejudice are still formidable barriers to communicating effectively with others.

Different Communication Codes

When Manny and Mary were on their vacation in Toronto, they visited a downtown market called Chinatown—a district populated with many Asian immigrants. When they tried to purchase some fruit, it was a frustrating experience for both Manny and Mary, as well as for the market salesclerk; Manny and Mary spoke no Chinese, and the clerk knew

ETHICAL PROBE

Following the September 11, 2001, terrorism attacks on the United States, there has been increased debate in Canadian media about the ethics of racial profiling—targeting a specific racial or ethnical group for questioning about possible terrorist activity. Even though we've identified the negative consequences of rigidly reacting to prejudices and stereotypes, are there situations that call for engaging in focusing on a specific group of people who may look suspicious because of their racial or ethnic background? Or, should any actions based on prejudging or stereotyping someone not occur?

stereotype
To place a person or group of persons into an inflexible, all-encompassing category.

prejudice
Judging someone before you know relevant facts or background information.

ETHICAL PROBE

Janice overheard her friend Lucy make a negative, bigoted comment about Asian Canadians that Janice found highly offensive. Is it appropriate for Janice to tell Lucy that she is offended by such comments? When should we voice our concerns and objections to racial, ethnic, or sexist slurs that offend us? Is it always appropriate to speak out when you hear others making prejudiced or bigoted remarks?

ReCAP

Barriers to Bridging Differences and Adapting to Others

Assuming Superiority	Becoming ethnocentric—assuming that our own culture and cultural traditions are superior to those of others
Assuming Similarity	Assuming that other people respond to situations as we respond; failing to acknowledge and consider differences in culture and background
Stereotyping and Prejudice	Rigidly categorizing others and prejudging others based upon limited information
Different Communication Codes	Differences in language and the interpretation of nonverbal cues, leading to misunderstanding

no English. It is not uncommon today, when you travel within Canada, to encounter people who do not speak your language. Obviously, this kind of difference poses a formidable communication challenge. Even when you do speak the same tongue as another, he or she may come from a place where the words and gestures have different meanings. Your ability to communicate will depend upon whether you can understand each other's verbal and nonverbal cues.

ADAPTING TO OTHERS WHO ARE DIFFERENT FROM YOU

It is not enough simply to identify some of the common barriers that highlight our differences. Although becoming "consciously competent" about what may keep us from adapting and connecting with others is important, there are also some strategies that can help in our quest to adapt to others. We need effective communication skills to overcome our differences. It is not enough just to point to the barriers we have identified and say, "Don't do that." Identifying the causes of misunderstanding is a good first step to adapting to others, but most people need more concrete advice with specific strategies to help them overcome these barriers. The underlying principle we develop in this chapter is one of adapting to others—acknowledging and responding to difference, with the goal of enhancing understanding.

⤳ Seek Information

Philosopher André Gide said, "Understanding is the beginning of approving." Prejudice often is the result of ignorance. Learning about another person's values, beliefs, and culture can help you understand his or her messages and their meaning. For example, as you speak to a person from another culture, think of yourself as a detective, watching for implied, often unspoken messages that provide information about the values, norms, roles, and rules of that person's culture.

You can also prepare yourself by studying the culture of others. If you are going to another country, start by reading a travel guide or another very simple, general overview of the culture. You may then want to learn more detailed information by studying the history, art, or geography of the culture. The Internet offers a wealth of information about the culture and traditions of others. In addition to reading books and magazines and using cyber sources, talk to people from other cultures. If you are trying to communicate with someone closer to home who is from a different background, you can learn about the music, food, and other aspects of the culture. Given the inextricable link between language and culture, the more you learn about another language, the better you will understand the traditions and customs of the culture.

As we discussed at the beginning of the chapter, the broad concept of culture also includes the notion of a co-culture, a cultural group within a larger culture. Learning how men and women, each a separate co-culture, communicate differently can help improve your communication with members of the opposite sex. Men, for example, are more likely to develop friendships through participating in common activities with other men (playing on a sports team or working together).[27] Women are more likely to develop friendships through talking together rather than working together.[28]

As you read about other cultures or co-cultures, it is important not to develop rigid categories or stereotypes for the way others may talk or behave. Proclaiming, "Oh, you're just saying that because you're a woman," or "You men are always saying things like that," can increase rather than decrease communication barriers. In this chapter and throughout this book, we will identify research-based gender differences in the way men and women communicate to improve your understanding of and communication with members of the opposite sex. But, as noted earlier, we don't recommend that you treat men and women as completely separate species from different planets and automatically assume you will be misunderstood. Such a stereotypical judgment does not enhance communication—it hinders it.

⤳ Listen and Ask Questions

When you talk with people who are different from you, you may feel some discomfort and uncertainty. This is normal. We are more comfortable talking with people we know and who are like us. Communication, through the give-and-take process of listening, talking, and asking questions, helps to reduce the uncertainty present in any relationship. When you meet people for the first time, you are typically not certain about their likes and dislikes, including whether they like or dislike you. When you communicate with a person from another culture or co-culture, the uncertainty level escalates. As you begin to talk, you exchange information that helps you develop greater understanding. If you continue to ask questions, eventually you will feel less anxiety and uncertainty. You will be more likely to predict how the person will behave. When you meet a person who is different from you, ask thoughtful questions, then pause to listen. This is a simple technique for gathering information and also for confirming the accuracy of your expectations and assumptions across cultural groups.

Just asking questions and sharing information about yourself is not sufficient to remove communication barriers and bridge differences in culture and background, but it is a good beginning. The skills of stopping (focusing on the message of the other person), looking (observing nonverbal cues), and listening (noting both details and major ideas) that we presented in the last chapter will serve you well in enhancing communication with people from a different cultural tradition than yours.

⤳ Tolerate Ambiguity

Many people become uncomfortable with uncertainty and ambiguity—especially if they are from a low-context culture such as that in North America. As we discussed earlier in the chapter, low-context cultures prefer a more direct approach to getting information. North Americans prefer direct messages and often say things like "Tell it to me straight," "Don't beat around the bush," "What is the bottom line?" or "Just tell me what you want."

Communicating with someone from another culture that does not value such directness produces uncertainty. It may take time and several exchanges to clarify a message. If you are from a cultural tradition that values certainty, and you are uncomfortable with uncertainty, you may have to acknowledge the cultural difference. Be patient and work at tolerating more ambiguity. Don't be in a hurry to have all of the details nailed down. Remind yourself that the other person does not have the same value of knowing the future or appreciating details.

⤳ Develop Mindfulness

To be **mindful** is to be aware of how you communicate with others. A mindful communicator puts into practice the first communication principle we presented in this book: *Be aware of your communication with yourself and others.* To be a mindful communicator, you should constantly remind yourself that other people are not like you. Also, you should be aware that other people see the world differently and therefore communicate differently; their different communication strategies are not intended to offend or to be rude, people just have different culturally based strategies of interacting with others. Intercultural communication scholar William Gudykunst suggests that being mindful is one of the best ways to approach any new cultural encounter.[29] Mindfulness is a conscious state of mind, a realization of what is happening to you at a given moment. If you are not mindful, you are oblivious to the world around you. You are on mental cruise control.

How can you cultivate the skill of being mindful? You can become more mindful through **self-talk,** something we discussed earlier in the book. Self-talk consists of rational messages you tell yourself to help you manage your discomfort, emotions, or negative thoughts about situations. When Manny and Mary tried to purchase the fruit in Toronto's Chinatown, they could have become offended and muttered, "Doesn't anyone speak English around here?" Instead, Mary reminded Manny, "You know, it's not surprising that only Chinese is spoken here. Yes, it would be more comfortable for us if the clerk spoke our language. But we have to realize that there is no intent to offend us." Mary was being

mindful
To be aware of what you are doing and how you are communicating with others.

self-talk
Inner speech; communication with the self; the process of mentally verbalizing messages that help a person become more aware or mindful of how he or she is processing information and reacting to life situations.

mindful of the cultural differences; by acknowledging the differences rather than emotionally and mindlessly becoming offended, she was able to maintain her composure and communicate in a manner appropriate to the circumstances.

⋯⟩ Become Other Oriented

Scholars of evolution might argue that it is our tendency to look out for number one that ensures the continuation of the human race. But if we focus exclusively on ourselves, it is very unlikely that we will be effective communicators. As we noted earlier, assuming superiority is a major barrier to communicating with others. Most of us are **egocentric**—focused on ourselves. Our first inclination is to focus on meeting our own needs before addressing the needs of others.

In this chapter we have emphasized the principle of adapting to others. If we fail to adapt our message to listeners, especially listeners who are different from us (and isn't everyone different from you?), it is less likely that we will achieve our communication goal. As we noted earlier, adapting messages to others doesn't mean that we tell others only what they want to hear. That would be unethical, manipulative, and ineffective. Nor does being considerate of others mean we abandon all concern for our own interests. **Other-oriented communication** suggests that we consider the needs, motives, desires, and goals of our communication partners while still maintaining our own integrity. The choices we make in forming the message and selecting the time and place to deliver it should consider the thoughts and feelings of others.

Becoming other oriented is not a single skill but a family of skills anchored in an attitude of attempting to understand others' thoughts and feelings. Research in emotional intelligence documents that focusing on the needs and interests of others is essential to adapting communication messages to others.[30]

How do you become other oriented? We suggest a two-stage process, using skills discussed previously. The first stage, which we previewed in Chapter 5, is called social decentring—consciously *thinking* about another's thoughts and feelings. The second stage moves to empathy, a set of skills we also discussed in the last chapter. To empathize is to respond *emotionally* to another's feelings and actions.

Social Decentring

Social decentring involves viewing the world from the other person's point of view. It is a *cognitive process* through which we take into consideration another person's thoughts, values, background, and perspectives. Throughout this chapter, we have identified some of the barriers that inhibit us from effectively communicating with another person. To socially decentre is not to be a mind reader but to use our past experiences and our ability to interpret the clues of others to understand what others may be thinking or "seeing." According to Mark Redmond, a scholar who has extensively studied the process of social decentring, there are three ways to socially decentre, to take another person's perspective.[31]

First, develop an understanding of the other person, based upon how you have responded when something similar has happened to you in the past.[32] You know what it's like when you've been late for a meeting or important appointment. When someone you know says he or she feels frazzled over being late for a major meeting, you can think about what would be going through your mind if the same thing happened to you.

A second way to socially decentre is to base your understanding of what another person might be thinking on your knowledge of how that person has responded in the past. In communicating with people who are different from you, the more direct experience you have in interacting with that person, the better able you usually are to make predictions about how that person will react and respond. Even if, for example, you have never seen a friend of yours be late for a meeting, you may know how generally punctual your friend is. You therefore suspect that your friend may be quite frustrated by being late for a meeting.

A third way we socially decentre is to use our understanding of how most people, in general, respond to situations. If your roommate is from France, you probably have some general sense of the cultural differences between you and your French friend. You may harbour some general theories or assumptions about other French people. The caution,

---

egocentric
A preoccupied focus on one's self and one's self-importance.

other orientation
Focusing on the needs and concerns of others while maintaining one's personal integrity, achieved through the processes of socially decentring and being empathic.

social decentring
Cognitive process in which we take into account another person's thoughts, values, background, and perspectives.

however, is to avoid rigid stereotypes or prejudices that confine or limit your perceptions. The more you can learn about others' cultural or gender perspectives, the more accurate you can become in socially decentring, or surmising what the other person may be thinking. It is important, however, not to develop inaccurate, inflexible stereotypes and labels of others or to base your perceptions of others only on those generalizations.

Empathy

To socially decentre involves attempting to think what another person may be thinking. **Empathy,** a second strategy for becoming other oriented, is feeling the *emotional* reaction that the other person may be experiencing. Empathy is feeling what another person feels.

As we discussed in the last chapter, you develop the ability to empathize by being sensitive to your own feelings and assessing how you feel during certain situations and then projecting those feelings onto others.[33] To develop empathy, we suggested that you first *stop* focusing on only your own messages and thoughts and focus instead on the messages of others. We also recommended that you *look* for information about the emotional meaning of messages by focusing on nonverbal cues. Then *listen* by concentrating on what someone is telling you. In addition, *imagine* how you would feel if you were in your partner's position. Then *ask* appropriate questions, if you need to, to gain additional information. Finally, *paraphrase* the message content and the feelings of your partner and monitor his or her reactions to what you communicate.

Some emotional reactions are almost universal and cut across cultural boundaries. The ravages of war, famine, and natural disasters such as floods or earthquakes evoke universal emotions. As you see pictures on the news of people who have experienced tragedy in their life, you empathize with them. If you've seen the now classic movie *E. T. the Extra Terrestrial,* you may remember when Elliott, the young boy who discovers E.T., experiences an emotional bond with the alien. Elliott feels what E.T. feels. Such extreme empathic bonding may only happen in the movies. It would be unusual, if not impossible, for us to develop such empathy in our everyday relationships with others. Yet it is possible to develop emotional connections to others, and some people are more skilled and sensitive than others in developing emotional, empathic bonds.

Empathy is different from sympathy. When you offer **sympathy,** you tell others that you are sorry that they feel what they are feeling. You buy a sympathy card to communicate that you are sorry to hear that a cherished friend or relative has died. When you sympathize, you acknowledge someone's feelings. When you empathize, however, you experience an emotional reaction that is similar to the other person's; as much as possible, you strive to feel what he or she feels.

The late author and theologian Henri J. M. Nouwen suggested that empathy lies at the heart of enhancing the quality of our relationships with others. As Nouwen phrased it, in order to bridge our differences we need to "cross the road for one another":

> We become neighbors when we are willing to cross the road for one another. There is so much separation and segregation: between black people and white people, between gay people and straight people, between young people and old people, between sick people and healthy people, between prisoners and free people, between Jews and Gentiles, Muslims and Christians, Protestants and Catholics, Greek Catholics and Latin Catholics.
>
> There is a lot of road crossing to do. We are all very busy in our own circles. We have our own people to go to and our own affairs to take care of. But if we could cross the road once in a while and pay attention to what is happening on the other side, we might indeed become neighbors.[34]

⤏ Adapt to Others

Adapting to others gets to the bottom line of this chapter. After you have thought about how you may be different from others, considered culture and gender differences, and even identified potential barriers to communication, you reach this question: So now what do I *do?* What you do is appropriately adapt. To **adapt** is to adjust your behaviour in response to the other person or persons you are communicating with. You don't just keep communicating by "default" or in the same way you always did. You make an effort to change how you communicate, to enhance the quality of communication.

empathy
The process of developing an emotional reaction that is similar to the reaction being experienced by another person. Feeling what another person is feeling, rather than just acknowledging that he or she feels a certain way.

sympathy
To acknowledge that someone may be feeling a certain emotion, often an emotion due to loss or grief; to be compassionate toward someone.

adapt
To adjust behaviour in accord with what someone else does.

When you interact with someone who is different from you, how you respond or adapt to that person is crucial to the kind of relationship you establish with that person. For example, imagine that you're meeting someone new. In that first conversation, you detect that the person is more reserved than you. Perhaps you notice that the person makes less direct eye contact, has a softer voice, and doesn't use as many gestures as you and your friends do. In this situation, if you want to be an effective communicator, you will adapt your behaviour in an attempt to adjust to the other person. Perhaps you won't use your normal volume level; or tell a joke, expecting uproarious laughter to follow; or reach over and touch the person on the arm. Those behaviours might communicate more familiarity than the person is comfortable with in a first conversation. You don't change the essence of who you are; you simply adapt your behaviour to create a positive impression and to enhance the success of the conversation. Socially skilled people appropriately adapt their behaviour toward others.

We adapt messages to others to enhance their understanding of the message, to help us achieve the goal or intended effect of our communication, to ensure that we are ethical in our communication with others, and to establish and develop satisfying relationships. To enhance understanding when presenting a speech, you may need to slow your rate of speech or talk faster than you normally do. You may need to use more examples or speak in a very structured, organized way. To ensure that you achieve your communication objectives, you may need to draw upon statistics and other forms of evidence to prove your point. Or your communication partner may not be impressed with statistics but might be quite moved by a story that poignantly illustrates your point. We also adapt messages to be ethical. Ethical communication gives your communication partner choices, rather than forcing or coercing him or her to do what you demand. Telling the truth, not withholding information, and identifying options are ways to adapt your message to be an ethical communicator. Finally, we adapt our communication to generate more positive feelings or regard for others, so as to enhance our relationships and improve our quality of life.

Can the skills and principles we have suggested here make a difference in your ability to communicate with others? The answer is a resounding "yes." Communication researcher Lori Carell found that students who had been exposed to lessons in empathy linked to a study of interpersonal and intercultural communication improved their ability to empathize with others.[35] There is evidence that if you master these principles and skills,

Re**CAP**

Adapting to Others

DEVELOP KNOWLEDGE

Seek Information	Learn about a culture's world view.
Ask Questions and Listen	Reduce uncertainty by asking for clarification and listening to the answer.

DEVELOP MOTIVATION

Tolerate Ambiguity	Take your time and expect some uncertainty.
Develop Mindfulness	Be consciously aware of cultural differences, rather than ignoring the differences.

DEVELOP SKILL

Become Other Oriented	Put yourself in the other person's mental and emotional frame of mind; socially decentre and develop empathy.
Adapt to Others	Listen and respond appropriately.

ReCAP ←····

How to Become Other Oriented

Socially Decentre	View the world from another person's point of view.
	• Develop an understanding of someone, based on your own past experiences.
	• Consider what someone may be thinking, based on your previous association with him or her.
	• Consider how most people respond to the situation at hand.
Develop Empathy	Consider what another person may be feeling.
	• Stop: Avoid focusing only on your own ideas or emotions.
	• Look: Consider nonverbal messages, especially the emotional meaning of messages.
	• Listen: Focus on what the other person says.
	• Imagine: Consider how you would feel.
	• Paraphrase: Summarize your understanding of the thoughts and feelings of your partner.
Adapt to Others	Appropriately respond to the messages of others, based upon your understanding of their thoughts (social decentring) and feelings (empathy).

you will be rewarded with greater ability to communicate with others who are different from you—which means everyone.

It is not possible to prescribe how to adapt to others in all situations. We can suggest that you draw on the other four communication principles for a lifetime that we have presented in this book. You will be more effective in adapting to others if you are aware of your own cultural traditions and gender-related behaviour, and how they are different from those of other people. Being able to use and interpret verbal and nonverbal symbols appropriately and effectively will also increase your ability to adapt and respond to others. The essential skills of listening and responding to others are key competencies in being able to adapt to others—to be other oriented. To interpret spoken information accurately (as well as "listening" with your eyes to unspoken messages) is a linchpin for competence in being able to adapt to others.

Adapting your messages to others does not mean you have to abandon your own ethical principles or personal positions. As with a politician who only tells his or her audience what they want to hear, it would be unethical to change your opinions and point of view just to avoid conflict and keep the peace. A spineless, wishy-washy approach to communication does not enhance the quality of your relationships with others. But you can be sensitive and mindful of how your comments may be received by others.

SUMMARY ⁞·

Human differences result in the potential for misunderstanding and miscommunication. Differences in culture and gender play a role in contributing to the challenge of communicating with others. The relevant communication principle is: *Effective communicators appropriately adapt their messages to others.* One concept that makes a difference when we communicate with others is taking into consideration cultural perspective or world view. Culture is a system of knowledge that is shared by a larger group of people. Our world view is the overarching set of expectations that helps us explain why events occur as they do and gives us a perspective for explaining what happens to us and others. Intercultural communication occurs when individuals or groups from different cultures communicate.

Culture and communication are clearly linked because of the powerful role culture plays in influencing our values. Cultural values reflect how individuals regard masculine (such as achieving results and being productive) and feminine (such as consideration for relationships) perspectives, the importance of tolerating uncertainty or preferring certainty, the preference for centralized or decentralized power structures, and the valuing of individual or collective accomplishment.

Two primary effects of gender on communication are the instrumental or masculine orientation, which involves assertiveness and action, and the expressive or feminine orientation, which emphasizes connection and the development of harmonious relationships and community. These orientations translate into communication behaviour that differs for the sexes. Women tend to attend to the relational dimension of communication; that is, they focus on *how* something is said more than *what*. Their purpose in communication typically is to establish and develop relationships and connections with others. In contrast, men tend to approach communication from a content perspective, meaning that they view communication as functioning primarily for information exchange. The principle of adaptation is quite useful in bridging gender differences in communication style. People can and should break out of sex-specific behaviour to choose the best approach to communicating in a given situation.

Several barriers inhibit effective communication. When one culture or gender assumes superiority, communication problems often occur. Ethnocentrism is the belief that our own cultural traditions and assumptions are superior to those of others. Sexism is the attitude that one sex is superior to the other. It is also not productive when individuals or groups from different backgrounds or cultures assume that others behave with similar responses. We stereotype by placing a group or person into an inflexible, all-encompassing category. A related barrier is prejudice. When we prejudge someone before we know all the facts about him or her, we also create a potential communication problem. Stereotyping and prejudice can keep us from acknowledging others as unique individuals and therefore can hamper effective, open, honest communication. Differences in language codes and the way we interpret nonverbal messages interfere with effective communication.

Strategies for adapting to others include developing knowledge, motivation, and skill to bridge differences of culture and gender. To enhance understanding, actively seek information about others who are different from you, ask questions, and listen to the responses. Motivational strategies include being tolerant of ambiguity and uncertainty and being more conscious or mindful when interacting with others who are different from you. Finally, to develop skills in adapting to others, become other oriented by socially decentring and emotionally empathizing with others. Then appropriately respond by adapting your messages to others; consider their thoughts and feelings.

Discussion and Review ⁂

1. What is intercultural communication?

2. Describe the differences between high-context and low-context cultures.

3. What are the characteristics and traits of masculine and feminine cultural values?

4. What are the differences between cultures that value certainty and those that hold a greater tolerance for uncertainty?

5. How are decentralized and centralized cultural perspectives different?

6. What are the differences between individualistic and collectivistic cultures?

7. How important is a person's gender in Canadian culture?

8. What are the primary differences between genders in terms of listening behaviour?

9. How can one adapt communication to bridge gender differences?

10. What are the characteristics of individualistic and collectivistic cultures?

11. Identify and describe the barriers that hinder intercultural communication.

12. What communication strategies will help bridge differences in communication and achieve the goal of adapting to others?

Developing Your Skills:
Putting Principles into Practice ⁂

1. Describe your perceptions of your cultural values, based upon the discussion of cultural values beginning on page 122 in this chapter. On a scale of 1 to 10, rate yourself in terms of the value of masculine (1) and feminine (10) perspective, individual (1) and group (10) achievement, tolerance of uncertainty (1) and need for certainty (10), and decentralized (1) and centralized (10) power. Provide an example of your reaction to an interpersonal communication encounter to illustrate each of these values. Share your answers with your classmates.

2. Role-play with someone of the opposite sex. Generate a hypothetical conversation topic, such as a first conversation or a conflict or disagreement among dating partners. First, enact the roles from the perspective of your own sex—in other words, both you and your partner play the roles of people of your own sex. Then enact the conversation again, but with the roles reversed. Note any differences that emerge in how the conversation plays out. Do you detect any overdrawn, stereotypical behaviours that emerge when you swap roles? Do you think an activity like this helps us better understand members of the opposite sex and their communication patterns?

3. This chapter presented five specific strategies or skills to help bridge differences in background and culture. Rank order these skills and strategies in terms of what you need to improve in your interactions with people from different backgrounds. Give a rank of 1 to the skill or strategy that you most need to develop, a rank of 2 to the next area you feel you need to work on, and so on. Rank yourself on all five strategies.

Seek information about the culture _____
Listen and ask questions of others _____
Tolerate ambiguity _____
Be mindful _____
Be other oriented _____

Write a journal entry about how you will develop skill in the areas in which you need greatest improvement. How will you put what you have learned in this chapter into practice?

4. As a group, go on an intercultural scavenger hunt. Your instructor will give you a time limit. Scavenge your campus or classroom area to identify influences of as many different cultures as you can find. For example, you could make note of ethnic foods that you find in the food court; or you could identify clothing, music, or architecture that is influenced by certain cultures.

5. In small groups, identify examples from your own experiences for each barrier to effective intercultural communication discussed in the text. Use one of the examples to develop a skit to perform for the rest of the class. See whether the class can identify which intercultural barrier your group is depicting. Also, suggest how the skills and principles discussed in the chapter might have improved the communication in the situation you role-played.

6. Try an exercise that will help clarify the different reasons men and women communicate. Ask the following questions of both men and women and then see whether you note any major differences.

1. What is the general purpose or function of communication?
2. Which of the following statements best summarizes your preferred approach to communication?
   A. It's better to get to the point when asking for information or making a request of someone.
   B. It's better to take some time to talk about the background of a situation rather than quickly trying to get to "the bottom line" of what you're saying.
3. What bothers you the most when you talk to someone of the opposite sex?
4. What general impressions do you have about the way men and women listen to each other?

Compare your answers with your classmates'. Do you note any general trends or differences and similarities in light of the research conclusions we've summarized in this chapter?

Diana Ong, "Sisy." © Diana Ong/SuperStock

The best of life is conversation, and the greatest
success is confidence, or perfect understanding
between sincere people.

— RALPH WALDO EMERSON

7 Understanding Interpersonal Communication

CHAPTER OUTLINE

···> What Is Interpersonal Communication?

···> Initiating Relationships

···> Maintaining Relationships through Interpersonal Communication

···> Summary

AFTER STUDYING THIS CHAPTER, YOU SHOULD BE ABLE TO

1. Define interpersonal communication and discuss its four unique attributes.

2. Distinguish interpersonal communication from impersonal communication.

3. Explain the difference between relationships of circumstance and relationships of choice.

4. Define interpersonal attraction and distinguish short-term initial attraction from long-term maintenance attraction.

5. Discuss three human needs that relate to complementarity in interpersonal relationships.

6. Provide examples of verbal and nonverbal ways we reveal our attraction to others.

7. Explain uncertainty reduction and describe three strategies of information seeking to reduce uncertainty.

8. Explain what is meant by the "art and skill" of asking great questions.

9. Describe some common verbal and nonverbal behavioural indicators of a self-absorbed communicator style.

10. Explain how to give and receive a compliment.

11. Define self-disclosure and explain its role in relationship maintenance.

12. Discuss what is meant by reciprocity, appropriateness, and risk in self-disclosure.

13. Clarify ways in which self-disclosure and intimacy are affected by gender.

14. Identify and explain two models of self-disclosure pertaining to relationship maintenance.

15. Discuss how emotional expression, as a form of self-disclosure, affects relationship maintenance.

"Hi. I'm _____. Nice to meet you." This simple statement can strike fear in the heart of even the most outgoing individual. Yet we know that meeting and getting to know people, as well as becoming known by them, is one of the most rewarding experiences in life. If we cannot break out of our comfort zones to communicate with others, we won't survive. As we said in Chapter 1, communication is inescapable. We communicate—intentionally and unintentionally, verbally and nonverbally—to accomplish things great and small throughout our lifetimes. And the most common, everyday kind of communication we accomplish comes in the form of simple conversations with loved ones, friends, co-workers, acquaintances, and even strangers as we go about the business of living.

Think about your best childhood friend for a moment. Perhaps you're still in touch with that person; maybe that person is still your closest friend. But can you remember the very first time you talked to that person? Maybe something the person did, versus said, is what you remember that formed your first impression. First conversations are fun to try to remember and reflect upon, as we grow with others and progress in our relationships. If you're dating someone that you've dated for a while or if you are married, think back to your very first conversation with your partner. Was it awkward? Exciting? Did you acknowledge the awkwardness and laugh about it? Was your first date so uncomfortable that you thought you'd never go out with that person again? Or was the conversation so engaging that you couldn't wait to see her or him again? Do you remember more of the nonverbal than verbal things that happened on that first date, like the way he smiled or how she looked at you when you talked?

These elements are part of what we call interpersonal communication, the form of communication we experience most often in our lives. Interpersonal communication involves all five of our principles for a lifetime (see Figure 7.1). *In the remaining chapters of the book, you will see a small version of the communication principles for a lifetime model in the margin to highlight our reference to one or more of the communication principles that we discuss.* First, effective interpersonal communication begins with an *awareness* of oneself. As you interact with people in your life, you make mental notes of what works well and not so well. You learn from these experiences and develop a personal style of communication. We continue this process by reassessing and reshaping our communication styles throughout our lives, with the goal of becoming better communicators. The second and third principles involve the *effective use of verbal and nonverbal messages.* We experiment with verbal and nonverbal communication as we interact with people, form relationships, develop those relationships, and, in some cases, let go of those relationships. A major element that enhances relationships is the ability to *listen carefully and respond sensitively* to others, our principle 4. And finally, few interpersonal relationships last without *adaptation.* We live in an extremely

FIGURE 7.1 Communication Principles for a Lifetime

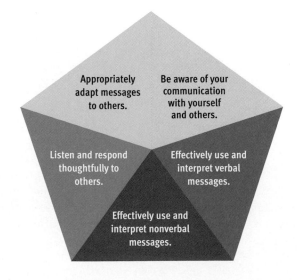

diverse world. It's imperative to learn to adapt our communication to others—their cultural backgrounds and values, personalities, communication styles, needs, and goals—so that we form satisfying relationships that help us enjoy our lives to the fullest.

In this chapter we examine interpersonal communication, distinguish it from other forms of human communication, and explore how interpersonal communication establishes and facilitates our relationships. As you work through this material, keep present in your mind those individuals who mean the most to you right now. Consider your communication with these valued people, assessing areas that are working well and areas that might need some attention. The more you personalize this information, the more you will gain from it.

WHAT IS INTERPERSONAL COMMUNICATION?

In Chapter 1 we looked at three contexts in which communication most commonly occurs: interpersonal communication, group communication, and public communication contexts. In this chapter we explore the interpersonal context in more depth. To review the definition provided in Chapter 1, **interpersonal communication** is a special form of unmediated human communication that occurs when we interact simultaneously with another person and attempt to mutually influence each other, usually for the purpose of managing relationships. Four unique attributes help us better understand the nature of interpersonal communication.

Effective communication can be the key to successful interpersonal relationships.

Interpersonal Communication Involves Quality

Imagine you're on a date and having dinner at a restaurant. Is the communication you have with your date different from the communication you have with the person who waits on your table? (We certainly hope so; if not, you're probably having a lousy date!) Most likely, the quality of communication differs between you and the restaurant staff and you and your date for the evening.

Interpersonal communication occurs not just when we interact with someone, but also when we treat the other as a unique human being. Conversely, **impersonal communication** occurs when we treat people as objects or respond to their roles rather than to who they are as unique people.[1] We engage in a good deal of impersonal communication each day. We may pass people on the sidewalk at our colleges or universities and say hello, whether or not we know the person. The first few days of a semester are always interesting because of the presence of so many people new to the campus, so we may find ourselves giving directions to various campus buildings. Giving directions or instructions is a common yet important form of impersonal communication. Many people's jobs involve a great deal of impersonal communication. For example, bank tellers, salespersons, utility workers, and emergency medical personnel rely on effective impersonal communication to function in their occupations.

Interpersonal Communication Occurs Simultaneously

When you communicate with someone interpersonally, both participants act on verbal and nonverbal information originating from the other person. While you are talking and your date is listening, for example, you are also observing your date's nonverbal cues—eye contact, clothing, body posture, and facial expressions. All of these nonverbal cues give you information about the other person and about how well the date is going. Remember Chapter 1's discussion of communication models? Communication is not a linear process of sending information to others, but a process in which both individuals simultaneously affect each other.

interpersonal communication
Communication that occurs simultaneously with another person in an attempt to mutually influence each other, usually for the purpose of managing relationships.

impersonal communication
Communication that treats people as objects or that only responds to their roles rather than who they are as unique people.

Verbal
Nonverbal

"Harrison, it's time we had a
face-to-face conversation — also known as
wireless communication."

Interpersonal Communication Involves Mutual Influence

Interpersonal communication also involves attempts at mutual influence. This means that both partners are affected by the interaction. We do not mean to imply that interpersonal communication exclusively involves persuasion—as in changing someone's mind or swaying someone to agree with your opinion. We simply mean that people who interact affect each other. For example, during dinner, you ask your date where he or she grew up, and you assume your date heard you. If so, you've both been affected by the question—there's something you want to know and information your date can provide. But what if your date doesn't hear you? In this case, interpersonal communication has not really occurred between you and your date because there is no mutual interaction; only you have been affected by your attempt at communication.

Every interpersonal communication interaction influences us. Sometimes it changes our lives dramatically, sometimes in small ways. Long-lasting interpersonal relationships are sustained not by one person giving and another taking, but by mutually satisfying communication.

Interpersonal Communication Helps Manage Relationships

When we move away from impersonal communication with others, we move toward interpersonal communication in relationships. **Relationships** are ongoing connections we make with others through interpersonal communication. For some people, the term *relationship* signals something serious and usually romantic, as in a serious dating relationship, a marriage, or other romantic partnering. But we use the term *relationship* in a much broader sense in this text. You probably have a wide variety of relationships that include family members, co-workers, classmates, friends, and romantic interests. We initiate and form relationships by communicating with those whom we find attractive in some way. We seek to increase our interactions with people we would like to know better, and we interpersonally communicate to maintain those relationships. We also use interpersonal communication to end relationships that we have decided are no longer viable.

Relationships form for different reasons. **Relationships of circumstance** form situationally—simply because our lives overlap with others' lives in some way or because a situation brings us into contact. Relationships with family members, teachers, classmates, and co-workers typically fall into this category. In contrast, when we seek out and intentionally develop relationships, those are termed **relationships of choice.** These relationships typically include friends, lovers, and spouses or relational partners (such as gay and lesbian partners in committed, monogamous relationships). These categories are not mutually exclusive.

---

relationship
An ongoing connection made with another person.

relationship of circumstance
A relationship that forms situationally, simply because one life overlaps with another in some way.

relationship of choice
A relationship that is sought out and intentionally developed.

ReCAP

What Is Interpersonal Communication?

- Interpersonal communication involves quality: The quality of communication within interpersonal relationships is superior to communication that occurs impersonally.

- Interpersonal communication occurs simultaneously: Both participants act on verbal and nonverbal information originating from the other person.

- Interpersonal communication involves mutual influence: Both interactants are affected by the interaction.

- Interpersonal communication helps manage relationships: Communication facilitates the initiation, maintenance, and, in some cases, termination of interpersonal relationships.

Relationships of circumstance can change into relationships of choice: Your sister or brother can turn out to be your best friend. Conversely, you may be extremely close to a certain family member, but over time that relationship becomes more distant and evolves into more of a relationship of circumstance than choice.

We communicate differently in these two types of relationships because the stakes are different. Generally, relationships of choice are more important to us and central to our sense of well-being than relationships of circumstance. Also, we tend to be more intimate in relationships of choice, choosing to reveal more delicate or sensitive things about ourselves only with our closest friends or lovers. We can "get away with" some behaviours among less intimate acquaintances or family members who have known us for some time; yet that same behaviour would be intolerable or a source of conflict within a relationship of choice.

INITIATING RELATIONSHIPS

For some people, it looks so easy; they just seem to meet people and make positive impressions effortlessly. For others, meeting and getting to know people is a huge challenge. We'll let you in on a little secret—it really isn't all that easy for anyone. Let's begin our discussion of relationship initiation by exploring the nature of attraction—what draws us into a conversation in the first place.

⋯⟩ Interpersonal Attraction: Why We Like Whom We Like

What does it mean to say that you are attracted to another person? Most of the time we tend to think of physical or sexual attraction. But there are many forms of attraction besides physical and sexual, including intellectual, spiritual, and personality attraction. **Attraction**, in general, is a motivational state that causes someone to think, feel, and behave in a positive manner toward another person.[2] More specifically, **interpersonal attraction** is the degree to which you desire to form and possibly maintain an interpersonal relationship with another person. Remember that interpersonal relationships imply some form of ongoing connection, so we're not talking here about those instances when you can't breathe because an incredibly attractive person walks by. Whenever we feel a positive regard for another person or when we like someone, we can say that we hold an interpersonal attraction for that person. However, the intensity of that attraction varies from relationship to relationship.

Interpersonal attraction occurs in both the early and later stages of relational development. **Short-term initial attraction** is the degree to which you sense a potential for developing an interpersonal relationship. For instance, you might find one of your classmates physically attractive but never move to introduce yourself. The information you gather in your first interaction with someone can also generate a short-term initial attraction for a relationship, which you may or may not pursue, depending upon the circumstances.

Long-term maintenance attraction, on the other hand, is the type that sustains relationships like your best friendships or a marriage. It refers to a level of liking or positive feeling that motivates you to maintain or escalate a relationship. Short-term attraction gives way to long-term attraction as a relationship progresses. Rarely do you maintain a long-term intimate relationship, such as marriage, solely because you find another person physically attractive.[3] You usually need something more as you develop an interpersonal attraction and deepen a relationship. Several factors come into play when you decide to act on your attraction and establish a relationship.

Similarity

Let's discuss the idea that "opposites attract." Opposites certainly do attract, and the differences between people can be interesting. They

attraction
A motivational state that causes someone to think, feel, and usually behave in a positive manner toward another person.

interpersonal attraction
The degree to which one desires to form or maintain an interpersonal relationship with another person.

short-term initial attraction
A degree of potential for developing an interpersonal relationship with someone.

long-term maintenance attraction
A level of liking or positive feeling that motivates one to maintain or escalate a relationship.

People often use many forms of communication to convey their attractiveness to another and to form relationships.

ETHICAL PROBE

A newspaper article discussed flirtations or minor obsessions people have with one another, more familiarly known as "crushes."[4] One view suggests that crushes come in three sizes, "small, medium, and totally-ruin-your-life." However, many people extol the virtues of crushes, contending that "Crushes are great because they're harmless and limited in scope. They're little ego boosts. Even if you're already in a happy relationship, it's always nice to have someone paying attention to you."

How should a person's relationship ethics pertain to a crush—that feeling of physical and sexual attraction for a person other than your partner in a monogamous relationship? Is it natural for people to be attracted to other people, even if they choose to have an intimate relationship with only one certain person? Are crushes harmless or are they a breach of faith, a misuse of trust?

can also form the basis for a good friendship or co-worker relationship—after all, we learn a great deal from people who are unlike us. But we like to add another phrase onto the "opposites attract" cliché: "Opposites attract, but opposites seldom last." People who are opposites or significantly different in dispositions and preferences may intrigue each other and teach each other something, but they don't typically progress into long-term relationships.

In general, you are attracted to people whose personality, values, upbringing, experiences, attitudes, and interests are **similar** to yours.[5] You may also be attracted more to persons who are similar to you in age, intelligence, and life goals. Interesting studies on dating partners and college roommates found that for both the partners and the roommates, similarity in the emotional dimensions of the relationship (such as comfort, ego support, conflict management, sincerity, and warmth) were more important than other dimensions of attraction and led to greater enjoyment of the relationship.[6]

In the initial stages of a relationship, we try to emphasize positive information about ourselves to create a positive and attractive image. We reveal those aspects of ourselves that we believe we have in common with the other person, and the other person does the same.[7] Think about your initial interactions with strangers; typically, you spend the first few minutes trying to find topics of mutual interest. You discover that the person is from a place near your hometown, has the same taste in music or sports, has the same attitude about school, and on and on. But the depth of this information is limited. You save your revelations about important attitudes and issues for later, as your relationship progresses. Attitude similarity is more likely to be a source of long-term maintenance attraction than of short-term initial attraction.

Physical and Sexual Attraction

Volumes have been written about the role that physical and sexual attraction play in the tendency to form relationships.[8] While these forms of attraction are often lumped together or viewed as the same thing, they actually are different. The degree to which we find another person's physical self appealing represents our **physical attraction** to him or her. That appeal might be based on height, size, skin tone and texture, clothing, hairstyle, makeup, vocal qualities, gestures, and so forth. By this definition, even if you are heterosexual, you can still be attracted to a person of your same sex because you admire her or his physical attributes. **Sexual attraction** has been defined as "the desire to engage in sexual activity with someone," a desire that "typically is accompanied by feelings of sexual arousal in the presence of the person."[9] You may be physically attracted to someone but not sexually attracted, as we stated before. But can you be sexually attracted but not physically attracted? We're not sure about the answer to that one because it may be a uniquely individual judgment. Suffice it to say that these two forms of attraction usually operate in tandem but do represent different kinds of appeal.

similarity
Having like characteristics, values, attitudes, interests, or personality traits with another person.

Aware

Nonverbal

physical attraction
The degree to which someone finds another person's physical self appealing.

sexual attraction
A desire to have sexual contact with a certain person.

⟨⟩ COMMUNICATION and DIVERSITY

What Attracts You?

Social psychologist Alan Feingold attempted to discover whether heterosexual women and men vary in terms of how much importance they place on physical appearance in the decision to date someone.[10] Looking for trends, Feingold surveyed a large number of studies conducted on the subject and discovered that, indeed, men and women look for different things when deciding to initiate and develop heterosexual romantic relationships. Approximately 50 studies determined that men value physical attractiveness most in a potential partner, while women value personality, intelligence, kindness and sensitivity, and a sense of humour more than looks.

This information doesn't have to be a "downer," meaning that heterosexuals are doomed because women and men look for and value very different attributes in each other. The sexes don't have to resent one other, claiming that men are superficial because they're drawn to looks while women are picky because they have "laundry lists" of qualifications for men. The information can be empowering, in that members of both sexes can understand and anticipate what attracts the other. Granted, there are exceptions; not everyone adheres to these sex-based findings on attraction. But in your experience, do men tend to emphasize a woman's looks over other aspects of her character? Do women prioritize psychological elements over physical ones in their interests in men?

The adage "Beauty is in the eye of the beholder" is particularly true in terms of explaining physical and sexual attraction. Each culture teaches and perpetuates its own definition of the physical ideal. In North America, for instance, advertisements and TV programs promote a slender ideal for both females and males. This seriously contributes to the North American fixation on (and obsession with) losing weight and getting fit.[11] However, in some cultures, and at various times throughout our history, physical attractiveness was synonymous with bulkiness.

Our perceptions about others' physical attractiveness reduces relationship possibilities. This means that, in general, although we may be attracted to a range of persons, we tend to seek out individuals who represent the same level of physical attractiveness as ourselves.[12] In nonverbal communication research, this is termed the **matching hypothesis.**[13] Perhaps you perceive yourself to be average looking, not model-beautiful but not unattractive either. You may be physically or sexually attracted to persons who are extremely good-looking; but if you are average-looking, you are more likely to seek someone to date, and even marry or partner with, who is also average-looking. Look around the next time you're at a public place, like an airport or a mall, and notice the couples—people who obviously look like they are together. Most couples will match each other in terms of physical attractiveness.

matching hypothesis
A tendency to seek out individuals who represent the same level of physical attractiveness as oneself.

Proximity

As social psychologist Sharon Brehm explains, "To meet people is not necessarily to love them, but to love them we must first meet them."[14] We are more likely to be attracted to people who are in closer **proximity** to us than those who are farther away.[15] In your classes, you are more likely to form relationships with classmates sitting on either side of you than with someone seated at the opposite end of the room. This is partly because physical proximity increases communication opportunities. We are more likely to talk, and therefore to feel attracted, to neighbours who live right next door than those who live down the block. Any circumstance that increases the possibilities for interacting is also likely to increase attraction.

proximity
The likelihood of being attracted to people who are physically close rather than to those who are farther away.

If you have ever been in a long-distance romantic relationship, you understand the principle of proximity first-hand. When you don't have close access to a significant other, you have to get creative and use as many channels for communication as you can so that the relationship develops. But this is a real challenge, isn't it? Do you know what the number one factor is in keeping long-distance relationships going? You might be thinking honesty, openness, or trust, but the answer is *money.* Money gives partners the means to get together

On the WEB ·····•

How do people meet other people, for the purposes of initiating romantic relationships? That's an age-old question with ever-evolving answers. Although singles bars and personal ads in newspapers are still around, people are turning increasingly to the Web to meet new people. Several Web sites have been created just for such purposes, and new ones will no doubt spring up as this approach gains popularity and more people become comfortable accessing the Web. There are pros and cons to cyber-connecting, so it's wise to employ the same precautions that you would use when meeting new people and deciding whom you'd like to date. If you're interested in meeting people via cyber-channels (or just curious to learn how these sites operate), here are a few addresses to try:

www.Match.com

www.Matchmaker.com

www.eCrush.com

intermittently and stay in touch over the telephone. Score another point for e-mail when it comes to long–distance relationships, because it does offer a relatively in-expensive way to communicate with a partner at a distance. But relationships that develop over distance generally face different challenges than those with more proximity.[16]

Complementarity

complementarity
The tendency to be attracted to persons with abilities, interests, and needs that differ from, but balance or round out, our own.

Although we tend to like people with whom we have much in common, most of us wouldn't find it very exciting to spend the rest of our lives with someone who has identical attitudes, needs, and interests. We may tend to be attracted to someone similar to us in impor-tant things like human values, but for other things we may be more interested in someone with **complementary** qualities and needs.[17] For example, if you are highly disorganized by nature (and that's fine by you), you might be attracted to someone who is very organized because you appreciate that person's sense of structure.

ReCAP ←····

Elements of Interpersonal Attraction

Short-Term Initial Attraction	This form of attraction involves a judgment that there is potential for an interpersonal relationship to develop with someone.
Long-Term Maintenance Attraction	This form is deeper and more long-lasting than short-term initial attraction and involves positive feelings that cause us to choose to maintain and escalate relationships.
Similarity	Attraction increases if we have like characteristics, values, attitudes, interests, and personality traits with another person.
Physical Attraction	This form of attraction relates to finding another person's physical self appealing.
Sexual Attraction	This form involves the desire to have sexual contact with a certain person.
Proximity	We are more likely to be interpersonally attracted to people who are physically close to us rather than farther away.
Complementarity	We may be attracted to persons with abilities, interests, and needs that differ from our own but that balance or round out our own.

Social psychologist Will Schutz identified three interpersonal needs that motivate us to form and maintain relationships with others: inclusion, control, and affection.[18] **Inclusion** represents the need to include others in our activities or to be included in theirs. **Control** represents the need to make decisions and take responsibility or the level of willingness to accept others' decision making. **Affection** represents the need to be loved and accepted by others or the willingness to give love and acceptance to others. Most people are attracted to those persons whose interpersonal needs complement their own.

If you have a high need to control and make decisions and a general disrespect or mistrust of others' decision making, you will be more compatible with someone who does not have similar needs—a person who wants others to make decisions for her or him. Many committed couples reflect this pattern regarding finances. The person who is better at keeping track of bills and balancing the chequebook pairs with someone who is good at maintaining a budget, to create a strong personal finance team. If you have high affection needs, you are likely to be less attracted to someone who is distant or aloof and who does not show affection. If you're dating someone and you resent it when that person spends time away from you with his or her friends, you are likely to be less attracted to that person over time because you may have different, noncomplementary inclusion needs. In essence, we can view pairs of individuals as teams in which each side complements the other side's weaknesses. In reality, there are no "perfect" matches, only degrees of compatibility.

⋯⟩ Communicating Our Attraction

In general, the more we are attracted to someone, the more we attempt to communicate with him or her. So the amount of interaction we have with someone indicates the level of attraction in the relationship.

When we are attracted to people, we use both indirect and direct strategies to communicate our liking, through nonverbal and verbal cues. Nonverbal cues are typically indirect and are often referred to as **immediacy**.[19] We discussed this briefly in Chapter 4: Immediacy behaviours work to reduce the physical and psychological distance between persons. For example, with people we are attracted to, we may sit closer, increase our eye contact and use of touch, lean forward, keep an open body orientation, use more vocal variety or animation, and smile more often than we normally do. Research also shows that individuals are more likely to preen in the presence of an attractive other.[20] For example, people may alter their posture to accentuate certain body parts, straighten or adjust their clothing, and fidget with their hair when interacting with someone they find attractive.

inclusion
The need to involve others in our activities or to be involved in the activities of others.

control
The need to make decisions and take responsibility; the level of willingness to accept others' decision making.

affection
The need to be loved and accepted by others; the willingness to give love and acceptance to others.

immediacy
Feelings of liking, pleasure, and closeness communicated by such nonverbal cues as eye contact, forward lean, touch, and open body orientation.

Nonverbal

⋯⟩•⟨⋯ **COMMUNICATION** and **TECHNOLOGY**

Cyber-Connecting: Dating on the Net

Do you know people who have met through electronic channels? Have you made any cyber-connections? More and more people these days are logging on to make a "love connection" in virtual reality. We know several colleagues who maintain regular cyber-relationships over the Internet. They claim that these relationships are just as intimate (and perhaps more intimate) than relationships established face to face.

Aspects of virtual relating that many people find attractive include the reduced importance of physical traits, the increased significance of rapport and similarity as factors in the decision to continue chatting with someone online, and a greater freedom from gender-role constraints.[21] Granted, there's a lot of role playing online, and the potential for deception is great. For instance, someone might describe herself online as being a beautiful but lonely woman who just wants a sexual connection with a special man. The reality might be that the initiator of that message is actually an adolescent boy, acting on his curiosity about gender identity and sexual activity. But if you do engage in an online relationship and believe that you can trust the truthfulness of the other person's communication, it can be a very beneficial way to explore some of the interpersonal communication strategies we discuss in this chapter. Maybe it helps to think of cyber-connecting as a rehearsal for the real thing.

Most often we communicate our attraction nonverbally. However, on occasion we may indirectly communicate our attraction verbally by using informal and personal language, addressing the person by her or his first name and often referring to "you and I" and "we." We ask questions to show interest, probe for details when our partner shares information, listen responsively, and refer to information shared in past interactions, in an attempt to build a history with the person. All of these behaviours demonstrate that we value what the other person is saying.

Listen and Respond

⋯⫶ Getting That First Conversation Going

Once you realize you're attracted to someone (and that realization usually happens very quickly), what do you do next? That's a question that we've all no doubt asked ourselves at times, when we feel that awkwardness about wanting to be around someone attractive, wanting to find a way to meet the person and get to know her or him. We have some practical suggestions for how you approach those first conversations, so that you feel confident and keep your self-esteem intact, while communicating effectively to impress the other person positively.

Reducing Uncertainty

Even though most of us like surprises from time to time, human beings are much more prone to certainty than uncertainty. We prefer the known to the unknown, the predictable to the chaotic. Over several years, a communication research team developed **uncertainty-reduction theory,** an explanation of how people use information as we endeavour to reduce our uncertainty, especially as it relates to communicating with persons we don't know (or know well). Communication researchers Berger, Calabrese, and Bradac contend that this driving motivation among humans to reduce our uncertainty prompts us to communicate.[22] We typically respond to uncertainty in three ways—using passive, active, and/or interactive strategies.

Aware

uncertainty-reduction theory
A driving human motivation to increase predictability by reducing the unknown in our circumstances.

To illustrate these strategies, let's consider an example. You're at a social gathering with some friends; a lot of people are there, some you know, some you don't. You spot an attractive person across the room and decide that you would like to know more about him or her. What's the first thing you would likely do in this situation? Charge right over to the person and introduce yourself? Maybe some of us would, but most of us respond less actively at first to an uncertain situation like this. The first thing most of us would do would be to scope out the situation, see who the "object of our affections" is talking with, watch to see if he or she seems to be with anyone at the party, and casually observe how the person communicates to get some sense of her or his personality. These are all **passive strategies;** we seek more information in order to reduce our uncertainty. Passive uncertainty reduction is related to principle 1 in this text—becoming more aware of yourself, your circumstances, and others.

passive strategy
A noncommunicative strategy of reducing uncertainty by observing others and situations.

After you've observed the person at the party, if you need more information before deciding what to do next, you might employ an **active strategy.** This approach involves getting information from a third party, such as asking your friends if they know the person, if he or she is dating anyone exclusively, what their opinions are about the situation or the person, and so forth. This is a form of perception checking, as we discussed in Chapters 2 and 4. Finding out what your friends think of the person at the party increases your information and helps you decide how to behave.

Verbal

active strategy
A communicative strategy of reducing uncertainty by getting information from a third party.

interactive strategy
A strategy of communicating directly to the source who has the greatest potential to reduce uncertainty.

The final approach is termed an **interactive strategy,** going directly to the source who has the greatest potential to reduce your uncertainty. In our example, an interactive strategy would involve actually going over to the person and starting a conversation or joining one in progress. In some situations, enough uncertainty can be reduced through passive and active strategies; there may be no cause for an interactive strategy. At the party, you may learn enough about the person you saw across the room by watching and talking to others about her or him that you decide against initiating a conversation. Also, these uncertainty-reduction strategies don't necessarily proceed in any order; you might surpass an active strategy and decide that the best way to cope with a situation is to get the information "straight from the horse's mouth." What's important is to understand that the need

ReCAP ⬅┈┈

Information-Seeking Strategies of Uncertainty Reduction

CATEGORY	DEFINITION	EXAMPLE
Passive	Observing and gathering useful information without interacting	While attending your first staff meeting at a new job, you observe colleagues and listen to their inter-action, noting verbal and nonverbal behaviours in an attempt to "get the lay of the land."
Active	Getting opinions and information from third parties	As a form of perception checking, you ask colleagues their views on the company and the people working there. You compare their perceptions with your own observations.
Interactive	Getting opinions and information from those parties most directly involved	You ask the boss directly for her or his opinion and for information about the company and your job.

to reduce our uncertainty, to make ourselves more comfortable in situations, is a prime motivating force in human communication.

What Do You Say First?

In some contexts, the first words you exchange with someone may be fairly scripted or expected, such as in a job interview situation in which introductions and ritualistic greetings are typically enacted in the first few minutes. (See Appendix A for helpful information on communicating in interviews.) But what about situations in which there are no prescribed, explicit rules or expectations for behaviour? Social situations, where you are meeting new people who may become friends or potential dating partners, create a level of anxiety for all of us—even the most confident person, who swears that he or she has absolutely no problem meeting new people. And probably no other situation gives us pause (and uncertainty) more than a social situation involving attraction, like the one we used to exemplify uncertainty-reduction theory. If someone you know can introduce you to the person you're attracted to, that can be helpful and serve as a bridge or a buffer for you. But what do you say if there's no one to introduce you?

Some interesting research has been conducted on just this kind of challenge. One study found that more than 90% of college students surveyed agreed that it was just as acceptable for a woman to initiate a first conversation with a man as the reverse.[23] Students also believed that cute or flippant opening lines were less effective than an honest, direct approach. A book from the 1970s, entitled *How to Pick Up Girls!* provides some laughs today in its suggestions for opening lines men could use to start conversations with women.[24] Here are a couple of memorable ones: "You're Miss Ohio, aren't you? I saw your picture in the paper yesterday." "Here, let me carry that for you. I wouldn't want you to strain that lovely body of yours." "Haven't I seen you here before?" (and the all-time favourite from the 1970s) "What's your sign?" We don't recommend the use of standard lines in opening conversations because that approach ignores the particular situation and the unique qualities of each person you will meet. Our principle 5 suggests that effective communicators adapt their messages to their listeners, so using the same type of communication in each new encounter is ill-advised. However, you should do some thinking about how you come across—and how you *want* to come across—when meeting new people.

One of the best strategies is to find something you perceive you might have in common with the person. We all give off a certain amount of "free" information that others can easily observe. If someone is wearing a T-shirt from a place you recognize or have visited, or carrying a book from a course you've taken or are taking, you can use that information as a starting point for conversation.

The Art and Skill of Asking Great Questions

When students ask us, as they frequently do, "What makes someone a good conversationalist?" a variety of things come to mind. All five of our principles for a lifetime could be reflected in our answer. But perhaps the most important element is the ability to ask a great question of another person. Research from the 1970s through the present shows that asking questions to generate conversation tends to be more of a woman's behaviour than a man's.[25] However, men and women alike need to develop this skill so that communication in initial encounters isn't necessarily one person's responsibility and so that we don't perpetuate sex-role stereotypes. The competency of asking great questions doesn't just magically appear—it takes time, maturity, and experience with a variety of people and relationships to develop fully.

It's impressive to show genuine interest and concern for someone you're talking to by learning to form great questions. What do we mean by "great questions"? We don't mean tossing rapid-fire, superficial questions at someone, as though you were in the first five minutes of a job interview. You don't want someone to think that you're gathering data for the census. Asking a great question means that, first, you tailor the question to the person as much as possible. Use what you've observed and learned from other sources to formulate your questions. You might ask basic information just to break the ice, but be careful not to use too many "yes/no" or one-word response types of questions that don't extend the conversation. Avoid questions that might be too personal or probing.

conversational narcissism
A communication style emerging from the view that we are the centre of the universe.

self-absorbed communicator style
A dominating communication style in which one focuses attention on the self.

A second, very critical skill to develop is to really listen to the person's answers to your questions. Then pose a follow-up question—one that is based on the person's response to your question. You can offer your opinion on something, but opinions work best when followed up with "Do you agree?" or "That's what I think, but what do you think?" Great conversationalists are great because they listen and then form responses that show they're listening—responses that are designed to draw other people out and let them shine.

Too many people think the best way to be conversationally impressive is by talking glibly, smoothly, confidently, and virtually nonstop *about themselves.* Terms for this behaviour include **conversational narcissism** and a **self-absorbed communicator style.**[26] For some people, this approach to communication is an outgrowth of a personality trait—a belief in themselves as the centre of the universe. Other times it is a state, not a trait, meaning a temporary style of interacting rather than a more pervasive characteristic of a person. We can all be self-absorbed from time to time, but if the self-absorbed communication continues, if it moves from a temporary state into a more permanent trait or style of a person, then the likelihood that the person will be positively perceived seriously declines.

You probably know what self-absorption sounds like and looks like in another communicator. Some verbal indications include the number of times the pronoun "I" is used, instead of "you" or "we." Narcissistic communicators converse mostly about themselves and typically provide more detail in their narratives than necessary (related to enjoying the sound of their own voices).[27] They talk more in statements than questions and constantly try to top someone's story or to draw the topic of conversation toward themselves, as in "Oh, you think *you're* tired, let me tell you about the kind of day *I* had." No one's day is as bad, no one's opinion as valuable nor information as correct as the self-absorbed communicator's. They may also feign empathy in a conversation, as in a response of, "Oh, I know exactly how you feel." This usually leads to a statement that begins, "The same thing happened to me," followed by a long story that takes attention away from the original communicator. Another indication of self-absorption is evidenced in people who talk ad nauseam on topics about which they have some particular knowledge or expertise but that bore the socks off of their listeners. Many times these types of communicators are driven by insecurity and uncertainty, rather than a belief that they are the centre of the universe.

Nonverbally, self-absorbed communicators use vocal cues (such as increasing volume) and dominant body postures to hold their turns at talk and stave off interruptions from others. They may even physically block another person from attempting to leave the conversation and are generally insensitive to others' nonverbal cues. People with self-absorbed personalities soon find themselves with few friends, because few of us can tolerate such an out-of-balance relationship.

Nonverbal

Listen
and
Respond

So, in sum, the best conversationalists aren't great talkers, they're great listeners and responders (as we've articulated in principle 4). In other words, it's not what *you* say, but how you respond to what *others* say that makes a good conversationalist.

The Art and Skill of Giving and Receiving Compliments

Sometimes it seems as though people don't comment about one another unless it's to criticize. That's unfortunate, because positive reinforcement and support from others is central to our self-esteem. So let's discuss the lost art of the compliment. First, think about yourself: Are you a person who compliments others? If so, what do you tend to compliment people for—their appearance, hard work, scholarly achievement, athletic prowess? If you are a person who tends not to compliment others, why is that the case? Do you believe you'll be sticking your nose into others' business if you comment, even positively, about their behaviour? Or are you somewhat oblivious to others, meaning that you tend not to notice or comment on things others do or how they look?

British linguistic scholar Janet Holmes calls compliments "social lubricants."[28] She explains that the most common purpose of a compliment is to make someone feel good by offering praise and encouragement, but an important by-product is a sense of increased goodwill and solidarity between the complimenter and the receiver of the compliment.

ETHICAL PROBE

A few years ago, one of your authors encountered one of the most memorable of students in her college teaching career. Unfortunately, the student was memorable because he epitomized the self-absorbed style of interpersonal communication. At first he seemed congenial, but it didn't take long to realize that all the guy could talk about was himself—his opinions on everything, his classes, how busy and stressful his life was, blah, blah, blah. He made everyone uncomfortable and was oblivious to others' nonverbal cues. The saddest thing of all was that

he didn't seem to have any friends. He brought about his own isolation because his communication style kept everyone at a distance.

What is a person's ethical obligation in a situation like this? In an instance like this, should you be "your brother or sister's keeper"? Granted, it's not our place to set about changing everyone's communication style to our liking. But when you see someone with potential, someone who might benefit from some honest advice and feedback about his or her communication patterns, should you offer it?

Giving compliments is a tricky business, because some attempts at flattery can be taken in ways other than you intend. For example, many female professionals tire of workplace compliments on their appearance, while their male co-workers are more often complimented on their work-related achievements. Some compliments are too personal and can make people feel uncomfortable. A pattern of personal compliments may be grounds for a claim of sexual harassment. But these are extreme examples. We encourage you to think about complimenting as a communication skill and a strategy particularly useful in first conversations. You don't want to come across as a phony, a predator, or just plain strange because you compliment someone you barely know, but a well-thought-out compliment can open the door to further conversation.

It's also important to know how to receive a compliment graciously—not by agreeing with the complimenter (and sounding cocky), or by disagreeing or attempting to talk the person out of his or her compliment, as in: "This old outfit? Had it for years—got a really great deal on it. I just threw it on today." The best response is a simple "thank you" that acknowledges that something nice was said about you.

MAINTAINING RELATIONSHIPS THROUGH INTERPERSONAL COMMUNICATION

Many forms of interpersonal communication are necessary to maintain successful, satisfying relationships. In this section, we explore a few of the most central forms, which represent some of the most heavily researched topics in the communication discipline.

⸺⸰ Self-Disclosure: Revealing Yourself to Others

Imagine that you're on a first date. (If you have been married for quite a while, this will take some work, but try it anyway.) Things are going fairly well. You find yourself liking the other person, and you become more comfortable as the evening progresses. But while you're engaged in conversation, your date manages to turn the topic of discussion to sex. The person starts describing sexual details about his or her last date or romantic partner—information that is just too intimate and private for a first date or, by some people's standards, for *any* date. Have you ever been in a situation where your date told you "more than you needed to know"? How did you feel about the person after that experience? Did the inappropriate disclosure stop the relationship from getting off the ground?

Self-disclosure, originally researched by psychologist Sidney Jourard, occurs when we voluntarily provide information to others that they would not learn if we did not tell them.[29] People can learn our approximate age, height, and weight by just observing us. But they can't learn our exact age, height, or weight unless we disclose it. Disclosing personal information not only provides a basis for another person to understand us better, but it also conveys our level of trust and acceptance of the other person.

self-disclosure
Voluntarily providing information to others that they would not learn if one did not tell them.

Reciprocity in Self-Disclosure

One expectation we have for self-disclosure is called **reciprocity,** meaning that when we share information about ourselves with other persons, we expect them to share information that is similar in risk or depth about themselves. If you introduce yourself to someone and give your name, you expect that person to respond by telling you his or her name. This cultural rule allows us to use disclosure as a strategy for gaining information and reducing uncertainty.

If the other person doesn't reciprocate, however, you might feel embarrassed or resentful. Sharing information about yourself gives others a certain amount of power over you. If the other person reciprocates and discloses similar information, it helps maintain an equal balance of power. But if one person shares information and the other doesn't, the resulting imbalance may cause discomfort. Over time, unreciprocated self-disclosure may cause someone to end a relationship.

Relationship experts John Harvey and Ann Weber describe relationship maintenance as "minding the close relationship," which they define as "thought and behaviour patterns

reciprocity
Sharing information about oneself with another person, with the expectation that the other person will share information that is similar in risk or depth.

that interact to create stability and feelings of closeness in a relationship."[30] In a "well-minded" relationship, partners facilitate self-disclosure by questioning one another about feelings and behaviours, using effective listener responses (such as head nods, eye contact, and vocalizations like "uh-huh"), accurately repeating or paraphrasing their partner's disclosure, and holding accurate and detailed knowledge of their partner's opinions and preferences. In contrast, partners who do not have a well-minded relationship exhibit poor listening behaviour, a lack of interest in their partner's disclosures, distorted repetitions or paraphrases of their partner's disclosures, and a general ignorance of their partner's opinions and preferences.

Appropriateness in Self-Disclosure

Appropriateness is another key variable related to self-disclosure. Certain kinds of information are inappropriate to disclose at an early stage, but appropriate at a later stage of relational development. However, people vary a good deal on this dimension. It's sometimes hard to gauge what is appropriate to talk about and what is not while you're in the process of discovering one another. Sometimes unwanted disclosures emerge because one person misjudges the nature of the relationship, assuming or wanting a greater level of intimacy than his or her partner assumes or wants.

Be sensitive to your partner when you choose what and when to disclose. Consider how the other person will react to the information. Although you may not feel certain information is intimate, the other person may. Conversely, when your partner reveals information, try to determine whether it is highly personal to her or him. You could upset the other person if you fail to treat the information appropriately.

Assessing the Risks of Self-Disclosure

Self-disclosure can be extremely rewarding because of its potential to deepen a relationship and enhance trust, but it is not without its risks.[31] When we disclose, we make ourselves vulnerable and forfeit control of information. We might hurt or insult the other person by saying things she or he finds offensive, signal an unintended level of intimacy, or damage the relationship with ill-timed and inappropriate disclosures. Typically, in relationships we seek a balance between the potential risks and rewards of disclosing personal information.

What is high self-disclosing for one person may be low self-disclosing for another. In judging what, when, and how much to disclose, it's important to realize that different people have different standards or expectations. For example, some individuals are quite comfortable talking about their personal problems with relative strangers, whereas others prefer such discussions only in the most intimate relationships, if at all.

Listen
and
Respond

appropriateness
An aspect of self-disclosure related to the propriety of revealing certain information to another person.

Adapt

On the WEB ⋯⋯●

Does self-disclosure, as a tool for enhancing intimacy in relationships, operate the same way in cyberspace as it does face to face? Apparently, according to research on Internet usage, people are telling other people all kinds of things about themselves over the Net. Revealing personal information isn't as threatening to many people when accomplished in separate locations, through machines, as compared to face-to-face encounters. What's your view of self-disclosure and relationship development in cyberspace? Have you shared personal information with an online user, or has someone shared personal information with you? If you haven't, but you're willing to try, here are a couple of sites to check out:

www.canadapersonals.com   This site allows you to look for a partner by indicating variables such as geographic location, age, and physical characteristics. There is an e-mail club, chat room, and many other useful links.

ca.personals.yahoo.com   This site, created by Yahoo!, contains information such as icebreakers that make flirting a breeze! Relationships can be explored by creating and publishing personal profiles in which you share information about yourself. You are able to connect with individuals through international sites in countries such as France, Germany, and China.

Relationships typically include periods of frequent self-disclosure early in the development process.[32] However, although the *level* of intimacy (or risk) in the information increases over time, the *amount* of disclosure tends to decrease as the relationship becomes more and more intimate. As a relationship proceeds, we share a good deal of low-risk information fairly rapidly, move on to share higher-risk information, and then, finally, to share our most intimate disclosures. The more intimate the relationship becomes, the more intimate the information that is disclosed. Holding back from sharing intimate information may signal a reluctance to develop a relationship.

Verbal

Self-Disclosure, Intimacy, and Gender

Interpersonal communication research is extensive on the topic of self-disclosure and the development of intimacy in a relationship. But just what is intimacy? Experts use such terms as bonding, closeness, and emotional connection, based on the sharing of personal, private information and experiences over time.[33] We especially like the definition developed by couples therapist Jeffrey Fine: "To be intimate is to be totally transparent, emotionally naked in front of another who is equally transparent. You want to see into the other's heart. What people should mean when they say *intimacy* is in-to-me-see."[34]

The conventional wisdom, borne out by early studies, contends that relationships cannot fully develop into intimacy without both partners sharing (ideally, with equal frequency and depth) information about themselves.[35] Without self-disclosure, we form only superficial relationships. However, research on gender and self-disclosure calls the wisdom and prior findings into question.[36]

Consider for a moment men's friendships with other men. Think about golfing buddies, a group of guys who gather over lunch a few times a week to shoot some hoops, or men who enjoy one another's company over a few beers. Do these relationships tend to be based on an intimate sharing of personal information? Or are they more likely based on shared experiences, on doing things together or having interests in common, rather than "deep" conversations? Now think about how women's friendships form, in general. Do they form more through shared activities or through communication? It's not a stereotype; women's friendships with other women are more often developed through interpersonal communication, particularly self-disclosure, than through common experiences.[37]

So, if men's friendships tend to form out of shared activities, are they any less meaningful than relationships that develop through communication? Research has attempted to discover what constitutes intimacy for men, how men's friendships form, and what makes them meaningful.[38] Most men describe their friendships with other men as forming quite differently than their friendships with women but as being just as satisfying and important.[39] Men's friendships more often develop by doing, while relationships with female friends involve more talking. Men who experience the terror of battle together form powerful

ReCAP ⬅┈┈

Self-Disclosure . . .

. . . is information you tell someone about yourself that she or he couldn't learn about you unless you revealed it.

. . . should be reciprocal, meaning that the person you reveal something to should respond with information about himself or herself—information similar in depth. The frequency with which partners self-disclose should be reciprocal as well.

. . . should be appropriate, meaning that it can be a mistake to reveal information that is too personal too soon in the development of a relationship.

. . . involves some risk, because knowledge is power. By revealing information to another person, you give that person a degree of power over you.

. . . is highly rewarding, in that it is a building block of relational intimacy.

bonds, developed more likely from shared moments than shared personal information down in the trenches. To suggest that only superficial relationships can be accomplished by doing, while deep ones must be accomplished by communicating, is to measure relational intimacy with a feminine yardstick.[40] However, communication scholars and teachers continue to be fascinated with the way self-disclosure generates intimacy in relationships, especially female–male romantic relationships.

⸺⸽ Two Models of Self-Disclosure

Research has explored the way in which self-disclosure works to move a relationship toward intimacy. Here, we examine two of the more prominent models that illustrate the process by which this happens.

The Social Penetration Model

A pair of researchers, Irwin Altman and Dalmas Taylor, developed a model of **social penetration** that illustrates how much and what kind of information we reveal in various stages of a relationship.[41] In their theory, interpersonal communication in relationships moves gradually from the superficial to the more intimate. Two aspects of this communication increase: the breadth of the information (the variety of topics discussed) and the depth (the personal significance of what is discussed).

   Their model is a configuration of rings, commonly referred to as concentric circles. The outermost circle represents breadth, or all the potential information about yourself that you could disclose to someone (see Figure 7.2). Some elements on this ring might include athletic activities, spirituality, family, school, recreational activities, political attitudes and values, and fears. Then there are a series of inner circles, which represent the depth of information you could reveal about yourself. The innermost circle represents your most personal information.

   As a relational partner interacts with you, that interaction can be seen as a wedge that begins narrowly (few topics are discussed) and shallowly (topics are fairly superficial). People who have just started dating might talk about commonalities (such as being students at the same college), hobbies, interests, and favourite activities. As the relationship progresses, the wedge becomes broader (as more topics are discussed) and deeper (as more personal topics are discussed). After several dates and conversations about hobbies and interests, topics might turn more to values, such as the importance of family and friendships or attitudes about politics or social issues. Self-disclosure causes your layers to be penetrated, as you penetrate the layers of the other person.

   Each of your relationships represents a degree of social penetration, or the extent to which the other person has entered your concentric circles. Some relationships, such as those with professors, distant family members, and acquaintances, may reflect a narrow, shallow wedge. The relationship does not involve a great deal of personal disclosure. A few

social penetration
A model of self-disclosure that depicts both the breadth and depth of information shared with another person.

FIGURE 7.2 Altman and Taylor's Concentric Circles and Wedge of Social Penetration

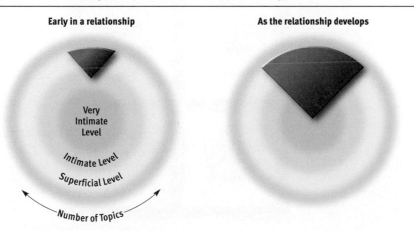

Early in a relationship

As the relationship develops

Very Intimate Level

Intimate Level

Superficial Level

Number of Topics

relationships represent almost complete social penetration, the kind you achieve in an intimate, well-developed relationship, in which a large amount of in-depth self-disclosure has occurred. But many contend that no one can ever completely know another person; there may be no such thing as complete social penetration. This model is a helpful way to assess your relationships, in terms of who you allow or encourage to get close to you and why. It may also help you diagram the level of intimacy you have in relationships with others, as you attempt to penetrate their layers.

The Johari Window

The **Johari Window** in Figure 7.3 is another model of how self-disclosure varies from relationship to relationship. It reflects various stages of relational development, degrees of self-awareness, and others' perceptions of us. Its name comes from the first names of the two men who developed it (Joe and Harry) and from its windowlike appearance.[42] The square window, like the circles in the social penetration model, represents yourself. This self encompasses everything about you, including things you don't see or realize. A vertical line divides the square into what you have come to know about yourself and what you don't yet know about yourself. A horizontal line divides the square into what another person knows about you and doesn't know about you. The intersection of these lines creates a four-paned window.

The *Open* quadrant represents that part of yourself that you know and have revealed to the other person. As a relationship becomes more intimate, the Open quadrant grows larger. The *Hidden* quadrant is information you know about yourself but have not shared with the other person. This quadrant is fairly large initially; but, as you self-disclose, it shrinks, and the Open quadrant grows. The information in the *Unknown* quadrant is that part of yourself which you have yet to discover or realize. As you learn and self-disclose more, or as others learn more about you, this quadrant becomes smaller and smaller. Individuals who are not very introspective and do not have a very well-developed sense of self will have larger Unknown areas than those who have made a concerted effort to come to know themselves.

Sometimes our friends observe things about us that we don't realize or perceive about ourselves. This kind of unintentional self-disclosure is represented by the *Blind* quadrant. This quadrant does not include misperceptions about us, but rather real aspects of ourselves that we fail to recognize. The Blind quadrant is usually small when someone doesn't know us very well; it grows larger as that person observes more and more information that is in our Unknown quadrant. However, as the relationship becomes more intimate, the other person is more likely to reveal his or her perceptions of us, so the Unknown and the Blind quadrants shrink as the information becomes known and accessible to us. As you can see, then, intimate relationships play an important role in the growth of self-knowledge.

Johari Window
A model that explains how self-disclosure varies from relationship to relationship; reflects various stages of relational development, degrees of self-awareness, and others' perceptions.

FIGURE 7.3 Johari Window

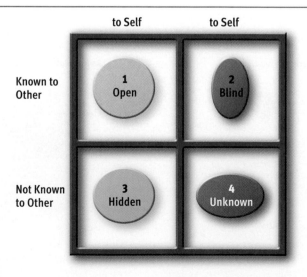

⤳ Expressing Emotions

Expressing emotions is another powerful way that we reveal ourselves to others and deepen our relationships. Such expression comes more easily to some people than others, but it is a skill that can be improved.[43] However, there are cultural barriers to achieving this skill, in that many cultures designate particular emotions as appropriate for only some people to display in certain situations.[44] If you placed emotional expression on a continuum according to cultural groups, with one end being an open approach to emotional display and the other end being the suppression of emotional display, Canadian culture would fall somewhere in the middle. Some cultural groups (such as Latin cultures) are comfortable with and accepting of emotional display, while other groups (such as Asian cultures) value emotional inhibition more than the Canadians.[45] People from countries where the norm is emotional inhibition often think that Canadians wear their hearts on their sleeves, while other cultures view Canadians as being "pent up" emotionally. One of your authors, while visiting Germany, was uncomfortable "hot tubbing it" with a group of foreign students (of course, nudity was the norm!). One German student responded, "You Canadians, you're so conservative. You need to let loose"!

Canadian families often teach children very specific rules about the appropriateness of emotional display. One fascinating nonverbal communication study found that, at very young ages, children learn to mask disappointment in order to be socially appropriate.[46] We also perpetuate gender distinctions regarding emotions.[47] Many Canadian men are taught to contain their emotions for fear that emotional expression may make them appear weak. Acquiring a "poker face" is a goal. Men are allowed to show anger and jealousy (short of physical violence), but it is frowned on for men to reveal sadness, fear, or great joy—unless they reveal it in a sporting context. (Some believe that this is one reason why so many men are drawn to sports; the sporting context allows them emotional release that would most likely be considered inappropriate or "unmanly" in other contexts.) In fact, the male tendency to suppress emotion is so pronounced, it led Sidney Jourard (who first studied self-disclosure) to entitle one of his book chapters, "The Lethal Aspects of the Male Role."[48] Jourard found that men who had difficulty expressing their feelings had high levels of stress-related disease. Research suggests that if and when men do disclose their feelings to someone, most seek women as listeners because they report feeling safer expressing emotions to women than to other men.[49]

Women in Canadian culture, in most settings, are allowed the emotional display of crying that can be prompted by sadness, fear, or joy. (Exceptions include some professional settings, where "keeping close to the vest" is valued and displaying emotion is deemed inappropriate.) But many women receive negative reactions when they display anger. The view persists that an angry woman is "out of control" or "hormonal," while an angry man is behaving more in line with societal expectations for members of his sex. Although these trends and expectations have changed somewhat with recent generations, there is still a significant tendency for men (and many women as well) to believe that emotional expression of any kind is more appropriate in women than men.

Many of us are reluctant or embarrassed to talk about our feelings or show our emotions, yet expressing feelings is a primary way we develop and deepen our relationships. We share feelings with our partners in two primary ways. First, we disclose more indirectly information about our past and current emotional states and experiences, such as sadness about the death of a family member or fear about what we will do after we graduate. This form of disclosure is more common in a growing relationship. The second way is the direct expression of emotions such as expressing attraction, love, or disappointment toward our partners. This form typically emerges later in the development of a relationship.[50]

As relationships become more intimate, we have a greater expectation that our partner will disclose emotions openly. The amount of risk associated with such emotional disclosure varies from person to person. Most of us are comfortable sharing positive emotions such as happiness and joy but are more reserved about

Nonverbal

Some researchers believe that men are drawn to sports because the sporting event allows them emotional release that might be considered inappropriate in other contexts.

Verbal

sharing negative emotions such as fear or disappointment. In a study of 46 committed, romantic couples, subjects reported that the number one problem in their relationship was an inability to talk about negative feelings.[51] For example, partners often made the following types of observations: "When she gets upset, she stops talking"; "He never lets me know when he's upset with something he doesn't like"; and "He just silently pouts." We generally want to know how our partners in intimate relationships are feeling, even if those feelings are negative.

SUMMARY

In this chapter we explored the important context of interpersonal communication—the form of communication that we have most frequently in our lives. Effective interpersonal communication is intricately related to our ability to enact the five communication principles of a lifetime. We first defined interpersonal communication as a special form of unmediated human communication that occurs when we interact simultaneously with another person and attempt to mutually influence each other, usually for the purpose of managing relationships. We then differentiated interpersonal from impersonal communication and relationships of circumstance from relationships of choice.

We all know that relationships are important, but just how do they begin? In this chapter we explored the concept of attraction in its various forms, distinguishing interpersonal attraction as being the form that causes us to forge ongoing connections with others. Four primary factors play a role in interpersonal attraction, including how similar we perceive ourselves to be with our relational partners, how physically and/or sexually attracted we are to them, what kind of proximity or access we can have to them, and whether our personality traits, values, and needs are complementary with theirs. We explored ways that we verbally and nonverbally communicate our attraction to others, as we attempt to form friendships, co-worker relationships, romances, and committed partnerships with key people in our lives.

Once you acknowledge that you are attracted to another person and desire a relationship with her or him, how do you use communication to get that relationship off the ground? Most of us face a degree of uncertainty when meeting new people and initiating relationships. We attempt to reduce that uncertainty by seeking information in passive, active, and interactive ways. We then must call on our best communication skills to meet and get to know the other person. Rather than communicating about ourselves in a self-absorbed or narcissistic fashion, it is better to learn to ask great questions of the other person that will draw him or her out and get a conversation going. Learning to give and receive compliments graciously and sincerely is a skill we can all benefit from, because the compliment is a unique form of interpersonal communication that can have a profoundly positive effect on a relationship.

One of the most important forms of interpersonal communication that facilitates our relationships is self-disclosure, defined as revealing something about yourself to another person that she or he would not otherwise know if you did not reveal it. The rate and depth of self-disclosure varies according to progression in a relationship, but we expect self-disclosure to be reciprocal. This means that if we share something about ourselves, we expect our partners to respond in kind, both in frequency and depth of information. Self-disclosure is also expected to be appropriate to the level of intimacy of the relationship. And self-disclosing involves a degree of risk.

One way to develop intimacy in a relationship is to disclose personal information, but research has determined that self-disclosure is not the only "road to intimacy." Gender affects how we develop relationships, in that men may develop close friendships with other men more through shared activities than shared information. Women, on the other hand, are more likely to deepen relationships by disclosing information than by sharing an experience. We discussed two models of self-disclosure: the social penetration model, which focuses on how personal layers are revealed to others; and the Johari Window, which illustrates self-awareness and relational partners' perceptions of us. Another form of disclosure is the expression of emotions to relational partners. The degree to which we feel safe discussing or displaying our emotions to others is a measure of intimacy in a relationship.

PRINCIPLES FOR A LIFETIME

Aware

Principle 1:   Be aware of your communication with yourself and others.

- Attraction emerges in several different forms; it's important to discover what traits in other persons are attractive to you.
- Early in a relationship, be aware of aspects of your personality that you want to emphasize to another person in order to create a positive and attractive image.
- One strategy to reduce uncertainty in interpersonal contexts is to be aware of your surroundings and situation as you passively observe others' interactions.
- The Johari Window is a device to help you become more aware of your relationships and your interpersonal communication.

Verbal

Principle 2:   Effectively use and understand verbal messages.

- Because unmediated interpersonal communication occurs simultaneously between two persons, realize that both persons act upon each other's verbal communication.
- In initial interactions, honest, direct approaches are preferable to "canned" opening lines.
- When initiating relationships, use questions that will engage and draw out another person.
- You may verbally reveal your liking for another person by using informal, personal, and inclusive language.
- You may verbally reveal your liking for another person by asking questions, probing for further information, and directly expressing your feelings.
- An active strategy to reduce uncertainty in interpersonal contexts is to ask third parties for their perceptions and knowledge.
- An interactive information-seeking strategy involves direct communication with the source who has the greatest potential for reducing your uncertainty.
- Asking great questions in a conversation draws a person out and helps a communicator avoid creating a perception of being self-absorbed.
- Practise giving sincere compliments generously and receiving others' compliments graciously.
- One of the key variables in relationship development is self-disclosure.
- As relationships grow more intimate, the expectation for deeper, more personal self-disclosure increases.
- Women's relationships tend to rely more on verbal communication, especially self-disclosure, while men's relationships with other men more often develop out of shared activities or common experiences.
- As relationships grow more intimate, the expectation for more emotional expression increases.

Nonverbal

Principle 3:   Effectively use and understand nonverbal messages.

- Because unmediated interpersonal communication occurs simultaneously between two persons, realize that both persons act upon each other's nonverbal communication.
- Physical attraction is the degree to which you find another person's physical self appealing, while sexual attraction is the desire to have sexual contact with a certain person.
- You may nonverbally reveal your liking for another person through the display of immediacy cues.
- Nonverbal behaviours, such as increasing your volume to keep someone from interrupting you, can signal a self-absorbed style of interpersonal communication.
- As children, we learn early on to mask our emotions—such as disappointment—so as to behave "appropriately."

Listen and Respond

Principle 4:   Listen and respond thoughtfully to others.

- Early in relationships, it's important to listen to your partner's answers to your questions, so you can offer an appropriate follow-up response.
- You may verbally reveal your attraction and liking for other people by listening, asking questions to elicit more detail, and then responding appropriately and sensitively to the added information.
- The best conversationalists aren't great talkers, they're great listeners and responders.
- The formulation of great questions in conversation requires listening carefully and responding appropriately to someone's communication.

- It's important to listen carefully to someone's self-disclosure, because there is an expectation of reciprocity, meaning that a receiver is expected to self-disclose in response to a sender's self-disclosure.

Adapt

Principle 5:   Adapt messages to others.

- Adapt to others' communication, especially in first conversations, by listening to what is said and following up with great questions.
- A self-absorbed style of communication involves very little adaptation to others.
- Adapt your self-disclosure to the other person and the context, so that your revelations are appropriate.

Discussion and Review

1. Why is interpersonal communication important in our lives?

2. What four components make up the definition of interpersonal communication?

3. Discuss three forms of attraction explained in this chapter. Then explore ways in which we verbally and nonverbally communicate our varying forms of attraction for others.

4. What are the three basic human needs, according to Will Schutz, whose research we reviewed in this chapter? How does the concept of complementarity in a relationship relate to these three needs?

5. Discuss uncertainty-reduction theory in the context of interpersonal relationships. What three information-seeking strategies do we typically use to reduce our uncertainty?

6. We've all no doubt met people who were, by trait, self-absorbed, or who exhibited self-absorbed communication styles. Explain, first, what is meant by self-absorption in interpersonal communication; then provide some examples that illustrate this style.

7. What is a "great" question? Provide examples of great questions versus poor questions that could be used to initiate conversations and relationships with others.

8. What is self-disclosure and how does it function to develop intimacy in a relationship?

9. What does the social penetration model teach us about relationship development?

10. Explain how the Johari Window reveals our view of self, as well as others' views of us. In what ways could the Johari Window be helpful in the assessment of our relationships?

Developing Your Skills: Putting Principles into Practice

1. Using a model of concentric circles (circles within circles), map out your interpersonal relationships. Put your name in the core circle, then write the names of those persons closest to you on the circle closest to the core, continuing outward on circles with the names of interpersonal relationships according to intimacy. Once you have completed your model, think about how your communication differs with people on the innermost circles versus those on the outermost circles. What kind of communication is required to move someone from an outer circle to an inner one; in other words, how do you communicate to increase relational closeness or intimacy with someone? Do you sense a need to "lighten up" with someone on an inner ring, possibly moving them to a more outer ring? How will you use interpersonal communication to accomplish this?

2. Think about someone in your life—either at present or in the past—to whom you were extremely attracted. Assess that attraction by considering these questions: How similar were you to that person, in terms of temperament, values, personality, and interests? Was your attraction to that person physical? Sexual? Intellectual? Psychological (meaning an attraction to the person's personality)? Spiritual? A combination of some of these? What kind of proximity did you have to the person? Did you have ready access to him or her? If not, what kind of effect did that have on your attraction? How complementary were your personality traits, abilities, and needs?

3. With a group of classmates, generate lists of the worst opening lines you can think of for getting a first conversation off the ground. Then discuss the use of canned opening lines as a strategy for initiating conversation. Should these types of lines be used? If someone uses a standard line to start a conversation, what happens to the ability to adapt one's communication to one's listeners?

4. Because we think that learning to ask great questions is so important, we want to provide you an opportunity to practise this art and skill. Below, we provide situations and snippets of conversations and ask you to generate effective follow-up questions that would deepen and extend the conversation. We've provided a complete example to get you started.

   a. *Sample Situation and Conversation:* The situation is a first conversation between two classmates who have never met; they are seated in the classroom before class begins.

      Bob: Hi; my name's Bob, what's yours?

      Sue: Hi; I'm Sue.

      Bob: I've never taken a philosophy course before, have you? What do you think this course will be like?

      Sue: Well, I've never taken a philosophy course either, but I expect there will be lots of reading. And I've heard that the professor's tests are pretty tough.

      Bob: Oh great; is it too late to drop?! When you say the tests are tough, tough in what way? Do you mean they cover lots of material, the prof's a hard grader, or what?

   b. *Sample Situation:* At a fraternity/sorority mixer, a woman and a man are introduced to each other for the first time by other members of their organizations.

   c. *Sample Situation:* After a staff meeting, two new co-workers who will be working on the same important project introduce themselves to each other.

5. As a class, develop a list of categories of information for self-disclosure. For example, categories could include academic achievement, religion, family background, cultural heritage, romantic experiences, and sexuality. Then have each class member write down (privately) something that pertains to each category that the person *would* and *would not* feel comfortable disclosing to another person. For example, under the category of family background, an item that might be disclosed could be that the person's parents were divorced; an item that might not be disclosed could be that the person suffered emotional or physical abuse in the family. This activity helps us clarify our own "rules" about self-disclosing personal information.

Romare Bearden, "The Family," collage on wood, 1988. Courtesy: National Museum of American Art, Washington, DC/Art Resource, NY.
© Romare Bearden Foundation/Licensed by VAGA, New York, NY.

Relationship is a pervading and changing mystery . . . brutal or lovely, the mystery waits for people wherever they go, whatever extreme they run to.

— EUDORA WELTY

8 Enhancing Relationships

AFTER STUDYING THIS CHAPTER, YOU SHOULD BE ABLE TO

1. Explain how the five principles for a lifetime apply to interpersonal communication among friends, family members, and co-workers.

2. Identify the most important interpersonal communication skills critical to job effectiveness.

3. Identify and describe the five stages of relational escalation.

4. Identify and describe the five stages of relational de-escalation.

5. Define interpersonal conflict and distinguish between constructive and destructive conflict.

6. Distinguish among complementary, symmetrical, and parallel interpersonal relationships, in terms of power dynamics.

7. Explain the difference between assertive and aggressive communication.

8. Explain the key characteristics of nonconfrontational, confrontational, and cooperative styles of conflict management.

9. Discuss the major ways to manage emotions, information, goals, and problems in conflict situations.

What makes you happy in this life? Think a bit before answering that question. What really gives you enjoyment? Staring at a computer screen? Working on a project for your job? Reading a great book? Playing a video game? Being by yourself, writing in your journal? Taking a long walk? Let us venture a guess: Although any one of these things might bring some level of pleasure into your life, none of them could be considered the thing in life that gives you the most enjoyment. Probably most of us would answer that question with some response that involves other people or, perhaps, only one other person.

To some degree, we all come from dysfunctional families—there is no such thing as a perfect or "functional" family. As Tolstoy said, "Happy families are all alike; every unhappy family is unhappy in its own way." But no matter how imperfect our families are, no matter how crazy our siblings used to make us (or still make us), or how far apart we feel we may have grown from family members, almost all of us would agree that family relationships are extremely important. Likewise, in the professional arena, when people talk about their jobs and what they like best about where they work, most often they talk about the people they work with. So, disregarding the few true hermits out there, most of us are "people who need people." It may sound corny, but we all know that our relationships with other people are what bring us great joy in this life.

In Chapter 7 we examined some fundamental aspects of interpersonal communication that facilitate relationships. We discussed attraction and those first conversations that can launch relationships or stop them dead in their tracks. In this chapter we move forward with interpersonal communication as it occurs in ongoing relationships. We attempt to answer the question: Now that I've initiated a relationship, how does it progress? What happens when relationships move backwards, even to the point of termination?

Our focus in this chapter is the face-to-face relationship—the kind that occurs in person, not through the wonders of technology. We realize that with ever-increasing frequency, people are connecting in cyberspace. But, for now, we ask that you be content to examine the good old average, everyday, face-to-face, unenhanced-by-technology kind of relationship.

First, let's reconsider our five communication principles for a lifetime as they pertain to certain relationships. Most of our examples in this chapter and the previous one tend to focus on romantic relationships, so we want to explore in some detail how communication principles apply to three other types of relationships most people experience: friendships, family, and colleagues.

THE IMPORTANCE OF FRIENDSHIP

One of the best definitions for a friend, attributed to Aristotle, is "a soul that resides in two bodies." A friend is someone we like and who likes us. We trust our friends and share good and bad times with them. We enjoy being with them, so we try to make time for that purpose. We expect a certain level of self-sacrifice from our friends. For example, you know you've got a good friend when that person gives up something (like a hot date) just to help you through a tough time.

Researchers have examined some differences among friendships at four stages in life: childhood, adolescence, adulthood, and old age.[1] When we start to talk (around the age of two), we begin to play and interact with others, and perceive playmates as those who can help meet our needs. Our first friendships are typically superficial, self-centred, and fleeting because they are based on momentary sharing of activities.[2] As we grow, we develop more of a give-and-take in friendships. During adolescence we move away from relationships with parents and toward greater intimacy with our peers. At this point in our development, peer relationships are the most important social influence on our behaviour. Adolescents are likely to join groups, such as a sports or debate team, or, unfortunately, less socially desirable groups bent on violence and destruction of property.

Adult friendships are among our most valued relationships, even though they may be few in number. Research has found that, on average, adults have ten to twenty casual friends, four to six close friends, and only one to two best friends.[3] But as North Americans continue to spend more hours at work each year, we often find that our closest friends are also our co-workers.[4] We share common interests, concerns, and schedules with co-workers, so it's natural when colleagues fulfil each others' social needs as well. No doubt some of you reading this text are working a job, taking classes that demand significant blocks of time, and juggling all of this with a home and family life. Given all this activity, you may find that friendships get squeezed in the mix. Unless we make maintaining friendships a priority, we may find ourselves becoming too busy to "work them in" and, sadly, losing them over time.

Finally, friendships are extremely important in old age.[5] During retirement, when many individuals have more time for socializing, friendships become increasingly critical. Older adults tend to rely on enduring friendships and to maintain a small, highly valued network of friends.

Many people find that the friendships they maintain over the years are among their most valuable.

···⟩ Communication Principles for a Lifetime: Enhancing Friendships

Noted author and motivational speaker Dale Carnegie suggests, "You can make more friends in two months by becoming interested in other people than you can in two years by trying to get other people interested in you."[6] Attraction is what draws you to potential friends, just like various forms of attraction draw you to potential dates or romantic partners. So how best do you reveal your interpersonal attraction to someone so as to form a friendship?

Like many other things, friendship development begins with an awareness of yourself—principle 1. Knowing your own interests, likes, and dislikes is a first step if you are trying to expand your circle of friends. If you consider yourself a spiritual person, then you're more likely to make new friends with those kinds of people at a church gathering or yoga and meditation class than some other setting.

Aware

We need communication to initiate, develop, deepen, and maintain friendships. Principles 2 and 3, which involve the effective use of verbal and nonverbal communication, are essential in friendship. Our verbal communication tends to become more frequent and to deepen as friendships develop. We also use immediacy cues to establish friendships, those behaviours we learned in Chapter 7 that reveal our liking of other people, such as leaning forward, moving closer, making eye contact, smiling, and nodding in response to others.

Verbal

Nonverbal

···⟩•⟨··· COMMUNICATION and TECHNOLOGY

Keeping up with Friends

Do you keep up with friends in distant places by crafting a good old-fashioned, handwritten, snail-mailed letter? If so, you may think that technological innovations—e-mail, telephone answering devices, and fax machines—have ruined the art of letter writing. Or perhaps you pride yourself on still being a letter writer amid a world of e-mailers.

No doubt the creators of all the forms of "instant access" available to us in the world today believe that their technologies bring people closer together. But there are those skeptics who ponder the difference between "virtual" friends and "in-person" friends. They also worry that the speed and ease of technology, such as e-mail, makes us lazy in our maintenance responsibilities to our friends. Do you put as much care into an e-mail message as you might a personal letter?

Do this little exercise: Think of friends you have who live at a distance from you (meaning that it takes a long-distance phone call to speak to them). Now think about the last time you were in contact with each of these people. What channel of interpersonal communication did you use? Were you face to face in a conversation, because you travelled to be in the same location? Was it over the phone? E-mail? Or did you send a card or letter? Finally, think about the quality of your communication with these friends. If you use technological innovations, such as e-mail, to stay in contact with these friends, has it improved your relationship?

Listen and Respond

Adapt

Listening and responding are important communication skills in friendship. Most of us don't stay friends with people who don't seem to listen to us, or who listen but respond inappropriately. With friends, it's important to be aware of what they *say* as well as what they *do,* as we attempt to read what's going on with them and determine the best response. That may be an empathic response, one in which you allow your friend to vent or emote while you merely attempt to feel what your friend is feeling. Your best response on other occasions may be to help a friend out of a bad spot by offering advice and counsel. Probably no other communication skill develops a friendship more than the ability to listen and respond appropriately.

Finally, we learn to adapt to our friends or they probably don't stay our friends for very long (principle 5). This doesn't mean that we become "social chameleons," changing our personalities as the wind blows. It means that we extend different parts of ourselves and communicate differently with various friends. You may enjoy your dancing buddies because you can let a creative, wilder side of yourself show with them, while you communicate more seriously as you study with a group of classmates who have become your friends.

THE IMPORTANCE OF FAMILY

Of all the relationships we develop in our lifetimes, none are more complicated than family relationships. Family members have the power to shape our self-concepts and affect self-esteem more than other people. Granted, at some point we can choose to stop or lessen the effect family members can have on our lives. But for most of us, those early messages we received as children, primarily from our parents and secondarily from our siblings, still remain in our psyches and affect who we are today.

To say that family life has changed is an understatement. Family units are dramatically different from the time when the predominant profile was a two-parent, father-as-bread-winner, mother-as-homemaker arrangement.[7] According to the 2001 census, the definition of "census family"[8] has changed significantly from earlier censuses:

- Two persons living in a same-sex common-law relationship, along with either partner's children, are now considered a census family.
- Children in a census family now may have been previously married. In previous censuses they had to be "never married."
- A grandchild living in a three-generation household where the parent is "never married" is now considered a child in the census family of his or her parent. In previous censuses, the census family consisted of the two older generations and the child was considered a non–census family person.
- A grandchild of another household member, where the middle generation is not present, will now be considered a child in the census family of his or her grandparent. In previous censuses, the grandchild was considered a non–census family person.

Aware

⋯⇥ Communication Principles for a Lifetime:
   Enhancing Family Relationships

Growing up in families, we begin to discover who we are and how we should communicate with others. If you were raised by the rule of "children should be seen and not heard,"

then you got clear messages about when it was appropriate to speak out and when to be silent. If you witnessed a good deal of conflict in your family, you no doubt have been affected by that experience. You may have turned out to be someone who avoids conflict at all costs, but research suggests that it is more likely that you will prefer the same form of conflict you witnessed or participated in as you grew up.[9] If you rarely argued with your parents or witnessed them arguing, you are more likely as an adult to be fearful and avoidant of disagreement, rather than to pick fights because you wish to experience a form of interaction you didn't get as a child.

Our earliest lessons about verbal and nonverbal communication come from our families. Virginia Satir has conducted extensive research on family communication.[10] She suggests that the following are found in healthy families: "the members' sense of self-worth is high; communication is direct, clear, specific, and honest; rules are flexible, humane, and subject to change; and the family's links to society are open and hopeful." In such families, Satir notes, people listen actively; they look *at* one another, not *through* one another or at the floor; they treat children as people; they touch one another affectionately regardless of age; and they openly discuss disappointments, fears, hurts, angers, and criticism, as well as joys and achievements. The degree to which parents and children can reveal what they are thinking and feeling is a measure of family cohesiveness. Another aspect Satir highlights corresponds to our principle 4, that of listening and responding. Family relationships are built upon foundations of trust, which involves listening to one another and responding helpfully. Many conflicts arise because family members don't listen to one another and respond based on that faulty listening.

Verbal
Nonverbal

Listen
and
Respond

Adapt

Finally, family relationships involve a good deal of adaptation, particularly when, as adults, we visit our parents. Here's an example: A colleague of ours describes the tension he feels when he visits his parents on certain holidays. His father was born in 1920, so he has very different experiences and values from his 40-something son. During key moments (such as over Thanksgiving dinner), when the father begins to talk in stereotypes (usually derogatory) about certain racial or ethnic groups, the son cringes. He must decide whether to engage his dad and risk ruining the occasion for his mother (which he has done at times) or squelch his own views, which could be seen as an act of cowardice and a tacit acceptance of racism. Most of the time now he says he "keeps the peace," adapting his communication for the higher goal of avoiding conflict and keeping the family holiday pleasant.

The Importance of Colleagues

For many of us, our work is our livelihood, our most time-consuming activity. According to the Business and Labour Market Analysis Division of Statistics Canada, between 1979 and 2000 hours per worker grew 2.2% in Canada, from 1669 to 1706 hours per year. In the U.S., hours per worker grew 9.6% from 1707 to 1871 hours per year.[11] Many things make a job worthwhile and rewarding, but most working persons say that relationships with people they work with make the most difference between job satisfaction and dissatisfaction.

When some co-workers interact, the relationship is all business. For others, the relationship becomes a friendship.

What are the most important skills people need to be successful on the job? Results from research are dramatically consistent. The number-one skill you need to perform your job well is the ability to communicate effectively with others.[12] You land your job through a face-to-face interview (in most situations). You keep your job based on your ability to do the work, which usually involves a large amount of interpersonal interaction. Studies have specifically asked employers to identify key skills to help college and university graduates obtain employment. One of the top skills continues to be speaking (meaning communicating interpersonally, not just giving presentations).[13] Nonverbal and listening skills are also high on the list of necessary, valued skills for job applicants. These research results suggest that interpersonal communication skills are more highly valued and considered than your grade-point average, the specific degree you hold, or the school you attended.

⋯⟩ Communication Principles for a Lifetime: Enhancing Workplace Relationships

Getting accustomed to a new job takes a while. There are the rudimentary things to discover and adjust to, such as finding out where to park, learning the procedures that make an organization function, and observing general office protocol. Then there are the more important things, such as ascertaining the chain of command and discovering which colleagues have the potential to develop into friends.

When most of us enter a new situation, such as a new job, we experience uncertainty. We discussed in Chapter 7 how the motivation to reduce uncertainty causes us to seek information. On the job, our uncertainty will be most likely reduced by those persons who hired us, those who are assigned to train or orient us to the new situation, and co-workers who are on our same level within the organization. We are most likely to use passive strategies first, meaning that we observe our surroundings and how people interact on the job, as a way of obtaining more awareness so that we will know how to behave appropriately (principle 1). Perception checking with colleagues also increases awareness. For example, after attending your first staff meeting, you might want to ask a few colleagues whether the gathering was typical of the kind of staff meetings the organization holds.

As we begin to interact with persons of varying status in the organization, we draw on our most effective verbal and nonverbal communication skills so that we make positive impressions on others (principles 2 and 3). The higher you go in an organization, the more your job involves communicating with others. In one research project, scholar Harvey Mintzberg observed chief executive officers for five weeks. He found that managers spend almost 80% of their day communicating orally with others.[14] In most organizations, working is communication; communicating is working.

One skill that makes for an effective worker—any worker, any organization—is the ability to listen and respond effectively to colleagues (principle 4). The best managers of other people are the best listeners. They listen patiently, fully, and nonjudgmentally. They also exercise caution before responding, so that they will respond appropriately.

Finally, our principle 5 about adaptation is critical to successful co-worker relationships. You cannot hope to be successful on the job if you communicate the same way to your boss as you do to your peers on the job, your subordinates, and others in your life— including long-term friends, intimates, and family members. This may seem obvious, but we find that people sometimes experience isolation on the job because they cannot get along with co-workers. Or they've trusted co-workers too much and revealed personal information, only to have that information used against them later. Some people don't realize that they can't talk at work about everything they talk about at home. They don't adapt to the situation, and it often costs them their jobs.

⋯⟩ Stages of Relationship Development

Researchers have determined that relationships develop in discernible stages, although they differ in their use of terms and the number of stages.[15] While the research on relational stages is most often applied to dating or romantic relationships, the information can also apply to friendships, co-worker relationships, and marriages or committed partnerships.

Understanding these stages is important. First, interpersonal communication is affected by the stage of the relationship. For instance, individuals in an advanced stage discuss topics and display nonverbal behaviours that rarely appear in the early stages of a relationship. Second, interpersonal communication facilitates movement between the various stages. Relationships change and are continually renegotiated by the persons involved. Interpersonal communication moves a relationship forward as we proceed from acquaintances, to friends, to lovers, and, possibly, to marital or committed partners. Ideally, communication should move a relationship back from partners to friends as well, although regressing a relationship is difficult to accomplish. Because of the potential for hurt feelings and conflict, the process often does not involve communication, but instead neglect or a decline in contact.

It's helpful to think of relational stages as floors in a high rise (see Figure 8.1). The bottom floor represents a first meeting; the penthouse is intimacy. Relational development

FIGURE 8.1 Relationship Stages

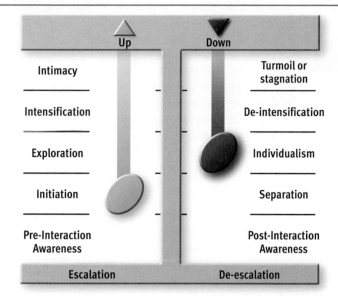

Source: From Steven A. Beebe, Susan J. Beebe, and Mark V. Richmond, *Interpersonal Communication: Relating to Others*, 3rd ed. Published by Allyn & Bacon, Boston, MA. Copyright © 2002 by Pearson Education. Reprinted by permission of the publisher.

is an elevator that stops at every floor. As you escalate to each floor, you might get off the elevator and wander around for a while before going to the next floor. Each time you get on, you don't know how many floors up the elevator will take you or how long you will stay at any given floor. In fact, sometimes you never get back on the elevator, electing instead to stay at a particular stage of relational development. This may represent stability or stagnation. Stability doesn't necessarily mean that a relationship is stagnant because it isn't moving through some stage or another; it may simply mean that a relationship has reached a comfortable point for both partners. But notice that we say *both* partners; if one partner feels the relationship has stabilized at an appropriate stage, but the other partner feels the relationship has stagnated, dissatisfaction and conflict are often the result.

If you fall head over heels in love, you might want to escalate quickly from floor to floor toward intimacy, possibly even skipping some floors. The process of de-escalating a relationship does not occur in every relationship, but if it does, it may be a slow or quick descent through various floors. The best approach to relationship development is to share this elevator with your partner, so that the two of you make decisions about how high you will ride the elevator, how long to stay at each floor, and whether to take the elevator back down. Often partners do not share decisions about movement within the relationship. Sometimes one of the partners rides the elevator alone. Let's explore in more depth this process of escalating and de-escalating relationships.

Relational Escalation

As depicted in Figure 8.1, the first level of relational development is termed the **pre-interaction awareness stage.** In this stage, you might observe a person or even talk with others about that person without having any direct interaction. You might not move beyond the pre-interaction awareness stage if your impressions of the person aren't favourable or the circumstances aren't right.

If you are attracted to the other person and the circumstances are right, you might proceed to the **initiation stage.** First conversations typically involve each person responding to the other's questions as they try to determine what they have in common. Try to ask engaging questions and then listen carefully to the answers. The answers suggest follow-up questions that can draw the person out and make you both more comfortable. Your nonverbal behaviour should also indicate your interest.

pre-interaction awareness stage
Becoming aware of one's attraction to another person; observing that person but not actually interacting.

initiation stage
The first actual contact with a person with whom one desires a relationship; usually characterized by asking and answering questions.

At the intensification stage, a couple's relationship becomes the central focus of their lives.

exploration stage
Stage that involves more in-depth interactions.

intensification stage
Stage in which partners begin to depend on each other for self-confirmation; characterized by increased shared activities, more time spent together, more intimate physical distance and contact, and personalized language.

intimacy stage
Stage in which partners provide primary confirmation of each other's self-concept; characterized by highly personalized and synchronized verbal and nonverbal communication.

If you decide to go to the next stage, **exploration,** you will begin to share more in-depth information. You will probably have minimal physical contact and limit the amount of time you spend together because you are building a relationship. But it's important to realize that some relationships move through stages very quickly. For example, we probably all know people whose relationships were extremely physical, and perhaps sexual, from the very start. Are those relationships doomed because they didn't follow set or prescribed paths for development? No; some relationships may just proceed through stages faster than others. However, relationships that are extremely physical or sexual may burn out quickly because they lack the emotional foundation necessary to survive.

If you proceed to the **intensification stage,** you will start to depend on each other for self-confirmation, meaning that your partner's opinion of or feelings about you weigh more heavily than those of others. Partners tend to spend more time together, increase the variety of activities they share, adopt more intimate physical distance and contact, and personalize their language. The frequency and level of shared personal information increases and deepens, and the couple may decide to label their connection.

The top level of relationship escalation is the **intimacy stage.** Here partners provide primary confirmation of each other's self-concept, meaning that your partner knows how you view yourself and accepts that view. Communication is highly personalized and synchronized. Partners talk about anything and everything, and a commitment to maintaining the relationship might even be formalized and socially recognized, such as a decision to marry. The partners share an understanding of each other's language and nonverbal cues and have a great deal of physical contact. They use fewer words to communicate effectively because they understand each other without words. Reaching this stage takes time—time to build trust, share personal information, observe each other in various situations, and create an emotional bond and commitment.

⤑ Relational De-escalation

Sometimes, for a variety of reasons, relationships begin to unravel. Some unravel to the point of termination. But as you may already know, ending a relationship is not as simple as going down the same way you came up; it is not a mere reversal of the escalation process.[16]

ReCAP ⟵⋯

Relational Escalation

STAGE	EXPLANATION
Pre-Interaction Awareness	You become aware of your attraction to someone and begin to observe that person.
Initiation	You engage in a first contact with the person with whom you want a relationship.
Exploration	Interactions deepen, as questions and answers elicit more information from partners.
Intensification	Partners begin to depend on each other for confirmation of their self-concepts. They spend more time together, engage in more intimate touch, and personalize their language.
Intimacy	Partners provide primary confirmation of each other's self-concept. Verbally, language is highly personalized; nonverbal behaviours are synchronized.

Students in an interpersonal communication class were discussing cyber-relationships, when one said a surprising thing: "I got a break-up notice over the Internet once. I couldn't believe it; this girl actually had the nerve to break up with me through an e-mail message. We never ever discussed it face to face or over the phone." No one in the class had heard of a "Dear John" message being conveyed electronically.

Breakups are tough, but what is a person's ethical obligation when she or he wishes to terminate a relationship? Granted, the Internet allows for a certain level of impersonality, but is this the right way to "dump" someone? Would you want someone to break up with you in such a "high-tech" way?

Communication scholar Mark Knapp provides a model for how relationships come apart.[17] When an intimate relationship is not going well, it usually enters either a turmoil or stagnation stage. The **turmoil stage** involves an increase in conflict, as one or both partners tend to find more faults in the other. The definition of the relationship seems to lose its clarity, and mutual acceptance declines. The communication climate is tense; interactions are difficult and forced. **Stagnation** occurs when the relationship loses its vitality and the partners become complacent, taking each other for granted. Communication and physical contact between the partners decrease; they spend less time together but don't necessarily engage in conflict. Partners in a stagnating relationship tend to go through the motions of an intimate relationship without the commitment or the joy; they simply follow their established relational routines. But a stagnating relationship can be salvaged. A relationship can remain in turmoil or stagnate for a long time, but the individuals can repair, redefine, or revitalize the relationship and return to intimacy.

If the turmoil or stagnation continues, however, the individuals will likely experience the **de-intensification stage.** This involves significantly decreased interaction; increased physical, emotional, and psychological distance; and decreased dependence on the other for self-confirmation. They might discuss the definition of their relationship, question its future, and assess each partner's level of dissatisfaction. The relationship can be repaired and the individuals can move once again toward intensification and intimacy, but it's more difficult to accomplish at this point.

turmoil or stagnation stage
Stage characterized by increased conflict, less mutual acceptance, a tense communication climate, an unclear relationship definition, and taking for granted one's partner.

de-intensification stage
Stage involving significantly decreased interaction, increased distance, and decreased dependence on one's partner for self-confirmation.

ReCAP

Relational De-Escalation

STAGE	EXPLANATION
Turmoil or Stagnation	Partners take each other for granted and have more conflict. They exhibit less mutual acceptance, their communication climate is tense, and their relationship definition is unclear.
De-intensification	Partners significantly decrease their interaction and their dependence upon each other for self-confirmation; they increase their physical distance.
Individualization	Partners define their lives more as individuals and less as a couple.
Separation	Partners make an intentional decision to minimize or eliminate further interpersonal interaction.
Post-Interaction	This is the bottom or final level in relational de-escalation; it represents the lasting effects of a relationship on the individuals.

individualization stage
Stage in which partners define their lives more as individuals and less as a couple.

After de-intensification, the **individualization stage** occurs. Partners tend to define their lives more as individuals and less as a couple or unit. Neither views the other as a partner or significant other any more. Interactions are limited, and the perspective changes from "we" and "us" to "you" and "me." Both partners tend to turn to others for confirmation of their self-concepts; physical intimacy is at an all-time low, if not nonexistent; and nonverbal distance is easily detected.

separation stage
Individuals make an intentional decision to minimize or eliminate further interpersonal interaction.

In the **separation stage,** individuals make an intentional decision to minimize or eliminate further interpersonal interaction. If they share custody of children, attend mutual family gatherings, or work in the same office, the nature of their interactions changes. They divide property, resources, and friends. Early interactions in this stage are often tense and difficult, especially if the relationship has been intimate.

post-interaction stage
The bottom or final level in relational de-escalation, which represents the lasting effects of a relationship on the self.

Although interaction may cease, the effect of a relationship is not over. Relationships—even failed ones—are powerful experiences in our lives. The final level in relational de-escalation is termed the **post-interaction stage.** This level represents the lasting effects the relationship has on the self and therefore on other interactions and relationships. Relationship scholar Steve Duck explains that in this final stage of terminating relationships, we engage in "grave-dressing"—we create a public statement for people who ask why we broke up or why we're no longer friends with someone. It also means that we come to grips with losing the relationship.[18] Sometimes our sense of self gets battered during the final stages of a relationship; we have to work hard to regain a healthy sense of self.

Research over several decades has shed light on how people prefer to end relationships, as well as how they prefer someone to end a relationship with them (in the unfortunate event that they are the "dumped" instead of the "dumper").[19] In most relationships, the breakup is unilateral (done by one party) rather than bilateral (done by both parties). Studies also show that most people use and prefer indirect breakup strategies, such as avoidance, requests for "distance" or "space" in the relationship, a general fading away rather than an abrupt or definite breakup, and the staging of a conflict that leads to blaming and relationship termination. Direct breakup strategies, typically accomplished face-to-face, are probably the most interpersonally communicative but not the most preferred by most people in relationships. Being told we're being dumped just isn't something too many of us prefer to experience.

Throughout the different relational stages of escalation and de-escalation, what typifies the stage is the communication—verbal and nonverbal—that is present or absent. Interpersonal communication facilitates movement through the stages of escalation; the lack of communication moves people through the stages of de-escalation.

MANAGING INTERPERSONAL CONFLICT

⇢ A World of Conflict

We live in a world full of conflict. You can hardly watch the news on television, catch a radio talk show, or read a newspaper headline without being confronted with another story of conflict. Whether it's the Middle East, a political coup in a country in Africa, or a disturbance generated by extremist groups right here at home, conflict on a global scale seems inevitable. While conflicts throughout the world have always existed, the events of September 11, 2001, launched a series of intense conflicts across the globe. How can we understand conflict on such a grand scale? What can we learn about conflict that might help mediate its destructive effect across the world? An understanding of conflict and the development of effective communication skills to manage conflict begins one on one, in our day-to-day relationships. Conflict is rooted in interpersonal communication.

Do you know what are the three most important words a person can say to someone? The answer isn't "I love you"; the answer is "I was wrong." These words are actually better to hear than "I'm sorry," because being sorry could mean that you're sorry you're having a disagreement, you're sorry you got caught doing something that caused the conflict, or it could be just something to say in an attempt to end the conflict. It's quite hard for most of us to admit that we were at fault, but it's very meaningful in a conflict situation when someone admits that she or he was wrong.

Interpersonal conflict is a struggle that occurs when two people cannot agree on a way to meet their needs. When needs are incompatible, if there are too few resources to satisfy them, or if individuals opt to compete rather than cooperate to achieve them, then conflict occurs. The intensity of a conflict usually relates to the intensity of the unmet needs. Conflict resolution researcher Sam Keltner developed the "struggle spectrum," shown in Figure 8.2, to describe conflicts ranging from mild differences to fights.[20] But at the bedrock of all conflict are differences—different goals, experiences, expectations, and so forth.

Humans are generally need driven and goal oriented, so it's not surprising that most conflict is goal driven. You want something; your partner wants something else. If your partner interferes with your achievement of your goal, there may be a conflict. Suppose you are trying to find a place to park in an overcrowded lot on campus. Just as you find an empty spot, another student zips into "your" space. Your blood boils and you get out of your car fighting mad. Or suppose you have had a difficult day at work or school (or both). All you want to do is hunker down with a bowl of popcorn and watch a game (*any* game). But your roommate announces that some mutual friends are coming over for dinner. "That's not what *I* feel like doing tonight. Why didn't you ask *me* before you invited them?" you shout. In both instances, your goals collide head-on with someone else's, and you feel as if you have lost control of the situation.

⋯⟩ How Conflict Functions in Relationships

Conflict is a normal, inevitable element within relationships. The more important the relationship, the greater the potential for conflict because we aren't as likely to voice disagreement with people who don't matter very much to us. Psychologist Phillip McGraw (better known as Dr. Phil, from *The Oprah Winfrey Show* and *The Dr. Phil Show*) contends that there is a third inevitability in life beyond death and taxes—conflict (or as he terms it, verbal fighting with the one you love).[21] McGraw describes three "fundamental truths" about fighting: (a) Fighting is unquestionably painful; (b) fighting is an unavoidable part of every relationship; and (c) there are right and wrong ways to fight—you just have to learn to conduct disagreements in ways that enhance your relationship.

It's surprising (and disconcerting) when people in relationships say, "We just get along so well; we belong together because we've never even had a fight." Although we don't advocate staging or picking a fight with a partner as an experiment, we do believe that it is worrisome to commit to a person when you don't know how she or he handles conflict. If your partner or close friend is a "screamer" and you prefer to walk away from a conflict in silent protest, your relationship is headed for very rough waters. Conflict, and people's responses to it, should be known quantities in any relationship.

interpersonal conflict
A struggle that occurs when two people cannot agree on a way to meet their needs.

FIGURE 8.2 The Struggle Spectrum

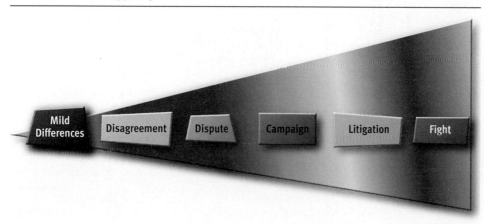

Mild Differences · Disagreement · Dispute · Campaign · Litigation · Fight

Conflict Can Be Constructive or Destructive

constructive conflict
Conflict characterized by cooperation in dealing with differences; helps build new insights and patterns in a relationship.

To construct something is to build or make something new. Characterized by greater cooperation in dealing with differences, **constructive conflict** can help identify which elements of a relationship need to change or be improved, so that new patterns are established. Here's an example:

Mike: You know, I'm getting tired of always going to your mother's on Sundays. It's like we're in a rut or something. Just one weekend, I'd like to have a Sunday with no schedule or agenda.

Claire: Mike, I thought you liked going over there, because my mom's such a good cook and you and Dad are working on that project together. Plus, it's one of the few times I get to spend time with my folks.

Adapt

Mike: Well, I do like going over there, but not every weekend.

Claire: I didn't realize that you were starting to resent it or feel like you were getting into a rut. Let's talk more about this and figure something out.

←·→ COMMUNICATION and DIVERSITY

Conflict and Culture

Conflict is difficult to manage, but when you start thinking about cross-cultural conflict, it becomes even more overwhelming. Some people are trained in negotiation and mediation techniques, so that they can facilitate peaceful relations between nations and peoples. But what if you're not planning on becoming an international negotiator? What if you simply want to know a few things to keep you from being tossed in jail in a foreign country?

Intercultural communication scholar Stella Ting-Toomey has written extensively on this subject and has produced some insightful information that can help you anticipate and avoid intercultural conflict.[22] Persons from individualistic cultures, such as Canada, emphasize the importance of the individual over the group. Collectivistic cultures, such as Japan, emphasize group rather than individual achievement. These differing values contribute to intercultural conflict.

So what should members of individualistic cultures (such as Canadians) know when working with members of collectivistic cultures? Note the seven assumptions about conflict that individualistic cultures hold; compare this list with the seven assumptions about conflict that collectivistic cultures hold. Then assess the differences.

Individualistic Cultures

1. The purpose of conflict is to air out major differences and problems.
2. Conflict can be both functional and dysfunctional.
3. Repressed, unconfronted problems can lead to dysfunctional conflict.
4. Conflict should be viewed as functional, because it provides an opportunity for solving problems.
5. Substantive and relational issues in conflict should be handled separately.
6. Conflict should be handled directly and openly.
7. Effective conflict management should be a win–win, problem-solving activity.

Collectivistic Cultures

1. Conflict is damaging to persons' self-respect and relational harmony; it should be avoided as much as possible.
2. For the most part, conflict is dysfunctional.
3. Conflict signals a lack of self-discipline and emotional immaturity.
4. Conflict provides a testing ground for skilful negotiation and "face-saving."
5. Substantive and relational issues are always intertwined.
6. Conflict should be handled discreetly and subtly.
7. Effective conflict management should be a win–win, face-saving, negotiation game.

Not only do members of different cultural groups have different views of conflict, they have vastly different ways of dealing with or managing conflict. It's wise to do some research on the country you will be visiting or moving to, so that you understand how basic cultural values differ from those of your home country.

Note that Claire recognizes that need for further dialogue about Mike's complaint. She transforms the issue of disagreement into a topic for discussion and relational adjustment. If Mike hadn't expressed his dissatisfaction, the issue might have taken on larger proportions. He might have expressed his feelings of being in a rut in a cruder, more hurtful way on the next drive over to the parents' house, for example. Many times these expressions contain more venom than we intend or actually feel. A well-managed disagreement that includes sharing personal needs or revising goals can lead couples or friends to first examine and then revitalize their relationship. Constructive conflict enables both people to view a disagreement from different perspectives, even if the information shared seems negative at first.

A rapidly spiralling **destructive conflict** can do as much damage as a tornado churning through a trailer park. A conflict may start over a seemingly small issue, but it increases in intensity as other issues and differences are brought into the discussion. Such destructive escalation blocks off options for managing differences and makes a win–win solution more elusive. The hallmark of destructive conflict is a lack of flexibility in responding to others.[23] Combatants view their differences from a win–lose perspective, rather than looking for solutions that allow each individual to gain. This form of conflict dismantles relationships without restoring them. If both individuals are dissatisfied with the outcome of the conflict, then it has been more destructive than constructive.

destructive conflict
Conflict characterized by a lack of cooperation in dealing with differences; dismantles relationships without restoring them.

In their book on interpersonal conflict, William Wilmot and Joyce Hocker provide six building blocks of constructive conflict, which involve analysis, adaptation, and effective interpersonal communication.[24]

1. *People change.* In relationships, people are involved with each other. In conflict, people must work hard to stay involved with each other, because an interaction that escalates into conflict can pull people apart. Flexibility and a willingness to change are key. Wilmot and Hocker explain that "rigid, insistent communication defeats the purpose of constructive conflict."

2. *People interact with an intent to learn instead of an intent to protect.* You can learn a great deal about yourself, your partner, and your relationship if you approach conflict as a learning experience—one that will take your relationship forward instead of allowing it to stagnate or regress. Protecting yourself against conflict doesn't help a relationship grow.

3. *People do not stay stuck in conflict when the conflict is constructive.* A destructive conflict, or series of conflicts, can make you feel stuck in one place within a relationship. Wilmot and Hocker point out that constructive conflict doesn't define who people are in a relationship; conflict is a dynamic process that emerges, plays out, and recedes.

4. *Constructive conflict enhances self-esteem in the participants.* You probably don't associate conflict with enhanced self-esteem, because most of us think of conflict as negative and destructive. However, constructive conflict brings energy and productivity to a relationship and provides a more honest, complete picture of ourselves.

5. *Constructive conflicts are characterized by a relationship focus instead of a purely individualistic focus.* If parties in a conflict focus on the relationship instead of themselves, then the conflict will more likely be constructive than destructive. Participants should emphasize the "we" over the "I," so that conflict is seen as an experience that builds the relationship. If individual winning is more important than the relationship winning, then conflict will erode the relationship.

6. *Constructive conflict is primarily cooperative.* Conflict built on competition, power struggles, and self interest will destroy a relationship. Conversely, a cooperative, win–win approach to conflict will open the door for greater growth in a relationship.

Conflict Involves Power

One of the most significant elements within interpersonal relationships is power. We might not realize it, but distributing power between partners requires a lot of subtle negotiation. Without this negotiation, conflict can become rampant. Furthermore, our ability to manage power successfully is a major factor in relational development. Power has been defined in a variety of ways, but for our purposes **interpersonal power** means the ability to influence another in the direction we desire—to get another person to do what we want.[25] It also

interpersonal power
The ability to influence another in the direction we desire; getting another person to do what we want.

involves our ability to resist others' influences on us.[26] Perhaps it is easier to think of it in terms of who has more control in a relationship, rather than to use the term *power*.

All interactions, including conflicts, involve power or control. If you ask a friend to go to a movie with you, you attempt to influence him or her. If the answer is no, your friend is mustering resistance and demonstrating power over you. If you don't like the negative response, you might attempt to assert control once more, perhaps by offering to buy your friend's ticket or to drive.

Romantic relationships can be typified by power dynamics.[27] For example, in what is termed a **complementary relationship,** one partner willingly and continuously cedes power to the other. For example, a couple may feel completely comfortable with only one partner planning most of the activities, controlling the purse strings, and making decisions for the future of the relationship. Some partners prefer this arrangement because conflict doesn't arise over who wants control. However, the out-of-power partner may come to resent this status over time.

Symmetrical relationships are characterized by similar control behaviours in each person. Both partners compete in order to dominate the other and assert control, or both relinquish control to the other to avoid making decisions or committing to something. In the first situation, partners may argue over which television program to watch. In the second couple type, partners don't express preferences but engage in endless exchanges of "I don't know; whatever you want." The negotiation process can be time-consuming, fatiguing, and ineffective when quick decisions are needed.

In a **parallel relationship,** power continually shifts from one partner to the other, depending on the nature of the interaction or situation. One partner may take control because he or she is more experienced or equipped to handle a particular circumstance. This doesn't mean that one partner is constantly in an out-of-power position, just that partners alternate being in control according to their strengths and weaknesses. For instance, if one partner is in charge of keeping the finances straight, she or he will have more power in budgetary decisions. If the other partner is a better cook, he or she probably will exert more power over decisions about diet and menus. This form of give and take works extremely well in intimate relationships, but partners need to agree on (and integrate into their self-concepts) who is really better suited to take control in certain situations. For example, when travelling by car, men and women often argue over directions to locations. (This may be a stereotype, but it's a stereotype many people experience.) Perhaps the man in the relationship believes that it is manly to be able to navigate, to know where one is going, and not to need to ask directions. However, in those situations where the couple ends up lost, the couple may find that the woman may be actually more adept at map-reading and navigating than the man. She may also be more comfortable stopping and asking for directions than the man.

Conflict May Involve Assertive or Aggressive Communication

Sometimes our emotions cause us to communicate aggressively, when assertive communication would be preferable. You may tend to think of assertive and aggressive communication as being the same thing, but they are actually quite different. The best way to distinguish

complementary relationship
A relationship in which one partner willingly and continuously cedes power to the other.

symmetrical relationship
A relationship characterized by similar control behaviours in partners; partners compete to dominate each other or both relinquish control to the other to avoid making decisions.

parallel relationship
A relationship in which power is shifted from one partner to the other.

Verbal

ReCAP ⟵┄┄

Relationship Types Based on Power Dynamics

RELATIONSHIP TYPE	SYMBOLS	EXPLANATION
Complementary	↑ ↓	One up, one down; one partner is almost always in power, the other is almost always out of power.
Symmetrical	↑ ↑ ↓ ↓	Both up or both down; partners compete for power and control.
Parallel	→ ←	Each one across; power alternates between partners, depending on who is better equipped or more adept in certain situations.

between the two is this: **Assertive communication** takes the listener's feelings and rights into account; **aggressive communication** does not. Let's say that you experience a mix-up with a close friend over when and where you were supposed to meet. You got your signals crossed and didn't get to go somewhere together. When next you see your friend, you have the choice of responding to the frustration over the situation in a passive, assertive, or aggressive manner. You could be passive, saying nothing about the mix-up and simply "go along to get along." Although this may sound like an unrealistic response, some people choose not to communicate even when they have been wronged. They are afraid of or unwilling to engage in any form of confrontation, no matter how benign or superficial, with strangers and intimates alike. A passive approach tends merely to internalize frustration, which may build into a destructive rage that at some point is bound to erupt.

Another option is to blow up at your friend. This is an aggressive, self-oriented approach because it does not take into account the rights of the recipient of such communication. Unfortunately, this is the tactic of choice for some people, especially if they have a great deal of anxiety and feel justified taking out their frustrations on others. An aggressive approach rarely achieves one's objectives.

Verbal aggression, also termed verbal abuse, has received much research attention in recent years, in an attempt to better understand the kind of threatening communication tactics persons in conflict occasionally resort to. Communication scholar Dominic Infante and various colleagues launched an interesting body of work on this topic, suggesting that verbal aggression is a form of communication violence because it attacks the heart of a person's being, her or his self-concept.[28] In persuasive speaking and argumentation literature, this phenomenon is called an "ad hominem" argument, which we discuss again in Chapter 15. Conflicts that degenerate into verbal aggression can be characterized by insults ("You wouldn't say that if you had half a brain"), ridicule ("You're just too selfish to understand"), merciless teasing (teasing that has an angry edge to it), character assassination ("You're low class"), and profanity.[29] Typically, the verbally aggressive person blames the other person as being the source or cause of the problem. Rather than focusing on the problem or the issues at hand, the focus shifts and becomes personal.

We can more easily fend off verbal aggression from those persons who don't matter much to us, but we can be deeply wounded, and the relationship can be permanently damaged, by verbal aggression from someone important to us, someone we care about a great deal.[30] Unfortunately, verbally aggressive tactics are used widely in conflicts, according to research. One study surveyed dating partners and found that more than 70% reported using or experiencing some form of verbal aggression in their relational conflicts.[31] When the verbally aggressive tactics were used only occasionally—as lapses into "bad" behaviour—partners were able to weather the aggression without much damage to the relationship. However, when the verbal aggression was more frequent, it signalled a relationship in trouble. Jennifer Connolly and her colleagues at the LaMarsh Centre for Research studied the abuse of power in relationships of Canadian children and youth.[32] After surveying teenagers about aggression they discovered the following:

- Approximately one in five students was a victim of major physical aggression in a dating relationship.
- One in four students was a victim of minor physical aggression.
- Half of the students were victims of verbal aggression.

Different forms of aggression often occurred simultaneously among these teenagers. Seventy-seven percent of students who were victims of physical aggression were also victims of verbal aggression.

Infante and his associates have developed a measure that determines a person's propensity toward verbal aggression. However, one interesting finding from his research is that many persons who are deemed "highly verbally aggressive," as determined by the scale, don't characterize their behaviour as such. Many believe their verbally aggressive comments in conflict situations to be humorous or benign kidding, not personal attacks that damage their relationships.[33] Research has also determined a connection between verbal aggression and physical aggression or abuse.[34]

assertive communication
Communication that takes a listener's feelings and rights into account.

aggressive communication
Self-serving communication that does not take a listener's feelings and rights into account.

Verbal

In most situations, assertive communication can be more effective than aggressive communication in getting the job done.

Probably all of us, at some time or another, have been in a conflict situation with someone we cared about, and we let a big, nasty, old "toad" fly out of our mouths. We probably felt terrible about it—maybe at the moment it flew out, or perhaps later, after we had time to reflect on the damage we'd done. As the research suggests, although not advisable or edifying for the relationship, occasional verbal aggression is likely to occur within a meaningful relationship. If you can remember some things you've said to someone that you wish you could take back, then you've had a moment of verbal aggression. But if you find yourself in a relationship—with a romantic partner, close friend, family member, or even a co-worker—and verbally aggressive communication typifies your approach to conflict with that person, then you definitely will want to spend some time thinking about why you tend to behave in an abusive manner. What is it about you—not the other person— that causes your communication to spiral downward and morph into a personal attack?

Clearly, an assertive approach is best for us and the people we interact with. It's important to assert yourself and express your perception of the problem to the person who can best correct or clear up the problem, rather than blowing off steam to an innocent bystander or third party. Communicating assertively means that you explain your concerns or cause for disagreement in a direct and firm manner, staying in control of your emotions but not allowing yourself to be bullied or discounted as you take the receiver's rights into account.

An assertive response to the timing mix-up with your friend might be something like this: "Hey, Joe, we were supposed to meet at five o'clock last night at the bowling alley, but you never showed up. What happened?" In this statement, you express your perception of the situation, but ask the person for his or her perception, rather than aggressively saying something in an angry tone that would make the other person defensive, such as, "Why did you leave me hanging when we made definite plans?" If the person offers a lame excuse for not showing up, another assertive follow-up comment might be as follows: "Well, whatever happened, I just want you to know that I don't like being stood up; it's no big deal, but I just hope this doesn't happen again." If you communicate in this manner, you're far more likely to reach a positive resolution to any conflicts than if you behave passively or aggressively, violating the receiver's right to be treated humanely.[35]

nonconfrontational style
A conflict management style of backing off, avoiding conflict, or giving in to the other person.

Aware

⸺⸽ Styles of Managing Conflict

Scholars in the communication discipline like to talk about conflict in terms of *management,* meaning that interpersonal communication can help people work through and handle conflict so that something positive results. What's your approach to managing interpersonal conflict: fight or flight? Do you tackle conflict head-on or seek ways to remove yourself from it? Most of us don't have a single way of dealing with disagreements, but we do have a tendency to manage conflict following patterns we learned early in life and have used before.[36] The pattern we choose depends on several factors, including our personality, the individuals with whom we are in conflict, and the time and place of the confrontation.

Researchers have attempted to identify styles of conflict management. One widely accepted approach organizes conflict styles into three types: (1) nonconfrontational; (2) confrontational or controlling; and (3) cooperative, also know as a solution orientation.[37]

Nonconfrontational Style

One approach to managing conflict is to back off, either avoiding the conflict or giving in to the other person. Placating, distracting, computing, withdrawing, and giving in are responses that typify a **nonconfrontational style.**

A *placating* response is an attempt to please; placaters are uncomfortable with negative emotions and may adopt this approach because they fear rejection if they rock the boat. Typically, they seek approval and try to avoid threats to their self-worth. Placaters never seem to get angry, are so controlled that they seem

"Well, if it doesn't matter who's right and who's wrong, why don't I be right and you be wrong?"

unresponsive to the intensity of the situation, quickly agree with others to avoid conflict, and try to avoid confrontation at all costs.

Another nonconfrontational style is called *distracting.* Distracters attempt to change the subject or make a joke to avoid conflict or stress, rather than face issues directly. They hope that eventually the problem will just go away if it can be put off long enough.

A third nonconfrontational style is called *computing;* computers remove themselves from conflict by remaining aloof and cool. They avoid emotional involvement and refuse to be provoked or ruffled, even under intense pressure. This detachment allows them to avoid expressing genuine feelings about issues and ideas. Instead, they respond to emotional issues with impersonal words and phrases, such as "One would tend to become angry when one's car is dented, wouldn't one?" The computing style is characterized by low empathy and minimal involvement with the issues at hand.

Withdrawing from conflict, either physically or psychologically, is another nonconfrontational approach. "I don't want to talk about it," "It's not my problem," or the one-word "whatever" are typical responses from someone who uses this style.

Finally, some people consistently *give in* when faced with conflict. They are so uncomfortable that they surrender before the conflict escalates. Skip hates romantic movies. Yet when his girlfriend wants to rent *Moulin Rouge,* Skip agrees, just to avoid a conflict. A nonconfrontational or avoidant style often leads to a perpetuating conflict cycle that has a chilling or silencing effect on a relationship.[38]

Confrontational Style

Each of us has some need to control others, but some people always want to dominate and make sure that their objectives are achieved. In managing conflict, **confrontational** people have a win–lose philosophy. They want to win at the expense of the other person, to claim victory over their opponents, and to control others. They focus on themselves and usually ignore the needs of others. Confronters often resort to *blaming* or seeking a scapegoat, rather than assuming responsibility for a conflict. "I didn't do it," "Don't look at me," and "It's not my fault" are typical responses. If this strategy doesn't work, confronters may try hostile name-calling, personal attacks, or threats.

confrontational style
A win–lose approach to conflict management in which one wants control and to win at the expense of others.

Cooperative Style

Those who take a **cooperative** approach to conflict management view conflict as a set of problems to be solved, rather than a competition in which one person wins and another loses. They work to foster a win–win climate by using the following techniques:[39]

- *Separate the people from the problem.* Leave personal grievances out of the discussion. Describe problems without making judgmental statements about personalities.

cooperative style
A conflict management style in which conflict is viewed as a set of problems to be solved, rather than a competition in which one person wins and another loses.

ReCAP

Conflict Management Styles

Nonconfrontational:	Avoids conflict by placating (agreeing), distracting, computing (becoming emotionally detached), or withdrawing from conflict
Confrontational:	Wants to manipulate others by blaming and making threats; sets up win–lose framework
Cooperative:	Seeks mutually agreeable resolutions to manage differences; works within a win–win framework
	• Separates people from problems
	• Focuses on shared interests
	• Generates many options to solve problems
	• Bases decisions upon objective criteria

- *Focus on shared interests.* Emphasize common interests, values, and goals by asking such questions as: What do we both want? What do we both value? Where do we already agree?
- *Generate many options to solve the problem.* Use brainstorming and other techniques to generate alternative solutions.
- *Base decisions on objective criteria.* Try to establish standards for an acceptable solution to a problem. These standards may involve cost, timing, and other factors.

···⟩ Conflict Management Skills

As we saw in the previous section, nonconfrontational and confrontational styles of conflict management do not solve problems effectively, nor do they foster healthy long-term relationships. The skills we review here are those we touched on in our discussion of the cooperative style.[40]

Managing conflict, especially emotionally charged conflict, is not easy. Even with a fully developed set of skills, you should not expect to melt tensions and resolve disagreements instantaneously. The following skills can, however, help you generate options that promote understanding and provide a framework for cooperation.

Manage Emotions

For weeks you have been working on a group project for an important class; your group has a firm deadline that the professor imposed. You submitted your portion of the project to your fellow group members two weeks ago. Today you check in with the group for a progress report and discover that very little has been done. The project is not much further along than when you completed your portion two weeks ago. Your grade is on the line; you feel angry and frustrated. How should you respond? You may be tempted to march into the next group meeting and scream at your classmates. You might consider going to the professor and complaining (loudly) about what has happened. Our best advice is this: Try to avoid taking action when you are in such an emotional state. You may regret what you say and you will probably escalate the conflict, making the situation worse.

Often the first sign that we are in a conflict situation is a combined feeling of anger, frustration, and fear, which sweeps over us like a tidal wave. In actuality, anger is not the predominant emotion generated by conflict. Many of us are unprepared for the aching,

On the WEB ·····•

Perhaps you've heard, in the news or with regard to some incident that might have happened at work or school, of someone "going to mediation." As a new cottage industry, centres for mediation services are springing up with increasing frequency across the country. When people are in conflict and cannot resolve that conflict, they may turn to mediation before taking a more formal (and expensive) step, such as going to court.

Many colleges and universities now offer mediation services for students, faculty, and staff members. The University of Windsor offers mediation services and defines mediation as follows: "Mediation involves a discussion of a dispute from both or all sides, with the intent to reach a solution that is mutually acceptable to both or all parties. The discussion between the parties is facilitated by a mediator. A mediator is a neutral third party, who does not take sides. A mediator will not decide the outcome or resolution, unlike a judge or an arbitrator, but will help each party to evaluate goals and options in order to find a solution that works for everyone." A number of community organizations also offer mediation services.

To read more about various mediation programs and services, here are a few Web addresses:

zeus.uwindsor.ca/mediation/Home.html (University of Windsor)
www.law.uwo.ca/mainSite (University of Western Ontario)
www.oafm.on.ca (Ontario Association for Family Mediation, a non-profit group)
www3.gov.ab.ca/hre/mediationservices/index.asp (Government of Alberta)
mrjc.ca (Mediation and Restorative Justice Center, a non-profit group)
www.ci.vancouver.wa.us/chservices/mediation (Community Mediation Services Vancouver, Washington)

lonely, sad, and forlorn feelings that can result from conflict.[41] If we feel powerless to control our own fate, then we'll have difficulty taking a logical or rational approach to managing the conflict. Expressing our feelings in an emotional outburst may make us feel better for the moment, but it may close the door to negotiation. Until we can tone down (not eliminate) and control our emotions, we'll find it difficult to use appropriate communication skills. Here are some specific strategies that you can draw upon when an intense emotional response to conflict clouds your judgment and decision-making skills.[42]

Aware

- *Select a mutually acceptable time and place to discuss a conflict.* If you're upset or tired, you're at risk for an emotion-charged confrontation. If you ambush someone with an angry attack, don't expect her or him to be in a productive frame of mind. Instead, give yourself time to cool off before you try to resolve a conflict. In the case of the group project, you could call a meeting for later in the week. By that time, you could gain control of your feelings and think things through. Of course, sometimes issues need to be discussed on the spot; you may not have the luxury of waiting. But whenever it's practical, make sure your conflict partner is ready to receive you and your message.

Verbal

- *Plan your message.* If you approach someone to discuss a disagreement, take care to organize your message, even if that means organizing ideas on paper. Identify your goal and determine what outcome you would like; don't barge in unprepared and dump your emotions on the other person. You might also consider sounding things out with a trusted friend or colleague first, to get a perception check and to help clarify the issues in the conflict.

- *Monitor nonverbal messages.* Your nonverbal communication plays a key role in establishing an emotional climate. Monitor nonverbal messages—yours and those of others—to help defuse an emotionally charged situation. Speak calmly, use direct eye contact, and maintain a natural facial expression and body position to signal that you wish to collaborate rather than control. Try also to place yourself at the same level of other people involved in the conflict. Standing while others sit, for example, can serve as a power cue and an impediment to resolving conflict.

Nonverbal

- *Avoid personal attacks, name-calling, profanity, and emotional overstatement.* Threats and derogatory language can turn a small conflict into an all-out war. When people feel attacked, they usually respond by becoming defensive in an effort to protect themselves. It's also important to avoid exaggerating your emotions. If you say you are irritated or annoyed rather than furious, you can still communicate your feelings, but you will take the sting out of your description. Avoid the bad habit of gunny-sacking—dredging up old problems and issues from the past (like pulling them out of an old bag or gunny sack) to use against your partner. As the Garth Brooks song goes, "We buried the hatchet; we left the handle sticking out." Gunny-sacking usually succeeds only in increasing tension, escalating emotions, and reducing listening effectiveness. It's more helpful to keep everyone's focus on the issues at hand, not on old hurts from the past.

Verbal

- *Use self-talk.* Back to the problem of the group project: At the next meeting, what if a member lashes out at you, suggesting that you're a big part of the problem? Instead of lashing back at that person, the best advice would be to pause, take a slow, deep breath, and say to yourself, "I could get really mad, but that won't make things better. I'll respond calmly and coolly, so we keep the problem in proportion." You may think that talking to yourself is an eccentricity, but nothing could be further from the truth. Thoughts are directly linked to feelings; the messages we tell ourselves play a major role in how we feel and respond to others.[43]

Aware

Manage Information

Because uncertainty, misinformation, and misunderstanding are often by-products of conflict and disagreement, skills that promote mutual understanding are important components of cooperative conflict management. The following suggested skills can help you reduce uncertainty and enhance the quality of communication during conflict.

- *Clearly describe the conflict-producing events.* Instead of blurting out complaints in random order, try to deliver a brief, well-organized minipresentation. Public speaking teachers recommend that, for certain speech topics, you describe events in chronological order. The same technique works well when describing a conflict. As in the group-project situation, you could offer your perspective on what created the conflict, sequencing the events and describing them dispassionately so that your fellow group members end up sharing your understanding of the problem.

Verbal

- *"Own" your statements by using descriptive "I" language.* In Chapter 3, we described the use of "I" language instead of "you" language in order to create a supportive climate. The same applies in conflict. "I feel upset when it seems like little is getting done and we're running the risk of not making our deadline." This is an example of an "I" statement that you could say to your group members. The statement describes your feelings as your own and keeps the issue manageable. Saying "You guys aren't pulling your weight and you're gonna blow our deadline" has an accusatory sting that will likely make members defensive, escalating the conflict. Also notice that, in the second statement, you don't take any responsibility for the problem but suggest that it belongs to several other people. This "ganging-up" approach almost always heightens people's defensiveness.

Listen
and
Respond

- *Use effective listening skills.* Managing information is a two-way process. Whether you are describing a conflict situation to someone or that individual is bringing a conflict to your attention, good listening skills are invaluable. Give your full attention to the speaker and make a conscious point of tuning out your internal messages. Sometimes the best thing to do after describing the conflict-producing events is simply to wait for a response. If you don't stop talking and give the other person a chance to respond, he or she will feel frustrated, the emotional pitch will go up a notch, and it will become more difficult to reach an understanding. Finally, not only should you focus on the facts or details, but you should also analyze them so you can understand the major points the speaker makes. As Stephen Covey suggests in his book *The Seven Habits of Highly Effective People,* it is wise to "seek to understand rather than to be understood."[44]

Aware

- *Check your understanding of what others say and do.* Checking perceptions is vital when emotions run high. If you are genuinely unsure about facts, issues, or major ideas addressed during a conflict, ask questions to help you sort through them instead of bar-relling ahead with solutions. Then summarize your understanding of the information; don't parrot the speaker's words or paraphrase every statement, but check key points to ensure that you comprehend the message. Your response and that of your conflict partner will confirm that you understand each other.

Manage Goals

As we have seen, conflict is goal driven. Both individuals involved in an interpersonal conflict want something. And, for some reason, be it competition, scarce resources, or lack of understanding, the goals appear to be in conflict. To manage conflict, it is important to seek an accurate understanding of these goals and to identify where they overlap. Here are a few techniques to help you accomplish just that.

Aware

- *Identify your goal and your partner's goal.* After you describe, listen, and respond, your next task should be to identify what you would like to have happen. What is your goal? Most goal statements can be phrased in terms of wants or desires. Continuing with the group project example, you express to your fellow group members your goal of turning the project in on time. Next, it's useful to identify the goals people involved in the conflict hold. Use effective describing, listening, and responding skills to determine what each conflict partner wants. Obviously, if goals are kept hidden, it will be difficult to resolve the conflict.

Adapt

- *Identify where your goals and your partner's goals overlap.* Authorities on conflict negotiation Roger Fisher and William Ury stress the importance of focusing on shared interests when seeking to manage differences.[45] Armed with an understanding of what you want and your partner want, you can then determine whether the goals overlap. So, after you explain your goal about the project deadline, another group member states that her or his goal is to make the project the best it possibly can be. These goals may be compatible, so you've identified a commonality that can help unify the group, rather than keep it splintered. But what if that goal of making the project the best means that your group will have to ask the professor for an extension on the deadline? Now you may have competing goals. But at least you've identified a central part of the problem. Framing the problem as "how can we achieve our mutual goal" rather than arguing over differences of opinion moves the discussion to a more productive level. If you focus on shared interests (common goals) and develop objective, rather than subjective, criteria for the solution, there is hope for finding a resolution that will satisfy everyone.

Manage the Problem

If you can view conflicts as problems to be solved rather than battles to be won or lost, you will better manage the issues that confront you in your relationships with others. Of course, not all conflicts can be magically managed and resolved. But using a rational, logical approach to conflict management is more effective than emotionally flinging accusations and opinions at someone. Structuring a disagreement as a problem to solve helps manage emotions that often erupt; a problem-solving orientation to conflict also helps keep the conversation focused on issues rather than personalities. Once conflict becomes personal, people become defensive and emotions flare.

In the chapters ahead we suggest that the groups and teams that function most effectively use a structured approach to solving problems; ideas shouldn't just tumble over one another. A logical, organized approach usually works best when trying to solve vexing problems.

The problem-solving process is one you've undoubtedly used in managing problems that have come your way. The approach is relatively simple: Define the problem, analyze the problem, generate possible solutions, evaluate the pros and cons of the solutions under consideration, and then select the solution that is agreeable to all concerned. The best solution is one that meets the goals of the persons involved in the conflict. To help you apply the problem-solving approach to managing conflict, consider the following suggestions.

- *Resist developing solutions to manage the conflict until you and the other person fully understand the precise nature of the problem as well as each other's goals.* When there is a problem to be solved, we typically want to head directly for solutions. Resist that temptation. Before blurting out solutions, realize that you're more likely to reach agreement on the solution to a problem if you each understand the specific issues that trigger the problem.
- *The more possible solutions you identify and consider, the greater the likelihood that the conflict will be managed successfully.* If you're just batting around one or two solutions, you're limiting your options in managing the conflict. Rather than making the conflict a tug of war with only two ends of the rope pulling against each other, consider many creative strategies for achieving what you both want. Many people find it helps to make a written list of many possible ways to achieve each other's goals. We'll talk more in Chapter 10 about how to brainstorm possible solutions to problems. For now, realize the powerful point that the more options you discuss, the more likely each of you will find common ground.
- *Systematically discuss the pros and the cons of the possible solutions together.* After you have a list of possible solutions, honestly identify advantages and disadvantages of each solution. How do you know which is the best solution? If you discussed the goals that each of you seek to achieve, you are well on your way to developing a vision of the future that can help you sort out the advantages and disadvantages of the potential solutions you're considering. Determine which solution, or combination of solutions, best achieves the goals you and your feuding partner are trying to accomplish.

We emphasize again that there are no sure-fire techniques that will manage or resolve the interpersonal conflicts that will inevitably occur even in the best of relationships. In reality, you don't simply manage your emotions and then march easily on to coolly communicate your ideas, followed by neatly sorting out goals and then rationally solving the problem that created the conflict. Conflict management is messier than this step-by-step process suggests. You may, for example, first try to manage your emotions, then communicate your ideas and feelings, only to find you need to go back and again manage your emotions. You are more than likely to bounce forward and backward from one step to another.

Our suggestions for managing emotions, information, goals, and the problem will not eliminate conflict from your life. Turning conflicts into problems to solve and seeking mutually agreeable solutions may, however, provide just the necessary structure to help you manage conflict constructively.

SUMMARY ⚓

In this chapter we focused on interpersonal communication that enhances relationships and discussed three types of relationships that have tremendous impact on our lives: friendships, family relationships, and workplace relationships. The five communication principles for a lifetime were reviewed in light of each of these three forms of important relationships.

Most relationships develop in stages that are characterized by the type and presence (or absence) of interpersonal communication. Once relationships are initiated, they begin to escalate if the partners want the relationship to develop and become more intimate. Relationships also de-escalate as they move away from intimacy.

Conflict is a significant element within interpersonal relationships. In this section of the chapter, we distinguished between constructive and destructive conflict in relationships and explored six building blocks of constructive conflict. Power and control work to create patterns that can lead to harmony or strife in relationships. We also contrasted assertive communication (that which takes receivers' rights into account) with aggressive communication (that which ignores the rights of receivers). Three conflict management styles were provided—nonconfrontational, confrontational, and cooperative—along with a discussion of the forms of communication that characterize these styles. In a final section on conflict management skills, we suggested that you view conflicts as manageable events rather than personal battles. We also offered suggestions for effective ways to manage emotions, information, goals, and problems, so that the resolution of conflict can actually make your relationships stronger.

⬠ PRINCIPLES FOR A LIFETIME

Aware

Principle 1:   Be aware of your communication with yourself and others.

- Know your own interests, likes, and dislikes as you expand your circle of friends.
- Awareness and an understanding of self begin in your family as you grow up.
- Perception checking with colleagues increases your awareness of yourself and your workplace.
- The first stage of relational escalation, the pre-interaction awareness stage, begins with an awareness of the self and the other person to whom you are attracted.
- Even after relationships terminate, they still have an effect on our self-concept; be aware of the effect of relationships (even failed ones) on your view of yourself.
- It's important to know your conflict management style, especially if your style is different from that of other people involved in the conflict.
- Self-talk is appropriate in conflict, because it can help you manage your emotions and think clearly.
- Check your perceptions of a conflict with trusted others.
- Be aware of your own goals, as well as the goals of others, in conflict situations.

Verbal

Principle 2:   Effectively use and interpret verbal messages.

- Language patterns we learn as children in our families transfer into adulthood.
- Persons in advanced stages of relationships tend to use verbal communication to discuss topics that typically are not discussed in early stages.
- Assertive communication takes the receiver's rights into account; aggressive communication does not.
- The management of the verbal expression of your emotions in conflict situations is an important skill.
- Plan your message carefully in a conflict situation.
- Avoid personal attacks, name-calling, profanity, and emotional overstatements in conflict situations.
- Use "I" language instead of "you" language in a conflict, so as to lessen defensiveness.

Nonverbal

Principle 3:   Effectively use and interpret nonverbal messages.

- Nonverbal immediacy behaviours, such as eye contact and forward body lean, are important in the maintenance of friendships, family relationships, and workplace relationships.

- Persons in advanced stages of relationships tend to display nonverbal behaviours that typically are not in evidence in early stages.
- Nonverbal skills are important in those first conversations with people, as you attempt to establish and escalate relationships.
- Nonverbal immediacy cues diminish when a relationship is in de-escalation.
- Monitor and adapt your nonverbal behaviours in conflict situations.
- Monitor the nonverbal behaviours of other persons involved in your disagreement.

Listen
and
Respond

Principle 4:   Listen and respond thoughtfully to others.

- Listening is important in friendships, family relationships, and workplace relationships.
- Listening and responding appropriately are key skills potential employers value.
- Destructive conflict is characterized by a lack of listening.
- Conflict often escalates because the parties don't listen to one another; continue to listen, even if you feel yourself becoming emotional in the conflict.

Adapt

Principle 5:   Adapt messages to others.

- It's important to learn to adapt our communication in friendships, family relationships, and workplace relationships.
- In conflict situations, partners often have to adapt to each other and admit that they were wrong.
- Destructive conflict often involves a reluctance to adapt to the other person and see the problem from her or his point of view.
- Be flexible and adapt to other cultures' approaches to conflict; don't assume that your home culture's approach to conflict management is applicable to members of other cultural groups.
- After checking your perceptions of a conflict with trusted others, adapt your communication accordingly.
- One way to adapt in a conflict is to look for overlaps in your goals and the goals of your conflict partner.

Discussion and Review ⁂

1. How does interpersonal communication facilitate the development of friendships? Family relationships? Workplace relationships?

2. What are the five stages of relational escalation? Do relationships necessarily have to follow these stages? What are the five stages of relational de-escalation? How do you prefer a relationship to end?

3. Define interpersonal conflict; provide examples of constructive and destructive conflicts.

4. A common issue among couples concerns shared activities, meaning who decides what the couple will and will not do together. How would a couple who have a complementary relationship (in terms of power) approach this issue? A symmetrical relationship? A parallel relationship?

5. What is the difference between assertive communication and aggressive communication? Provide an example of an aggressive response to someone's communication; then demonstrate how an assertive response would be preferable in the example.

6. What characterizes nonconfrontational, confrontational, and cooperative styles of conflict management?

Developing Your Skills: Putting Principles into Practice ⁂

1. Think about your best friend, your closest family member, and a colleague (or classmate) with whom you feel exceptionally close. Put the names of these three individuals across the top of a sheet of paper, forming columns down the page. Next, indicate, under each column, which forms of communication are most critical to the maintenance of each of these relationships. Finally, look for overlapping skills across the columns.

2. Work with a small group of classmates. Have each person think of a relationship—a friendship or romance—that has undergone the process of relational escalation and de-escalation. Discuss these processes and listen for commonalities across classmates' experiences. How did the presence or absence of interpersonal communication move the relationship through the stages?

3. Sometimes it's hard to discern the difference between assertive and aggressive communication. To give you some practice, use the following situations to generate, first, aggressive and inappropriate communication. Then rethink the situation and generate an assertive form of communication that would be more effective. We've provided an example to get you started.

Situation: You are expecting a raise at work but find out that another co-worker, who has less time on the job than you, received a raise and you did not.

Aggressive Communication: You interrupt a staff meeting that your boss is holding, storming about the room and demanding (loudly) an explanation for why you did not receive the expected raise.

Assertive Communication: You make an appointment with your boss for a meeting outside the office. At the meeting, you calmly ask the boss to assess your value to the company, leading up to the question of why you did not receive the expected raise.

Situation: Two people have been in a monogamous dating relationship for several months, when one partner finds out that the other person has cheated.

Situation: A student receives a disappointing grade on a paper. After reading the papers of a few fellow classmates, finding that lesser quality papers received higher grades, the student decides to confront the teacher about the grade.

4. Generate an example of a common source of conflict among romantic couples. Then brainstorm for ways that persons with nonconfrontational, confrontational, and cooperative styles of conflict management would approach the situation.

Patricia Ossa, "Citizens." © SuperStock

The best way to have a good idea is to have a lot of ideas.

— LINUS PAULING

9 Understanding Group and Team Performance

CHAPTER OUTLINE

AFTER STUDYING THIS CHAPTER, YOU SHOULD BE ABLE TO

1. Define and note similarities and differences between a group and a team.

2. Identify and describe types of small groups.

3. Identify and appropriately perform task and social roles in groups and teams.

4. Avoid performing individual roles in a group.

5. Describe group rules and norms.

6. Define and differentiate between status and power.

7. List strategies to enhance group cohesiveness.

8. Recognize group and team interaction patterns.

9. Identify the four stages of group development.

10. Identify strategies to adapt to cultural differences in groups and teams.

Do you like working with others in groups? Although you may be one of those people who relish working on team projects and going to meetings, many people don't like collaborating with others. Here are some typical sentiments people sometimes have about working in groups:

On judgment day the Lord will divide people by telling those on his right hand to enter his kingdom and those on his left to break into small groups.

To be effective, a committee should be made up of three persons. But to get anything done, one member should be sick and another absent.

A committee is a group of people who individually can do nothing and who collectively decide nothing can be done.

A group task force is a collection of the unfit chosen from the unwilling by the incompetent to do the unnecessary.

Whether you are one of those people who likes group work or one who finds it frustrating and a waste of time, the evidence suggests that groups are here to stay. Human beings collaborate. We are raised in groups, are educated in groups, worship in groups, are entertained in groups, and work in groups. Today's technology makes it easier for us to collaborate in teams, even when we're not meeting face to face. There is evidence that most of you reading this book will spend about one-third of your time on the job working in groups or teams and attending meetings or preparing for meetings.[1] And if you aspire to upper-management leadership positions, you'll spend up to two-thirds of your time in meetings.[2] Your work will revolve around that kindergarten category called "getting along with others."

To help you with the inevitable group and team projects that will come your way, this chapter offers insights *describing* how groups and teams work. In the next chapter, we'll offer specific strategies for *improving* group and team performance. As we examine concepts and strategies of group skills and theories, we'll remind you how the core of group communication research can be discussed with the five principles we've used to frame our presentation of human communication:

Adapt   Aware
Listen and Respond   Verbal
Nonverbal

1. *Be aware of your communication with yourself and others.* Your awareness of your own behaviour and the behaviour of other group members is often the first step to understanding why you and other group members behave as you do and to adjusting your behaviour for improved group performance.
2. *Effectively use and interpret verbal messages.* The verbal messages you and other group members use are pivotal in shaping what roles you assume and how the group accomplishes its work.
3. *Effectively use and interpret nonverbal messages.* The social climate of a group is influenced by the way other group members behave nonverbally; eye contact, tone of voice, facial expression, and the use of space and time influence what it feels like to be in a group.
4. *Listen and respond thoughtfully to others.* The quintessential skill of listening and responding to others is vital for an effectively functioning group; how group members interact (or don't interact) is directly shaped by group members' skill in listening and responding to what others say and do.
5. *Appropriately adapt messages to others.* The ability to modify messages and adjust to the behaviour of others is especially important when communicating with three or more people in a small group.

GROUPS AND TEAMS DEFINED

What makes a group a group? Is a collection of people waiting for the elevator a group? How about students assigned to a class project—do they meet the technical definition for a group? And what about the term "team"? Teams are often viewed as the management innovation that can improve both productivity and morale. Is there a difference between a group and a team? By exploring these questions, you can better understand what groups and teams do and develop strategies for improving group and team performance.

Communicating in Small Groups

A **small group** consists of three to fifteen people who share a common purpose, who feel a sense of belonging to the group, and who exert influence on one another.[3] Let's look at this definition more closely.

Many important workplace decisions are made within small groups of co-workers.

A Group Consists of a Small Number of People

How many people does it take to be a group? We suggest at least three people. Two people do not usually exhibit the characteristics of group behaviour that we will present later in this chapter, such as the formation of group member roles and norms. If a group becomes too large, it typically operates as a collection of sub-groups rather than a single body. When more than fifteen people meet together, it is difficult for all members to participate; usually, when the group gets too big for everyone to talk, a few people monopolize the discussion. Large groups need formal rules, such as parliamentary procedure, to provide structure that will help the group stay focused on the task at hand.

A Group Has a Common Purpose

In order to be a group, people need to be united by a common goal or purpose. They must all seek the same thing. A collection of people waiting for an elevator may all want to go somewhere, but they probably haven't organized their efforts so they are going the same place. If you are assigned to a class project by an instructor, your classmates do have a common goal—to complete the project and earn a good grade. This class-project group would meet our definition of a group.

small group
Three to fifteen people who share a common purpose, feel a sense of belonging, and exert influence on one another.

Group Members Feel a Sense of Belonging

In order to be a group, the members must realize that they are part of the group. Again, people waiting for the elevator doors to open probably do not feel an obligation to others around them. Group members develop a sense of identity with their group. They know when they are in the group or not in the group.

Group Members Exert Influence on Others in the Group

When you are in a group, your presence and participation influences other people in the group. Group members are interdependent; what one group member says or does affects other group members. Your comments and even your silence help shape what the group does next. As you learned in Chapter 5, your nonverbal messages have a powerful effect on personal relationships. Each member of a group potentially has some influence on others. Even nonverbalized silence, facial expression, and eye contact (or lack of it) affect what the group does.

Small-group communication is the transactive process of creating meaning among three to fifteen people who share a common purpose, who feel a sense of belonging to the group, and who exert influence on each other. Communicating in small groups is sometimes a challenge because of the potential for misunderstanding. But don't assume it is inevitable that working in a group will be a frustrating experience. People accomplish much when working together. It was anthropologist Margaret Mead who said, "Never doubt that a small group of concerned citizens can change the world. Indeed, it's the only thing that ever has." In this chapter and the next chapter, we'll provide concepts and strategies to enhance the quality of your collaborations with others.

small-group communication
The transactive process of creating meaning among three to fifteen people who share a common purpose, feel a sense of belonging to the group, and exert influence on each other.

Communicating in Teams

Most of us have participated on a sports team at some time. Whether it is soccer, baseball, football, or a competitive water sport, the goal of a sports team is usually to win the game or competition. A work team has some of the same characteristics as a sports team. Instead of winning the game, the goal may be to get the contract, build the best mousetrap, or achieve a host of other objectives. A **team** is a coordinated group of people organized to work together to achieve a specific, common goal.[4]

team
A coordinated small group of people organized to work together to achieve a specific common goal.

On the WEB ·····•

Teams are becoming an integral part of today's workforce. How to become an efficient, productive team is among the most popular training seminars presented to Canadian workers. The following site offers additional information about the nature and function of teams and offers links to other sites that provide interesting information about the power of teamwork.
www.workteams.unt.edu

Often the terms "team" and "group" are used interchangeably. Is there a difference? Yes. Given the increased importance teams have in the workforce today, it's important to know precisely how groups and teams are different from each other. Although both groups and teams are made up of a small number of people who work to achieve a goal, teams are often structured deliberately to achieve the goal. Also, teams spend a great deal of time coordinating their efforts to accomplish the goal. Every team is a group, but not every group is highly organized or coordinated enough to meet the definition of a team. Let's consider several specific characteristics of teams.

Teams Develop Clearly Defined Responsibilities for Team Members

On a sports team, most team members have specifically assigned duties, such as shortstop, pitcher, quarterback, or fullback. On a work team, team members' duties and roles are usually explicitly spelled out. Team members may perform more than one function or role, but they nonetheless have well-defined duties.

Teams Have Clearly Defined Rules for Team Operation

Team members develop explicit rules for how the work should be done. As we learned in Chapter 1, a rule is a followable prescription for acceptable behaviour.[5] Just as there are written rules in the game of Monopoly, teams usually develop explicit rules for how the team will function. For example, a team may establish a rule that a member who is going to be absent should tell another team member beforehand. Team members know what the rules are and know how those rules affect the team.

Teams Develop Clear Goals

A third way to characterize a team is to look at the importance and specificity of the team goal. A team goal is usually stated in such a way that the goal can be measured, such as to win the game, to sell more cornflakes than the competition, or to get to the North Pole before anyone else.

Teams Develop a Way of Coordinating Their Efforts

Team members spend time discussing how to accomplish the goals of the team. Their work is coordinated to avoid duplication of effort. A sports team spends considerable time practising how to work together. Watching a sports team at work is like watching a choreographed dance. Team members have developed a system of working together rather than at cross-purposes. Just as a football team develops a list of the plays to get the ball down the field, a work team also develops collaborative strategies to achieve its goal.

Although we have differentiated between groups and teams, don't get the idea that they are completely exclusive entities. Both groups and teams are made up of a small number of people striving to achieve a goal. Since every team is a small group, whenever we refer to a team we are also suggesting that it's a group as well. Think of groups and teams as existing on a continuum; some deliberations will be more like a group, while others will be closer to our description of a team—a more coordinated and structured process, with clear rules and explicit goals.

Characteristics of Effective Team Members

Now that you understand what a team is, you may still wonder, "What do effective team members do? What are some of the attributes that make team members effective?" Communication researchers Frank LaFasto and Carl Larson sought to answer those questions by surveying more than 6000 team members and leaders.[6] They specifically wanted to know what seasoned team members consider to be the characteristics of an excellent team. They found six characteristics that seemed to set effective team members apart from ineffective members.

1. *Experience.* Effective team members have "been there and done that." They have practical experience in collaborating with others. More experienced team members were better able to see the big picture; less experienced members tended to lack the technical background needed to be successful at their collaborative work.

ETHICAL PROBE

Teams have a strong sense of purpose and a well-structured, coordinated plan to achieve the goals of the team. If you disagree with the goal of the team, is it appropriate to voice your concern, even if it means diverting the team from its stated objective? What are your responsibilities to ensure that your own behaviour in a team meets your personal standards of ethics?

Re CAP ←···

Comparing Groups and Teams

	GROUPS	TEAMS
Roles and Responsibilities	Individual responsibilities may not always be explicitly defined for group members.	Team member expectations, roles, and responsibilities are clearly developed and discussed.
Rules	Rules are often not formally written down and developed; rules evolve, depending on the group's needs.	Rules and operating procedures are clearly identified to help the team work efficiently and effectively.
Goals	Group goals may be discussed in general terms.	Clearly spelled out goals are the focus of what the team does.
Methods	Group members may decide to divide the work among group members.	Team members develop clear methods of collaborating and coordinating their efforts to achieve the team goal.

2. *Problem-Solving Ability.* Team members who were effective were perceived as decisive. It wasn't that they just made quick decisions; they carefully analyzed information and issues while staying focused on the problem. Their ability to examine a problematic situation and select effective strategies for managing problems set skilled team members apart from less skilled collaborators.

3. *Openness.* Have you ever worked in a team and found one or more members not willing to express ideas and opinions honestly, yet tactfully? LaFasto and Larson found that openness was an essential characteristic for team success. Effective team members were willing to discuss delicate and sensitive issues and topics in an appropriate way that didn't make people defensive. Team members who were more secretive and participated less were perceived as less important to team success.

4. *Supportiveness.* Supportive team members listened to others. They didn't just stand by and watch someone else work; they found out what needed to be done, then pitched in and did it. Nonsupportive team members tended to focus on their individual agendas, rather than being aware of the needs of the team as a whole.

Listen and Respond

5. *Action Oriented.* "Just do it!" That advertising slogan sold a lot of tennis shoes for a sports equipment company. It's also a good motto for effective team members. Ineffective team members hung back and watched others do the work.

6. *Positive Personal Style.* There's the story about a boy on Christmas morning who awoke to find only a large pile of manure under the tree. But undaunted, he smiled and said, "With this much horse manure, there's got to be a pony here somewhere!" Effective team members were optimistic. Even in bad times, they found something positive. Their encouraging, patient, enthusiastic, and friendly attitude contributed to their being well liked by other team members. Here's how to be perceived as an ineffective team member: Argue with others frequently, be intolerant and impatient, and cultivate skills that will help you win the "pain-in-the-neck" award.

UNDERSTANDING TYPES OF GROUPS AND TEAMS

Groups and teams are formed for a variety of reasons. The type of group is determined by its purpose. The following group descriptions focus on the different goals or purposes groups have.

DILBERT reprinted by permission of United Feature Syndicate, Inc.

Primary Groups

primary group
A group that exists to fulfil basic human needs, such as a family.

A **primary group** exists to fulfil the basic human need of associating with others. One of the best examples of a primary group is your family. Although some families may have a family business or have other goals, in most family discussions, one person does not whip out an agenda while the rest of the group follows a process to achieve a specific outcome. Like other primary groups, family communication is informal. People talk just because they are together.

Study Groups

study group
A group that exists to help group members learn new information and ideas.

As a student, you probably don't need this type of group defined for you. A **study group** meets to learn new ideas. Learning theory suggests you are more likely to learn when you actively participate in the learning process. Students sometimes form study groups because they know that by participating in the give and take of a discussion, they'll be more likely to remember what is discussed. Teachers, too, often assign groups as a method of learning called collaborative learning. Breaking students into small groups and inviting participation is a time-proven strategy to help students learn. It is also a training ground for the groups and teams they will participate in during their careers.

Therapy Groups

therapy group
A group that provides treatment for problems that group members may have.

Therapy means providing treatment to solve a personal concern or problem, or to resolve an issue. A **therapy group** exists to provide treatment for the personal problems that

---

COMMUNICATION and TECHNOLOGY

Finding Virtual Groups to Learn Online

Even with the increasing use of distance learning and Web-based or Web-assisted learning, most people have more experience in learning in live, real-time classrooms. One of the advantages to learning with others is the use of interaction and group association with other students to reinforce learning. When you are learning online, consider some of the following tips and strategies for recreating the advantages of learning with others in groups and teams.[7]

• Seek out online courses that have real-time chat groups.
• Enrich your online class experience by joining a related Listserv, a group of people who receive information on related topics. You will then have a virtual support group to reinforce your learning.

• Read the e-mail postings from other students in your class to learn from the questions and comments of your classmates.
• Use e-mail or your membership in a Listserv to determine whether someone taking the same class lives near you and plan to meet for study sessions.

With thought and ingenuity, you can enjoy the advantages of distance-learning experiences while using the technology to work with others in groups to reinforce what you learn.

group members may have. Weight Watchers, Alcoholics Anonymous, and Gamblers Anonymous are examples of therapy groups. People gain insight by being in a group with others who have similar needs. Also, the feedback people receive from the therapy group leader and other group members is an important part of the treatment. We learn about ourselves from the perceptions of others.

Problem-Solving Groups

A **problem-solving group** exists to resolve an issue or overcome an unsatisfactory situation or obstacle to achieve a goal. Problem-solving teams are the most common type of groups in businesses and other organizations. In business, the problem often focuses on, "How can we overcome an obstacle to make more money?" A problem-solving team in a hospital or health clinic will focus on ways to make people healthy. Most problems boil down to something you want more of or less of. The problem-solving group goal is often to figure out how to get more or less of something (time, money, help from others) in order to achieve the goal of the group or organization.

Focus Groups

A **focus group** is a small group of people who are asked to discuss a particular topic or issue so that others can better understand how these group members respond to the topics or issues presented. One person usually acts as the moderator or facilitator asks open-ended questions, and then gives group members a chance to share their views on the issues at hand. Many advertising agencies will show a group a new advertising campaign and then listen to the responses of the group members to assess the impact or effectiveness of the campaign. For example, before launching a new kind of potato chip, an advertising agency may use reactions from a focus group to guide them in marketing the new product. Politicians often use focus groups to determine the effectiveness of a political strategy or new policy. In some ways, a focus-group discussion is like a group interview. The purpose is to listen to the issues, ideas, and responses group members may have toward whatever is being discussed.

Social Groups

Some groups exist just for the joy of socializing with others. Such is the case with a **social group.** Travel groups, dinner clubs, or music groups are often formed because group members enjoy the fellowship of interacting and meeting with others. They also like the activity that the group supports. In most cases, people could still do the activity (eat, travel, play music) without a group—but a group makes the experience more enjoyable. Social groups exist because of the fun group members have when interacting with others.

UNDERSTANDING GROUP AND TEAM DYNAMICS

Groups and teams are dynamic; their structure changes. Those dynamic or changing factors that fuel the energy for groups to achieve goals include how group members interact with and relate to one another. The study of group dynamics includes a discussion of the roles, norms, status, power, and cohesiveness of groups. We'll examine each concept and note how it is related to the five principles of communication.

Roles

How you communicate with others in a group is a function of your role. Your **role** is the consistent way you communicate with others in a group. It is based on your expectations of yourself and the expectations others place on you. Do you often become a leader of

problem-solving group
A group that meets to seek a solution to a problem.

focus group
A group that is asked to discuss a particular topic or issue so that others can better understand how the group members respond to the topics or issues presented to them.

social group
A group that exists to provide opportunities for group members to enjoy the company of others.

role
The consistent way a person communicates with others in a small group.

A therapy group can be more effective than an individual therapy session for treating many personal problems.

a group, or are you more comfortable just blending in and taking directions from others? Or are you the one who makes sure the group gets the work done instead of just having a good time? And then there are those group members who seem especially gifted at smoothing conflict and disagreement. Or perhaps you have no typical pattern to what you do in a group; your role depends on the group and who else is in it.

There are three classic categories of group roles. **Task roles** are behaviours that help the group achieve its goal and accomplish its work; gathering and sharing research conclusions with the group, taking minutes of meetings, or writing ideas on a chalkboard are examples of task-role behaviours.

Social roles focus on behaviour that manages relationships and affects the group climate; these roles help resolve conflict and enhance the flow of communication. Smoothing hurt feelings and helping the group celebrate its accomplishments are examples of social-role behaviour.

Finally, **individual roles** focus attention on the individual rather than on the group. These are roles that do *not* help the group; they emphasize individual accomplishments and issues rather than those of the entire group. Dominating group discussions to talk about personal issues or concerns, telling frequent jokes that routinely get the group off track, and constantly complaining or whining about how one's individual needs aren't being met are examples of individual roles.

All five of the communication principles we've presented throughout the book are involved in influencing whether the role you assume from moment to moment in a group is primarily about the task, relationship maintenance, or individual concerns. Effective group members are aware of the roles they are assuming, rather than oblivious to how their communication affects the groups. The role behaviour is communicated by the verbal and nonverbal messages expressed. Roles are not static. We adjust our behaviour by listening and responding to other group members and then adapting our behaviour accordingly.

More than 50 years ago, Kenneth Benne and Paul Sheats identified a list of group roles that remains a classic way of dividing up the group and individual roles that group and team members typically assume.[8] Table 9.1 presents a summary of these roles. As you review the list of roles and their descriptions, note whether you usually assume roles in the task, social, or individual category. Or perhaps you'll "see yourself" in a variety of roles in all three categories.

As you look at the list of roles in Table 9.1, you may think, "Yes, that's what I usually do. That's the role I usually take." You can probably see roles that fit other group members. Most group members don't assume only one or two roles during group meetings. Most of us assume several roles when we interact in a group. A role is worked out jointly between us and the group, and the roles we assume change depending on which group we're in. Effective group members adapt their behaviour to what is happening or needed in the group. In some groups, your expertise may give you the confidence to give information and share your opinions freely. In other groups, you may assume a role to maintain social harmony and peace.

What are the best or worst roles to assume? We don't recommend that you assume any individual role; by definition, these roles focus attention on an individual rather than the group. The group needs a balance of task and social roles, not attention drawn to an individual.

What is the proper balance between task and social concerns? Some experts recommend a 60:40 balance between task and social roles.[9] What is clear is that groups seem to operate most effectively when it's not all work and no play. Conversely, an out-of-balance group that focuses just on having a good time is not going to achieve its task goals. In general, more comments need to be about getting the work done than about having fun or managing the social climate, but don't neglect making sure that there are good working relationships among group members.

The action step for you: Monitor what roles are being assumed and not assumed in your group. Be aware of your communication. Then help meet a need. Adapt your behaviour to the needs of the group. If your group seems unduly focused on the task without sensitivity to the harmony of the group relationships, the group will wobble.

⋯⟩ Rules

As we noted both in Chapter 1 and earlier in this chapter, rules are followable prescriptions that indicate what behaviour is expected or preferred.[10] Rules also clearly specify what

task role
A role that helps the group achieve its goal and accomplish the work.

social role
A role that helps the group manage relationships and affect the group climate.

individual role
A role that focuses attention on the individual rather than on the group.

TABLE 9.1 A Classification of Group Roles

Task Roles	Description	Example
Initiator/contributor	Offers new ideas or approaches to the group; suggests ways of getting the job done or offers new ideas to the group.	"How about developing an agenda to help us organize our work?"
Information seeker	Asks for additional clarification, facts, or other information that helps the group with the issues at hand.	"Can anyone tell me how many times the university has threatened to close the fraternities and sororities on campus because of the problem of underage drinking?"
Opinion seeker	Asks for group members to share opinions or express a personal point of view.	"So, what do you guys think of the new dress code the school board is proposing?"
Information giver	Provides facts, examples, statistics, or other evidence that relates to the task confronting the group.	"Within the past year, the Vice-President for Student Affairs has given a special award to three fraternities and one sorority for developing a program to combat underage drinking."
Opinion giver	Offers opinions or beliefs about what the group is discussing.	"I think the new school dress code proposed for students in Grade 1 is unworkable."
Elaborator	Provides comments or examples to extend or add to the comments of others.	"Oh, Tom, that's a good point. I had the same thing happen to me when my children were attending a private school last year."
Coordinator	Clarifies and notes relationships among the ideas and suggestions that have been offered by others.	"Tyrone, your ideas sound a lot like Juanita's suggestion. Juanita, why don't you elaborate on your idea and then see if Tyrone agrees or disagrees with you?"
Orienter	Summarizes what has occurred and seeks to keep the group focused on the task at hand.	"I think we're getting a bit off track here. Let's go back to the issue on the agenda."
Evaluator/critic	Assesses the evidence and conclusions that the group is considering.	"How recent are those statistics? I think there are newer figures for us to consider."
Procedural technician	Helps the group accomplish its goal by handling tasks such as distributing reports, writing ideas on a chalkboard, or performing other tasks that help the group.	"I'll write your ideas on the board as you suggest them. After they are written down, I'll copy them and summarize them in an e-mail message to each of you."
Recorder	Makes a written record of the group's progress by writing down specific comments, facts, or the minutes of the meeting.	"I'll take the minutes of today's meeting."

TABLE 9.1   *(continued)*

Social Roles	Description	Example
Encourager	Offers praise and support, and confirms the value of other people and the ideas they contribute.	"You're doing a wonderful job."
Harmonizer	Manages conflict and mediates disputes among group members.	"Tynesha, you and Mandy seem to be agreeing more than you are disagreeing. Both of you want the same goal. Let's brainstorm some strategies that can help you both get what you want."
Compromiser	Resolves conflicts by trying to find an acceptable solution. Seeks new alternatives.	"Jane, you want us to meet at 7:00 pm and Sue, you'd like us to start at 8:00. What if we started at 7:30? Would that work?"
Gatekeeper	Encourages people who talk too much to contribute less and invites those who are less talkative to participate.	"Tim, we've not heard what you think. What do you suggest we do?"
Follower	Goes along with the suggestions and ideas of other group members.	"I can support that option. You have summarized the issues about the same way I see them."
Emotion expresser	Verbalizes how the group may be feeling about a specific issue or suggestion.	"We seem to be frustrated that we are not making more progress."
Group observer	Summarizes the group's progress or lack of progress.	"We are making great progress on all of the issues except how much salary we should offer."
Tension reliever	Monitors stress within the group and offers suggestions for breaks, using humour or other appropriate strategies.	"Hey, what we need is a good laugh. Here's a joke I saw on the Internet today."
Individual Roles	**Description**	**Example**
Aggressor	Deflates or disconfirms the status of other group members or tries to take credit for the work of others.	"Lee, your idea is the pits. We all know that what I suggested two meetings ago is the only way to go."
Blocker	Is negative, stubborn, and disagreeable without an apparent reason.	"I just don't like it. I don't have to tell you why. I just don't like it."
Recognition seeker	Seeks the spotlight by dwelling on his or her personal accomplishments. Unduly seeks the praise of others.	"Don't you remember this was my idea? And, say, did you see my picture in the paper? I won the grand prize at the science fair."
Self-confessor	Uses the group as a forum to self-disclose unnecessary personal feelings and personal problems unrelated to the group's task.	"Let me tell you how my parents are so unfair. They won't let me live off campus next year. My parents just don't understand me."

TABLE 9.1   *(continued)*

Individual Roles	Description	Example
Joker	Wants to crack jokes, tell stories, and just have fun without focusing on the task or what the group needs.	"Hey, let's forget this project and go to the mall. Then I'll tell you the gossip about Professor Smith. What a kook!"
Dominator	Tries to take control of the group, talks too much, and uses flattery or aggression to push his or her ideas off on the group.	"Now, here's what we're going to do: Marcie, you will take notes today; Phil, you go get us some pizza; and Russ, I want you to just sit there in case I need you to run an errand."
Special-interest pleader	Seeks to get the group to support a pet project or personal agenda.	"My service club would like it if we would support the new downtown renovation project. I'll stand a good shot at group president if I can get you on board."
Help seeker	Seeks to evoke a sympathetic response from others. Often expresses insecurity stemming from feelings of low self-worth.	"I don't know if I can participate in this project. I'm not very good with people. I just feel like I don't relate well to others or have many friends."

behaviour is inappropriate. Rules are especially important when working in groups and teams because leaders or members often develop rules that specify how people should behave. Think of rules as serving the same function as provincial law and the Canadian constitution.

Teams, in particular, often develop **team ground rules** that help a team function more smoothly. Team ground rules are just another way of talking about the prescribed behaviours that are expected of group members. They are important to help manage uncertainty when working with others. Imagine playing on a sports team if there were no written rules; it would be chaos. Highly structured teams need rules to ensure that the team is both efficient and effective. While most informal groups may not develop explicit, written rules, more formal teams may take time to develop such rules as the following: Everyone should attend all meetings; meetings will start on time; each team member should follow through on individual assignments. By making the rules explicit, it's easier to enforce what is either appropriate or inappropriate.

team ground rules
A way of talking about the prescribed behaviours that are expected of group members; team members work together to develop explicit rules of acceptable behaviour.

norms
Standards that determine what is appropriate and inappropriate behaviour in a group.

---> Norms

Although not all groups develop explicit rules, most every group and team develop norms. **Norms** are general standards that determine what is appropriate and inappropriate behaviour in a group. Is it normal for group members to raise their hands before speaking in your group? Is it okay to move around while the group is in session or to go get a cup of coffee while someone is talking? Norms reflect what's normal behaviour in the group; they influence how group members are supposed to behave—such as the type of language that is acceptable, the casualness of the clothes they wear (or don't wear), or whether first names are used.

How do you know what the norms of any group are? Watch the group. Listen and observe any repeated verbal or nonverbal behaviour

©1997 Tribune Media Services, Inc. All rights reserved.

"The problem boils down to this — Harrison *woulda*, Reynolds *coulda* and Sorenson *shoulda*."

ETHICAL PROBE

If a group member is enacting an individual role that keeps the group from achieving its goal, is it appropriate to confront the group member and tell him or her to modify the behaviour so that it does not inhibit the group? Is it ethical to point out behaviour that is distracting the group from achieving the task?

Adapt   Aware
Listen   Verbal
and
Respond   Nonverbal

Verbal

Nonverbal

status
An individual's importance and prestige.

patterns. Note, for example, consistencies in the way people talk or dress. Consider the following questions:

- What are group members' attitudes toward time (do meetings start and stop on time)?
- How do group members dress?
- Is it acceptable to use informal, slang terms or to use obscenity?
- What kind of humour is acceptable?
- How does the group treat the leader?

Noting when someone breaks a norm can also help you spot a norm. If a member waltzes into a meeting 20 minutes late and several folks grimace and point to their watches, that's a sure sign that a norm has been violated. The severity of the punishment corresponds to the significance of the norm.[11] Mild punishment is usually unspoken—such as nonverbal glances or a frowning stare. More serious punishment can be a negative comment about the behaviour in front of other group members or even expulsion from the group. You don't have to worry about whether your group will have norms or not; norms happen. You should, however, monitor the group norms to ensure that your behaviour doesn't distract from the work of the group, or to note the possible development of an unproductive group norm that the group should talk about.

How do norms differ from rules? Rules are more explicit. Group and team rules are either written down or at least verbalized. Here's an example of a rule: If you have more than three absences in this course, you lose one-third of a letter grade. Here's another: Any member of this team who does not pay his or her dues on time will pay an extra $5 in dues. Norms, on the other hand, are more general standards or expectations that are not as clearly spelled out. It may be a norm in your group that no one uses four-letter words; there's probably no written policy that prohibits expletives, or group members may never have said, "No one should ever use a curse word during our discussions." But even without such specific admonitions, group members don't use offensive or obscene words. Norms develop based upon those norms that you and other team members have experienced in other groups, as well as when the behaviour just seems to occur. If after a couple of meetings no one is telling off-colour jokes or stories, then a norm has begun to gel.

⋯⟩ Status

As she walks into the room, all eyes are fixed on her. Group members watch every move. As the chairperson, her influence is important. Without her support, no new issues will come before the board. She has high status. **Status** refers to an individual's importance and prestige. Your status in a group influences who you talk to, who talks to you, and even what you talk about. Your perceived importance affects both your verbal and your nonverbal messages. A person with high status typically

- Talks more than low-status members.
- Directs comments to other high-status group members.
- Has more influence on the decision the group makes.
- Is listened to by group members.
- Usually makes more comments to the entire group.[12]

Because high-status people enjoy more privileges, most people want to be in the "in group"—the group with status and influence. Being aware of status differences can help you predict who talks to whom. If you can discern status differences, you'll also be better able to predict the type of messages communicated.

But just because a person has status does not mean that his or her ideas are good. Don't let status difference influence your perceptions of the value of the ideas contributed. Some groups get into trouble because they automatically defer to the person with more status, without reviewing the validity of the ideas presented. Status influences group communication, but don't let status differences influence your critical thinking about the merit of the ideas presented. Conversely, don't dismiss ideas out-of-hand because the person who suggested them doesn't have status or prestige. Focus on the quality of the message, not just on the messenger.

···❯ Power

Status refers to perceived importance, while power refers to whether the status influences behaviour. **Power** is the ability to influence others' behaviour. Although status and power often go hand in hand, a group member could have status and still not be able to influence how others behave. People have power if they can affect what others do. Their power stems from the resources available to them to influence others. Who does and doesn't have power in a group influences how people relate to one another.

A power struggle often creates ripples of conflict and contention through the group. Power struggles also often focus attention on individual group members rather than on the group as a whole. People with less power tend to participate less in group discussion unless they're trying to gain power. A group that is not power balanced may have problems; the "power people" may dominate the discussion. In any group or team, when one or more members dominate the discussion, the group loses the contributions and insights of others. Research supports the conclusion that groups with equal power distribution usually have better quality outcomes.[13]

According to a classic discussion of how individuals become powerful, there are five power bases: legitimate, referent, expert, reward, and coercive power. These power bases explain why certain people have power and why others don't.[14]

Legitimate Power

You have **legitimate power** if someone elected or appointed you to a position of power. Your power source comes from holding a position of responsibility. The president of your university or college has the legitimate power to establish and implement school policy. Canadian politicians, police officers, and parent/teacher association (PTA) presidents are other examples of people who have legitimate power. A group or team member who has been elected chair or president of the group is given legitimate power to influence how the group operates.

Referent Power

You have **referent power** if people like you. Put simply, people we like have more power over us than people we do not like. If you are working on a committee with your best friend, your friend exerts power over you in the sense that you will tend to give more credence to what your friend recommends. Just the opposite occurs if you are working with someone you don't like; you will be more likely to ignore the advice that comes from someone you don't admire.

Expert Power

Knowledge is power. People who have **expert power** are perceived as informed or knowledgeable. They will have more influence in a group or team than people who are perceived as uninformed. Suppose you are working with a group to develop strategies to clean up the river that runs through your town. Your colleague who is majoring in aquatic biology will probably have more power than other, less knowledgeable group members.

Reward Power

People who can grant favours, money, or other rewards have more power than people who can't provide such rewards; those who can bestow rewards have **reward power.** People who have greater power to reward are typically sent more positive, supportive messages than people who don't have the ability to reward others. Someone has reward power if he or she can also take away a punishment or other unpleasant experience. But reward power is effective only if the person being rewarded finds the reward satisfying or useful. What is rewarding to one person may not be rewarding to another person.

power
The ability to influence other people's behaviour.

legitimate power
Power base that stems from being elected or appointed to a position of authority.

referent power
Power that stems from being liked and able to influence the behaviour of others.

expert power
Power derived from having expertise and information that can influence the behaviour of others.

reward power
Power that comes from the ability to provide rewards or favours.

What group roles do you see occurring in this picture? Who has legitimate power and who has referent power?

Re**CAP** ←····

Types of Power

Legitimate Power	Being elected, appointed, or ordained to lead or make decisions for a group or a team.
Referent Power	Being popular and well liked.
Expert Power	Having information or being exceptionally knowledgeable about issues or ideas.
Reward Power	Having the resources to bestow gifts, money, recognition, or other rewards that are valued by group members.
Coercive Power	Having the ability to punish others.

coercive power
Power that stems from being able to punish others.

Coercive Power

You have coercive power if you can punish others. **Coercive power** is the flip side of reward power. The ability to influence comes from the ability to make others uncomfortable. If someone can cut your salary, lower your grade, demote you, or force you to do unpleasant jobs, then that person has coercive power. The power results from the perception that the person with the power will actually use the power. If a person has the authority to punish, but group members don't perceive that the person will use this power, then there really is no coercive power.

Even though we have categorized power into five different types, don't get the idea that group members may exert just one type of power. In reality, group or team members' power often stems from more than one source. For example, because a group member may be the elected leader (legitimate power), he or she may also be able to offer more rewards (reward power) or punishments (coercive power).

Listen
and
Respond

cohesiveness
The degree of attraction members feel toward one another and toward their group.

····→ Cohesiveness

If you have ever read about the Three Musketeers or have seen a movie about them, you know that their motto is "One for all, and all for one." They are a cohesive group. They like to be around one another. Group **cohesiveness** is the degree of attraction that members of a group feel toward one another and the group. In a highly cohesive group, the members feel a high degree of loyalty to one another; the goal of the group is also the goal of the individual. Cohesive group members listen to one another.

Groups become cohesive because of a variety of forces that attract people to the group and to one another. Similarity of goals, feelings of genuine liking, and similarity of backgrounds and culture are variables that influence group cohesion. Cohesiveness also is more likely to occur when group members' needs are satisfied by participating in the group. In the case of the Three Musketeers, the desire to do good deeds and assist those in need provided the clear, elevating goal from which the musketeers derived satisfaction. Think of a group you belong to in which there is a high degree of *esprit de corps* and cohesiveness. You will also probably find that you like both the group members and the overall goals and objectives that the group is trying to accomplish.

What makes groups and teams cohesive? Table 9.2 summarizes some of the strategies that enhance group cohesiveness and those that make a group less cohesive. The common element in cohesive groups is the manner in which group members communicate with one another. Cohesiveness is more likely to occur if group members have the opportunity to talk with one another freely about a goal all members have in common and if this interaction increases affection and liking toward one another.

TABLE 9.2 Suggestions for Enhancing Group Cohesiveness[15]

Cohesive Groups	Uncohesive Groups
Talk about the group in terms of "we" rather than "I."	Tend to emphasize the individual contributions of group members.
Reinforce good attendance at group meetings.	Make little effort to encourage group members to attend every meeting.
Establish and maintain group traditions.	Make little effort to develop group traditions.
Set clear short-term as well as long-term goals.	Avoid setting goals or establishing deadlines.
Encourage everyone in the group to participate in the group task.	Allow only the most talkative or high-status members to participate in the group task.
Celebrate when the group accomplishes either a short-term or long-term goal.	Discourage group celebration; group meetings are all work and little or no fun.
Stress teamwork and collaboration.	Stress individual accomplishment.

Can a group be too cohesive? Yes. If group members are focused only on developing a positive, cohesive relationship to the exclusion of getting their work done, group productivity can suffer. There is a curvilinear relationship between cohesiveness and amount of work a group produces. This means that rather than a direct, linear relationship between cohesiveness and work output, after a certain level of group cohesiveness, group productivity actually decreases. If you think about it, this makes perfect sense. If the group becomes obsessed primarily with having fun and enjoying one another's company, they will produce *less* work. Although usually cohesiveness is a good thing, a group can have too much of a good thing. Strive for group cohesiveness, but balance it with concern for accomplishing the group's task.

⋯⟩ Communication Interaction Patterns

When you participate in a group or a team meeting, do you even notice that you frequently talk with some people but hardly speak to others? It is normal for most of us to develop preferences for whom we do and don't talk with. Group communication scholars have studied and classified the various distinct patterns that emerge when people talk to one another in groups. A **communication interaction pattern** is a pattern of communication that identifies the frequency of who talks to whom. Some groups have an equal distribution of interaction among members, while others develop distinct patterns of interaction between two or more people.

In most groups, we often speak to specific people in the group rather than to the group as a whole. We tend to speak to people who have more power and status. In addition, we talk to people we like more than people we don't like. There will also, however, be more communication directed toward someone in the group who holds an opinion different from that of the rest of the group. This person is called a **group deviate.** Other group members may spend considerable talk time trying to change his or her opinion.

A group in which everyone talks to everyone else is called an all-channel network. All channels are open and used, as you can see in the first model in Figure 9.1 on page 206. There is considerable interaction, and no cliques or small subgroups emerge. A **clique** is a smaller group of people within a larger group who form a common bond among one another. Perhaps in your social, service, or religious groups you have special friends whom you seek out and who seek you out when you attend meetings. During meetings you probably sit together, share private jokes and stories, and talk about other members.

Verbal

communication interaction pattern
A consistent pattern of who talks to whom.

group deviate
A group member who holds an opinion, attitude, or belief that is different from that of other group members.

clique
A smaller, cohesive group within a larger group.

FIGURE 9.1 Small Group Communication Networks

All-Channel Network

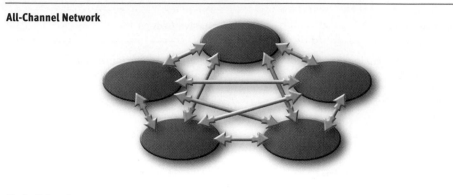

Chain Network

Wheel Network

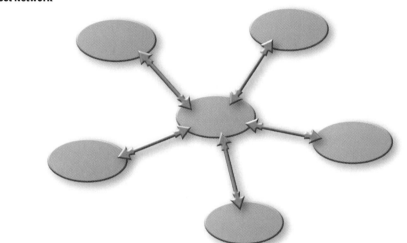

Although there is nothing wrong with having special friends and colleagues, cliques can become detrimental to a group or team if they foster rivalries within the group or if they overly inhibit the flow of communication with others. Groups should avoid subgroups or cliques that can develop divisive power plays that foster conflict. You don't want cliques or groups to ratchet up the emotional tension as the group seeks to deliberate rationally.

The chain network in Figure 9.1 involves people who convey a message through one person at a time rather than with all group members at once. In organizations, it is typical for a hierarchical chain communication pattern to exist. Here's an example: The president of the company sends a message to the vice-president, who talks to the director. The director then talks to the manager, who eventually gives the message to the other employees. As you might suspect, passing a message through many different ears and minds often results in communication misunderstanding by the time it reaches the last person in the chain.

The wheel network pattern occurs when one person receives most of the messages from a central person. This pivotal communicator is also the prime source of information to other group members. Perhaps one member of your family always seems to know what's going on. The wheel pattern emerges when there is a strong leader or when the group members do individual tasks and need someone to keep them informed of what others are doing, without interacting with those others.

What's the best interaction pattern? It depends. Sometimes, the efficiency and structured nature of the chain or wheel pattern may be called for. For example, during the huddle before a football play, the quarterback usually does most of the talking while others listen (wheel network). But most teams function best if there is an all-channel expectation of communication, especially when the group is trying to generate new, creative ideas. Breaking into smaller groups can be a useful divide-and-conquer strategy and enhances efficiency for some tasks. If the group is not too large, the all-channel pattern serves most groups well. As you participate in or lead group meetings, be aware of the general pattern of communication. Are all members participating? Do some people whisper their ideas only to a few and not share with the rest of the group? Is a group deviate monopolizing the conversation? By being observant of interaction patterns, you can help the group enhance cohesiveness and develop appropriate roles to get the work done.

UNDERSTANDING GROUP AND TEAM PHASES OF DEVELOPMENT

Sometimes, small-group communication can be a disorganized, messy process—especially if the all-channel network is the predominant communication pattern. Although the free flow of ideas is a good thing, it may seem as though there is no order or structure to the way group members interact. But what may look like chaotic talk may, in fact, be just a normal aspect of how groups behave.

Researchers have found that some groups go through certain phases or sequences of talk when they meet to solve a problem or make a decision. Some researchers have found three phases; most have found four. One of the most descriptive four-phase models was developed by Aubrey Fisher.[16] His four phases of group talk are (1) **orientation,** (2) **conflict,** (3) **emergence,** and (4) **reinforcement.** To understand the sequence of these four phases can be like having a group map. By listening to what people are saying, you can identify where the group is. We will describe these phases so that you can identify them when they occur in your group.

Verbal

⌁⟩ Orientation

As you might suspect, when people first get together in a group, they take time to become oriented to at least two things: who's in the group (group process) and what they will be doing (group task).

When you join a group for the first time, you have high uncertainty about how the group will be organized, who will be in charge, and exactly how things will work. The research on the orientation phases suggests that your earliest communication is directed at orienting yourself to others, as well as to the group's task. Another name for what happens during this first phase is **primary tension.** This is the tension that results from the uncertainty and discomfort people experience when they meet for the first time. Just as you may have some tension and anxiety when you give a speech, some tension and anxiety occur in a group when group members are trying to figure out who is supposed to do what, who's in charge, and why they are there. Some group members who don't like uncertainty at all and are eager to start sorting things out will suggest an agenda: "Hello, my name is Steve. Let's each introduce ourselves." Other group members are quite content to sit quietly in the background and let others take the lead. As people begin to become acquainted and group members start talking about the purpose of the meeting, typical groups experience the second phase—conflict.

⌁⟩ Conflict

People are different. That common sense observation has powerful implications for human communication, and nowhere is it more evident than in a group discussion after the group gets down to business. As the group becomes more comfortable and oriented toward the task and one another, they start asserting opinions about what the group should be doing and who should be doing it. They have tested the water in the first phase and are now ready to jump in. This second phase, which is characterized by increased disagreement, is

orientation
The first phase of group interaction, in which members become adjusted to one another and to the group's task.

conflict
The second phase of group interaction, in which group members experience some degree of disagreement about social and task issues.

emergence
The third phase of group interaction, in which conflict or disagreement is managed, decisions are made, and the work plan and group problems begin to be solved or managed.

reinforcement
The fourth phase of group interaction, in which group members express positive feelings toward each other and toward the group.

primary tension
Anxiety and discomfort that occurs when a group first meets.

secondary tension
Conflict that occurs over group norms, roles, leadership, and differences among member opinions; develops after the members of the group have become acquainted with one another.

sometimes called **secondary tension.** This tension or conflict occurs when there may be a struggle for leadership or when group members disagree with each other.

Conflict is not always bad—it occurs when people are honest about sharing their opinions. If there is no conflict, it usually means people aren't honest about how they really feel. As journalist Walter Lippman once said, "When we all think alike, then no one is thinking." The conflict phase is necessary for solving problems and maintaining group relationships. When ideas aren't challenged and tested, groups are more likely to make unwise decisions. Also, honest yet tactful expressions of personal disagreement are more likely to foster genuine cohesiveness than phony relationships. So conflict and disagreement are not necessarily bad, especially if the disagreement is about issues, rather than a personal or relationship conflict. Conflict that results in attacking people rather than ideas is not productive. We are not suggesting that you celebrate when you have conflict, only that you take some comfort in knowing that conflict is an expected part of group deliberations. The amount and intensity of the conflict varies, depending on how important the issues are to the group. The more important the issues are to group members, the more likely conflict will emerge with greater intensity.

⋯⟩ Emergence

You know you are in the emergence phase when the group begins to solidify a common point of view. Decisions emerge; conflict is reduced. Though conflict is still evident in this third phase, what sets the emergence phase apart from the conflict phase is the way in which group members manage conflict. Norms, roles, and leadership patterns that have been established in the group now help the group get work accomplished. In the emergence phase, the group settles on norms and moves closer toward agreement. The group begins to get a clearer glimpse of how issues will be resolved and what the group outcome will be.

Not all of what emerges may be productive. The group could decide that the conflict is so intense that the best decision is to disband the group. Or an individual could decide to leave the group.

⋯⟩ Reinforcement

Group members become more unified in the fourth phase. During the orientation, conflict, and emergence phases, group members struggled through getting acquainted, developing cohesiveness, competing for status and prominence, and puzzling over action the group could take. The group eventually emerges from those struggles and develops a new sense of direction. This accomplishment results in a more positive feeling about the

---

ReCAP ⟨⋯

A Map of Group Phases

Phase One: Orientation	• What are we doing here? • What is our goal? • Who are these people? • What is my role?
Phase Two: Conflict	• I see the goal differently. • Who put him/her in charge? • I have different ideas. • I have different strategies.
Phase Three: Emergence	• Something happens. • Decisions are made. • Issues are managed. • The group moves forward.
Phase Four: Reinforcement	• The group is aware it is making progress. • Members seek to justify their actions. • Members reward others. • The team celebrates its success or rationalizes its failure.

group. The group more clearly develops a sense of "we." In fact, one of the ways you can identify the reinforcement phase is when group members use more collective pronouns to talk about the group *(we, us, our)* than personal pronouns *(I, me, my).*

The Process Nature of Group Phases

Even though we have identified four distinct phases that groups can experience, don't get the idea that all groups neatly progress through these phases in exactly the same way. They don't. Some researchers have found that only about one-third of all groups experience these distinct stages.[17] Other studies have difficulty identifying all four phases but find just one or two. Even if you have trouble identifying these phases in your group, you will probably see some elements of these four types of talk during your group meetings. Some groups may simply get stuck in one of the phases. For example, have you ever participated in a group that could never quite figure out what it was supposed to do? It was stuck in the orientation phase.

Some groups remain in the conflict phase for long periods of time, perhaps bouncing between orientation and conflict. The group either seems torn by personal conflict between group members, or it just can't reach agreement or make a decision.

Eventually something will emerge (phase three) from the group, even if it is not a wise decision or quality solution. The group may decide, for example, to disband and never meet again because the members are so dysfunctional. Although not the original objective of the group, something emerged—the group members quit.

Reinforcement is likely to occur because we like to make sense out of what happens to us. Even if the group disbands, we are likely to celebrate its demise or reinforce the decision to disband. Because of our culture's emphasis on efficiency and productivity, many groups quickly gloss over the reinforcement aspects of group celebration. Wise group leaders and participants make sure that accomplishments are celebrated and both group and individual efforts are recognized. The cohesiveness and positive feelings that result from such celebrations will be helpful as the group prepares for its next task.

UNDERSTANDING DIVERSITY IN GROUPS AND TEAMS: ADAPTING TO DIFFERENCES

As we emphasized in Chapter 6, at the heart of any discussion of diversity is the fact that we are different from one another. The effects of diversity are particularly noticeable when working with others in a group or on a team. By definition, groups and teams involve people united by a common goal. Differences in culture and other perspectives make it more challenging to be united as a group and to foster cohesiveness. Among the differences that have an impact on groups and teams are the concepts of individualism and collectivism, culture differences in our use of time, and differences in the use of personal space and touching. Learning about these differences can help you adapt your messages to enhance understanding.

Differences in Working Collectively or Individually

We introduced the concept of individualism and collectivism in Chapter 6. We return to these concepts here because of the profound effect these cultural mindsets have on group and team communication. **Individualism** is the tendency to focus on individual achievement.[18] Most North Americans value individual accomplishment over group or team achievement. Canada, Great Britain, and Australia are nations that savour and celebrate individual accomplishment.

Collectivism emphasizes group or team accomplishment rather than individual achievement. Research suggests that the collectivist mindset is prevalent in Asian countries such as Japan, China, and Taiwan. Venezuela, Colombia, and Pakistan are other countries where people value collective accomplishments more than individual success.

These two perspectives have important implications for group and team collaboration. People who hold individualist cultural values may find it more challenging to work

Adapt

individualism
The tendency or preference to focus on individual achievement rather than on group or team accomplishments.

collectivism
The tendency or preference to focus on group, team, or collaborative achievement rather than on individual accomplishments.

TABLE 9.3   A Comparison of Individualism and Collectivism in Small Groups

Individualistic Assumptions	Collectivistic Assumptions
The best decisions are made by individuals.	The most effective decisions are made by teams.
Planning should be done by the leaders.	Planning is best done by the entire group.
Individuals should be rewarded.	Groups or teams should be rewarded.
Individuals should work primarily for themselves.	Individuals should work primarily for the team.
Healthy competition among group and team members is more important than teamwork.	Teamwork is more important than competition.
Meetings are for sharing information with individuals.	Meetings are for making group or team decisions.
To get something accomplished, you should work with individuals.	To get something accomplished, you should work with the entire group or team.
The prime objective of meetings is to advance your own ideas.	The prime objective of meetings is to reach consensus or agreement.
Group or team meetings are often perceived as a waste of time.	Group or team meetings are the best way to achieve a quality goal.

Source: Adapted from John Mole, *Mind Your Manners: Managing Business Cultures in Europe*, reprinted with permission of Nicholas Brealey Publishing. Copyright 1995.

collaboratively than people from collectivist cultures. Table 9.3 compares individualist and collectivist approaches to working in groups and teams.

⤏ Differences in the Use of Time

Mark was frustrated. He was sure the meeting was supposed to start at 11:00 A.M. He double-checked his notes. Yes, he was in the right place. And yes, the meeting was supposed to start at 11:00 A.M. But it was now 11:15 A.M., and no one else was there. Finally, about five minutes later, Gilbert arrived. Samantha arrived a few minutes later. Then Joe showed up about 11:30. "Where were you guys?" an exasperated Mark asked. "Oh, I thought you knew. When we say 11:00 A.M. in our organization, that means we'll actually start 20 or 30 minutes after that," said Joe. Gilbert chimed in with, "Yeah, doesn't everybody know that?" "Yes," said Samantha, "I'm sorry; we should have made it clear. The time for starting is just a general goal." Although Mark now had at least some insight, he was still somewhat frustrated and puzzled. Mark and his colleagues had different cultural assumptions about time.

Some people are **monochronic;** they like to do only one thing at a time, give more attention to deadlines and schedules, and make plans to use time efficiently. Others are more **polychronic;** they think about doing many things at a time, don't worry about deadlines and schedules, believe relationships are more important than work, change plans more frequently, and are less concerned about deadlines than are monochronic individuals.

People from North America and Northern Europe tend to be more monochronic; deadlines and timelines are valued. Latin Americans, Southern Europeans, and Middle Easterners are often more polychronic; deadlines and strict adherence to schedules are less important. Western cultures have a tendency to approach a discussion of problems in groups or teams in a more linear, step-by-step manner. Structuring, scheduling, and agendas are important. In Eastern cultures, such as China and Japan, problem-solving approaches follow a less structured, more narrative approach. One team of scholars found that North Americans tend to view time as having a definite beginning and ending, and

monochronic
Use of time that emphasizes doing one thing at a time, giving attention to deadlines and schedules, and using time efficiently.

polychronic
Use of time in which people may do many things at once, are not very concerned about deadlines and schedules, and consider relationships to be more important than work and meeting deadlines.

Verbal

COMMUNICATION and DIVERSITY

Gender Differences and Team Communication

Do men or women make better team leaders? This is an intriguing question. The answer is less intriguing: It depends. As in most of our discussion of diversity throughout this book, there are rarely instances when one group always outperforms another. A principle we have stressed throughout our discussion is that effective communicators adapt. Our research conclusions are also adapting to fit the times. More than 40 years ago, researchers claimed women were less likely to take on leadership positions; men were perceived to be more influential and confident in group leadership situations than women. Research in the late 1970s found that women were more open than men in accepting new ideas, nurturing interpersonal relationships within a group, and being attentive to and concerned about others. Males were viewed as being more dominant and controlling of the group conversation. Females, however, were

viewed as having a leadership style in sync with contemporary human-resource approaches to leadership. By the late 1980s differences in leadership between men and women were vanishing in the research. The research was making distinctions between biological gender (sex differences) and psychological gender (style of interacting with others). Research suggested that the most effective leader was the most adaptable and not locked into a specific set of expectations.[19] Recent research suggests that communication in groups and teams that is "task-relevant" (talk that is on task and helps the group accomplish its goal) is a key to perceived leadership effectiveness, regardless of a person's gender.[20] Who are better leaders, men or women? Evidence to support your answer depends on from which decade you draw your research support. Today, the most effective leaders are believed to be those who adapt to the situation.

believe that only one thing can or should be done at a time.[21] People from Latin American cultures, in contrast, are more comfortable working on multiple tasks simultaneously.

What should you do if you are in a group and you realize that group members have different assumptions about deadlines and getting the work done? Talk about it. Rather than seething and eventually becoming upset, talk with other group members about your observations. Don't attack or pounce on other team members and accuse them of being laggards, but do let them know some of your assumptions about how the work should be done.

Differences in the Use of Personal Space

Anthropologist Edward Hall noted that people from some cultures are more comfortable interacting at close distances and being touched; these are people from **high-contact cultures.** People from high-contact cultures tend to be from warmer climates, including Arabic, Hispanic, Indonesian, Mediterranean, Eastern European, and some Russian cultures. If you are from a cooler climate, you'll have a tendency to prefer less personal contact. People from Norway, Finland, Sweden, Germany, England, and Japan, and Anglo-Saxon North Americans fit the profile of low-contact cultures. Although being touched is a basic human need, people from **low-contact cultures** generally prefer less touch, like more space around them, and would rather talk to others from greater distances than people from high-contact cultures.[22] The preference people have for personal space is yet another difference to which we may need to adapt.

Edward Hall defined the different zones, or "bubbles," of personal space that we carry around us. These zones vary from culture to culture; the measures below apply to people from Canada, the United States, and Northern and Central Europe.[23]

- *The intimate zone (0 to 45 cm).* Because this zone is so close to our bodies, we reserve it for people we are intimate with. At this range we can touch each other and whisper to each other. Intrusions into this zone are generally experienced as unpleasant and disturbing, if not threatening.
- *The personal zone (45 cm to 1.2 m).* The personal zone is less intimate, but still within arm's length. It is reserved for family members and close personal friends.
- *The social zone (1.2 m to 3.6 m).* Most social and business interaction takes place in this zone. There are cultures (for example,

high-contact culture
Cultural preference for closer personal distances and personal touch when communicating with others.

low-contact culture
Cultural preference for greater personal distances and less personal touch when communicating with others.

Nonverbal

Hall's research about culture and personal space would predict that these friends prefer to keep a bit of distance betweeen them while talking.

ReCAP ←┈┈

Understanding Diversity in Groups and Teams: Adapting to Differences

PREFERENCES FOR WORKING TOGETHER OR ALONE	PREFERENCES FOR USING TIME	PREFERENCES FOR USING PERSONAL SPACE
Individualist: People prefer to work for individual accomplishment.	*Monochronic:* People are more comfortable doing one thing at a time and are sensitive to deadlines and schedules.	*High Contact:* People prefer closer distances and are more comfortable with touch.
Collectivist: People champion and prefer teamwork and team rewards.	*Polychronic:* People can do many things at once and are less sensitive to deadlines and schedules.	*Low Contact:* People prefer more personal space around them and are less comfortable with touch.

most Arab countries) where people prefer to conduct social and business interaction at closer range and do not distinguish between the personal and social zones.

- *The public zone (3.6 m and outward).* Not much interaction occurs in this zone. At 3.6 metres or more, people usually try to ignore each other. For instance, watch how people choose where to put their towel at a public outdoor swimming pool or on a beach. They keep their distance as long as possible because they are not planning to communicate with each other.

How does your preference for being touched or for personal space affect your communication in groups and teams? Preferences for use of personal space affect preferred seating arrangements in group and team meetings. Research suggests, for example, that Chinese people often prefer sitting side by side rather than across from one another.[24] North Americans usually like to have more personal space when interacting than do Latin Americans, Arabs, and Greeks.[25] And in some Middle Eastern countries, it is normal for many people to stand close enough to someone to smell his or her breath.[26]

The diverse nature of Canada calls for greater sensitivity to people's individual preferences regarding personal space. An effective communicator will become aware of these preferences and incorporate them into her or his communication style. Be aware of and sensitive to people's preferences for space and seating arrangement if you are leading a meeting or have some control of who sits where. It may be best to let group members determine their own seating preferences, rather than dictating who will sit where. Or, if during a group meeting you sense that the seating arrangement may be negatively affecting the discussion, either feel free to move or to ask others to make themselves more comfortable. In considering these research summaries, remember that not all people from a cultural or ethnic group communicate in the same way. Be mindful of these generalizations, but avoid making rigid stereotypical judgments about others.

Adapt

Aware

SUMMARY ⬇

Groups and teams are an ever-present aspect of our lives. Small-group communication is the transactive process of creating meaning among a small number of people (three to fifteen people) who share a common purpose, who feel a sense of belonging to the group, and who exert influence on one another. Groups and teams are similar in that they are a collection of a small number of people who meet to achieve a goal. A team can be differentiated from a group in that it is more highly organized, and the collaborative efforts are more coordinated to achieve the team goal. Groups exist for a variety of reasons. Some primary groups, such as families, exist to meet basic human needs; other types of groups include study groups, therapy groups, focus groups, problem-solving groups, and social groups.

Groups and teams are dynamic. This means that a variety of factors influence the ever-changing nature of what occurs when you interact with others in groups and teams. The role you assume in a group, the consistent way you communicate with others, influences your behaviour and the behaviour of others. There are three primary types of roles in small groups and teams: task roles—those that help the group do its work; social roles—those that help the group members relate to one another; and individual roles—roles that inappropriately focus on individual concerns rather than group concerns. Other aspects that affect the dynamic nature of groups and teams include norms (standards of what is normal or expected), rules (explicit statements about appropriate and inappropriate behaviour), status (a person's importance or prestige), power (the ability to influence others), cohesiveness (the degree of loyalty and attraction the group members feel toward one another), and interaction patterns (the consistent communication networks that emerge based upon who talks to whom).

Groups may sometimes seem to carry on a chaotic discussion of ideas, but researchers have noted that many (not all) groups experience predictable phases of what is discussed. During the orientation phase, group members get acquainted with both the task and one another. The second phase, conflict, occurs when group members recognize that they have differing ideas and opinions about both the group's task and procedures for accomplishing the task. The third phase, emergence, is evident when the group begins to make decisions and starts completing the task. The reinforcement phase occurs when the group has accomplished its task and takes some time to recognize and confirm the group's actions; the reinforcement phase may be brief, especially in groups that don't take time to celebrate their success or attend to the social dynamics of the group.

We ended the chapter by returning to one of our foundation principles: Effective communicators adapt. Because of the differences in cultural expectations, specifically in the emphasis on the individual or team, use of time, and use of space, group members and leaders need to be sensitive to these differences and adapt accordingly. In the next chapter we identify practical strategies to help you make decisions and solve problems as a group member, lead a group, or organize a meeting. Throughout our discussion, we will continue to interweave the five foundation principles that are fundamental to communicating with others, including in groups and teams.

PRINCIPLES FOR A LIFETIME

Aware

Principle 1: Be aware of your communication with yourself and others.

- Be knowledgeable of the definitions of and differences between groups and teams.
- Be aware of your role and the roles of others in groups and teams.
- Be aware of how you and your group develop and maintain group norms.
- Be mindful of how your power and the power of others influence group interaction.
- Be aware of the forces that affect group and team cohesiveness.
- Be aware of and sensitive to the stages of orientation, conflict, emergence, and reinforcement that influence group interaction.

Verbal

Principle 2: Effectively use and interpret verbal messages.

- Your use of verbal messages affects whether you perform task, social, or individual roles in a group.
- Verbal messages affect the establishment and maintenance of group rules and norms.
- Verbal messages shape and reflect a person's status in a group or team.
- A group member's power is reflected in the verbal messages a person uses.
- The stages of orientation, conflict, emergence, and reinforcement can be detected by listening to the verbal messages sent and received in a group.
- Verbal messages are the primary indicators of group interaction patterns.

Nonverbal

Principle 3: Effectively use and interpret nonverbal messages.

- Many norms in group and team interaction are unspoken; normative group behaviour is typically enacted nonverbally.
- A person's status in a group is reflected in the way the person uses space, touch, and eye contact.

- A cohesive group is evident from the way group members interact nonverbally; more enthusiastic vocal cues, closer personal distances, and eye contact often signify a cohesive group.
- Group members' use of time (monochronic or polychronic) is an important nonverbal element of a group's culture.
- Use of space and touch (high-contact or low-contact culture) is a reflection of group members' cultural preferences.

Listen
and
Respond

Principle 4: Listen and respond thoughtfully to others.

- A group member's role emerges from listening to others and interacting with other group members.
- Group norms are more easily recognized if group members listen to others.
- Cohesive group members reflect their loyalty and concern for others by listening and appropriately responding to other group members.
- Interaction patterns emerge as group members both speak and listen appropriately.

Adapt

Principle 5: Appropriately adapt messages to others.

- Be sensitive to the needs of your group so that you can adapt your messages to help the group achieve its goal.
- A group member's role is worked out jointly between the group member and the group by adapting to the needs of the group.
- Group members who adapt to group norms are more likely to be cohesive.
- Effective group members adapt to help the group become oriented to the task, manage conflict, facilitate emergent decisions, and reinforce appropriate group behaviour.
- Effective group members are sensitive and adapt to cultural differences of group members.

Discussion and Review

1. Define small-group communication and team communication. What are the differences and the similarities between the two?
2. Describe and provide examples of task, social, and individual group roles.
3. Identify and describe group norms.
4. Differentiate between the concepts of *status* and *power*.
5. What are the five bases of power discussed in this chapter?
6. What are strategies for enhancing group cohesiveness?
7. Define the communication patterns "wheel," "chain," and "all channel." What are the implications of these patterns on group productivity?
8. What are the stages of group development discussed in this chapter?
9. Identify how groups and teams have culturally different approaches to working individually and collectively, using time, and using space.

Developing Your Skills: Putting Principles into Practice

1. "Ice-Breaker" Activities: The following activities are designed to help you "break the ice" at initial group or team meetings.

   A. If you were in a gift shop, what gift would you buy for each member of the group? Discuss why you would buy the gift.

   B. If you could invite a famous person to join your group, whom would you invite and why?
   C. Draw or symbolize your "lifeline." Use symbols and pictures to illustrate the high and low points in your life; not only show your past, but also make some predictions about your future.
   D. Tell three things about yourself, one of which is false. Group members should guess which of the things you've disclosed about yourself is false. After the group has guessed, reveal what is true and not true about you.

   After you have completed one or more of these ice breakers, consider the following questions:

   1. How did your group experience the orientation phase? Did these activities help the group become oriented to one another?
   2. What norms emerged as group members participated in these activities?
   3. Can you identify the role or roles you assumed (task, social, individual) and the roles of other group members?
   4. What interaction patterns were evident in your group?

2. Agree–Disagree Statements: Read each statement once. Take four or five minutes to do this. Then, in small groups, try to reach consensus about each statement. Try especially to find reasons for differences of opinions. If your group cannot reach agreement or disagreement,

you may change the wording in any statement enough to promote unanimity. Mark as follows: "A" if you agree, "D" if you disagree.[27]

_____ 1. Despite its flaws, a meeting is the *best* way to get work done in an organization.

_____ 2. There are often occasions when an individual who is a part of a working team should do what he or she thinks is right, regardless of what the group has decided to do.

_____ 3. Sometimes it is necessary to change people in the direction you yourself think is right, even if they object.

_____ 4. It is sometimes necessary to ignore the feelings of others in order to reach a group decision.

_____ 5. When the leader is doing his or her best, one should not openly criticize or find fault with his or her conduct.

_____ 6. In most team conflicts, someone must win and someone must lose. That's the way conflict is.

_____ 7. Much time is wasted in talk, when everybody in the group has to be considered before making a decision.

_____ 8. Almost any job that can be done by a committee can be done better by having one individual responsible for the job.

_____ 9. Body language and nonverbal messages are more important than verbal messages when communicating with others in team meetings.

_____ 10. If people spend enough time together, they will find something to disagree about and will eventually become upset with one another.

_____ 11. Most hidden agendas are probably best kept hidden to ensure a positive social climate and manage conflict.

_____ 12. If you disagree with someone in a group, it is usually better to keep quiet than to get the group off-track with your personal difference of opinion.

_____ 13. When a team can't reach a decision, members should abide by the decision of the group leader if the leader is qualified and competent.

_____ 14. Some people produce more conflict and tension than others. These people should be restricted from decision-making meetings.

Source: Adapted from Steven A. Beebe and John T. Masterson, *Communicating in Small Groups: Principles and Practices* (Boston, MA: Allyn & Bacon, 2003).

3. Losing Your Job[28]

Your group represents a family with a take-home income of $65 000. You hear through the grapevine at work that because of organizational restructuring your entire department will be laid off within four months. It is probable that you will be without your monthly salary cheque in the very near future. You do have skills that could lead to income from consulting. You have $3000 in a bank savings account and a $5000 stock portfolio, but you also have $1500 charged to your credit cards. Because of the nature of your job, you pay Canada Customs and Revenue quarterly rather than in monthly payroll deductions. You have the following monthly budget:

20-year fixed mortgage	$1 000
Food	$600
Bank-financed car payment	$300
Clothing and personal items	$400
Miscellaneous	$500
University savings fund	$200
Pension fund	$300
Medical bills	$300

You are sure you will get a good job recommendation from your boss, yet it may take you four to six months to find work at a comparable salary. Rank the following strategies from the most- to least-important actions you should take immediately to prepare for the impending loss of your income.

A. Change your mortgage from a 20-year to a 15-year term. _____

B. Start a dramatic increase in your savings plan by re-evaluating your budget. _____

C. Transfer your car bank loan to a home equity loan. _____

D. Pay off charge cards. _____

E. Borrow more money from the bank. _____

F. Charge most of your food and living expenses to your credit card to help you save. _____

G. Quit adding money to your pension plan now. _____

H. Switch investments from stocks into a money market fund. _____

I. Skip your next income tax payment. _____

J. Increase your purchases of items you find on sale, such as clothes and food. _____

K. Start your own consulting practice. _____

L. Use this opportunity to go back to school and retrain for a higher-paying job. _____

Following the group discussion, consider one or more of the following questions:

- Did our group go through the phases of orientation, conflict, emergence, or reinforcement? Or did the group go through only one or two of these phases? Did the group get bogged down in one of the phases?
- What was the predominant pattern of communication? Did we use all channel, chain, or wheel? Were there any group deviates who influenced the communication pattern?
- What roles did group members assume? Were the roles appropriate for the group's task?
- What norms developed? Were the norms useful or unproductive?

4. Norms are standards for acceptable behaviour. Even though there are certain cultural standards of appropriate and inappropriate behaviour, acceptable conduct may vary from group to group. Several group member behaviours are listed below. For each behaviour, indicate the appropriateness or inappropriateness of the behaviour as a group norm. Use the following scale:

5 = Definitely appropriate as a norm
4 = Probably appropriate as a norm
3 = Uncertain whether appropriate as a norm
2 = Probably inappropriate as a norm
1 = Definitely inappropriate as a norm

_____ 1. Did not talk or participate in group discussion.
_____ 2. Talked about fight he or she had with roommate.
_____ 3. Disagreed with another group member.
_____ 4. Challenged the evidence used by another group member.
_____ 5. Interrupted two other group members who were talking.
_____ 6. Was often absent.
_____ 7. Asked for additional information to help clarify the purpose of the meeting.
_____ 8. Told other group members about a great movie that he or she saw last weekend.
_____ 9. Used obscene language and shouted at another group member.
_____ 10. Wore dressy clothes (dress shirt and tie for men or fashionable tailored dress for women).
_____ 11. Told group members that he or she did not have to abide by the decision of the group.
_____ 12. Told another group member that he or she was being rude and disruptive.
_____ 13. Brought research from an Internet search to provide evidence for a decision the group was making.
_____ 14. Frequently got up and walked around the room while other group members were talking.
_____ 15. Brought food to the group meeting but did not offer to share it with other group members.
_____ 16. Was usually 15 minutes late to group meetings.

Compare your responses with those of other group members to see whether you agree about what would be appropriate group norms.

Source: Adapted from Steven A. Beebe and John T. Masterson, *Communicating in Small Groups: Principles and Practices*. Boston, MA: Allyn & Bacon, 2003).

Never doubt that a small group of concerned citizens can change the world; it's the only thing that ever has.

— MARGARET MEAD

10 Enhancing Group and Team Performance

AFTER STUDYING THIS CHAPTER, YOU SHOULD BE ABLE TO

1. Identify five functions that effective group members perform.

2. List and describe the five steps of group problem solving (reflective thinking).

3. Compare and contrast trait, functional, styles, situational, and transformational group leadership.

4. Develop and use an agenda to ensure that meetings have appropriate structure.

5. Use strategies to maintain appropriate discussion and dialogue to ensure that meetings have appropriate interaction.

What's so great about groups? Why does every organization, from the Canadian government to the local parent/teacher association, use groups, teams, and committees to get something done? The simple fact is: Groups work. Collaborating with others produces clear benefits that just don't happen when you give a task to an individual. Research clearly supports the following conclusions:

- Groups and teams come up with more creative solutions to problems than a person working alone.
- Working with others in groups improves the comprehension of the ideas presented.
- Group and team members are more satisfied with the conclusions and recommendations if they participated in the discussion.
- Groups have more available information by tapping the experiences of group members.[1]

All of these advantages sound wonderful. But these benefits of collaboration don't just automatically happen when people work in groups and teams. And sometimes there are significant disadvantages to working collaboratively.[2] Overly talkative or insensitive, overbearing people may speak too long and dominate the discussion. There is also pressure to conform to what other group members are doing and saying—it can be challenging to stick up for your own ideas when everyone else sees issues differently. Some group members, for fear of not wanting to be either "weird" or wrong, will go along with the majority opinion, even if they know majority opinion is wrong. Another disadvantage to working in groups: Some group members will just sit back and wait for others to do the work. Finally, and perhaps the biggest disadvantage for many people, working in groups takes much more time than working individually. It takes time to talk and listen.

This chapter is designed to help you achieve the advantages of working in groups and minimize the disadvantages of working collaboratively. We can't claim that if you follow all of the strategies we suggest, your life will be free of unpleasant and unproductive group experiences. We do believe that group members who both understand how groups work (see Chapter 9) and know principles and strategies for enhancing the quality of group work are much more likely to avoid the pitfalls and reap the benefits of working in groups. Most groups will involve more time than working by yourself, but the benefit of improved quality of decision can far outweigh the time invested.

WHAT EFFECTIVE GROUP MEMBERS DO

"I hate groups," mutters an exasperated group member who has just finished a two-hour meeting in which nothing was accomplished. "Not me," chirps another group member. "Meetings and team projects are fun. I like the energy and productivity that occurs when we work together." What is it the second group member knows that the first one doesn't? As we noted at the start of the last chapter, working in groups can be frustrating, but it doesn't have to be if you and other group members learn some fundamental ways in which effective group members perform.

Underpinning all of the suggestions we offer in this chapter are the same five communication principles for a lifetime that we introduced in Chapter 1 and have been discussing throughout the book. Effective group members are aware of what they are doing. They effectively use verbal and nonverbal messages, listen and respond, and then appropriately adapt their messages to others.

Researchers have found that effective group members put these principles into practice by performing certain functions or behaviours that enhance the overall quality of a group. When these specific functions are not performed, the group is less effective. This **functional approach** to group communication attempts to describe the kinds of behaviours or functions that lead to better quality solutions and decisions in group deliberations.[3]

Researchers have spent several years trying to identify the key functions of high-performing groups and teams so that you can make sure you do them in your group. The primary means by which researchers have identified these functions is by comparing the way group members talk in high-performing groups with the way group members talk in low-performing groups.

functional approach
Leadership approach that identifies key communication functions or behaviours that should be performed during group discussion.

The essence of these functions involves group members being vigilant thinkers.[4] **Vigilant thinkers** pay attention to the *process* of how problems are solved. A vigilant thinker assesses, evaluates, and tests ideas; he or she effectively uses verbal messages and listens to what others are saying. Communication researcher Randy Hirokawa and his colleagues identified four essential questions that vigilant-thinking group members should consider:

1. What goal does the group want to achieve?
2. Does something in the present situation need to be changed?
3. What choices does the group have that will help achieve the goal?
4. What are the positive and negative implications of the choices?[5]

Even though these questions are usually discussed in the order listed, some productive, vigilant-thinking groups don't always follow this sequence.[6] What is clear, however, is that if one or more of these critical questions is not discussed, the group is less effective in solving problems and making wise decisions. These questions lead to the achievement of the following five critical functions that effective groups need to consider.

···⟩ Identify a Clear, Elevating Goal

What are we trying to do? Note that the first question that a vigilant-thinking group asks relates to the group's goal. Articulating a clear and elevating goal is one of the early functions that group members should ensure occurs in their group. According to one research team, the goal should not only be clear, but it should also be *elevating* or exciting to the group.[7] As we noted in Chapter 9, one of the hallmarks of an effectively functioning team is that the goal is clear and is something that could not be accomplished without team effort. It is important, therefore, for group members to ask and answer the question: "What's our clear, important goal?" The group needs to know that it is pursuing a goal that is significant; the group goal needs to be more exciting and important than an individual could achieve on his or her own. A professional baseball team during spring training camp may hang up signs in the locker room that say "World Series Champs!" A professional football team may see itself as a Grey Cup contender at the beginning of summer training camp. Groups, too, need to identify a clear, exciting, yet realistic goal that drives all aspects of what the group does. Without a goal and a results-driven structure to achieve the goal, group performance sputters.[8] A results-driven structure is one in which the actions of the group are on target to accomplish the goal rather than off topic and off target.

···⟩ Gather and Use Information Effectively

Computer programmers are familiar with the acronym GIGO: garbage in, garbage out. If you develop a computer program using bad information or a bad program command (garbage), you're likely to receive low-quality output (more garbage). Information is the fuel that makes a group function well. High-performing groups and teams don't just rely upon the unsupported opinions of group members; group members should conduct research and find relevant information to accomplish the goal. Effectively functioning groups ask, "Does something need to be changed?" They gather information and analyze the situation to answer that question.

If the group or team's purpose is to solve a problem, it gathers information to help analyze the problem. To analyze an issue, an effective group should do at least three things:

1. Gather the data, information, or evidence the group members need in order to make a decision.
2. Effectively communicate information and data to all group and team members.
3. Draw accurate conclusions from the data, evidence, and information for other group members.

As is true of other group-communication functions, group members who don't gather and use information effectively are more likely to make bad decisions. Having too little evidence— or no evidence at all—is one of the reasons groups sometimes fail to analyze their current situation correctly. Even if group members do have plenty of evidence, it may be bad evidence or they may not have tested the evidence to see whether it is true, accurate, or relevant.

vigilant thinker
A group member who pays attention to the process of how problems are solved, is sensitive to the need to make changes, identifies the goal of the group, identifies choices the group needs to make, and evaluates the positive and negative implications of the choices.

Verbal

Some tasks, such as creating a smooth concrete floor, cannot be completed without the cooperation of all the group members involved in the task.

⋯⟩ Develop Options

Another hallmark of an effectively functioning group is that group members generate many ideas and potential solutions *after* gathering information and analyzing a situation. Effective groups don't just settle on one or two ideas and then move on. They list multiple creative approaches.

Sometimes groups get stuck and ideas just don't flow. Rather than continuing to hammer away at the problem, the group may want to take a break from the stymying issues or knotty problems. Perhaps you've had a great idea come to you when you were taking a walk, driving, or doing some other mindless activity. Taking a break gives your mind a chance to thrash through some of the issues and generate a breakthrough solution. The principle of self-awareness operates here; become aware of the group's ability to generate high-quality ideas. Be sensitive to the group's need to take a fresh look at the problem or issue.

Aware

⋯⟩ Evaluate Ideas

High-performing groups know a good idea when they see it. They are able to evaluate evidence, opinions, assumptions, and solutions to separate good ideas from bad ideas. Low-performing groups are less discriminating. A group that is too eager to make a decision just to do the job without critically evaluating ideas usually comes up with lower-quality decisions.

An effectively functioning group examines the advantages and disadvantages of an idea, issue, or opinion.[9] When the group is zeroing in on a particular course of action, the effective group has at least one member who suggests, "Let's consider the positive and negative consequences of this decision." Research suggests that it's especially important to talk about the negative consequences of a specific proposal.[10] Some groups use a chalkboard or flip chart and make a written list of the pros and the cons. Groups that do this are more likely to come up with a better decision than groups that don't systematically evaluate the good and the bad aspects of a potential solution or decision.

⋯⟩ Develop Sensitivity toward Others

Most of the functions we've described so far focus on getting the work done effectively and efficiently; but group success is about more than just focusing on the task. Effectively

ReCAP ⟨⋯

What Effective Group and Team Members Do

GROUP FUNCTION	DESCRIPTION OF FUNCTION
Develop a Clear, Elevating Goal	Ensure the group has developed a clear, elevating, or important goal that anchors the purpose of group discussion.
Gather and Use Information Effectively	Conducting research and using accurate information is an important element in the deliberation of any group or team.
Generate Many Options	Effective groups expand the number of alternatives or options before choosing a course of action.
Evaluate Ideas	Effective groups or teams examine the pros or cons of an option before implementing the strategy.
Develop Sensitivity toward Others	Group members do more than focus on the task; they express sensitivity to the needs and concerns of group members by using appropriate verbal and nonverbal messages, listening, responding, and adapting messages to others.

functioning groups also are sensitive to the needs of group members. They listen and are sensitive to one another. They are aware of how the comments they make might be perceived by group members. Effectively functioning group members also make comments that confirm the value of others' contributions and nonverbally show that they are genuinely interested in what others are saying. In Chapters 7 and 8, we presented several skills and concepts that can enhance the quality of interpersonal relationships.

Effective group members balance concern for the task with concern for the feelings of others. Being too task-oriented is not beneficial to the functioning of a group. Group members also listen to what each group member has to say—even members who may hold a minority opinion. One of the benefits of working in a group comes from hearing a variety of ideas. If opinions of others are quickly squelched because they are not what most other groups think or believe, the group loses the power of many different points of view.

Being sensitive to others also involves effectively interpreting nonverbal messages. The group climate is influenced by the positive support expressed through eye contact, responsive facial expressions, and a positive tone of voice.

STRUCTURING GROUP AND TEAM PROBLEM SOLVING

"Just tell me what to do. What I want to know is, what techniques will help me solve the problem? Make it simple." We usually want simple techniques or steps that will help us achieve our goal. The truth is, however, that there are no magic techniques that will enable a group or team always to come up with the right solution to a problem.

The functional approach to group problem solving that we just discussed is based on the assumption that high-performing groups and teams perform certain functions or communication behaviours that ineffective groups and teams don't enact. We now turn our attention to a more structured, prescriptive approach to solving problems. You will note some obvious similarities between the two approaches. But the more prescriptive approach to group problem solving we present now offers a sequence of steps and techniques to help your group stay on task and remain productive while still being sensitive to group members. Just as a prescription from your doctor is a specific dose of medicine that is given to help solve a specific ailment, a prescriptive approach to problem solving is based on the assumption that there are specific things you can do to enhance the communication health of the group.

Communication researcher Arthur Van Gundy suggests that problems can be classified on a continuum of *structured* to *unstructured*.[11] A structured problem is one to which there is a single best correct solution. A math problem is structured in the sense that there is one right answer. An unstructured problem is one in which there is high uncertainty about how to solve the problem; there is little information about how to proceed, and the group is confused. Problems such as how to "save" social security, how to solve the parking problem on campus, or how to increase teachers' salaries without raising taxes are examples of unstructured problems; there is more than one way to tackle the problem. The more uncertainty there is (or the more unstructured the nature of the problem), the greater the need for a structured approach to help the group manage its uncertainty. Leaders who give the group structure by setting goals, keeping track of the time, and suggesting procedures enhance the group's perceived effectiveness.

More than 70 methods or sequences of prescriptive steps and techniques have been identified for structuring problem solving in groups and teams.[12] Several researchers have sought to identify the sequence that works best. Their conclusion? *No one single prescriptive method or step works best in every situation. But having some structured sequence of steps or questions works better than having no structure.*[13]

Structure is the way a group or team discussion is organized to follow a prescribed agenda. Because of the number of people working together to solve a problem, groups need structure to avoid hopping from topic to topic. According to one researcher, groups left to their own free-ranging discussion change topics about once a minute.[14]

Can a group have too much structure? Yes. If you've been to a meeting or group discussion that seemed more like a seminar than an interactive discussion, then there was too

structure
The way a group or team discussion is organized, focusing on the group's agenda and the task that needs to be achieved.

much structure. If the meeting is so controlled that one or two people do most of the talking, you're not at a meeting, you're at a speech. The goal is to balance the amount of structure with group interaction.

Interaction includes give-and-take discussion and the responsiveness group members have to the comments of others. In an interactive group, there are fewer long utterances; more people are contributing; more people are taking turns to talk. In a highly structured meeting, there is more control over who talks, about what, and for how long; overly structured meetings have less interaction. As suggested in Figure 10.1, the key is to find the right balance between structure and interaction. Too much interaction, and the group experiences the chaos of unbridled talk that may not be focused; group and team members may need help in structuring or focusing on one idea at a time, rather than bouncing from topic to topic. Too much structure, however, and the group loses the freedom to listen and respond with sensitivity to what others are saying. An overly structured meeting occurs when one or only a handful of people controls who says what; there's not much reaction to what is said.

What follows is a standard agenda of steps that can help you develop a sequence of things group members should be talking about. These five steps are inspired by educator and philosophy John Dewey, who in 1910 wrote a book called *How We Think*.[15] His book described how individuals go about the problem-solving process; in essence, he described the scientific method of defining and analyzing a problem, identifying solutions, picking a solution, and putting the solution into practice that scientists still use to solve problems. He called this process **reflective thinking.** We present these steps here, not as a one-size-fits-all prescription that you should always follow, but as a way of structuring the problem-solving process to manage uncertainty and also to ensure that the key functions we talked about earlier are included in your discussion. In addition to describing each step of the reflective thinking process, we present several techniques to help you structure discussion.

⋯⟩ Step 1: Identify and Define the Problem

"What's your problem?" Groups work best when they have identified a clear, elevating goal that unites their problem-solving effort. To reach a clear statement of the problem, consider asking the following questions:

- What is the specific problem that concerns us?
- What do we want more of, or less of?
- What terms, concepts, or ideas do we need to define in order to understand the problem?
- Who is harmed by the problem?
- When do the harmful effects of the problem occur?

Most group experts recommend that an effective way to give your problem-solving task appropriate structure is to phrase your problem in the form of a policy question. A policy question is phrased so that the group will recommend some action (policy) to eliminate,

interaction
The talk or give-and-take dialogue that occurs during group discussion.

Verbal

reflective thinking
Steps that describe how to structure a problem-solving process based on the scientific method of investigating a problem.

FIGURE 10.1 Groups Need a Balance of Structure and Interaction

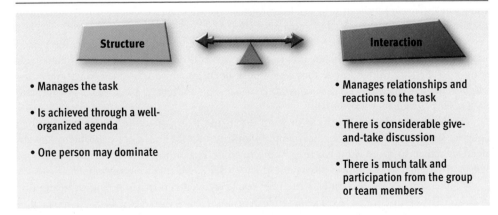

reduce, or manage the problem. Policy questions begin with the words "What should be done about…" or "What could be done to improve…"

Here are some examples:

- What should be done to lower the cost of tuition at our university?
- What could be done to decrease property taxes in our city?
- What should be done to make prescription drugs more affordable for all Canadian citizens?

One specific technique for structuring the discussion to identify a problem is to use the Journalist's Six Questions method.[16] Most news reporters are taught to include the answers to six questions when writing a news report. The questions are Who? What? When? Where? Why? and How? Using a chart like the one in Figure 10.2, the group poses these six questions about the problem the group has identified and then writes a response to each question. This method can help further define and limit the problem, and can also help the group move to the next step in the process—analyze the problem. Whatever method or technique a group uses, it is essential that it knows precisely what problem it is trying to solve.

⋯⟩ Step 2: Analyze the Problem

To analyze something is to break it down into smaller pieces; to analyze a problem is to consider the causes, effects, symptoms, history, and other information that will inform the group about how to best solve the problem. Many groups want to cut to the chase quickly and start spinning out solutions, without taking the time to analyze the problem thoroughly. Resist this temptation. Analyzing the problem well is an important prerequisite to an effective solution. When analyzing a problem, group members will need to spend time in the library or on the Internet to gather information and determine how experts view the problem. Essential questions that can help you analyze problems include the following:

- How long has the problem been in existence?
- How widespread is the problem?
- What are the causes of the problem?
- What are the effects of the problem?
- What are the symptoms of the problem?
- Who is harmed by the problem?
- What methods already exist for managing the problem?
- What are the limitations of existing methods?
- What obstacles keep the group from achieving the goal?

In addition to considering these questions, group members should develop criteria for an acceptable solution. **Criteria** are standards or goals for an acceptable solution to the problem. Identifying clear criteria can help you spot a good solution when you see one. Sample criteria for problems include the following:

criteria
Standards for an acceptable solution.

- The solution should be inexpensive, not to exceed 5% of our budget.
- The solution should be implemented by a certain date.
- The solution should be agreed on by all group members.
- The solution should be agreed on by all persons affected by our recommendations.

FIGURE 10.2 Journalist's Six Questions

Who?	
What?	
When?	
Where?	
Why?	
How ?	

force field analysis technique

A method of analyzing a problem or issue by identifying (1) those forces that increase the likelihood that the desired goal will occur (driving forces) and (2) those forces that decrease the probability that the goal will occur (restraining forces).

Don't rely on your memory when you verbalize criteria. Write the list of criteria your group has identified; include it in the minutes or notes that summarize the meeting, or write them on a chalkboard or flip chart.

After you have gathered information and developed criteria, your group may need to develop a systematic way of analyzing the information you've gathered. One technique that can help structure the analysis of your problem and also help your team identify criteria is the **force field analysis technique.**[17] This technique works best when your group has identified a clear goal and needs to assess what is happening now that would increase the probability that the goal will be achieved.

Here's how to conduct a force field analysis. After identifying a goal, the group lists all of the forces currently at work that would help attain the goal. Then the group does just the opposite: It identifies forces that are keeping the group from achieving the goal. When complete, the analysis can help the group see what needs to be increased (the forces that currently favour attaining the goal) and what needs to be decreased (the forces working against the goal). Figure 10.3 shows an example of a group that wanted to increase the number of students who volunteer for community projects; the goal is written on the top. On the left side of the diagram is a list of all of the factors that the group identified as increasing the chances of achieving the goal—getting more students to volunteer. On the right side is a list of the restraining forces, or forces that keep the group from achieving the goal. The task of the group in developing solutions is now clear: increase the driving forces and decrease the restraining forces.

One final observation: Be careful not to spend so much time overanalyzing data that you forget the purpose of the group—to solve the problem. Beware of "the killer inch" problem. This occurs when group members agree on the major points but are distracted by minor details; they've travelled a long way to reach their goal but get distracted in the last inch of the journey. Avoid analysis paralysis.

Step 3: Generate Creative Solutions

brainstorming

A method of helping a group generate many possible solutions to a problem by withholding evaluation while group members suggest ideas; ideas are evaluated after suggestions have been offered.

You've now identified a specific problem, analyzed its causes and history, and are ready to identify possible ways to solve the problem. The classic technique to identify possible solutions is called **brainstorming.** It was developed by an advertising executive more than 40 years ago to encourage a group to be creative.[18] You've probably already used this technique before. Many groups, however, don't use the technique effectively.

FIGURE 10.3   Force Field Analysis

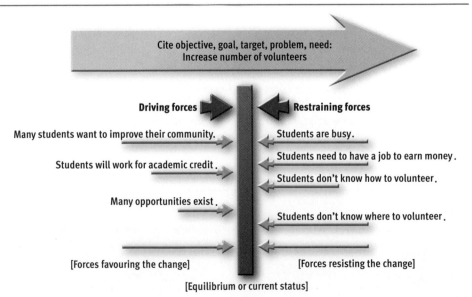

The key to make brainstorming work—to generate many creative ideas—is to *separate the generation of ideas from the evaluation of ideas.* This means group members are supposed to feel free to offer ideas without fear of criticism, snickering, or being made to feel foolish. Reality, however, may be quite different. When group members start suggesting ideas, there may be either verbal or, more likely, nonverbal evaluation of ideas. People may laugh at the more offbeat suggestions; or, when someone announces a suggestion, others may frown, sneer, or voice an editorial comment. Another subtle form of evaluation occurs when some group ideas are praised and some are not. Group members whose ideas are not praised may feel disconfirmed, that their idea was stupid. Clearly, when ideas are evaluated, brainstorming doesn't work well. Members may be reluctant to share ideas if those ideas will be evaluated. This is especially true of group members who are shy or uncomfortable talking in a group; these people, however, may have great ideas that need to be shared. The key to making brainstorming work is to separate the generation of ideas from the evaluation of ideas.

Barry loves to go around brainstorming.

EALLARD STREET copyright © Van Amarongen. Reprinted with permission of Creators Syndicate.

One solution to this problem is to have a period of **silent brainstorming** before members share their ideas verbally. Another name for silent brainstorming is **nominal group technique.**[19] For a few moments, people work individually so they are a group in name only (hence the name *nominal group technique*). After group members have identified some responses individually, they share them with the group.

The same rules of brainstorming still apply. Those rules include the following:

Verbal
Nonverbal

- Set aside judgments and criticism when people offer ideas.
- Think of as many ideas as possible; volume is important.
- Piggyback off of someone else's idea.
- Try to identify one or more zany or wild ideas—this triggers creativity and may lead to someone else adapting or taming down the idea.
- Record the ideas on a flip chart or chalkboard when people share them. It's usually best to go around the group one at a time to have group members share what they have written down.
- Evaluate the ideas after all of the group members have finished sharing.

silent brainstorming
A method used to generate creative ideas; group members follow the brainstorming method except that they write ideas on paper before sharing their ideas with the group.

nominal group technique
Group members work individually to write down creative ideas before meeting together face to face to share their ideas.

ReCAP

Brainstorming Steps

1. Select a problem that needs to be solved.
2. Discuss the history, causes, and background of the problem. Make sure the group knows precisely what options are needed.
3. Tell the group to develop a creative mindset.
   - Put aside judgments and evaluations.
   - Stress quantity of ideas.
   - Avoid criticizing ideas, including your own ideas.
   - Try to come up with one or more wild ideas—stretch your imagination; it's easier to modify wild ideas.
   - It's okay to piggyback off someone else's ideas.
4. Start brainstorming. Give the group a time limit. To reduce the possibility of evaluating ideas, consider using a period of silent brainstorming.
5. Write all of the ideas on the board or flip chart.
6. Keep reminding the group not to evaluate the ideas of others when first expressed.
7. Evaluate the ideas after all ideas have been presented.

→•← COMMUNICATION and TECHNOLOGY

E-Brainstorming

Computer technology makes electronic applications of brainstorming possible. Electronic brainstorming (e-brainstorming) is a technique that helps a team or group to creatively generate many solutions by typing ideas at a computer keyboard. The ideas typed by the electronically linked group are displayed on a screen so that all group members can see the ideas that have been generated and can piggyback off those ideas. The screen can be a small area of the individual computer screen or one large screen that is visible to all team members; electronic brainstorming can occur when all group members are in the same room or computer lab or when they are at computers in other places such as at home or in different offices.

Is e-brainstorming effective? Research suggests it is.[20] E-brainstorming groups come up with more ideas than do groups that meet face to face. Some researchers surmise that electronic brainstorming results in more ideas because the ideas are generated anonymously; group members don't have to worry about being criticized for suggesting a wacky or wild idea.[21] They're less likely to be criticized because group members don't have to know whether they are critiquing an idea that was suggested by the boss or by the newest member of the organization. One of the chief virtues of electronic brainstorming is that more ideas are likely to be generated. When brainstorming, it is desirable to have many ideas, even the wild and wacky ones that can be tamed down later.

One of the disadvantages to electronic brainstorming is the need to have access to the appropriate software and a networked computer system. But when the goal is to generate lots of ideas, electronic brainstorming seems to be an effective method of helping groups and teams develop creative options.

You may ask group members to do some individual brainstorming before they come to the group meeting. For example, you could say, "Each group member should bring five or ten suggestions for solving our problem." Or you could just invite group members to brainstorm ideas silently for a few minutes and then get into small groups to share ideas and piggyback off of the ideas. If everyone has e-mail access, ask for group members to do some private brainstorming and e-mail their responses to either the leader or other group members. Another creative way to have group members generate ideas is to have group members first write each idea or suggestion on a Post-it Note®, those small, self-sticking pieces of paper.[22] Once the ideas are on the Post-it Notes®, group members could stick them to the wall and then arrange them in groups. Seeing the ideas of other group members may trigger additional creative ideas from the group. The goal is to separate generating or listing ideas from critiquing the ideas. When those two parts of brainstorming get mixed together, fewer ideas flow because of the concern group members may have of being criticized.

→ Step 4: Select the Best Solution

The next step is to evaluate the ideas your group has identified and pick the best solution. The group now takes the long list of ideas generated and determines which ones best meet the criteria you identified when you analyzed the problem. You also determine which solutions best achieve the clear, elevating goal you identified. This means it's really important that you have both a clear goal and specific criteria—without them, it will be difficult to spot a good solution when you see it.

It is usually easier for groups to expand alternatives (brainstorm) than it is to narrow alternatives. The methods used by groups to whittle a long list down to a manageable number for more serious debate include these five:

1. *Decision by expert.* Let someone who has high credibility narrow the list.
2. *Rank.* Tell group members to rank their top five choices from 1 to 5.
3. *Rate.* Ask group members to evaluate each solution on a scale from 1 to 5; the solutions rated best get the most serious discussion.
4. *Majority vote.* Group members simply vote for the ones they like.
5. *Consensus.* Group members seek a solution that all group or team members can accept.

consensus
An agreement that all members of a group or team support an idea, proposal, or solution.

Consensus occurs when there is enough support so that group members will abide by the decision. Consensus doesn't mean everyone agrees enthusiastically and completely with what the group has decided—but at least group members won't stand in the way of what the group has decided. Reaching a consensus decision has the advantage that all group members can verbalize support for the decision. But reaching consensus takes time.

Three primary strategies can help groups reach consensus:

1. *Be goal oriented.* Keep the outcomes in mind as you talk. Because groups often bounce from topic to topic, it's important to keep the group oriented toward the goal. When you see the group starting to stray from its task, remind the group what the goals are. It also helps to write ideas and facts on a flip chart or chalkboard; this helps keep groups focused.
2. *Listen.* Work to clarify misunderstandings. When you do agree with something that is said, say so. Maintain eye contact with the speaker and give him or her your full attention.
3. *Promote honest dialogue and discussion.* A true consensus is more likely to occur if many ideas are shared and group members don't just give in to avoid conflict.

Listen and Respond

Table 10.1 compares what effective group members should do to achieve consensus with ineffective strategies for reaching agreement.

Be cautious if all group members agree too quickly. You may be experiencing groupthink instead of consensus. **Groupthink** occurs when group members seemingly agree but they primarily just want to avoid conflict. On the surface, it seems as though group members have reached consensus—but it's an illusion of agreement. Another way of describing groupthink is as an ineffective consensus; too little disagreement often reduces the quality of group decisions. If a group does not seriously examine the pros and cons of an idea, it's likely that the quality of the decision will suffer because the group has not used its full power to analyze and evaluate ideas.

Failure to test ideas and the resulting groupthink can have serious consequences. Wrong, dangerous, or stupid decisions can be the result. As reported by CBC News in January 2002, "according to a judicial inquiry report about Walkerton, Ontario's fatal

groupthink
A faulty sense of agreement that occurs when members of a group fail to challenge an idea; a false consensus; conflict is minimized and group members do not express concerns or reservations about an idea or proposal.

TABLE 10.1 Suggestions for Reaching Group and Team Consensus

Effective Group Members	Ineffective Group Members
Keep the Group Oriented toward Its Goal	
Remind the group what the goal is.	Go off on tangents and do not stay focused on the agenda.
Write facts and key ideas on a flip chart or chalkboard.	Rely on oral summaries or use no summaries to keep group members focused on the goal.
Talk about the discussion process; ask questions that keep the group focused on the agenda.	Do little to help summarize or clarify group discussion.
Listen to the Ideas of Others	
Clarify misunderstandings.	Do not clarify misunderstandings or check to see whether their message is understood.
Emphasize areas of agreement.	Ignore areas of agreement.
Maintain eye contact when listening to someone and remain focused on the speaker.	Do not have eye contact with the speaker and do not focus attention on the speaker.
Promote Honest Dialogue and Discussion	
Seek out differences of opinion.	Do not seek other opinions from group members.
Do not change their minds quickly to avoid conflict.	Quickly agree with other group members to avoid conflict.
Try to involve everyone in the discussion.	Permit one person to talk too much and dominate the conversation.

Source: Adapted from Steven A. Beebe and John T. Masterson, Communicating in *Small Groups: Principles and Practices* (New York: Longman, 2003).

"All those in favor say 'Aye.'"
"Aye."
"Aye."
"Aye."
"Aye."
"Aye."

E. coli outbreak, the most serious case of water contamination in Canadian history could have been prevented by proper chlorination of drinking water. According to this news coverage a number of things occurred: a lack of chlorine testing and reporting promoted contamination; the Ontario Government failed to make reporting of positive tests for contamination mandatory when water testing was privatized in 1996; Government cuts at the province's Environment Ministry made it less capable of identifying and dealing with problems at Walkerton's water utility."[23] During discussions on this issue, groupthink occurred—no one challenged the decisions being made. Tragically, seven people died and more than 2300 became ill. Some people, particularly children, may endure lasting effects as a result of the water contamination.

What causes groupthink? Sometimes it occurs because group members may not be particularly interested in the topic, or the group may just be tired and wants to get on with other work. If a group has a highly revered leader, someone with high status whom all group members respect, the group is more likely to agree with the leader, rather than test and challenge the leader's ideas. Groupthink also occurs when group members feel they can do no wrong; they feel invincible. So rather than taking time to test and evaluate ideas, the group may quickly decide that their decision is a good one. In summary, groupthink is most likely to occur when (1) the group feels apathetic about its task; (2) group members don't expect to be successful; (3) one group member has very high credibility—group members tend to believe what he or she says; (4) one group member is very persuasive; and (5) group members don't usually challenge ideas—it's expected that group members will agree with one another.[24] Be on the lookout for these symptoms in your groups and teams.

To overcome groupthink, consider the following strategies:[25]

- Don't agree with someone just because he or she has high status; examine the ideas of others carefully, regardless of their position.
- Consider asking someone from outside the group to evaluate the group's decisions and decision-making process.

ETHICAL PROBE

Ashley doesn't like to disagree with other group members. She consistently tries to find something positive or pleasant to say about others' comments. When she does disagree with an idea or suggestion of another group member, she usually doesn't voice her opinion. Is it ethical to remain silent when you actually disagree with an idea suggested? How can such disagreement lead to groupthink? Are there times when it is best to keep quiet, rather than express disagreement that could escalate to conflict?

ReCAP

Top Six Reasons Groups and Teams Sometimes Make Stupid Decisions

No Common Goal	Group does not begin with the end in mind—no collective vision.
Analysis Paralysis	Team members may overanalyze unimportant, off-task details; talk is valued more than action.
Jumping to Solutions	People propose solutions before the facts are known.
Groupthink	Group and team members agree too quickly just to "get on with it"—ideas are not questioned or challenged.
Topic Hopping	There is a lack of agenda and structure; discussion is not focused on the goal.
Killer Inch	Group and team members agree on major points, but argue over minor details.

- Assign someone to be a devil's advocate—to look for disadvantages to a proposed idea.
- Ask group members to break into smaller teams or dyads to consider both the pros and the cons of a proposed solution.

An easy way to structure this discussion is to use a T chart like the one in Figure 10.4. Simply write the possible solution at the top of the chart (on a flip chart, chalkboard, or transparency using an overhead projector) and then list both the pros and the cons. This technique will help you look at the positive and negative consequences of an action before you leap into a specific recommendation.

Step 5: Take Action

Once you have identified your solution(s), your group needs to consider the question "Will it work?" You may want to do a pilot test (practice test) or ask a small group of people what they think of your idea before you "go public" with it. Bouncing your proposed solution off of an expert and checking to see whether the solution has been successful when others may have adopted it can help you test the solution's effectiveness.

If your group not only has to identify a solution, but also has to put it into action, your group will need structure to make sure that details don't fall through the cracks in getting the job done. Perhaps you know the people in the following story:

> This is a story about four people: Everybody, Somebody, Anybody, and Nobody. There was an important job to be done and Everybody was asked to do it. Everybody was sure Somebody would do it. Anybody could have done it but Nobody did it. Somebody got angry about that because it was Everybody's job. Everybody thought Anybody could do it but Nobody realized that Everybody wouldn't do it. It ended up that Everybody blamed Somebody when actually Nobody asked Anybody.

Make a written list of who should do what. Follow up at the next group meeting to see whether the assignments have been completed. Effective groups and teams develop an action plan and periodically review it to make sure Anybody asked Somebody.

ENHANCING GROUP AND TEAM LEADERSHIP

Leadership is the ability of a person to influence others through communication. Some view a leader as someone who delegates and directs the group. Others see a leader as someone who is primarily responsible for ensuring that whatever task is assigned or

Verbal

ETHICAL PROBE

Ann liked to volunteer to work on community projects. She enjoyed working with others to solve important problems that affected people's lives. During group meetings she would often volunteer to do a specific task or project but would not always carry through on the work. She thought that because she was a volunteer, she would do what she could, but not be overly worried if she didn't finish her task. She wasn't being paid, so she figured there was no major harm done if she didn't do the work. Have you worked on a team project with people like Ann? If you were a member of Ann's group, would you talk with her about her lack of follow-through? What would you say to her that doesn't dampen her enthusiasm for volunteering but also addresses the need to follow through on what she volunteers to do?

leadership
Communication that influences the behaviour of others toward a desired goal.

FIGURE 10.4 T-Chart

Pros	Cons

Although Beverley McLachlin, Chief Justice of the Supreme Court of Canada, may have been born with many of the traits that make her an effective leader, she also has to work at maintaining communication skills that facilitate teamwork.

trait approach to leadership
Leadership approach that identifies specific qualities or characteristics of effective leaders.

functional approach to leadership
Leadership approach that identifies the key task and process duties that need to be performed in a group.

task functions
Leadership behaviours that help accomplish the job the group is doing.

designed by the group is completed. Actually, most groups have many leaders—not just one person who influences others. In fact, each group or team member undoubtedly influences what the group does or does not achieve. The following five approaches present the prevailing insights about how effective leaders lead.

····⟩ Trait Approach

Are leaders born or made? The **trait approach to leadership** suggests that there are certain attributes or traits that make leaders. According to this approach, if you are born with these traits or if you cultivate leadership skills, then you will be a leader. Researchers have identified intelligence, confidence, social skills, general administrative skill, physical energy, and enthusiasm as some of the traits effective leaders possess.[26] Although many leaders do seem to have traits or special skills that can enhance their ability to influence others, just having these traits does not mean you will be an effective leader. Many of these attributes that researchers have found may be important, but they are not sufficient to make a leader effective. If you are looking for someone to be a leader, you may want to find someone who is intelligent, confident, and has good verbal skills; but these traits alone will not ensure effective leadership behaviour. Leadership is more complicated than that.

····⟩ Functional Approach

Rather than identifying personality characteristics or other traits, the **functional approach to leadership** categorizes the essential leadership behaviours or functions that need to be performed to enhance the workings of the group. According to the functional approach, there are two broad leadership functions: (1) task functions and (2) process functions. These two functions should look familiar. They are similar to the types of group roles that we discussed in the last chapter.

Task functions include behaviours that help the group or team get the work done. Whether the leader is appointed or elected, one of the responsibilities of leaders is to ensure that the group completes the task it is tackling. The functional approach to leadership suggests that several people can perform leadership functions.

One of the task functions of a leader is to process the work; groups need leaders to help the group get the job done. These are some of the jobs that often need to be done:

- Helping to set the group's agenda
- Recording what the group does
- Determining when the meeting begins and ends
- Preparing and distributing handouts
- Initiating or proposing new ideas
- Seeking and giving information
- Suggesting options
- Elaborating on the ideas of others
- Evaluating ideas

Listen and Respond   Nonverbal

In most groups, these key functions are assumed by many if not most group members. A group member who rarely helps with any of these tasks often earns the uncoveted title of "slacker."

The second major function leaders assume in groups are **process functions.** Process leaders help maintain a harmonious group climate by encouraging amiable relationships in a group. They seek to maintain a friendly environment that also promotes honest, frank discussion. As we noted in Chapter 9, conflict is a normal and expected part of working with others. It would be unusual if there were no conflict. Process leaders are skilled at "people skills." They sensitively listen to others and are observant of nonverbal cues. They focus on managing relationships by adapting to the needs of individual members, whereas task leaders focus on the work. A single person can perform both essential functions. But just as with task leadership, more than likely, several people will help maintain the group's process. Specific process roles include the following:

process functions
Leadership behaviours that help maintain a positive group climate.

- Energizing the team by encouraging team members to keep at it
- Mediating conflict
- Compromising or helping others to compromise
- Gatekeeping: monitoring discussion to ensure that some members don't talk too much and others too little

In most groups or teams, these process roles are not formally assigned. Although some of the task group functions may be explicitly assigned to others ("Daria, would you make copies of this report?"), process roles are assumed when needed. These roles usually emerge, based on the needs of the group and the personality, skills, sensitivity, and past experiences of the group members who are present. It is unlikely that you will start a meeting by saying, "Okay, Janice, you're in charge of settling the arguments between Ken and Anwar. And Vijay, you try to encourage Nadia and Russell to talk more." Effective leaders are on the lookout for opportunities to enhance the overall climate of the group; they try to catch people doing something right and then offer sincere praise and recognition.

⋯⟩ Styles Approach

The **styles approach to leadership** suggests that leaders operate in one of three primary styles: (1) authoritarian, (2) democratic, and (3) laissez-faire. The methods used to influence group members usually fall into one of these broad categories, outlined in Table 10.2 on page 234.[27]

Authoritarian leaders influence by giving orders and controlling others. Dictators and military officers assume this leadership style. However, you don't have to be in the military or in a dictatorship to experience an authoritarian leadership style. Perhaps you've been in a group and mumbled, "Who put *her* in charge?" Or maybe you have been in a group, observed that action needed to be taken, and asked someone to do what you thought was needed. As we discussed, groups need a certain amount of structure. The authoritarian leader assumes he or she knows the type and amount of structure the group needs and proceeds to tell others what to do. Authoritarian leaders may be self-aware and use appropriate verbal and nonverbal messages, but they are not always known for listening and responding to others; they also may not be worried about adapting their messages to those whom they lead. They often speak and expect others to follow.

styles leadership
Leadership approach that identifies three methods of interacting when leading others: authoritarian or directive, democratic, and laissez-faire.

authoritarian leader
One who leads by directing, controlling, telling, and ordering others.

Adapt   Aware
Listen and   Verbal
Respond   Nonverbal

TABLE 10.2   Leadership Styles

Authoritarian	Democratic	Laissez-Faire
The leader makes all policy decisions.	The leader discusses all policy decisions with group members. The group makes decisions by consensus.	The leader gives minimal direction to discussions of policy decisions. Group members must initiate discussions about policy and procedures.
The leader determines what will happen one step at a time; future steps are unclear or uncertain.	The group discusses what steps need to be taken. Group members work together to develop both short-term and long-term actions.	The leader may supply information about what steps to be taken, if asked. The leader does not volunteer information.
The leader tells people what to do.	The leader serves as a facilitator to develop a collaborative approach to how work should be accomplished.	The leader does not participate in making work assignments.

democratic leader
A person who leads by developing a consensus among group members; asks for input and uses the input of others when leading and making decisions.

laissez-faire leader
A person who fails to lead, or who leads or exerts influence only when asked or directed by the group.

Adapt

situational leader
A leader who gauges how to lead based on such factors as the quality of the relationship among group members, the power of the leader, the nature of the task, and the maturity of the group.

The **democratic leader,** as you might guess from the name, consults with the group before issuing edicts. The democratic leader listens and adapts messages to others. This type of leader seeks to join in the process of influencing without bulldozing or shoving the group into action it may resent. Sometimes formal votes are taken in larger groups or assemblies; but in smaller groups, the leader or leaders will gauge the reaction of the group through dialogue and nonverbal cues. The democratic leader will lead by developing a consensus decision, rather than telling people what to do or think.

The **laissez-faire leader** takes a hands-off, laid-back approach to influencing. This type of leader shies away from actively influencing the group. He or she influences only when pushed to lead. Like the authoritarian leader, this type of leader often does not adapt to the needs of the group. This leadership approach is easiest to spot when there is an elected or appointed leader who won't lead. Sometimes the laissez-faire leader fears making a mistake. Other times this leader just wants to be liked and doesn't want to ruffle anyone's feathers. But as the slogan goes: Not to decide is to decide. The laissez-faire leader is influencing the group by his or her silence or inactivity. The team may have uncertainty to unravel, but the laissez-faire leader is reluctant to act.

Which leadership style works best? It depends. During times of crisis, the group needs a decisive leader who can help manage uncertainty and provide appropriate structure. During a military battle, the commander doesn't usually ask for a democratic vote; someone needs to lead the group to take decisive action. If the group's task is to solve a problem or make a decision collaboratively, then the democratic leadership style is what the group needs. An authoritarian or dictatorial leader may squelch the free flow of ideas needed to analyze issues and identify a solution. And if a group's goal is primarily social or creative, a laissez-faire leader may be best. Rather than structure and agendas, when trying to come up with a creative idea, the group may function best with no direct influence from a leader.

The effective leader adapts his or her style to fit the needs of the group and the task at hand. Drawing upon the principle of adapting to others gives rise to the situational approach to leadership. Remember, leadership in groups and teams is usually shared by several people. Even when someone has been appointed or elected to be "the leader," leadership roles are often assumed by several group members.

⋯⟩ Situational Approach

The **situational approach** views leadership as an interactive process that links a particular style of leadership with such factors as culture, time limitations, group member personalities, and the work the group needs to do. Sometimes a group needs a strong, authoritarian leader to make decisions quickly so that the group can achieve its goal. A military commander under fire does not have time to hold a meeting of the troops and make a democratic decision. Although a democratic leadership style is preferred by most groups, leaders sometimes need to be more assertive, especially in times of crisis or high uncertainty.

ETHICAL PROBE

The following guidelines present strategies to be an ethical communicator in group and team discussions.

- Give credit to your evidence and other information sources.
- Use sound reasoning and evidence.
- Be honest in reporting information and communicating with others.
- Be tolerant of others' ideas.
- Follow through on your commitments to the group and group members; if you say you will do something, make sure you do it.

- Be supportive of other group and team members.
- Admit personal biases you may have.
- Don't form cliques that disrupt group cohesion.
- Don't abandon your own ethical principles if the group makes a decision you consider unethical.

Do you agree with this list? Are there other suggestions you could offer as guidelines for an ethical group communicator?

One of the most popular situational leadership models used to train managers in corporate settings was developed by Paul Hersey and Kenneth Blanchard.[28] Their model, shown in Figure 10.5 on page 236, considers three key factors: (1) relationship behaviour, (2) task behaviour, and (3) the maturity of the group members. Relationship behaviour involves whether group members like one another and work together easily. Task behaviour includes whether the work is highly structured or not highly structured. Maturity refers to how experienced and skilled the members are in working together—it does not depend on age. An immature group, for example, could consist of senior managers who have just started working together on a new project and who lack focus and direction. An example of a mature group could be a team of computer programmers in their mid-20s who have worked together for two years, have developed a sense of how other team members operate, and are highly skilled in performing their task. Quadrant S1 represents a group that needs high structure: They need to be told what to do, because the task behaviour is important (they need to act), there is low relationship skill, and they are an immature group. The leader would do well to provide clear agendas and tell group members what to do. As relationship skill develops and trust evolves, the group's behaviour falls into quadrant S2. The leader can ease up a bit and sell, rather than tell. Structure is needed, but the group is beginning to find its way without rigid direction. In quadrant S3, a more mature group with high relationship skills can participate in the process with even less structure; a participatory, democratic style will work best. If trust and relational comfort decline and the task is more unstructured, the leader can best help the group by delegating—giving assignments to specific people to get the job done.

One simple rule of determining your leadership style is this: When the leader emerges naturally from the group or leads a one-time-only group, then the group will permit him or her to be more directive. If the group will be together for some time and the quality of group relations is important to the functioning of the group, a more participative, democratic leadership style is in order.[29]

Transformational Leadership

One of the newest leadership approaches to emerge from the leadership literature is called **transformational leadership**.[30] The transformational leader influences the group or organization by *transforming* the group—giving it a new vision, energizing or realigning the culture, or giving the group a new structure. The leader leads by helping the group see all the possibilities within the group. The transformational leader also develops a relationship with those whom he or she leads. Author Peter Senge suggests three fundamental skills of transformational leadership: (1) Build a shared vision, (2) challenge existing ways of thinking, and (3) be a systems thinker—help a group or team see that everything is connected to everything else.[31]

transformational leader
A person who leads by shaping the vision of the group based on developing trust through quality interpersonal relationships with group members.

FIGURE 10.5   Hersey and Blanchard's Situational Leadership Model

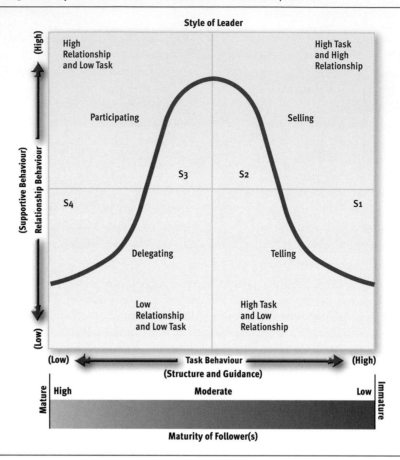

Source: Paul Hersey and Ken Blanchard, *Management of Organizational Behavior: Utilizing Human Resources,* 6th Ed. (Englewood Cliffs, NJ: Prentice-Hall, 1992), 249. Reprinted by permission.

Articulating a collective vision is an important part of what a transformational leader does. An authoritarian leader would just tell the group, "Here's your vision; now get to work." The democratic leader would say, "What vision do you want?" The laissez–faire leader would do nothing about a vision unless asked to do something. The situational leader would say, "Let me see what type of group I'm leading and listen to group members, and then I'll share a vision." The transformational leader paints a picture of the future for the group by knowing individual members in the group. Drawing on the approaches of both the democratic leader and the situational leader, the transformational leader leads by establishing quality interpersonal relationships with others. Transformational leaders provide inspiration, motivation, and intellectual stimulation for the group by being aware of individual needs.

Transformational leadership is less a set of prescribed skills or techniques. It is more like a general philosophy that says people can be trusted; people can be motivated to achieve important goals if they have someone they can trust to help them see the possibilities. Transformational leaders like to think of themselves more as coaches or mentors rather than as leaders who will dictate or even just facilitate interaction; they are sometimes viewed as "the guide on the side" rather than "the sage on the stage." This ancient description of a wise leader offers insight into what makes a leader great:

> The wicked leader the people despise
> The good leader the people revere
> The great leader the people say
> "We did it ourselves."
>
> —Lao Tsu

ENHANCING GROUP AND TEAM MEETINGS

Humour columnist Dave Barry said, "If you had to identify, in one word, the reason why the human race has not achieved, and never will achieve, its full potential, that word would be 'meetings.'"[32] Meetings are an inescapable fact of life for most people and will undoubtedly be inescapable for you as well.

Why does meeting participation inspire such a negative reaction—not only from Dave Barry, but from many people? Often, it's because meeting leaders and participants have not mastered the principles we've stressed as fundamental to communication success in any context. Meetings are more productive if participants are aware of their behaviours and the behaviour of others. Using and interpreting verbal and nonverbal symbols is also vital for meeting effectiveness, as well as listening and responding to messages with sensitivity. Because of the complexity and uncertainty of several people collaborating, being able to adapt message content and message structure is essential. We conclude this chapter by revisiting strategies we've offered in Chapter 9 and in this chapter and applying them to one of the most likely collaborative contexts you'll encounter—working in meetings.

What specific problems occur most frequently in meetings? Based on a survey of meeting participants, the most common meeting "sin" is getting off the subject.[33] The second biggest problem is not having clear goals or a meeting agenda. Meeting goers also

---

⟨⟨⟩⟩ COMMUNICATION and DIVERSITY

Men, Women, and the Effect of Their Nonverbal Messages in Groups and Teams

As we noted in Chapter 4, nonverbal messages play a major role in the total communication process. They are especially important in communicating feelings, emotions, and attitudes. Given the importance of unspoken messages in communicating with others, you may wonder: Are there differences between the way men and women use nonverbal communication messages when communicating in groups and teams? Research suggests the answer is yes. And because of the different ways men and women express themselves nonverbally, you may make the wrong assumption about issues of leadership and interaction management when working in a group or team with people of the opposite sex. Here's a summary of some of the research conclusions about the nonverbal messages of men and women, applied to working in groups and teams.[34]

Use of Personal Space and Seating Arrangement in Groups and Team Meetings

- Most people, whether male or female, tend to move closer to women than to men.
- Women will generally move closer to other people than will men when participating in groups; men will be less comfortable than women if the meeting room is small and cramped.

Eye Contact

- Men tend to have less eye contact with others than do women; eye contact is a key regulator of communication interaction in groups and teams. We use eye contact to signal when we want to talk and not talk to others.

Gestures

- Men tend to use more gestures when expressing themselves than do women; in groups and teams, gestures may provide cues about interest in the topic.

Touch

- Men usually initiate touch with others more often than women; the person who initiates touch is often perceived as the most powerful or influential.

Voice

- Women typically speak with less volume than do men; volume may communicate information about team leadership perceptions and amount of engagement in the discussion topic.

After reading this brief summary of the differences between the ways men and women tend to communicate nonverbally in groups, you may be left with yet another question: So what? What difference does it make if men and women have different ways of using nonverbal messages when working in groups and teams? Knowing these differences can help you understand how to interpret nonverbal cues and avoid misunderstandings. Understanding these differences can also increase your sensitivity and enhance your tolerance when you experience these differences. These are research generalizations, and we don't claim that all men or women behave according to these generalizations.

On the WEB ·····•

When you facilitate a meeting, you need all the help you can get. A Web site called The Virtual Meeting Assistant can give you some additional tips and tools for helping you prepare for and run a quality meeting: **www.ukans.edu/cwis/units/coms2/vma/vms.htm**.

agenda
The written plan for achieving the goals during a group meeting; typically includes items for discussion, action, and information.

The participants at this meeting will likely accomplish all three of the most common goals of meetings: giving information, discussing information, and taking action.

reported that meetings were often too long, people weren't prepared, nothing really happened, meetings started late, and there were often no follow-up action plans.

Meetings need two essential things in order to be effective: *structure* and *interaction*. Sound familiar? As we noted earlier in the chapter, groups also need a balance of these two things.

Many of the meeting problems we've described stem from a lack of clear structure—no clear written agenda or no one helping to keep the group on track. You can also see that too many unstructured interactions lead to unfocused discussion. Consequently, nothing gets done. Being able to adapt to the need for structure and interaction is a fundamental principle of meeting management. The essential tool for giving a meeting structure is the agenda. To manage interaction, meeting participants need to be good facilitators of talk. We'll look more closely at how to provide these two essential needs.

···⟩ Manage Meeting Structure

As we just noted, the essential weapon to combat disorganized, rambling meetings is a clear, well-developed agenda. An **agenda** is a list of the key issues, ideas, and information that will be discussed, in the order of discussion. How do you develop a well-crafted agenda? Consider these three steps.

Step 1: Determine Your Meeting Goals

Every meeting seeks to accomplish something. (If not, don't hold a meeting!) Most meeting goals include one or more of the following three goals: (1) giving information, (2) discussing information, and (3) taking action.

An information-giving meeting is like a briefing or a series of short speeches. If the only task is to share information, you may not really need a meeting at all—a written memo or an e-mail message will suffice. But if you want to share information live and in-person to emphasize its importance, then it is appropriate to give information as a primary meeting goal.

An information-discussion meeting is one in which there is considerable interaction and give-and-take discussion. The key in this type of meeting is not to let it become a series of long-winded speeches. Also, if you're not careful, discussions digress off the topic. The meeting leader or meeting participants should be aware of what the goals of the discussion are so that the comments remain relevant.

A meeting to take action often involves making a decision, solving a problem, or implementing a decision or solution. If the purpose of the meeting is to take action, it's helpful if group members know before they arrive for the meeting that they will be asked to take some action.

Step 2: Identify What Needs to be Discussed to Achieve the Goal

After you have determined your goal(s), you need to determine how to structure the meeting to achieve the goal. What topics need to be covered to achieve the goal? What information do we need? What issues do we need to focus on? Brainstorm answers for these questions, but don't worry about the precise order of the items yet; focus on organizing the agenda after you know what you need to discuss.

Step 3: Organize the Agenda

Once you have identified your meeting goals (giving information, discussing information, taking action) and assessed what you need to talk about, take time to arrange the items in the most effective way to achieve your goals. There are several strategies for organizing effective meetings.[35]

Consider organizing the agenda around your meeting goals. When your meeting goal is to solve a problem, don't forget about the five steps we discussed earlier in the chapter. Agenda items should include how to (1) identify and define the problem, (2) analyze the problem, (3) generate creative solutions, (4) select the best solution, and (5) take action. A single meeting may focus on only one or two of those steps; don't feel you have to cram all five problem-solving steps into every meeting.

Realize, too, that the three primary meeting goals may all occur during the same meeting. Consider using subheadings of "Information Items," "Discussion Items," and "Action Items" as you construct your agenda to signal to group members the goal of the discussion, as shown in the sample agenda below. Before making final decisions about which items you will discuss, estimate how long you think the group will need to discuss each item. Most groups take more time than you would expect to talk about issues and ideas.

There are several strategies for organizing an effective meeting. Some meeting management experts suggest putting your most important item first, because usually what is introduced first takes the most time. You may want to string together several small issues so that you can dispense with them before getting into the meat of the meeting. One research team suggests that you place the most challenging issues for discussion in the middle of the meeting, thus giving the group a chance to get oriented at the beginning and ease out of the discussion at the end.[36] Another strategy is to make your first agenda item something that will immediately involve all meeting participants in active discussion. Starting the meeting with announcements and routine reports, a very common organizational pattern, sets a climate of passivity, and boredom is the usual product. One way to start your meeting is to involve members in actively finalizing the agenda; ask them for reactions to how you have structured the discussion. Here's a suggested agenda:

Sample Meeting Agenda

Meeting Goals:

1. Discuss new product proposal: evaluate the pros and cons
2. Decide whether to implement the personnel policy and mentor program
3. Receive updates from committees

    I. Discussion Items
       A. Revise today's agenda
       B. Identify new problems: What new issues or problems have you identified?
       C. React to new product team proposal (distributed by e-mail): What are the pros and cons of the proposal?
   II. Action Items
       A. Approval of new personnel policy (distributed by e-mail)
       B. Issue: Should we implement new mentor program?
  III. Information Items
       A. New employee orientation report
       B. Planning committee report
       C. Finance committee report
       D. Announcements

When your job is to lead the meeting, there are several specific tasks to perform, which include the following:

1. Call the group together; find out when is the best time to meet (often a major problem for busy people).
2. Develop an agenda, using the just-mentioned steps.
3. Determine whether there is a quorum—the minimum number of persons who must be present at a meeting to conduct business.
4. Call the meeting to order.
5. Use a flip chart, chalkboard, or dry-erase board to summarize meeting progress; written notes of the meeting become the "group mind" and help keep the group structured.
6. Decide when to take a vote.
7. Prepare a final report or delegate that the report or minutes be made.

⇢ Manage Meeting Interaction

Interaction, as you recall, is the back-and-forth dialogue and discussion in which participants engage during meetings. Without interaction, meetings would be like a monologue, a speech, or a seminar, rather than a lively discussion. But too much unfocused interaction can result in a disorganized, chaotic discussion that rambles and wobbles. To keep a meeting on track, meeting leaders and participants need facilitation skills. The most important facilitation skills include being a gatekeeper, using metadiscussion, monitoring discussion time, and structuring discussion techniques to keep discussion focused.

Listen
and
Respond

Verbal

metadiscussion
Discussion about the discussion process; comments that help the group remain focused on the goals of the group, or that comment about how the group is doing its work.

"I" message
A message in which you state your perspective or point of view.

"you" message
A message that is likely to create defensiveness in others because it emphasizes how the other person has created a problem, rather than describing the problem from your perspective ("I" message).

- *Use gatekeeping skills.* A gatekeeper helps encourage less-talkative members to participate and tries to limit long-winded contributions by other group members. Gatekeepers need to be good listeners so that they can help manage the flow of conversation. Gatekeepers make such comments as, "Ashley, we haven't heard your ideas yet. Won't you share your thoughts with us?" Or, "Mike, thanks for sharing, but I'd like to hear what others have to say." Polite, tactful invitations to talk or limit talk usually work. You may need to speak privately with an unruly ororverbalizer to let him or her know that you'd appreciate a more balanced discussion.
- *Use metadiscussion.* **Metadiscussion** literally means "discussion about discussion."[37] It's a comment about the discussion process rather than about the topic under consideration. Metadiscussional statements include, "I'm not following this conversation. What is our goal?" Or, "Can someone summarize what we've accomplished so far?" "Peggy, I'm not sure I understand how your observation relates to our meeting goal." These comments contain information and advice about the communication *process*, rather than about the issues that are being discussed.

    Metadiscussional phrases are helpful ways to keep the team or group focused on the task. We're not suggesting that you personally attack others. Don't just blurt out, "You're off task" or "Oh, let's not talk about that any more." Instead, use tactful ways of letting other group members know you'd like to return to the issues at hand. Use "I" messages rather than "you" messages to bring the group back on track. An **"I" message** begins with the word "I," such as "I am not sure where we are in our discussion" or "I am lost here." A **"you" message** is a way of phrasing a message that makes others feel defensive. Here are examples of "you" messages: "You're not following the agenda" or "Your

ReCAP ◄┈┈

Making Meeting Agendas Useful

POTENTIAL MEETING AGENDA PROBLEM	SUGGESTED MEETING AGENDA STRATEGY
Meeting participants tend to spend more time on the first or second agenda item.	Make sure the early agenda items are something the group needs to spend time on.
Meeting participants will want to talk, even if the meeting leader just wants them to listen.	Take advantage of the desire to participate by inviting input and discussion early in the meeting, rather than trying to squelch or interrupt group members.
Meeting participants aren't prepared. They haven't done their "homework."	Take a few minutes to have silent reading. Let members get up to speed by reviewing information or quickly looking at key pieces of data.
Meeting participants won't stick to the agenda.	Continue to remind the group what the agenda is and what the overall goal of the meeting is. Make sure you have a written agenda that is distributed ahead of the meeting.
There is an agenda item that may produce conflict and disagreement.	Help the group develop a track record of success by putting one or more noncontroversial items on the agenda ahead of the item that may produce conflict. Build on the group's ability to reach agreement.

point doesn't make any sense." Another way to express these same ideas, but with less of a negative edge, is to use "I" messages such as "I'm not sure where we are on the agenda" or "I'm not sure I understand how your point relates to the issue we are discussing." Metadiscussion is an exceptionally powerful skill because you can offer metadiscussional statements even if you are not the appointed leader.

- *Monitor time.* Being sensitive to the time the group is spending on an issue is yet another skill necessary to manage meeting interaction. Think of your agenda as a map, helping you plan where you want to go. Think of the clock as your gas gauge, telling you the amount of fuel you have to get where you want to go. In a meeting, keeping one eye on the clock and one eye on the agenda is analogous to focusing on the map and the gas gauge on a car trip. If you are running low on fuel (time), you will either need to get more gas (budget more time) or recognize that you will not get where you want to go. Begin each meeting by asking how long members can meet. If you face two or three crucial agenda items, and one-third of your group has to leave in an hour, you may need to reshuffle your agenda to make sure you can achieve your goals.

- *Use structure to manage interaction.* Another way to manage interaction is to use some of the prescriptive structures that we talked about earlier. For example, using silent brainstorming is a way to gain maximum participation from everyone. Yet another strategy is to ask people to come to the meeting with written responses to questions that you've posed in your pre-meeting agenda. This signals that you want people to prepare for the meeting rather than having meeting participants do their homework at the meeting. An essential task of the meeting facilitator is to orchestrate meaningful interaction during the meeting so that all group or team members have opportunity to share. Structured methods of inviting involvement work by having group members first write individually and then share their ideas with the group. Having members write before speaking is like providing them with a script that can be effective in garnering contributions from *all* group members—not just the people who talk the most or who aren't shy about speaking up.

One of the best ways to ensure appropriate interaction as a meeting participant when you are not assigned the specific role of leader is to consider the following suggestions from Mosvic and Nelson in their book *We've Got to Start Meeting Like This!*:[38]

Verbal

- Organize what you say. Don't ramble.
- Speak to the point. Make sure your contributions are relevant to the goal.
- Make one point at a time.
- Speak clearly and forcefully. Weak, timid suggestions mumbled to the group will probably not be listened to.
- Support your ideas with evidence. Don't just assert opinion without data or expert opinion backing you up.
- Listen. Listen. Listen. Connect your comments to those of others.

Listen and Respond

What are the best strategies to make yourself a valuable meeting leader or participant? The five communication principles for a lifetime that we've emphasized throughout the book will serve you well, and Table 10.3 outlines the necessary steps to an effective meeting.

TABLE 10.3   The Necessary Steps to an Effective Meeting

Before the Meeting

Leader	**Participants**
1. Define the objective.	1. Block time on schedule.
2. Select participants.	2. Confirm attendance.
3. Make preliminary contact with participants to confirm availability.	3. Define your role.
	4. Determine leader's needs from you.
4. Schedule meeting room and arrange for equipment and refreshments.	5. Suggest other participants.
	6. Know the objective.
5. Prepare agenda.	7. Know when and where to meet.
6. Invite participants and distribute agenda.	8. Do any required homework.
7. Touch base with nonparticipants.	
8. Make final check of meeting room.	

During the Meeting

Leader	**Participants**
1. Start promptly.	1. Listen and participate.
2. Follow the agenda.	2. Be open-minded/receptive.
3. Manage the use of time.	3. Stay on the agenda and subject.
4. Limit/control the discussion.	4. Limit or avoid side conversations and distractions.
5. Elicit participation.	5. Ask questions to assure understanding.
6. Help resolve conflicts.	6. Take notes on your action items.
7. Clarify action to be taken.	
8. Summarize results.	

After the Meeting

Leader	**Participants**
1. Restore room and return equipment.	1. Evaluate meeting.
2. Evaluate effectiveness as meeting leader.	2. Review memorandum of discussion.
3. Send out meeting evaluations.	3. Brief others as appropriate.
4. Distribute memorandum of discussion.	4. Take any action agreed to.
5. Take any action you agreed to.	5. Follow up on action items.
6. Follow up on action items.	

Source: From Marion E. Haynes, *Effective Meeting Skills* (Los Altos, CA: Crisp Publications, 1988).

ReCAP ←····

HOW TO GIVE A MEETING STRUCTURE	**HOW TO ENSURE MANAGED INTERACTION**
Prepare an effective agenda by	Keep discussion on track by
• Determining your meeting goals	• Using effective gatekeeping skills
• Identifying what needs to be discussed to achieve the goals	• Using metadiscussion to help the group focus on the goals
• Organizing the agenda to achieve the goals	• Helping the group be sensitive to elapsed time and time remaining for deliberation
	• Using strategies to manage interaction (for example, writing before speaking, nominal group technique, or silent brainstorming)

Stucture   Interaction

In general, be aware of your own behaviour and the behaviour of others. Monitor your verbal and nonverbal messages to make sure you are making comments relevant to the task at hand but are also sensitive to the needs of the people in your group. You develop that sensitivity by listening to others and thoughtfully responding. Ineffective meeting participants make little effort to link their comments to what others are saying. They also don't adapt to the messages of others. Effective communicators adapt what they say and do to help achieve the goals of the group.

SUMMARY

Specific strategies can help groups and teams operate at peak performance levels. Research has identified several essential functions that, when performed in a group, enhance the group performance. Effective group members describe the goal, analyze information, generate creative ideas, evaluate ideas, and are sensitive to group social and relationship concerns.

Groups also perform best if they have appropriate structure to make an often bumpy process smooth. Although there are many different steps, methods, and procedures that group communication researchers have identified, there is no single best series of steps that will ensure high performance. In his book *How We Think,* John Dewey described five problem-solving steps: (1) Identify and define the problem, (2) analyze the problem, (3) generate creative solutions, (4) select the best solution, and (5) take action.

High-performing groups have competent group leaders. Researchers have sought to find which leadership approach works best. The trait approach to leadership seeks to identify certain characteristics or traits that all leaders possess. Leadership is more complicated than finding leaders with just the right traits, however. The functional approach to leadership suggests that leaders need to be concerned for both the task and the group process. The functional leadership approach identifies specific roles that leaders should perform. A third approach to leadership, leadership styles, identifies leaders as being authoritarian, democratic, or laissez-faire. No one style seems to work best all of the time. The situational leadership approach suggests that the best leadership style depends on a variety of factors, including the maturity of the group, the urgency of the problem, and the type of issue the group is discussing. Finally, transformational leadership is an approach that encourages leaders to help shape the vision and goals of the group through being in touch with followers. Groups can be transformed if the leaders help articulate a vision for the future that takes the group in new directions, yet builds upon the vision and goals of the group.

Groups need a balance of structure and interaction. Groups can gain appropriate structure if meeting planners develop and use an agenda to keep the discussion focused and on track. Meetings also need appropriate amounts of dialogue and discussion. Effective meeting participants monitor the amount of participation from other group or team members, and serve as gatekeepers to ensure that oververbalizers don't monopolize the discussion or quiet members don't feel intimidated.

PRINCIPLES FOR A LIFETIME

Aware

Principle 1: Be aware of your communication with yourself and others.

- Be sensitive to the need of your group for appropriate structure to organize and focus the discussion or interaction and to encourage dialogue.
- Know whether the essential functions of group communication (set clear goals, analyze information, generate creative ideas, evaluate ideas, be sensitive to others) are present in your group.
- Be aware of the appropriate leadership style to meet your group's needs.

Verbal

Principle 2: Effectively use and interpret verbal messages.

- Use appropriate verbal messages to identify and define the problem, analyze the problem, generate creative solutions, select the best solution, and take action.
- Clearly describe the goal of the group.
- Evaluate the merits of ideas by verbalizing both the pros and the cons.
- Use verbal messages to express your sensitivity to other group members about their feelings and need for information.
- Use verbal messages to articulate a vision and motivate a team.
- Develop and use a written agenda for group meetings to give the meeting structure.

- Manage the amount of interaction in a group by encouraging quiet members to participate and overly dominant members to let others express ideas.
- Use metadiscussion to keep a meeting on track.

Nonverbal

Principle 3:   Effectively use and interpret nonverbal messages.

- Use appropriate nonverbal messages to establish and maintain a positive group climate.
- Do your best to avoid nonverbally expressing your evaluation of others' ideas when brainstorming.
- Communicate your sensitivity to other group members through your nonverbal expressions.
- Use eye contact and other nonverbal regulatory cues to regulate the flow of interaction in group and team meetings.

Listen and Respond

Principle 4:   Listen and respond thoughtfully to others.

- Listen to other group members to determine whether your group is including the appropriate group functions.
- Listen and respond to others to express your sensitivity to others' ideas and opinions.
- Listen and respond to others to provide appropriate leadership.
- Listen and respond to provide appropriate contributions to group meetings and problem-solving discussions.

Adapt

Principle 5:   Appropriately adapt messages to others.

- Adapt your comments to ensure that your group spends an appropriate amount of time on the five functions of effective groups.
- Adapt your leadership and followership styles to achieve the goals of the group.
- Adapt your messages to help the group identify goals and define, analyze, create solutions, select the best solution, or take action.
- Adapt your messages to give group meetings appropriate structure or interaction.

Discussion and Review ⁑

1. What are the five essential functions that groups should perform?

2. What are the five steps to structure group problem solving?

3. What is the trait approach to leadership?

4. Describe the functional leadership approach.

5. What are the differences among authoritarian, democratic, and laissez-faire leadership styles?

6. Identify the assumption underlying the situational-leadership approach.

7. What is the transformational-leadership approach?

8. How can you provide appropriate structure for a group meeting?

9. What are strategies or techniques for ensuring appropriate interaction during group or team meetings?

Developing Your Skills: Putting Principles into Practice ⁑

1. *Winter Power Failure*[39]

   Although you have idly watched news reports of winter power failures in places such as Quebec and Newfoundland and Labrador, you have not given any serious thought to the possibility that a winter power failure could occur where you live. However, you have just heard that an unprecedented snow and ice storm will hit your community. Forecasters are predicting the storm's arrival in nine to twelve hours. Having taken no precautions, you are stunned by the amount of work you have to do to secure your three-bedroom suburban home, which is about three kilometres from any conveniences. You have enough food in the house for two days. You also have one candle and a transistor radio with one weak battery. Remembering the terrible ice storm that ravaged eastern Ontario and southern Quebec in January 1998, you realize that you have no other sources of power or heat! Your task is to rank the following items in terms of importance for ensuring your survival and the safety of your property. Place number 1 by the first thing you should do, 2 by the second, and so on through number 11. Please work individually on this task.

Fill your car with gas _____

Buy antifreeze to protect plumbing _____

Fill your bathtub with water _____

Construct storm shutters for
your windows _____

Buy enough food for a week _____

Buy batteries and candles _____

Bring in patio furniture from outside _____

Purchase CSA-approved emergency
heating equipment, such as camp stoves
kerosene heaters, or a wood stove _____

Invite friends over for a
ice storm party _____

Listen to TV and radio for further
bulletins before doing anything _____

Make sure you have an
evacuation plan _____

After you have made your individual decisions, work in small groups with others and seek to reach consensus. Your group's task is to rank these items according to their importance.

2. *Stranded in the Desert Situation*[40]

You are a member of a geology club that is on a field trip to study unusual formations in the New Mexico desert. It is the last week in July. You have been driving over old trails, far from any road, in order to see out-of-the-way formations. At about 10:30 A.M., your club's specially equipped minibus overturns, rolls into a six-metre ravine, and burns. The driver and professional adviser to the club are killed. The rest of you are relatively uninjured.

You know that the nearest ranch is approximately 70 kilometres east of where you are. There is no closer habitation. When your club does not report to its motel that evening, you will be missed. Several people know generally where you are but will not be able to pinpoint your whereabouts.

The area around you is rather rugged and dry. There is a shallow waterhole nearby, but the water is contaminated by worms, animal feces and urine, and several dead mice. Before you left, you heard on a weather report that the temperature would reach 42 degrees Celsius, making the surface temperature 53 degrees Celsius. All of you are dressed in lightweight summer clothing, and all have hats and sunglasses.

While escaping from the minibus, each group member salvaged a couple of items; there are 12 items in all. Your group's task is to rank these items according to their importance to your survival, starting with 1 for the most important and proceeding to 12 for the least important. You may assume that the number of club members is the same as the number of persons in your group and that the group has agreed to stick together.

_____ Magnetic compass

_____ A piece of heavy-duty, light-blue
canvas, two square metres in size

_____ Book, *Plants of the Desert*

_____ Rear-view mirror

_____ Large knife

_____ Flashlight

_____ One jacket per person

_____ One transparent, plastic ground cloth
(1.8 metres by 1.2 metres) per person

_____ A .38-calibre loaded pistol

_____ One two-litre plastic canteen of water per person

_____ An accurate map of the area

_____ A large box of kitchen matches

3. *Assessing Group and Team Problem-Solving Competencies*[41]
Use the following evaluation form to assess the presence or absence of small-group communication competencies in a group or team discussion. Competencies are specific behaviours that group and team members perform. This assessment form includes nine competencies organized into four general categories. Here's how to use this form.

a. Observe a group or team that is attempting to solve a problem. Write the names of the group members at the top of the form. (If the group includes more than five group members, photocopy the form so that each group member can be evaluated.)

b. When using the form, first decide whether each group member has performed each competency. Circle "NO" if the group member was not observed performing the competency. Circle "YES" if you did observe the group member performing the competency (e.g., defining the problem, analyzing the problem, identifying criteria, and so on).

c. For each competency for which you circled "YES," determine how effectively the competency was performed. Use the scale, which ranges from 0–3.

0 = This competency was performed, but it was inappropriately or inadequately performed. For example, the person observed tried to define the problem but did so poorly.

1 = Overall, there was an adequate performance of this competency.

2 = Overall, there was a good performance of this competency.

3 = Overall, there was an excellent performance of this competency.

d. Total the score for each group member in each of the four categories.

The first category, *Problem-Oriented Competencies,* consists of items 1 and 2. These are behaviours that help the group or team member define and analyze the problem. If the competency was performed, the total number of points will range from 0 to 6. The higher the number of points, the better the individual performed this competency.

Solution-Oriented Competencies include items 3, 4, and 5, with a point range from 0 to 9. These competencies focus on how well the group or team member helped develop and evaluate a solution to the problem.

Discussion Management Competencies, competencies that helped the group or team remain focused or helped the group manage interaction, are items 6 and 7. The points for this category range from 0 to 6.

Relational Management Competencies are behaviours that focus on dealing with conflict and developing a positive, supportive group climate. Items 8 and 9 reflect this competency; points range from 0 to 6.

e. You can also assess the overall group's or team's ability to perform these competencies. The column marked "Group Assessment" can be used to record your overall impressions of how effectively the group or team behaved. Circle "NO" if no one in the group performed this competency. Circle "YES" if at least one person in the group or team performed this competency. Then evaluate how well the entire group

Competent Group Communicator Problem-Solving Group Communication Competencies	Group Member	Group Member	
Problem-Oriented Competencies			
1. Defined the problem the group attempted to solve.	NO YES 0 1 2 3	NO YES 0 1 2 3	
2. Analyzed the problem the group attempted to solve. Used relevant information, data, or evidence, discussed the causes, obstacles, history, symptoms, or significance of the problem.	NO YES 0 1 2 3	NO YES 0 1 2 3	
Solution-Oriented Competencies			
3. Identified criteria for an appropriate solution to the problem.	NO YES 0 1 2 3	NO YES 0 1 2 3	
4. Generated solutions or alternatives to the problem.	NO YES 0 1 2 3	NO YES 0 1 2 3	
5. Evaluated solution(s): Identified positive or negative consequences of the proposed solutions.	NO YES 0 1 2 3	NO YES 0 1 2 3	
Discussion Management Competencies			
6. Maintained task focus: Helped the group stay on or return to the task, issue, or topic the group was discussing.	NO YES 0 1 2 3	NO YES 0 1 2 3	
7. Managed group interaction: Appropriately initiated and terminated discussion, contributed to the discussion, or invited others to contribute to the discussion. Didn't dominate or withdraw.	NO YES 0 1 2 3	NO YES 0 1 2 3	
Relational Management Competencies			
8. Managed conflict: Appropriately and constructively helped the group stay focused on issues rather than personalities when conflict occurred.	NO YES 0 1 2 3	NO YES 0 1 2 3	
9. Maintained climate: Offered positive verbal comments or nonverbal expressions that helped maintain a positive group climate.	NO YES 0 1 2 3	NO YES 0 1 2 3	

Scoring: NO = Not observed   YES   0 = Overall inappropriate or inadequate performance of competency   1 = Overall adequate performance of competency

Problem-Oriented Competencies (0–6)
Solution-Oriented Competencies (0–9)
Discussion Management Competencies (0–6)
Relational Management Competencies (0–6)

performed this competency, using the 0 to 3 scale (0 = the competency was observed but was not performed appropriately or effectively).

Sometimes it is difficult to make so many judgments about group competencies by just viewing a group discussion once. Many people find that it's easier to videotape the group discussion so that you can observe the group discussion more than once.

Group Member	Group Member	Group Member	Group Assessment
NO YES 0 1 2 3	NO YES 0 1 2 3	NO YES 0 1 2 3	NO YES 0 1 2 3
NO YES 0 1 2 3	NO YES 0 1 2 3	NO YES 0 1 2 3	NO YES 0 1 2 3
NO YES 0 1 2 3	NO YES 0 1 2 3	NO YES 0 1 2 3	NO YES 0 1 2 3
NO YES 0 1 2 3	NO YES 0 1 2 3	NO YES 0 1 2 3	NO YES 0 1 2 3
NO YES 0 1 2 3	NO YES 0 1 2 3	NO YES 0 1 2 3	NO YES 0 1 2 3
NO YES 0 1 2 3	NO YES 0 1 2 3	NO YES 0 1 2 3	NO YES 0 1 2 3
NO YES 0 1 2 3	NO YES 0 1 2 3	NO YES 0 1 2 3	NO YES 0 1 2 3
NO YES 0 1 2 3	NO YES 0 1 2 3	NO YES 0 1 2 3	NO YES 0 1 2 3
NO YES 0 1 2 3	NO YES 0 1 2 3	NO YES 0 1 2 3	NO YES 0 1 2 3

2 = Overall good performance of competency

3 = Overall excellent performance of competency

"Offering Cloth." Korea, 19th c. Silk gauze patchwork. 25 1/8" x 23 3/8". Copyright The Newark Museum/Art Resource, NY.

Everyone has the fundamental freedoms:

(b) Freedom of thought, belief, opinion and expression, including freedom of the press, and other media of communication.

THE CANADIAN CHARTER OF
RIGHTS AND FREEDOMS, CONSTITUTION ACT, 1982

11 Developing Your Presentation

CHAPTER OUTLINE

AFTER STUDYING THIS CHAPTER, YOU SHOULD BE ABLE TO

1. Explain the practical value of presentational speaking skills.

2. List the nine components of the audience-centred public speaking model.

3. Suggest three questions and three strategies that can help a speaker discover a topic.

4. List the three general purposes for presentations.

5. Explain how to write an audience-centred specific-purpose statement.

6. List and explain four criteria for a central idea.

7. Explain how to generate main ideas from a central idea.

8. Describe three sources and five types of supporting material for a presentation, and offer guidelines for using each type effectively.

9. List six types of library resources.

10. List and explain five strategies for organizing main ideas in a presentation.

11. Define the principles of primacy, recency, and complexity and explain how each can be applied to organizing main ideas.

12. List and explain four strategies for organizing supporting material in a presentation.

13. Explain three ways to organize a presentation.

14. List and explain the five functions of a presentation introduction.

15. Suggest at least five strategies for getting an audience's attention in a presentation introduction.

16. List and explain the four functions of a speech conclusion.

17. Outline a presentation according to standard outline format.

18. Define a delivery outline and explain how a speaker would use one.

The 5th Wave   By Rich Tennant

public speaking or presentational speaking
A teachable, learnable process of developing, supporting, organizing, and presenting ideas.

Have you had a public speaking experience that could have been more polished? When we study the public speaking process and learn its component skills and principles, we certainly increase the likelihood that our presentations will be successful experiences.

Far from being a rare talent possessed only by an inspired few, **public speaking** or **presentational speaking** is a teachable, learnable process—a process of developing, supporting, organizing, outlining, and presenting ideas. It is important to remember that the more you practise, the easier and more "natural" the public speaking process will become.

Perhaps you will feel motivated if you consider that the skills you will develop as you study presentational speaking will be of practical use to you in the future. They will give you an edge in other college or university courses that require oral presentations. They may help you convince some current or future boss that you deserve a raise. And they may even land you a job. As we noted in Chapter 1, the Employability Skills profile reveals that employers consider communication skills an important factor in helping graduating college and university students obtain employment.[1]

Oral communication skills are grounded in the five communication principles for a lifetime and can be learned and practised in the various stages of the public speaking process. Let's begin our discussion of presentational speaking with an overview of that process. We will focus more closely on the first five stages of the public speaking process, which involve generating, exploring, and developing ideas for presentations. The first four stages of the speech preparation process will be reviewed: selecting and narrowing a topic, identifying a general and specific purpose, determining a central idea, and generating main ideas. Finally, we will explore how to organize, support, and outline a presentation. Once speech preparation, organization, and outlines are complete, it will be time to rehearse and deliver your presentation (Chapter 12).

AN OVERVIEW OF THE PRESENTATIONAL SPEAKING PROCESS

Chances are that you didn't complete a driver-education course before you got behind the wheel of a car for the first time. Similarly, you don't have to read an entire book on public speaking before you give your first presentation. An overview of the public speaking process can help you with your early assignments, even if you have to speak before you have a chance to read Chapters 11 through 13.

Figure 11.1 illustrates the public speaking process. Viewing the model as a clock, you find "Select and narrow topic" at 1 o'clock. From this stage, the process proceeds clockwise in the direction of the arrows, to "Deliver presentation." Each stage is one of the tasks of the public speaker:

1. Select and narrow topic.
2. Identify purpose.
3. Develop central idea.
4. Generate main ideas.
5. Gather supporting material.
6. Organize presentation.
7. Rehearse presentation.
8. Deliver presentation.

Note that a ninth component, "Consider the audience," appears at the centre of the model. Double-headed arrows connect this centre with every other stage, illustrating that at any point, you may revise your ideas or strategies as you seek out and learn more about your audience. Your audience influences every decision you make.

Audience-centred presentational speakers are inherently sensitive to the diversity of their audiences. While guarding against generalizations that might be offensive, they acknowledge that cultural, ethnic, and other traditions affect the way people process messages. They apply the fundamental principle of appropriately adapting their messages to

Adapt

audience-centred presentational speaker
Someone who considers and adapts to the audience at every stage of the public speaking process.

FIGURE 11.1   An Audience-Centred Model of the Presentational Speaking Process

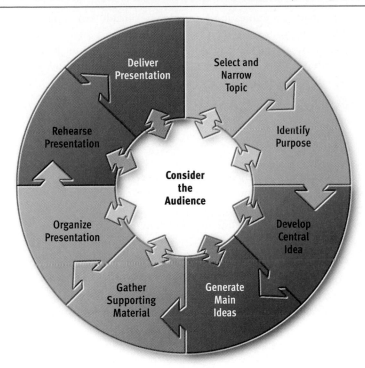

others. How? They might choose to use pictures to help them communicate. They might select topics and use illustrations with universal themes such as family and friendship. They might adjust the formality of their delivery and even their dress to whatever is expected by the majority of the audience members. The fundamental communication principle of adapting to the audience is the key to the success of any presentation.

SELECTING AND NARROWING YOUR TOPIC

Sometimes a speaker is invited or assigned to speak on a certain topic and doesn't have to think about selecting one. At other times, however, a speaker is given some guidelines—such as time limits and perhaps the general purpose for the presentation—but otherwise allowed freedom to choose a topic. When this happens to you—as it almost certainly will in your communication class—you may find your task made easier by exploring three questions: Who is the audience? What is the occasion? What are my interests and experiences?

⋯⟩ Who Is the Audience?

As we have noted several times throughout this book, the principle of appropriately adapting messages to others is central to the communication process. In presentational speaking, that adaptation begins with topic selection. Who are the members of your audience? What interests and needs do they have in common? Why did they ask you to speak? Your classmates are likely to be interested in such topics as student loans and the job market. Older adults might be more interested in such topics as the cost of prescription drugs and pension plan benefits. Thinking about your audience can often yield an appropriate topic.

Adapt

⋯⟩ What Is the Occasion?

You might also consider the occasion for which you are being asked to speak. A Remembrance Day address calls for such topics as patriotism and service to one's country. A university centennial address will focus on the successes of the institution's past and a vision for its future.

What Are My Interests and Experiences?

Self-awareness, another communication principle you already know, can also help you discover a topic. Exploring your own interests, attitudes, and experiences may suggest topics about which you know a great deal and feel passionately, and result in a presentation that you can deliver with energy and genuine enthusiasm. One speaker thinking about her own interests and experiences quickly produced the following list of possible topics:

Toronto, Ontario: city of cultural diversity
Are world climates really changing?
Working at Canada's Wonderland
What a sociologist does

Even after considering audience, occasion, and personal interests and experiences, you may still find yourself facing a speaking assignment for which you just cannot come up with a satisfactory topic. When that happens, you might try silent brainstorming, scanning Web directories and Web pages, or listening and reading for topic ideas.

Silent Brainstorming

silent brainstorming
A technique used to generate creative ideas.

Silent brainstorming, discussed in Chapter 10 as a technique used to generate creative ideas, is a useful strategy for generating possible topics for presentations. A silent brainstorming session of about three minutes yielded the following list of 10 potential topics:

Gargoyles
Gothic architecture
Notre Dame
French food
Disney's *The Hunchback of Notre Dame*
Collecting Disney movie celluloids
Grammy Award winning movie themes
Famous Canadians Matthew Perry, Shania Twain
Sudbury, Ontario

You may now go back to your list and eliminate topics that don't have much promise or about which you know you would never speak. For example, you may not have any real interest in or reason for discussing Sudbury, Ontario. However, you think that your film course has given you good background for discussing famous Canadians. Keep the topics you like in your class notebook. You can reconsider them for future assignments.

Scanning Web Directories and Web Pages

You know how addicting it can be to surf the Web—to follow various categories and links out of interest and curiosity. What may seem an idle pastime can actually be a good way to discover potential speech topics. For example, a recent random search starting with the general category of Society & Culture on the Web directory Yahoo! (**www.yahoo.ca**) yielded the following subcategories and possible broad topics:

Disabilities
Etiquette
Mythology & Folklore
Pets
Religion & Spirituality

An additional advantage of this strategy is that you now have both a broad topic and one or more potential sources for your presentation. We will talk more about electronic and other sources in more detail later in this chapter.

Listening and Reading for Topic Ideas

Listen
and
Respond

It is not unusual to see on television or read in a newspaper something that triggers an idea for a presentation. For example, the following list of quite varied topics was suggested by the headlines in a recent daily newspaper:

Corporate accounting scandals
Canada's declining health-care system
Diagnosing breast cancer
Canadian government aid to foreign nationals

The nightly news is not the only media source of potential topics. You might also get topic ideas from television talk shows or from general interest or news magazines. Or you might get an idea from a non-fiction book. Perhaps you have just read Daniel Goleman's *Working with Emotional Intelligence*. You might decide to give a speech on what emotional intelligence is and why it is important in the workplace.

You might also find a topic in material you have studied for a class. Perhaps you recently had an interesting discussion of minimum mandatory sentencing in your criminology class. It might make a good topic for a presentation. And your instructor would probably be happy to suggest additional resources.

Even a topic that comes up in casual conversation with friends may make a good speech topic. Perhaps everyone in your dorm seems to be sniffling and coughing all at once. "It's sick-building syndrome," gasps one. Sick-building syndrome might be an interesting topic for a presentation.

The point is to keep your eyes and ears open. You never know when you might see or hear a potential topic. If you do, write it down. Nothing is so frustrating as to know you had a good idea for a topic but not to be able to remember what it was!

If you discover potential topics through brainstorming, surfing the Web, or listening or reading, you should still consider the communication principles of adapting to your audience and being aware of your own interests and experiences before you make your final topic selection. And you will also need to consider the time limits of the speaking assignment. Many good topics need to be narrowed before they are viable for a given assignment. Be realistic. Although many beginning speakers worry about how they will ever fill three minutes, in reality, more speakers run over their time limits than under.

One strategy for narrowing topics is to construct the kinds of categories and subcategories created by Web directories. Write your general topic at the top of a list, making each succeeding word or phrase more specific and narrow. For example, in order to narrow the topic "animals," write it down and then write an increasingly specific list of topics under it:

Animals
Pets
Reptiles
Bearded dragons
Caring for a bearded dragon

If you have 10 minutes for your presentation, you might decide that the last topic is too narrow. If so, just go back one step. In 10 minutes, you may be able to discuss characteristics and habits of bearded dragons, as well as how to care for them.

ReCAP

Select and Narrow Your Topic

- Consider the audience, the occasion, and your interests and experiences.
- Practise silent brainstorming.
- Scan Web directories and Web pages.
- Listen and read for topic ideas.
- Narrow your topic by generating increasingly specific categories and subcategories.

IDENTIFYING YOUR PURPOSE

With topic in hand, you now need to clarify your purpose for your presentation. If you are unclear about exactly what you hope to accomplish, you probably won't accomplish anything, except to ramble about your topic in some sort of vague way. Clear objectives, on the other hand, can help you select main ideas, an organizational strategy, and supporting material, and can even influence the way in which you deliver the presentation. You should determine both your general purpose and your specific purpose for every presentation that you give.

⋯⟩ General Purpose

general purpose
The broad reason for giving a presentation: to inform, to persuade, or to entertain an audience.

Your **general purpose** will be either to inform, to persuade, or to entertain. When you inform, you teach. You define, describe, or explain a thing, person, place, concept, or process. You may use some humour in your presentation; you may encourage your audience to seek out further information about your topic. But your primary purpose for speaking is to give information.

If you are using information to try to change or reinforce your audience's ideas or convictions or to urge your audience to do something, your general purpose is persuasive. The insurance representative who tries to get you to buy life insurance, the candidate for you preferred political party who asks for your vote, and the coordinator of Habitat for Humanity who urges your church group to get involved in building homes, all have persuasive general purposes.

Aware

The speaker whose purpose is to entertain tries to get the members of his or her audience to smile, laugh, and generally enjoy themselves. For the audience members, learning something or being persuaded about something is secondary to having a good time. Most after-dinner speakers speak to entertain. So do most stand-up comedians and storytellers.

In your speech class, the general purpose for each assignment will probably be set by your instructor. Because the general purpose influences the way you develop and organize your presentation, as well as the way you deliver it, it is important that you be aware of your general purpose throughout the process of developing and delivering your presentation.

⋯⟩ Specific Purpose

Knowing whether you want to inform, persuade, or entertain clarifies your general purpose for speaking. You also need to determine your **specific purpose.** A specific purpose is a concise statement of what your listeners should know or be able to do or how they should feel by the time you finish your presentation. In other words, a specific purpose is an audience-centred goal for your presentation. You can begin every specific purpose for every presentation with the words:

specific purpose
A concise statement of what listeners should know or be able to do, or how they should feel, by the time the speaker finishes the presentation.

> At the end of my presentation, the audience will . . .

And then specify a behaviour. For example, if you are giving an informative presentation on eating disorders, you might state:

Verbal

> At the end of my presentation, the audience will be able to explain the causes and most successful treatments for anorexia and bulimia.

Every subsequent decision you make while preparing and delivering your presentation should be guided by your specific purpose. As soon as you have formulated it, write it on a note card and keep it with you while you are working on your presentation. Think of it as a compass pointing true north—toward your audience. Refer to it often.

DEVELOPING YOUR CENTRAL IDEA

central idea
The thesis statement of a presentation.

Although your specific purpose indicates what you want your audience to know or do by the end of your presentation, your **central idea** specifies the topic of the presentation and makes some definitive statement about it. If you have taken a writing course in college or university, you may have used the term *thesis statement* for the central idea. Sometimes, as

ReCAP ⟵┈┈

Identify Your Purpose

GENERAL PURPOSE

• To inform	To define, describe, or explain a thing, person, place, concept, or process
• To persuade	To change or reinforce audience members' ideas or convictions, or to urge them to do something
• To entertain	To amuse an audience

SPECIFIC PURPOSE

- Specifies what you want audience members to know, feel, or do by the end of your presentation
- Uses the words, "At the end of my presentation, the audience will . . ."

EXAMPLES OF GENERAL PURPOSES

EXAMPLES OF GENERAL PURPOSES	EXAMPLES OF SPECIFIC PURPOSES
To inform	At the end of my presentation, the audience will be able to list two benefits for adults who learn to play a musical instrument.
To persuade	At the end of my presentation, the audience will enrol in a music appreciation course.
To entertain	At the end of my presentation, the audience will be laughing at my misadventures as an adult cello student.

Effective speakers state their central idea during their introductory remarks to help their audience focus on the main points covered in the body of the speech.

in the following example, wording the central idea can be as simple as copying the part of the specific purpose statement that specifies what the audience should know, feel, or do.

TOPIC:	Foreign-language education
SPECIFIC PURPOSE:	At the end of my presentation, the audience will be able to explain two reasons foreign-language education should begin in the elementary grades.
CENTRAL IDEA:	Foreign-language education should begin in the elementary grades.

Even though they may seem similar, the specific purpose and central idea are used quite differently. The specific purpose guides you as you prepare your presentation; the central idea will guide the audience as they listen to the presentation. Although the specific purpose never actually appears in the presentation itself, the central idea does, usually at or near the end of the speaker's introduction. It provides the focus for the body of the presentation.

The most successful central ideas meet the following criteria: They are audience centred; they reflect a single topic; they are complete declarative sentences; and they use specific language. Let's consider each of these criteria in turn.

┈┈⟩ Audience Centred

If your specific purpose is audience centred, your central idea probably will be, too. It should reflect a topic in which the audience has a reason to be interested and should provide some knowledge they do not already have or make some claim about the topic that they may not have previously considered. The second of the following central ideas is more appropriate to an audience of college and university students than the first.

INAPPROPRIATE:	Taking Advanced Placement classes in high school can help fulfil your general education requirements. *(Inappropriate because taking Advanced Placement classes is something college and university students either did or did not do in the past. They cannot make any decisions about them at this point.)*

Adapt

| APPROPRIATE: | Taking Web-based classes can help fulfil your general studies requirements. *(Appropriate because students are probably looking for various options for completing required courses. They can still choose to take courses on the Web.)* |

⤳ A Single Topic

A central idea should reflect a single topic. Trying to cover more than one topic, even if multiple topics are related, only muddles your presentation and confuses the audience.

| MULTIPLE TOPICS: | Clubbing and running in marathons are two activities that appeal to many college and university students. |
| SINGLE TOPIC: | Clubbing appeals to many college and university students. |

⤳ A Complete Declarative Sentence

declarative sentence
A complete sentence that makes a statement, as opposed to asking a question.

Your central idea should be more than just the word or phrase that is your topic—it should make a claim about your topic. Questions may help you come up with a central idea, but questions themselves are not good central ideas, because they don't make any kind of claim. A central idea should be a complete **declarative sentence**—not a topic and not a question.

TOPIC:	Study abroad
QUESTION:	Should students consider opportunities to study abroad?
CENTRAL IDEA:	Study abroad provides significant advantages for students in most fields of study.

⤳ Specific Language

A good central idea should use specific rather than general, vague, or abstract language.

| VAGUE: | Crop circles are not what they seem to be. |
| SPECIFIC: | Although they have been variously attributed to alien forces and unknown fungi, crop circles are really just a clever hoax. |

GENERATING MAIN IDEAS

Getting from the central idea to related but more specific main ideas can seem a challenging task, but actually you can use the central idea to generate main ideas. Here's how.

Write the central idea at the top of a clean sheet of paper or your computer screen. Then ask yourself two questions:

1. Does the central idea have *logical divisions?*
2. Can you support the central idea with a series of *steps* or a *chronological sequence?*

You should be able to answer yes to one of these questions and to write down the corresponding divisions, reasons, or steps. Let's apply this strategy to several examples.

Re**CAP** ⬅

The Central Idea Should . . .

Be audience centred

Reflect a single topic

Be a complete declarative sentence

Use specific language

⋯⋗ Does the Central Idea Have *Logical Divisions*?

Suppose that your central idea is "Most accomplished guitarists play three types of guitars." The phrase "three types" is a flag that indicates that this central idea does indeed have logical divisions—those being, in this case, the three types of guitars. You list the three that come to mind:

1. Acoustic   2. Classical   3. Electric

Right now you are simply trying to generate main ideas. You may revise them—and your central idea—several times before you actually deliver the presentation. For example, you may decide that you need to include steel guitars in your list. So you revise your central idea to read "four types of guitars" and add "steel" to your list.

⋯⋗ Can You Support the Central Idea with a Series of *Steps* or a *Chronological Sequence*?

"After you graduate from college or university, you will want to find employment directly related to your field of study." This seemed liked a good central idea when you came up with it. However, it doesn't have any logical divisions, so now what do you do? You can support this central idea with a chronological sequence of the problem—looking for employment. You jot down the following points:

1. Research employment opportunities directly related to your field of study.
2. Research employers who hire graduates in your field of study.
3. Write a resumé and covering letter that incorporate researched information, targeting specific employer needs.
4. Preview and edit your written materials.
5. Have your written materials proofread by others.
6. Mail your resumé and covering letter to targeted employers.
7. Create a job search journal incorporating employer feedback.
8. Follow up with specific employers.

These eight steps, arranged in chronological order, could become the main ideas of your speech.

How many main ideas should you have? Your topic and time limit will help you decide. A short presentation (three to five minutes) might have only two main ideas. A longer one (eight to ten minutes) might have four or five. If you find that you have more potential main ideas than you can use, decide which main ideas are likely to be most interesting, relevant, and perhaps persuasive to your audience. Or combine two or more closely related ideas.

GATHERING SUPPORTING MATERIAL

By the time you have decided on your main ideas, you have a skeleton presentation. Your next task is to flesh out that skeleton with **supporting material,** both verbal and visual. Verbal supporting material includes illustrations, explanations, descriptions, definitions, analogies, statistics, and opinions— material that will clarify, amplify, and provide evidence to support your main ideas and your thesis. Visual supporting material includes objects, charts, graphs, posters, maps, models, and all kinds of computer-generated graphics. You can also support your speech with audio aids such as music or sounds from a CD-ROM or DVD. We will discuss strategies for using presentation aids in Chapter 12. The speaker who seeks out strong verbal and visual supporting material is adhering to the fundamental communication principles of effectively using both verbal and nonverbal messages.

Verbal
Nonverbal

supporting material
Verbal illustrations, explanations, descriptions, definitions, analogies, statistics, and opinions; and objects, charts, graphs, posters, maps, models, graphics, and other presentation aids.

⋯⋗ Sources of Supporting Material

Like a chef who needs to know where to buy quality fresh fruits and vegetables for gourmet recipes, you need to know where to turn for supporting material that will effectively develop your presentation and achieve your specific purpose. We will discuss three potential sources of supporting material: you and people you know, the Internet, and the library.

Listen
and
Respond

Aware

Internet
A vast collection of hundreds of thousands of computers accessible to millions of people all over the world.

World Wide Web
The most popular information delivery system of the Internet.

directory
An Internet site that offers the user ever-more-specific categories through which to search the World Wide Web.

search engine
An Internet site that works much like a traditional card catalogue or index, allowing the user to perform a subject or keyword search of the World Wide Web.

hit
A Web site or Web page discovered as a result of a search; also refers to any single access of a site or page.

Web site
A location on the World Wide Web that includes a number of related Web pages.

Web page
An individual file or screen that is part of a larger Web site.

advanced or Boolean search
A Web search that ties words together so that a search engine can hunt for the resulting phrase.

You and People You Know

You needn't look far for at least some of the supporting material for your presentation. You may wish to include some personal experience, such as undergoing plastic surgery or negotiating a favourable apartment lease. Or you may have discovered your topic through listening to others. For example, your roommate may have confided in you about her mother's treatment for melanoma. The point is that you don't necessarily need to use the Internet or run to the library for every piece of supporting material for every topic on which you speak. It's true that most well-researched presentations will include some objective material gathered from the Internet or from library resources, but don't overlook the expertise and experience of yourself or the people you know. As an audience-centred speaker, realize that personal knowledge or experience can heighten your credibility in the minds of your listeners. They will respect your authority if they realize that you have first-hand knowledge of the topic on which you are speaking.

The Internet

The **Internet** is the first place many of us turn when faced with a research task. The most popular Internet information-delivery system is the **World Wide Web.** You have probably accessed material on the Web through a **directory** or **search engine** such as Yahoo!, AltaVista, or another of the sites listed in Table 11.1.

You can use directories and search engines in two ways: by clicking on subject categories that are in turn broken down into ever-more-specific subcategories, or by entering key words or phrases into a designated space, clicking on a "Find" command, and then sorting through the **hits**, or resulting list of **Web sites** and **Web pages** that deal with the topic you entered.

The Web sites and Web pages you discover may include personal pages, books, periodicals, newspapers and wire services, reference material, and government documents. In addition, you may discover indexes and catalogues for accessing these various kinds of resources. You may even find sites designed to help you prepare and deliver your presentations. Although the sheer volume of material may be overwhelming for even the most experienced researchers, two strategies can help.

First, explore the **advanced or Boolean search** capabilities of your directory or search engine. Most offer directions on how to limit your search to those sites that are most relevant to what you are looking for. Boolean searches allow you to enclose phrases in quotation marks or parentheses so that a search yields only those sites on which all words of the phrase appear together, rather than sites that contain any word in the phrase. You

TABLE 11.1   **Popular World Wide Web Directories and Search Engines***

AltaVista	**www.altavista.ca** Alta Vista is both a directory and a keyword search engine.
Google	**www.google.ca** In addition to providing both a directory and a keyword search engine, Google enables the user to conduct specific image searches.
Lycos	**www.lycos.ca** "Lycos," the Greek word for "spider," is also an Internet term for an automated program that scans the Web in order to index sites.
WebCrawler	**www.webcrawler.com** A metasearch engine that searches other search engines simultaneously.
Yahoo!	**www.yahoo.ca** Both a directory and a search engine, Yahoo! is one of the best for browsing a wide-ranging topical list of sites. Each topic branches to additional topical subcategories.

*If some of these or other URLs provided in this chapter change or become unavailable at a later date, you may be automatically forwarded to new sites. If not, you can search for the sites by name. And if you still can't find a site, chances are that several new and better ones have taken its place.

can also insert the word *or* between two parenthetical phrases, directing your search to include documents in which either phrase appears. Or you can insert the word *and* between parenthetical phrases to indicate that you wish to see results that contain both phrases. These relatively simple strategies can help you narrow a list of hits from, in some cases, millions to a more workable number.

A second strategy for consideration regarding information you discover on the World Wide Web has to do with appropriately interpreting the accuracy of Web sites. When deciding whether the material you have discovered is usable, keep in mind the following criteria:

1. *Accountability.* Find out what organization or individual is responsible for the Web site. Is the sponsor or organization legitimate? If the sponsor is an individual, what are the person's qualifications for writing on this topic? If you cannot discover an author, be wary of the site.
2. *Accuracy.* Sources of facts should be documented on a Web site just as they are in a print source. Web sites should also be relatively free of errors in usage and mechanics. If a site contains such errors, it might also contain errors in content.
3. *Objectivity.* As noted above, you need to know who has posted the site. Consider the philosophies and possible biases of the organization or individual responsible for the site. Are those beliefs, interests, and biases likely to slant the information? The more objective the author, the more credible the facts and information.
4. *Date.* Many sites will include a statement of when the site was posted and when it was last updated. In most cases, when you are concerned with factual data, the more recent, the better.
5. *Usability.* Frames, graphics, and multimedia resources can enhance a site, or they can complicate it by increasing the time it takes to load. Consider the practical efficiency of the sites you explore.

The Library

Despite the explosion of World Wide Web resources in recent years, the library remains a rich source of supporting material. Most libraries, from the largest research university library to the smallest village public library, house the following kinds of resources:

Books
Periodicals
Full-text databases
Newspapers
Reference resources
Government documents
Special services

Books   A library's books are housed in the **stacks,** often several floors of seemingly endless shelves of books. Books are organized in the stacks according to **call number,** a reference number assigned to each book, which encodes the subject or topic, as well as the author. Most libraries use the **National Library of Canada classification system** of call numbers.

stacks
The collection of books in a library.

call number
The numerical code by which books are organized in a library.

National Library of Canada classification system
The most commonly used system of call numbers.

ReCAP

Using the World Wide Web as a Source of Supporting Material

1. Use a directory or search engine to find relevant sites.

2. Expect to discover a wide variety of sites: personal pages, books, periodicals, newspapers and wire services, reference material, government documents, and indexes and catalogues.

3. Evaluate Web sites according to these five criteria: accountability, accuracy, objectivity, date, and usability.

card catalogue
A file of information about the books in a library; may be an index-card file or a computerized system.

A library's central catalogue of all its books is called the **card catalogue.** Today, most card catalogues are electronic ones. Banks of monitors in a central location in the library provide directions for looking up the books you need. Many college and university card catalogues these days are also accessible from remote locations, meaning that you can search them online and build preliminary bibliographies of books and call numbers before ever coming to the library building itself.

If your presentation addresses a current topic, or if you want to use current examples, you probably will not find the information you need in books, as books generally are written two to three years before they are published. If you decide to use books, card catalogue records have all the necessary information, such as the author's name, title of the book, publisher, and date of publication (see Figure 11.2). For up-to-date information, periodicals and newspapers are available both online and in hard copy.

periodical
A popular magazine or professional journal.

periodical index
A listing of bibliographical data for articles published in a group of magazines or journals during a given time period.

Periodicals   The term **periodicals** refers both to magazines, such as *Time, People,* and *Sports Illustrated,* and to professional journals, such as *College English* and the *Quarterly Journal of Economics.* Both types of periodicals can be useful for presentations.

Periodical indexes are the equivalent of card catalogues in helping you locate information you need. A number of such indexes cover many topics and most of the thousands of periodicals published. Many periodical indexes are available on CD-ROM, and many can be accessed either from the library or from remote locations. In most periodical indexes, entries are indexed alphabetically according to both subject and author. Most people use them by searching for subjects or keywords, much as they would conduct a World Wide Web search. Some periodical indexes are **full-text databases,** meaning that you can access not only bibliographical information but the texts of the articles themselves.

full-text database
A World Wide Web or CD-ROM indexing system that provides not only bibliographic data but full texts of entries.

newspaper index
A listing of bibliographical data for articles published in a newspaper (or group of newspapers) during a given time period.

Newspapers   You can find information that is only hours old by reading the latest edition of a daily newspaper. Newspapers also offer the most detailed coverage available of current events.

Newspapers today exist in three formats: traditional newsprint, microfilm, and online. As with books and periodicals, you need a subject index to help you find newspaper articles of potential value to the topic you are researching. **Newspaper indexes** are published for a number of medium-to-large newspapers. Your library may subscribe to several of these.

reference resources
Material housed in the reference section of a library; may include encyclopedias, dictionaries, directories, atlases, almanacs, yearbooks, books of quotations, and biographical dictionaries.

Reference Resources   A library's **reference resources** include encyclopedias, dictionaries, directories, atlases, almanacs, yearbooks, books of quotations, and biographical dictionaries. As a speaker, you may at one time or another use most of these types of materials. Like periodicals, newspapers, and microfilm, reference resources are usually available only for in-house research and cannot be checked out.

FIGURE 11.2 Entry from an Electronic Card Catalogue

AUTHOR: Powers, M. Fishback

TITLE: Footprints: The True Story Behind the Poem
That Inspired Millions

PUBLISHER: HarperCollins Publishers Ltd., 1993

SUBJECTS: Life stories, fulfilment and happiness

LIBRARY HOLDINGS:
Floor 5 (A-J), 6 (K-Q)

1. ISBN: 0-00-647425-X–BOOK–Available

Government Documents   The federal government publishes information on almost every conceivable subject and keeps records of most official federal proceedings. Once a dauntingly complex collection of pamphlets, special reports, and texts of speeches and debates, **government documents** today are much more readily accessible through the World Wide Web.

Canadian statistics can be found online at **www.statcan.ca/start.html.** An informative Web site filled with Canadian government documents is **www.canada.gc.ca/publications/publication_e.html.** Canadian issues are highlighted in the official newspaper of the Government of Canada, the *Canada Gazette.* The government's daily news bulletin, *The Wire,* reports on news items and provincial, territorial, municipal, and private sector matters. You can read it online at **www.canada.gc.ca/wire/wire_e.html.**

Special Services   Interlibrary loan and **reciprocal borrowing privileges** are among the special services that can help you find resources not otherwise available through your own library or online.

Say you are reading an article and discover a reference to a book you would like to see. Your library does not own the book. You might be able to use interlibrary loan to locate the book at another library and have it sent to your library within a few days. Or, if your library has reciprocal borrowing privileges with another nearby library, you may be able to go yourself to that library and locate the book.

⤑ Types of Supporting Material

If you have explored the knowledge and insights of yourself and people you know, discovered material on the Internet, and examined a variety of library resources, you probably have a wealth of potential supporting material. Now you will need to decide what to use in your presentation. Keeping in mind your audience's knowledge, interests, and expectations will help you determine where an illustration might stir their emotions, where an explanation might help them understand a point, and where statistics might convince them of the significance of a problem. Let's discuss these and other types of supporting material and consider suggestions for using them effectively.

Illustrations

Illustrations offer an example of or tell a story about an idea, issue, or problem a speaker is discussing. They can be as short as a word or phrase or as long as a well-developed paragraph. Sometimes speakers will offer a series of brief illustrations, as Stephanie did in her speech on the failure of network television to reflect multiculturalism:

> Today TV seems determined to wear a cosmopolitan yuppified face in pursuit of viewers who flock to *Friends, Frasier,* and *Dharma and Greg.*[1]

Other speakers may offer longer and more detailed illustrations:

> In a small town in eastern Canada, a young woman sits devastated. The snowstorm has been worse than expected. She is trapped in her stalled car and the snowdrifts now cover the top of its roof, reducing visibility to zero. As minutes turn into hours, she begins to numb. Then, she hears people calling her name. As she pokes her snow scraper through the cracked window of the car and the snow above, she hears, "Look, something in the snow drift ... over there!" Within two hours of her rescue, her thoughts turn from terror to immense relief and gratitude toward those neighbours she never knew.

Illustrations may be true examples of past events or **hypothetical illustrations**—ones that have not actually occurred. If you decide to use a hypothetical illustration, it is important to make clear to your audience that the scene you describe never really happened.

Whether you choose to use brief or extended illustrations, true or hypothetical ones, remember this principle: Everybody likes to hear a story. An illustration almost always ensures audience interest. In addition, the following suggestions should help you use illustrations effectively in your presentations.

---

government documents
Material published by the government, including records of official proceedings, pamphlets and brochures, and statistical data.

interlibrary loan
A borrowing/lending arrangement between one library and another.

reciprocal borrowing privileges
A borrowing/lending arrangement among libraries that allows patrons of any one library to use the resources of the others.

Verbal

illustration
A story or anecdote that provides an example of an idea, an issue, or a problem the speaker is discussing.

hypothetical illustration
An example or story that has not actually occurred.

This speaker effectively uses an electronic presentation aid to complement his use of descriptions and explanations.

Verbal

description
A statement that provides a word picture of something.

explanation
A statement that makes clear how something is done or why it exists in its present or past form.

definition
A statement of what something means.

classification
A definition constructed by first placing a term in the general class to which it belongs and then differentiating it from all other members of that class.

operational definition
A statement that shows how a term works or what it does.

analogy
A comparison between two ideas, things, or situations that demonstrates how something unfamiliar is similar to something the audience already understands.

literal analogy
A comparison between two similar things.

figurative analogy
A comparison between two seemingly dissimilar things that share some common feature on which the comparison depends.

statistics
Numerical data that summarize examples.

- Be sure that your illustrations are directly relevant to the idea or point they are supposed to support.
- Choose illustrations that are typical, not exceptions.
- Make your illustrations vivid and specific.
- Use illustrations with which your listeners can identify.
- Remember that the most effective illustrations are often personal ones.

Descriptions and Explanations

Probably the most commonly used forms of supporting material are **descriptions** and **explanations.** To describe is to provide detailed images that allow an audience to see, hear, smell, touch, or taste whatever you are describing. Descriptions can make people and scenes come alive for an audience, and will heighten their interest in your speech. Explanations of how something works can promote understanding of events or processes.

Although descriptions and explanations are part of most presentations, they lack the inherent interest factor that illustrations have. The following suggestions may help you prevent audiences from yawning through your descriptions and explanations:

- Avoid too many descriptions and explanations.
- Keep your descriptions and explanations brief.
- Describe and explain in specific and concrete language.

Definitions

Speakers should offer **definitions** of all technical or little-known terms in their presentations. However, they do not need to define terms with which most or all audience members are likely to be familiar. If you determine that you should define a word or phrase for your audience, consider whether you can best define it by **classification,** the format of a standard dictionary definition, or by an **operational definition,** explaining how the word or phrase works or what it does.

To use definitions effectively, consider the following suggestions:

- Use definitions only when necessary.
- Be certain that your definitions are understandable.
- Be sure that any definition you provide accurately reflects your use of the word or phrase throughout the presentation.

Analogies

Analogies demonstrate how unfamiliar ideas, things, and situations are similar to something the audience already understands. Speakers can use two types of analogies in their presentations. The first is a **literal analogy,** or comparison of two similar things. Kyle uses a literal analogy to compare the African slave trade to other historical travesties:

> The trans-Atlantic slave trade was one of the greatest tragedies in human history, rivaled by such horrible events as the Jewish Holocaust and the Spanish invasion of the Americas.[2]

The second type of analogy is a **figurative analogy,** or comparison of two seemingly dissimilar things that in fact share a significant common feature. Stephen compares the human body to a car in this figurative analogy dealing with the impact of water deficiency on the human body:

> We chug along until our "motors" burn up.[3]

Two suggestions can help you use analogies more effectively in your presentations:

1. Be certain that the two things you compare in a literal analogy are very similar.
2. Make the similarity between the two objects in a figurative analogy apparent to the audience.

Statistics

Statistics or numbers can represent hundreds or thousands of illustrations, helping a speaker express the significance, magnitude, reliability, and validity of a situation. Statistics can also help a speaker express the relationship of a part to the whole.

Statistics Canada uses both types of statistics in its 2001 census analysis series: Canada's labour force consisted of almost 15.6 million people, up 9.5% from 14.2 million a decade earlier. The number of women in the labour force grew at twice the pace of men, increasing 13.8% to 7.3 million.[4]

You can use statistics more effectively if you consider the following three suggestions:

1. Round large numbers.
2. Use visual aids to present your statistics.
3. Cite the sources of your statistics.

Opinions

The opinions of others can add authority, drama, and style to a presentation. A speaker can use three types of opinions: **expert testimony, lay testimony,** and **literary quotations.**

Expert testimony is perhaps the most frequent type of opinion employed by speakers. If you lack recognized authority in the area of your topic, cite someone who can offer such expertise. In his speech on Canada's official policy of multiculturalism, David realized that his audience might not accept the argument that emphasizing differences among Canadians promotes the notion of being separate rather than a sense of belonging. Therefore, David quoted an expert:

> Citizenship, whether through birth or naturalization, implies belonging. It implies a basic commitment of intellectual and emotional loyalty. It is a thing of value. And yet, in recent years, the diminishing value of Canadian citizenship—the creation of the hyphenated Canadian with divided loyalties, the perception that immigration policy now permits the rich to buy their way into the country, the idea that citizenship is a matter of rights and not of obligations—means that the opposite has also come to be true. Canadian citizenship is frequently seen not as a means of committing oneself to the country but simply as a way of abandoning it with an assurance of safety.[5]

Few speakers will have eyewitnesses at hand when they present. However, they can quote first-hand witnesses of dramatic or traumatic events. Such lay testimony can stir an audience's emotions and provide the most memorable moments of a presentation.

Finally, speakers may wish to include literary quotations in their presentations. Such quotations add to the validity of the speaker's topic. Concluding David's speech on Canada's official policy of multiculturalism with a quote from Pierre Elliott Trudeau would likely have an impact on the audience.

Whether you use expert testimony, lay testimony, or literary quotations, consider the following suggestions for using opinions effectively in your presentations:

- Be certain that any authority you cite is actually an expert on the subject you are discussing.
- Identify your sources.
- Cite unbiased authorities.
- Cite opinions that are representative of prevailing opinion. If you cite a dissenting viewpoint, identify it as such.
- Quote or paraphrase your sources accurately and within the context in which the remarks were originally made.
- Use literary quotations sparingly.

Now that you have gathered supporting material for your speech, it is time to organize your main ideas. Now watch your presentation take shape!

ORGANIZING YOUR MAIN IDEAS

You have already completed the first five stages of audience-centred speech preparation:

- Select and narrow a topic.
- Determine your purpose.
- Develop your central idea.

Verbal

expert testimony
The opinion of someone who is an acknowledged expert in the field or area under discussion.

lay testimony
The opinion of someone who experienced an event or situation first-hand.

literary quotation
The words spoken by a famous person or written in literature that add validity to a presentation.

- Generate main ideas.
- Gather supporting material.

Organizing the ideas and information you have generated and discovered will take some time and effort. There are a number of ways of doing this:

- Logically
- Chronologically
- Topically
- Showing cause and effect
- By problems and solutions

Let's talk first about strategies for organizing the main ideas and then about organizing supporting material and developing transitions in the body of the presentation. Next, we will talk about effectively introducing and concluding your presentations. Finally, we will discuss how to outline the entire presentation structure.

⋯⟩ Organizing Ideas Logically

logical organization
Organization involving a logical sequence of thought presented as introduction, body, and conclusion.

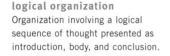
Verbal

Logical organization is one way you can communicate your verbal message effectively. A logically organized presentation has three major divisions—an introduction, a body, and a conclusion. The introduction catches the audience's attention and previews the body. The body presents the main content of the presentation. The conclusion summarizes the main ideas and provides memorable closure to the presentation.

⋯⟩ Organizing Ideas Chronologically

chronological organization
Organization by time or sequence.

If you determine that you can best develop your central idea through a series of steps, you will probably organize those steps—your main ideas—chronologically. **Chronological organization** is sequential order, according to when each step or event occurred or should occur. If you are explaining a process, you will want to organize the steps of that process from first to last. If you are providing a historical overview of an event, movement, or policy, you might begin with the end result and trace its history backwards in time.

⋯⟩ Organizing Ideas Topically

topical organization
Organization according to the speaker's discretion, recency, primacy, or complexity.

If your main ideas are natural divisions of your central idea, you will probably arrange them according to **topical organization.** Topical organization may organize main ideas that are fairly equal in importance. For example, if you are giving an informative presentation on tips for a job search, your main ideas probably will be dress, speech, nonverbal communication, research, and interview skills.

recency
Arranging ideas from the least to the most important.

The principle of **recency** suggests that audiences remember best what they hear last. If you want to emphasize interview skills, you will purposefully place that tip last in your presentation.

If you intend to describe a series of different types of procedures in your presentation, you may find that it works well to organize your main ideas topically.

Another principle that can help guide your topical organization is the principle of **primacy.** Primacy suggests that you discuss first your most convincing or least controversial idea. To adapt to an audience who may be skeptical of some of your ideas, discuss first those points on which you all agree, for example, the importance of finding a job.

One other type of topical organization is organization according to **complexity,** moving from simple ideas and processes to more complex ones. Many skills you have learned in life have been taught by order of complexity. If you are giving a presentation on how to maintain employment, you might discuss verbal communication, teamwork, and specific knowledge needed to do your job.

Organizing Ideas to Show Cause and Effect

Cause-and-effect organization actually refers to two related patterns: identifying a situation and then discussing the resulting effects (cause–effect), and presenting a situation and then exploring its causes (effect–cause).

A speaker who discusses the consequences of being fired from a job might use a cause–effect pattern, establishing first that good communication skills are necessary to maintain employment and then discussing various consequences or effects. On the other hand, a speaker who speaks on the same topic, but chooses to explore the reasons for being fired, will probably use an effect–cause pattern, discussing being fired first as an effect and then exploring its various causes. As the recency principle would suggest, a cause–effect pattern emphasizes effects; an effect–cause pattern emphasizes causes.

Organizing Ideas by Problem and Solution

If, instead of exploring causes or consequences of a problem or issue, you want either to explore how best to solve the problem or to advocate a particular solution, you will probably choose **problem-and-solution organization.** For example, if you were speaking on how to protect yourself from grizzly bear attacks in Canada's national parks, you might first establish that a significant problem exists, then talk about solutions to that problem. Although you can use problem-and-solution organization for either informative or persuasive presentations, you are more likely to use it when your general purpose is to persuade— to urge your audience to support or adopt one or more of the solutions you discuss.

ORGANIZING YOUR SUPPORTING MATERIAL

Once you have organized your main ideas, you are ready to organize the supporting material for each idea. The same organizational patterns you considered as you organized your main ideas can also help you organize your supporting material. For example, you might arrange a group of brief illustrations chronologically. At other times, you might find it

Adapt

primacy
Arranging ideas from the strongest or least controversial to the weakest or most controversial.

complexity
Arranging ideas from the simple to the more complex.

cause-and-effect organization
Organization by discussing a situation and its causes or a situation and its effects.

problem-and-solution organization
Organization by discussing first a problem and then various solutions.

ReCAP

Organizing Your Main Ideas

STRATEGY	DESCRIPTION
Logical	Organization involving a logical sequence of thought presented as introduction, body, and conclusion
Chronological	Organization by time or sequence
Topical	Arbitrary arrangement or organization according to recency, primacy, or complexity
Cause and effect	Organization by discussing a situation and its causes, or a situation and its effects
Problem and solution	Organization by discussing a problem and then various solutions

COMMUNICATION and DIVERSITY

Acknowledging Cultural Differences in Organizing Messages

What's the shortest distance between two points? Why, going in a straight line, of course. In organizing a message, it may seem that the most logical strategy is to develop a structure that moves from one idea to the next in a logical, "straight" way of thinking. But not every culture organizes ideas using that logic. In fact, each culture teaches its members unique patterns of thought and organization that are considered appropriate for various occasions and audiences. In general, Canadian speakers tend to be more linear and direct than do Semitic, Asian, Romance, or Russian speakers.[6] Semitic speakers support their main points by pursuing tangents that might seem "off topic" to many Canadian listeners. Asians may allude to a main point only through a circuitous route of illustrations and parables. And speakers from Romance and Russian cultures tend to begin with a basic principle and then move to facts and illustrations that only gradually are related to a main point. The models in Figure 11.3 illustrate these culturally diverse patterns of organization.[7] Of course, these are very broad generalizations. It should be noted that assigning characteristics by nationality is used as a general guideline to compare and learn from communication preferences when organizing messages. As an effective speaker who seeks to adapt to your audience, you should investigate and perhaps acknowledge or even consider adopting the customary organizational strategy of your particular audience. In addition, when you are listening to a presentation, recognizing the existence of cultural differences can help you appreciate and understand the organization of a speaker from a culture other than your own. In the Canadian context, family life preferences and traditions relating to cultural background would be an acceptable approach when organizing your message.

FIGURE 11.3 Organizational Patterns by Culture

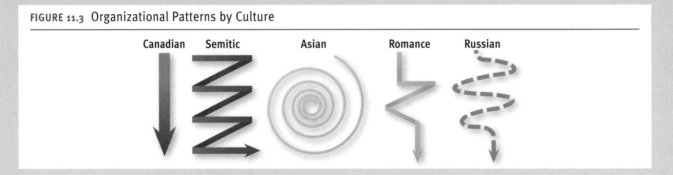

more useful to organize supporting material according to the principles of recency, primacy, or complexity. You would employ the principle of recency if you saved your most convincing statistic for last. You would use primacy if you decided to present first the opinion with which you were certain your audience would agree. And you might arrange two explanations according to the principle of complexity, presenting the simplest one first and working up to the more complex one. Two additional principles that may help you organize supporting material are **specificity** and arrangement from **"soft"** to **"hard" evidence**.

Sometimes your supporting material includes both very specific illustrations and a more general explanation. The principle of specificity suggests that you group your specific information and either offer it first, followed by your general explanation; or make your general explanation first and then support it with your specific illustrations.

Another principle that can help you organize your supporting material is moving from "soft" to "hard" evidence. Hypothetical illustrations, descriptions, definitions, analogies, and opinions are usually considered soft. "Hard" evidence consists of facts and statistics. David moves from a soft opinion to a harder factual illustration as he discusses Canada's official policy of multiculturalism:

> Canada welcomes immigrants with open arms and has become increasingly multi-ethnic and multicultural. According to Statistics Canada, Canada has welcomed 13.4 million immigrants since 1901. In 2001, 61% of immigrants who came to Canada in the 1990s used a nonofficial language as their primary home language. More than 200 different ethnic origins were reported in response to the 2001 census question on ethnic ancestry.

specificity
Organization from specific information to a more general statement, or from a general statement to specific information.

soft evidence
Supporting material based primarily on opinion or inference, including hypothetical illustrations, descriptions, explanations, definitions, analogies, and opinions.

hard evidence
Factual examples and statistics.

ReCAP

Organizing Your Supporting Material

STRATEGY	DESCRIPTION
Chronology	Sequential or reverse sequential order
Recency	Most important material last
Primacy	Most convincing or least controversial material first
Complexity	From simple to more complex material
Specificity	From specific information to general overview or from general overview to specific information
"Soft" to "hard" evidence	From hypothetical illustrations and opinions to facts and statistics

Acknowledgment of Supporting Material

Once you have supporting material in hand, you must decide whether it must be credited to a source. Some information is so widely known that you may not need to acknowledge a source. For example, you need not credit a source if you say that Lucien Bouchard played a major role during the October 1995 referendum campaign on Quebec independence. This fact is general knowledge and is widely available in a variety of reference sources. However, if you decide to use any of the following, then you must give credit:

- Direct quotations, even if they are only brief phrases
- Opinions, assertions, or ideas of others, even if you paraphrase them rather than quote them verbatim
- Statistics
- Any nonoriginal visual materials, including graphs, tables, and pictures

To cite your source, you can integrate an **oral citation** into your presentation. For example, you might say,

oral citation
The oral presentation of such information about a source as the author, title, and publication date.

> Quoting from an article entitled "Underweight Canadians," published by Statistics Canada in 2002, "According to the 1998–99 National Public Health Survey, almost one in 10 (9%) Canadians ages 15 and over, 2.2 million people, were underweight (i.e. they have a body mass index, or BMI, of less than 20). While the proportion of overweight individuals has increased steadily over time (from 17% in 1985 to 30% in 1998–99), that of underweight Canadians has dropped from 13% to 9% during these years."[8]

As you select your illustrations, descriptions, explanations, definitions, analogies, statistics, and opinions, be guided not only by the suggestions provided in this chapter for each type of supporting material but by the five communication principles for a lifetime. The best supporting material reflects self-awareness, taking advantage of your own knowledge and experience. Effective verbal supporting material is appropriately worded, concrete, and vivid enough that your audience can visualize what you are talking about. Effective visual supporting material enhances, rather than detracts from, your verbal message. Sensitivity to your audience will help you choose the verbal and visual supporting material that is most appropriately adapted to them. If a presentation is boring, it is probably because the speaker has not used the fundamental principles of communication as criteria for selecting supporting material.

ORGANIZING YOUR PRESENTATION—
THE FINAL TOUCHES

You now have a fairly complete, logically organized plan for your presentation. But if you tried to deliver it at this point, your audience would probably become confused. What are

ReCAP ⟵⋯

Supporting Your Speech

TYPE OF SUPPORTING MATERIAL	GUIDELINES FOR USE
Illustrations	• Make illustrations directly relevant to the idea or point. • Choose illustrations that are typical. • Make illustrations vivid and specific. • Use illustrations with which your listeners can identify. • Remember that the most effective illustrations are often personal ones.
Descriptions and Explanations	• Avoid too many descriptions and explanations. • Keep descriptions and explanations brief. • Describe and explain in specific and concrete language.
Definitions	• Use definitions only when necessary. • Be certain that definitions are understandable. • Be sure that a definition accurately reflects your use of the word or phrase.
Analogies	• Be certain that the two things you compare in a literal analogy are very similar. • Make the similarity between the two objects in a figurative analogy apparent to the audience.
Statistics	• Round large numbers. • Use visual aids. • Cite your sources.
Opinions	• Be certain that any authority you cite is actually an expert on the subject you are discussing. • Identify your sources. • Cite unbiased authorities. • Cite representative opinions, or identify dissenting viewpoints as such. • Quote or paraphrase accurately and in context. • Use literary quotations sparingly.

signpost
A verbal or nonverbal organizational signal.

preview
A statement of what is to come.

transition
A word, phrase, or nonverbal cue that indicates movement from one idea to the next.

summary
A recap of what has been said.

Adapt

initial preview
First statement of the main ideas of the presentation, usually presented with or near the central idea.

your main ideas? How is one main idea related to the next? What supporting material develops which main idea? To adapt your logically organized message to your audience, you need to provide organizational cues for their ears. You do this by adding **signposts—previews, transitions,** and **summaries**—that allow you to move smoothly from one idea to the next throughout the presentation. Once you have provided organizational cues, it is time to rehearse and look for areas that need improvement to ensure that your message is clearly understood. Once feedback from others has been incorporated into your message, you will be ready to present.

⋯⟩ Previews

A preview "tells them what you're going to tell them." It is a statement of what is to come. Previews help your audience members anticipate and remember the main ideas of your presentation. They also help you move smoothly from the introduction to the body of your presentation and from one main idea to the next. The **initial preview** is usually presented in conjunction with, and sometimes as part of, the central idea. Note how Blake states his central idea and then previews his three main ideas near the end of the introduction to his presentation on employment preparation:

> Finding a job upon graduation directly related to your field of study can be a difficult process. Preparation and persistance are key to success in the job search. Today, we will first examine the concept of networking, then review employment documentation, and finally discuss interview skills.

In addition to offering an initial preview, a speaker may also offer **internal previews** at various points throughout a presentation. These previews introduce and outline ideas that will be developed as the presentation progresses. An internal preview lets listeners know what the speaker is going to talk about. Their anticipation increases the likelihood that they will hear and later remember the speaker's solutions.

⤏ Verbal and Nonverbal Transitions

Effectively using and understanding verbal messages includes using **verbal transitions,** words or phrases that show relationships between ideas in your presentation. They include simple enumeration *(first, second, third);* repeated words or synonyms or pronouns that refer to earlier key words or ideas (the word *they* at the beginning of this sentence refers to the phrase "verbal transitions" in the previous sentence); and words and phrases that show relationships between ideas *(in addition, not only . . . but also, in other words, in summary, therefore, however).* As you begin to rehearse your presentation, you might need to experiment with various verbal transitions to achieve coherence that seems natural and logical to you. If none of the verbal alternatives seems quite right, consider a **nonverbal transition.**

Nonverbal transitions are sometimes used alone and sometimes in combination with verbal transitions. An effective nonverbal transition might take the form of facial expression, a pause, a change in vocal pitch or speaking rate, or movement. Most good speakers will use a combination of verbal and nonverbal transitions to help them move from one idea to the next throughout their presentations.

If this speaker carefully uses signposts, previews, transitions, and summaries, his presentation will be easier for his audience to follow.

internal preview
Preview within the speech that introduces ideas still to come.

verbal transition
A word or phrase that indicates the relationship between two ideas.

⤏ Summaries

Like previews, summaries provide an additional opportunity for the audience to grasp a speaker's most important ideas. Most speakers use two types of summaries: **internal summaries** and a **final summary.**

Internal summaries, like internal previews, occur within and throughout a presentation. You might want to use an internal summary after you have discussed two or three main ideas, to ensure that the audience keeps them firmly in mind as you move into another main idea.

You may also want to provide your audience with a final opportunity to hear and remember your main ideas, in the form of a final summary in your conclusion. Although your initial preview gave your audience their first exposure to your main ideas, your final summary will give them their last exposure to those ideas.

Adding previews, transitions, and summaries to your well-organized presentation applies the fundamental principles of using both verbal and nonverbal messages effectively and of adapting your message to others, increasing the likelihood that your audience will grasp your main ideas and the logic of your organizational strategy.

nonverbal transition
Facial expression, vocal cue, or physical movement that indicates a speaker is moving from one idea to the next.

internal summary
A recap of what has been said so far in the presentation.

final summary
A recap of all the main points of a presentation, usually occurring just before or during the conclusion.

INTRODUCING AND CONCLUDING YOUR PRESENTATION

At this point, you have pretty well developed the ideas and content of the body of your presentation, and you have strategies for organizing that material. But you have not yet given much thought to how you are going to begin and end the presentation. That's okay. Even though you will deliver it first, you usually plan your introduction last. You need to know first what you're introducing—especially your central idea and main ideas. Once you do, it is time to plan how you are going to introduce and conclude your presentation. Although they make up a relatively small percentage of the total presentation, your **introduction** and **conclusion** provide your audience with first and final impressions of you and your presentation. They are important considerations in adapting your message to others.

introduction
Opening lines of a presentation, which must catch the audience's attention and introduce the speaker's topic.

conclusion
Closing lines of a presentation, which leave a final impression.

···> Introductions

Your introduction should convince your audience to listen to you. More specifically, it must perform five functions: get the audience's attention, introduce the topic, give the audience a reason to listen, establish your credibility, and preview your main ideas. Let's briefly consider each of these five functions.

Get the Audience's Attention

If an introduction does not capture the audience's attention, the rest of the presentation may be wasted on them. You have to use verbal messages effectively to wake up your listeners and make them want to hear more.

There are several good ways to gain an audience's attention. One commonly used and quite effective one is to open with an illustration, as April does in her presentation on the link between children's vaccines and autism:

Verbal

> When Alanna Gallagher began to constantly spin in circles and obsessively line up her toys, her mother knew it wasn't normal two-year-old behavior. When her obsession was finally diagnosed, Alanna's parents were horrified to find their little girl was showing early signs of autism.[9]

Other strategies are to ask a rhetorical question, to draw an analogy, to relate a startling fact or statistic, to quote an expert or a literary text, to tell a humorous story, to refer to historical or recent events of note, or to use statements that will promote an emotional response from the audience.

In May 1991, the leader of the Reform Party, Preston Manning, provoked an emotional response with the following speech:

> Canada's mission in the 21st century will be to create by evolution, not revolution, a more balanced society on the northern half of the North American continent...
>
> New Canada must be a balanced federation, not an unbalanced federation where one province has special status or a special deal; not an unbalanced federation where all the provinces have special status and Canada has no status; not an unbalanced federation where one generation centralizes all the power in Ottawa, and the next generation centralizes it all in the provincial capitals in the name of decentralization...[10]

Verbal

Speakers might get their audience's attention by referring to a personal experience, referring to the occasion, or referring to something said by a preceding speaker. Although not all of these strategies will work for all presentations, at least one of them should be an option for any presentation you make. And with a little practice, you may find yourself being able to choose from several good possibilities for a single presentation.

Introduce the Topic

Within the first few seconds of listening to you, your audience should have a pretty good idea of what your topic is. The best way to achieve this objective is to include a statement of your central idea in your introduction.

Give the Audience a Reason to Listen

Not only do you have to get your audience's attention and introduce your topic, you also have to motivate your listeners to continue to listen. Show the audience how your topic affects them directly. By the end of your introduction, your audience should be thinking, "This concerns *me!*"

Establish Your Credibility

A credible speaker is one whom the audience judges to be believable, competent, and trustworthy. Be aware of the skills, talents, and experiences you have had that are related to your topic. You can increase your credibility by telling your audience about your expertise. For example, in your introduction to a persuasive presentation on studying abroad, you might say:

I know first-hand how studying abroad can broaden your world view, increase your understanding of another culture, and enrich your academic studies. Last fall, I studied at the Sorbonne in Paris.

Preview Your Main Ideas

As we discussed above, you should provide an initial preview of your main ideas at or near the end of your introduction, to allow your listeners to anticipate the main ideas of your presentation.

⋯⟩ Conclusions

While your introduction creates a critically important first impression, your conclusion leaves an equally important final impression. Long after you finish speaking, your audience will hear the echo of effective final words. An effective conclusion serves four functions: to summarize the presentation, to re-emphasize the main idea in a memorable way, to motivate the audience to respond, and to provide closure. Let's consider each of these functions.

Summarize the Presentation

As we noted when we discussed final summaries, the conclusion offers a speaker a last chance to repeat his or her main ideas. Most speakers summarize their main ideas between the body of the presentation and its conclusion or in the first part of the conclusion.

Re-emphasize the Central Idea in a Memorable Way

The conclusions of many famous speeches contain many of the lines we remember best:

> Canada has no cultural unity, no linguistic unity, no religious unity, no economic unity, no geographic unity. All it has is unity.
> *(Kenneth Boulding)*[11]

> To agree to disagree, to harness diversity, to respect dissent; perhaps this is the real essence of Canada.
> *(Robert L. Perry)*[12]

Use your final verbal message effectively. Word your thoughts so that your audience cannot help but remember them.

Motivate the Audience to Respond

Think back to your specific purpose. What do you want your audience to be able to do by the end of your presentation? If your purpose is to inform, you may want your audience to think about your topic or to seek more information about it. If your purpose is to persuade, you may want your audience to take some sort of action—to write a letter, make a phone call, or volunteer for a cause. Your conclusion is where you can motivate your audience to respond. Travis closes his presentation on sleep deprivation with this admonition:

> Before we are all, literally, dead on our feet, let's take the easiest solution step of all. Tonight, turn off your alarm, turn down your covers, and turn in for a good night's sleep.[13]

On the WEB ⋯•

We've emphasized the importance of catching your listeners' attention when you begin your presentation. The Internet can be a good place to find an attention-gaining quote, story, statistic, or illustration. Here are some Web addresses that may help you find what you need to begin your presentation in a memorable way:

Famous Quotations
reference.startpage.com/html/quotations.html
Humorous Quotations
www.yahoo.com/text/Reference/Quotations/Humorous
Stories From Literature
www.literature.org/Works
Statistics Canada's Web site
www.statcan.ca

Verbal

Re**CAP** ⟨⋯

The Purposes of Introductions and Conclusions

Your introduction should	1. Get your audience's attention.
	2. Introduce your topic.
	3. Give your audience a reason to listen.
	4. Establish your credibility.
	5. Preview your main ideas.
Your conclusion should	1. Summarize your presentation.
	2. Re-emphasize your central idea in a memorable way.
	3. Motivate your audience to respond.
	4. Provide closure.

Provide Closure

You may have experienced listening to a presentation and not being certain when it was over. That speaker did not achieve the last purpose of an effective conclusion: providing **closure.**

One good way to provide closure is to refer to your introduction by finishing a story, answering a rhetorical question, or reminding your audience of the startling statistic you presented in your introduction. David concludes his presentation on issues surrounding Canada's policy of multiculturalism with a finishing story:

> At a coffee house in January 2004, I asked my diverse group of friends about their feelings on being immigrants to Canada. Some of them have lived in Toronto for only a few months and others immigrated here over the past six years. Recent arrivals did express a sense of separateness, while those who have lived here for a longer period stressed a progressive sense of belonging. Except for First Nations people, all Canadians are immigrants, some arriving in this great land of ours many years ago and some arriving more recently. Government policies on multiculturalism are simply guidelines to help integrate new immigrants into Canada's "mainframe." As Canadians, it is our job to promote a sense of belonging.

You can also achieve closure by using verbal and nonverbal signposts. For example, you might use such transitions as "finally" and "in conclusion" as you move into your conclusion. You might pause before you begin the conclusion, slow your speaking rate as you deliver your final sentence, or signal by falling vocal inflection that you are making your final statement. Experiment with these strategies until you are certain that your presentation "sounds finished."

Verbal
Nonverbal

Aware

OUTLINING YOUR PRESENTATION

With your introduction and conclusion planned, you are almost ready to begin rehearsing your presentation. By this point, you should have your **preparation outline** nearly complete. The preparation outline is a fairly detailed outline of central idea, main ideas, and supporting material and may also include the specific purpose, introduction, and conclusion. A second outline, which you will prepare shortly, is a **delivery outline,** the notes from which you will eventually deliver your presentation.

···⟩ Preparation Outline

Most speakers develop a fairly detailed preparation outline that helps them ensure that their main ideas are clearly related to their central idea, and that their main ideas are logically and adequately supported. A speaker who creates a preparation outline is applying the first fundamental principle of communication: becoming increasingly aware of his or her communication. In addition to helping the speaker judge the unity and coherence of the presentation, the preparation outline also serves as an early rehearsal outline and is usually the outline handed in as part of a class requirement.

Almost certainly, your instructor will require that you use **standard outline format.** Standard outline format lets you become more aware of the exact relationships among

closure
The sense that a presentation "sounds finished."

preparation outline
Detailed outline that includes main ideas, subpoints, and supporting material, and that may also include specific purpose, introduction, blueprint, internal previews and summaries, transitions, and conclusion.

delivery outline
Condensed and abbreviated outline from which speaking notes are developed.

standard outline format
Conventional use of numbered and lettered headings and subheadings to indicate the relationships among parts of a presentaton.

···⟩•⟨··· COMMUNICATION and TECHNOLOGY

Using Outlining Software

Many word processing programs have an outlining feature. Such features allow you to set the style of an outline and the levels within the outline. If you need to rearrange sections, the outliner will move subpoints along with major headings.

If you have access to computer software with an outlining feature, try using it to prepare either your preparation outline or your delivery outline for your next presentation. Then evaluate the software. Did it make outlining easier or harder for you than doing it by hand?

various main ideas, subpoints, and supporting material in your presentation. When reviewing the sample preparation outline, note the use of standard numbering; the number of subdivisions, if any, for each point; and the consistency of format, for example, use of complete sentences or phrases. Using the standard outline format will help you find your exact place when you glance down at your speaking notes. You will know, for example, that your second main idea is indicated by "II."

A SAMPLE PREPARATION OUTLINE

Purpose

By the end of my presentation, the audience will be aware of issues surrounding Severe Acute Respiratory Syndrome (SARS).[14]

Writing the purpose statement at the top of the outline helps the speaker keep it in mind. But always follow your instructor's specific directions regarding how to format your preparation outline.

Introduction

Perhaps it was mother's intuition that sent Susan Chung into her five-year-old son Edward's room to check on him. His temperature was 100.4°F and he appeared to be having difficulty breathing. Susan rushed Edward to the hospital, where doctors found radiographic evidence of pneumonia. After further examination, the doctor on call discovered that Edward met the clinical criteria for severe respiratory illness of unknown etiology and the epidemiological criteria for exposure to SARS.

Sarah catches her audience's attention by opening her presentation with an illustration. Other strategies for effectively getting audience attention were discussed earlier in this chapter.

Central Idea

The potentially deadly respiratory health concern known as Severe Acute Respiratory Syndrome must be understood, qualified, and contained to avoid further contamination and deaths.

Sarah writes out and labels her central idea. Again, follow your instructor's requirements.

Body Outline

I. The problem of SARS is multifaceted.
   A. Laboratory Criteria
      1. Definition—SARS is a respiratory illness caused by a novel coronavirus
      2. Confirmed
      3. Negative
      4. Undetermined
   B. Case Classification
      1. Probable case—meets the clinical criteria for severe respiratory illness and the epidemiological criteria for exposure
      2. Suspect case—meets the clinical criteria for moderate respiratory illness and the epidemiological criteria for exposure
      3. Exclusion criteria—testing results for serum previously collected between 22 and 28 days after onset of symptoms are acceptable and will not require collection of an additional sample
II. There is the issue of communicability.
   A. Update: Panel concludes that lab was source of infection in Singapore patient
      1. Worldwide—first recognized in Asia in February 2003 and then spread to more then two dozen countries in North and South America, Europe, and Asia. For more information refer to the World Health Organization or the Centers for Disease Control and Prevention
      2. Canada—144 cases in Toronto, 73 (51%) were HCWs (5)
III. The problem has been caused in two ways.
   A. Close contact within 10 days of onset of symptoms with a person known or suspected to have SARS
   B. Travel within 10 days of onset of symptoms to an area with current or previously documented or suspected community transmission of SARS
IV. Precautions: Upon a SARS patient being admitted to hospital, infection control personnel should be notified immediately.

The first main idea of the presentation is indicated by the Roman numeral I. This main idea has two subpoints, indicated by A and B.

Subpoints 1 and 2 provide supporting material for A.

Sarah identifies the World Health Organization and the Centers for Disease Control and Prevention, to add credibility to her presentation.

Moving from soft to hard evidence, Sarah follows up opinion with statistics.

Sarah moves now from a discussion of the problem to a discussion of its two causes, A and B of main idea III.

Having established the problem and discussed its causes, Sarah turns to solutions.

A SAMPLE PREPARATION OUTLINE

Sarah draws on personal experience to convince her audience members that precautions are taken seriously.

    A. Standard precautions—hand washing and protective eyewear. During my visit to a hospital in December 2003, washing hands at the entrance to the hospital was still a common practice.

    B. Contact precautions—wearing a gown and gloves

    C. Airborne precautions—isolation room with negative pressure relative to the surrounding area and use of N.95 filtering disposable respirator mask for people entering the room

  V. Second is the problem of community-level preparedness and response to SARS

     1. October 23, 2003, Webcast

     2. Webcasts from September 23 and 30, "Preparing for the Return of SARS: Are We Ready?"

Conclusion

In her conclusion, Sarah summarizes her main ideas and completes the illustration with which she began the presentation.

Today we have looked at the SARS problem and have discussed possible causes of the emergence of this respiratory condition. The Centers for Disease Control and Prevention (CDC) and the World Health Organization (WHO) have issued information concerning infection control precautions in health-care and community settings. If enacted, these precautions would minimize, if not eradicate, this problem. Susan Chung's five-year-old son, Edward, has demonstrated some health improvement since being diagnosed with SARS. Given proper attention and respect, this problem will not reach us or those we love. All it takes is an understanding of the problem and a combined effort and we will not fall victim to SARS.

It may have been easier for this student to deliver an effective message, if she had prepared a concise delivery outline on note cards.

⋯⟩ Delivery Outline

As you rehearse your presentation, you will find yourself needing to look at your preparation outline less and less. You have both the structure and the content the of your presentation pretty well in mind. At this point, you are ready to develop a shorter delivery outline.

Your delivery outline should provide all the notes you will need to make your presentation as you have planned, without being so detailed that you will be tempted to read it rather than speak to your audience. Here are a few suggestions for developing a delivery outline:

- *Use single words or short phrases whenever possible.*
- *Include your introduction and conclusion in abbreviated form.* Even if your instructor did not require your introduction and conclusion on your preparation outline, include an abbreviated version of them on your delivery outline. You might even feel more comfortable delivering the presentation if you have your first and last sentences written out in front of you.
- *Include supporting material and signposts.* Write out in full any statistics and direct quotations and their sources. Write your key signposts—your initial preview, for example—to ensure that you will not have to grope awkwardly as you move from one idea to another.
- *Do not include your purpose statement.* Because you will not actually deliver your purpose statement, do not put it on your delivery outline.

note card
A 10 × 15 cm card on which your delivery outline is written.

Nonverbal

delivery cue
A reminder of how to speak or move during a presentation, which is often written on a speaker's note cards.

Although you may write the first version of your delivery outline on paper, eventually you will probably want to transfer it to **note cards**. They don't rustle as paper does, and they are small enough to hold in one hand. Two or three note cards will probably give you enough space for your delivery outline. Type or print neatly on one side only, making sure that the letters and words are large enough to read easily. Plan your note cards according to logical blocks of material, using one note card for your introduction, one or two for the body of your presentation, and one for your conclusion. Number your note cards to prevent getting them out of order while you are speaking.

A final addition to your note cards as you rehearse your presentation will be **delivery cues** such as "Louder," "Pause," or "Walk two steps left." These will remind you to communicate the nonverbal messages you have planned. Write your delivery cues in a different colour ink so that you don't confuse them with your verbal content.

A SAMPLE DELIVERY OUTLINE

Introduction

- Susan Chung—her five-year-old son, Edward—temperature was 100.4°F, difficulty breathing
- hospital—found radiographic evidence of pneumonia
- Edward met the clinical criteria for severe respiratory illness otherwise known as SARS

For the delivery outline, Sarah does not need to write her purpose statement, as she will not actually deliver it in the presentation.

Sarah bullets the three parts of her introduction she wants to be certain to remember.

Central Idea

The potentially deadly respiratory health concern known as Severe Acute Respiratory Syndrome must be understood, qualified, and contained to avoid further contamination and deaths.

Preview

- Examine the problem of SARS
- Discuss classification of SARS
- Look at communication of this problem
- Understand the causes
- Note the suggested precautions
- Look at opportunities available to stop this danger

Previews, transitions, and summaries are added to the delivery outline and labelled so that the speaker can find them quickly, as with this initial preview.

Body Outline

I. SARS = multifaceted.
   A. Laboratory Criteria
       1. Definition—SARS is a respiratory illness caused by a novel coronavirus
       2. Confirmed
       3. Negative
       4. Undetermined
   B. Case Classification
       1. Probable Case = clinical criteria for severe respiratory illness and epidemiological criteria for exposure
       2. Suspect Case = clinical criteria for moderate respiratory illness and epidemiological criteria for exposure
       3. Exclusion Criteria = testing results for serum previously collected between 22 and 28 days after onset of symptoms are acceptable and will not require collection of an additional sample

Part of the "shorthand" of delivery outlines may include symbols such as the "equals" sign here.

Transition

Not so long ago, we would not have worried about finding a treatment for Edward's respiratory condition. However, now, by our own creation, many will suffer unnecessary pain and death due to this problem. We have promoted this domino effect and its causes throughout the world.

II. Communicability
   A. Update: Panel concludes that lab was source of infection in Singapore patient
       1. Worldwide = First recognized in Asia, February 2003—spread to more then two dozen countries in North and South America, Europe, and Asia. (For more information refer to the World Health Organization or The Centers for Disease Control and Prevention.)
       2. Canada = 144 cases in Toronto, 73 (51%) HCWs (5)
III. Causes
   A. Close contact within 10 days of onset of symptoms with a person known or suspected to have SARS
   B. Travel within 10 days of onset of symptoms to an area with current or previously documented or suspected community transmission of SARS

Sarah's transition from main idea I to main idea II of her presentation includes a preview of II.

Transition

When you or someone you love is sick, the most natural solution is to go to the doctor and ask for a prescription. However, we have seen how this action may actually amplify the problem. We need

Sarah provides a transition from main idea II to main idea III, again previewing III.

A SAMPLE DELIVERY OUTLINE

to uncover solutions that won't leave us vulnerable to this condition. The first solution is simply education, and the second is the continuation and expansion of preparedness and immediate response.

IV. Precautions—upon a SARS patient being admitted to hospital, infection control personnel should be notified immediately

    A. Standard precautions: hand washing and protective eyewear. During my visit to a hospital in December 2003, washing hands at the entrance to the hospital was still a common practice.

    B. Contact precautions: wearing a gown and gloves

    C. Airborne precautions: isolation room with negative pressure relative to the surrounding area and use of N.95 filtering disposable respirator mask for people entering the room.

V. Second is the problem of community-level preparedness and response to SARS

    A. October 23, 2003, Webcast

    B. Webcasts from September 23 and 30, "Preparing for the Return of SARS: Are We Ready?"

Sarah writes out her final summary.

Final Summary

Today we have looked at the SARS problem and have discussed possible causes of the emergence of this respiratory condition. The Centers for Disease Control and Prevention (CDC) and the World Health Organization (WHO) have issued information concerning infection control precautions in health-care and community settings. If enacted, these precautions would minimize, if not eradicate, this problem.

Conclusion

Sarah writes out her final sentence, to ensure that she can end her presentation fluently.

1. Susan Chung's five-year-old son, Edward, has demonstrated some health improvement since being diagnosed with SARS.
2. Given proper attention and respect, this problem will not reach us or those we love. All it takes is an understanding of the problem and a combined effort and we will not fall victim to SARS.

ReCAP

Two Types of Presentation Outlines

TYPE	PURPOSE
Preparation Outline	Allows speaker to examine presentation for completeness, unity, coherence, and overall effectiveness. May serve as first rehearsal outline.
Delivery Outline	Serves as speaking notes. Includes delivery cues.

SUMMARY

Learning to speak in public is a teachable, learnable process of developing, supporting, organizing, and presenting ideas. Presentational speaking skills can help you in other courses and in the workplace.

The stages of the public speaking process centre on consideration of the audience, which influences every decision a speaker makes. A speaker's tasks include selecting and narrowing a topic, identifying a general and specific purpose for speaking, developing the central idea of the presentation, generating main ideas, gathering supporting material, organizing the presentation, and finally, rehearsing and delivering the presentation.

Nearly everyone feels some anxiety about speaking in public. Speaker anxiety triggers physiological responses that may be worrisome but are actually your body's attempt to help you. Focusing on your audience and message and thinking positively can help you manage speaker anxiety, as can knowing how to develop a presentation, being well prepared, and seeking out opportunities to speak. Professional help is available for those few who continue to suffer debilitating speaker anxiety.

As you begin to prepare your presentation, you will first have to select and narrow your topic, keeping in mind the audience, the occasion, and your own interests and experiences. You may find helpful such strategies as silent brainstorming, scanning Web directories and Web pages, and listening and reading for topic ideas. Once you have a topic, you need to identify both your general purpose and your specific purpose. General purposes include to inform, to persuade, and to entertain. Specific purposes are determined by the general purpose, the topic, and the audience. You will also need to decide on the central idea for the presentation. You can use that central idea to help you generate your main ideas, which are usually logical divisions of the central idea, reasons the central idea is true, or a series of steps or chronological sequence that develops the central idea.

Next, you will need to discover support for your main ideas. As a presentational speaker, you have at least three potential sources of supporting material: yourself and people you know, the Internet, and the library. Personal knowledge and experience increase the likelihood that the audience will find you a credible speaker. To supplement your own knowledge and experience, you might turn to the vast resources available on the Internet. And most likely, you will still use library resources—books, periodicals, newspapers, reference resources, government documents, and various special services—as sources of supporting material.

The types of supporting material you can use in a presentation include illustrations, descriptions, explanations, definitions, analogies, statistics, and opinions. Simple guidelines can help you use each of these types of supporting material effectively and cite your sources correctly.

Once you have found supporting material, you are ready to organize your ideas and information. Depending on your topic, purpose, and audience, you can organize the main ideas of your presentation logically, chronologically, topically, by cause and effect, or by problem and solution. You can sometimes organize supporting material according to one of these same patterns, or you can organize it according to the principles of recency, primacy, complexity, specificity, or "soft" to "hard."

With your presentation organized, you will want to add signposts—previews, transitions, and summaries—to make your organization clearly apparent to your audience. A carefully planned introduction will get your audience's attention, introduce your topic, give the audience a reason to listen, establish your credibility, and preview your main ideas. In an equally carefully planned conclusion, you can summarize your presentation, re-emphasize the central idea in a memorable way, motivate your audience to respond, and provide closure.

A final step before beginning to rehearse your presentation is to prepare a detailed preparation outline and a delivery outline that eventually will become your speaking notes.

PRINCIPLES FOR A LIFETIME

Aware

Principle 1:   Be aware of your communication with yourself and others.

- Understand that learning to speak in public will be a valuable lifelong skill.
- Be mindful of the central role of the audience in the public speaking process.
- Consider your own interests and experiences when searching for a topic.
- Remember that the most effective illustrations are often personal ones.
- Use your presentation introduction to help establish your own credibility; be aware of the skills, talents, and experiences you have that can enhance your credibility with your listeners.
- Use a preparation outline to demonstrate to yourself that your main ideas are clearly related to your central idea and are logically and adequately supported.

Verbal

Principle 2:   Effectively use and interpret verbal messages.

- Search for topics on the Web, in the media, and in non-fiction books.
- Wording your specific purpose in terms of your audience will help you keep your focus on them.
- A central idea should reflect a single topic, be a complete declarative sentence, and use specific language.
- Consider the accountability, accuracy, objectivity, date, and usability of verbal material you find on Web sites.
- Be sure that your illustrations are directly relevant to the idea or the point they are supposed to support.
- Make your illustrations vivid and specific.
- Avoid too many descriptions and explanations.

- Keep descriptions and explanations brief.
- Describe and explain in specific and concrete language.
- Make your definitions readily understandable, and be certain they accurately reflect how you use the word or phrase in the speech.
- Round off large statistics to make them more readily understandable.
- Cite unbiased authorities.
- Cite opinions that are representative of prevailing opinion.
- Quote or paraphrase accurately and in context.
- Use literary quotations sparingly.
- Integrate oral citations of your sources into your presentation.
- Logical organization is one way you can communicate your verbal message effectively.
- Use verbal transitions to show relationships between ideas in your presentation.
- Introduce your topic and preview your main ideas in your introduction.
- Use stories, examples, illustrations, statistics, a quotation, or other technique to capture your listeners' attention when you begin your talk.
- In your conclusion, summarize your presentation and re-emphasize your main idea in a memorable way.

Nonverbal

Principle 3:   Effectively use and interpret nonverbal messages.

- Consider the accountability, accuracy, objectivity, date, and usability of pictures and graphics you find on Web sites.
- Use visual aids to present statistics.
- Nonverbal transitions—pauses, facial expression, altered vocal pitch or speaking rate, and movement—can help indicate when you are moving from one idea to the next.
- Use nonverbal cues, such as pausing, slowing your rate of speech, and letting your vocal inflection fall, to signal that you are approaching the end of your presentation.
- Add delivery cues and reminders to your final delivery outline.

Listen
and
Respond

Principle 4:   Listen and respond thoughtfully to others.

- The more you know about your audience and how they are likely to respond to your message, the more comfortable you will feel about speaking in public.
- Listen for topic ideas in the course of casual conversation with friends.
- As you listen to presentations, recognize the cultural differences in the organization of speakers from cultures other than your own.

Adapt

Principle 5:   Appropriately adapt messages to others.

- At any point in the presentation-preparation process, you may revise your ideas or strategies as you seek out and learn more about your audience.
- Audience-centred speakers are sensitive to and adapt to the diversity of their audiences.
- Consider your audience's interests and expectations as you select the topic for your presentation.
- Keep in mind your audience's knowledge, interests, and expectations as you select supporting material for your presentation.
- Use illustrations with which your audience can identify. Consider making your audience members part of the scenario in a hypothetical illustration.
- Make the similarity between the two objects in a figurative analogy apparent to your audience.
- Investigate and consider using the customary organizational strategy of your audience's culture.
- Discuss last the idea that you most want your audience to remember.
- If you know your audience will be skeptical of some of your ideas, present first those ideas on which you can agree.
- Provide signposts as organizational cues for your audience.
- Use your introduction and conclusion to help adapt your presentation to your audience.

Discussion and Review ⁞

1. Explain how presentational speaking skills can be of practical use, both while you are in college or university and afterwards.

2. Sketch and label the stages of the audience-centered public speaking model.

3. Suggest both criteria and strategies for discovering a good presentation topic.

4. What are the three general purposes for presentations?

5. With what phrase should an audience-centred, specific-purpose statement begin?

6. In what ways does a central idea differ from a specific purpose?

7. What are the characteristics of a good central idea?

8. List the three questions that you can apply to generate main ideas from a central idea.

9. Where might you find supporting material for a presentation?

10. List and explain the five criteria for evaluating Web sites.

11. What resources are available in most libraries?

12. What types of supporting material might you use in your presentations?

13. List and explain five strategies for organizing the main ideas in a presentation.

14. List and explain five strategies for organizing supporting material in a presentation.

15. How can you make a nonverbal transition?

16. List and explain five functions of a presentation introduction.

17. How can you get your audience's attention in your introduction?

18. List and explain four functions of a presentation conclusion.

19. What is included on most preparation outlines? What are they used for?

20. What is included on most delivery outlines? What are they used for?

Developing Your Skills: Putting Principles into Practice ⁞

1. Interview someone who regularly speaks in public as part of his or her job. Ask that person what stages or steps he or she goes through in developing a speech.

2. Brainstorm a list of at least 10 possible topics for an informative classroom presentation.

3. Write an informative specific purpose and a persuasive specific purpose for each of the following topics:

   Rap music
   Employability
   Ethnicity
   Athletes as role models
   Tuition fees

4. Generate at least three main ideas from each of the following central ideas. Apply the questions suggested in this chapter: Does the central idea have *logical divisions*? Can you support the central idea with a series of *steps* or a *chronological sequence*?

   Students who commute have at least three advantages over students who live on campus.
   Sleep deprivation is dangerous.
   Three specific strategies can help you deal with unsolicited telemarketers.
   Women should have annual mammograms.

5. Read a news story in a newspaper or national news magazine. See how many different types of supporting material you can identify in the story.

6. Take notes as you listen to a presentation, either live or on audiotape or videotape. Then organize your notes into an outline that you think reflects both the speaker's organization and the intended relationship among ideas and supporting material.

7. Read one of the speeches in Appendix B. Answer the following questions:

   a. How are the main ideas organized?
   b. Look closely at the supporting materials. If two or more are used to support any one main idea, what strategy do you think the speaker used to organize them?
   c. Is there an initial preview statement? If so, what is it?
   d. Is there a final summary? If so, what is it?
   e. Find at least one example of each of the following:

      A transition word or phrase
      An internal preview
      An internal summary

8. Draft an introduction for a presentation on one of the following topics:

   New strategies for surviving a blackout
   Private-school uniforms
   Multiculturalism
   Celebrities and the press

   In addition to introducing the topic and previewing your main ideas, be sure to plan strategies for getting your audience's attention and giving them a reason to listen. Also devise a way to establish your own credibility as a speaker on that topic.

Steve Dininno, "Audience of Ears." © Images.com/CORBIS

O the orator's joys!

To inflate the chest, to roll the thunder of the
voice out from the ribs and throat,

To make the people rage, weep, hate, desire . . .

— WALT WHITMAN

12 Delivering Your Presentation

AFTER STUDYING THIS CHAPTER, YOU SHOULD BE ABLE TO

1. List and describe the four methods of delivery and provide suggestions for effectively using each one.

2. Define and explain what causes speaker anxiety and offer at least three suggestions for managing speaker anxiety.

3. List and explain five criteria for using words well.

4. Identify and illustrate characteristics of effective delivery.

5. List 11 types of visual aids from which a speaker might select, and provide suggestions for effectively using each type.

6. Offer four general guidelines for preparing and using effective presentation aids.

Which is more important: the content of a presentation or the way it is delivered? Speakers and speech teachers have argued about the answer to this question for thousands of years. In the 4th century BC, the Greek rhetorician Aristotle declared delivery "superfluous." On the other hand, when his contemporary and fellow Athenian Demosthenes was asked to name the three most important elements for a speaker to master, he is reported to have replied, "Delivery, delivery, delivery."

Nonverbal

The debate continues. Which is more important: content or delivery? It is clear that the way you deliver a speech influences the way listeners respond to you and to your message. In a now-classic study, Alan H. Monroe found that audience members equate effective presentational speaking with such nonverbal factors as direct eye contact, alertness, enthusiasm, a pleasant voice, and animated gestures.[1] Another researcher concluded that delivery was almost twice as important as content when students gave self-introduction presentations, and three times as important when students gave persuasive presentations.[2] Other scholars have found that delivery provides important information about a speaker's feelings and emotions and will in turn affect listeners' emotional responses to the speaker.[3] Most speech teachers today believe that both content and delivery contribute to the effectiveness of a presentation. As a modern speechwriter and communication coach suggests,

> In the real world—the world where you and I do business—content and delivery are always related. And woe be to the communicator who forgets this.[4]

Adapt   Aware

Listen   Verbal
and
Respond   Nonverbal

In this chapter, we will discuss how you can apply the five communication principles for a lifetime to delivery. As delivery is an essential part of the public speaking process, we will define and explain speaker anxiety and offer suggestions for managing anxiety and developing confidence. We will also talk about both verbal and nonverbal delivery skills. We will consider how important it is to be aware of the words you use and of such nonverbal cues as gestures, eye contact, and facial expression. We will discuss how to determine what presentation aids might be effective for your audience, and we'll offer guidelines for both the preparation and the use of various types of presentation aids.

METHODS OF DELIVERY

Audiences today generally expect speakers to use clear, concise, everyday language and conversational delivery style, as opposed to the flowery language and dramatic, choreographed gestures used by speakers a century ago. However, different audiences expect and prefer variations of this delivery style. For example, if you are using a microphone to speak to an audience of 1000 people, your listeners may expect a relatively formal delivery style. On the other hand, your communication class would probably find it odd if you delivered a formal oration to your 25 classmates.

People from different cultures also have different expectations of speakers' delivery. Listeners from Japan and China, for example, may prefer subdued gestures to a more flamboyant delivery style. British listeners might expect a speaker to stay behind a lectern and use relatively few gestures.

Speakers should consider and adapt to their audience's expectations, their topic, and the speaking situation as they select from four basic methods of delivery: manuscript speaking, memorized speaking, impromptu speaking, and extemporaneous speaking. Each is more appropriate to some speaking contexts and audiences than to others, and each requires a speaker to use a slightly different delivery style. Let's consider each of these four delivery methods in more detail.

Adapt

⋯⟩ Manuscript Speaking

Perhaps you remember the first presentation you ever had to give—maybe as long ago as elementary school. Chances are that you wrote your speech out and read it to your audience.

manuscript speaking
Reading a speech from a written text.

Unfortunately, **manuscript speaking** is rarely done well enough to be interesting. Most speakers who rely on a manuscript read it in either a monotone or a pattern of vocal inflection that "sounds read." They are so afraid of losing their place that they keep their eyes glued to the manuscript and seldom look at the audience. These challenges are significant enough that most speakers should avoid reading from a manuscript most of the time.

However, there are some exceptions. Sometimes effective verbal messages depend on careful and exact phrasing. For example, because an awkward statement made by the Canadian Minister of Foreign Affairs could cause an international crisis, he or she usually has remarks on critical issues carefully scripted. A company manager or administrator presenting a new, potentially controversial company policy to employees or customers might also deliver that announcement from a manuscript.

If you ever have to speak on a sensitive, critical, or controversial issue, you too might need to deliver a manuscript speech. If so, consider the following suggestions:[5]

Verbal

- Type your manuscript in short, easy-to-scan phrases on the upper two-thirds of the paper so that you do not have to look too far down into your notes.
- Use appropriate nonverbal messages. Try to take in an entire sentence at a time so that you can maintain eye contact throughout each sentence.
- Do not read the speech too quickly.
- Vary the rhythm, inflection, and pace of your delivery so that the speech does not "sound read."
- Use gestures and movement to add further nonverbal interest and emphasis to your message.

Nonverbal

Memorized Speaking

After that first speech you read in elementary school, you probably became a more savvy speaker and decided that you would memorize the speech you had written out. You thought that no one would be able to tell you had written it out first. What you didn't know then, but probably do now, is that most **memorized speaking** sounds stiff and recited. In addition, you run the risk of forgetting parts of your speech and having to search awkwardly for words in front of your audience. And you forfeit the ability to adapt to your audience while you are speaking.

memorized speaking
Delivering a speech word for word from memory without using notes.

However, speaking from memory is occasionally justifiable. Memorized speeches might be appropriate in the same instances as manuscript speaking, when exact wording is critical to the success of the message and when the speaker has time to commit the speech to memory. If you must deliver a short presentation within narrowly proscribed time limits, memorizing and rehearsing the speech will allow you to time it more accurately. Three guidelines can help you use nonverbal messages effectively when you deliver a speech from memory:

- Do not deliver your memorized speech too rapidly.
- Avoid patterns of vocal inflection that make the speech sound recited. Focus on what you are saying, and let your voice rise and fall to emphasize key words and phrases and to reflect the structures of your sentences. Consider recording your presentation and listening to it to ensure that your vocal delivery sounds like a conversation rather than a recitation.
- Use gestures and movement to add interest and emphasis to your message.

Nonverbal

Impromptu Speaking

Although you can usually plan your presentations, there are times—such as when a teleprompter fails—when the best plans go awry. In other, more likely instances, you may be asked to answer a question or respond to an argument without advance warning or time to prepare a presentation. At such times, you will have to call upon your skills in **impromptu speaking,** or speaking "off the cuff." Five guidelines can help you avoid fumbling for words or rambling:

impromptu speaking
Delivering a speech without advance preparation.

Adapt

- Consider your audience. A quick mental check of who your audience is and what their interests, expectations, and knowledge are can help ensure that your impromptu remarks are audience centred.
- Be brief. As one leadership consultant points out,

You're not the star—not this time, anyway. If you were the luminary, they would not have asked you to speak without warning. You're merely expected to hit a theme, say a few nice words, and then depart.[6]

Nonverbal

One to three minutes is probably a realistic time frame for most impromptu presentations.

- Organize. Think quickly about an introduction, body, and conclusion. If you want to make more than one point, use a simple organizational strategy such as chronological order—past, present, and future. Or construct an alphabetical list, in which your main ideas begin with the letters A, B, and C.[7]

Aware

- Draw on your personal experience and knowledge. Audiences almost always respond favourably to personal illustrations, so use any appropriate and relevant ones.
- Use gestures and movement that arise naturally from what you are saying.
- Be aware of the potential impact of your communication. If your subject is at all sensitive or your information is classified, be noncommittal in what you say.

⤳ Extemporaneous Speaking

We have saved for last the method of speaking that is the most appropriate choice for most circumstances: **extemporaneous speaking.** This is the speaking style taught today in most public speaking classes and preferred by most audiences. When you speak extemporaneously, you develop your presentation according to the various stages of the audience-centred public speaking model, stopping short of writing it out. Instead, you speak from an outline and rehearse the presentation until you can deliver it fluently. Your audience will know that you have prepared, but will also have the sense that the presentation is being created as they listen to it—and to some extent, it is. In short, the extemporaneous presentation is a well-developed and well-organized message delivered in an interesting and vivid manner. It reflects your understanding of how to use both verbal and nonverbal messages effectively, and your ability to adapt these messages to your audience.

Verbal

Nonverbal

Although the presentational speaking chapters in this book offer numerous guidelines for extemporaneous speaking, consider these four when you reach the rehearsal and delivery stages:

- Use a full-content preparation outline when you begin to rehearse your extemporaneous presentation. Be aware of your growing confidence in delivering it and rely increasingly less on your notes.

Aware

- Prepare an abbreviated delivery outline and speaking notes. Continue to rehearse, using this new outline.
- Even as you become increasingly familiar with your message, do not try to memorize it word for word. Continue to vary the ways in which you express your ideas and information.
- As you deliver your presentation, adapt it to your audience. Use gestures and movement that arise naturally from what you are saying.

Adapt

UNDERSTANDING SPEAKER ANXIETY

The overview of the stages of the public speaking process provided in Chapter 11 and knowledge of delivery methods should help increase your understanding of how to prepare for your first speaking assignment. However, if you still feel nervous at the prospect, you are definitely not alone. One study found that more than 80% of the population feel anxious when they speak to an audience.[8] Another survey discovered that people are more afraid of public speaking than of death![9]

speaker anxiety
Also known as stage fright; involves physiological symptoms such as rapid heartbeat, butterflies, shaking knees and hands, quivering voice, and increased perspiration.

You might be surprised at the names of some of the people who have admitted to experiencing **speaker anxiety,** also known as stage fright or communication apprehension. John F. Kennedy and Winston Churchill, among the greatest orators of the 20th century, were anxious about speaking in public. More contemporary public figures who have talked about their speaker anxiety include Katie Couric, Conan O'Brien, Jay Leno, and Oprah Winfrey.[10] In fact, almost everyone feels at least some anxiety about speaking or performing in public. Why?

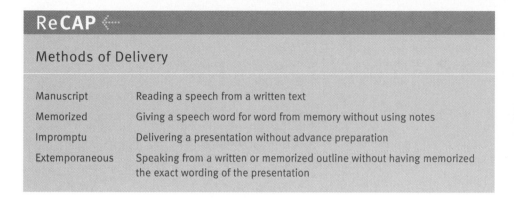

Even performers like Matthew Perry suffer from communication anxiety; we all need to take positive steps to control anxiety before a performance.

To answer this question and to manage your own anxiety, you need both accurate information and practical advice. Even if the prospect of giving a presentation makes you feel only a sense of heightened excitement, rather than fear, you can use these suggestions to make your excitement help you, rather than distract you.

It is important to understand that speaker anxiety results from your brain signalling your body to help with a challenging task. The body responds by increasing its breathing rate and blood flow and by pumping more adrenalin, which in turn results in the all-too-familiar symptoms of a rapid heartbeat, butterflies in the stomach, shaking knees and hands, quivering voice, and increased perspiration.

Although these physical symptoms may annoy and worry you, remember that they indicate that your body is trying to help you with the task at hand. The same increased oxygen, blood flow, and adrenalin that cause the uncomfortable symptoms can actually be helpful. You may find that you speak with heightened enthusiasm. Your brain thinks faster and more clearly than you would have believed possible. Your state of increased physical readiness can help you speak better.

Keep in mind, too, that most speakers feel more nervous than they look. Although the antiperspirant advertising slogan "Never let 'em see you sweat" suggests that our increased perspiration, along with our shaking hands and knocking knees, is likely to be visible to our audience, rarely is this true. A study by three communication researchers found that student speakers in introductory-level communication classes report higher levels of speaker anxiety than their audiences detect.[11]

Speaker anxiety is a normal, physiological reaction. It can actually help us in our speaking tasks. Its physical symptoms are seldom apparent to anyone else; rarely does it become so severe that it is actually debilitating. Still, it can be uncomfortable. Some practical tips can help you manage that discomfort and further build your confidence in your speaking ability.

MANAGING SPEAKER ANXIETY

Perhaps you've read popular paperbacks or magazine articles that address the topic of speaker anxiety with such advice as "Look over the audience's heads, rather than at them,"

and "Imagine that your audience members are naked." Interesting though they may be, these techniques are not particularly helpful in reducing speaker anxiety. After all, wouldn't you be pretty anxious if you had to talk to a group of naked people? In addition, these strategies create new problems. Gazing at the back wall robs you of eye contact with your audience, an important source of information about how they are responding to your speech. And your audience can tell if you are looking over their heads instead of at them. Rather than pay attention to your speech, they may begin to glance surreptitiously over their shoulders to find out what in the world you're staring at.

If these techniques won't help, what will? Fortunately, several proven strategies exist for managing anxiety.

Know How to Develop a Presentation

If you have read Chapter 11, you have already taken this first step toward managing anxiety—learning about the public speaking process. Just knowing what you need to do to develop a presentation can boost your confidence in being able to do it.

Be Prepared

Being well prepared will also mean less anxiety. Being prepared includes selecting an appropriate topic, researching that topic thoroughly, and organizing your ideas logically. But perhaps most important, it also includes rehearsing your presentation. Research suggests that people who experience high speaker anxiety typically spend less time rehearsing than do those who report lower speaker anxiety.[12]

When you rehearse your presentation, imagine that you are giving it to the audience you will actually address. Stand up. If you cannot rehearse in the room where you will deliver the presentation, at least imagine that room. Practise rising from your seat, walking to the front of the room, and beginning your presentation. Speak aloud, rather than rehearsing silently. Thorough preparation that includes realistic rehearsal will increase your confidence when it comes time to deliver your presentation.

Adapt

Focus on Your Audience

The fundamental communication principle of being audience centred is key to reducing speaker anxiety. As you are preparing your presentation, consider the needs, goals, and interests of your audience members. As you rehearse your presentation, visualize your audience and imagine how they may respond; practise adapting your presentation to the responses you imagine. The more you know about your audience and how they are likely to respond to your message, the more comfortable you will feel about delivering that message. And as you finally deliver your presentation, focus on connecting to your listeners. The more you concentrate on your audience, the less you can attend to your own nervousness.

Verbal

Focus on Your Message

Focusing on your message can also be a constructive anxiety-reducing strategy. Like focusing on your audience, it keeps you from thinking too much about how nervous you are. In the few minutes before you begin your presentation, think about what you are going to say. Mentally review your main ideas. Silently practise your opening lines and your conclusion. Once you are speaking, maintain your focus on your message and your audience, rather than on your fears.

Think Positively

Aware

Even if you focus primarily on your audience and your message, you are bound to have some lingering thoughts about your performance. Rather than dwelling on how worried or afraid you are, make a conscious effort to think positively. Remind yourself that you have chosen a topic you know something about. Give yourself a positive mental pep talk before getting up to speak: "I know I can give this presentation. I have prepared and practised, and I'm going to do a great job." This kind of positive thinking can help you manage your anxiety.

→ Use Deep-Breathing Techniques

Two of the physical symptoms of nervousness are shallow breathing and rapid heart rate. To counter these symptoms, take a few slow, deep breaths before you get up to speak. As you slowly inhale and exhale, try to relax your entire body. These simple strategies will increase your oxygen intake and slow your heart rate, making you feel calmer and more in control.

→ Take Advantage of Opportunities to Speak

As you gain public speaking experience, you will feel more in control of your nervousness. Past successes build confidence. This course will provide opportunities for frequent practice and corresponding skill and confidence.

→ Seek Available Professional Help

For a few people, the above strategies may not be enough help. These people may still experience a level of speaker anxiety that they consider debilitating. If you feel that you may be such a person, ask your communication instructor where you might turn for additional help. Some college or university departments of communication maintain communication labs that teach students various additional strategies to help manage counterproductive anxiety.

One such strategy is **systematic desensitization,** in which you learn to manage anxiety through a combination of general relaxation techniques and visualization of successful and calm preparation and delivery of a presentation.

Another proven strategy is **performance visualization**. Introduced in Chapter 2 as a means to enhance self-esteem, performance visualization is a process of relaxing: viewing a videotape of a successful, effective speaker, becoming familiar enough with the videotaped presentation that you can imagine it, and eventually visualizing yourself as the speaker.[13] This process may offer one of the best long-term strategies for managing speaker anxiety. Studies suggest that student speakers who practise performance visualization view themselves as more positive, vivid, and in-control speakers both immediately after performance visualization and up to several months later.[14]

Additional services may be available through college or university counselling or other student support services. If you think that you might benefit from professional help, find out what is available and use it.

Knowledge of well-researched and well-designed presentation and delivery methods will help alleviate feelings of speaker anxiety. Let's examine effective verbal and nonverbal delivery methods that also lend themselves to an effective presentation.

systematic desensitization
An anxiety management strategy that includes general relaxation techniques and visualization of success.

performance visualization
An anxiety management strategy in which a person views a videotape of a successful presentation and imagines himself or herself delivering that presentation.

EFFECTIVE VERBAL DELIVERY

Although you will not write out most presentations word for word, you will want to think about and rehearse words, phrases, and sentences that accurately and effectively communicate your ideas. At the same time, you will want to give your message a distinctive and memorable style. Let's examine some guidelines for effectively using and understanding words and word structures in a presentation.

Re**CAP** ←⋯

Managing Speaker Anxiety

- Know how to develop a presentation.
- Be prepared.
- Focus on your audience.
- Focus on your message.

- Think positively.
- Use deep-breathing techniques.
- Take advantage of opportunities to speak.
- Seek available professional help.

Verbal

---> **Using Words Well**

The most effective words are specific and concrete, unbiased, vivid, simple, and correct. Building on our discussion in Chapter 3 of the power of verbal messages, we'll examine each of these characteristics in turn.

Specific, Concrete Words

A **specific word** refers to an individual member of a general class—for example, *ammonite* as opposed to the more general term *fossil*, or *sodium* as opposed to *chemical*. Specific words are often **concrete words,** appealing to one of the five senses and clearly communicating an image. For example, which of the following pairs of words creates a more specific mental picture: *Dog* or *poodle? Utensil* or *spatula? Toy* or *Lego?* In each case, the second word is more specific and concrete than the first and better communicates the image the speaker intends. For maximum clarity in your communication, use more specific, concrete words than general, abstract ones in your presentations.

specific word
A word that refers to an individual member of a general class.

concrete word
A word that refers to an object or describes an action or characteristic in the most specific way possible.

Unbiased Words

Unbiased words are those that do not offend, either intentionally or unintentionally, any sexual, racial, cultural, or religious group—or any audience member who may belong to one of these groups. Although a speaker can fairly easily avoid overtly offensive language, it is more difficult to avoid language that more subtly stereotypes or discriminates. As we noted in Chapter 3, the once-acceptable usage of a masculine noun *(man, mankind)* to refer generically to all people may now be offensive to many audience members. Other words that reflect gender bias include *chairman, waiter,* and *councilman.* Even if you yourself do not consider these terms offensive, a member of your audience might. When possible, you should adapt to your audience by choosing instead such unbiased gender-neutral alternatives as *chairperson* or *chair, server,* and *Member of Parliament.*

unbiased word
A word that does not offend, either intentionally or unintentionally, based on sexual orientation, gender, culture, religion, physical disability, or other features.

Adapt

Vivid Words

Vivid words add colour and interest to your language. Like concrete words, they help you communicate mental images more accurately and interestingly. Most speakers who try to make their language more vivid think first of adding adjectives to nouns—for example, *distressed oak table* instead of *table,* or *scruffy tabby cat* instead of *cat.* And certainly the first phrase of each example is more vivid. However, speakers less frequently consider the potential power of substituting vivid verbs for "blah" verbs—for example, *sprout* instead of *grow,* or *devour* instead of *eat.* When searching for a vivid word, you might want to consult a **thesaurus,** or collection of synonyms. But do not feel that the most obscure or unusual synonym you find will necessarily be the most vivid. Sometimes a simple word can evoke a vivid image for your audience.

vivid word
A colourful word.

thesaurus
A list of synonyms.

simple word
A short word known to most people who speak the language.

Simple Words

In fact, **simple words** are generally an asset to you as a speaker. They will be immediately understandable to your audience. In his essay "Politics and the English Language," George Orwell includes this prescription for simplicity:

> Never use a long word where a short one will do. If it is possible to cut a word out, always cut it out. Never use a foreign phrase, a scientific word, or a jargon word if you can think of an everyday English equivalent.[15]

Selected thoughtfully, simple words can communicate with both accuracy and power.

correct word
A word that means what the speaker intends and is grammatically correct in the phrase or sentence in which it appears.

Correct Words

Finally, and perhaps most obviously, you should use **correct words** when you speak. Grammatical and usage errors communicate a lack of preparation and can lower your credibility with your audience. Be aware of any errors you make habitually. If you are uncertain of how to use a word, look it up in a dictionary or ask someone who knows. If you are stumped by whether to say, "Neither the people nor the president *knows* how to solve the problem" or "Neither the people nor the president *know* how to solve the problem," seek assistance from a good English handbook. (By the way, the first sentence is correct!)

THE FAR SIDE® BY GARY LARSON

"Hang him, you idiots! Hang him! ... 'String him up' is a figure of speech!"

ReCAP

Using Words Well

Use concrete words to communicate clearly and specifically.

Use unbiased words to avoid offending any sexual, racial, cultural, or religious group.

Use vivid words to add colour and interest to your language.

Use simple words to be understood readily.

Use correct words to enhance your credibility.

EFFECTIVE NONVERBAL DELIVERY

At this point, you know how important it is to deliver your presentation effectively and what delivery style is preferred by most audiences today. You are familiar with the four methods of delivery and know how to maximize the use of each one. And you have some ideas about how to use effective and memorable language. But you may still be wondering, "What do I do with my hands?" "Is it all right to move around while I speak?" "How can I make my voice sound interesting?" To help answer these and other similar questions, and to help you use nonverbal messages more effectively, we will examine five major categories of nonverbal delivery: eye contact, physical delivery, facial expression, vocal delivery, and personal appearance. This next section further develops the fundamental principle of using and interpreting nonverbal messages that we introduced in Chapter 4.

⋯⟩ Eye Contact

Of all the nonverbal delivery variables discussed in this chapter, the most important one in a presentational speaking situation for North Americans is **eye contact.** Eye contact with your audience lets them know that you are interested in them and ready to talk to them. It also permits you to determine whether they are responding to you. And most listeners will think that you are more capable and trustworthy if you look them in the eye. Several studies document a relationship between eye contact and speaker credibility, as well as between eye contact and listener learning.[16]

How much eye contact do you need to sustain? One study found that speakers with less than 50% eye contact are considered unfriendly, uninformed, inexperienced, and even dishonest by their listeners.[17] Is there such a thing as too much eye contact? Probably not, for North American audiences. Be aware, though, that not all people from all cultures prefer as much eye contact. Asians, for example, generally prefer less.

The following suggestions can help you use eye contact effectively when you speak in public:

- Establish eye contact with your audience before you say anything. Eye contact sends the message, "I am interested in you. I have something I want to say to you. Tune me in."

eye contact
Looking at an audience during a presentation.

Nonverbal

Adapt

- Maintain eye contact with your audience as you deliver your opening sentence without looking at your notes.
- Try to establish eye contact with people throughout your audience, not just with the front row or only one or two people. Briefly look into the eyes of an individual, then transfer your eye contact to someone else. Do not look over your listeners' heads! They will be able to tell and may even turn around to try to find out what you are looking at.

Nonverbal

physical delivery
A person's gestures, movement, and posture, which influence how a message is interpreted.

gestures
Movements of the hands and arms to communicate ideas.

···> Physical Delivery

Gestures, movement, and posture are the three key elements of **physical delivery.** A good speaker knows how to use effective gestures, make meaningful movements, and maintain appropriate posture while speaking to an audience.

Gestures

The hand and arm movements you use while speaking are called **gestures.** Nearly all people from all cultures use some gestures when they speak. In fact, research suggests that gesturing is instinctive and that it is inherently related to speaking and thinking.[18] Yet even if you gesture easily and appropriately in the course of everyday conversation, you may feel awkward about what to do with your hands when you are in front of an audience. To minimize this challenge, consider the following guidelines:

- Focus on the message you want to communicate. As in ordinary conversation, when you speak in public, your hands should help to emphasize or reinforce your verbal message. Your gestures should coincide with what you are saying.
- Be conversational. Let your gestures flow with your message. They should appear natural, not tense or rigid.
- Be definite. If you want to gesture, go ahead and gesture. Avoid minor hand movements that will be masked by the lectern or that may appear to your audience as accidental brief jerks.
- Vary your gestures. Try not to use the same hand or one all-purpose gesture all the time. Think of the different gestures you can use, depending on whether you want to enumerate, point, describe, or emphasize ideas.
- Don't overdo your gestures. You want your audience to focus not on your gestures, but on your message.
- Make your gestures appropriate to your audience and situation. When you are speaking to a large audience in a relatively formal setting, use bolder, more sweeping, and more dramatic gestures than when you are speaking to a small audience in an informal setting. Consider, too, the culture-based expectations of your audience. As noted earlier, Canadians in general tend to use more gestures than do speakers from other cultures. If you are speaking to a culturally diverse audience, you might want to tone down your gestures.

Adapt

movement
Change of location during a presentation.

Movement

Another element of physical delivery is **movement.** You may have wondered, "Should I walk around during my presentation, or should I stay in one place?" "Should I stay behind the lectern, or could I stand beside or in front of it?" "Can I move around among the audience?" The following criteria may help you determine the answers to these questions:

By walking close to her audience, this speaker establishes a connection with her listeners.

- Like gestures, any movement should be purposeful. It should be consistent with the verbal content of your message, rather than appear as aimless wandering. You might signal the beginning of a new idea or major point in your speech with movement. Or you might move to signal a transition from a serious idea to a more humorous one. The bottom line is that your use of movement should make sense to your listeners. No movement at all is better than random, distracting movement.
- If such physical barriers as a lectern, row of chairs, or an overhead projector make you feel cut off from your audience, move closer to them. Studies suggest that physical proximity enhances learning.[19]

- Adapt to the cultural expectations of your audience. British listeners, for example, have commented to your authors that North American lecturers tend to stand too close to an audience when speaking. If you think that movement will make your audience uncomfortable, stay in one carefully chosen spot to deliver your presentation.

Adapt

Posture

Posture is the third element of physical delivery you should consider when delivering a presentation. One study suggests that your posture may reflect on your credibility as a speaker.[20] Certainly, slouching lazily across a lectern does not communicate enthusiasm for or interest in your audience or your topic. On the other hand, you should adapt your posture to your topic, your audience, and the formality or informality of the speaking occasion. For example, it may be perfectly appropriate, as well as comfortable and natural, to sit on the edge of a desk during a very informal presentation. In spite of the fact that few speech teachers or texts attempt to advocate specific speaking postures, speakers should observe some basic common sense guidelines about their posture:

posture
A speaker's stance.

Adapt

- Avoid slouching, shifting from one foot to the other, or drooping your head.
- Unless you have a disability, do not sit while delivering a presentation. The exception might be perching on the edge of a desk or stool (which would still elevate you slightly above your audience) during a very informal presentation.

Like your gestures and movement, your posture should not call attention to itself. It should reflect your interest in and attention to your audience and your presentation.

⋯⟩ Facial Expression

Your **facial expression** plays a key role in expressing your thoughts, emotions, and attitudes.[21] Your audience sees your face before they hear what you are going to say, giving you the opportunity to set the tone for your message even before you begin speaking. Throughout your presentation, your facial expression, like your body language and eye contact, should be appropriate to your message. Present sombre news with a serious expression on your face. Relate a humorous story with a smile. To communicate interest in your listeners, keep your expression alert and friendly. Social psychologist Paul Ekman has found that facial expressions of primary emotions are virtually universal, so that even a culturally diverse audience will be able to read your facial expressions clearly. To help ensure that you are maximizing your use of this important nonverbal delivery cue, consider rehearsing your speech in front of a mirror, or, better yet, videotaping yourself practising your speech. Consider as objectively as possible whether your face is reflecting the emotional tone of your ideas.

facial expression
Use of the facial muscles to communicate.

Nonverbal

⋯⟩ Vocal Delivery

We have already discussed the importance of selecting words and word phrases that will most effectively communicate your ideas, information, and images. We referred to this element of delivery as verbal delivery. **Vocal delivery,** on the other hand, involves nonverbal vocal cues—not the words you say, but the way you say them. Effective vocal delivery requires that you speak so that your audience can understand you and will sustain interest in what you are saying. Nonverbal vocal elements include volume, pitch, rate, and articulation.

Nonverbal

vocal delivery
Nonverbal voice elements, including pitch, rate, volume, and articulation.

Volume

Volume is the softness or loudness of your voice. It is the most fundamental determinant of audience understanding. If you do not speak loudly enough, even the most brilliant presentation will be ineffective, because the audience simply will not hear you. In addition, you can use volume to signal an important idea in your presentation, by delivering the key idea either more loudly or more softly than the level at which you have been speaking. Consider these guidelines to help you appropriately adapt the volume of your voice to your audience's needs:

volume
The softness or loudness of a speaker's voice.

Adapt

- Speak loudly enough that the members of your audience farthest from you can hear you without straining. This will ensure that everyone else in the room can hear you, too.

⟨⋯⟩ COMMUNICATION and DIVERSITY

Adapting Your Delivery to a Diverse Audience

Most of the suggestions we've presented in this chapter assume that your listeners will be expecting a typical North American approach to delivery. Because the research conclusions used to support our advice are based predominantly on responses from college and university students who are mostly white and between 18 and 25 years of age, realize that our prescriptions may not be applicable to every audience. As we have stressed throughout the book, effective communicators appropriately adapt their message to the expectations of their listeners, especially those from different cultural backgrounds. Consider the following suggestions to help you develop strategies for adapting your nonverbal messages to a culturally diverse audience.

- *Avoid an ethnocentric mindset.* Ethnocentrism is the attitude that your own cultural approaches are superior to those from other cultures. When considering how to adapt your delivery style to your audience, try to view different approaches and preferences not as right or wrong but merely as different from your own.
- *Consider using a less dramatic delivery style for predominantly high-context listeners.* As you recall from Chapter 6, a high-context culture places considerable emphasis on unspoken messages. Therefore, you need not be overly expressive for a high-context audience. For example, for many Japanese people, a delivery style that includes exuberant gestures, overly dramatic facial expressions, and frequent movements seems overdone. A more subtle, less demonstrative approach would create less "noise" and be more effective.
- *If you know that you will be speaking to a group of people from a cultural background different from your own, find out as much as you can about your audience's expectations for delivery.* Don't assume that your own expectations are necessarily universal. For example, if you were to speak to an audience in or predominantly from India, you would want to know that in India, a sideways movement of the head signals understanding or agreement rather than misunderstanding or disagreement.[22] This insight could keep you from misinterpreting your audience's feedback. Also for some Aboriginal audiences, you would never point with a single finger.[23] Aboriginals use this gesture only with inferiors. A pointing gesture should be made with the full hand.

Even such variables as the timing and length of a presentation can have cultural variations. When speaking at a Polish university, one of your authors expected to begin promptly at 11:00 A.M., as announced in the program and on posters. By 11:10 it was clear that the speech would not begin on time, and your author began to despair of having any audience at all. In Poland, it turns out, both students and professors expect to adhere to the "academic quarter." This means that most lectures begin at least 15 minutes, or a quarter hour, after the announced starting time. If your author had asked another professor about the audience's expectations, he would have known this custom in advance. Solutions to such misunderstandings include talking with people you know who are familiar with the cultural expectations. Try to observe other speakers presenting to that audience. Ask specific questions, including the following:

1. What are the audience expectations about where I should stand while speaking?
2. Do listeners expect direct eye contact?
3. When will the audience expect me to start and stop my talk?
4. Will listeners find movement and gestures distracting or welcome?
5. Do listeners expect the use of presentation aids, such as displaying key ideas on an overhead projector or using a PowerPoint, computer-supported presentation?
6. Know the code. Communication occurs when both speaker and listener share the same code system—both verbal and nonverbal. One of your authors became very embarrassed after speaking to a Caribbean audience because he used a circled-thumb-and-finger gesture to signal "okay." Later he discovered that this was an obscene gesture—like extending a middle finger to a Canadian audience.

Although we cannot provide a comprehensive description of each cultural expectation you may face in every educational and professional setting, we can remind you to keep cultural expectations in mind when you rehearse and deliver a presentation. We are not suggesting that you totally abandon your own cultural expectations about delivery. Rather, we urge you to become sensitive and responsive to cultural difference.

On the WEB ⋯⋯•

There are several sites on the Web that can let you both see and hear famous speeches from both the past and today. Here are several places to find speeches on the Internet:

C-SPAN Online (Real Audio)	**www.c-span.org/watch**
History Channel Archive of Speeches	**www.historychannel.com/speeches/index.html**
Webcorp Historical Speeches Archive	**www.webcorp.com/sounds**
MSU Vincent Voice Library	**www.lib.msu.edu/vincent**

- Vary the volume of your voice in a purposeful way. Indicate important ideas by turning your volume up or down.
- Be aware of whether you need a microphone to amplify your volume. If you do and one is available, use it.

There are three kinds of microphones, only one of which demands much technique. The *lavaliere microphone* is the clip-on type often used by newspeople and interviewees. Worn on the front of a shirt or dress, it requires no particular care other than not thumping it or accidentally knocking it off.

The *boom microphone* is used by makers of movies and TV shows. It hangs over the heads of the speakers and is remote controlled, so the speakers need not be particularly concerned with it.

The third kind of microphone, and the most common, is the *stationary microphone.* This is the type that is most often attached to a lectern, sitting on a desk, or standing on the floor. Generally, the stationary microphones used today are multidirectional. You do not have to remain frozen behind a stationary mike while speaking. However, you will have to keep your mouth about the same distance from the mike at all times to avoid distracting fluctuations in the volume of sound. You can turn your head from side to side and use gestures, but you will have to limit other movements.

Under ideal circumstances, you will be able to practise before you speak with the type of microphone you will use. If you have the chance, figure out where to stand for the best sound quality and how sensitive the mike is to extraneous noise. Practice will accustom you to any voice distortion or echo that might occur so that these sound qualities do not surprise you during your presentation.[24]

Pitch

While volume is the loudness or softness of your voice, **pitch** refers to how high or low your voice is. To some extent, pitch is determined by physiology. The faster the folds in your vocal cords vibrate, the higher the habitual pitch of your voice. In general, female vocal folds vibrate much faster than do those of males. However, you can raise or lower your habitual pitch within a certain range. This ability to vary your pitch, called **inflection,** is a key factor in communicating the meaning of your words. You know that saying a startled "Oh!" in response to something someone has told you is quite different from questioning, "Oh?" Your vocal inflection indicates your emotional response to what you have heard. Vocal inflection also helps keep an audience interested in your presentation. If your pitch is a monotone, the audience will probably become bored quickly. To help you monitor and practise your pitch and inflection as you prepare to speak, record and play back your presentation at least once as you rehearse. Listen carefully to your pitch and inflection. If you think you are speaking in too much of a monotone, practise the presentation again with exaggerated variations in pitch.

Rate

Another vocal variable is **rate** or speed. How fast do you talk? Most speakers average between 120 and 180 words per minute but vary their rate to add interest to their delivery and to emphasize key ideas. To determine whether it is appropriate and purposeful, consider becoming consciously aware of your speaking rate. Record your presentation during rehearsal and listen critically to your speech speed. If it seems too fast, make a conscious effort to slow down. Use more **pauses** after questions and before important ideas. If you are speaking too slowly, make a conscious effort to speed up.

Articulation

Articulation is the enunciation of sounds. As a speaker, you want to articulate distinctly to ensure that your audience can determine what words you are using. Sometimes we fall into the habits of mumbling or slurring—saying *wanna* instead of *want to,* or *chesterdrawers* instead of *chest of drawers.* Some nonstandard articulation is actually part of a speaker's **dialect,** a speech style common to an ethnic group or a geographic region. One dialect with which most of us are probably familiar is the dialect of Newfoundland and Labrador,

pitch
How high or low a speaker's voice is.

inflection
Variation in vocal pitch.

Aware

rate
How fast or slow a speaker speaks.

pause
A few seconds of silence during a presentation; can both slow a fast pace and signal a key idea.

articulation
The process of producing speech sounds clearly and distinctly.

dialect
A consistent style of pronunciation and articulation that is common to an ethnic group or geographic region.

characterized by adding "b'y" to the end of sentences, dropping and adding letters to words, and speaking quickly so that words flow into each other. Although most native speakers of English can understand English dialects, studies have shown that North American listeners assign more favourable ratings to, and can recall more information presented by, speakers with dialects similar to their own.[25] If your dialect is significantly different from that of your listeners, or you suspect that it could be potentially distracting, you may want to work to improve or standardize your articulation. To do so, be aware of key words or phrases that you have a tendency to drawl, slur, or chop. Once you have identified them, practise saying them distinctly and correctly.

appearance
A speaker's dress and grooming.

⸱⸱⸱⸱⸱> Appearance

What would you wear to deliver a presentation to your class? To address your city council? The fact that you probably would wear something different for these two occasions suggests that you are already aware of the importance of a speaker's **appearance.** There is considerable evidence that your personal appearance affects how your audience will respond to you and your message. If you violate your audience's expectations, you will be less successful in achieving your purpose. The following guidelines might help make your wardrobe selection a bit easier the next time you are called on to speak:

- Never wear anything that would be potentially distracting—for example, a T-shirt with writing on it. You want your audience to listen to you, not read you.
- Consider wearing appropriate clothing as a presentation aid. For example, if you are a nurse or emergency technician, wear your uniform when you speak about your profession. (We will discuss presentation aids in more detail shortly.)
- Take cues from your audience. If you know that they will be dressed in business attire, dress similarly. If anything, you want to be a bit more dressed up than members of your audience.
- When in doubt about what to wear, select something conservative.

presentation aid
Any tangible item—including objects, models, people, drawings, photographs, maps, graphs, charts, videotapes, CD-ROMs and DVDs, and audiotapes and CDs—used to help communicate ideas to an audience.

EFFECTIVE PRESENTATION AIDS

We have already discussed two elements of delivery: verbal delivery and nonverbal delivery. A third element used with increasing frequency in this era of sophisticated computer presentation software is the **presentation aid.** The term *presentation aid* refers to anything your audience can listen to or look at to help them understand your ideas. Charts, photographs, posters, drawings, graphs, videos, and CDs are some of the types of presentation aids frequently used by speakers.

Re**CAP** ⸱⸱⸱⸱<

Characteristics of Effective Nonverbal Delivery

- Gestures should be relaxed, definite, varied, and appropriate to your audience and the speaking situation.
- Movement should be purposeful.
- Posture should feel natural and be appropriate to your topic, your audience, and the occasion.
- Eye contact should be established before you say anything and sustained as much as possible throughout your presentation.
- Facial expression should be alert, friendly, and appropriate to your message.
- Volume should be loud enough that you can be easily heard and should be purposefully varied.
- Pitch should be varied so that the inflection in your voice helps sustain your audience's interest.
- Rate should be neither too fast nor too slow and can be varied to add interest and emphasize key ideas.
- Articulation should be clear and distinct.
- Appearance should conform to what the audience expects.

Rehearsing on Videotape

There is no feedback more total or more objective than video-tape. First, it reproduces your total image, both visual and aural; and second, it lets you see for yourself. If friends or colleagues tell you that you are a good speaker, you may not respect their judgment, you may think they're being nice rather than honest, or you may think they're biased in your favour. Bruce, a pharma-ceutical salesman, simply couldn't believe it when people told him he was a good speaker because an unpleasant high school speaking experience had convinced him he would never be able to speak well. Seeing himself on videotape was a revelation to him: He saw for himself how good he was. Another person could never have convinced him of it.

By the same token, if someone tells you your voice is too high, that you slouch, or that you need to loosen up your body, you may not be convinced. A videotape has the inherent reassurance of a machine: It has no ulterior motive, and it lets you see it like it is.

People are constantly amazed when they see themselves on videotape. Time and again, it's as if they were seeing and hearing themselves for the first time. They really see the extra 10 kilograms they've been lugging for 10 years; they see the stiff way they stand; they hear the lack of energy in their voices, the *ums*, the *you sees*, the *you knows*, the *likes*.

Becoming aware of the kind of image you project is the first step toward controlling it or altering it.[26]

Presentation aids can be invaluable to you as a speaker. They help you gain and main-tain your audience's attention.[27] They communicate your organization of ideas. They illus-trate sequences of events or procedures. And they help your audience understand and remember your message. In addition, chances are that, for at least one of the assignments in your communication class, you will be required to use a presentation aid. Because pre-sentation aids are valuable supplements to your speeches and because they are so often required, let's discuss first the types of presentation aids that are available to you, including computer-generated ones. Then we will discuss guidelines for preparing presentation aids, and finally provide some general suggestions for using your presentation aids effectively.

···≻ Types of Presentation Aids

If you are required to use a presentation aid for an assignment, or you think a presentation aid might enhance your message, you have a number of options from which to select. You might decide to use an object or model; a person; such two-dimensional presentation aids as drawings, photographs, maps, graphs, or charts; or a videotape, CD-ROM, DVD, audio-tape, or audio CD.

Objects

The first type of presentation aid you ever used—perhaps as long ago as preschool "show and tell"—was probably an object. You took to school your favourite teddy bear or the new remote-control car you got for your birthday. Remember how the kids crowded around to see what you had brought? Objects add interest to a talk because they are real. Whether the members of your audience are in preschool or college, they like tangible, real things. If you use an object as a presentation aid, consider these guidelines:

- Make certain the object can be handled easily. If it is too large, it may be unwieldy; if it is too small, your audience won't be able to see it.
- Don't use dangerous or illegal objects as presentation aids. They may make your audi-ence members uneasy or actually put them at risk.

Models

If it is impossible to bring an object to class, you may be able to substitute a model. You cannot bring a 1965 Ford Thunderbird into a classroom, but you may be able to construct and bring a model. You could probably not acquire and bring to class a dog's heart, but you might be able to find a model to use for your explanation of how heartworms damage that vital organ. If you use a model as a presentation aid, remember this guideline:

- Be sure that the model is large enough to be seen by all members of your audience.

People

You might not think of people as potential presentation aids, but they can be. People can model costumes, play a sport with you, or demonstrate a dance. Consider the following guidelines if you are going to ask someone to assist you as a presentation aid for a speech:

- Rehearse with the person who will be helping you.
- Don't have the person stand beside you doing nothing. Wait until you need your presentation aid to have him or her come to the front.
- Don't let your presentation aid steal the show. Make his or her role specific and fairly brief. As the speaker, you should remain the "person of the hour."

Drawings

You can use simple drawings to help illustrate or explain ideas that you are talking about. For example, you could sketch the tunnels of a fire ant mound to show your audience why it is so difficult to eradicate the entire colony, rather than just drive them underground. You could sketch the life cycle of plants and animals. If you use a drawing as a visual aid, consider these suggestions:

- Keep your drawings large and simple. Line drawings are often more effective than more detailed ones.
- Consider drawing or photocopying your drawing onto an overhead transparency and use an overhead projector to show the drawing to your audience.
- Your drawing does not have to be original artwork. If you need help, you could ask a friend to help you prepare a drawing, or you could use computer software to generate a simple image. Just be sure to credit your source if you use someone else's sketch.

Photographs

If you are giving a speech on urban forestry, you might want to show your audience good colour pictures of trees appropriate for urban sites in your area. In this case, photographs would show colour and detail that would be nearly impossible to achieve with drawings. The biggest challenge to using photographs as presentation aids is size; most photos are simply too small to be seen clearly from a distance. If you want to use a photograph, you will usually have to enlarge it. Consider the following options for making photographs into viable presentation aids:

- Many copy centres or photo shops can produce poster-size colour photocopies.
- Transfer your photograph to a slide and project it onto a screen.
- Use a digital camera to record your picture on a computer disk. Then, when you want to use it, bring it up on your computer screen and use a video projection system to enlarge it for your audience.

Maps

Like photographs, most maps are too small to be useful as presentation aids unless you enlarge them in some way. Consider these suggestions for using maps effectively in a presentation:

bar graph
A pictorial representation of statistical data; typically shows the relationship between sets of data.

- Enlarge your map by photocopying it or by transferring it to a slide. An outline map with few details could be copied or drawn on an overhead transparency.
- Highlight on your map the areas or routes you are going to talk about in your presentation.

Graphs

pie graph
A circular graph that shows the distribution of data in proportion to other data.

Graphs are effective ways to present statistical relationships to your audience. They help to make data more concrete. You are probably already familiar with the three main types of graphs. A **bar graph** consists of bars of various lengths to represent numbers of things or people. It is useful for making comparisons. A round **pie graph** shows how data are distributed out of a total number. And a **line graph** can show both trends over a period of time and relationships among variables. Figure 13.1 illustrates all three types of graphs. The following guidelines will help you use graphs more effectively in your presentations:

line graph
A graph that shows trends over a period of time and relationships among variables.

FIGURE 13.1   Three Types of Graphs

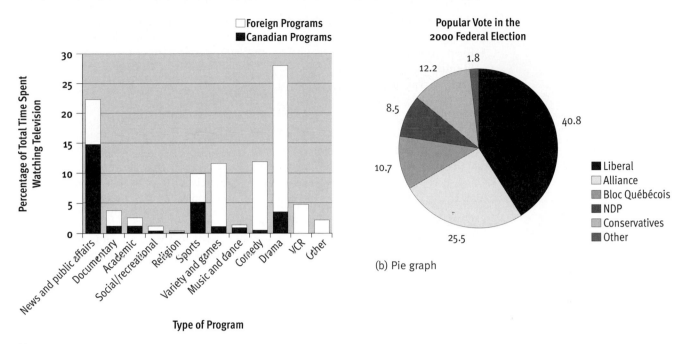

(a) Bar graph

(b) Pie graph

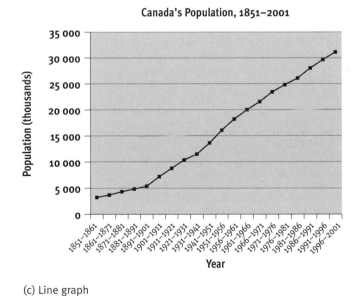

(c) Line graph

Sources: (a) Adapted from Statistics Canada Web site, ‹http://www.statcan.ca/english/freepub/87F0006XIE/87F0006XIE.xls, table 2; (b) Elections Canada, "Thirty-seventh General Election 2000: Official Voting Results," Table 9 ‹http://www.elections.ca/gen/rep/37g/table9_e.html› Courtesy of Elections Canada; (c) Adapted from Statistics Canada Web site, "Population and Growth Components," 1851–2001 Censuses ‹http://www.statcan.ca/english/Pgdb/demo03.htm›.

- Make your graphs big, by drawing them on a large piece of paper, by drawing or copying them on an overhead transparency, or by putting them on a computer disk for projection.
- Keep your graphs simple and uncluttered.
- Remember that many computer programs will generate graphs from statistics. You don't usually need to draw your own.

Charts

Charts can summarize and organize a great deal of information in a small space. Consider using a chart any time you need to present information that could be organized under several headings or in several columns. You can prepare charts by drawing them or by generating them with a computer. Whichever method you use, remember these guidelines:

- Whether you use a large flip chart, transfer your chart to an overhead transparency, or use a computer presentation program, be certain your chart is big enough to be seen easily.
- Keep your chart simple. Do not try to put too much information on one chart. Eliminate any unnecessary words.
- Print or type any lettering on a chart, instead of writing in script.

Videotapes

A VCR will allow you to show scenes from a movie, an excerpt from a training film, or a brief original video to an audience. Modern VCRs have good picture and sound quality and permit stop-action freeze-frame viewing. They also allow you to rewind and replay a scene several times if you want your audience to watch different specific elements of the film. If you plan to use a videotape in a presentation, consider these suggestions:

- If you have an audience of 25 to 30 people, you can use a 25-inch television screen. For larger audiences, you will need a large-screen projection TV or several monitors.
- Use only brief clips and excerpts. Video should always supplement, rather than take over, your speech.

CD-ROMs and DVDs

CD-ROMs and DVDs (digital video discs) allow a speaker to retrieve audio and visual information easily and quickly. One CD-ROM can contain hundreds of words, pictures, or sounds. If you were talking about Prime Minister Paul Martin, you could click your mouse to let your audience hear Martin speak. If you wanted to show various images of Monet's garden, you could retrieve and project those pictures with ease. One DVD can hold an entire movie and can be stopped and started at precise places. Both CD-ROMs and DVDs can be used in combination with a large-screen video projector or a liquid crystal display (LCD) panel connected to an overhead projector. If you plan to use a CD-ROM or DVD, remember these guidelines:

- Be certain that the equipment you will need will be available in the room in which you are going to speak.
- Have the equipment set up and ready to go before you speak.

Audiotapes and Audio CDs

If you want to supplement your speech with audio presentation aids—say, music or excerpts from speeches or interviews—you might want to use cassette audiotapes or audio CDs. Both are readily available and can be amplified to fill rooms of various sizes. A cassette tape has the advantage of your being able to tape and play back original material, such as an interview you did with the dean of students. A CD has better fidelity and can be more easily cued to begin in a specific place. If you use one of these audio presentation aids, consider these suggestions:

- Be certain that your tape or CD is amplified so that your audience can hear it without straining.
- Use audio presentation aids sparingly. You do not want them to interfere with or "become" the speech.

⤳ Computer-Generated Presentation Aids

Not too many years ago, if you wanted to use a drawing or graph as a visual aid, you had to draw it by hand on a blackboard, flip chart, or overhead transparency. If you wanted to use a photograph or map, you had to have it professionally enlarged. Although speakers still use overheads, blackboards, flip charts, and posters, today they also have another option: computer graphics programs. Using these programs, available for both Windows and Macintosh operating systems, you can both create and present professional-looking visual aids inexpensively and easily.

Using a graphics program such as Microsoft's popular PowerPoint, you can develop an outline to emphasize your main points as you speak. You can create graphs and charts. You can use clip art, or you can scan in photographs, maps, or drawings. You can even incorporate video and audio clips. If you have computer-projection equipment available in the room in which you will speak, you can display your presentation by connecting a computer to a special large-screen projector or an LCD panel that fits on top of an overhead projector. You can then run your program with a keyboard or mouse, or even set it to run automatically. If you do not have such equipment available, you can transfer the images you have created to slides, overhead transparencies, or paper.

Among the advantages of learning to use computer graphics programs such as PowerPoint for classroom presentations is that they are an important way to adapt your message to audiences who increasingly expect sophisticated technical support. You will undoubtedly encounter and be expected to use these programs again in the business world. Experience with them now can give you an edge in seeking employment and in making your earliest business presentation more effective.

Adapt

However, such programs also have inherent risks. As one consultant points out,

> When you darken the room and give the audience a preprogrammed, oh-so-beautiful, PowerPoint presentation, the audience will say, "I'm not part of this experience. That guy up there has done it all." The result: Your colleague will mentally go on vacation. . . . [28]

The solution? As with other presentation aids we have discussed, don't let your PowerPoint slides become your presentation—use them to supplement it. Don't use too many slides. Make certain that the ones you do use contain significant information in a simple, uncluttered style. Don't overuse bulleted text. Instead, take advantage of the ease with which you can create and show such visual elements as graphs, charts, and photos on PowerPoint slides. Finally, practise with your PowerPoint slides so that you can time them to coincide with your oral presentation.

⸱⸱⸳> Guidelines for Preparing Presentation Aids

In addition to the specific guidelines we have provided for preparing and using various types of presentation aids, four general guidelines can help you prepare all types of presentation aids more effectively.

Select the Right Presentation Aids

As is evident from the above discussion, you have a number of options for presentation aids. If you are trying to decide which to use, consider these suggestions:

1. Adapt to your audience. Let their interests, experiences, and knowledge guide your selection of presentation aids. For example, an audience of accountants would readily understand arbitrage charts that might be incomprehensible to a more general audience. If you will be speaking to a large audience, be certain that everyone will be able to see or hear your presentation aid.
2. Be constantly aware of your specific purpose. Be certain that your presentation aid contributes to its achievement.
3. Consider your own skill and experience. Use equipment with which you have had experience or have ample time to practise. It may be easier to make an overhead transparency of your PowerPoint image than fumble with an unfamiliar computer and LCD projector.
4. Take into account the room in which you will speak. If it has large windows and no shades, for example, do not plan to use a visual presentation aid that will require a darkened room. If you plan to run a PowerPoint presentation, be sure that both hardware and software are available and in good working order.

Make Your Presentation Aids Easy to See

You have probably experienced the frustration of squinting and straining to read a speaker's too-small presentation aid. If you are going to remember only one thing about using a presentation aid, remember this: Make it big!

Steve Jobs, chief executive officer of Apple Computers, uses a large-screen projector to make sure his audience can see his PowerPoint presentation and the product he used to create it.

Keep Your Presentation Aids Simple

Don't cram too much information on any single presentation aid. Limit words to keywords or phrases. Leave plenty of white space.

Polish Your Presentation Aids

Especially in this day of readily available, professional-looking computer graphics, audiences have high expectations for the appearance of presentation aids. A sloppy, hand-drawn visual will detract from even the best verbal message. Prepare your presentation aids well in advance of your speaking date and make them as attractive and professional as possible. Even if you can't run a PowerPoint presentation in the room in which you are speaking, consider using such a program to produce your presentation aids.

⋯⟩ Guidelines for Using Presentation Aids

Once you have prepared potentially effective presentation aids, you will want to use them effectively as well. In addition to the guidelines offered earlier in this chapter for using specific types of presentation aids, the following general suggestions will help you more effectively adapt various types of presentation aids to your audience.

1. **Rehearse with your presentation aids.** Your speaking day should not be the first time you deliver your presentation while holding up your chart, turning on your projector, or cueing your CD. Practise setting up and using your presentation aids until you feel at ease with them. Consider during rehearsal what you would do at various stages of the speech if you had to carry on without your presentation aid. Electricity fails, equipment fails to show up, and bulbs burn out. Have contingency plans.

2. **Maintain eye contact with your audience, not your presentation aids.** You can glance at your presentation aids during your talk, but do not talk to them. Keep looking at your audience.

3. **Explain your presentation aids.** Always talk about and explain your presentation aids. Do not assume that the audience will understand their relevance and how to interpret them.

4. **Time your presentation aids to coincide with your discussion of them.** Don't put a presentation aid in front of your audience until you are ready to use it. Likewise, remove your presentation aid after you are finished with it. Keeping presentation aids in front of an audience before or after you use them will only serve to distract from your message.

5. **Do not pass objects, pictures, or other small items among your audience.** Passing things around distracts audience members. People are either focused on whatever they are looking at or counting the number of people who will handle the object before it reaches them. If the item is too small for everyone to see, it is not a good presentation aid.

6. **Use handouts effectively.** Handing out papers during your presentation can also distract audience members. If possible, wait to distribute handouts until after you have spoken. If your audience needs to refer to the material while you're talking about it, go ahead and pass out the handouts and tell them at various points in your presentation where in the handout they should focus.

7. **Use small children and animals with caution.** Small children and even the best-trained animals are unpredictable. In a strange environment, in front of an audience, they may not behave in their usual way. The risk of having a child or animal detract from your presentation may be too great to make planning a presentation around one a good idea.

8. **Use technology thoughtfully.** Computer-generated graphics, LCDs, and DVDs will probably become increasingly common components of presentations as more and more classrooms and seminar rooms are equipped for them. However, resist the temptation to use them just because they are glitzy. Be sure that they help you communicate your message. And be sure that you know how to operate the hardware and that you rehearse with it.

Re**CAP** ←····

Preparing and Using Presentation Aids

TIPS FOR PREPARING AND USING SPECIFIC TYPES OF PRESENTATION AIDS	GENERAL TIPS FOR PREPARING AND USING PRESENTATION AIDS

TIPS FOR PREPARING AND USING SPECIFIC TYPES OF PRESENTATION AIDS

- Use objects that you can handle easily and that are safe and legal.
- Be sure that any models are large enough to be seen easily.
- Rehearse with people who will serve as presentation aids, and don't let them steal the show.
- Keep drawings simple and large.
- Be sure photographs are large enough to be seen easily.
- Highlight on a map the geographic areas you will discuss.
- Keep graphs simple and uncluttered.
- Limit the amount of information you put on any single chart.
- Use only brief excerpts and clips from videotapes.
- Have CD-ROM, DVD, or VCR equipment set up and ready to go before you speak.
- Amplify any audiotapes and CDs so they can be heard easily.

GENERAL TIPS FOR PREPARING AND USING PRESENTATION AIDS

Preparing Presentation Aids

- Select the right presentation aid.
- Make your presentation aids easy to see.
- Keep your presentation aids simple.
- Polish your presentation aids.

Using Presentation Aids

- Rehearse with your presentation aids.
- Maintain eye contact with your audience, not your presentation aids.
- Explain your presentation aids.
- Time your presentation aids to coincide with your discussion of them.
- Do not pass objects, pictures, or other small items among your audience.
- Use handouts effectively.
- Use small children and animals with caution.
- Use technology thoughtfully.

SOME FINAL TIPS FOR REHEARSING AND DELIVERING YOUR PRESENTATION

Throughout this chapter, we have described and offered suggestions for effective verbal and nonverbal delivery and use of presentation aids. In addition to the tips offered throughout the chapter, the following suggestions will help you make the most of your rehearsal time and ultimately deliver your presentation successfully.

1. **Finish your full-content outline several days before you must deliver the presentation.** Begin to rehearse from the full-content outline. Revise the presentation as necessary so that you can deliver it within your given time limits. Prepare your speaking notes. Continue to rehearse and to modify your speaking notes as necessary.
2. **Practise, practise, practise. Rehearse aloud as often as possible.** Only by rehearsing will you gain confidence in both the content of the presentation and your delivery of it.
3. **Practise good delivery skills while rehearsing.** Rehearse your presentation standing up. Pay attention to your gestures, posture, eye contact, facial expression, and vocal delivery, as well as the verbal message. Rehearse with your presentation aids.

The 5th Wave   By Rich Tennant

Gesundheit.

4. **If possible, practise your presentation for someone.** Seek and consider feedback from someone about both the content and your delivery.

5. **Tape record or videotape your presentation.** Becoming more aware of your delivery can help you make necessary adjustments.

6. **Re-create the speaking situation in your final rehearsals.** Try to speak in a room similar to the one in which you will deliver the presentation. Use the set of speaking notes you will use the day you deliver the presentation. Give the presentation without stopping. The more realistic the rehearsal, the more confidence you will gain.

7. **Get plenty of rest the night before you speak.** Being well rested is more valuable than frantic, last-minute rehearsal.

8. **Arrive early.** If you don't know for certain where your room is, give yourself plenty of time to find it. Rearrange any furniture or equipment and check and set up your presentation aids.

9. **Review and apply the suggestions offered in Chapter 11 and this chapter for becoming a more confident speaker.** As the moment for delivering your presentation nears, remind yourself of the effort you have spent preparing it. Visualize yourself delivering the presentation effectively. Silently practise your opening lines. Think about your audience. Breathe deeply, and consciously relax.

10. **After you have delivered your presentation, seek feedback from members of your audience.** Use this information to improve your next presentation.

SUMMARY

Once you have developed, supported, and organized your presentation, you are ready to begin to rehearse aloud in preparation for delivering it. The way in which you deliver your presentation will determine in large part your success as a speaker.

As you begin to consider how you will deliver your presentation, you will select from four methods of delivery: manuscript speaking, memorized speaking, impromptu speaking, or extemporaneous speaking. Extemporaneous speaking is the style taught today in most presentational speaking classes and preferred by most audiences.

Once you know what method of delivery you will use, you should begin to think about and rehearse words, phrases, and sentences that will best communicate your intended message and give it a distinct and memorable style. The most effective language is concrete, unbiased, vivid, simple, and correct.

Nearly everyone feels some anxiety about speaking in public. Speaker anxiety triggers physiological responses that may be worrisome but are actually your body's attempt to help you. Focusing on your audience and message and thinking positively can help you manage speaker anxiety, as can knowing how to develop a presentation, being well prepared, and seeking out opportunities to speak. Professional help is available for those few who continue to suffer debilitating speaker anxiety.

Nonverbal variables are also critical to effective delivery. Physical delivery includes a speaker's gestures, movement, and posture. Eye contact is perhaps the most important delivery variable, determining to a large extent your credibility with your audience. Facial expression plays a key role in expressing thoughts, emotions, and attitudes. Vocal delivery includes such elements as volume, pitch, rate, and articulation. And finally, your personal appearance can also affect how your audience will respond to you and your message.

Presentation aids may not always be necessary, but they are used with increasing frequency. Presentation aids may include objects or models, people, drawings, photographs, maps, graphs, charts, videotapes, CD-ROMs, DVDs, audiotapes, and audio CDs. Today, many presentation aids can be created and displayed by computer graphics programs such as PowerPoint. Guidelines for using any type of presentation aid include selecting the right one for the audience, occasion, and room; and making the presentation aid simple, easy to see (or hear), and polished. As you prepare to use any presentation aid, be sure that you rehearse with it, maintain eye contact with your audience, explain your presentation aid, time your use of your presentation aid, refrain from passing things around or using handouts indiscriminately, remember that small children and animals are unpredictable presentation aids, and use technology thoughtfully.

Final suggestions for rehearsing your presentation include allowing ample time for and conducting realistic rehearsals, audiotaping or videotaping your presentation, and practising your presentation for someone who will offer feedback. Final tips for delivering your presentation include getting plenty of rest the night before you speak, arriving early, and applying the suggestions offered in Chapter 11 and this chapter for becoming a more confident speaker.

PRINCIPLES FOR A LIFETIME

Aware

Principle 1: Be aware of your communication with yourself and others.

- If your subject is sensitive or your information classified, be cautious and noncommittal in any impromptu remarks you might be asked to make.
- As you feel increasingly comfortable rehearsing an extemporaneous presentation, prepare and use successively less detailed notes.
- Understand that speaker anxiety is a normal physiological response and can help you perform better.
- Give yourself a positive pep talk before getting up to speak.
- Grammatical and usage errors communicate a lack of preparation. If you are uncertain of how to use a word or phrase, look it up or ask someone.
- Use a microphone if you need one and one is available. Be sure to rehearse with it.
- Be aware of your speaking rate, and adjust it if necessary.
- Identify keywords or phrases that you have a tendency to drawl, slur, or chop. Practise saying them distinctly and clearly.
- Be certain that your presentation aids, including those that use technology, contribute to your specific purpose.
- Pay attention to your nonverbal delivery when you rehearse your presentation.
- During rehearsal, tape record or videotape your presentation; objectively and critically observe your gestures, posture, eye contact, facial expression, and vocal delivery, as well as your verbal message; and make necessary adjustments.
- When you deliver your presentation, apply the suggestions offered in Chapter 11 and this chapter for becoming a more confident speaker.

Verbal

Principle 2: Effectively use and interpret verbal messages.

- Give a manuscript or memorized speech when exact wording is critical.
- Focus on your message to help manage speaker anxiety.
- Phrase your ideas so that they will be clear, accurate, and memorable.
- Do not try to memorize an extemporaneous presentation word for word; vary the ways in which you express ideas and information.
- The most effective words are concrete, unbiased, vivid, simple, and correct.

Nonverbal

Principle 3: Effectively use and interpret nonverbal messages.

- The physical symptoms of speaker anxiety are rarely visible to an audience.
- Audience members equate the effectiveness of a presentation with various nonverbal delivery variables.
- Nonverbal delivery provides important information about a speaker's feelings and emotions, and affects listeners' emotional responses to the speaker.
- When you deliver a manuscript speech, try to look at an entire sentence at a time so that you can maintain eye contact throughout the sentence.
- Do not read a manuscript speech too rapidly; vary the rhythm, inflection, and pace of delivery so that the speech does not "sound read."
- Do not deliver a memorized speech too rapidly, and avoid patterns of vocal inflection that make the speech "sound recited."
- Use gestures and movement to add interest and emphasis to both manuscript and memorized speeches.
- Use gestures to emphasize or reinforce your verbal message.
- Move during your presentation to signal the beginning of a new idea or major point, or to signal a transition from a serious idea to a humorous one or vice versa.
- Your posture may reflect on your credibility as a speaker.
- To heighten your credibility and to increase listener learning, use eye contact to let your audience know that you are interested in them and ready to talk to them.
- Speak loudly enough to be heard easily by all members of your audience.
- Vary the volume of your voice to emphasize ideas and sustain the audience's interest.

- Vocal inflection is a key factor in communicating the meaning of words.
- Vary your speaking rate to add interest to your delivery and to emphasize key ideas.
- Articulate your words clearly.
- Your personal appearance affects how your audience will respond to you and your message.

Listen and Respond

Principle 4:   Listen and respond thoughtfully to others.

- Eye contact can help you determine how your audience members are responding to you.
- If possible, rehearse your presentation for someone and seek feedback about both your content and your delivery.

Adapt

Principle 5:   Appropriately adapt messages to others.

- Although audiences today generally expect speakers to use everyday language and a conversational delivery style, you will need to adapt your delivery to audiences of different sizes and from different cultures.
- Consider your audience and speaking context when you select a method of delivery.
- Consider your audience's interests, expectations, and knowledge to ensure that your impromptu presentation is audience centred.
- As you deliver an extemporaneous presentation, adapt it to your audience.
- Being audience centred is key to reducing speaker anxiety.
- Avoid any language that might be offensive to a member of your audience.
- Adapt your gestures to your audience. Use bolder, more sweeping, and more dramatic gestures with large audiences. Tone down gestures if you are speaking to a culturally diverse audience who might prefer a more subdued style.
- Adapt your movement during a presentation to the cultural expectations of your audience. Better to stay in one carefully chosen spot than to make your audience uncomfortable.
- Deliver your presentation with a posture that seems natural to you in light of your topic, your audience, and the formality of the occasion.
- Adapt the amount of eye contact you use to the expectations of your audience. North Americans prefer as much eye contact as possible; Asians generally prefer less.
- To communicate your interest in your listeners, keep your facial expression alert and friendly.
- Adapt the volume of your voice to your audience's needs.
- Adapt to your audience's expectations for your appearance.
- Let your audience's interests, experiences, and knowledge guide your preparation and selection of presentation aids.

Discussion and Review

1. In what way(s) does delivery contribute to the success of a presentation?

2. What style of delivery do most North American audiences expect?

3. Give an example of how culture can influence audience expectations for speaker delivery.

4. Under what circumstances might a speaker want to deliver a manuscript or memorized speech?

5. How does an extemporaneous presentation differ from an impromptu presentation?

6. Explain what causes the symptoms of speaker anxiety.

7. Offer at least three suggestions for managing speaker anxiety.

8. List and explain five criteria for effective words in a presentation.

9. List and define the three key elements of physical delivery and provide suggestions for effectively using each one.

10. What is the most important nonverbal delivery variable for most North American audiences?

11. What can facial expression communicate during a presentation?

12. List and define four nonverbal elements of vocal delivery and provide suggestions for using each one effectively.

13. How should you dress when you are going to deliver a presentation?

14. List 11 types of presentation aids from which a speaker might select, and provide suggestions for effectively using each type.

15. Offer four general guidelines for preparing effective presentation aids.

16. Provide eight general guidelines for using presentation aids effectively in a presentation.

17. Offer nine general guidelines for rehearsing and delivering a presentation.

Developing Your Skills: Putting Principles into Practice ⚜

1. Consult either a print thesaurus or the electronic thesaurus on your word processing program and find a more concrete or specific word to express each of the following:

go	happy
say	green
big	cat
dark	street
good	car

2. Attend or watch on television a political campaign speech. Pay particular attention to the politician's delivery. Critique his or her use of gestures, movement, posture, eye contact, facial expression, vocal delivery, and appearance. What advice would you give this politician?

3. Videotape one of your presentations, during either rehearsal or delivery to your class. Analyze your strengths and weaknesses based on the principles and suggestions offered in this chapter.

4. You are a speech consultant to the superintendent of your local school district. She is about to begin working on her annual "State of the District" address, which she gives to an audience of about 250 teachers, parents, and community members. This year, she wants to enliven her presentation of enrolment statistics, student achievement facts, and the state of the physical plant with some presentation aids. Write an advisory memo to the superintendent, in which you suggest what types of presentation aids she might employ and offer suggestions for using each one effectively.

5. You will need the following materials to complete this assignment:

   One or two pieces of paper or poster board measuring at least 37 by 50 centimetres
   At least two different-coloured felt-tipped markers or a set of marking pens
   A ruler or straightedge
   A pencil with an eraser

   Three speech topics are given below, each with a brief description and information that could be communicated with the help of a presentation aid. Design one or more presentation aids for one of the three speeches.

   a. A speech about various kinds of organizing tools that students could use to help them keep track of assignments and projects. These tools include paper wall calendars, paper daytimers, personal information-manager software, handheld electronic organizers, and Internet-based calendars.[29]

   b. A speech about the spread of AIDS. New HIV infections in 2000 for various continents include the following:[30]

      North America: 45 000
      Caribbean and Latin America: 210 000
      Europe and Central Asia: 280 000
      North Africa and Middle East: 80 000
      Sub-Saharan Africa: 3 800 000
      East Asia and Pacific: 130 000
      South Asia: 780 000
      Australia and New Zealand: 500

   c. A speech that discusses Web sites offering useful information about nutrition and diet. Sites might include the following:[31]

      - **www.hc-sc.gc.ca/hpfb-dgpsa/onpp-bppn/ food_guide_rainbow_e.html**—Health Canada's food guide to healthy eating
      - **www.dietsite.com**—allows users to enter recipes to obtain a calorie count
      - **www.mealsforyou.com**—offers thousands of healthy recipes

Diana Ong, "The Defense." © Diana Ong/SuperStock.

Give me the right word and the right accent and I will move the world.

— JOSEPH CONRAD

13 Speaking to Inform and Persuade

CHAPTER OUTLINE

AFTER STUDYING THIS CHAPTER, YOU SHOULD BE ABLE TO

1. Identify three goals of speaking to inform.

2. Describe and illustrate five types of informative speaking.

3. Identify and use strategies for making an informative presentation clear.

4. Identify and use strategies for making an informative presentation interesting.

5. Identify and use strategies for making an informative presentation memorable.

6. Define persuasion and describe four strategies for motivating listeners.

7. Define attitudes, beliefs, and values, and explain why a speaker should know which one he or she is targeting in a persuasive message.

8. Define credibility; analyze its three factors; and describe how to enhance initial, derived, and terminal credibility.

9. Define and provide an example of inductive, deductive, and causal reasoning.

10. Explain three ways to make emotional appeals in a persuasive presentation.

11. List and explain four ways to organize a persuasive message.

12. List and explain the five steps of the motivated sequence.

13. Provide specific suggestions for adapting to receptive audiences, neutral audiences, and unreceptive audiences.

This is the information age. With the help of today's technology, we are immersed in facts, data, and words. The Internet is an overflowing fount of information on every conceivable topic. Information is a good thing: It is necessary to help us live our lives. But the volume of information makes it difficult to use and interpret.

A challenge of speaking to inform is to keep your informative message from becoming a persuasive one. It cannot be denied that informing and persuading are interrelated. Information alone may persuade someone to think or do something in a different way. However, if you intentionally try to change or reinforce your listeners' feelings, ideas, or behaviour, your speech may become more persuasive than informative.

In this chapter, we will suggest ways to build on your experience and enhance your skill in informing others. We will examine different types of informative tasks, and identify specific strategies to help you make your messages clear, interesting, and memorable. We also define persuasion, noting how it is similar to and different from informing others, and then describe how persuasion works by explaining how to motivate an audience. We'll also offer suggestions for developing a persuasive speech; present ideas to help you organize your persuasive message; and provide methods to help you move an audience because of your credibility, use of logic, and use of emotional appeals. Finally, although we hope that all of the audiences you face are receptive to your persuasive speeches, we'll help you adapt your message not only to receptive audiences but also to those who are neutral or unreceptive. Throughout our discussion we will remind you to keep the five communication principles for a lifetime in mind.

SPEAKING TO INFORM

inform
To share information with others to enhance their knowledge or understanding of the information, concepts, and ideas you present.

The purpose of a message to **inform** is to share information with others to enhance their knowledge or understanding of the information, concepts, and ideas you present. When you inform someone, you assume the role of a teacher by defining, illustrating, clarifying, or elaborating on a topic.

A recent survey of both speech teachers and students who had taken a communication course found that the single most important skill taught in a presentational speaking class is how to give an informative presentation.[1] This is not surprising, given the importance of sending and receiving information in our lives.

Speaking to inform others can be a challenging task. The information you communicate to someone else is rarely, if ever, understood exactly as you intend it. As we noted in Chapter 2, and further elaborated on in Chapter 6, we're each different from one another. We literally experience the world in different ways. As a student, you have first-hand experience that just because a teacher presents information, you don't always soak up knowledge like a sponge. Informing or teaching others is a challenge because of a simple fact: *Presenting information does not mean that communication has occurred.* Communication happens when the listeners make sense of the information.

TYPES OF INFORMATIVE PRESENTATIONS

When preparing an informative presentation, your first task, after considering the needs and backgrounds of your audience, is to select a topic. Although you may be assigned a topic based upon your job, experience, or expertise, there are times (such as in a communication class) when you are given a free hand in determining what you will talk about. Identifying the type of informative presentation you will deliver can help you select and narrow your topic, as well as organize your message. For general tips on selecting a topic and organizing a message, review the information we've included in Chapter 11.

As you will see in the following discussion, the demands of your purpose will often dictate a structure for your presentation. As you look at these suggestions about structure, however, keep in mind that a clear organization is only *one* factor in your audience's ability to process your message. Remember these fundamental communication principles: Adapt your message to your listeners (be audience centred), and use verbal and nonverbal messages to communicate your ideas clearly.

⋯⟩ Presentations about Objects

A speech about an object might be about anything tangible—anything you can see or touch. Chapter 12 provides suggestions for using objects as visual aids to illustrate your ideas.

The time limit for your speech will determine the amount of detail you can share with your listeners. Even in a 30- to 45-minute presentation, you cannot talk about every aspect of any object listed. So you will need to focus on a specific purpose. Here's a sample outline for a speech about an object:

TOPIC:	Nuclear power plant
GENERAL PURPOSE:	To inform
SPECIFIC PURPOSE:	At the end of my presentation, the audience should be able to describe two major parts and functions of a nuclear power plant.

I. The reactor core
   A. The nuclear fuel in the core
   B. The placement of the fuel in the core
II. The reactor vessel
   A. The walls of a reactor vessel
   B. The function of the coolant in the reactor vessel

When speaking about Indian rock art, this speaker may find it helpful to organize her speech either topically, spatially, or chronologically.

As in the above example, presentations about objects may be organized *topically*; a topical pattern is structured around the logical divisions of the object you're describing. Presentations about objects may also be organized *chronologically*. A speaker might, for example, focus on the history and development of nuclear power plants. That presentation would probably be organized chronologically. If a how-to discussion becomes the central focus of the speech, it then becomes a presentation about a *procedure*.

⋯⟩ Presentations about Procedures

A presentation about a procedure discusses how something works (for example, the human circulatory system), or describes a process that produces a particular outcome (such as how grapes become wine). At the close of such a presentation, your audience should be able to describe, understand, or perform the procedure you have described. Here are some examples of procedures that could make effective informative presentations:

How to surf the Internet
How provinical laws are made
How to refinish furniture

Notice that all of these examples start with the word *how*. A presentation about a procedure usually focuses on how a process is completed or how something can be accomplished. Presentations about procedures are often presented in workshops or other training situations in which people learn skills. The best way to teach people a skill is to remember the acronym T-E-A-C-H, which stands for Tell-Example-Apply-Coach-Help:[2]

- *Tell:* Describe what you want your listeners to know.
- *Example:* Show them an example of how to perform the skill.
- *Apply:* Give them an opportunity to apply the knowledge by performing the skill.
- *Coach:* Provide positive coaching to encourage them.
- *Help:* Help them learn by correcting mistakes.

Describing how to develop a new training curriculum in teamwork skills, Anita grouped some of her steps together like this:

I. Conduct a needs assessment of your department.
   A. Identify the method of assessing department needs.
   B. Implement the needs assessment.

II. Identify the topics that should be presented in the training.
   A. Specify topics that all members of the department need.
   B. Specify topics that only some members of the department need.
III. Write training objectives.
   A. Write objectives that are measurable.
   B. Write objectives that are specific.
   C. Write objectives that are attainable.
IV. Develop lesson plans for the training.
   A. Identify the training methods you will use.
   B. Identify the materials you will need.

Her audience will remember the four general steps much more easily than they could have hoped to recall the curriculum development process if each task were listed as a separate step.

Many presentations about procedures include visual aids. Whether you are teaching people how to install a computer modem or how to give a presentation, showing them how to do something is almost always more effective than just telling them how to do it.

⋯⟩ Presentations about People

A biographical presentation could be about someone famous or about someone you know personally. Most of us enjoy hearing about the lives of real people, whether famous or not, living or dead, who have some special quality about them. The key to making an effective biographical presentation is to be selective. Don't try to cover every detail of your subject's life. Relate the key elements in the person's career, personality, or other significant life features so that you are building to a particular point, rather than just reciting facts about an individual. Perhaps your grandfather was known for his generosity, for example. Mention some notable examples of his philanthropy. If you are talking about a well-known personality, pick information or a period that is not widely known, such as the person's private hobby or childhood. One speaker gave a memorable presentation about his friend:

> To enter Charlie's home was to enter a world of order and efficiency. His den reflected his many years as an Air Force officer; it was orderly and neat. He always knew exactly where everything was. When he finished reading the morning paper, he folded it so neatly by his favourite chair that you would hardly know that it had been read. Yet for all of his efficiency, you knew the minute you walked into his home that he cared for others, that he cared for you. His jokes, his stories, his skill in listening to others drew people to him. He never met a stranger. He looked for opportunities to help others.

Note how these details capture Charlie's personality and charm.

Presentations about people should give your listeners the feeling that the person is a unique, authentic individual. One way to talk about a person's life is in chronological order—birth, school, career, family, achievements, death. However, if you are interested in presenting a specific theme, such as, "Canada's multicultural environment as envisioned by Pierre Elliott Trudeau," you may decide instead to organize those key experiences topically.

⋯⟩ Presentations about Events

Most Canadians remember where they were and what they were doing on September 11, 2001, the day terrorists attacked the World Trade Center and the Pentagon. Major events punctuate our lives and mark the passage of time.

A major event can form the basis of a fascinating informative presentation. You can choose to talk about an event that you have either witnessed or researched. Your goal is to describe the event in concrete, tangible terms and to bring the experience to life for your audience members so that they can visualize the scene.

Most speeches built around an event follow a chronological arrangement. But a presentation about an event might also describe the complex issues or causes behind the event and be organized topically. For example, if you were to talk about the Quebec referendum, you might choose to focus on three aspects:

   I. Political ramifications

  II. Economic impact

 III. Social changes

Although these main points are topical, specific subpoints may be organized chronologically. However you choose to organize your speech about an event, your audience should be enthralled by your vivid description.

⤍ Presentations about Ideas

Presentations about ideas are usually more abstract than the other types of presentations. The following principles, concepts, and theories might be topics of idea presentations:

Principles of time management

Freedom of speech

Theories of communication

Most presentations about ideas are organized topically (by logical subdivisions of the central idea) or according to complexity (from simple ideas to more complex ones). The following example illustrates how Thompson organized a presentation about philosophy into an informative speech:

TOPIC:	Philosophy
GENERAL PURPOSE:	To inform
SPECIFIC PURPOSE:	At the end of my presentation, the audience should be able to define the study of philosophy and describe three branches of the study of philosophy.

   I. Definition of philosophy

     A. Philosophy as viewed in ancient times

     B. Philosophy as viewed today

  II. Three branches of the study of philosophy

     A. Metaphysics

       1. The study of ontology

       2. The study of cosmology

     B. Epistemology

       1. Knowledge derived from thinking

       2. Knowledge derived from experiencing

     C. Logic

       1. Types of reasoning

       2. Types of proof

Thompson decided that the most logical way to give an introductory talk about philosophy was first to define it and then to describe three branches of philosophy. He used a topical organizational pattern to organize his message. When you look at his outline, you may say, "That topic sure looks boring." The key to gaining and maintaining interest is in your selection of supporting material. As we discussed in Chapter 11, a good speaker can select stories, examples, and illustrations that can make an abstract message about an idea both exciting and relevant to the audience.

STRATEGIES FOR MAKING YOUR INFORMATIVE PRESENTATION CLEAR

Think of the best teacher you ever had. He or she was probably a great lecturer with a special talent for making information clear, interesting, and memorable. Like teachers, some speakers are better than others at presenting information clearly. In this section, we will review some of the principles that can help you become this kind of speaker.[3]

A message is clear when it is understood by the listener in the way the speaker intended. How do you make your messages clear to others? First, be aware (mindful) of what you intend to communicate. Is the message clear to you? Say to yourself, "If I heard this message for the first time, would it make sense to me?"

ReCAP ◀┄┄

Types of Informative Presentations

PRESENTATION TYPE	DESCRIPTION	TYPICAL ORGANIZATIONAL PATTERNS	SAMPLE TOPICS
Presentations about objects	Present information about tangible things	Topical Chronological	The Rosetta Stone MP3 players The Ottawa Parliament buildings
Presentations about procedures	Review how something works or describe a process	Chronological Topical Complexity	How to . . . Clone an animal Operate a nuclear power plant Use a computer Trap lobsters
Presentations about people	Describe either famous people or personal acquaintances	Chronological Topical	Pierre Elliott Trudeau Mike Myers Your grandmother Your favourite teacher
Presentations about events	Describe an actual event	Chronological Topical Complexity	Chinese New Year Canada Day St. Jean Baptiste Day
Presentations about ideas	Present abstract information or information about principles, concepts, theories, or issues	Topical Complexity	Communism Economic theory Tao Te Ching

If the message makes sense to you, select appropriate words that are reinforced with appropriate nonverbal cues to express your ideas. If you detect that your listeners are puzzled by what you say, stop and try another way to express your ideas.

Adapt your message to your audience. Be audience centred. Keep your listeners in mind as you select and narrow a topic, fine-tune your purpose, and complete each preparation and presentation task. Here are several additional specific strategies to make your message clear.

┄┄> Simplify Ideas

Your job as a presentational speaker is to get your ideas over to your audience, not to see how much information you can cram in. The simpler your ideas and phrases, the greater the chance that your audience will remember them.

Let's say you decide to talk about state-of-the-art personal computer hardware. Fine, but just don't try to make your audience as sophisticated as you are about computers in a five-minute presentation. Discuss only major features and name one or two leaders in the field. Don't load your presentation with details. Edit ruthlessly.

As we noted in Chapter 11, your audience will more readily understand your information if you organize your major points logically. Regardless of the length or complexity of your message, you must always follow a logical pattern in order to be understood.

┄┄> Pace Your Information Flow

Organize your message so that you present an even flow of information, rather than bunch up a number of significant details around one point. If you present too much new information too quickly, you may overwhelm your audience. Their ability to understand may falter.

COMMUNICATION and DIVERSITY

Using an Interpreter

It is quite possible that someday you may be asked to speak to an audience that does not understand English. In such a situation, you will need an interpreter to translate your message so that your audience can understand you. When using an interpreter, consider the following tips:

1. Realize that a presentation that may take you 30 minutes to deliver without an interpreter will take at least an hour to present with an interpreter. Edit your message to make sure it fits within the time limit.
2. Even with an experienced interpreter, you'll need to slow your speaking rate a bit. Also, be sure to pause after every two or three sentences to give the interpreter time to translate your message.
3. Don't assume that your audience doesn't understand you just because you are using an interpreter. Don't say anything that you don't want your audience to hear.
4. If you have many facts, figures, or other detailed summary of data, write this information down before you speak, and give it to your interpreter.
5. Humour often doesn't translate well. Be cautious of using a joke that was a real knee-slapper when you told it to your colleagues in your office; it may not have the same effect on people with a different cultural background and different language. Also, even a very skilled interpreter may have difficulty communicating the intended meaning of your humour.
6. Avoid using slang, jargon, or any terms that will be unfamiliar to your listeners or interpreter.
7. When possible, talk with your interpreter before you deliver your presentation. Tell him or her the general points you will present. If possible, give the interpreter an outline or a transcript if you are using a manuscript.

Make sure that your audience has time to process any new information you present. Use supporting material to help the pace of your presentation.

Relate New Information to Old

Most of us learn by building on what we already know. We try to make sense of our world by associating the old with the new. When you meet someone for the first time, you may be reminded of someone you already know. Your understanding of calculus is based on your knowledge of algebra.

When presenting new information to a group, help your audience associate your new idea with something that is familiar to them. Use an **analogy.** Tell bewildered first-year students how their new academic life will be similar to high school and how it will be different. By building on the familiar, you help your listeners understand how your new concept or information relates to their experience.

analogy
A comparison between two ideas, things, or situations, that demonstrates how something unfamiliar is similar to something the audience already understands.

STRATEGIES FOR MAKING YOUR INFORMATIVE PRESENTATION INTERESTING

He had them. Every audience member's eyes were riveted on the speaker. It was as quiet as midnight in a funeral home. Audience members were also leaning forward, ever so slightly, not wanting to miss a single idea or brilliant illustration. No one moved. They hung on every word. How can you create such interest when *you* speak? Here are several strategies that can help you keep your audiences listening for more.

Relate to Your Listeners' Interests

Your listeners may be interested in your topic for a variety of reasons. It may affect them directly; it may add to their knowledge; it may satisfy their curiosity; or it may entertain them. If your audience feels that they will benefit from your presentation in some way, your presentation will interest them.

Throughout this book, we have encouraged you to adapt—to develop an audience-centred approach to presentational speaking. Being an audience-centred informative

Adapt

speaker means that you are aware of information that your audience can use. Specifically, what factors help maintain audience interest? Consider the following strategies:[4]

- *Activity and movement:* We are more likely to listen to a story that is action packed than to one that listlessly lingers on an idea too long.
- *Issues and events close to an audience:* To capture your listeners' attention, relate your information to what is happening in your school, community, or province. Not surprisingly, most people are interested in themselves. Therefore, one of the secrets to making a presentation interesting is to use examples with which your audience can relate. Make it personal. When appropriate, mention specific audience members' names.
- *Conflict:* Clashes of ideas; stories that pit one side against another; or opposing forces in government, religion, or interpersonal relationships grab attention. The Greeks learned long ago that the essential ingredient of any play, be it comedy or tragedy, is conflict.

Another way you can make your message interesting is to think about why you are interested in the topic. Once you are aware of your own interests and background, you can often find ways to establish common bonds with your audience.

⋯⟩ Use Attention-Catching Supporting Material

Supporting material is effective if it both clarifies your ideas and keeps your listeners' attention. One classic type of supporting material often used in informative speaking is definitions. But, if you are trying to tell your listeners about a complex or abstract process, you will need more than definitions to explain what you mean. When describing abstract ideas or processes, it's usually more difficult to hold listeners' attention. Research suggests that you can demystify a complex process and increase audience interest if you first provide a simple overview of the process with an analogy, model, picture, or vivid description.[5]

Before going into great detail, first give listeners the "big picture" or convey the gist of what the process is about. *Analogies* (comparisons) are often a good way to do this. For example, if you are describing how a personal computer works, you could say that it stores information like a filing cabinet or that computer software works like a piano roll on an old-fashioned player piano. In addition to using an analogy, consider using a *model* or other *visual aid* to show relationships among the parts of a complex process, following the guidelines we presented in Chapter 12.

You can also describe the process, providing more detail than you do when you just define something. Descriptions answer questions about the *who, what, where, why,* and *when* of the process. Who is involved in the process? What is the process, idea, or event that you want to describe? Where and when does the process take place? Why does it occur, or why is it important to the audience? (Of course, not all of these questions apply to every description.)

⋯⟩ Establish a Motive for Your Audience to Listen to You

Most audiences will probably not be waiting breathlessly for you to talk to them. You will need to motivate them to listen to you.

Some situations have built-in motivations for listeners. A teacher can say, "There will be a test covering my lecture tomorrow. It will count as 50% of your semester grade." Such threatening methods may not make the teacher popular, but they certainly will motivate the class to listen. You will rarely have the power to motivate your listeners with such strong-arm tactics, and you will therefore need to find more creative ways to get your audience to listen to you. Don't assume that your listeners will be automatically interested in what you have to say.

The 5th Wave   By Rich Tennant

...which reminds me of a story about a dyslexic mathematician...

Oh no. Not the perturbation of transient time-independent theory joke again!

QUANTUM FEST

© The 5th Wave. www.the5thwave.com

One way to arouse the interest of your listeners is to ask them a *question*. Speaking on the high cost of tuition, you might ask, "How many of you are interested in saving tuition dollars this year?" You'll probably capture their attention. Motivate them to listen to you. Tell them how the information you present will be of value to them. Proceed to tell your audience that you will talk about several approaches to seeking low-cost loans and grants. "Who would like to save money on their income taxes?" "How many of you would like to have a happier home life?" "How many of you would like to learn an effective way of preparing your next speech?" These are other examples of questions that could stimulate your listeners' interest and motivate them to give you their attention. Besides using rhetorical questions, you can begin with an *anecdote*, a *startling statistic*, or some other attention-grabbing device.

Ontario Premier Dalton McGuinty's use of memorable word pictures helps his audience visualize change.

⋯⋗ Use Word Pictures

As we noted in Chapter 12, words have the power to create powerful images that can gain and hold an audience's attention. Consider using a **word picture** to make your message vivid and interesting. Word pictures are lively descriptions that help your listeners form a mental image by appealing to their senses of sight, taste, smell, sound, and touch. The following suggestions will help you construct effective word pictures:

word picture
A vivid use of words to describe a situation that invites listeners to draw on their senses.

- Form a clear mental image of the person, place, or object before you try to describe it.
- Describe the appearance of the person, place, or object. What would your listeners see if they were looking at it? Use lively language to describe the flaws and foibles, bumps and beauties of the people, places, and things you want your audience to see.
- Describe what your listeners would hear. Use colourful, onomatopoetic words, such as *buzz, snort, hum, crackle,* or *hiss.* These words are much more descriptive than the more general term *noise.* Imitate the sound you want your listeners to hear with their "mental ear." For example, instead of saying, "When I walked in the woods, I heard the sound of twigs breaking beneath my feet and wind moving the leaves above me in the trees," you might say, "As I walked in the woods, I heard the *crackle* of twigs underfoot and the *rustle* of leaves overhead."
- Describe smells, if appropriate. What fragrance or aroma do you want your audience to recall? Such diverse subjects as Thanksgiving, nighttime in the tropics, and the first day of school all lend themselves to olfactory imagery. No Thanksgiving would be complete without the rich aroma of roast turkey and the pungent, tangy odour of cranberries. And the first day of school evokes for many the scents of new shoe leather, unused crayons, and freshly painted classrooms. In each case, the associated smells greatly enhance the overall word picture.
- Describe how an object feels when touched. Use words that are as clear and vivid as possible. Rather than saying that something is rough or smooth, use a simile, such as "the rock was rough as sandpaper" or "the pebble was as smooth as a baby's skin." These descriptions appeal to both the visual and the tactile senses.
- Describe taste, one of the most powerful sensory cues, if appropriate. Thinking about your grandmother may evoke for you memories of her rich, homemade noodles and her light, flaky, buttery pie crust. Descriptions of these taste sensations would be welcome to almost any audience, particularly your fellow students subsisting mainly on dormitory food or their own cooking! More important, such description can help you paint an accurate, vivid image of your grandmother.
- Describe the emotion that a listener might feel if he or she were to experience the situation you relate. If you experienced the situation, describe your own emotions. Use specific adjectives rather than general terms such as *happy* or *sad.* One speaker, talking about receiving her first speech assignment, described her reaction with these words: "My heart stopped. Panic began to rise up inside. Me? . . . For the next five days I lived in dreaded anticipation of the forthcoming event."[6]

Note how effectively her choice of such words and phrases as "my heart stopped," "panic," and "dreaded anticipation" describes her terror at the prospect of giving a speech—much more so than if she had said simply, "I was scared." The more vividly and accurately you can describe emotion, the more intimately involved in your description the audience will become. One final word of caution: Don't overdo horrific graphic images. You will risk alienating your audience, rather than engaging them.

⋯⟩ Create Interesting Presentation Aids

Nonverbal

Research about learning styles suggests that many of your listeners are more likely to remember your ideas if you can reinforce them with presentation aids. As we discussed in Chapter 12, pictures, graphs, posters, and computer-generated graphics can help you gain and maintain audience members' attention, as well as increase their retention. Today's audiences are exposed daily to a barrage of messages conveyed through highly visual electronic media—CD-ROM, DVD, the World Wide Web, and video. They have grown to depend on more than words alone to help them remember ideas and information. When you present summaries of data, a well-crafted line graph or colourful pie chart can quickly and memorably reinforce the words and numbers you cite.

⋯⟩ Use Humour

"Humour is the spice of speeches," said comedian Michael Klepper. "Too little and your message may be bland or lifeless, too much and it can burn the mouth."[7] The challenge is to use just the right kind of humour in the right amounts. Use humour wisely by considering the following ideas:"[8]

- *Use humour to make a point:* Don't just tell jokes for the sake of getting a laugh. Make sure your story or punch line relates to your message. Here's an example of how a brief joke was used to make a point about the value of teamwork:

  > I read recently about a veterinarian and a taxidermist who decided to share a shop in a small town in Alberta. The sign in the front window read: "Either way, you get your dog back."
  >
  > There is an important lesson there. We need to work together to solve our problems. People from marketing need to work with operations people. Designers need to work with engineers. Then, when we find a problem that one part of the organization can't solve, someone else may suggest a solution. It doesn't matter who comes up with the solution. The important thing is to "get your dog back."[9]

- *Make yourself the butt of the joke:* Audiences love it when you tell a funny or embarrassing story about yourself. If the joke's on you, then also you don't have to worry about whether you will offend someone else.
- *Use humorous quotations:* You don't have to be a comedy writer to be funny. Quote humorous lines of proverbs, poetry, or sayings from others. But remember, what may be funny to you may not be funny to your audience. Try out your quotes and jokes on others before you present them from behind the lectern. Also, don't try to pass off a quotation from others as one of your own; always give credit for quotations you use.
- *Use cartoons:* Using an overhead projector to display a cartoon or scanning a cartoon into your computer presentation may be just the right way to make your point. Make sure your cartoon is large enough to be seen by everyone in the audience. As with any humour, don't overdo your use of cartoons.

STRATEGIES FOR MAKING YOUR INFORMATIVE PRESENTATION MEMORABLE

If you've made your message clear and interesting, you're well on your way to ensuring that your audience members remember what you say. The goal is for your ideas to stick to your listeners' minds like Velcro, rather than slide off like Teflon. As we discussed in Chapter 5, one day after hearing your presentation, most audiences will remember only about half of what you told them. And they will recall only about 25% two weeks later.

People remember what is important to them. So one of the keys to making a message memorable is, again, to adapt your message to your listeners. Presenting a well-organized message, following the strategies we discussed in Chapter 11, will also go a long way toward helping your listeners remember what you say. Here are several strategies for making your presentation memorable.

Adapt

⋯⟩ Build in Redundancy

You need to build in redundancy to make sure that the information you want to communicate will get across. Most speech teachers advise their students to structure their presentations as follows:

1. *Tell them what you're going to tell them.* In the introduction of your presentation, provide a broad overview of the purpose of your message. Identify the major points you will present.
2. *Tell them.* In the body of your presentation, develop each of the main points mentioned during your introduction.
3. *Tell them what you've told them.* Finally, in your conclusion, summarize the key ideas discussed in the body.

⋯⟩ Use Adult Learning Principles

If your audience consists of adult listeners, you will need to ensure that you deliver your message in the way that adults learn best. **Adult learners** prefer the following:[10]

- To be given information they can use immediately
- To be involved actively in the learning process
- To connect their life experiences with the new information they learn
- To know how the new information is relevant to their busy lives
- To receive information that is relevant to their needs

Most people who work in business have an in-basket on their desk to receive letters that must be read and work that must be done. Each of us also has a kind of mental in-basket, an agenda for what we want or need to accomplish. And don't forget about the important principle of adapting your message to others. You will make your message memorable, and also have more success in informing your audience, if you tailor your information to address *their* agenda.

Adapt

Re**CAP** ⟨⋯

Strategies for Informative Speaking

MAKE YOUR PRESENTATION CLEAR

Simplify ideas.
Pace the information flow.
Relate new information to old.

MAKE YOUR PRESENTATION INTERESTING

Relate to your listeners' interests.
Use attention-catching supporting material.
Establish a motive for your audience to listen to you.
Use word pictures.
Use humour.
Use interesting presentation aids.

MAKE YOUR PRESENTATION MEMORABLE

Build in redundancy.
Use adult learning principles.
Reinforce key ideas verbally.
Reinforce key ideas nonverbally.

---> Reinforce Key Ideas Verbally

Verbal

You can reinforce an idea by using such phrases as "This is the most important point" or "Be sure to remember this next point; it's the most compelling one," or "Of all the suggestions I've given you, this last tip is the most important one." Be careful not to overuse this technique. If you claim that every other point is a key point, soon your audience will not believe you.

---> Reinforce Key Ideas Nonverbally

Nonverbal

You can also signal the importance of a point with nonverbal emphasis. Gestures serve the purpose of accenting or emphasizing key phrases, as italics do in written communication.

A well-placed pause can provide emphasis and reinforcement to set off a point. Pausing just before or just after you make an important point will focus attention on your thought. Raising or lowering your voice can also reinforce a key idea.

Movement can help emphasize major ideas. Moving from behind the lectern to tell a personal anecdote can signal that something special and more intimate is about to be said. As we discussed in Chapter 12, your movement and gestures should be meaningful and natural, rather than seemingly arbitrary or forced. Your need to emphasize an idea can provide the motivation to make a meaningful movement.

SPEAKING TO PERSUADE

From ancient times to the present, accused criminals, advertisers, and politicians have all highly valued the skill of persuasion. But you don't have to be an attorney, an advertiser, or a politician to draw upon the highly valued skill of persuasion. Whether you're asking your roommate to help you clean the kitchen, seeking an extension on your term paper, or trying to convince the school board not to raise taxes, you too will need to wield the power to persuade.

In 333 BC, Aristotle was among the first to write a comprehensive guide to persuasion. His work, *The Rhetoric,* was used by other Greek and Roman writers who sought to summarize principles and strategies of persuasion. The material that follows draws upon some of that more-than-2000-year-old classic advice that has been updated with contemporary research.

PERSUASION DEFINED

persuasion
The process of attempting to change or reinforce a listener's attitudes, beliefs, values, or behaviour.

Persuasion is the process of attempting to change or reinforce attitudes, beliefs, values, or behaviour. When we persuade, we are inviting someone to modify or maintain the way he or she thinks, feels, or behaves.

In the first half of this chapter, we described strategies for informing others—presenting new information to others so that they will understand and remember what is communicated. Because informative speaking and persuasive speaking are related, we will build on the suggestions we offered for informing others. Your presentation will still need to be well organized; have a clear beginning, middle, and end; use interesting supporting material; have smooth transitions; and be skilfully delivered. As a persuasive speaker, you will need to develop arguments supported with evidence. But in a persuasive presentation, the speaker invites the listener to make an explicit choice, rather than just offering information about the options. Also, when you persuade, you will do more than teach; you will ask your audience to respond thoughtfully to the information you present. Persuasive speakers intentionally try to change or reinforce their listeners' feelings, ideas, or behaviour.

coercion
Using unethical force to get another person to think or behave as you wish; takes away free choice.

Coercive communication, unlike persuasive communication, takes away an individual's free choice. In the opening pages of this book we suggested that an effective communicator not only is understood and achieves his or her goal, but also is ethical. Using force to achieve your goal would be **coercion,** not persuasion. Weapons, threats, and other unethical strategies may momentarily achieve what you want, but it certainly would not be appropriate or ethical to use such means. Efforts to persuade should be grounded in giving people options rather than forcing them to respond in a certain way. To be ethical, the persuader has an obligation to be honest and forthright in crafting messages.

Now that you have an understanding of what persuasion is and isn't, you undoubtedly have questions about how to begin to develop a persuasive message. You start your preparation for a persuasive presentation as you begin any speech, by considering the needs, interests, and background of your audience. Ethically adapting to listeners is important in any communication situation but is especially important when persuading others.

The audience-centred model of public speaking, introduced in Chapter 11 and shown again in Figure 13.1, can be used to help you design and deliver a persuasive presentation just as it can an informative one. Audience analysis is at the heart of the speech-making process; it affects every choice you make as a speaker. Before we talk about the nuts and bolts of developing a persuasive presentation, we'll describe the audience psychology of persuasion—what motivates an audience to respond to your persuasive appeal. Understanding how an audience is likely to respond to your message not only can help you to develop your presentation but also can help you be a smarter consumer of persuasive messages that come your way.

MOTIVATING YOUR AUDIENCE:
THE PSYCHOLOGY OF PERSUASION

How does persuasion work? What makes you watch a commercial for a sizzling, spicy pizza on TV and then dial the phone number to have a piping hot cheese-and-pepperoni pizza delivered to your door? What motivates people to do things that they wouldn't do unless they were persuaded to do so? Let's look at four explanations of why people respond to efforts to persuade.

⋯❯ Motivating with Dissonance

When you are presented with information that is inconsistent with your current thinking or feelings, you experience a kind of discomfort called **cognitive dissonance.** For example, if you frequently drive while drowsy, and then you learn that drowsy driving is a major contributor to traffic accidents, dissonance theory predicts that you will experience

cognitive dissonance
The sense of disorganization or imbalance that prompts a person to change when new information conflicts with previously organized thought patterns.

FIGURE 15.1 An Audience-Centred Model of the Presentational Speaking Process

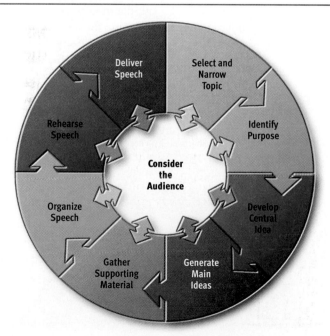

cognitive dissonance. The incompatibility between your behaviour and your new knowledge will make you feel uncomfortable. And your discomfort may prompt you to change your thoughts, likes or dislikes, feelings, or behaviour so that you can restore your comfort level or sense of balance—in this case, by not driving when drowsy.

Skilled persuasive speakers can effectively use verbal messages. They know that creating dissonance and then offering their listeners a way to restore balance is an effective persuasive strategy. For example, Sean wants to persuade his listeners to take greater safety precautions in preparing food. He begins by focusing on the health threat posed by bacteria in even the cleanest kitchens:

> Right now, as you sit and listen to me speak about kitchen bacteria, millions of them are probably reproducing in your kitchen, simply waiting for the perfect opportunity to join you for lunch.[11]

Sean is deliberately creating dissonance. He knows that his audience members value their health and that they have always assumed their kitchens to be relatively clean. His next task is to restore the audience's sense of balance. He assures them that solutions exist and "that they are simple and you can start them as early as today."[12] If the audience implements such simple actions as washing hands frequently, using paper towels, and washing sponges and dishcloths along with the dishes, then they can resolve their dissonance and once again feel secure about their kitchen safety. The need to resolve dissonance provides one explanation of why people may respond to a speaker's attempts to persuade.

Verbal

Adapt

hierarchy of needs
Abraham Maslow's classic theory that humans have five levels of need arranged in such a manner that lower-level needs must be met before people can be concerned about higher-level needs.

⋯⟫ Motivating with Needs

Need is one of the best motivators. As a speaker, the better you understand what your listeners need, the better you can adapt to them and the greater the chances that you can persuade them to change an attitude, belief, or value, or get them to take some action.

The classic theory that outlines our basic needs was developed by Abraham Maslow.[13] If you've taken a psychology course, you have undoubtedly encountered this theory, which has important applications for persuasion. Maslow suggests that a **hierarchy of needs** motivates the behaviour of all people. Basic physiological needs (such as food, water, and air) have to be satisfied before we attend to any other concern. Once our physiological needs are met, we think next about safety needs. We need to feel safe and to be able to protect those we love. Comfortable and secure, we attend next to social needs, including the needs to be loved and to belong to a group. The next level of need is self-esteem, or thinking well of ourselves. Finally, if these first four levels of need have been satisfied, we may attend to the need for self-actualization, or achieving our highest potential. Figure 13.2 illustrates Maslow's classic five levels of needs, with the most basic at the bottom.

As a persuasive speaker, understanding and applying the hierarchy of needs helps you adapt to your audience. One practical application is to do everything in your power to

FIGURE 13.2   Maslow's Hierarchy of Needs

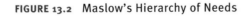

Self-actualization needs

Self-esteem needs

Social needs

Safety needs

Physiological needs

ensure that your audience's physiological and safety needs are met. For example, if your listeners are sweating and fanning themselves, they are unlikely to be very interested in whether Bigfoot exists or whether the city should re-open River Park. If you can turn on the air conditioning or fans, you will stand a greater chance of persuading them.

Another way in which you can apply the need hierarchy is to appeal to an audience's basic needs. For example, Mike knows that most of his audience members have young friends or family members who routinely ride school buses. As he begins to talk about the problem of safety hazards on school buses, he appeals to the audience's need to protect those they love.

⋯⟩ Motivating with Fear Appeals

Verbal

One of the oldest ways to convince people to change their minds or their behaviour is by scaring them into compliance. Fear works. The appeal to fear takes the form of a verbal message—an "if-then" statement. *If* you don't do X, *then* awful things will happen to you. "If you don't take a flu shot, then you will probably catch the flu." "If you don't wear a seat belt, then you are more likely to die in an automobile accident." "If you don't vote for me, then my opponent in this election will ruin the country." These are examples of fear appeals. A variety of research studies support the following strategies for effectively using fear as a motivator.[14]

- *A strong threat to a family member or someone whom members of the audience care about will often be more successful than a fear appeal directed at the audience members themselves.* Here's an example: "If your parents don't have a smoke alarm in their house, they are 10 times more likely to die in a house fire."
- *The more respected the speaker, the greater the likelihood that the appeal to fear will work.* If you're trying to motivate your audience with fear, you may not have the credibility to convince them that the threat will harm them, but you could use the opinion of someone who is highly believable, competent, and trustworthy. Quoting a doctor if you're talking about a health issue, or an award-winning teacher if you're talking about an education issue, will probably be more effective than just stating your own opinion when trying to motivate with fear. Of course, you have an ethical responsibility not to overstate your case or fabricate evidence when using a fear appeal.
- *Fear appeals are more successful if you convince your audience that the threat is real and will affect them unless they take action.* In trying to convince her audience to eat less fat and exercise more, Doreen said, "An overly fatty diet coupled with lack of exercise is the primary cause of heart disease in North America. Eat less fat and get more exercise, or you may die prematurely."
- *Increasing the intensity of a fear appeal increases the likelihood that the fear appeal will be effective; this is especially true if the listener can take the action the persuader is suggesting.*[15] Recent research findings suggest that the more fear and anxiety produced by the message, the more likely it is that the listener will respond. Strong, credible fear appeals seem to work better than mild fear appeals if evidence exists to support the claim. The persuader always has an ethical responsibility to be truthful when trying to arouse fear in the listener.

Fear appeals work based on the theory of cognitive dissonance and Maslow's need theory. The fear aroused creates dissonance. Taking action reduces the fear and can meet a need—such as to live a long life, to be safe from harm, to have good friends, or to have a fulfilling career.

⋯⟩ Motivating with Positive Appeals

Verbal

From a political candidate's TV ad: "Vote for me and you'll have lower taxes and higher wages, and your children will be better educated." Does this politician's promise have a familiar ring to it? It sounds like what most politicians offer—better days ahead if you'll vote for the person you see on your TV screen. Politicians, salespersons, and most other successful persuaders know that one way to change or reinforce your attitudes, beliefs, values, or behaviour is to use a positive motivational appeal. Positive motivational appeals are verbal messages promising that good things will happen if the speaker's advice is followed. The key to using positive motivational appeals is to know what your listeners value. Most Canadians value a comfortable, prosperous life; stimulating, exciting activity; a sense of accomplishment; world, community, and personal peace; and overall happiness and contentment. In a persuasive presentation, you can motivate your listeners to respond to your message by describing what good, positive things will happen to them if they follow your advice.

SELECTING AND NARROWING YOUR PERSUASIVE TOPIC

With a basic understanding about how persuasion works, we're ready to focus on the specifics of developing a persuasive talk. As with any presentation, after you've thought about your audience, the next step is to select and narrow your topic. In a communication class, you may be given some latitude in selecting your topic. The best persuasive topic is one about which you feel strongly. If your listeners sense that you are committed to and excited about your topic, the chances are greater that they will be interested and involved as well. In most non-classroom persuasive-speaking situations, you probably won't be asked just to pick a persuasive topic; your topic will stem from your personal convictions. When you have the flexibility of selecting your own topic, the principle of appropriately adapting messages to others can also guide your choice of a persuasive topic. Know the local, provincial, national, and international issues that interest and affect your listeners. Should the city build a new power plant? Should convicted child molesters be permitted to live in any neighbourhood they like? Should the United States drop economic sanctions against Cuba? These and other controversial issues make excellent persuasive speech topics. Avoid frivolous topics, such as "why you should make your own potholders," when so many important issues challenge the world and your listeners.

For a persuasive presentation, you can use any of the strategies for selecting and narrowing topics that were discussed in Chapter 11. Pay particular attention to verbal messages in the print and in the electronic media to help keep you current on important issues of the day. Daily newspapers such as *The Toronto Star* or *The Winnipeg Free Press* and national weekly news magazines such as *Maclean's* can suggest potential persuasive topics. Another interesting source of controversial issues is talk radio; both local and national programs can provide ideas for persuasive topics. Chat rooms on the Internet and home pages of print and broadcast media can also provide ideas for persuasive presentations.

After you have chosen a topic for your persuasive message, keeping up with the media can give you additional ideas for narrowing your topic and for finding interesting and appropriate supporting material for your presentation.

IDENTIFYING YOUR PERSUASIVE PURPOSE

Once you have a topic for your persuasive presentation, your next step is to identify both a general and a specific purpose. The general purpose is easy—to persuade. The specific purpose requires more thought. The way you word your specific purpose will help you focus your message. When your general purpose is to persuade, your specific purpose will target your audience's attitudes, beliefs, values, or behaviour. You can, as you recall from our definition of persuasion, try to *reinforce* attitudes, beliefs, values, and behaviour the audience already holds; or you can try to *change* their attitudes, beliefs, values, or behaviour. Reinforcing what an audience already knows or thinks is relatively easy, but it is more of a challenge to change their minds. To increase your chances for success, it is important to be aware of the differences among attitudes, beliefs, and values and to know which one you are targeting in your specific purpose statement. Let's examine the terms *attitudes, beliefs,* and *values* in more detail.

An **attitude** is a learned predisposition to respond favourably or unfavourably to something. In other words, attitudes represent likes and dislikes. Because many attitudes are formed quickly and often with little evidence, they are relatively susceptible to change

attitude
A learned predisposition to respond favourably or unfavourably to something; a like or dislike.

through additional evidence and experience. For example, we may like a song we hear on the radio, then decide after we buy the single that we don't really like it so well after all. We may think that we don't like spinach, then discover that a friend's Florentine dip is delicious. As a persuasive speaker, you would probably have a good chance to succeed if your specific purpose targeted one of the following attitudes:

- At the end of my presentation, the audience will favour making downtown streets one way to regulate traffic flow.
- At the end of my presentation, the audience will agree that the community needs a new elementary school.

A **belief** is the way in which we structure our perception of reality—our sense of what is true or false. Perhaps you believe that the earth is round, that God exists, and that your local bank is a financially sound institution. We base our beliefs on our own past experiences and on the experiences of other people. Beliefs are more difficult to alter than attitudes. If your audience were skeptical, you would need a great deal of evidence to succeed with these specific purpose statements:

- At the end of my presentation, the audience will testify that ghosts exist.
- At the end of my presentation, the audience will acknowledge that the increase in highway traffic deaths is related to the increase in the speed limit for large trucks.

A **value** is an enduring conception of right or wrong, good or bad. If you value something, you classify it as good or desirable. If you do not value something, you think of it as bad or wrong. Values determine your behaviour and goals. For example, because you value honesty, you refuse to cheat on a test. Because you value freedom, you support asylum for political refugees. Values are stable and deeply ingrained. Although it is not impossible to change the values of an audience, it is much more difficult than trying to change attitudes or beliefs. Political and religious points of view are especially difficult to modify. If you were speaking to a right-wing conservative audience, you would find it difficult to achieve these specific purposes:

- At the end of my presentation, the audience will campaign for the New Democratic Party in the upcoming election.
- At the end of my presentation, the audience will support the right of art museums to show whatever kinds of art the museum directors deem appropriate.

Figure 13.3 illustrates that attitudes lie fairly close to the surface of our convictions, with values the most deeply ingrained in the centre of the model. Be aware of whether your

belief
A sense of what is true or false.

value
An enduring conception of right or wrong, good or bad.

FIGURE 13.3 Comparing Attitudes, Beliefs, and Values

Attitudes—our likes and dislikes—are more likely to change than are our beliefs or values. Our sense of what is right and wrong—our values—are least likely to change.

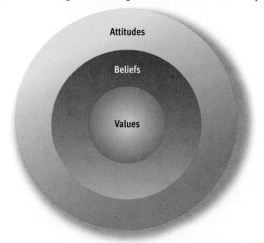

specific purpose aims to change or reinforce an attitude, a belief, a value, or a behaviour and be realistic in assessing what you will need to do in your presentation to effect change.

SUPPORTING YOUR PRESENTATION WITH CREDIBILITY, LOGIC, AND EMOTION: STRATEGIES FOR PERSUADING YOUR AUDIENCE

Aristotle defined *rhetoric* as the process of "discovering the available means of persuasion."[16] What are those "available means"? They are the various strategies you can use to support your message. Aristotle suggested three: (1) emphasizing the credibility or ethical character of a speaker (he called this **ethos**); (2) using logical arguments (**logos**); and (3) using emotional appeals to move an audience (**pathos**).

⤷ Ethos: Establishing Your Credibility

ethos
The credibility or ethical character of a speaker.

If you were going to buy a new computer, to whom would you turn for advice? Perhaps you would consult your brother, the computer geek, or your roommate, the computer science major. Or you might seek advice from *Consumer Reports,* the monthly publication of studies of various consumer products. In other words, you would turn to a source that you consider knowledgeable, competent, and trustworthy—a source you think is credible.

logos
Logical arguments.

Credibility is an audience's perception of a speaker's competence, trustworthiness, and dynamism. It is not something a speaker inherently possesses or lacks; rather, it is based on the listeners' mindset regarding the speaker. Your listeners, not you, determine whether you have credibility.

pathos
Emotional appeals.

credibility
An audience's perception of a speaker's competence, trustworthiness, and dynamism.

Teachers and researchers have for centuries sought to understand the factors audiences consider in regarding a speaker to be credible. Aristotle thought that a public speaker should be ethical, possess good character, display common sense, and be concerned for the well-being of his audience. Quintilian, a Roman teacher of public speaking, advised that a speaker should be "a good man speaking well." These ancient speculations about the elements that enhance a speaker's credibility have been generally supported by modern research.

competence
The factor in a speaker's credibility that refers to his or her being perceived as informed, skilled, or knowledgeable.

One clear factor in credibility is **competence.** A speaker should be informed, skilled, or knowledgeable about the subject he or she is discussing. You will be more persuasive if you can convince your listeners that you know something about your topic. How? You can use verbal messages effectively by talking about relevant personal experience with the topic. If you have taken and enjoyed a cruise, you can tell your audience about the highlights of your trip. You can also cite evidence to support your ideas. Even if you have not taken a cruise yourself, you can be prepared with information about what a good value a cruise is—how much it costs and what is included, versus how much the same tour would cost if your audience were to travel by air and stay and eat in hotels.

Verbal

trustworthiness
The factor in a speaker's credibility that refers to his or her being perceived as believable and honest.

A second factor in credibility is **trustworthiness.** While delivering a speech, you need to convey honesty and sincerity to your audience. You can't do this simply by saying, "Trust me." You have to earn trust. You can do so by demonstrating that you are interested in and experienced with your topic. Again, speaking from personal experience makes you seem a more trustworthy speaker. Conversely, having something to gain by persuading your audience may make you suspect in their eyes. That's why salespersons and politicians often lack credibility. If you do what they say, they will clearly benefit from sales commissions or public office.

Nonverbal

dynamism
The factor in a speaker's credibility that refers to his or her being perceived as energetic.

A third factor in credibility is a speaker's **dynamism** or energy. Dynamism is often projected through delivery. Applying the communication principle of effectively using and understanding nonverbal messages, a speaker who maintains eye contact, has enthusiastic vocal inflection, and moves and gestures purposefully is likely to be seen as dynamic. **Charisma** is a form of dynamism. A charismatic speaker possesses charm, talent, magnetism, and other qualities that make the person attractive and energetic. Prime Minister Pierre Trudeau and the Princess of Wales, Diana, were considered charismatic speakers by many people.

charisma
Characteristic of a talented, charming, attractive speaker.

A speaker has opportunities throughout a presentation to enhance his or her credibility. The first such opportunity results in **initial credibility.** This is the impression of your credibility your listeners have even before you begin speaking. They grant you initial credibility based on such factors as your appearance and your credentials. Dressing appropriately and having a brief summary of your qualifications and accomplishments ready for the person who will introduce you are two strategies for enhancing your initial credibility.

The second credibility-building opportunity is called **derived credibility.** This is the perception your audience forms as you deliver your presentation. If you appropriately adapt your message to your audience, you will enhance your derived credibility. Specific strategies include establishing common ground with your audience, supporting your arguments with evidence, and presenting a well-organized message.

The last phase of credibility, called **terminal credibility,** is the perception of your credibility your listeners have when you finish your presentation. A thoughtfully prepared and well-delivered conclusion can enhance your terminal credibility, as can maintaining eye contact through and even after your closing sentence. Also, apply the communication principle of listening and responding thoughtfully to others. Be prepared to answer questions after your presentation, regardless of whether there is a planned question-and-answer period.

⋯→ Logos: Using Evidence and Reasoning

In addition to being considered a credible speaker, you will gain influence with your audience if you can effectively use logically structured arguments supported with evidence. As we noted earlier, Aristotle called this *logos,* which, translated from Greek, means *the word.* Using words effectively to communicate your arguments to your listeners is vital to persuading thoughtful and informed listeners. The goal is to provide logical **proof** for your arguments. Proof consists of both **evidence** and **reasoning.** *Evidence* is another word for the illustrations, definitions, statistics, and opinions that are your supporting material. We discussed each of these types of evidence in Chapter 11. *Reasoning* is the process of drawing conclusions from your evidence. There are three major ways to draw logical conclusions: inductively, deductively, and causally.

Inductive Reasoning

Reasoning that arrives at a general conclusion from specific instances or examples is known as **inductive reasoning.** You reason inductively when you claim that a conclusion is probably true because of specific evidence.

initial credibility
The impression of a speaker's credibility that listeners have before the speaker begins to speak.

derived credibility
The impression of a speaker's credibility based on what the speaker says and does during the presentation.

terminal credibility
The final impression listeners have of a speaker's credibility after the presentation has been concluded.

Adapt

Listen and Respond   Verbal
Nonverbal

Verbal

proof
Evidence plus reasoning.

evidence
Material used to support a point or premise.

reasoning
The process of drawing a conclusion from evidence.

inductive reasoning
Using specific instances or examples to reach a probable general conclusion.

Holocaust survivor, author, and human rights activist Elie Wiesel uses the rhetorical devices of evidence and reasoning to appeal to his audiences.

ReCAP ←⋯

Enhancing Your Credibility

ENHANCING YOUR INITIAL CREDIBILITY: BEFORE YOU SPEAK

- Dress appropriately.
- Have a brief summary of your qualifications and accomplishments ready for the person who will introduce you.

ENHANCING YOUR DERIVED CREDIBILITY: AS YOU SPEAK

- Establish common ground with your audience.
- Support your arguments with evidence.
- Present a well-organized message.

ENHANCING YOUR TERMINAL CREDIBILITY: AFTER YOU SPEAK

- Prepare your conclusion, and deliver it well.
- Maintain eye contact through and even after your closing sentence.
- Be prepared to answer questions after your presentation.

Verbal

On the WEB

Besides teaching you how to become more persuasive, one of our goals in this chapter is to help you become a better consumer of persuasive messages that come your way. One of the most important skills a consumer of persuasive messages can have is the ability to spot poorly constructed persuasive messages. Being able to identify faulty reasoning is especially important. On the following Web site, you'll find several reasoning fallacies, along with examples to help you identify them: **www.philosophypages.com/lg/index.htm.**

ETHICAL PROBE

Can you think of how an over-reliance on emotional appeals may be unethical? Is it appropriate for a speaker to try to convince an audience by using only emotional appeals?

Deductive Reasoning

Reasoning from a general statement or principle to reach a specific conclusion is called **deductive reasoning**. Contemporary logicians note that when you reason deductively, your conclusion is certain rather than probable. The certainty of the conclusion rests primarily on the validity of the major premise and secondarily on the truth of the minor premise. For example, if you can prove that keeping schools in good repair extends the useful life of the buildings, and it is true that the proposed bond issue provides money for school repairs, then your conclusion will be certain.

Causal Reasoning

You use **causal reasoning** when you relate two or more events in such a way as to conclude that one or more of the events probably caused the others. For example, you might argue that public inoculation programs during the 20th century eradicated smallpox. The key to developing any causal argument is to be certain that a causal relationship actually exists between the two factors you are investigating.

⤳ Pathos: Using Emotion

People often make decisions based not on logic but on emotion. Advertisers know this. Think of the soft-drink commercials you see on television. There is little rational reason that people should spend any part of their food budget on soft drinks. They are "empty calories." So soft-drink advertisers turn instead to emotional appeals, striving to connect feelings of pleasure with their product. Smiling people, upbeat music, and good times are usually part of the formula for selling soft drinks.

One way to make an emotional appeal is with emotion-arousing verbal messages. Words such as *mother, flag, freedom,* and *slavery* trigger emotional responses in listeners. The patriotic slogan "I am Canadian" is an example of a phrase that has successfully aroused emotions in listeners.

Another way to appeal to emotions is through concrete illustrations and descriptions. Although illustrations and descriptions are themselves types of evidence or supporting material, their impact is often emotional, as in the following example:

> Michelle Hutchinson carefully placed her three-year-old daughter into her child safety seat. She was certain that Dana was secure. Within minutes Michelle was involved in a minor accident,

ReCAP ⬅

Inductive, Deductive, and Causal Reasoning

TYPE OF REASONING	REASONING BEGINS WITH ...	REASONING ENDS WITH ...	CONCLUSION IS ...	EXAMPLE
Inductive	specific examples	a general conclusion	probable or not probable	Dell, Gateway, and IBM computers are all reliable. Therefore, PCs are reliable.
Deductive	a general statement	a specific conclusion	certain or not certain	All professors at this university have advanced degrees. Tom Bryson is a professor at this university. Therefore, Tom Bryson has an advanced degree.
Causal	something known	a speculation about causes or effects of what is known	likely or not likely	The number of people with undergraduate degrees has risen steadily since 1960. This increasing number has caused a glut in the job market for people with degrees.

and the seat belt that was never designed to hold a child safety seat allowed the seat to lunge forward, crushing the three-year-old's skull on the dash. Dana died three days later. . . . [17]

Effective use of nonverbal messages can also appeal to an audience's emotions. Visual aids—pictures, slides, or video—can provide emotion-arousing images. A photograph of a dirty, ragged child alone in a big city can evoke sadness and pain. A video clip of an airplane crash can arouse fear and horror. A picture of a smiling baby makes most of us smile, too. As a speaker, you can use visual aids to evoke both positive and negative emotions.

Nonverbal

When you use emotional appeals, you do have an obligation to be ethical and forthright. Making false claims, misusing evidence or images, or relying exclusively on emotion without any evidence or reasoning violates standards of ethical presentational speaking.

ORGANIZING YOUR PERSUASIVE MESSAGE

You already know that how you organize a presentation can have an impact on your listeners' response to your message. Some speakers gather stories, examples, facts, and statistics to achieve their persuasive goal, and then develop an organizational structure for these materials. Other speakers organize the presentation first and then develop supporting material. In reality, the organization of your presentation usually emerges after you have done at least some initial research and thinking about both your message and your audience. An audience-centred speaker adapts the organizational structure of the presentation based upon the needs, attitudes, beliefs, behaviours, and background of the audience. Most persuasive presentations are organized according to one of four strategies: problem and solution, cause and effect, refutation, and the motivated sequence—a special variation of the problem-and-solution format.

Adapt

⇢ Problem and Solution

Even though we discussed **problem-and-solution organization** in Chapter 11, we mention it again here as the most basic organizational pattern for a persuasive presentation. The problem-and-solution strategy works best when a clearly evident problem can be documented and a solution or solutions proposed to deal with the evils of the problem.

problem-and-solution organization
Organization by discussing first a problem and then its various solutions.

When you use problem-and-solution organization, apply the principle of appropriately adapting messages to others. If you are speaking to an apathetic audience or one that is not even aware that a problem exists, you can emphasize the problem portion of the message. If your audience is already aware of the problem, you can emphasize the solution or solutions. In either case, your challenge will be to provide ample evidence that your perception of the problem is accurate and reasonable. You'll also need to convince your listeners that the solution or solutions you advocate are the most appropriate ones to solve the problem.

Adapt

⇢ Cause and Effect

Like the problem-and-solution strategy, **cause-and-effect organization** was introduced in Chapter 11. We noted there that a speaker could either identify a situation and then discuss the resulting effects (cause–effect), or present a situation and then explore its causes (effect–cause).

cause-and-effect organization
Organization by discussing a situation and its causes, or a situation and its effects.

ReCAP ⇠⋯

Tips for Using Emotion to Persuade

- Use emotion-arousing words.
- Use concrete illustrations and descriptions to create emotional images.
- Use visual aids to evoke both positive and negative emotions.
- Be ethical and forthright. Avoid making false claims, misusing evidence or images, or relying exclusively on emotion.

Aware

Regardless of which variation you choose, you should apply the fundamental principle of being aware of your communication with yourself and others. Specifically, you must analyze and then convince your listeners of the critical causal link. An effect may have more than one cause. For example, standardized test scores may be low in your province both because of low per-pupil expenditures and because of a lack of parental involvement in the schools. To argue that only one of the two factors causes the low test scores would not be accurate. It is also possible to have two situations that coexist but are not causally related. Perhaps standardized test scores are indeed low in your province, and your province has a lottery. Both situations exist, but one does not cause the other. However, if you do have causally related situations, a cause-and-effect strategy can work well for a persuasive presentation.

⋯⟩ Refutation

refutation
Organization according to objections your listeners may have to your ideas and arguments.

A third way to organize your efforts to persuade an audience is especially useful when you are facing an unreceptive audience—one that does not agree with your point of view or your specific proposition. **Refutation** is an organizational strategy by which you identify objections to your proposition and then refute those objections with arguments and evidence. You will be most likely to organize your persuasive message by refutation if you know your listeners' chief objections to your proposition. In fact, if you do not acknowledge such objections, the audience will probably think about them during your presentation, anyway. Credible facts and statistics will generally be more effective than emotional arguments in supporting your points of refutation.

⋯⟩ The Motivated Sequence

motivated sequence
Alan H. Monroe's five-step plan for organizing a persuasive message: attention, need, satisfaction, visualization, and action.

Like refutation, the fourth organizational strategy is often applied to persuasive speaking. The **motivated sequence,** devised by Alan Monroe, is a five-step organizational plan.[18] This simple yet effective strategy integrates the problem-and-solution organizational method with principles that have been confirmed by research and practical experience. The five steps involved are attention, need, satisfaction, visualization, and action.

Attention

Adapt

Your first task, and the first stage in appropriately adapting your message to others, is to get your listeners' attention. In Chapter 11, we discussed specific attention-getting strategies for introductions: rhetorical questions, illustrations, startling facts or statistics, quotations, humorous stories, and references to historical or recent events.

Joyce began her presentation about racial profiling with this attention-catching true story:

> Dr. David Watson, a 42-year-old African-Canadian dentist says his gold BMW has been pulled over by police more than 50 times, and each time he is asked the same question: "Do you have any drugs or weapons in your car?"

Need

Adapt

After getting your audience's attention, establish why your topic, problem, or issue should concern your listeners. Tell your audience about the problem. Adapt your message to them by convincing them that the problem affects them directly. Argue that there is a need for change. During the need step (which corresponds to the problem step in a problem-and-solution strategy), you should develop logical arguments backed by evidence. It's during the need step that you create dissonance or use a credible fear appeal to motivate listeners to respond to your solution. Joyce develops her need step as follows:

> Minority motorists are routinely stopped, questioned, and searched, even though no violation of the law has occurred. These activities are, at a minimum, inconvenient and embarrassing. However, in too many of these cases, the victims of this misconduct are subject to physical harm and on some occasions deadly force.

Satisfaction

After you explain and document a need or problem, identify your plan (or solution) and explain how it will satisfy the need. You need not go into painstaking detail. Present enough information so that your listeners have a general understanding of how the problem may be solved.

Joyce presents her satisfaction step with these three proposals:

> First, withdraw federal funding from all departments with high level of unresolved brutality cases. Second, all law enforcement agencies must go through mandatory sensitivity training and race relations courses. Third, we must ban racial profiling in all federally funded drug interdiction programs.

She goes on to explain briefly each of the three solutions she has proposed. You need not go into great detail yet. Save for the end of your message the specific action you want your listeners to take.

Visualization

Now you need to give your audience a sense of what it would be like if your solution were adopted or, conversely, if it were not adopted. **Visualization** applies the fundamental principle of effectively using and understanding verbal messages. An appropriate presentation aid can also help your audience visualize the implications of your persuasive message. With a **positive visualization** approach, you paint a rosy picture of how wonderful the future will be if your satisfaction step is implemented. With a **negative visualization** approach, you paint a bleak picture of how terrible the future will be if nothing is done; you use a fear appeal to motivate your listeners to do what you suggest to avoid further problems. Or you might combine both approaches: The problem will be solved if your solution is adopted, but things will get increasingly worse if it is not. An ethical speaker takes care to ensure that the positive or negative visualization message is accurate and not overstated.

Joyce provides a positive visualization in the closing moments of her presentation:

> Today, by assessing the magnitude of the problem, uncovering the reasons, and conceiving a sound plan of action, I challenge all of us to dream of a day when a black man can drive along a highway in a nice car and not be afraid of being stopped because of his skin colour.

Action

The final step of the motivated sequence requires that you adapt your solution to your audience. Offer them some specific action they can take to solve the problem you have discussed. Identify exactly what you want them to do. Give them simple, clear, easy-to-follow steps. Provide a phone number to call for more information, an address to which they can write a letter of support, or a petition to sign at the end of your presentation.

Joyce suggests a specific action step her listeners can take to solve the problem she has identified:

> Your provincial Human Rights Commission needs your help in making sure that departments are aware of these policies. So, I advise us all to contact our local enforcement agencies and make sure they are cognizant of Canada's human rights guidelines.

The action step is your conclusion. You remind your audience of the problem (need step), give them the solution (satisfaction step), and remind them what great things will happen if they follow your advice (positive visualization) or what bad things will happen if they don't do what you say (negative visualization). Finally, unless they are unreceptive to your ideas, tell them what they need to do next (action step).

You can adapt the motivated sequence to the needs of your topic and your audience. For example, if you are speaking to a knowledgeable, receptive audience, you do not have to spend a great deal of time on the need step. Your listeners already know that the need is serious. They may, however, feel helpless as to what they can do about it. Clearly, you would want to emphasize the satisfaction and action steps.

On the other hand, if you are speaking to a neutral or apathetic audience, you will need to spend time getting their attention and proving that a problem exists, that it is significant, and that it affects them personally. You will emphasize the attention, need, and visualization steps. In the final section of this chapter, we will offer additional strategies for persuading receptive, unreceptive, and neutral audiences.

visualization
A word picture of the future.

positive visualization
A word picture of how much better things will be if a solution is implemented.

negative visualization
A word picture of how much worse things will be if a solution is not implemented; a fear appeal.

ReCAP ⟨····

Organizational Patterns for Persuasive Presentations

ORGANIZATIONAL PATTERN	DEFINITION	EXAMPLE
Problem and Solution	Organization by discussing a problem and then its various solutions	I. Tooth decay threatens the dental health of children. II. Inexpensive, easy-to-apply sealants make teeth resistant to decay.
Cause and Effect	Organization by discussing a situation and its causes, or a situation and its effects	I. Canadian medicare will not pay for treatment deemed "experimental." II. Patients die who might have been saved by "experimental" treatment.
Refutation	Organization according to objections your listeners may have to your ideas and arguments	I. Although you may think that university hockey players get too much financial aid, they work hard for it, spending 20 to 30 hours a week in training and on the ice. II. Although you may think that university hockey players don't spend much time on academics, they have two hours of enforced study every weeknight.
Motivated Sequence	Alan H. Monroe's five-step plan for organizing a persuasive message; the five steps are attention, need, satisfaction, visualization, and action	I. Attention: "An apple a day keeps the doctor busy." What has happened to the old adage? Why has it changed? II. Need: Pesticides are poisoning our fresh fruits and vegetables. III. Satisfaction: Growers must seek environmentally friendly alternatives to pesticides. IV. Visualization: Remember the apple poisoned by Snow White's wicked stepmother? You may be feeding such apples to your own children. V. Action: Buy fruits and vegetables grown organically.

Adapt

HOW TO ADAPT IDEAS TO PEOPLE AND PEOPLE TO IDEAS

As we have emphasized throughout our discussion of presentational speaking, analyzing your audience and adapting to it is at the heart of the speech-making process; it's one of the fundamental communication principles for a lifetime. In a persuasive presentation, that adaptation begins with identifying your specific purpose and understanding whether you are trying to change or reinforce attitudes, beliefs, values, or behaviour. It continues with your selection of an organizational strategy. For example, if your audience members are unreceptive toward your ideas, you might choose to organize your speech by refutation, addressing the audience's objections head-on. Both research studies and experienced speakers can offer other useful suggestions to help you adapt to your audience. Let's look at some specific strategies for persuading receptive, neutral, and unreceptive audiences.

···⟩ The Receptive Audience

It is usually a pleasure to address an audience that already supports you and your message. You can explore your ideas in depth and can be fairly certain of a successful appeal to action if your audience is receptive.

One suggestion that may help you make the most of such a speaking opportunity is to identify with your audience. Emphasize your similarities and common interests. The introduction of your message may be a good place in which to do this.

Another suggestion is to be overt in stating your speaking objective, telling your audience exactly what you want them to do, and asking audience members for an immediate show of support.

A third suggestion for persuading a receptive audience is to use emotional appeals. If your audience already supports your position, you can spend less time providing detailed evidence. Rather, you can focus on moving your receptive audience to action with strong emotional appeals.

···⟩ The Neutral Audience

Many audiences will fall somewhere between being wildly enthusiastic and being hostile. They will simply be neutral. Their neutrality may take the form of indifference: They know about the topic or issue, but they don't see how it affects them, or they can't make up their minds about it. Or their neutrality may take the form of ignorance: They just don't know much about the topic. Regardless of whether your neutral audience is indifferent or ignorant, your challenge is to get them interested in your message.

A Radio Shack sales associate tries to persuade a customer that this hands-free device will be easy to use with his cellphone.

One way to get a neutral audience interested is to "hook" them with an especially engaging introduction or attention step. Quebec-based journalist Trish Snyder hooked her audience with statements related to the terrible ice storm of January 1998 that devastated eastern Ontario and southern Quebec:

> "Everything is caked with ice. Branches look like they are draped in diamonds. It is beautiful, pristine, but also scary. Trees are hunched under the weight of the ice and foot-long icicles dangle from the roof…I'm starting to feel powerless. I think about how grimy I feel without a shower; wonder how we'll get cash when ours runs out, with most bank machines dead."[20]

Another strategy for persuading neutral audiences is to refer to universal beliefs and concerns. These could include such common interests as protecting the environment and having access to good health care.

A third strategy for neutral audiences is to show how the topic affects not only them but also people they care about. For example, parents will be interested in issues and policies that affect their children.

Finally, be realistic about what you can accomplish. People who are neutral at the beginning of your presentation are unlikely to change in just a few minutes to wildly enthusiastic. Persuasion is unlikely to occur all at once or after a first hearing of arguments and issues.

···⟩ The Unreceptive Audience

One of your biggest challenges as a speaker is to persuade audience members who are unreceptive toward you or your message. If they are unreceptive toward you personally, your job is to seek ways to enhance your credibility and persuade them to listen to you. If they are unreceptive toward your point of view, several strategies may help.

First, don't immediately announce your persuasive purpose. If you immediately and overtly tell your listeners that you plan to change their minds, it can make them defensive. Focus instead on areas of agreement. As you would with a neutral audience, refer to universal beliefs and concerns. Instead of saying to your unreceptive audience, "I'm here this morning to convince you that we should raise city taxes," you might say, "I think we can agree that we have an important common goal: the best quality of life possible here in our small community."

Second, if you think your audience may be unreceptive, advance your strongest arguments first. This is the principle of primacy, which we discussed in Chapter 11. If you save your best argument for last (the recency principle), your audience may already have stopped listening.

Third, acknowledge the opposing points of view that members of your audience may hold. Summarize the reasons they may oppose your point of view; then cite evidence and use arguments to refute the opposition and support your conclusion. In speaking to students seeking to hold down tuition costs, a dean might say, "I am aware that many of you struggle to pay for your education. You work nights, take out loans, and live frugally." Then the dean could go on to identify how the university could provide additional financial assistance to students.

Finally, as with a neutral audience, don't expect a major shift in attitude from an unreceptive audience. Set a realistic goal. It may be enough for an eight- to ten-minute presentation just to have your listeners hear you out and at least think about some of your arguments.

ReCAP ←···

Adapting Ideas to People and People to Ideas

PERSUADING THE RECEPTIVE AUDIENCE	PERSUADING THE NEUTRAL AUDIENCE	PERSUADING THE UNRECEPTIVE AUDIENCE
• Identify with your audience. • Emphasize common interests. • Provide a clear objective; tell your listeners what you want them to do. • Appropriately use emotional appeals.	• Gain and maintain your audience's attention. • Refer to beliefs and concerns that are important to the listener. • Show how the topic affects people your listeners care about. • Be realistic about what you can accomplish.	• Don't tell listeners that you are going to try to convince them to support your position. • Present your strongest arguments first. • Acknowledge opposing points of view. • Don't expect a major shift in attitudes on behaviour.

SUMMARY ↓

Informative and persuasive speeches are interrelated but serve different functions in the presentation process. To inform is to teach someone something you know. In this chapter, you have studied the goals, principles, and strategies that presentational speakers use to inform others.

There are five basic types of informative presentations. Messages about ideas are often abstract and generally discuss principles, concepts, or theories. Messages about objects discuss tangible things. Messages about procedures explain a process or describe how something works. Messages about people can be about either the famous or the little known. Messages about events describe major occurrences or personal experiences.

To make your message clear, use simple rather than complex ideas, pace the flow of your information, and relate old information to new ideas. For the sake of increasing interest in your presentation, relate information to your

listeners, find and use attention-catching supporting material, establish a motive for your audience to listen to you, use vivid word pictures, use humour appropriately, and create intriguing and clear presentation aids. Finally, to make messages memorable, build in some redundancy (tell them what you're going to tell them; tell them; tell them what you've told them), use principles of adult learning, and reinforce key ideas, both verbally and nonverbally.

Persuasion is the process of attempting to change or reinforce attitudes, beliefs, values, or behaviours. Several theories suggest how persuasion works—how listeners may be motivated to respond to a persuasive message. Cognitive dissonance involves developing a sense of disorganization or imbalance to prompt a person to change when new information conflicts with previously organized thought patterns. Maslow's classic hierarchy of needs is another approach that attempts to explain why people may be motivated to respond to persuasive appeals to various levels of need. Both fear appeals and positive motivational appeals can also motivate listeners to respond to your persuasive message.

Preparing and presenting a persuasive message require the same general approach as preparing any other kind of presentation. When you have a choice of persuasive topics, select a topic that is of interest to you and your listeners. Your specific purpose will target your audience's attitudes, beliefs, values, or behaviour. Attitudes are learned ways to respond favourably or unfavourably toward something. A belief is one's sense of what is true or false. Values are enduring conceptions of right or wrong, good or bad. Of the three, attitudes are most susceptible to change; values are least likely to change.

Ways to organize your persuasive message include problem and solution, cause and effect, refutation, and the motivated sequence. The motivated sequence includes five steps: attention, need, satisfaction, visualization, and action.

A key to persuading others is to establish your credibility as a speaker. Credibility is an audience's perception of a speaker's competence, trustworthiness, and dynamism.

You should try to enhance your initial credibility—what you do before you speak; derived credibility—what you do during your presentation; and terminal credibility—what you do after your presentation, to improve your overall credibility as a presentational speaker.

Reasoning, the process of drawing a conclusion from evidence, is integral to the persuasive process. The three primary types of reasoning are inductive, deductive, and causal.

In addition to persuading others because of who you are (ethos) or how well you structure your logical arguments (logos), you can also move an audience to respond by using emotional appeals (pathos).

Finally, be prepared to adapt your persuasive messages to receptive, neutral, and unreceptive audiences. Throughout the persuasive speaking process, being aware of your messages and others' messages, effectively using verbal and nonverbal messages, listening and responding to your audience, and adapting to your listeners can enhance your skill as a persuasive speaker.

⬡ PRINCIPLES FOR A LIFETIME

Aware

Principle 1:   Be aware of your communication with yourself and others.

- When developing an informative talk, be mindful of the ideas you wish to express before formulating your message.
- Be conscious of the type of informative message you are developing (presentation about objects, procedures, people, events, or ideas).
- Clearly formulate your presentation objective before you begin organizing your ideas.
- Be consciously aware of using strategies that would make your informative messages clear, interesting, and memorable.
- As a persuasive speaker, the more you understand what your listeners need, the greater the chances that you can persuade them to change an attitude, belief, or value, or get them to take some action.
- The best topics for persuasive presentations are those about which you as a speaker feel strongly.
- Know whether your specific purpose aims to change or reinforce an attitude, a belief, a value, or a behaviour, and be realistic in assessing what you will need to do in your presentation to effect change.
- When you use cause-and-effect organization, you must analyze and then convince your listeners of the critical causal link.
- Speaking from personal experience will make you seem a more competent and trustworthy speaker.
- Having a brief summary of your qualifications and accomplishments ready for the person who will introduce you can help enhance your initial credibility.

Verbal

Principle 2:   Effectively use and interpret verbal messages.

- Use concrete supporting material, such as stories, examples, and illustrations, to gain and maintain attention.
- Use word pictures to make images and stories interesting and memorable.
- Pace the flow of the information you present to enhance message clarity.
- Relate new information to old information to increase clarity and retention.
- Verbally reinforce ideas to help make your message memorable.
- Use simple ideas rather than complex ideas to make your message clear.

- Build in message redundancy to enhance message retention.
- Creating dissonance and then offering listeners a way to restore balance is an effective persuasive strategy.
- To create negative visualization, describe in detail how bleak or terrible the future will be if your solution is not implemented.
- To create positive visualization, describe in detail how wonderful the future will be if your solution is implemented.
- To select and narrow a topic for a persuasive presentation, pay attention to print and electronic media to help keep you current on important issues of the day.
- To make yourself seem more competent to your audience, cite evidence to support your ideas.
- A thoughtfully prepared conclusion can enhance your terminal credibility.
- Persuasive speakers who provide logical proof (evidence and reasoning) for their arguments heighten their chances for success with their audience.
- Use emotion-arousing words to appeal to an audience's emotions.
- Use concrete illustrations and descriptions to appeal to an audience's emotions.

Nonverbal

Principle 3:   Effectively use and interpret nonverbal messages.

- Use presentation aids to make messages clear, interesting, and memorable.
- Observe the nonverbal messages of your audience to help you determine whether your message has been communicated clearly.
- Nonverbally reinforce ideas to make your message memorable.
- If you maintain eye contact, have enthusiastic vocal inflection, and move and gesture purposefully, your audience is likely to view you as dynamic.
- Dressing appropriately will help enhance your credibility.
- Maintaining eye contact through and even after your closing sentence can help enhance your terminal credibility.
- Use presentation aids to help evoke both positive and negative emotions as well as positive and negative visualization.

Listen
and
Respond

Principle 4:   Listen and respond thoughtfully to others.

- Before you deliver your presentation to an audience, talk and listen to audience members to help you customize your message to them.
- To help enhance your terminal credibility, be prepared to answer questions after your presentation, regardless of whether there is a planned question-and-answer period.

Adapt

Principle 5:   Appropriately adapt messages to others.

- Effective informative speakers are audience centred when developing a message for listeners.
- Adapt the structure and flow of your presentation to your listeners to enhance message clarity.
- Adapt your examples and illustrations to your listeners to help gain and maintain interest and attention.
- Develop a motivation for your audience to listen to you.
- Adapting to your audience is especially important when persuading others.
- The better you understand what your listeners need, the better you can adapt to them.
- Do everything possible to ensure that your audience's physiological and safety needs are met.
- To motivate an audience, appeal to their basic needs.
- The principle of appropriately adapting messages to others can guide your choice of a persuasive topic.
- If you are speaking to an apathetic audience or one that is not even aware that a problem exists, you can emphasize the problem portion of your problem-and-solution presentation.
- If your audience is aware of the problem you are discussing, you can emphasize the solution or solutions in your problem-and-solution presentation.
- Acknowledge and then refute the opposing points of view held by an unreceptive audience.
- Your first task in any presentation is to get your audience's attention.

- In the need step of your motivated-sequence presentation, establish why your topic, problem, or issue should concern your listeners. Convince your audience that the problem affects them directly.
- In the action step of the motivated sequence, offer your audience members specific action they can take to solve the problem you have discussed.
- If you are speaking to a knowledgeable, receptive audience, you do not need to spend a great deal of time on the need step of the motivated sequence; instead, you can emphasize the satisfaction and action steps.
- If you are speaking to a neutral audience, you will want to emphasize the attention, need, and visualization steps of the motivated sequence.
- One strategy for enhancing derived credibility is to establish common ground with your audience.
- Effective strategies for developing your persuasive purpose depend on the background and cultural expectations of your listeners.
- Make the most of your opportunity to speak to a receptive audience by identifying with them.
- If your audience is receptive, state your speaking objective overtly, tell your audience exactly what you want them to do, and ask audience members for an immediate show of support.
- Use emotional appeals with a receptive audience.
- Appeal to universal beliefs and concerns to persuade a neutral audience.
- Show a neutral audience how your topic affects both them and those they love.
- Be realistic about what you can accomplish with neutral and unreceptive audiences.
- Focus on areas of agreement with an unreceptive audience.
- If your audience is unreceptive, advance your strongest arguments first.

Discussion and Review ⸪

1. What is informative speaking?

2. What are the three goals of speaking to inform?

3. Describe the five types of informative speaking.

4. What are three strategies to make your informative message clear?

5. Identify six strategies that can enhance interest in your informative talk.

6. What are four strategies that can make your presentation memorable?

7. Where might you turn if you needed ideas for a topic for a persuasive presentation?

8. Define attitudes, beliefs, and values. Why is it important that a persuasive speaker know which one he or she is targeting in a persuasive presentation?

9. List and explain four ways to organize a persuasive presentation.

10. When would you be most likely to organize a presentation by refutation?

11. List and explain the five steps of the motivated sequence.

12. What is credibility?

13. Define initial, derived, and terminal credibility, and explain how to enhance each one.

14. Define and provide an example of inductive reasoning.

15. Define and provide an example of deductive reasoning.

16. Define and provide an example of causal reasoning.

17. How can you appeal to your listeners' emotions in a persuasive presentation?

18. What is cognitive dissonance? How can you apply the theory in a persuasive presentation?

19. List and explain the five levels of Maslow's hierarchy of needs. How can you apply the theory in a persuasive presentation?

20. Provide specific suggestions for adapting to receptive audiences, neutral audiences, and unreceptive audiences.

Developing Your Skills:
Putting Principles into Practice ⸪

1. From the following list of suggested topics for an informative presentation, select five and develop a specific purpose sentence for each. For one of those topics, identify two to four major ideas. Organize them topically, chronologically, or according to some other logical pattern of organization.

   How to get a better grade in your communication class
   The spread of terrorism in the world
   How the Canadian Charter of Rights and Freedoms was developed

A historical person I wish I could meet
What makes a good teacher
The best way to lose weight
How to buy a digital camera
Surrogate parenthood
Safe-driving principles
How the stock market works
Social security

2. Replace each of the following words with a livelier one:

cat   work
airplane   light
house   eat
walk   study

3. Look up the origin of the following words in a comprehensive dictionary, such as the *Canadian Oxford Dictionary* or the *Etymological Dictionary of Modern English*.

logic   teacher
pillow   dance
love   amateur
communication   disciple

4. Write a word picture—a vivid, colourful description that appeals to the senses—for one of the following scenes:

Your first day learning how to drive
Visiting your father or mother at work
A holiday when you were six
A visit to your grandparents' house
Your first day at college or university
Your most frightening experience
Your most memorable birthday celebration

5. Watch a broadcast of a politician arguing for or against a particular proposition. Identify the organizational pattern and the persuasive strategies the speaker uses.

6. Identify three nationally or internationally known speakers whom you consider to be credible. Analyze why these speakers are credible, according to the three components of credibility.

7. Develop a specific purpose statement and central idea for a persuasive message. Describe strategies you would use if you were to give this presentation to a receptive audience. Identify strategies you would use if you were to give this presentation to a neutral audience. Finally, suggest strategies you would use if you were to give this presentation to an unreceptive audience.

A Appendix: Interviewing

AFTER STUDYING THIS APPENDIX, YOU SHOULD BE ABLE TO

1. Describe what an interview is.

2. Identify five different kinds of interview goals.

3. Identify and discuss the important elements of being interviewed for a job.

4. Develop a clear, well-worded resumé.

5. Identify and discuss the important elements of participating in an information-gathering interview.

6. Explain how to conduct an interview.

The stakes are often high when you participate in an interview. If you are interviewing for a job, your career and perhaps your future rest on the impression you make. If someone is interviewing you to gather information, the accuracy of what you say can have a powerful impact on others. Or if you are the person who is conducting the job interview, you have much to gain or lose; your choice of a new employee will affect the success of the organization. If you're interviewing someone to gather information, your credibility is at stake if you pass on or publish information that later proves to be false or inaccurate.

In this introduction to interviewing, we'll discuss communication strategies that can enhance your job interview skills, as well as offer tips about how to participate in an information-gathering interview. We conclude the appendix by identifying strategies that can help you polish your talents if you are the person interviewing others. Whether you are a recent high school graduate or have been in the workforce for several years and have come back to school to finish your degree and pursue a new career, the principles for a lifetime that we've emphasized in this book can help you enhance your interviewing skills. In this appendix we offer specific tips and techniques to enhance the impression you make on others in an interview.

THE NATURE AND TYPES OF INTERVIEWS

interview
A form of oral interaction structured to achieve a goal; involves two or more people, who take turns speaking and listening.

An **interview** is a form of oral interaction structured to achieve a goal, which often involves just two people but could include more than two people, who take turns speaking and listening. An effective interview is not a random conversation but occurs when the person conducting the interview has carefully framed the objectives of the interview and developed a structured plan for achieving the objectives. The person being interviewed should also prepare by considering the kinds of questions he or she may be asked and being ready to give appropriate responses.

When many people think of the term "interview," the most common image that comes to mind is a job interview. Yet interviews can also include the goals of gathering information, sharing job performance feedback, solving problems, and persuading others. Even though we are focusing primarily on employment and information-gathering interviews, the strategies we present can help you with *any* interview situation.

⋯⟩ Information-Gathering Interview

information-gathering interview
An interview in which the purpose is to seek information from another person, such as an opinion poll.

Information-gathering interviews, just as the name suggests, are designed to seek information from the person being interviewed. Public-opinion polls are one type of information-gathering interview. When you leave an organization, you may be asked to participate in an exit interview, an interview designed to assess why you are leaving the company. A reporter for a newspaper, radio, or TV station interviews people to gather information for a story or broadcast.

Those most skilled at conducting information-gathering interviews do their homework before the interview. They come prepared with specific questions and have already conducted background research. In addition to prepared questions, a skilled information-gathering interviewer listens and develops questions that stem from the information that is shared during the interview.

⋯⟩ Appraisal Interview

appraisal interview
An interview during which a supervisor or employer shares information with an employee about his or her job performance.

An **appraisal interview,** sometimes called a performance review, occurs when a supervisor or employer shares information with you about your job performance. Such an interview enables you to see how others perceive your effectiveness and helps you determine whether you are likely to get a promotion or a "pink slip." During an appraisal interview you can typically express your observations about the organization and your goals for the future. Usually a supervisor begins by preparing a written report summarizing your strengths and weaknesses, then meets with you to review it.

When receiving feedback from a supervisor, the best approach is to listen and gather as much objective information about his or her perceptions as possible. Most appraisal interviews involve evaluating or rating employees. As we learned in Chapter 3, in an evaluation situation it is easy to become defensive; try to manage your emotions and use the information to your benefit instead. If you disagree with your supervisor's evaluation, consider using the conflict management skills we discussed in Chapter 8. In addition, provide specific examples to support your position. Just saying you don't like the review is likely to do more harm than good.

⇢ Problem-Solving Interview

A **problem-solving interview** is designed to resolve a problem that affects one or both parties involved in the interview. A disciplinary interview to consider corrective action toward an employee or a student is one type of problem-solving interview. Grievance interviews are also problem-solving interviews; one person brings a grievance or complaint against another person, and solutions are sought to resolve the problem or conflict.

The strategies for structuring a problem-solving group discussion that we presented in Chapter 10 can also help you organize a problem-solving interview. Before seeking to solve or manage a problem, first define the issues and then analyze the causes, history, and symptoms of the problem. Rather than focusing on only one solution, brainstorm several possible solutions and then evaluate the pros and the cons of the potential solutions before settling on a single solution.

problem-solving interview
An interview designed to solve a problem, such as a grievance or disciplinary interview.

⇢ Persuasion Interview

During a **persuasion interview,** one person seeks to change or reinforce the attitudes, beliefs, values, or behavior of another person. The sales interview is a classic example of an interview in which the goal is to persuade. A political campaign interview is another example of a persuasion interview.

Our discussion in Chapter 13 of the principles and strategies of persuading others can help you prepare for a persuasion interview. The advantage you have in persuading someone during an interview rather than a speech is the size of the audience; during a persuasive interview, you may have an audience of one. It is especially important to analyze and adapt to your listener when seeking to persuade.

persuasion interview
An interview that attempts to change or reinforce attitudes, beliefs, values, or behaviour, such as a sales interview.

⇢ Job Interview

A **job interview** is a focused, structured conversation in which the goal of the interview is to assess the credentials and skills of a person for employment. The job interview may involve elements of each of these types of interviews we've discussed. Information is both gathered and shared; it will certainly solve a problem if you're the one looking for a job and you are hired. Elements of persuasion are also involved in a job interview. If you are seeking a job, you're trying to persuade the interviewer to hire you; if you are the interviewer and you're interviewing an exceptionally talented person, your job is to persuade the interviewee to join your organization.

The planned or structured nature of an interview sets it apart from other communication situations. Yet interviews may sometimes include elements of interpersonal, group, and public speaking situations. Interviews embody interpersonal communication in that there are two or more people participating in the interview who must establish a relationship. If the goal of the interview is to find a solution to a vexing problem, the interview may resemble elements of a group discussion in which a problem is to be defined and analyzed and solutions are generated, evaluated, and then solved. Preparing for some interviews is like a public speaking situation; you focus on your audience (the interviewers), keep your purpose in mind as you research the company you're interviewing with, organize your ideas, and even rehearse your responses to questions you think you may be asked.

Regardless of the purpose or format of an interview, the five communication principles for a lifetime that we've used to organize our discussion of interpersonal, group and team, and public speaking situations will serve you well when you participate in an interview. Whether you are the interviewer or interviewee, it is important to be aware of how you are coming across to others. Using and interpreting verbal and nonverbal messages are critical to

job interview
A focused, structured conversation in which the goal of the interview is to assess the credentials and skills of a person for employment.

participating in a successful interview. In our definition of an interview, we noted that all individuals involved talk and listen. Unless you can adapt your messages to others, you won't be successful. Effective interview participants are able to listen, respond, and speak extemporaneously, rather than deliver overly scripted, planned messages. Adapting to others is essential.

INTERVIEW STRUCTURE

Just as a speech or term paper has a beginning, middle, and end, so does a well-structured interview. Most interviews have three phases:

1. *The opening:* The interviewer tries to put the interviewee at ease and presents an overview of the interview agenda.
2. *The body:* During the longest part of an interview, the interviewer asks questions, and the interviewee listens and responds. The interviewee may also ask questions.
3. *The conclusion:* The interviewer summarizes what will happen next and usually gives the interviewee an opportunity to ask any final questions.

It is the responsibility of the person leading the interview to develop a structure for the interview. But it's helpful for the interviewee to understand the overall structure of an interview in advance in order to know what to expect and how to prepare for the interview experience. So, whether you're the interviewer (regardless of the type of interview) or interviewee, the interview structure we discuss should be of value to you.

The Opening

The opening of any interview is crucial because it can create a climate for positive and open communication. A skilled interviewer begins by trying to put an interviewee at ease. He or she briefly discusses the weather, recent events attended by both parties, or other light topics such as something about their hobbies or extracurricular activities. These "openers" are used in an attempt to ease some of the anxiety an interviewee may feel. The interviewer also promotes a degree of rapport and diplomacy with the interviewee. Making direct eye contact, smiling, and offering a firm handshake all help establish a warm atmosphere.

A skilled interviewer states that he or she is glad to see the other person and looks forward to talking with her or him. In addition, the interviewer provides an orientation to an interview. Even though an interviewee will usually know why he or she is there, clarifying a meeting's purpose helps both parties get their bearings and check their understandings. To pave the way for both parties, know the purpose of the interview and be sure that everyone is on the same wavelength before the actual questioning begins.

Arrive for the interview a few minutes ahead of the scheduled hour. Be prepared, however, to wait patiently, if necessary. If you are the interviewer and you are going to take written notes, get out your paper and pen. Now you are ready to begin asking your prepared questions. If you are the interviewee, you may also want to get out paper and pen to record any questions that may arise during the interview process that you want to ask at its conclusion.

The Body: Asking Questions

Once the interviewee is at ease during the opening of the interview, the bulk of the interview will consist of the interviewer asking the interviewee questions. If an interviewer has done a good job of identifying and clarifying his or her objectives and gathering information, the key questions to be asked usually are fairly obvious. But what kinds of questions are they?

Question Types

An interview is conducted as a series of questions and responses. Even though both parties will listen and speak, the interviewer has the primary responsibility for questioning. Interview questions fall into one of four categories: open, closed, probing, or hypothetical.[1]

Open Questions   Open questions are broad and basically unstructured. Often they indicate only the topic to be considered and allow interviewees considerable freedom to determine the amount and kind of information they will provide.

Because they encourage the interviewee to share information almost without restriction, open questions are useful to determine opinions, values, and perspective. Such questions as "What are your long- and short-term career goals?" or "Why do you seek employment here?" or "How do you feel about shift work?" prompt personal and wide-ranging responses.

Closed Questions   Closed questions limit the range of possible responses. They may ask for a simple yes or no—Do you enjoy working in teams?—or they may allow interviewees to select responses from a number of specific alternatives—How often do you upgrade your skills? (1) Less than once a month, (2) Once a month, (3) Once every six months, (4) Once a year. Closed questions enable the interviewer to gather specific information, by restricting interviewees' freedom to express personal views or elaborate on responses. Closed questions are most often used when the maximum amount of information is required in a relatively short period of time.

Probing Questions   Probing questions encourage interviewees to clarify or elaborate on partial or superficial responses. Through the use of these questions, interviewers attempt to direct responses. Such questions as "Could you elaborate on your coursework in the area of communication?" "Do you mean to say that you changed jobs three times in six months?" and "Will you tell me more about your relationship with your supervisor?" seek further information in a particular area. Often spontaneous, probing questions follow up on the key questions that interviewers have prepared in advance.

Hypothetical Questions   Interviewers use hypothetical questions to describe a set of conditions and ask interviewees what they would do if they were in specific situations. Such questions are generally used either to gauge reactions to emotion-arousing or value-laden circumstances or to discover responses to real or imaginary situations. Hypothetical questions are used in behavioural-based interviews. Employers may assume that if you reacted in a particular way in the past, chances are you will respond to a future occurrence in a similar

ReCAP

Types of Interview Questions

	USES	EXAMPLE
Open Question	Prompts wide-ranging responses	Tell me about your previous job duties.
	Determines opinions, values, perspectives	How would you describe your son's problems in school?
Closed Question	Requests simple yes or no response	Have you been skiing in the past month?
	Forces a response from limited options	Which one of the following drinks would you buy? (a) Coke (b) Pepsi (c) 7-Up
Probing Question	Encourages clarification of or elaboration on previous responses	Would you tell me more about the pain in your side?
	Directs responses in a specific direction	We've talked about your mother. Can you describe how you felt about your father's long absences from home when you were a child?
Hypothetical Question	Gauges reactions to emotional or value-laden situations	How would you support your opponent if she were elected chairperson of the board?
	Elicits response to a real or imaginary situation	What would you do if your secretary lost an important file?

manner. An example would be, "Tell me about a time when you dealt with conflict in the workplace. What was the situation and how did you handle it?" A job-specific question may also be asked, such as, "As a bank teller, you would be dealing with the general public on a daily basis. How would you handle an irate customer who is claiming you lost her deposit?"

Questioning Sequences

Open, closed, probing, and hypothetical questions may be used in any combination, as long as their sequence is thoughtfully planned. Depending on the purpose, these questions may be arranged into four basic sequences: funnel, inverted funnel, quintamensional, and tunnel.

funnel sequence
A questioning sequence that begins with broad, open questions and proceeds toward more closed questions.

The Funnel Sequence   The **funnel sequence** begins with broad, open questions and proceeds to more closed questions (see Figure A.1). The advantage of this format is that it allows an interviewee to express views and feelings without restriction, at least early in an interview. For example, it may be more useful to begin a grievance interview with the question, "How would you describe your relationship with your supervisor?" instead of asking, "What makes you think your supervisor treats you like an idiot?" The first question allows the free expression of feelings, while the second question clearly reflects an interviewer's bias, immediately forcing the discussion in a negative direction. The following series of questions provides an example of a funnel sequence that might be used for an information-gathering interview.

1. Why do you find communication interesting?
2. What is your primary interest in the study of communication?
3. How long have you studied interpersonal communication?
4. Why do you think interpersonal attraction theory is useful?
5. What would you do to test interpersonal attraction theory?

Notice that the questions start asking for general information and then focus on more specific ideas.

The funnel sequence is appropriate when an interviewer believes that an interviewee is more comfortable with questions that allow him or her to choose general or specific responses.

inverted funnel sequence
A questioning sequence that begins with closed questions and proceeds with more open questions, intended to encourage an interviewee to respond easily early in the interview.

The Inverted Funnel Sequence   Just the opposite of the funnel sequence, the **inverted funnel** begins with closed questions and proceeds to more open questions (Figure A.2). An interview designed to gather information about a worker grievance and based on the inverted funnel might include the following series of questions:

1. Do you believe that your supervisor wants to fire you?
2. What makes you think you'll be fired soon?

FIGURE A.1   The Funnel Sequence

Broad, open questions

Increasingly closed questions

Getting at specific pieces of
information needed through use of
direct questioning

FIGURE A.2   The Inverted Funnel Sequence

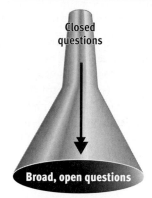

Building the "big picture" with
repeated questioning, intergrating
previous responses

3. What do you think has caused this problem between you and your supervisor?
4. How has this problem developed?
5. How would you describe the general working climate in your department?

The relatively closed questions that begin the inverted funnel sequence are intended to encourage an interviewee to respond easily, because they require only brief answers (yes or no, short lists, and the like). As the sequence progresses, the questions become more open and thus require more elaborate answers and greater disclosure.

The inverted funnel sequence is appropriate when an interviewer wants to direct the interview along specific lines and encourage an interviewee to respond with short, easily composed answers. An interviewer can follow up with more general questions to provide increasingly broad information—the "big picture," so to speak.

The Quintamensional Design Sequence   Quintamensional means "five dimensions." The **quintamensional design sequence** is a five-step series of questions intended to assess an individual's attitudes toward a particular topic and the strength of his or her feelings about the relevant issues. The first step assesses a respondent's knowledge about an issue (awareness). Next, an interviewer asks for an interviewee's general perspective—for example, a description of the nature of the controversy or the important and unimportant elements (uninfluenced attitudes). Third, an interviewer asks for a respondent's personal stand (specific attitude). Fourth, an interviewer wants to know the respondent's reasons for his or her specific attitude or opinion (reason why). Finally, an interviewer assesses the strength of an interviewee's feelings about his or her opinion (intensity of attitude). The five steps and sample questions can proceed as follows:

1. *Awareness:* Tell me what you know about the race for the Student Federation Association's November elections.
2. *Uninfluenced attitudes:* What are the issues in this race as you see them?
3. *Specific attitude:* Which candidate do you plan to vote for in this race?
4. *Reason why:* What led you to favour this candidate?
5. *Intensity of attitude:* How strongly do you feel about your choice—strongly, very strongly, definitely not willing to change your mind?

The Tunnel Sequence   Finally, the **tunnel sequence** consists of a series of parallel open or closed questions or a combination of the two. This sequence has no probing questions; it goes into less depth than the other three sequences. An interviewer may use the tunnel sequence to gather information about attitudes and opinions without regard for the reasons behind an interviewee's answers or the intensity of his or her feelings. The following is a typical tunnel sequence:

1. What are the three major issues in the student elections this year?
2. Which candidate would you vote for if the election were held today?

quintamensional design sequence
A five-step questioning sequence intended to assess both what an interviewee's attitudes are and how strongly he or she feels about the relevant issues. The five steps are (1) awareness, (2) uninfluenced attitudes, (3) specific attitudes, (4) reason why, and (5) intensity of attitude.

tunnel sequence
A way of structuring interview questions so that parallel open or closed questions (or a combination of open and closed questions) are asked to gather a large amount of information in a short amount of time; no probing questions are asked.

3. For whom do you think you will vote in the race for council president?
4. Are you a registered voter in this school?
5. What do you think of the proposition to set up a free tutoring service on campus?

The tunnel sequence is most appropriate when an interviewer wants some general information on a variety of topics in a relatively short period of time.

Although these sequences have been discussed as if they were independent and easily distinguishable, good questioning strategy will probably combine one or more question sequences. The key to effective interviewing is to prepare a set of questions that will get the needed kinds and amount of information. An interviewer should remain flexible enough to add, subtract, and revise questions as a discussion proceeds. Such an approach ensures accomplishing interviewing objectives.

As you conduct the interview, use the questions you have prepared as a guide but not a rigid schedule. If the person you are interviewing mentions an interesting angle you did not think of, don't be afraid to pursue the point. Listen carefully to the person's answers, and ask for clarification of any ideas you don't understand.

⤳ The Conclusion

Opinion polls, marketing surveys, and sales pitches often end rather abruptly with a "Thank you for taking the time to help me out." Many other kinds of interviews require follow-up meetings or some form of future contact, however. For this reason, and for reasons of common courtesy, the conclusion of an interview is very important.

A primary function of the conclusion is to summarize the proceedings. All parties should be aware of and agree on what happened during the meeting. To ensure understanding and satisfaction, an interviewer summarizes the highlights of the discussion, asking for and offering clarification, if necessary.

Another function of the conclusion is to encourage continued friendly relations. The positive communication climate developed during the interview should be carried into the conclusion. You may need to establish interpersonal harmony if you asked questions that resulted in conflict or made the interviewee uncomfortable. Comments such as "I'm so glad we had a chance to talk about this problem" or "It's been a pleasure to serve" enable both parties to feel that they have had a positive and productive encounter. An interviewer can tell the other person when to expect further contact or action, if appropriate. A job applicant wants to know when to expect a phone call about a follow-up interview or a job offer. An expert, interviewed by a journalist, wants to know what will be done with her comments and when the story is likely to be published.

Re**CAP** ⤎⋯

Organizing an Interview

STEP	GOALS
Opening	Put the interviewee at ease. Review the purpose. Establish rapport and diplomacy. Provide an orientation.
Body	Use questions appropriate to the interview type and objectives. Design questioning sequences appropriate to interview purpose and information needs.
Conclusion	Summarize the proceedings. Encourage friendly relations. Arrange further contact(s). Exchange thank-yous.

At the end of virtually any interview, both the interviewer and the interviewee are expected to say thank you. Because an interview is a mutual effort, both parties deserve recognition. Do not prolong the interview beyond the time limits of your appointment.

HOW TO BE INTERVIEWED FOR A JOB

It's been said that a major element in being successful in life is just showing up—but we suggest that you do more than just "show up" for a job interview. As you learned in Chapter 11, giving a speech involves considerable preparation. Like a speech, a successful job interview involves thoughtful preparation and careful planning.

⋯⟩ Be Aware of Your Skills and Abilities

The first communication principle we introduced in this book is to be aware of your communication. Before you interview for a job, it is important to be aware not only of your communication as you interact with others, but also of your unique skills, talents, and abilities. Many people select a career because they think they might like to *be* a lawyer, doctor, or teacher. But rather than thinking about what you want to be, we suggest considering what you like to *do*. Ask yourself these questions:

Aware

- What do I like to do in my free time?
- What are my best skills and talents?
- What special education and training do I have?
- What experiences or previous jobs have I had?

In addition to these questions, write down responses to complete this statement: "I can . . ." For example, you might respond: "I can cook, write, relate well to others." List as many answers as possible. Here's another statement to complete: "I have . . ." "I have travelled, worked on a farm, sold magazine subscriptions." Responding to the "I can" and "I have" statements will help you develop an awareness of your skills and experiences to keep on tap when you are asked about them during the interview. Reflecting on your interests can help you decide which career will best suit your talents; you will also be able to develop a resume that reflects your best abilities. Further reflection will allow you to set realistic goals that may require upgraded skills and continued education.

Verbal

⋯⟩ Prepare Your Resumé

A **resumé** is a written, concise, well-organized description of your qualifications for a job. How long should a resumé be? Many employers don't expect a resumé to be longer than two pages; some will look only at a one-page resumé. Resumés of experienced career professionals may be longer than two pages. Although your resumé is important in helping you land a job, its key function is to help you get an interview and then use the interview to get the job. Employers rarely hire someone for a job based only on a resumé. Most employers spend less than a minute—and some only a few seconds—looking at each resumé. Therefore, your resumé should be clear, easy to read, and focus on the essential information an employer seeks.

Most employers will be looking for standard information on your resumé. Note the sample resumé on page 349.[2] Here's a list of the essential pieces of information that should be included on your resumé.

- *Personal information:* Employers will look for your name, address, phone numbers, e-mail, and a Web page address (if you have one). Provide phone numbers where you can be reached during both day and evening.
- *Career objective:* Many employers will want to see your career objective. Make it brief, clear, and focused. You may need to customize your career objective for the different positions you seek.
- *Education:* Include your major, your degree or diploma, your graduation date, and the institution.

resumé
A written, concise, well-organized description of a person's qualifications for a job.

- *Experience:* Describe your relevant work experience. Include the names of employers, dates when you worked, and a very brief description of your duties.
- *Honours and special accomplishments:* List any awards, honours, offices held, or other leadership responsibilities.
- *Optional information:* If you have volunteer experience, have travelled, or have computer skills or other pertinent experience, be sure to include it if it is relevant to your objective and the job.
- *References:* List the names, phone and fax numbers, and e-mail addresses of people who can speak positively about your skills and abilities. Or you may indicate that your references are available upon request.

Verbal

When developing your resumé, be sure to use specific action verbs when describing your experience. Also use these action words during your interview. Rather than using a general verb such as "I *worked* on a project," use more descriptive action words that clarify the role you assumed. Use the following words to make a list of four or five activities or accomplishments:

accelerated	evaluated	planned
accomplished	expanded	promoted
achieved	expedited	proposed
adapted	facilitated	provided
administered	found	recommended
analyzed	generated	reduced
approved	guided	researched
building	increased	resulted in
built	influenced	reviewed
coordinated	initiated	revised
conceived	instructed	selected
conducted	interpreted	solved
completed	improved	stimulated
controlled	maintained	structured
created	managed	supervised
delegated	mastered	tested
developed	motivated	trained
demonstrated	negotiated	translated
designed	operated	travelled
directed	originated	updated
effected	organized	used
eliminated	participated	won

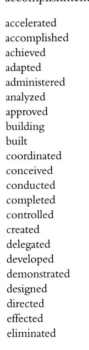

⤍ Identify the Needs of Your Employer

After you have analyzed your skills and abilities and prepared a well-crafted resumé, you need to be audience centred, to anticipate the needs and goals of your potential employer. A good interviewee adapts his or her message to the interviewer.

Adapt

How do you find out information about an organization that will help you adapt your message to fit the needs of the organization? In a word, research. Gather as much information as you can about not only the person who will interview you but the needs and goals of the organization or company where you seek a job. Aside from the wealth of company information available on the Internet, most libraries include books and articles about organizations both large and small. Typical library resources that include information about major corporations include the following:

- *The Information Please Business Almanac and Sourcebook*
- *Louis Rukeyser's Business Almanac*
- *Standard and Poor's Register of Corporations, Directors, and Executives*
- *The Job Vault: The One-Stop Job Search Resource*

Virtually every organization these days has a Web page. Explore the information available on the Web. Do more than just look at the home page of an organization; explore the various hyperlinks that help you learn about what the organization does.

What determines whether you are hired for the job? The short answer to this question is "the way you communicate." By the time you get to an interview, your interviewer has already determined that you have at least minimum qualifications for the job. Your ability to apply the communication principles for a lifetime that we've reiterated throughout the book is key to making a good impression on your interviewer. In Chapter 1, when discussing why it's important to learn about communication, we noted the key factors that employers look for in a job applicant; the top three factors focus on your communication skills.[3] Your ability to listen, respond, and relate to your interviewer is one of the best predictors of whether you will be hired for a job.

As you prepare for the interview, don't forget about the power of nonverbal messages in making a good impression, which we discussed in Chapter 4. Dressing for success is important. Most experts suggest you dress conservatively and give special attention to your grooming. For most professional positions, men will be expected to wear a coat and tie or a suit and well-polished shoes. Women will be expected to wear a dress, suit, or other co-ordinated attire that makes them look their best.

Besides assessing your appearance and your ability to communicate, other traits interviewers consider include the following:

- *Self-expression:* Are you clear or vague when you respond to questions? Do you have effective eye contact? Do you talk too much or too little?
- *Maturity:* Can you make good judgments and effective decisions?
- *Personality:* What's your overall style of relating to people? Are you outgoing, shy, quiet, overbearing, enthusiastic, warm, friendly?
- *Experience:* Can you do the job? Do you have a track record that suggests you can effectively do what needs to be done?
- *Enthusiasm:* Do you seem interested in this job and the organization? Do you seem to be genuine and authentic, or is your enthusiasm phony?
- *Goals:* Where are you heading in life? Are your short-term and long-term goals compatible with the needs of the organization?

Listen, Respond, and Ask Appropriate Questions

Because an interview is a structured, planned discussion, it will be important to demonstrate the effective listening and responding skills that we presented in Chapter 5. Stay focused on what your interviewer is asking you. Remember to stop, look, and listen for both the details of the questions and the major points of the questions.

When you respond to questions, you should project genuine enthusiasm and competence. Don't put on an act: Be yourself while being professional. Be friendly and pleasant without being overly effusive or giddy.

One of the best ways to prepare for an interview is to anticipate the interviewer's questions. Table A.1 on page 348 lists typical questions that may be asked during an interview. We don't recommend that you memorize "canned" or overly rehearsed answers, but it may be helpful to think about possible responses to these questions. Also be prepared to answer questions about special activities in your background, such as volunteer experience, vocational training, sports teams, and the like. During the opening part of the interview, your interviewer will probably ask general questions seeking to establish rapport and a friendly, positive interview climate. Be sure to get a good night's sleep and eat well so that you can stay alert. Long interviews can be physically demanding.

Consider the interview an opportunity to ask questions as well as to answer them; toward the end of the interview, most interviewers will give you an opportunity to ask whatever questions you'd like. Asking questions about an organization is a way to display enthusiasm for the job, as well as a means of assessing whether you really want to join the organization. You will want to know the following:

- Will there be any job training for this position?
- What are the opportunities for advancement?
- What is the atmosphere like in the workplace? (You will also observe this during the interview.)

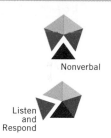

Nonverbal

Listen and Respond

Listen and Respond

TABLE A.1   Typical Questions and Follow-up Questions for Job Interviews[6]

I. Education

1. Why did you select your major area of study?
2. Why did you select your college/university?
3. What subjects were most and least interesting? Useful? Directly related to the job you are applying for?
4. Other than the courses you studied, what is the most important thing you learned from your college/university experience?
5. How did you finance your college/university education?

II. Experience

6. What do you see as your strengths and weaknesses as an employee?
7. You say that a strength you have is _____. Give me some indication, perhaps an example, that illustrates this strength.
8. What special skills would you bring to this position?
9. Describe your last few work experiences. Why did you leave each one?
10. What were the best and worst aspects of your last job?
11. What were some of your achievements and disappointments in your last job?
12. Do you see yourself as a leader/manager of people? Why?
13. What kinds of work situations would you like to avoid? Why?
14. What frustrations have you encountered in your work experience? How have you handled these frustrations?
15. What do you look for in a boss?
16. Most employees and bosses have some disagreements. What are some things that you and your boss have disagreed about? How did you settle these desagreements?

III. Position and Company

17. Why did you select this company?
18. Why did you decide to apply for this particular position?
19. How do you see yourself being qualified for this position?
20. Are you willing to relocate?

IV. Self-Evaluation

21. Tell me a little bit about yourself. Describe yourself.
22. What do you see as your personal strengths? Talents? How do you know that you possess these? Give examples of each.
23. What do you see as your weak points? Areas for improvement? Things you have difficulty doing? What have you done to deal with these?
24. Describe a specific work problem you had. Tell what you did to solve this problem.
25. What do you consider to be your greatest work achievement? Why?

V. Goals

26. Where do you see yourself being in your profession in five years? In ten years? How did you establish these goals? What will you need to do to achieve these goals?
27. What are your salary expectations for this position? Starting salary? Salary in five years?

- What hours do people work?
- Is there flexibility in scheduling the work day?
- When do you anticipate making a decision about this position?

The very first question you ask should *not* be, "How much does this job pay?" Usually the interviewer will discuss salary and benefits with you during the interview. If this is a preliminary interview, and you may be called back for another visit, you may want to defer

SAMPLE RESUMÉ

MARK SMITH
1075 Yonge Street
Toronto, Ontario
M2N 5T7
(416) 226-0102
(416) 226-0010

PROFESSIONAL OBJECTIVE:
Seeking a position in human resources as a Human Resources Officer.

EDUCATION:
Corporate Communication Diploma
Seneca College of Applied Arts & Technology
Graduation date: May 20XX

PROFESSIONAL EXPERIENCE:
20XX–Present, Co-op, ABC Technologies, Toronto, Ontario
- Assist in creating a leadership training program.
- Write copy for flyers and display ads.
- Make cold calls to prospective clients.

20XX–August 20XX, Co-op, Target Market, Barrie, Ontario.
- Developed sales training seminar.
- Coordinated initial plan for introducing advertising company for Crest Inc.'s advertising campaign.

20XX–20XX, Supervisor, S&B Associates, Pickering, Ontario.
- Supervised three employees editing training materials.

20XX–20XX, Advertising Sales and Reporter, *College Star*, Toronto, Ontario.
- Sold ads for college paper and worked as social events reporter.

OTHER EXPERIENCES:
20XX–XX, Summer jobs and part-time work.

SKILLS:
20XX–XX, Team Leadership, Photography, Computer Proficiency, Research and Analysis, Public Speaking, Customer Service.

ACCOMPLISHMENTS AND HONOURS:
Paid for majority of my college education while maintaining a 3.5 grade point, Presidential Scholarship, Vice-President of Seneca College Communication Club, Editor/Historian of MortarBoard, John Marshall High School Vice-President of Junior Class, Yearbook Coordinator.

PROFESSIONAL ORGANIZATIONS:
Canadian Marketing Association, Advertising Club, National Communication Association.

INTERESTS:
Photography, tennis, softball, theatre.

REFERENCES:
Available at your request.

questions about salary, benefits, and flexible work hours until you know that the organization is seriously considering you for the position.

During the interview, maintain eye contact and speak assertively. The goal in an interview is to project a positive attitude to the interviewer. As motivational speaker Zig Ziglar once noted, "Your attitude, not your aptitude, will determine your altitude."

⇢•⇠ COMMUNICATION and TECHNOLOGY

The Growth of E-Resumés

More and more job applicants are sending resumés to prospective employers via the Internet. The number of job-related Web sites grew from around 200 in the late 1990s to more than 1200 by the year 2002.[4] Is this a useful practice? From the job applicant's standpoint, the answer seems to be "yes" in terms of convenience. But there is evidence that many employers are not enamoured with the quantities of e-resumés they receive. Employers are finding it difficult to keep up with the volume of resumés that come their way; many people are indiscriminately sending a resumé via monster.ca rather than carefully targeting an organization or company to make sure their talents match the needs of the employer. Another problem with electronic resumés: The attachments applicants send along aren't always compatible with the employer's software. So if you send an electronic resumé, don't hold your breath waiting for an answer. Use electronic resumés, but don't rely on them to be your *only* method of making contact with employers; your resumé could end up in a stack with thousands of others. Support your electronic contact with a more personal connection between you and your prospective employer.

⇢ Follow up after the Interview

After the interview, it is wise to write a brief letter to thank the interviewer and to provide any additional information that he or she requested. You may also want to send a thank-you note to others in the organization, such as a secretary or administrative assistant, for helping you arrange the interview. If the interviewer asked for references, make sure you contact your references quickly and ask them to send letters of recommendation to the organization. Expedite this process by providing addressed, stamped envelopes and a copy of your resumé so that they can personalize their letters with specific information.

Is it appropriate to call the person who interviewed you to ask when a decision will be made about hiring someone? Some employers abide by the philosophy, "Don't call us, we'll call you." But many others would interpret your call as a sign of your interest in the position and a testament to your ability to follow through. You may want to take the direct approach and simply ask your employer toward the end of the interview, "Would it be all right if I called you in a few days to see if you have made a decision or if you need additional information?" If the date on which the interviewer told you a decision would be made passes by, it is probably okay to call and find out whether they've offered the job to someone else and to express your continued interest in the position if it hasn't been filled.

HOW TO BE INTERVIEWED FOR AN INFORMATION-GATHERING INTERVIEW

The bulk of the responsibility for an effective information-gathering interview falls on the shoulders of the person who is doing the interviewing. If you are the interviewer for an

Frank and Ernest

© Thaves. Reprinted with permission. Newspaper dist. by NEA, Inc.

information-gathering interview, review the suggestions we offered earlier in this appendix for structuring the interview; most information-gathering interviews follow the general structure we outlined.

If you are being interviewed, however, being prepared, listening carefully, and appropriately responding to questions are your primary responsibilities. In addition, a good interviewee knows what to expect in an information-gathering interview. You should prepare responses for anticipated questions, pay close attention to requests for specific information, and answer questions directly and accurately.

⋯⟩ Prepare for the Interview

In most cases, interviewees have some advance knowledge of the purpose and objective of interviews, especially if someone is seeking specific information or advice. You can therefore anticipate probable topics of discussion. If you are uncertain what the interview is about, it is appropriate to ask the person who will interview you how best to prepare for the questions he or she plans to ask you. Yes, sometimes news programs have an interviewer pop up in an office, thrust a microphone in the interviewee's face, and ask a pointed question; in most cases, however, Mike Wallace of *60 Minutes* fame is not going to ambush you.

Depending upon the nature of the questions you will be asked, you may want to brush up on the facts you may be asked. Jot down a few notes to remind you of names, dates, and places you may be asked about. In some cases, you may want to do some background reading on the topic of the interview.

Finally, think about not only what you will say in the interview, but how you will respond nonverbally. Be on time. Maintain an attitude of interest and attentiveness with eye contact, attentive body positions, alert facial expressions, and an appropriately firm handshake.

⋯⟩ Listen Effectively

Interviewing situations require you to listen for the amount and depth of information desired. For responses to be appropriate and useful, you must know what is being requested. If questions are unclear, ask for clarification or elaboration. By doing so, you can respond more fully and relevantly.

Listen
and
Respond

Successful interviewees also practise empathy. Interviewers are people, and interviewing situations are interpersonal encounters. Effective interviewees consider situations from interviewers' points of view, listen for unintentional messages, and watch for nonverbal cues. When interviewees listen to all facets of the communication, they can better adapt to the situation.

⋯⟩ Respond Appropriately

Just as questioning is the primary responsibility of an interviewer, responding is the primary responsibility of an interviewee. Keep answers direct, honest, and appropriate in depth and relevance. For example, in response to the question "How would you describe the quality of your relationship with your co-workers?" don't give a 15-minute speech about your problems with your ex-boss, keeping everyone's on target with project completion, and finding dependable co-workers to work in teams. To make sure that you give the best possible answer, listen carefully when a question is posed and, if necessary, take a few moments to think before you answer. A response that is well thought out, straightforward, and relevant will be much more appreciated than one that is hasty, evasive, and unrelated to the question. Remember, the real question being asked behind all other questions is, "Why should we hire you?"

Verbal

Using language and vocabulary appropriate to the situation is also important. The use of too much slang or technical terminology in an attempt to impress an interviewer can easily backfire by distracting from or distorting clear and open communication. Direct and simple language promotes understanding and sharing.

Finally, be adaptable and flexible to the needs of the interviewing situation. Some interviewers will ask questions to throw you off guard. When this happens, take a moment to think before you respond. Try to discover the reason for the question and respond to the best of your ability. Listen carefully for content *and* intent of questions so that you provide the information requested, especially when the interviewer changes topics. Flexibility and adaptability depend on good listening, empathy, accurate reading and interpretation of nonverbal communication, and practice. Just remember, "Engage brain before opening mouth!"

THE RESPONSIBILITIES OF THE INTERVIEWER

So far we've emphasized how to behave when you are the person being interviewed. As you assume leadership positions in your profession and community, you will undoubtedly be called on to interview others. In addition to knowing how to structure the opening, body, and conclusion of an interview, which we discussed earlier, there are several other characteristics of effective interviewers, whether you are seeking a future employee or simply gathering information.

┈┈> Be Aware of Biases and Prejudices

First and foremost, an interviewer must be aware of his or her own biases and prejudices. Each person has a set of experiences, beliefs, attitudes, and values through which that person receives, interprets, and evaluates incoming stimuli. If accurate and useful information is to be shared in an interview, an interviewer must be aware of his or her own perceptual processes in order to make accurate and objective interpretations. An otherwise qualified candidate for a job shouldn't be eliminated from consideration just because the interviewer has a bias against redheads.

┈┈> Adapt to an Interviewee's Behaviour

Adapt

Skilled interviewers observe, evaluate, and adapt to the communication behaviour of their interviewees. Because no two interviews—and no two interviewees—are exactly alike, interviewers adapt their communication behaviour accordingly. A flexible communication style is a necessity. Interviewers should have predetermined plans, but they should not be thrown off balance if an interviewee suddenly turns the tables and asks, "How much money do *you* make for this job?"

Adaptability also includes the use of appropriate language and vocabulary. You should consciously choose language and vocabulary that interviewees will understand. Little is gained by the use of technical, ambiguous, or vague terms. Words should be straightforward, simple, and specific, but not so simple that interviewees feel "talked down" to. Empathy is important in determining the most appropriate language and vocabulary.

┈┈> Deal Wisely with Sensitive Content

Verbal

When planning questions for an interview, consider possible sensitive topics and topics to be avoided. A question such as "Why were you fired from your last job?" will provoke a defensive reaction in a grievance interview.

Good judgment and choice of words play crucial roles. One ill-chosen question can destroy the positive and open communication developed in an opening. Effective interviewers avoid potentially troublesome topics and attempt to put interviewees at ease. They discuss sensitive issues *if and only if* they are related to the purpose of the interviews. When a sensitive subject must be discussed, experienced interviewers choose their words carefully; thus, the question, "Why were you fired?" might be rephrased as "How would you describe your relationship with your previous supervisor?"

┈┈> Listen Effectively

Listen and Respond

The admonition to listen effectively has appeared frequently in this appendix. Effective listening is at the heart of any interview. No matter how well interviewers have prepared, the time will have been wasted if they are poor listeners. They need strong listening skills to make sure that they are receiving the kind and amount of information they need. They must be able to identify partial or irrelevant responses.

Highly developed listening skills also increase the ability to accurately perceive and interpret unintentional messages and beliefs, attitudes, and values. Interviewers learn a great deal from nonverbal, as well as verbal, communication.

⋯⟩ Record Information

The information accumulated from an interview is useless if it is not recorded completely and accurately. A partial or inaccurate report can lead to poor decisions and mistaken actions.

⋯⟩ Ask Appropriate Questions

Verbal

The success of most interviews will be determined by the quality of the questions asked during the conversation. Think of questions as "mental can openers" designed to understand how the other person thinks and behaves. Earlier we discussed question types (open, closed, probing, and hypothetical) and question sequences (funnel, inverted funnel, and the quintamensional design). Some of your questions should be planned. Other questions may evolve from the discussion. Famed TV interviewer Larry King suggests that the best questions during an interview emerge from simply listening to what the other person is saying and then probing or following up on information and ideas verbalized. It is important to note that if you work in a unionized environment, the same standard questions for every candidate are the norm. Probing of answers is limited to ensure that all interviewers receive a fair interview.

If you are interviewing a job applicant, you should be aware that there are certain questions you should *not* ask. These are questions that are inappropriate because they ask for information that either laws or court interpretations of laws suggest could lead to illegal discrimination. Here's a list of topics you should not bring up during an employment interview when you're asking the questions.[5]

arrest records	insurance claims
less-than-honourable discharges	judgments
gender and marital status	citizenship or national origin
maiden name	mother's maiden name
number of children	place of birth
ages of children	disabilities
number of preschool children	handicap
spouse's name	prior illnesses or accidents
spouse's education	hospitalizations
spouse's income	current or prior medication/treatment
form of birth control	workers' compensation claims
family plans	weight
child care arrangements	religion
car accidents	church affiliation
lawsuits	social organizations
legal complaints	loans
ownership of home	wage assignments or garnishments
rental status	bankruptcy
length of residence	credit cards
date of high school graduation	form of transportation
age	ownership of car
sexual orientation	

SUMMARY

An interview is a form of oral interaction structured to achieve a goal and involving two or more people who take turns speaking and listening. In this appendix, we have focused on tips and strategies for being interviewed, as well as offered strategies for interviewing others. The five types of interview situations we've identified include information-gathering interview, job interview, appraisal interview, problem-solving interview, and persuasion interview. This appendix focused primarily on job interviews and information-gathering interviews.

All interviews have an opening, in which the interviewee is put at ease; a body, during which questions are asked and answered; and a conclusion, which brings the interview to a comfortable close.

When you are seeking employment, start by becoming aware of your skills and abilities, and use your personal inventory to help you develop a well-written resumé. Focus on the needs of your prospective employer: Research the organization to which you are applying for a job. During the interview, listen carefully to the questions asked by the interviewer and respond appropriately. After the interview, it may be appropriate to send a thank-you note to the interviewer.

When preparing to be interviewed for an information-gathering interview, remember three primary tasks. First, prepare for the interview by reviewing information you think the interviewer will ask you. Second, listen closely to the questions that you are being asked. Finally, respond appropriately by keeping answers direct and honest. Don't ramble. Observe the nonverbal responses of the interviewer to determine whether you are appropriately answering the questions.

We concluded this appendix by summarizing the essential requirements when you interview others. Don't let your own biases and prejudices interfere with your job of listening and responding to the interviewee. Although it's useful to have a prepared list of questions to ask, be prepared to adapt to the interviewee's behaviour if the work environment permits this type of flexibility. The best interviews have a spontaneous flow to them rather than a rigid structure. Don't ask illegal questions during a job interview, and handle sensitive questions with tact and diplomacy. Listening well is the hallmark of an effective interviewer. Develop a strategy to record the information you gather from the interview. Finally, the key to any interview is the quality of the questions asked. As the interviewer, you have prime responsibility for asking clear, appropriate, and answerable questions.

PRINCIPLES OF INTERVIEWING

Aware

Principle 1: Be aware of your communication with yourself and others.

- Take inventory of your skills and abilities to help you determine the best job opportunities and careers for you.
- Use your analysis of your talents to help you develop your resumé.
- During an interview, monitor your messages to ensure you are communicating clearly and effectively.

Verbal

Principle 2: Effectively use and interpret verbal messages.

- Speak clearly and respond to each question you are asked during an interview.
- Use action-oriented words on your resumé and during an interview to describe your accomplishments.
- Organize your resumé to include key elements of your education, experience, and special qualifications.
- Don't ask illegal or unethical questions during an employment interview.

Nonverbal

Principle 3: Effectively use and interpret nonverbal messages.

- Pay special attention to your appearance when you interview for a job; dress conservatively, and appear neat and well groomed.
- Speak with confidence, use appropriate eye contact, and communicate interest and enthusiasm during the interview.
- When you interview someone, monitor your interviewee's nonverbal messages for clues about the individual's personality and ability to work with people.
- Skilled interviewers observe, evaluate, and then appropriately adapt to the communication behaviour of their interviewees.

Listen and Respond

Principle 4: Listen and respond thoughtfully to others.

- When you are interviewed for a job, be sure to stop, look, and listen to the questions and comments of the interviewer.
- Listen for both the details of the message and the major points or key ideas.
- When interviewing others, among your most important tasks is to listen.

Adapt

Principle 5: Appropriately adapt messages to others.

- Learn as much as you can about any prospective employer so that you can describe how your abilities best fit with the needs of the organization to which you are applying.

B

Appendix: Sample Speeches for Discussion and Evaluation

---> On the Occasion of a Tribute to the Prime Minister

---> On the Occasion of the Presentation of the Governor General's Awards in Commemoration of the Persons Case

ON THE OCCASION OF A TRIBUTE TO THE PRIME MINISTER[1]

Prime Minister Jean Chrétien
Toronto, Ontario,
November 13, 2003

My friends,

That video brought me back a long way. A very long way. So many memories. So many bonds and so many friendships. So much road travelled. For a young man born in a large working class family in Shawinigan.

And I am very proud to say it is a road we have travelled together.

Because if—as I have always said—Canada is my life, it is the Liberal Party that has been like family to me.

It is the Liberal Party that gave me the chance to grow. To meet people in every part of Canada. To learn the true meaning of democracy and public service. That opened my horizons and my world.

I began as president of the Young Liberals Association at Laval University. But it is in April 1963 that I proudly entered Parliament as MP for St. Maurice-Laflèche under the exceptional leadership of Lester B. Pearson.

He did so many things of lasting benefit for Canadians. He showed me so much kindness and confidence especially when he sent me to Mitchell Sharp to be trained to be the first francophone Minister of Finance.

Mitchell, still young at 92 years old, is here tonight. He proved to me, at an early age, that Liberalism is about heart and passion, yes, but it is also about responsibility, and balance, and creating growth and opportunity.

And Pierre Trudeau. Larger than life. And a presence so powerful that he forever changed the way we see ourselves as Canadians.

I was very proud to be part of Mr. Trudeau's team and of the confidence he had in me to do the challenging jobs that needed to be done, from transforming aboriginal policy, creating national parks, to the Quebec referendum in 1980, to bringing home the constitution and negotiating the Charter of Rights and Freedoms.

That is Liberalism in action, my friends. The spirit and vision of governments like those of Lester Pearson and Pierre Trudeau.

That built the modern Canada we love so deeply.

That built the social programs that Canadians cherish. That gave our country its own flag.

That gave birth to national Medicare. To the Charter of Rights and Freedoms. To the Canada Pension Plan.

To a truly bilingual Canada that has become home to people from every corner of the world—and a shining model of how the human race can live together in peace, progress and prosperity.

It was these governments—under these two great Canadians—that cemented Canada as the champion of a multilateral approach on the international scene. Also as a trusted peacekeeper. As an honest voice in the world. A force for peace and stability.

My friends, that is what we are celebrating at this convention: the vision, the passion, and the spirit of Liberalism.

In June 1990, in Calgary, you gave me the great honour and responsibility of carrying the Liberal torch. Of succeeding a great Liberal, John Turner. Of upholding our timeless principles and traditions.

And adapting them to new times and new challenges as every leader must do. And that is what I have tried to do.

Because, my friends, when this country is in a time of need, in crisis, when things need to be righted, Canadians have always turned to Liberal governments.

And that is the way it was in Canada ten years ago.

We remember the state of the nation ten years ago. Canadians remember it. I know I will never forget it.

We were in a crisis, all right. The worst crisis Canada had seen in more than half a century. An economic crisis. A fiscal crisis. A national unity crisis. And even more troubling, a crisis of confidence.

Canadians had given up believing Canada could ever work again.

We were virtually broke. Almost bankrupt. Against the wall. The annual deficit was $42 billion, by far the largest in our entire history. Thirty-seven cents of every tax dollar went to servicing the national debt. Unemployment and interest rates were far too high, both above 11 percent.

The International Monetary Fund was knocking at the door. *The Wall Street Journal* was saying we were a candidate to become a Third World economy.

And that malaise went much, much deeper than the economy. The dice had been rolled on our national unity. And Canada was on the brink of disaster. Of falling apart. In Quebec, support for separatism was at its highest in history.

Western Canadians were turning their backs on national parties for a narrow regional party. It is hard to believe now, but people were giving up—actually giving up—on the very idea of Canada.

Canadians gave us a job to do. They gave us a mission. A solemn responsibility. They wanted their country back. They wanted it turned around. They wanted to be proud again.

And my friends, that is what we set out to do. Together, with our team. Members of Parliament. Ministers. A professional public service. A skilled, committed team of men and women. Who cared deeply about their country and were eager to work hard, very hard.

I want to thank them—all of them—personally tonight for their contribution and their dedication.

Think of what we have accomplished with Canadians in ten years. Well, everyone knows—the whole world knows—how we turned the finances of this country around. It was hard. It hurt. Canadians made sacrifices. But we took that $42 billion deficit and turned it into six consecutive balanced budgets.

Today we are the only G-7 country with a balanced budget. Today we lead the industrial world in fiscal responsibility.

We in Canada are entering our seventh year in balance. And not only that, we have also paid down more than ten percent of the national debt.

In ten years, our economy has created three million new jobs. Interest rates are at their lowest levels in decades. Young families can afford to finance their homes. We have been able to pass on to the Canadian people the biggest tax cut in the history of Canada.

We have been able to invest large sums of money in health care.

And we have created the National Child Benefit which is the most important new social programme since Medicare.

My friends, we understood that our young people need to be liberated to make their dreams come true, to make their contribution to our country and to our future.

As soon as we eliminated the deficit, our first priority was to make massive investments in education, in our young people, in their brains and in their capacity.

From the Millennium Scholarships, to the Canada Research Chairs, from graduate scholarships, to the Canada Foundation for Innovation, to the Canadian Institutes of Health Research, and so much more, we are making Canada the place to be for young people in the 21st century.

We have restored an activist, progressive national government. That speaks and acts for the whole country. As only the national government can do. And we have done so in accordance with timeless Liberal principles and traditions.

Just as it took time to restore our fiscal health, it took several years to rebuild the unity of this country.

But slowly, carefully, deliberately, we took the steps to strengthen the bonds that tie our country together. It was not easy to fight years of myths that had been created by those who wanted to break up Canada.

But it was worth the fight. Yes, my friends, it was worth the fight. We vowed that we would never again run the risk of losing Canada through ambiguity and misunderstanding and lack of presence.

Ladies and gentlemen, make no mistake about it, the Clarity Act has secured the future of Canada.

Again, it wasn't easy. All the pundits, the elites, thought we were crazy to take such a risk. But the people of Canada—and the people of the province of Quebec in particular—knew better.

We did it by telling the truth to Quebeckers. We did not make unrealistic, empty promises. We refused to pander. We were frank and direct. And we governed well.

Today we as Liberals can hold our heads up high in Quebec.

Let me tell you, it was tough, my friends. It was tough for all of us who stood for Canada. It was very tough for me personally. It hurt me deeply. It hurt my family. To be vilified in my home province—the province I love—just for standing up for Canada.

Because I believed so profoundly, as I still believe today, that being part of Canada is best for Quebec.

But no matter how lonely it was—we never gave up.

And, tonight, I can tell you, my friends, that nothing gives me greater satisfaction than the knowledge that we have prevailed in Quebec. That we have earned the respect of the people of Quebec. That we have turned the page and are working on real solutions to real problems.

From the bottom of my heart, I thank my fellow citizens of Quebec.

And let me tell you that we would not have succeeded without the patience and understanding and commitment of Canadians across the land during a very difficult period. It made me so proud to be a Canadian.

Restoring the pride, restoring the faith of Canadians has been a big job, my friends.

And it has not stopped with the economy or with national unity.

We have worked hard to ensure that our values—Canadian values—are what have guided our government and its policies.

That is why we have one of the toughest gun control laws in the world. As a Canadian, that makes me very, very proud.

And we have restored the pride in who we are. Look at the cultural vitality of Canada today. We saw the wonderful artists here tonight.

The magic of Le Cirque du Soleil is seducing audiences around the world, and transforming entertainment in the 21st Century.

Taking their cue from two great friends of mine, Paul Anka and Oscar Peterson, who led the way many years ago, today Canadian women are the biggest phenomenon in the history of the recording industry. From Céline Dion to Shania Twain to Diana Krall to Alanis Morrissette to Avril Lavigne, they are taking over the world, and doing it in a very Canadian way.

Our authors are winning prestigious awards around the globe. It is nothing short of a renaissance of Canadian literature.

My friends, in every field, the Canadian arts are the most vibrant and celebrated they've ever been.

And of course, Canadians have been proud to once again reassert our independence on the world stage.

We have a wonderful story to tell the world. About how to live together in peace and diversity. About how to resolve differences with civility. About mutual respect. About building bridges. You might say the world could use a little more Canada.

And we've been delivering. The Land Mines Treaty. The International Criminal Court. New hope for Africa, NEPAD.

The effort to narrow the gap between the richest and poorest nations has been important to Canadians.

We have worked hard at it. Because we Canadians know how these disparities fuel hatreds and violence in the most troubled corners of our world.

We have not been afraid to confront those hatreds. That is why our brave Canadian troops went to Bosnia and Kosovo with NATO. That is why they are in Afghanistan today.

And that is why we stood shoulder to shoulder with our closest friend and ally, the United States when they were targeted on that terrible September day. We are with them and all civilized nations in the fight against terrorism. Canadians are making a vital contribution in that struggle—and we are very proud of it.

But we also have known when we must go our own way internationally. In a manner that is consistent with our values. Doing the right thing, no matter how difficult.

And it was because of our deep belief as Canadians in the values of multilateralism and the United Nations that we did not go to war in Iraq.

It was the same with the Kyoto Protocol. When it comes to a decision as important as the very preservation of our planet, you don't look over your shoulder to see what your neighbour is doing. You don't wait for others to decide first. You don't duck your head.

You do the right thing. For today, and above all the right thing for the future. For our kids. For their kids. For this planet. It was the same when we confronted the Europeans in the Turbot war in 1995.

That is what Canadians want. And that is what we as Liberals have provided.

That is not all that we did. We took historic action to limit the influence in elections of big business and big unions. Because that's what Liberalism is about. Giving power to the people, not to special interests. About opening up democracy. About ensuring that all Canadians are free to exercise their human rights.

And you know, when we speak of human rights, we are admired around the world for our social liberalism.

We have taken those classic Liberal values I spoke about earlier, and adapted them for a new era.

The world has changed in the past 40 years, and it continues to change. And we have to keep up with it. We recognize that issues respecting same sex must be dealt with, because the Charter of Rights is a precious heritage for Liberals. Any time we are asked to choose between fewer rights and more rights, we Liberals, and we Canadians, will always choose more rights, and especially for minorities.

My friends, all this is some of what we have accomplished. Together as Liberals. Together with Canadians.

Ten years ... Ten years. From *The Wall Street Journal* calling us a candidate for the Third World to *The Economist*, a few weeks ago, telling the world that Canada is cool!!

We are proud of what we have accomplished. But tonight I want to let you in on a secret. I want to tell you what makes me happiest by far. It's not simply what we have done in government. It's not just our economy. It's not just the problems we solved.

It is the new spirit in the land. You can see it. You can feel it. The new pride of Canadians. Our sense of confidence. Our can-do spirit. We have never been more confident. We have never been more proud. We have never been more united. We have never been more sure of who we are. We have never been more eager, more prepared to take on the world.

My friends, that is the Canada of 2003. That is how far we have travelled in ten years. And I am honoured to have had the opportunity to play a part in it.

When the question is asked, are Canadians better off today than we were ten years ago? The answer is clear and unmistakable. Yes. Yes. Yes.

It has been a good time to be a Liberal. It is a good time to be a Liberal. And it is a great time to be a Canadian.

And as I leave as leader of our Party, I can say with pride, that with our record, we are in a very, very good position to win a fourth consecutive Liberal majority government.

Yes, we must celebrate our accomplishments. But we must not be satisfied with them.

We must remember, my friends, we do not govern by divine right. We do not have a permanent lease on office. It is not something that is owed to us.

We govern with the power and trust invested in us by the Canadian people. We must never, never forget that. We must never take them, or their support, for granted. We must earn it every day.

Being a Liberal means always, always thinking about the future. So tonight I would like to challenge us as a party, as I pass on the torch.

Tonight I want to ask you, my Liberal family, what can we do to ensure that our country is even better off ten years from now than it is today?

To govern is to lead. We define ourselves by the hard choices we make. By the decisions we make. We saw that with the deficit. We saw it with the Clarity Act. We saw it with Iraq. We saw it every time we stood tall for Canada.

Not just for the headlines of today, but for the world of tomorrow.

There is no substitute for doing the right thing at home or abroad.

The rest of the world looks to us as a model, as a beacon. Look at the people in this great hall. You see in this one location all the faces, all the races, and the colours, and religions that make up this planet. This is the Canada of today.

And this is our mission to the world. To show how it is possible to live together in diversity and in harmony. But to fulfill this mission, we have a solemn responsibility to speak to the world in our own voice—an independent voice.

It is not something to barter or give away, not for economic gain, commercial advantage or anything else.

My friends, we cannot be complacent, at a time when the opposition is getting together. When in a country of the centre, the opposition is moving to the right.

Canadians should beware of those on the right who put the interests of Bay Street over the interests of Main Street.

Canadians should beware of those on the right who put profit ahead of community ... beware of those on the right who put the narrow bottom line ahead of everything else.

Canadians should beware of those on the right who would reduce taxes at the expense of necessary public services ... beware of those on the right who do not care about reducing social and environmental deficits.

Canadians should beware of those on the right who would weaken the national government because they do not believe in the role of government.

My friends, my fellow Canadians, my fellow Liberals, if you remember only one thing that I say tonight, remember this ... we must never ever lose our social conscience.

My final message for you is simple. Trust Canadians. They are wise. They are generous. They care.

And above all, trust the young generation of Canadians that is coming up. I have a lot of faith in young Canadians today. There has never been a generation in history more sure of itself and its Canadian identity, and yet more in touch and involved in every corner of the world. They care. And they understand.

My friends, I am passing on the leadership of our Party to a new leader. A new prime minister.

A great Liberal. Who has been a big part of our record. Of the Liberal record. Of the record we are so proud of.

Although we have accomplished so much, there is still so much more to do. Paul Martin will need all our support, the support of all of us. And I can assure Paul that he has my support.

And when he has some lonely moments, as I know he will, he should remember, as I have, how each successive leader has been strengthened by our Liberal values. He should remember Laurier, remember King, remember St-Laurent, remember Pearson, remember Trudeau, remember Turner.

There is no greater privilege than to be able to serve your country. To be Prime Minister of the most wonderful country in the world. I have always felt a special love of this country. With all my fellow citizens. Regardless of their political views.

So from the bottom of my heart, I want to thank the people of Canada for the confidence they have shown in me over so many years. I will be forever grateful.

I want to thank the Liberal Party for the great confidence you have shown in me since you chose me as your leader 13 years ago.

And for the privilege I have had in leading the greatest political party in the world.

When I first announced my candidacy for the leadership of the Liberal Party back in 1984, I said: "Fasten your seat belts—it's going to be a helluva ride".

Well my friends, it has been a hell of a ride.

Now I finish my career as I began, as an ordinary Liberal. I will be there to support our new team. I will be there to encourage young Canadians to continue to be engaged. And I will be there to support our new leader.

I want to thank tonight, the people of St. Maurice who have shown their confidence in me for the last 40 years, as well as the people of Beauséjour for three years. Without them, I would not be here tonight.

And, my friends, I will be there side-by-side with Aline, my rock of Gibraltar for almost the last 50 years…

Vive le Canada!

ON THE OCCASION OF THE PRESENTATION OF THE GOVERNOR GENERAL'S AWARDS IN COMMEMORATION OF THE PERSONS CASE[2]

Her Excellency the Right Honourable Adrienne Clarkson
Rideau Hall
October 20, 2003

I'm delighted to welcome you to Rideau Hall for what has become one of my favourite ceremonies.

It was one of the first over which I presided after being appointed Governor General, when we inaugurated the statue for the Famous Five in Calgary in October 1999. And I continue to marvel ever since at the strength, the wisdom, and the downright artfulness of the women who get these awards each year. The original Famous Five—Emily Murphy, Nellie McClung, Louise McKinney, Irene Parlby and Henrietta Muir Edwards—would have been, I feel, quite happy in their company, drinking a cup of tea and, yes, wearing hats!

One of the earliest and most read feminists, Mary Wollstonecraft, said that she did not wish women "to have power over men but over themselves". I think she got to the essence of the matter, because she realized that you can't overcome societal attitudes—whether in the form of men or the structures that men have made—without first developing a very strong sense of worth, a self-esteem, an ability to feel strong.

It is this manifestation of strength to which Susan B. Anthony alluded when she said: "The only question left to be settled now is, are women persons?" In 1928, some years after she made that statement, they were declared persons in Canada. That was what the Famous Five settled for us; and that is what we are celebrating today—that women are, in the eyes of society and all its institutions, indeed persons. They are indeed truly human.

To have taken well into the previous century for this recognition of women's humanity is appalling for a society like ours. Not only for the egregious and outrageous discrimination it represented and perpetuated. But also because of what it denied to our own society. It denied the full contribution and full participation of half of the population from being truly human. For to be truly human is to be someone who helps to create the things that could be, not accept the way things are. Denying it robbed our society of that element, that potential, of creating progress and public good.

To work for the things that could be is to work with hope, with optimism, with joy. Yet hoping and working for social change as you have done is extremely demanding and often misunderstood and misinterpreted. It is an uphill struggle, because people are simply afraid of change. Thank goodness, however, we have women who can put their minds to it. They know in their hearts that change is incremental, that progress means making sudden leaps ahead, only to be pushed back by the inevitable riptide of reaction and vested interest.

I've only just returned from State Visits to Russia, Finland and Iceland. And they were successful because we had roundtables on federalism, governance, minority languages, literature—all participated in by women who were outstanding on our trip. And we met outstanding women on these visits who have taken their place in public life—like the President of Finland, Tarja Halonen, as well as various ministers of important portfolios in both Finland and Iceland who are the driving forces behind their social and cultural policy. The Nordic countries have a great place for women in their societies—and we are a Nordic country. So let's take our place.

On the Canadian side, I was particularly happy to bring with us Senator Landon Pearson, Senator Mira Spivak, Member of Parliament Karen Kraft-Sloan, and five women from the Inuit and Aboriginal communities who are playing such a vital role in helping their northern culture to be maintained and strengthened through international cooperation. There was Fibbie Tatti, a Dene, who is the Languages Commissioner for the Northwest Territories, engaged in substantive discussion in Russia with Mrs. Lyudmila Putina, who takes a personal interest in this because Russia has 120 indigenous languages. Norma Kassi—a Gwi'chen, who speaks out on the dangers caused to the Porcupine caribou herds' migration patterns by oil pipelines going through the Yukon—was discussing sustainable development with Russian environmental specialists in a public roundtable.

And with us through the whole trip were two absolutely superb women whose names you should know—Sheila Watt-Cloutier, the elected President of the Inuit Circumpolar Conference, the international organization for all Inuit of all northern countries, and Mary Simon, our Ambassador for Circumpolar Affairs and former Ambassador to Denmark.

You can imagine how proud I was as a Canadian to present these outstanding women, whose lives—as Sheila herself pointed out—stretch from travelling exclusively by dog-team up until the time they were almost teenagers to taking their seat in discussions in Russia, Finland and Iceland, as well as in Canada of course, on the future of our northern hemisphere. Their knowledge of the indigenous communities of the north, their experience in governance, their contacts with people throughout the circumpolar world through their languages—this background and credibility contributed hugely to the success of our mission and to the many discussions we had with Russians, Finns, Sámi people, and Icelanders. I wish you could have been there.

Seeing the strength of these women, their perseverance and hard work makes me even more hopeful that we are continuing in a long line of women who have helped to shape Canadian society. The women we are honouring today with the Persons Awards have also driven change in our society, just as the women delegates on my circumpolar trip have done. They haven't waited for others to take the lead—they have seized it themselves by virtue of an unshakeable commitment to social justice, a fundamental belief in rights for all human beings, and a consummate ability to represent the people of their country *and* their own gender.

This is particularly important. For it seems to me that the next step in the struggle for progress and equality for women is to bind the two together wherever possible. So that all Canadians increasingly grasp that the interests of their own country are served and advanced to the extent that equality of gender is achieved at home. Home meaning Canada as well as in the home.

So our country will be served by the progress of women.

We always have to remember Nellie McClung, who fought so hard for all women and for the right to vote. She met the most vicious and personally wounding opposition from the then-Premier of Manitoba, to whom she said so memorably: "We are not here to ask for a reform or a gift or a favour but for a right—we are here not for mercy but for justice."

As we all know, Nellie and her friends won a very important victory for all of us women and ultimately for Canadian society. Yet all the battles have not yet been won, even though everything seems to open to women, particularly in higher education, in the professions and, yes, in certain hockey leagues. There was a documentary about Haley Wickenheiser while we were in Finland and we were very proud—there she was on her men's team. It would be foolish to think that the struggle was over. Each battle fought and won is simply the battle. The outcome is not yet certain. Temporary truces are exactly that: they shouldn't be mistaken for a final peace accord.

And when we've thought about ourselves and our rights in this comfortable country in the northern hemisphere, we have to think about the women of Africa, of Afghanistan, of Pakistan, who seem to make some progress and then are turned back in the most brutal and vicious and controlling of ways. While we make our progress as a middle-class society in the developed world, we must never forget them.

Some of you might recall the wasps' nest I managed to stir up last February at the Law Society of Upper Canada when I asked where all the women were who are now managing partners of the large law firms? Yes, there are now perhaps slightly more women in law schools across the country than men. And there have been an increasingly number of women in law firms over the past two decades. And we have outstanding women judges and three in the Supreme Court, including our Chief Justice. So I asked why this was not represented at the top levels of the top law firms. That's all I asked. The reaction to this question was, shall we say, strident and often indignant, but did not answer the question. However, between you and me in this room, I want to tell you that since then, many men from large law firms have sidled up to me and said, "You were right."

We could ask the question of other professions. Where are the women who are heads of the departments of surgery, internal medicine and so forth in the medical profession? The fact is, we have still not reached the final stage of truth that the philosopher Schopenhauer identified. My husband is a philosopher, you know, so I read a lot of philosophy. As he said: "... Truth passes through three states. First it is ridiculed. Second, it is violently opposed. Third, it is accepted as being self-evident." In the glacial way in which progress is made in women's rights, we're between the second—that is, the violently opposing phase—and the third, the acceptance as being self-evident. Let's all keep working so that we can progress to the self-evident stage of truth in our own lifetimes.

That is why these awards are so important. In honouring the spirit of the Famous Five, we are inspired to fight unpopular battles and to continue to improve the lives of all women. You will hear in a moment from Senator Maheu the detailed citations of this year's recipients. So I will just mention them by name—because these are names that honour all women, names that we will, I am sure, hear time and again whenever and wherever the cause of women's equality is at stake: Nicole Demers, Eira Friesen, Joyce Hayden, Marilou McPhedran, Jayanti Negi—and Jennifer Hustwitt, a role model for other young women. As Nellie McClung said: "I am a firm believer in women—in their ability to do things and in their influence and power." As Governor General of Canada and as a woman, I share that belief and I am delighted to have the opportunity to celebrate it with you today.

Thank you.

Notes

Chapter 1 Notes

1. E. T. Klemmer and F. W. Snyder, "Measurement of Time Spent Communicating," Journal of Communication 20 (June, 1972): 142.
2. F. E. X. Dance and C. Larson, *Speech Communication: Concepts and Behavior* (New York: Holt, Rinehart and Winston, 1972).
3. Dance and Larson, *Speech Communication*.
4. J. T. Masterson, S. A. Beebe, and N. H. Watson, *Invitation to Effective Speech Communication* (Glenview, IL: Scott, Foresman, 1989).
5. This section is based on J. T. Masterson, S. A. Beebe, and N. H. Watson. We are especially indebted to J. T. Masterson for this discussion.
6. For an excellent discussion of comparative religions and the common principle of being other oriented see: W. Ham, *Man's Living Religions* (Independence, MO: Herald Publishing House, 1966), 39–40.
7. For additional discussion of the ethical values taught in the world's religions, see: H. Smith, *The World's Religions* (San Francisco: HarperSanFrancisco, 1991).
8. National Communication Association, "NCA Credo for Communication Ethics," 1999 (June 27, 2001) <http://www.natcom.org/conferences/Ethics/ethicsconf-credo99.htm>.
9. We thank Tom Burkholder, University of Nevada, Las Vegas, for this idea.
10. D. Quinn, *My Ishmael* (New York: Bantam Books, 1996).
11. The Conference Board of Canada <http://www.conferenceboard.ca/education/learning-tools/pdfs/esp2000.pdf>.
12. See: J. C. McCroskey and M. Beatty, "The Communi-biological Perspective: Implications for Communication in Instruction," *Communication Education* 49 (2000): 1. Also see: J. C. McCroskey, J. A. Daly, M. M. Martin, and M. J. Beatty, eds., *Communication and Personality: Trait Perspectives* (Cresskil, NJ: Hampton Press, 1998).
13. The Conference Board of Canada <http://www.conferenceboard.ca/education/learning-tools/pdfs/esp2000.pdf>.
14. The Conference Board of Canada <http://www.conferenceboard.ca/education/learning-tools/pdfs/esp2000.pdf>.
15. The Conference Board of Canada <http://www.conferenceboard.ca/education/learning-tools/pdfs/esp2000.pdf>.
16. K. E. Davis and M. Todd, "Assessing Friendship: Prototypes, Paradigm Cases, and Relationship Description." In *Understanding Personal Relationships*, edited by S. W. Duck and D. Perlman (London: Sage, 1985); B. Wellman, "From Social Support to Social Network." In *Social Support: Theory, Research and Applications*, edited by I. G. Sarason and B. R. Sarason (Dordrecht, Netherlands: Nijhoff, 1985); R. Hopper, M. L. Knapp, and L. Scott, "Couples' Personal Idioms: Exploring Intimate Talk," *Journal of Communication 31* (1981): 23–33.
17. M. Argyle and M. Hendershot, *The Anatomy of Relationships* (London: Penguin Books, 1985), 14.
18. D. Goleman, "Emotional Intelligence: Issues in Paradigms Building." In *The Emotionally Intelligent Workplace,* edited by C. Cherniss and D. Goleman (San Francisco: Jossey Bass, 2001), 13.
19. V. Satir, *Peoplemaking* (Palo Alto, CA: Science and Behavior Books, 1972).
20. M. Argyle, *The Psychology of Happiness* (London: Routledge, 2001).
21. J. J. Lynch, *The Broken Heart: The Medical Consequences of Loneliness* (New York: Basic Books, 1977).
22. D. P. Phillips, "Deathday and Birthday: An Unexpected Connection." In *Statistics: A Guide to the Unknown*, edited by J. M. Tanur (San Francisco: Holden Day, 1972). Also see: F. Korbin and G. Hendershot, "Do Family Ties Reduce Mortality: Evidence from the United States 1968," *Journal of Marriage and the Family 39* (1977): 737–746; K. Heller and K. S. Rook, "Distinguishing the Theoretical Functions of Social Ties: Implications of Support Interventions." In *Handbook of Personal Relationships* 2e, edited by S. W. Duck, K. Dindia, W. Ickes, R. Milardo, R. S. L. Mills, and B. R. Sarason (Chichester: Wiley, 1997); B. R. Sarason, I. D. Sarason, and R. A. R. Gurung, "Close Personal Relationships and Health Outcomes: A Key to the Role of Social Support." In *Handbook of Personal Relationships*; Duck, et al. Also see: S. Duck, *Relating to Others* (Buckingham, England: Open University Press, 1999), 1.
23. H. Lasswell, "The Structure and Function of Communication in Society." In *The Communication of Ideas*, edited by L. Bryson (New York: Institute for Religious and Social Studies, 1948), 37.
24. See: V. E. Cronen, W. B. Pearce, and L. M. Harris, "The Coordinated Management of Meaning: A Theory of Communication." In *Human Communication Theory: Comparative Essays*, edited by F. E. X. Dance (New York: Harper & Row, 1982), 61–89.
25. L. Barker, R. Edwards, C. Gaines, K. Gladney, and F. Holley, "An Investigation of Proportional Time Spent in Various Communication Activities of College Students," *Journal of Applied Communication Research 8* (1981): 101–109.
26. See: D. Barnlund, *Interpersonal Communication: Survey and Studies* (Boston: Houghton Mifflin Company, 1968).
27. O. Wiio, *Wiio's Laws—and Some Others* (Espoo, Finland: Welin-Goos, 1978).

28. T. Watzlawick, J. Beavin Bavelas, and D. Jackson, *The Pragmatics of Human Communication* (New York: W. W. Norton, 1967).

29. S. B. Shimanoff, *Communication Rules: Theory and Research* (Beverly Hills: Sage, 1980).

30. For an excellent review of intrapersonal communication theory and research, see: D. Voate, *Intrapersonal Communication: Different Voices, Different Minds* (Hillsdale, NJ: Lawrence Erlbaum, 1994).

31. Quinn, *My Ishmael.*

32. Barker et al., "An Investigation . . ."

33. We appreciate and acknowledge our friend and colleague M. Redmond for his contributions to our understanding of interpersonal communication. For more information, see: S. A. Beebe, S. J. Beebe, and M. V. Redmond, *Interpersonal Communication: Relating to Others* 3e (Boston: Allyn & Bacon, 2002).

34. For an excellent discussion of the power of dialogue to enrich the quality of communication, see: D. Yankelovich, *The Magic of Dialogue: Transforming Conflict into Cooperation* (New York: Simon & Schuster, 1999).

35. S. A. Beebe and J. T. Masterson, *Communicating in Small Groups: Principles and Practices* 7e (Boston: Allyn & Bacon, 2003).

Chapter 2 Notes

1. S. R. Covey, *The Seven Habits of Highly Effective People* (New York: Simon & Schuster, 1989), 67.

2. R. A. Baron and D. Byrne, *Social Psychology* 10e (Boston: Allyn & Bacon, 2003).

3. K. Horney, *Neurosis and Human Growth* (New York: W. W. Norton & Co., 1950), 17.

4. B. Goss, *Processing Communication* (Belmont, CA: Wadsworth, 1982), 72.

5. J. T. Masterson, S. A. Beebe, and N. H. Watson, *Invitation to Effective Speech Communication* (Glenview, IL: Scott, Foresman and Company, 1989).

6. W. James, *Principles of Psychology* (New York: Henry Holt and Company, 1890).

7. D. M. Garner, "The 1997 Body Image Survey Results," *Psychology Today* (January/February, 1997): 30–44, 74–75, 78, 80, 84.

8. G. B. Forbes, L. E. Adams-Curtis, B. Rade, and P. Jaberg, "Body Dissatisfaction in Women and Men: The Role of Gender-Typing and Self-Esteem," *Sex Roles 44* (2001): 461–484.

9. J. Che, "Underweight Canadians," *Canadian Social Trends 67* (Winter 2002). Catalogue no. 11-008-XPE.

10. A. N. Markham, *Life Online: Researching Real Experience in Virtual Space* (Walnut Creek, CA: AltaMira Press, 1998), 135; 202–203.

11. C. H. Cooley, *Human Nature and the Social Order* (New York: Scribner's, 1912).

12. G. H. Mead, *Mind, Self, and Society* (Chicago: University of Chicago Press, 1934).

13. D. K. Ivy and P. Backlund, *GenderSpeak: Personal Effectiveness in Gender Communication* 3e (New York: McGraw-Hill, 2004).

14. J. C. Pearson, L. Turner, and W. T. Mancillas, *Gender & Communication* 3e. (Dubuque, IA: William C. Brown, 1995).

15. J. E. Stake, "Gender Differences and Similarities in Self-Concept within Everyday Life Contexts," *Psychology of Women Quarterly 16* (1992): 349–363.

16. G. Steinem, *Revolution from Within: A Book of Self-Esteem* (Boston: Little, Brown and Company, 1993), 26.

17. Ivy and Backlund, *GenderSpeak.*

18. See: C. Gilligan, *In a Different Voice: Psychological Theory and Women's Development* (Cambridge, MA: Harvard University Press, 1982); P. Orenstein, *Schoolgirls: Young Women, Self-Esteem, and the Confidence Gap* (New York: Doubleday, 1994).

19. Statistics Canada, Health Indicators, December 2001, Catalogue No. 82-221-XIE.

20. R. A. Josephs, H. R. Markus, and R. W. Tafarodi, "Gender and Self-Esteem," *Journal of Personality and Social Psychology 63* (1991): 391–402.

21. K. Meyer, "Kids Self Esteem May Not Be Evident to Parents, Teachers," February 12, 2003 <http://www.uoguelph.ca/research/news/articles/2003/Feb/kids_self_esteem_may_not_be_evident.shtml>.

22. G. J. Carter, "The New Face: As Women's World Cup Soccer Kicks Off This Weekend, Girls around the Globe Finally Get the Role Model They Deserve: Mia Hamm," *USA Weekend* (June 18–20, 1999): 6–7.

23. J. Hattie, *Self-Concept* (Hillsdale, NJ: Lawrence Erlbaum, 1992).

24. A. Chatham-Carpenter and V. DeFrancisco, "Pulling Yourself Up Again: Women's Choices and Strategies for Recovering and Maintaining Self-Esteem," *Western Journal of Communication 61* (1997): 164–187.

25. Goss, *Processing Communication.*

26. L. Costigan Lederman, "The Impact of Gender on the Self and Self-Talk." In *Women and Men Communicating: Challenges and Changes* 2e, edited by L. P. Arliss and D. J. Borisoff (Prospect Heights, IL: Waveland, 2001), 78–89; J. R. Johnson, "The Role of Inner Speech in Human Communication," *Communication Education 33* (1984): 211–222; C. R. Streff, "The Concept of Inner Speech and Its Implications for an Integrated Language Arts Curriculum," *Communication Education 33* (1984): 223–230; J. L. McFarland, "The Role of Speech in Self-Development, Self-Concept, and Decentration," *Communication Education 33* (1984): 231–236; J. Ayres, "The Power of Positive Thinking," *Communication Education 37* (1988): 289–296.

27. C. J. Mruk, *Self-Esteem: Research, Theory, and Practice* (New York: Springer, 1995).

28. See: J. Ayres and T. S. Hopf, "The Long-Term Effect of Visualization in the Classroom: A Brief Research Report," *Communication Education 39* (1990): 75–78; J. Ayres and T. S. Hopf, "Visualization: Is It More Than Extra-Attention?" *Communication Education 38* (1989): 1–5.

29. J. Ayres, T. S. Hopf, and D. M. Ayres, "An Examination of Whether Imaging Ability Enhances the Effectiveness of an Intervention Designed to Reduce Speech Anxiety," *Communication Education 43* (1994): 252–258.

30. Covey, *The Seven Habits of Highly Effective People*, 105.

31. P. R. Hinton, *The Psychology of Interpersonal Perception* (New York: Routledge, 1993).

32. U. Neisser, *Cognition and Reality: Principles and Implications of Cognitive Psychology* (San Francisco: W. H. Freeman and Company, 1976).

33. D. J. Schneider, A. H. Hastorf, and P. C. Ellsworth, *Person Perception* 2e (Reading, MA: Addison-Wesley, 1979).

34. D. T. Kenrick, S. L. Neuberg, and R. B. Cialdini, *Social Psychology: Unraveling the Mystery* 2e (Boston: Allyn & Bacon, 2002), 399.

35. C. N. Macrae, G. V. Bodenhausen, A. B. Milne, and J. Jetten, "Out of Mind but Back in Sight: Stereotypes on the Rebound," *Journal of Personality and Social Psychology 67* (1994): 808–817.

36. Macrae et al., "Out of Mind," 808.

Chapter 3 Notes

1. D. Spender, *Man Made Language* 2e (London: Routledge & Kegan Paul, 1985).

2. To explore further examples of Newfoundland English, see: G. M. Story, W. J. Kirwan and J. Widdowson (eds.), *The Dictionary of Newfoundland English* (Toronto: University of Toronto Press, 1982).

3. *Webster's New World Dictionary* (New York: Warner Books, 1990), 526.

4. D. K. Ivy and P. Backlund, *GenderSpeak: Personal Effectiveness in Gender Communication* 3e (New York: McGraw-Hill, 2004).

5. A. Ellis, *A New Guide to Rational Living* (North Hollywood, CA: Wilshire Books, 1977).

6. C. Peterson, M. E. P. Seligman, and G. E. Vaillant, "Pessimistic Explanatory Style Is a Risk Factor for Physical Illness: A 35-Year Longitudinal Study," *Journal of Personality and Social Psychology 55* (1988): 23–27.

7. <http://www.cbc.ca/storyview/CBC/200211/25/barghi021125>.

8. J. Barlow, "E-Mail Etiquette Has Its Own Rules," *Houston Chronicle* (March 11, 1999): C1.

9. D. A. Lieberman, *Public Speaking in the Multicultural Environment* 2e (Boston: Allyn & Bacon, 1997), 34–35.

10. Senior Analyst, Demography Division of Statistics Canada, "Canada's Aboriginal Languages," *Canadian Social Trends* (Winter 1998). Catalogue no. 11-008.

11. Senior Analyst, Demography Division of Statistics Canada, "Canada's Aboriginal Languages."

12. Senior Analyst, Demography Division of Statistics Canada, "Canada's Aboriginal Languages."

13. See: J. Briere and C. Lanktree, "Sex-Role Related Effects of Sex Bias in Language," *Sex Roles 9* (1983): 625–632; L. Brooks, "Sexist Language in Occupational Information: Does It Make a Difference?" *Journal of Vocational Behavior 23* (1983): 227–232; A. Stericker, "Does This 'He or She' Business Really Make a Difference? The Effect of Masculine Pronouns as Generics on Job Attitudes," *Sex Roles 7* (1981): 637–641.

14. H. S. O'Donnell, "Sexism in Language," *Elementary English 50* (1973): 1067–1072, as cited by J. C. Pearson, L. Turner, and W. Todd Mancillas, *Gender & Communication* 3e (Dubuque, IA: William C. Brown, 1995).

15. See: J. L. Stinger and R. Hopper, "Generic *He* in Conversation?" *Quarterly Journal of Speech 84* (1998): 209–221; J. Gastil, "Generic Pronouns and Sexist Language: The Oxymoronic Character of Masculine Generics," *Sex Roles 23* (1990): 629–641; D. K. Ivy, L. Bullis-Moore, K. Norvell, P. Backlund, and M. Javidi, "The Lawyer, the Babysitter, and the Student: Inclusive Language Usage and Instruction," *Women & Language 18* (1994): 13–21; W. Martyna, "What Does 'He' Mean? Use of the Generic Masculine," *Journal of Communication 28* (1978): 131–138.

16. L. Madson and R. M. Hessling, "Does Alternating between Masculine and Feminine Pronouns Eliminate Perceived Gender Bias in a Text?" *Sex Roles 41* (1999): 559–576; D.

Kennedy, "Review Essay: She or He in Textbooks," *Women and Language 15* (1992): 46–49.

17. See: R. Maggio, *The Nonsexist Word Finder: A Dictionary of Gender-Free Usage* (Boston: Beacon, 1988); C. Miller, K. Swift, and R. Maggio, "Liberating Language," *Ms.* (September/October, 1997): 50–54.

18. C. H. Palczewski, "'Tak[e] the Helm,' Man the Ship . . . and I Forgot My Bikini! Unraveling Why Woman Is Not Considered a Verb," *Women & Language 21* (1998): 1–8; Maggio, *The Nonsexist Word Finder*.

19. Ivy and Backlund, *GenderSpeak*.

20. D. O. Braithwaite and C. A. Braithwaite, "Understanding Communication of Persons with Disabilities as Cultural Communication." In *Intercultural Communication: A Reader* 8e, edited by L. A. Samovar and R. E. Porter (Belmont, CA: Wadsworth, 1997), 154–164.

21. J. R. Gibb, "Defensive Communication," *Journal of Communication 11* (1961): 141–148. Also see: R. Bolton, *People Skills* (New York: Simon & Schuster, 1979), 14–26; O. Hargie, C. Sanders, and D. Dickson, *Social Skills in Interpersonal Communication* (London: Routledge, 1994); O. Hargie, ed., *The Handbook of Communication Skills* (London: Routledge, 1997).

Chapter 4 Notes

1. A. Mehrabian, *Nonverbal Communication* (Chicago: Aldine-Atherton, 1972).

2. R. L. Birdwhistell, *Kinesics and Context* (Philadelphia: University of Pennsylvania Press, 1970).

3. J. H. Bert and K. Piner, "Social Relationships and the Lack of Social Relations." In *Personal Relationships and Social Support*, edited by S. W. Duck with R. C. Silver (London: Sage, 1989).

4. W. F. Chaplin, J. B. Phillips, J. D. Brown, N. R. Clanton, and J. L. Stein, "Handshaking, Gender, Personality, and First Impressions," *Journal of Personality and Social Psychology 79* (2000): 110–117.

5. J. K. Burgoon, L. A. Stern, and L. Dillman, *Interpersonal Adaptation: Dyadic Interaction Patterns* (Cambridge, England: Cambridge University Press, 1995).

6. P. Ekman, "Communication through Nonverbal Behavior: A Source of Information about an Interpersonal Relationship." In *Affect, Cognition, and Personality*, edited by S. S. Tomkins and C. E. Izard (New York: Springer, 1965).

7. M. Argyle, *Bodily Communication* (New York: Methuen & Company, 1988).

8. P. Ekman and W. V. Friesen, "Constants across Cultures in the Face and Emotion," *Journal of Personality and Social Psychology 17* (1971): 124–129; Argyle, *Bodily Communication*, 157; I. Eibl-Eibesfeldt, "Similarities and Differences between Cultures in Expressive Movements." In *Nonverbal Communication*, edited by R. A. Hinde (Cambridge, England: Royal Society and Cambridge University Press, 1972); P. Collett, "History and Study of Expressive Action." In *Historical Social Psychology*, edited by K. Gergen and M. Gergen (Hillsdale, NJ: Lawrence Erlbaum, 1984); E. T. Hall, *The Silent Language* (Garden City, NY: Doubleday, 1959); R. Shuter, "Proxemics and Tactility in Latin America," *Journal of Communication 26* (1976): 46–55; E. T. Hall, *The Hidden Dimension* (New York: Doubleday, 1966).

9. R. E. Porter and L. A. Samovar, "An Introduction to Intercultural Communication." In *Intercultural Communication:*

A Reader 8e, edited by L. A. Samovar and R. E. Porter (Belmont, CA: Wadsworth, 1997), 19.

10. See: Burgoon et al., *Interpersonal Adaptation;* J. K. Burgoon and S. B. Jones, "Toward a Theory of Personal Space Expectations and Their Violations," *Human Communication Research 2* (1976): 131–146; J. K. Burgoon, "A Communication Model of Personal Space Violations: Explication and an Initial Test," *Human Communication Research 4* (1978): 129–142; J. K. Burgoon and L. Aho, "Three Field Experiments on the Effect of Violations of Conversation Distance," *Communication Monographs 49* (1982): 71–88; J. K. Burgoon and J. L. Hale, "Nonverbal Expectancy Violations: Model Elaboration and Application to Immediacy Behaviors," *Communication Monographs 55* (1988): 58–79.

11. J. Fast, *Body Language* (New York: M. Evans, 1970).

12. "Style Experts," *Entertainment Weekly* (July 12, 1999): 30.

13. G. B. Forbes, L. E. Adams-Curtis, B. Rade, and P. Jaberg, "Body Dissatisfaction in Women and Men: The Role of Gender-Typing and Self-Esteem," *Sex Roles 44* (2001): 461–484; R. A. Botta, "Television Images and Adolescent Girls' Body Image Disturbance," *Journal of Communication 49* (1999): 22–37; M. Wiederman and S. Hurst, "Body Size, Physical Attractiveness, and Body Image among Young Adult Women: Relationships to Sexual Experience and Sexual Esteem," *Journal of Sex Research 35* (1998): 272–281.

14. E. Hatfield and S. Sprecher, *Mirror, Mirror . . . : The Importance of Looks in Everyday Life* (Albany: SUNY Press, 1986); C. M. Marlowe, S. L. Schneider, and C. E. Nelson, "Gender and Attractiveness Biases in Hiring Decisions: Are More Experienced Managers Less Biased?" *Journal of Applied Psychology 81* (1998): 11–21; W. R. Zakahi, R. L. Duran, and M. Adkins, "Social Anxiety, Only Skin Deep? The Relationships between Ratings of Physical Attractiveness and Social Anxiety," *Communication Research Reports 11* (1994): 23–31; L. A. Zebrowitz, *Reading Faces: Window to the Soul?* (Boulder, CO: Westview, 1997).

15. J. Gorham, S. H. Cohen, and T. L. Morris, "Fashion in the Classroom III: Effects of Instructor Attire and Immediacy in Natural Classroom Interactions," *Communication Quarterly 47* (1999): 281–299; K. D. Roach, "Effects of Graduate Teaching Assistant Attire on Student Learning, Misbehaviors, and Ratings of Instruction," *Communication Quarterly 45* (1997): 125–141; S. E. White, "A Content Analytic Technique for Measuring the Sexiness of Women's Business Attire in Media Presentations," *Communication Research Reports 12* (1995): 178–185; J. M. Townsend and G. D. Levy, "Effects of Potential Partners' Costume and Physical Attractiveness on Sexuality and Partner Selection," *Journal of Psychology 124* (1990): 371–389; F. B. Furlow, "The Smell of Love." In *The Nonverbal Communication Reader: Classic and Contemporary Readings* 2e, edited by L. K. Guerrero, J. DeVito, and M. L. Hecht (Prospect Heights, IL: Waveland, 1999), 118–125; R. K. Aune, "The Effects of Perfume Use on Perceptions of Attractiveness and Competence." In Guerrero, *The Nonverbal Communication Reader,* 126–132.

16. J. T. Molloy, *New Dress for Success* (New York: Warner Books, 1988); J. T. Molloy, *New Woman's Dress for Success Book* (New York: Warner, 1996).

17. L. Averyt, "Casual-Attire Fridays Are Spreading to Rest of Week in Many Companies," *Corpus Christi Caller Times* (August 31, 1997): A1, A6; M. G. Frank and T. Gilovich, "The Dark Side of Self- and Social Perception: Black Uniforms and Aggression in Professional Sports," *Journal of Personality and Social Psychology 54* (1988): 74–85; P. A. Andersen, *Nonverbal Communication: Forms and Functions* (Mountain View, CA: Mayfield, 1999).

18. Birdwhistell, *Kinesics and Context;* D. G. Leathers, *Successful Nonverbal Communication: Principles and Applications* 3e (Boston: Allyn & Bacon, 1997).

19. P. Ekman and W. V. Friesen, "The Repertoire of Nonverbal Behavior: Categories, Origins, Usage, and Coding," *Semiotica 1* (1969): 49–98.

20. G. Beattie and H. Shovelton, "Mapping the Range of Information Contained in the Iconic Hand Gestures That Accompany Spontaneous Speech," *Journal of Language & Social Psychology 18* (1999): 438–462; J. Streeck, "Gesture as Communication I: Its Coordination with Gaze and Speech," *Communication Monographs 60* (1993): 275–299.

21. W. G. Woodall and J. P. Folger, "Nonverbal Cue Context and Episodic Memory: On the Availability and Endurance of Nonverbal Behaviors as Retrieval Cues," *Communication Monographs 52* (1985): 320–333; A. A. Cohen and R. P. Harrison, "Intentionality in the Use of Hand Illustrators in Face-to-Face Communication Situations," *Journal of Personality and Social Psychology 28* (1973): 276–279.

22. C. Darwin, *Expression of Emotions in Man and Animals* (London: Appleton; reprinted University of Chicago Press, 1965).

23. M. Thunberg and D. Dimberg, "Gender Differences in Facial Reactions to Fear-Relevant Stimuli," *Journal of Nonverbal Behavior 24* (2000): 44–50; D. LaPlante and N. Ambady, "Multiple Messages: Facial Recognition Advantage for Compound Expressions," *Journal of Nonverbal Behavior 24* (2000): 211–221; D. Keltner, "Signs of Appeasement: Evidence for the Distinct Displays of Embarrassment, Amusement, and Shame," *Journal of Personality and Social Psychology 68* (1995): 441–453.

24. M. F. Abrahams, "Perceiving Flirtatious Communication: An Exploration of the Perceptual Dimensions Underlying Judgments of Flirtatiousness," *Journal of Sex Research 31* (1994): 283–292; K. Grammer, "Strangers Meet: Laughter and Nonverbal Signs of Interest in Opposite-Sex Encounters," *Journal of Nonverbal Behavior 14* (1990): 209–235.

25. M. M. Moore, "Nonverbal Courtship Patterns in Women: Context and Consequences," *Ethology and Sociobiology 6* (1985): 237–247; D. Knox and K. Wilson, "Dating Behaviors of University Students," *Family Relations 30* (1981): 255–258.

26. A. Abbey, "Sex Differences in Attributions for Friendly Behavior: Do Males Misperceive Females' Friendliness?" *Journal of Personality and Social Psychology 42* (1982): 830–838; L. B. Koeppel, Y. Montagne, D. O'Hair, and M. J. Cody, "Friendly? Flirting? Wrong?" In Guerrero, *The Nonverbal Communication Reader,* 290–297.

27. H. J. Delaney and B. A. Gluade, "Gender Differences in Perception of Attractiveness of Men and Women in Bars," *Journal of Personality and Social Psychology 16* (1990): 378–391.

28. A. E. Scheflen, "Quasi-Courtship Behavior in Psychotherapy," *Psychiatry 28* (1965): 245–257; K. Grammer, K. B. Knuck, and M. S. Magnusson, "The Courtship Dance: Patterns of Nonverbal Synchronization in Opposite Sex Encounters," *Journal of Nonverbal Behavior 22* (1998): 3–25.

29. J. A. Daly, E. Hogg, D. Sacks, M. Smith, and L. Zimring, "Sex and Relationship Affect Social Self-Grooming," *Journal of Nonverbal Behavior* 7 (1983): 183–189.

30. M. L. Knapp and J. A. Hall, *Nonverbal Communication in Human Interaction* 5e (Fort Worth, TX: Harcourt Brace, 2002), 390–391.

31. S. A. Beebe, "Eye Contact: A Nonverbal Determinant of Speaker Credibility," *Speech Teacher* 23 (1974): 21–25.

32. Cited in R. Caldwell, "Where Have All the Orators Gone?" *The Globe and Mail*, January 23, 2002 <www.engr.usask.ca/dept/techcomm/globe.html>.

33. D. Goleman, "Can You Tell When Someone Is Lying to You?" In Guerrero, *The Nonverbal Communication Reader*, 358–366; T. H. Feeley and M. A. deTurck, "The Behavioral Correlates of Sanctioned and Unsanctioned Deceptive Communication," *Journal of Nonverbal Behavior* 22 (1998): 189–204; L. A. Zebrowitz, L. Voinescu, and M. A. Collins, "'Wide-Eyed' and 'Crooked-Faced': Determinants of Perceived and Real Honesty across the Life Span," *Personality and Social Psychology Bulletin* 22 (1996): 1258–1269.

34. P. Ekman and W. Friesen, *Unmasking the Face* (Englewood Cliffs, NJ: Prentice-Hall, 1975).

35. Ekman and Friesen, *Unmasking the Face*.

36. V. Lee and H. Wagner, "The Effect of Social Presence on the Facial and Verbal Expression of Emotion and the Interrelationships among Emotion Components," *Journal of Nonverbal Behavior* 26 (2002): 3–23; M. T. Motley, "Facial Affect and Verbal Context in Conversation," *Human Communication Research* 20 (1993): 3–40; D. S. Berry, "Accuracy in Social Perception: Contributions of Facial and Vocal Information," *Journal of Personality and Social Psychology* 61 (1991): 298–307.

37. Ekman and Friesen, *Unmasking the Face*.

38. P. M. Cole, "Children's Spontaneous Control of Facial Expression," *Child Development* 57 (1986): 1309–1321.

39. S. Dang, "Abused Kids More Sensitive to Anger: Study Shows Victims Identify More Faces as 'Angry' Than Non-Abused," *Corpus Christi Caller Times* (June 23, 2002): A26.

40. L. E. Boone and D. L. Kurtz, *Contemporary Business* (New York: Dryden Press, 1997); V. Quercia, *Internet in a Nutshell* (Cambridge, MA: O'Reilly, 1997).

41. S. E. Jones and A. E. Yarbrough, "A Naturalistic Study of the Meanings of Touch," *Communication Monographs* 52 (1985): 19–56.

42. A. Montague, *Touching: The Human Significance of the Skin* (New York: Harper & Row, 1978).

43. M. S. Remland, T. S. Jones, and H. Brinkman, "Proxemic and Haptic Behavior in Three European Countries," *Journal of Nonverbal Behavior* 15 (1991): 215–231; M. S. Remland, T. S. Jones, and H. Brinkman, "Interpersonal Distance, Body Orientation and Touch: Effect of Culture, Gender, and Age," *Journal of Social Psychology* 135 (1995): 281–295; S. M. Jourard, "An Exploratory Study of Body-Accessibility," *British Journal of Social and Clinical Psychology* 26 (1966): 235–242; D. C. Barnlund, "Communicative Styles in Two Cultures: Japan and the United States." In *Organization of Behavior in Face-to-Face Interaction*, edited by A. Kendon, R. M. Harris, and M. R. Key (The Hague: Mouton, 1975).

44. J. W. Lee and L. K. Guerrero, "Types of Touch in Cross-Sex Relationships between Coworkers: Perceptions of Relational and Emotional Messages, Inappropriateness, and Sexual Harassment," *Journal of Applied Communication Research* 29 (2001): 197–220; M. S. Remland, *Nonverbal Communication in Everyday Life* (Boston: Houghton Mifflin, 2000); J. D. Murphy, D. M. Driscoll, and J. R. Kelly, "Differences in the Nonverbal Behavior of Men Who Vary in the Likelihood to Sexually Harass," *Journal of Social Behavior and Personality* 14 (1999): 113–128; D. K. Ivy and S. Hamlet, "College Students and Sexual Dynamics: Two Studies of Peer Sexual Harassment," *Communication Education* 45 (1996): 149–166.

45. L. M. Kneidinger, T. L. Maple, and S. A. Tross, "Touching Behavior in Sport: Functional Components, Analysis of Sex Differences, and Ethological Considerations," *Journal of Nonverbal Behavior* 25 (2001): 43–62; L. K. Guerrero and P. A. Andersen, "Public Touch Behavior in Romantic Relationships between Men and Women." In Guerrero, *The Nonverbal Communication Reader*, 202–210; S. E. Jones, "Sex Differences in Touch Communication," *Western Journal of Speech Communication* 50 (1986): 227–241; A. Hall and E. M. Veccia, "More 'Touching' Observations: New Insights on Men, Women, and Interpersonal Touch," *Journal of Personality and Social Psychology* 59 (1990): 1155–1162; F. N. Willis, Jr., and L. F. Briggs, "Relationship and Touch in Public Settings," *Journal of Nonverbal Behavior* 16 (1992): 55–63; B. Major, A. Schmidlin, and L. Williams, "Gender Patterns in Social Touch: The Impact of Setting and Age," *Journal of Personality and Social Psychology* 58 (1990): 634–643.

46. A. N. Markham, *Life Online: Researching Real Experience in Virtual Space* (Walnut Creek, CA: AltaMira Press, 1998), 76.

47. M. Mahal, "Culture Shock—Exploring Cross-Cultural Diversity" <http://www.malkam.com/CultureShock/Issue02.htm>.

48. T. DeGroot and S. J. Motowidlo, "Why Visual and Vocal Interview Cues Can Affect Interviewers' Judgments and Predict Job Performance," *Journal of Applied Psychology* 84 (1999): 986–993; L. L. Carli, S. J. LaFleur, and C. C. Loeber, "Nonverbal Behavior, Gender, and Influence," *Journal of Personality and Social Psychology* 68 (1995): 1030–1041; N. Christenfeld, "Does It Hurt to Say Um?" *Journal of Nonverbal Behavior* 19 (1995): 171–186; J. K. Burgoon, T. Birk, and M. Pfau, "Nonverbal Behaviors, Persuasion, and Credibility," *Human Communication Research* 17 (1990): 140–169; R. L. Street, Jr., R. M. Brady, and R. Lee, "Evaluative Responses to Communicators: The Effects of Speech Rate, Sex, and Interaction Context," *Western Journal of Speech Communication* 48 (1984): 14–27.

49. A. Jaworski, "The Power of Silence in Communication." In Guerrero, *The Nonverbal Communication Reader*, 156–162.

50. D. D. Henningsen, D. Dryden, M. G. Cruz, and M. C. Morr, "Pattern Violations and Perceptions of Deception," *Communication Reports* 13 (2000): 1–10; M. A. deTurck, T. H. Feeley, and L. A. Roman, "Vocal and Visual Cue Training in Behavioral Lie Detection," *Communication Research Reports* 14 (1997): 249–259; T. H. Feeley and M. A. deTurck, "Global Cue Usage in Behavioral Lie Detection," *Communication Quarterly* 43 (1995): 420–430.

51. S. J. Baker, "The Theory of Silence," *Journal of General Psychology* 53 (1955): 145–167.

52. D. R. Peterson, "Interpersonal Relationships as a Link between Person and Environment." In *Person–Environment Psychology*, edited by W. B. Walsh, K. H. Craig, and R. H. Price (Hillsdale, NJ: Lawrence Erlbaum, 1991), 154.

53. A. Rapoport, *The Meaning of the Built Environment: A Nonverbal Communication Approach* (Beverly Hills: Sage, 1982).

54. A. H. Maslow and N. L. Mintz, "Effects of Esthetic Surroundings: I," *Journal of Psychology 41* (1956): 247–254.

55. M. H. Eaves and D. G. Leathers, "Context as Communication: McDonald's vs. Burger King," *Journal of Applied Communication Research 19* (1991): 263–289; E. J. Langan, "Environmental Features in Theme Restaurants." In Guerrero, *The Nonverbal Communication Reader,* 255–263.

56. Hall, *The Hidden Dimension.*

57. R. Sommer, "Studies in Personal Space," *Sociometry 22* (1959): 247–260; L. Smeltzer, J. Waltman, and D. Leonard, "Proxemics and Haptics in Managerial Communication." In Guerrero, *The Nonverbal Communication Reader,* 184–191.

58. J. A. Hall, *Nonverbal Sex Differences: Communication Accuracy and Expressive Style* (Baltimore: Johns Hopkins University Press, 1984); P. A. Bell, L. M. Kline, and W. A. Barnard, "Friendship and Freedom of Movement as Moderators of Sex Differences in Interpersonal Distancing," *Journal of Social Psychology 128* (1998): 305–310; M. Remland, T. S. Jones, and H. Brinkman, "Interpersonal Distance, Body Orientation and Touch: Effect of Culture, Gender, and Age," *Journal of Social Psychology 135* (1995): 281–295.

59. S. M. Lyman and M. B. Scott, "Territoriality: A Neglected Sociological Dimension." In Guerrero, *The Nonverbal Communication Reader,* 175–183.

60. A. L. S. Buslig, "'Stop' Signs: Regulating Privacy with Environmental Features." In Guerrero, *The Nonverbal Communication Reader,* 241–249.

61. R. L. Paetzold and A. M. O'Leary-Kelly, "Organizational Communication and the Legal Dimensions of Hostile Work Environment Sexual Harassment." In *Sexual Harassment: Communication Implications,* edited by G. L. Kreps (Cresskill, NJ: Hampton Press, 1993), 63–77.

62. Mehrabian, *Nonverbal Communication.* For interesting applications of Mehrabian's immediacy principle to the instructional context, see S. D. Johnson and A. N. Miller, "A Cross-Cultural Study of Immediacy, Credibility, and Learning in the U.S. and Kenya," *Communication Education 51* (2002): 280–292; M. A. Jaasma and R. J. Koper, "Out-of-Class Communication between Female and Male Students and Faculty: The Relationship to Student Perceptions of Instructor Immediacy," *Women's Studies in Communication 25* (2002): 119–137; J. L. Chesebro and J. C. McCroskey, "The Relationship of Teacher Clarity and Immediacy with Student State Receiver Apprehension, Affect, and Cognitive Learning," *Communication Education 50* (2001): 59–68; P. L. Witt and L. R. Wheeless, "An Experimental Study of Teachers' Verbal and Nonverbal Immediacy and Students' Affective and Cognitive Learning," *Communication Education 50* (2001): 327–342; D. K. Baringer and J. C. McCroskey, "Immediacy in the Classroom: Student Immediacy," *Communication Education 49* (2000): 178–186; J. W. Neuliep, "A Comparison of Teacher Immediacy in African-American and Euro-American College Classrooms," *Communication Education 44* (1995): 267–277; J. F. Andersen, "Teacher Immediacy as a Predictor of Teaching Effectiveness." In *Communication Yearbook 3,* edited by D. Nimmo (New Brunswick, NJ: Transaction Books, 1979), 543–559.

63. Argyle, *Bodily Communication.*

64. Andersen, *Nonverbal Communication.*

65. Mehrabian, *Nonverbal Communication.*

Chapter 5 Notes

1. H. van Bommel, *Hospice Care Handbook,* 2002 <http://www.legacies.ca/Hospice%20Handbook_3.htm#Verbal%20Communication>.

2. J. Brownell, "Perceptions of Effective Listeners: A Management Study," *The Journal of Business Communication* (Fall, 1990): 401–415; D. A. Romig, *Side by Side Leadership* (Austin, TX: Bard, 2001).

3. Adapted from the International Listening Association's definition of listening, which may be found on their Web site <http://www.listen. org>.

4. O. E. Rankis, "The Effects of Message Structure, Sexual Gender, and Verbal Organizing Ability upon Learning Message Information," doctoral dissertation, Ohio University, 1981.

5. Rankis, "The Effects of Message Structure, Sexual Gender, and Verbal Organizing Ability upon Learning Message Information"; C. H. Weaver, *Human Listening: Process and Behavior* (New York: The Bobbs-Merrill Company, 1972); R. D. Halley, "Distractibility of Males and Females in Competing Aural Message Situations: A Research Note," *Human Communication Research 2* (1975): 79–82. Our discussion of gender-based differences and listening is also based on a discussion by S. A. Beebe and J. T. Masterson, *Family Talk: Interpersonal Communication in the Family* (New York: Random House, 1986).

6. M. Booth-Butterfield, "She Hears . . . He Hears: What They Hear and Why," *Personnel Journal 44* (1984): 36–42.

7. D. K. Ivy, and P. Backlund, *Genderspeak: Personal Effectiveness in Gender Communication* 3e (New York: McGraw-Hill, 2004).

8. W. Winter, A. J. Ferreira, and N. Bowers, "Decision-Making in Married and Unrelated Couples," *Family Process 12* (1973): 83–94.

9. R. Montgomery, *Listening Made Easy* (New York: Amacon, 1981). Also see: O. Hargie, C. Sanders, and D. Dickson, *Social Skills in Interpersonal Communication* (London: Routledge, 1994); O. Hargie, ed., *The Handbook of Communication Skills* (London: Routledge, 1997).

10. R. G. Owens, "Handling Strong Emotions." In *The Handbook of Communication Skills,* edited by O. Hargie (London: Croom Helm/New York University Press, 1986).

11. D. Goleman, *Emotional Intelligence: Why It Can Matter More Than IQ* (New York: Bantam Books, 1995). Also see: D. Goleman, "Emotional Intelligence: Issues in Paradigms Building." In *The Emotionally Intelligent Workplace,* edited by C. Cherniss and D. Goleman (San Francisco: Jossey Bass, 2001), 13.

12. J. L. Gonzalez-Balado, ed., *Mother Teresa: In My Own Words* (New York: Gramercy Books, 1997).

13. R. G. Nichols, "Factors in Listening Comprehension," *Speech Monographs 15* (1948): 154–163; G. M. Goldhaber and C. H. Weaver, "Listener Comprehension of Compressed Speech when the Difficulty, Rate of Presentation, and Sex of the Listener Are Varied," *Speech Monographs 35* (1968): 20–25.

14. M. Fitch-Hauser, D. A. Barker, and A. Hughes, "Receiver Apprehension and Listening Comprehension: A Linear or Curvilinear Relationship?" *Southern Communication Journal* (1988): 62–71.

15. Fitch-Hauser et al., "Receiver Apprehension and Listening Comprehension."

16. K. Watson, L. Barker, and J. Weaver, "The Listening Styles Profile (LPP16): Development and Validation of an Instrument

to Assess Four Listening Styles," *Journal of the International Listening Association* (1995). Research cited on *20/20* ABC Television broadcast September 1998.

17. M.V. Redmond, "The Functions of Empathy (Decentering) in Human Relations," *Human Relations 42* (1993): 593–606.

18. A. Mehrabrian, *Nonverbal Communication* (Chicago; Aldine Atherton, 1970). A. Mehrabian, *Silent Messages* (Belmont: Wadsworth, 1981). Also see: D. Lapakko, "Three Cheers for Language: A Closer Examination of a Widely Cited Study of Nonverbal Communication," *Communication Education 46* (1997): 63–67.

19. M. Argyle and M. Cook, *Gaze and Mutual Gaze* (Cambridge, MA: Cambridge University Press, 1976).

20. Hargie, Sanders, and Dickson, *Social Skills in Interpersonal Communication*; Hargie, *The Handbook of Communication Skills*.

21. See R. G. Nichols and L. A. Stevens, "Listening to People," *Harvard Business Review 35* (September–October, 1957): 85–92.

22. K. K. Halone and L. L. Pecchioni, "Relational Listening. A Grounded Theoretical Model," *Communication Reports 14* (2001): 59–71.

23. J. B. Weaver and M. B. Kirtley, "Listening Styles and Empathy," *The Southern Communication Journal 60* (1995): 131–140.

24. Goleman, "Emotional Intelligence."

25. Goleman, "Emotional Intelligence."

26. H. J. M. Nouwen, "Listening as Spiritual Hospitality." In *Bread for the Journey* (New York: HarperCollins, 1997).

27. J. C. McCroskey and M. J. Beatty, "The Communibiological Perspective: Implications for Communication in Instruction," *Communication Education 49* (2000): 1–6; M. J. Beatty and J. C. McCroskey, "Theory, Scientific Evidence and the Communibiological Paradigm: Reflections on Misguided Criticism," *Communication Education 49* (2001): 36–44.

28. For a review of information about listening styles see: Watson, Barker, and Weaver, "The Listening Styles Profile (LPP16): Development and Validation of an Instrument to Assess Four Listening Styles"; Weaver and Kirtley, "Listening Styles and Empathy"; K. W. Watson, L. Barker, and J. Weaver, *The Listener Style Inventory* (New Orleans: Spectra, Inc., 1995).

29. Also see: Goleman, "Emotional Intelligence."

30. C. Y. Cheng, "Chinese Philosophy and Contemporary Communication Theory." In *Communication Theory: Eastern and Western Perspectives,* edited by D. L. Kincaid (New York, 1987).

31. T. S. Lebra, *Japanese Patterns of Behavior* (Honolulu: University Press of Hawaii, 1976).

32. A. Yugi, (trans. N. Chung), *Ilbon-in ye usik koo-jo (Japanese Thought Patterns)* (Seoul: Baik Yang Publishing Co. [in Korean], 1984).

33. "Personality Typing," *Wired* (July, 1999): 71.

34. "Personality Typing."

35. Hargie, Sanders, and Dickson, *Social Skills in Interpersonal Communication*; R. Boulton, *People Skills* (New York: 1981). We also acknowledge others who have presented excellent applications of listening and responding skills in interpersonal and group contexts: D. A. Romig and L. J. Romig, *Structured Teamwork* (D Guide) (Austin, TX: Performance Resources, 1990); S. Deep and L. Sussman, *Smart Moves* (Reading, MA: Addison-Wesley, 1990); P. R. Scholtes, *The Team Handbook* (Madison, WI: Joiner Associates, 1988); Hargie, Sanders, and Dickson, *Social Skills in Interpersonal Communication*; Hargie, *The Handbook of Communication Skills*.

36. L. B. Comvber and T. Drollinger, "Active Empathic Listening and Selling Success: A Conceptual Framework," *Journal of Personal Selling & Sales Management 19* (1999): 15–29; S. B. Castleberry, C. D. Shepherd, and R. Ridnour, "Effective Interpersonal Listening in the Personal Selling Environment: Conceptualization, Measurement, and Nonmological Validity," *Journal of Marketing Theory and Practice* (Winter, 1999): 30–38.

Chapter 6 Notes

1. Adapted from *Information Please Almanac* (Boston: Houghton Mifflin, 1990) and *World Almanac and Book of Facts* (New York: World Almanac, 1991), as cited by Lustig and Koester, *Intercultural Competence*, 11.

2. A. G. Smith, ed., *Communication and Culture* (New York: Holt, Rinehart & Winston, 1966).

3. E. T. Hall, *Beyond Culture* (Garden City, NY: Doubleday, 1976).

4. G. Hofstede, *Culture's Consequences: International Differences in Work-Related Values* (Beverly Hills: Sage 1980); G. Hofstede, *Cultures and Organizations: Software of the Mind* (London: McGraw-Hill, 1991).

5. For an excellent discussion of world view and the implications for intercultural communication, see: C. H. Dodd, *Dynamics of Intercultural Communication* (New York: McGraw Hill, 1998).

6. Hall, *Beyond Culture.*

7. L. A. Samovar, R. E. Porter, and L. A. Stefani, *Communication between Cultures* (Belmont, CA: Wadsworth, 1998).

8. Hofstede, *Culture's Consequences*; *Cultures and Organizations.* For an excellent summary of Geert Hofstede's cultural values, see: Lustig and Koester, *Intercultural Competence*, 111–125.

9. G. Hofstede, "Cultural Dimensions in Management and Planning," *Asia Pacific Journal of Management* (January, 1984): 81–98; Hofstede, *Cultures and Organizations.*

10. Hofstede, *Culture's Consequences*; Hofstede, *Cultures and Organizations.*

11. Hofstede, *Culture's Consequences*; Hofstede, *Cultures and Organizations.*

12. Hofstede, *Culture's Consequences*; Hofstede, *Cultures and Organizations.*

13. W. B. Gudykunst, *Bridging Differences: Effective Intergroup Communication* (Newbury Park, CA: Sage, 1998).

14. Gudykunst, *Bridging Differences.*

15. Statistics Canada <http://www.statcan.ca/english/Pgdb/labor05.htm>.

16. E. E. Maccoby, "Gender and Relationships: A Developmental Account," *American Psychologist 45* (1990): 513–520.

17. J. Gray, *Men Are from Mars, Women Are from Venus* (New York: Harper Collins, 1992).

18. D. K. Ivy and P. Backlund, *GenderSpeak: Personal Effectiveness in Gender Communication* 3e. (New York: McGraw Hill, 2004); D. J. Canary and T. R. Emmers-Sommer, *Sex and Gender Differences in Personal Relationships* (New York, Guilford, 1997).

19. D. Tannen, *You Just Don't Understand* (New York: William Morrow, 1990).

20. T. Parsons and R. F. Bales, *Family, Socialization, and Interaction Processes* (New York: Free Press of Glencoe, 1955). Also see: D. Bakan, *The Duality of Human Existence* (Chicago: McNally, 1966).

21. A. C. Selbe, *Are You from Another Planet or What?* Workshop presented at Joint Service Family Readiness Matters Conference, Phoenix, AZ, July 1999.

22. R. B. Rubin, E. M. Perse, and C. A. Barbato, "Conceptualization and Measurement of Interpersonal Communication Motives," *Human Communication Research 14* (1988): 602–628; D. Tannen, *That's Not What I Meant!* (London: Dent, 1986).

23. E. Comack, *Women in Trouble* (Halifax: Fernwood Publishing, 1996).

24. D. G. Dutton, *The Domestic Assault of Women: Psychological and Criminal Justice Perspectives* (Vancouver: UBC Press, 1995).

25. C. Kluckhohn and S. Murry, 1953, as quoted by J. S. Caputo, H. C. Hazel, and C. McMahon, *Interpersonal Communication* (Boston: Allyn & Bacon, 1994), 304.

26. S. Kamekar, M. B. Kolsawalla, and T. Mazareth, "Occupational Prestige as a Function of Occupant's Gender," *Journal of Applied Social Psychology 19* (1988): 681–688.

27. J. T. Wood, *Communication Mosaics: A New Introduction to the Field of Communication* (Belmont, CA: Wadsworth, 1997), 207; C. C. Inman, "Men's Friendships: Closeness in the Doing." In *Gendered Relationships,* edited by J. T. Wood (Mountain View, CA: Mayfield, 1996), 95–110.

28. Ivy and Backlund, *GenderSpeak.*

29. W. B. Gudykunst and Y. Kim, *Communicating with Strangers* (New York: Random House, 1984); Gudykunst, *Bridging Differences.*

30. S. DeTurk, "Intercultural Empathy: Myth, Competency, or Possibility for Alliance Building?" *Communication Education 50* (2001): 374–384.

31. M. V. Redmond, "The Functions of Empathy (Decentering) in Human Relations," *Human Relations 42* (1993): 593–606. Also see: M. V. Redmond, "A Multidimensional Theory and Measure of Social Decentering," *Journal of Research in Personality* (1995); for an excellent discussion of the role of emotions in establishing empathy, see: D. Goleman, *Emotional Intelligence* (New York: Bantam, 1995).

32. See: B. J. Broome, "Building Shared Meaning: Implications of a Relational Approach to Empathy for Teaching Intercultural Communication," *Communication Education 40* (1991): 235–249. This discussion is based on our treatment of social decentring and empathy from: S. A. Beebe, S. J. Beebe, and M. V. Redmond, *Interpersonal Communication: Relating to Others* 3e (Boston: Allyn & Bacon, 2002).

33. For an excellent discussion of empathy related to intercultural communication, see: D. W. Augsburger, *Pastoral Counseling Across Cultures* (Philadelphia: The Westminister Press, 1986), 28–30.

34. H. J. M. Nouwen, *Bread for the Journey* (New York: HarperCollins, 1997).

35. L. J. Carrell, "Diversity in the Communication Curriculum: Impact on Student Empathy," *Communication Education 46* (1997): 234–244.

Chapter 7 Notes

1. K. M. Galvin and C. Wilkinson, "The Communication Process: Impersonal and Interpersonal." In *Making Connections: Readings in Relational Communication*, edited by K. M. Galvin and P. Cooper (Los Angeles, CA: Roxbury, 1996): 4–10.

2. E. Berscheid, "Interpersonal Attraction." In *The Handbook of Social Psychology*, edited by G. Lindzey and E. Aronson (New York: Random House, 1985), 413–484, as reported in J. A. Simpson and B. A. Harris, "Interpersonal Attraction." In *Perspectives on Close Relationships*, edited by A. L. Weber and J. H. Harvey (Boston: Allyn & Bacon, 1994), 45–66.

3. W. Stoebe, "Self-Esteem and Interpersonal Attraction." In *Theory and Practice in Interpersonal Attraction*, edited by S. Duck (London: Academic Press, 1977).

4. D. Garner, "Harmless Crushes Can Be Uplifting," *Corpus Christi Caller Times* (December 3, 1996): H1, H4.

5. See: D. T. Kenrick, S. L. Neuberg, and R. B. Cialdini, *Social Psychology: Unraveling the Mystery* 2e (Boston: Allyn & Bacon, 2002); L. K. Guerrero, P. A. Andersen, and W. A. Afifi, *Close Encounters: Communicating in Relationships* (Mountain View, CA: Mayfield, 2001); E. Berscheid and H. T. Reis, "Attraction and Close Relationships." In *The Handbook of Social Psychology* 4e, Vol. 2, edited by D. T. Gilbert, S. T. Fiske, and G. Lindzey (New York: McGraw-Hill, 1998), 193–281; V. Sharma and T. Kaur, "Interpersonal Attraction in Relation to Similarity and Help," *Psychological Studies 39* (1995): 84–87; T. Shaikh and S. Kanakar, "Attitudinal Similarity and Affiliation Need as Determinants of Interpersonal Attraction," *Journal of Social Psychology 134* (1994): 257–259; S. S. Brehm, *Intimate Relationships* 3e (New York: McGraw-Hill, 2001); M. Sunnafrank, "Interpersonal Attraction and Attitude Similarity: A Communication-Based Assessment." In *Communication Yearbook 14*, edited by J. A. Andersen (Newbury Park, CA: Sage, 1991), 451–483; J. E. Lydon, D. W. Jamieson, and M. Zanna, "Interpersonal Similarity and the Social and Intellectual Dimensions of First Impressions," *Social Cognition 6* (1988): 269–286.

6. B. R. Burleson, A. W. Kunkel, and J. D. Birch, "Thoughts about Talk in Romantic Relationships: Similarity Makes for Attraction (and Happiness, Too)," *Communication Quarterly 42* (1994): 259–273; A. E. Varnadore, S. C. Howe, and S. Brownlow, "Why Do I Like You? Students' Understanding of the Impact of the Factors That Contribute to Liking." Paper presented at the meeting of the Southeastern Psychological Association, March 1994.

7. Sunnafrank, "Interpersonal Attraction and Attitude Similarity."

8. J. H. Harvey and A. L. Weber, *Odyssey of the Heart: Close Relationships in the 21st Century* 2e (Mahwah, NJ: Lawrence Erlbaum, 2002); Kenrick et al., *Social Psychology*; M. L. Knapp and J. A. Hall, *Nonverbal Communication in Human Interaction* 5e (Belmont, CA: Wadsworth, 2002); M. Crawford and R. Unger, *Women and Gender: A Feminist Psychology* 3e (New York: McGraw-Hill, 2000).

9. Guerrero, *Close Encounters*, 59.

10. A. Feingold, "Gender Differences in Effects of Physical Attractiveness on Romantic Attraction: A Comparison across Five Research Paradigms," *Journal of Personality and Social Psychology 59* (1990): 981–993.

11. See: A. Botta, "Television Images and Adolescent Girls' Body Image Disturbance," *Journal of Communication 49* (1999): 22–37; M. Wiederman and S. R. Hurst, "Body Size, Physical Attractiveness, and Body Image among Young Adult Women: Relationships to Sexual Experience and Sexual Esteem," *Journal of Sex Research 35* (1998): 272–281; L. Lazier and A. Gagnard Kendrick, "Women in Advertisements: Sizing Up the Images, Roles, and Functions." In *Women in Mass Communication* 2e, edited by P. Creedon (Newbury Park, CA: Sage, 1993), 199–219; A. Gagnard, "From Feast to Famine: Depiction of Ideal Body Type in Magazine Advertising: 1950–1984." In *Proceedings of the Nineteen Eighty-Six Conference of the American Academy of Advertising,* edited by E. F. Larkin

(Charleston, SC: American Academy of Advertising, 1986), R46–R50; B. Silverstein, L. Perdue, B. Peterson, and E. Kelly, "The Role of Mass Media in Promoting a Thin Standard of Bodily Attractiveness for Women," *Sex Roles 14* (1986): 519–532.

12. S. W. Duck, *Personal Relationships and Personal Constructs: A Study of Friendship Formation* (New York: John Wiley & Sons, 1973).

13. E. H. Walster, V. Aronson, D. Abrahams, and L. Rottmann, "Importance of Physical Attractiveness in Dating Behavior," *Journal of Personality and Social Psychology 4* (1966): 508–516; V. B. Hinsz, "Facial Resemblance in Engaged and Married Couples," *Journal of Social and Personal Relationships 6* (1989): 223–229.

14. Brehm, *Intimate Relationships*.

15. Guerrero, *Close Encounters*; Kenrick, *Social Psychology*; Knapp, *Nonverbal Communication in Human Interaction*.

16. K. R. Van Horn, A. Arnone, K. Nesbitt, L. Desilets, T. Sears, M. Giffin, and R. Brudi, "Physical Distance and Interpersonal Characteristics in College Students' Romantic Relationships," *Personal Relationships 4* (1997): 15–24; M. E. Rohlfing, "'Doesn't Anybody Stay in One Place Anymore?' An Exploration of the Understudied Phenomenon of Long-Distance Relationships." In *Understudied Relationships: Off the Beaten Track*, edited by J. T. Wood and S. Duck (Thousand Oaks, CA: Sage, 1995), 173–196; L. Stafford and J. R. Reske, "Idealization and Communication in Long-Distance Premarital Relationships," *Family Relations 39* (1990): 274–279; T. Stephen, "Communication and Interdependence in Geographically Separated Relationships," *Human Communication Research 13* (1986): 191–210.

17. Guerrero, *Close Encounters*; Brehm, *Intimate Relationships*.

18. W. Schutz, *FIRO: A Three-Dimensional Theory of Interpersonal Behavior* (New York: Holt, Rinehart, and Winston, 1960).

19. A. Mehrabian, *Nonverbal Communication* (Chicago: Aldine-Atherton, 1972).

20. J. A. Daly, E. Hogg, D. Sacks, M. Smith, and L. Zimring, "Sex and Relationship Affect Social Self-Grooming." In *The Nonverbal Communication Reader: Classic and Contemporary Readings* 2e, edited by L. K. Guerrero, J. DeVito, and M. L. Hecht (Prospect Heights, IL: Waveland, 1999), 56–61.

21. A. Cooper and L. Sportolari, "Romance in Cyberspace: Understanding Online Attraction," *Journal of Sex Education & Therapy 22* (1997): 7–14.

22. C. R. Berger and R. J. Calabrese, "Some Explorations in Initial Interaction and Beyond: Toward a Developmental Theory of Interpersonal Communication," *Human Communication Research 1* (1975): 99–112; C. R. Berger and J. J. Bradac, *Language and Social Knowledge: Uncertainty in Interpersonal Relations* (Baltimore: Edward Arnold, 1982).

23. C. L. Kleinke, F. B. Meeker, and R. A. Staneski, "Preference for Opening Lines: Comparing Ratings by Men and Women," *Sex Roles 15* (1986): 585–600.

24. E. Weber, *How to Pick Up Girls!* (New York: Bantam Books, 1970).

25. For research on sex roles and interaction, see: A. E. Lindsey and W. R. Zakahi, "Perceptions of Men and Women Departing from Conversational Sex Role Stereotypes during Initial Interaction." In *Sex Differences and Similarities in Communication*, edited by D. J. Canary and K. Dindia (Mahwah, NJ: Lawrence Erlbaum, 1998), 393–412; A. E. Lindsey and W. R. Zakahi, "Women Who Tell and Men Who Ask: Perceptions of Men and Women Departing from Gender Stereotypes during Initial Interaction," *Sex Roles 34* (1996): 767–786; L. A. McCloskey, "Gender and Conversation: Mixing and Matching Styles." In *Current Conceptions of Sex Roles and Sex Typing: Theory and Research*, edited by D. B. Carter (New York: Praeger, 1987), 139–153; J. Coates, *Women, Men, and Language* 2e (New York: Longman, 1993); V. Derlega, B. Winstead, P. Wong, and S. Hunter, "Gender Effects in an Initial Encounter: A Case Where Men Exceeded Women in Disclosure," *Journal of Social and Personal Relationships 2* (1985): 25–44; R. Lakoff, *Language and Woman's Place* (New York: Harper & Row, 1975); P. M. Fishman, "Interaction: The Work Women Do," *Social Problems 25* (1978): 397–406; J. D. Davis, "When Boy Meets Girl: Sex Roles and the Negotiation of Intimacy in an Acquaintance Exercise," *Journal of Personality and Social Psychology 36* (1978): 684–692.

26. A. L. Vangelisti, M. L. Knapp, and J. A. Daly, "Conversational Narcissism," *Communication Monographs 57* (1990): 251–274.

27. C. Derber, *The Pursuit of Attention: Power and Ego in Everyday Life* (New York: Oxford University Press, 2000).

28. J. Holmes, "Complimenting—A Positive Politeness Strategy." In *Language and Gender: A Reader*, edited by J. Coates (Malden, MA: Blackwell, 1998), 100–120.

29. S. Jourard, *The Transparent Self* (Princeton, NJ: Van Nostrand, 1971); J. C. Pearson and B. H. Spitzberg, *Interpersonal Communication: Concepts, Components, and Contexts* 2e (New York: McGraw-Hill, 1990).

30. Harvey, *Odyssey of the Heart*, 105–106.

31. S. Petronio, "The Boundaries of Privacy: Praxis of Everyday Life." In *Balancing Secrets of Private Disclosure*, edited by S. Petronio (Mahwah, NJ: Lawrence Erlbaum, 2000), 37–49; L. B. Rosenfeld, "Overview of the Ways Privacy, Secrecy, and Disclosure Are Balanced in Today's Society." In Petronio, *Balancing Secrets of Private Disclosure*, 3–17; C. A. Wilkinson, "Expressing Affection: A Vocabulary of Loving Messages." In Galvin, *Making Connections*, 150–157; Guerrero, *Close Encounters*.

32. C. A. Vanlear, Jr., "The Formation of Social Relationships: A Longitudinal Study of Social Penetration," *Human Communication Research 13* (1987): 299–322.

33. Harvey, *Odyssey of the Heart*.

34. J. Fine, "Intimacy," *O: The Oprah Winfrey Magazine* (October, 2001), 225.

35. For research on the role of self-disclosure in relationship development, see: J. H. Berg, "Responsiveness and Self-Disclosure." In *Self-Disclosure: Theory, Research, and Therapy*, edited by V. Derlega and J. Berg (New York: Plenum, 1987); J. Honeycutt, "A Model of Marital Functioning Based on an Attraction Paradigm and Social-Penetration Dimensions," *Journal of Marriage and the Family 48* (1986): 651–667; G. J. Chelune, E. Waring, B. Yosk, F. Sultan, and J. Ogden, "Self-Disclosure and Its Relationship to Marital Intimacy," *Journal of Clinical Psychology 40* (1984): 216–219; M. Knapp, *Interpersonal Communication and Human Relationships* 2e (Boston: Allyn & Bacon, 1992); C. R. Berger and J. J. Bradac, *Language and Social Knowledge: Uncertainty in Interpersonal Relations* (London: Edward Arnold, 1982); S. S. Hendrick, "Self-Disclosure and Marital Satisfaction," *Journal of Personality and Social Psychology 40* (1981): 1150–1159; G. J. Chelune and associates, *Self-Disclosure: Origins, Patterns, and Implications of Openness in Interpersonal Relationships* (San Francisco: Jossey-Bass, 1979); G. R. Miller

and M. Steinberg, *Between People: A New Analysis of Interpersonal Communication* (Chicago: Science Research Associates, 1975); G. Levinger and D. Senn, "Disclosure of Feelings in Marriage," *Merrill-Palmer Quarterly 13* (1967): 237–249.

36. D. Borisoff, "The Effect of Gender on Establishing and Maintaining Intimate Relationships." In *Women and Men Communicating: Challenges and Changes* 2e, edited by L. P. Arliss and D. J. Borisoff (Prospect Heights, IL: Waveland, 2001), 15–31; K. Galvin and C. Bylund, "First Marriage Families: Gender and Communication." In Arliss, *Women and Men Communicating,* 132–148; H. T. Reis, "Gender Differences in Intimacy and Related Behaviors: Context and Process." In Canary, *Sex Differences and Similarities in Communication,* 203–231; J. T. Wood and C. C. Inman, "In a Different Mode: Masculine Styles of Communicating Closeness," *Journal of Applied Communication Research 21* (1993): 279–295; K. Dindia and M. Allen, "Sex Differences in Self-Disclosure: A Meta-Analysis," *Psychological Bulletin 112* (1992): 106–124.

37. D. J. Canary and T. M. Emmers-Sommer, with S. Faulkner, *Sex and Gender Differences in Personal Relationships* (New York: Guilford, 1997).

38. E. L. Paul and K. M. White, "The Development of Intimate Relationships in Late Adolescence," *Adolescence 25* (1990): 375–400; J. M. Reisman, "Intimacy in Same-Sex Friendships," *Sex Roles 23* (1990): 65–82; S. Swain, "Covert Intimacy in Men's Friendships: Closeness in Men's Friendships." In *Gender in Intimate Relationships: A Microstructural Approach* (Belmont, CA: Wadsworth, 1989), 71–86; R. J. Barth and B. N. Kinder, "A Theoretical Analysis of Sex Differences in Same-Sex Friendships," *Sex Roles 19* (1988): 349–363; B. A. Winstead, "Sex Differences in Same-Sex Friendships." In *Friendship and Social Interaction,* edited by V. J. Derlega and B. A. Winstead (New York: Springer-Verlag, 1986), 81–99.

39. W. K. Rawlins, "Times, Places, and Social Spaces for Cross-Sex Friendship." In Arliss, *Women and Men Communicating,* 93–114.

40. Wood, "In a Different Mode."

41. I. Altman and D. Taylor, *Social Penetration: The Development of Relationships* (New York: Holt, Rinehart and Winston, 1973); Brehm, *Intimate Relationships;* B. M. Montgomery, "Communication in Close Relationships." In Weber, *Perspectives on Close Relationships,* 67–87.

42. J. Luft, *Group Process: An Introduction to Group Dynamics* (Palo Alto, CA: Mayfield, 1970).

43. P. Mehta and M. S. Clark, "Toward Understanding Emotions in Intimate Relationships." In Weber, *Perspectives on Close Relationships,* 88–109.

44. A. Hochschild, "The Economy of Gratitude." In *The Sociology of Emotions: Original Essays and Research Papers,* edited by D. Franks and E. D. McCarthy (Greenwich, CT: JAI Press, 1989), 95–113.

45. E. R. McDaniel, "Nonverbal Communication: A Reflection of Cultural Themes." In *Intercultural Communication: A Reader* 8e, edited by L. A. Samovar and R. E. Porter (Belmont, CA: Wadsworth, 1997), 256–265.

46. P. M. Cole, "Children's Spontaneous Control of Facial Expression," *Child Development 57* (1986): 1309–1321.

47. L. K. Guerrero and R. L. Reiter, "Expressing Emotion: Sex Differences in Social Skills and Communicative Responses to Anger, Sadness, and Jealousy." In Canary, *Sex Differences and Similarities in Communication,* 321–350; Canary, *Sex and Gender Differences in Personal Relationships.*

48. Jourard, *The Transparent Self.*

49. B. B. Burleson, "Introduction to the Special Issue: Psychological Mediators of Sex Differences in Emotional Support," *Communication Reports 15* (2002): 1–4; W. E. Snell, R. S. Miller, and S. S. Belk, "Development of the Emotional Self-Disclosure Scale," *Sex Roles 18* (1988): 59–73.

50. Galvin, "First Marriage Families"; F. Dickson-Markman, "How Important is Self-Disclosure in Marriage?" *Communication Research Reports 1* (1984): 7–14.

51. A. L. Vangelisti, "Communication Problems in Committed Relationships: An Attributional Analysis." In *Attributions, Accounts, and Close Relationships,* edited by J. H. Harvey, T. L. Orbuch, and A. L. Weber (New York: Springer-Verlag, 1992), 144–164.

Chapter 8 Notes

1. W. Rawlins, *Friendship Matters: Communication, Dialectics, and the Life Course* (Hawthorne, NY: Aldine de Gruyter, 1992); W. J. Dickens and D. Perlman, "Friendship over the Life-Cycle." In *Personal Relationships 2: Developing Personal Relationships,* edited by S. W. Duck and R. Gilmour (London: Academic Press, 1981).

2. R. Blieszner, "Close Relationships over Time," as reported in J. A. Simpson and B. A. Harris, "Interpersonal Attraction." In *Perspectives on Close Relationships,* edited by A. L. Weber and J. H. Harvey (Boston: Allyn & Bacon, 1994), 1–18.

3. J. Yager, *Friendshifts: The Power of Friendship and How It Shapes Our Lives* (Stamford, CT: Hannacrois Creek Books, 1999); W. Rawlins, "Being There for Friends." In *Making Connections: Readings in Relational Communication,* edited by K. M. Galvin and P. Cooper (Los Angeles: Roxbury, 1996), 258–260; R. Blieszner and R. Adams, *Adult Friendships* (Newbury Park, CA: Sage, 1992).

4. P. M. Sias and D. J. Cahill, "From Coworkers to Friends: The Development of Peer Friendships in the Workplace," *Western Journal of Communication 62* (1998): 273–299; G. A. Fine, "Friendships in the Workplace." In Galvin, *Making Connections,* 270–277.

5. M. Monsour, *Women and Men as Friends: Relationships across the Life Span in the 21st Century* (Mahwah, NJ: Lawrence Erlbaum, 2002).

6. D. Carnegie, *How to Win Friends and Influence People* (New York: Simon & Schuster, 1937).

7. K. Galvin and C. Bylund, "First Marriage Families: Gender and Communication." In *Women and Men Communicating: Challenges and Changes* 2e, edited by L. P. Arliss and D. J. Borisoff (Prospect Heights, IL: Waveland, 2001), 132–148; V. Satir, "The Rules You Live By." In Galvin, *Making Connections,* 168–174; S. S. Brehm, *Intimate Relationships* 3e (New York: McGraw-Hill, 2001).

8. Statistics Canada, 2001 Census <http://www12.statcan.ca/english/census01/products/analytic/companion/inc/method.cfm>.

9. M. M. Kern, "Fighting the Fight." In Galvin, *Making Connections,* 247–249.

10. V. Satir, *The New Peoplemaking* (Mountain View, CA: Science & Behavior Books, 1988), 4.

11. A. Heisz and S. LaRochelle-Cote, *Working Hours in Canada and the U.S.* Statistics Canada, Business & Labour Market Analysis Division.

12. National Association of Colleges and Employers, "Job Outlook 2002" (July 2002) <http://www.jobweb.com>.

13. M. S. Peterson, "Personnel Interviewers' Perceptions of the Importance and Adequacy of Applicants' Communication Skills," *Communication Education 46* (1997): 287–291; D. B. Curtis, J. L. Winsor, and R. D. Stephens, "National Preferences in Business and Communication," *Communication Education 38* (1989): 6–14.

14. H. Mintzberg, "The Manager's Job: Folklore and Fact," *Harvard Business Review 53* (1975): 26–41.

15. J. H. Harvey and A. L. Weber, *Odyssey of the Heart: Close Relationships in the 21st Century* 2e (Mahwah, NJ: Lawrence Erlbaum, 2002); L. K. Guerrero, P. A. Andersen, and W. A. Afifi, *Close Encounters: Communicating in Relationships* (Mountain View, CA: Mayfield, 2001); M. L. Knapp and A. Vangelisti, "Relationship Stages: A Communication Perspective." In Galvin, *Making Connections,* 134–141.

16. S. W. Duck, "A Topography of Relationship Disengagement and Dissolution." In *Personal Relationships 4: Dissolving Relationships,* edited by S. W. Duck (New York: Academic Press, 1982); Guerrero, *Close Encounters.*

17. M. L. Knapp, *Social Intercourse: From Greeting to Goodbye* (Boston: Allyn & Bacon, 1978).

18. Duck, "A Topography of Relationship Disengagement and Dissolution."

19. For research on relationship termination, see: L. A. Baxter, "Accomplishing Relational Disengagement." In *Understanding Personal Relationships: An Interdisciplinary Approach,* edited by S. Duck and D. Perlman (London: Sage, 1985), 243–265; L. A. Baxter, "Trajectories of Relationship Disengagement," *Journal of Social and Personal Relationships 1* (1984): 29–48; L. A. Baxter, "Strategies for Ending Relationships: Two Studies," *Western Journal of Speech Communication 46* (1982): 223–241; S. Metts, "Face and Facework: Implications for the Study of Personal Relationships." In *Handbook of Personal Relationships: Theory, Research, and Interventions,* edited by S. Duck (Chichester, UK: Wiley, 1997), 373–390; G. M. Phillips and J. T. Wood, "The Deterioration Stages in Human Relationships." In Galvin, *Making Connections,* 213–218; T. L. Morton, J. F. Alexander, and I. Altman," Communication and Relationships Definition." In *Explorations in Interpersonal Communication,* edited by G. R. Miller (Newbury Park, CA: Sage, 1976), 105–125.

20. J. W. Keltner, *Mediation: Toward a Civilized System of Dispute Resolution* (Annandale, VA: Speech Communication Association, 1987).

21. P. C. McGraw, "Couples Combat: The Great American Pastime," *O: The Oprah Winfrey Magazine* (August, 2002): 42–43.

22. S. Ting Toomey and L. Chung, *Understanding Intercultural Communication* (Los Angeles: Roxbury, 2003); S. Ting-Toomey and J. G. Oetzel, *Managing Intercultural Conflict Effectively* 2e (Newbury Park, CA: Sage, 2001); S. Ting-Toomey, "Managing Intercultural Conflicts Effectively." In *Intercultural Communication: A Reader* 8e, edited by L. A. Samovar and R. E. Porter (Belmont, CA: Wadsworth, 1997), 392–404.

23. M. Deutsch, *The Resolution of Conflict* (New Haven: Yale University Press, 1973).

24. W. W. Wilmot and J. L. Hocker, *Interpersonal Conflict* 6e (New York: McGraw-Hill, 2001).

25. C. R. Berger, "Social Power and Interpersonal Communication." In Miller, *Explorations in Interpersonal Communication.*

26. Brehm, *Intimate Relationships.*

27. P. J. Kalbfleisch and M. J. Cody, eds., *Gender, Power, and Communication in Human Relationships* (Hillsdale, NJ: Lawrence Erlbaum, 1995); L. P. Arliss, "When Myths Endure and Realities Change: Communication in Romantic Relationships." In Arliss, *Women and Men Communicating,* 115–131; F. E. Millar and L. E. Rogers, "Relational Dimensions of Interpersonal Dynamics." In *Interpersonal Processes: New Directions in Communication Research,* edited by M. E. Roloff and G. R. Miller (Newbury Park, CA: Sage, 1987), 117–139.

28. D. A. Infante and A. S. Rancer, "Argumentativeness and Verbal Aggressiveness: A Review of Recent Theory and Research," *Communication Yearbook 19* (1995): 319–351; D. A. Infante, B. L. Riddle, C. L. Horvath, and S. A. Tumlin, "Verbal Aggressiveness: Messages and Reasons," *Communication Quarterly 40* (1992): 116–126; D. A. Infante, K. C. Hartley, M. M. Martin, M. A. Higgins, S. D. Bruning, and G. Hur, "Initiating and Reciprocating Verbal Aggression: Effects on Credibility and Credited Valid Arguments," *Communication Studies 43* (1992): 182–190; D. A. Infante, T. C. Sabourin, J. E. Rudd, and E. A. Shannon, "Verbal Aggression in Violent and Nonviolent Marital Disputes," *Communication Quarterly 38* (1990): 361–371; D. A. Infante and C. J. Wigley III, "Verbal Aggressiveness: An Interpersonal Model and Measure," *Communication Monographs 53* (1986): 61–69. For extensions of this line of research on verbal aggression, see: S. A. Myers and K. A. Rocca, "Perceived Instructor Argumentativeness and Verbal Aggressiveness in the College Classroom: Effects on Student Perceptions of Climate, Apprehension, and State Motivation," *Western Journal of Communication 65* (2001): 113–137; C. M. Anderson and M. M. Martin, "The Relationship of Argumentativeness and Verbal Aggressiveness to Cohesion, Consensus, and Satisfaction in Small Groups," *Communication Reports 12* (1999): 21–32; D. E. Ifert and L. Bearden, "The Influences of Argumentativeness and Verbal Aggression on Responses to Refused Requests," *Communication Reports 11* (1998): 145–154; J. J. Teven, M. M. Martin, and N. C. Neupauer, "Sibling Relationships: Verbally Aggressive Messages and Their Effect on Relational Satisfaction," *Communication Reports 11* (1998): 179–186.

29. Wilmot, *Interpersonal Conflict.*

30. C. M. Carey and P. A. Mongeau, "Communication and Violence in Courtship Relationships." In *Family Violence from a Communication Perspective,* edited by D. D. Cahn and S. A. Lloyd (Hillsdale, NJ: Lawrence Erlbaum, 1996), 127–150.

31. P. Yelsma, "Couples' Affective Orientations and Their Verbal Aggressiveness," *Communication Quarterly 43* (1995): 100–114.

32. LaMarsh Centre for Research <http://www.yorku.ca/lamarsh/projects/trp/trp_ww105.html>.

33. Infante, "Verbal Aggressiveness: Messages and Reasons."

34. L. N. Olson, "Exploring 'Common Couple Violence' in Heterosexual Romantic Relationships," *Western Journal of Communication 66* (2002): 104–128; T. C. Sabourin and G. H. Stamp, "Communication and the Experience of Dialectical Tensions in Family Life: An Examination of Abusive and Nonabusive Families," *Communication Monographs 62* (1995): 213–242; J. W. White and J. A. Humphrey, "Women's Aggression in Heterosexual Conflicts," *Aggressive Behavior 20* (1994): 195–202.

35. M. M. Martin, C. M. Anderson, and C. L. Horvath, "Feelings about Verbal Aggression: Justifications for Sending, and Hurt

from Receiving, Verbally Aggressive Messages," *Communication Research Reports 13* (1996): 19–26; D. Cloven and M. E. Roloff, "The Chilling Effect of Aggressive Potential on the Expression of Complaints in Intimate Relationships," *Communication Monographs 60* (1993): 199–219.

36. Satir, *The New Peoplemaking;* Wilmot, *Interpersonal Conflict.*

37. L. L. Putnam and C. E. Wilson, "Communicative Strategies in Organizational Conflicts: Reliability and Validity of a Measurement Scale." In *Communication Yearbook 6,* edited by M. Burgoon (Beverly Hills: Sage, 1982).

38. Cloven, "The Chilling Effect of Aggressive Potential on the Expression of Complaints in Intimate Relationships"; Wilmot, *Interpersonal Conflict.*

39. R. Fisher and W. Ury, *Getting to Yes: Negotiating Agreement without Giving In* (Boston: Houghton Mifflin, 1988).

40. This information is based on several excellent discussions of conflict management skills. We acknowledge: Wilmot, *Interpersonal Conflict;* O. Hargie, ed., *The Handbook of Communication Skills* (London: Routledge, 1997); O. Hargie, C. Saunders, and D. Dickson, *Social Skills in Interpersonal Communication* (London: Routledge, 1994); W. A. Donahue and R. Kolt, *Managing Interpersonal Conflict* (Newbury Park, CA: Sage, 1992); D. A. Romig and L. J. Romig, *Structured Teamwork© Guide* (Austin: Performance Resources, 1990); S. Deep and L. Sussman, *Smart Moves* (Reading, MA: Addison-Wesley, 1990); Fisher, *Getting to Yes;* M. D. Davis, E. L. Eshelman, and M. McKay, *The Relaxation and Stress Reduction Workbook* (Oakland, CA: New Harbinger, 1982); R. Boulton, *People Skills* (New York: Simon & Schuster, 1979).

41. B. M. Gayle and R. W. Preiss, "Language Intensity Plus: A Methodological Approach to Validate Emotions in Conflicts," *Communication Reports 12* (1999): 43–50; Wilmot, *Interpersonal Conflict.*

42. A. Ellis, *A New Guide to Rational Living* (North Hollywood, CA: Wilshire Books, 1977).

43. L. Costigan Lederman, "The Impact of Gender on the Self and Self-Talk." In *Women and Men Communicating: Challenges and Changes* 2e, edited by L. P. Arliss and D. J. Borisoff (Prospect Heights, IL: Waveland, 2001), 78–89; Ellis, *A New Guide to Rational Living.*

44. S. R. Covey, *The Seven Habits of Highly Effective People* (New York: Simon & Schuster, 1989), 67.

45. Fisher, *Getting to Yes.*

Chapter 9 Notes

1. R. K. Mosvick and R. B. Nelson, *We've Got to Start Meeting Like This!* (Glenview, IL: Scott, Foresman, 1987).

2. Mosvick and Nelson, *We've Got to Start Meeting Like This!*

3. S. A. Beebe and J. T. Masterson, *Communicating in Small Groups: Principles and Practices* 7e. (New York: Longman, 2003).

4. Our discussion of teams and teamwork is from Beebe and Masterson, *Communicating in Small Groups.*

5. S. B. Shimanoff, *Communication Rules: Theory and Research* (Beverly Hills: Sage, 1980).

6. F. LaFasto and C. Larson, *Teamwork* (Thousand Oaks, CA: Sage, 2001).

7. C. Santo, "Teaching the Teachers: Online Training Helps Educators Integrate Technology into the Classroom," *Family PC* (June/July, 1999): 107.

8. K. D. Benne and Paul Sheats, "Functional Roles of Group Members," *Journal of Social Issues 4* (1948): 41–49. For a good review of role development in groups, see: A. P. Hare, "Types of Roles in Small Groups: A Bit of History and a Current Perspective," *Small Group Research 25* (1994): 433–438, and A. J. Salazar, "An Analysis of the Development and Evolution of Roles in the Small Group," *Small Group Research 27* (1996): 475–503.

9. R. F. Bales, *Interaction Process Analysis* (Chicago: University of Chicago Press, 1976).

10. Shimanoff, *Communication Rules.*

11. M. Shaw, *Group Dynamics: The Psychology of Small Group Behavior* (New York: McGraw-Hill, 1981), 281.

12. J. I. Hurwitz, A. F. Zander, and B. Hymovitch, "Some Effects of Power on the Relations among Group Members." In *Group Dynamics: Research and Theory,* edited by D. Cartwright and A. Zander (New York: Harper & Row, 1953), 483–492; D. C. Barnlund and C. Harland, "Propinquity and Prestige as Determinants of Communication Networks," *Sociometry 26* (1963): 467–479; G. C. Homans, *The Human Group* (New York: Harcourt Brace and World, 1992); H. H. Kelly, "Communication in Experimentally Created Hierarchies," *Human Relations 4* (1951): 36–56.

13. M. R. Singer, *Intercultural Communication: A Perceptual Approach* (Englewood Cliffs, NJ: Prentice-Hall, 1987), 118.

14. J. R. P. French and B. H. Raven, "The Bases of Social Power." In Cartwright and Zander, *Group Dynamics,* 607–623.

15. Adapted from E. G. Bormann and N. C. Bormann, *Effective Small Group Communication* (Minneapolis: Burgess Publishing Company, 1980), 70–72.

16. B. A. Fisher, "Decision Emergence: Phases in Group Decision-Making," *Speech Monographs 37* (1970): 60.

17. M. S. Poole, "Decision Development in Small Groups III: A Multiple Sequence Model of Group Decision Development," *Communication Monographs 50* (1983): 321–341; also see: C. Pavitt and K. Kline Johnson, "Scheidel and Crowell Revisited: A Descriptive Study of Group Proposal Sequencing," *Communication Monographs 69* (2002): 19–32.

18. For a discussion of individualism and collectivism see: E. T. Hall, *Beyond Culture* (Garden City, NY: Doubleday, 1976); G. Hofstede, *Culture and Organizations: Software of the Mind* (London: McGraw-Hill, 1991); H. C. Triandis, *The Analysis of Subjective Culture* (New York: Wiley, 1972); and C. H. Hui and H. C. Triandis, "Individualism-Collectivism: A Study of Cross-Cultural Researchers," *Journal of Cross-Cultural Psychology 17* (1986): 225–248.

19. E. T. Hall and M. R. Hall, *Understanding Cultural Differences* (Yarmouth, ME: Intercultural Press, 1989).

20. See, for example, the review of literature in P. H. Andrews, "Sex and Gender Differences in Group Communication: Impact on the Facilitation Process," *Small Group Research 23* (1992): 74–94; E. I. Megargee, "Influence of Sex Roles on the Manifestation of Leadership," *Journal of Applied Psychology 53* (1969): 377–382; C. Nemeth, J. Endicott, and J. Wachtler, "From the 50's to the 70's: Women in Jury Deliberations," *Sociometry 39* (1976): 293–304; J. E. Baird and P. H. Bradley, "Styles of Management and Communication: A Comparative Study of Men and Women," *Communication Monographs 46* (1979): 101–111; B. Spillman, R. Spillman, and K. Reinking, "Leader Emergence: Dynamic Analysis of the Effects of Sex and Androgyny," *Small Group Behavior 12* (1981): 139–157; J. R.

Hoktepe and C. E. Schneier, "Sex and Gender Effects in Evaluating Emergent Leaders in Small Groups," *Sex Roles 19* (1988): 29–36. See also: E. Kushell and R. Newton, "Gender, Leadership Style, and Subordinate Satisfaction: An Experiment," *Sex Roles 14* (1986): 203–209; V. P. Hans and N. Eisenberg, "The Effects of Sex Role Attitudes and Group Composition on Men and Women in Groups," *Sex Roles 12* (1985): 477–490; J. A. Kolb, "Are We Still Stereotyping Leadership? A Look at Gender and Other Predictors of Leader Emergence," *Small Group Research 28* (1997): 370–393.

21. K. W. Hawkins, "Effects of Gender and Communication Content on Leadership Emergence in Small, Task-Oriented Groups," *Small Group Research 26* (1995): 234–249.

22. Hall, *Beyond Culture*.

23. E. T. Hall, *The Silent Language* (New York: Anchor, 1973). Analysis and description of Edward Hall's theory of personal space, http://www.e-lisa.at/journale/englisch/secure/aktuell/thema/2003_2/part6.asp.

24. C. H. Dodd, *Dynamics of Intercultural Communication* (Dubuque, IA: Wm. C. Brown, 1991).

25. Hall, *The Silent Language*.

26. Hall, *The Silent Language*.

27. Beebe and Masterson, *Communication in Small Groups*.

28. Beebe and Masterson, *Communication in Small Groups*.

Chapter 10 Notes

1. See: N. R. F. Maier, "Assets and Liabilities in Group Problem Solving: The Need for an Integrative Function," *Psychological Review 74* (1967): 239–249; M. Argyle, *Cooperation: The Basis of Sociability* (London: Routledge, 1991); H. A. M. Wilke and R. W. Meertens, *Group Performance* (London: Routledge, 1994).

2. Maier, "Assets and Liabilities in Group Problem Solving"; Argyle, *Cooperation*; Wilke and Meertens, *Group Performance*.

3. R. Y. Hirokawa, "Discussion Procedures and Decision-Making Performance: A Test of a Functional Perspective," *Human Communication Research 12* (1985): 203–224.

4. R. Y. Hirokawa, "Why Informed Groups Make Faulty Decisions: An Investigation of Possible Interaction-Based Explanations," *Small Group Behavior 18* (1987): 3–29.

5. R. Y. Hirokawa and K. Rost, "Effective Group Decision-Making in Organizations: Field Test of the Vigilant Interaction Theory," *Management Communication Quarterly 5* (1992): 267–288; R. Y. Hirokawa, "Why Informed Groups Make Faulty Decisions: An Investigation of Possible Interaction-Based Explanations," *Small Group Behavior 18* (1987): 3–29; R. Y. Hirokawa, "Group Communication and Decision-Making Performance: A Continued Test of the Functional Perspective," *Human Communication Research 14* (1988): 487–515; M. O. Orlitzky and R. Y. Hirokawa, "To Err Is Human, to Correct for It Divine: A Meta-Analysis of Research Testing the Functional Theory of Group Decision-Making Effectiveness." Paper presented at the meeting of the National Communication Association, Chicago, November, 1997.

6. Hirokawa, "Discussion Procedures and Decision-Making Performance."

7. C. E. Larson and F. M. J. LaFasto, *Teamwork: What Must Go Right / What Can Go Wrong* (Beverly Hills: Sage, 1989). Also see: D. D. Chrislip and C. E. Larson, *Collaborative Leadership* (San Francisco: Jossey-Bass, 1994); D. A. Romig, *Breakthrough Teamwork: Outstanding Results Using Structured Teamwork*

(Chicago: Irwin, 1996); M. A. Marks, J. E. Mathieu, and S. J. Zaccaro, "A Temporally Based Framework and Taxonomy of Team Processes," *Academy of Management Review 26* (2001): 356–376; N. Katz, "Sports Teams as a Model for Workplace Teams: Lessons and Liabilities," *Academy of Management Executive 15* (2001): 56–67.

8. Larson and LaFasto, *Teamwork*; Chrislip and Larson, *Collaborative Leadership*; Romig, *Breakthrough Teamwork*.

9. Orlitzky and Hirokawa, "To Err Is Human, to Correct for It Divine."

10. Orlitzky and Hirokawa, "To Err Is Human, to Correct for It Divine"; B. L. Smith, "Interpersonal Behaviors That Damage the Productivity of Creative Problem Solving Groups," *Journal of Creative Behavior 27* (1993): 171–187.

11. See: A. B. VanGundy, *Techniques of Structured Problem Solving* (New York: Van Nostrand Reinhold Company, 1981), 4; Romig, *Breakthrough Teamwork*.

12. Beebe and Masterson, *Communicating in Small Groups*; VanGundy, *Techniques of Structured Problem Solving*.

13. J. K. Brilhart and L. M. Jochem, "Effects of Different Patterns on Outcomes of Problem-Solving Discussion," *Journal of Applied Psychology 48* (1964): 174–179; W. E. Jurma, "Effects of Leader Structuring Style and Task Orientation Characteristics of Group Members," *Communication Monographs 49* (1979): 282–295; S. Jarboe, "A Comparison of Input–Output, Process–Output, and Input– Process–Output Models of Small Group Problem-Solving Effectiveness," *Communication Monographs 55* (1988): 121–142; VanGundy, *Techniques of Structured Problem Solving*.

14. D. M. Berg, "A Descriptive Analysis of the Distribution and Duration of Themes Discussed by Task-Oriented Small Groups," *Speech Monographs 34* (1967): 172–175; E. G. Bormann and N. C. Bormann, *Effective Small Group Communication* 2e (Minneapolis: Burgess Publishing, 1976), 132; M. S. Poole, "Decision Development in Small Groups III: A Multiple Sequence Model of Group Decision Development," *Communication Monographs 50* (1983): 321–341.

15. J. Dewey, *How We Think* (Boston: D. C. Heath, 1910).

16. This discussion of the journalist's six questions is based on a discussion by J. E. Eitington, *The Winning Trainer* (Houston: Gulf Publishing, 1989), 157.

17. Based on the research of K. Lewin, "Frontiers in Group Dynamics," *Human Relations 1* (1947): 5–42.

18. A. F. Osborn, *Applied Imagination* (New York: Scribner's, 1962).

19. A. L. Delberg, A. H. Van de Ven, and D. H. Gustason, *Group Techniques for Program Planning: A Guide to Nominal Group and Delphi Processes* (Glenview, IL: Scott, Foresman, 1975), 7–16.

20. M. C. Roy, S. Gauvin, and M. Limayem, "Electronic Group Brainstorming: The Role of Feedback on Productivity," *Small Group Research 27* (1996): 215–247.

21. J. J. Sosik, B. J. Avolio, and S. S. Kahai, "Inspiring Group Creativity: Comparing Anonymous and Identified Electronic Brainstorming," *Small Group Research 29* (1998): 3–31; W. H. Cooper, R. B. Gallupe, S. Pollard, and J. Cadsby, "Some Liberating Effects of Anonymous Electronic Brainstorming," *Small Group Research 29* (1998): 147–177.

22. D. Straker, *Rapid Problem Solving with Post-It® Notes* (Tucson: Fisher Books, 1997).

23. CBC News, "Walkerton Report Highlights," January 2002 <http://www.cbc.ca/news/features/walkerton_report.html>.

24. J. F. Veiga, "The Frequency of Self-Limiting Behavior in Groups: A Measure and an Explanation," *Human Relations 44* (1991): 877–895.

25. I. L. Janis, *Victims of Groupthink* (Boston: Houghton Mifflin, 1973).

26. See: B. M. Bass, *Stodgill's Handbook of Leadership* (New York: The Free Press, 1981).

27. R. White and R. Lippitt, "Leader Behavior and Member Reaction in Three 'Social Climates'." In *Group Dynamics* 3e, edited by D. Cartwright and A. Zander (New York: Harper & Row, 1968), 319.

28. P. Hersey and K. Blanchard, *Management of Organizational Behavior: Utilizing Human Resources* 6e (Englewood Cliffs, NJ: Prentice-Hall, 1992).

29. F. Fiedler, *A Theory of Leadership Effectiveness* (New York: McGraw-Hill, 1967), 144.

30. B. M. Bass and M. J. Avolio, "Transformational Leadership and Organizational Culture," *International Journal of Public Administration 17* (1994): 541–554. Also see: F. J. Yammarino and A. J. Dubinsky, "Transformational Leadership Theory: Using Levels of Analysis to Determine Boundary Conditions," *Personnel Psychology 47* (1994): 787–809.

31. P. M. Senge, "The Leader's New Role: Building Learning Organizations," *Sloan Management Review 32*, no. 1 (1990).

32. D. Barry, *Dave Barry Turns 50* (New York: Ballantine Books, 1998), 182.

33. R. K. Mosvick and R. B. Nelson, *We've Got to Start Meeting Like This!* (Glenview, IL: Scott, Foresman, 1987).

34. G. Leventhal and M. Matturro, "Differential Effects of Spatial Crowding and Sex on Behavior," *Perceptual Motor Skills 50* (1980): 111–119; R. Sommer, "Studies in Personal Space," *Sociometry 22* (1959): 247–260; P. C. Ellsworth and L. M. Ludwig, "Visual Behavior in Social Interaction," *Journal of Communication 22* (1972): 375–403; N. M. Henley, *Body Politics: Power, Sex and Nonverbal Communication* (Englewood Cliffs, NJ: Prentice-Hall, 1977); N. N. Markel, J. Long, and T. J. Saine, "Sex Effects in Conversational Interaction: Another Look at Male Dominance," *Human Communication Research 2* (1976): 356–364.

35. Suggestions about organizing meeting agendas are based on M. Doyle and D. Straus, *How to Make Meetings Work* (New York: Playboy Press, 1976); Mosvick and Nelson, *We've Got to Start Meeting Like This!*; G. Lumsden and D. Lumsden, *Communicating in Groups and Teams: Sharing Leadership* (Belmont, CA: Wadsworth, 1993); D. B. Curtis, J. J. Floyd, and J. L. Winsor, *Business and Professional Communication* (New York: HarperCollins, 1992); Romig and Romig, *Structured Teamwork Guide*; T. A. Kayser, *Mining Group Gold* (El Segundo, CA: Serif Publishing, 1990); J. E. Tropman and G. Clark Morningstar, *Meetings: How to Make Them Work for You* (New York: Van Nostrand Reinhold, 1985): 56; Beebe and Masterson, *Communicating in Small Groups.*

36. J. E. Tropman, *Making Meetings Work* (Thousand Oaks, CA: Sage, 1996).

37. See: D. S. Gouran, "Variables Related to Consensus in Group Discussions of Questions of Policy," *Speech Monographs 36* (1969): 385–391; T. J. Knutsun, "An Experimental Study of the Effects of Orientation Behavior on Small Group Consensus," *Speech Monographs 39* (1972): 159–165; J. A. Kline, "Orientation and Group Consensus," *Central States Speech Journal 23* (1972): 44–47.

38. Mosvick and Nelson, *We've Got to Start Meeting Like This!*

39. Beebe and Masterson, *Communicating in Small Groups*; Environment Canada, "Winter Power Failure" <http://www.pnrrpn.ec.gc.ca/air/wintersevere/power.en.html>.

40. D. W. Johnson and F. P. Johnson, *Joining Together* (Englewood Cliffs, NJ: Prentice-Hall, 1975), 114.

41. An earlier version of this instrument appeared in S. A. Beebe, J. K. Barge, and C. McCormick, *The Competent Group Communicator*, presented at the meeting of the National Communication Association, New York, November, 1998. Also published in Beebe and Masterson, *Communicating in Small Groups.*

Chapter 11 Notes

1. S. Aduloju, "Whitewashed." In *Winning Orations 2000* (Mankato, MN: Interstate Oratorical Association, 2000), 83.

2. K. Clanton, "African American History." In *Winning Orations 2000*, 55.

3. S. Barnett, "Dying for a Drink of Water." In *Winning Orations 1999*, 53.

4. *2001 Census: Analysis Series: The Changing Profile of Canada's Labour Force*, Catalogue no. 96F003OXIE 2001009 (Ottawa: Minister of Industry, 2003).

5. N. Bissoondath, *Selling Illusions: The Cult of Muliculturalism in Canada* (Toronto: Penguin Books, 2002).

6. D. A. Lieberman, *Public Speaking in the Multicultural Environment*, 2e (Boston: Allyn & Bacon, 1997), 23.

7. Lieberman, *Public Speaking in the Multicultural Environment.*

8. J. Che, "Underweight Canadians," *Canadian Social Trends 67* (Winter 2002). Catalogue no. 11-008-XPE.

9. A. Kinney, untitled speech. In *Winning Orations 2000*, 134.

10. Cited in M. Kingwell and C. Moore, *Canada Our Century* (Toronto: Doubleday, 1999).

11. Cited in L. J. Peter, *Peter's Quotations: Ideas for Our Time* (New York: William Morrow & Co., 1977): 94.

12. Cited in L. J. Peter, *Peter's Quotations: Ideas for Our Time* (New York: William Morrow & Co., 1977): 93.

13. T. Kirchhefer, "The Deprived." In *Winning Orations 2000*, 151.

14. Information on SARS from the Centers for Disease Control and Prevention <http://www.cdc.gov/ncidod/sars/>.

Chapter 12 Notes

1. A. H. Monroe, "Measurement and Analysis of Audience Reaction to Student Speakers' Studies in Attitude Changes," *Bulletin of Purdue University Studies in Higher Education 22* (1937).

2. P. Heinbert, "Relationship of Content and Delivery to General Effectiveness," *Speech Monographs 30* (1963): 105–107.

3. A. Mehrabian, *Nonverbal Communication* (Hawthorne, NY: Aldine, 1972).

4. J. Detz, "Delivery Plus Content Equals Successful Presentation," *Communication World 15* (1998): 34.

5. Adapted from R. Ailes, *You Are the Message* (New York: Doubleday, 1989), 37–38.

6. J. Wareham, "Doing It Off-the-Cuff," *Across the Board 35* (1998): 49–50.

7. Wareham, "Doing It Off-the-Cuff."

8. S. B. Butterfield, "Instructional Interventions for Situational Anxiety and Avoidance," *Communication Education 37* (1988): 214–223.

9. Survey conducted by R. H. Bruskin and Associates, *Spectra 9* (December, 1973): 4.

10. L. Fletcher, *How to Design & Deliver Speeches* (New York: Longman, 2001), 3.

11. R. R. Behnke, C. R. Sawyer, and P. E. King, "The Communication of Public Speaking Anxiety," *Communication Education 36* (1987): 138–141.

12. J. Ayres, "Speech Preparation Processes and Speech Apprehension," *Communication Education 45* (1996): 228–235.

13. J. Ayres and B. Huett, "An Examination of the Long-Term Effect of Performance Visualization," *Communication Research Reports 17* (2000): 229–236.

14. J. Ayres and B. Huett, "An Examination of the Impact of Performance Visualization," *Communication Research Reports 16* (1999): 29–39; Ayres and Huett, "An Examination of the Long-Term Effect of Performance Visualization."

15. G. Orwell, "Politics and the English Language," reprinted in *About Language,* edited by W. H. Roberts and G. Turgeson (Boston: Houghton Mifflin, 1986), 282.

16. S. A. Beebe, "Eye Contact: A Nonverbal Determinant of Speaker Credibility," *Speech Teacher 23* (1974): 21–25; S. A. Beebe, "Effects of Eye Contact, Posture and Vocal Inflection Upon Credibility and Comprehension," *Australian Scan Journal of Nonverbal Communication 7–8* (1979–80): 57–70; M. Cobin, "Response to Eye Contact," *Quarterly Journal of Speech 48* (1963): 415–419.

17. Beebe, "Eye Contact."

18. E. Adler, "Gestures May Give You a Hand with Speaking," *Austin American-Statesman* (November 25, 1998): E6.

19. J. C. McCroskey, V. P. Richmond, A. Sallinen, J. M. Fayer, and R. A. Barraclough, "A Cross-Cultural and Multi-Behavioral Analysis of the Relationship between Nonverbal Immediacy and Teacher Evaluation," *Communication Education 44* (1995): 281–290.

20. M. J. Beatty, "Some Effects of Posture on Speaker Credibility," library paper, Central Missouri State University, 1973.

21. P. Ekman, W. V. Friesen, and S. S. Tomkins, "Facial Affect Scoring Technique: A First Validity Study," *Semiotica 3* (1971).

22. W. B. Chapel, "Advising Graduate Students for Successful International Internships," *Business Communication Quarterly 61* (1998): 92–104.

23. "Business Tips for India." 1998–2001 (July 15, 2002). <http://www.morebusiness.com/running_your_business/management/d930585271.brc?highlightstring=Business+Tips+for+India>.

24. Adapted from S. A. Beebe and S. J. Beebe, *Public Speaking: An Audience-Centered Approach* 5e. (Boston: Allyn & Bacon, 2003), 292–293.

25. M. M. Gill, "Accents and Stereotypes: Their Effect on Perceptions of Teachers and Lecture Comprehension," *Journal of Applied Communication Research 22* (1994): 348–361.

26. Adapted from S. Linver, *Speak Easy: How to Talk Your Way to the Top* (New York: Summit Books, 1978), 204–205.

27. E. Bohn and D. Jabusch, "The Effect of Four Methods of Instruction on the Use of Visual Aids in Speeches," *Western Journal of Speech Communication 46* (1982): 253–265.

28. P. S. Sochaczewski, "How Can We Put Intimacy into Presentations?" *Consulting to Management 12* (2001): 37–38.

29. R. Raskin, "Have Your Calendar Call Mine," *Family PC* (June/July, 1999): 21–26.

30. Statistics from the World Health Organization, as reported by CBS News. July 9, 2002 (July 9, 2002) <http://www.cbsnews.com/sections/world/main202.shtml>.

31. S. P. Mermelstein, "Nutrition on the Net," *Good Housekeeping* (July 1999): 149.

Chapter 13 Notes

1. J. R. Johnson and N. Szczupakiewicz, "The Public Speaking Course: Is It Preparing Students with Work-Related Public Speaking Skills?" *Communication Education 36* (1987): 131–137.

2. For an excellent discussion about teaching someone to perform a skill, especially a social skill, see: M. Argyle, *The Psychology of Interpersonal Behavior* (London: Penguin, 1990).

3. For an excellent discussion of strategies for informing others, see. K. E. Rowan, "A New Pedagogy for Explanatory Public Speaking: Why Arrangement Should Not Substitute for Invention," *Communication Education 44* (1995): 236–250.

4. For an excellent discussion of factors of attention in public speaking, see: D. Ehninger, B. E. Gronbeck, R. E. McKerrow, and A. H. Monroe, *Principles and Types of Speech Communication* (Glenview, IL: Scott, Foresman, 1986), 43.

5. This suggestion is based on an excellent review of the literature found in Rowan, "A New Pedagogy for Explanatory Public Speaking."

6. M. Groover, "Learning to Communicate: The Importance of Speech Education in Public Schools." In *Winning Orations 1984* (Mankato, MN: Interstate Oratorical Association, 1984), 7.

7. M. Klepper and R. Gunther, *I'd Rather Die than Give a Speech* (New York: Carol Publishing Group, 1995).

8. Our discussion of using humour is adapted from Klepper and Gunther, *I'd Rather Die than Give a Speech.*

9. Klepper and Gunther, *I'd Rather Die than Give a Speech.*

10. M. Knowles, *Self-Directed Learning* (Chicago: Follett Publishing, 1975).

11. S. McLaughlin, "The Dirty Truth about Your Kitchen: Using Common Sense to Prevent Food Poisoning." In *Winning Orations 1996* (Northfield, MN: Interstate Oratorical Association), 73.

12. McLaughlin, "The Dirty Truth about Your Kitchen," 75.

13. A. Maslow, "A Theory of Human Motivation." In *Motivation and Personality* (New York: Harper & Row, 1954), Chapter 5.

14. See: I. L. Janis and S. Feshback, "Effects of Fear Arousing Communications," *Journal of Abnormal and Social Psychology 48* (1953): 78–92; F. A. Powell and G. R. Miller, "Social Approval and Disapproval Cues in Anxiety Arousing Situations," *Speech Monographs 34* (1967): 152–159; and K. L. Higbee, "Fifteen Years of Fear Arousal: Research on Threat Appeals, 1953–1968," *Psychological Bulletin 72* (1969): 426–444.

15. P. A. Mongeau, "Another Look at Fear-Arousing Persuasive Appeals." In *Persuasion: Advances through Meta-Analysis,* edited by M. Allen and R. W. Preiss (Creskill, NJ: Hampton Press, 1998), 65.

16. Aristotle, *Rhetoric* (L. Cooper, trans.). (New York: Appleton-Century-Crofts, 1960).

17. A. Bogeajis, "The Danger of Child Safety Seats: Why Aren't They Safe?" In *Winning Orations 1996*, 10.

18. D. Ehninger, B. E. Gonbeck, R. E. McKerrow, and A. H. Monroe, *Principles and Types of Speech Communication* (Glenview, IL: Scott, Foresman, 1986), 15.

19. Adapted from J. Olsen, "The Long Road Home." In *Winning Orations 2000,* 25.

20. T. Snyder, "Notes from the Heart of Darkness," *Chatelaine* (April 1998).

Appendix A Notes

1. Our discussion of interview questions is based on J. T. Masterson, S. A. Beebe, and N. Watson, *An Invitation to Effective Speech Communication* (Glenview, IL: Scott Foresman and Company, 1989). We especially acknowledge the contributions of Norm Watson for this discussion.

2. This resumé and our suggestions for developing a resumé are based on the *2002 Southwest Texas State University Career Services Manual* (San Marcos, TX: Office of Career Services, 2002).

3. J. L. Winsor, D. B. Curtis, and R. D. Stephens, "National Preferences in Business and Communication Education: A Survey Update," *Journal of the Association for Communication Administration 3* (1997): 174.

4. S. Armour, "Employers: Enough Already with the E-Resumes," *USA Today* (July 15, 1999): B1.

5. *2002 Southwest Texas State University Career Services Manual.*

Appendix B Notes

1. Source: "Notes for an address by Prime Minister Jean Chretien on the occasion of a Tribute to the Prime Minister" http:www.pco-bcp.gc.ca/defaultasp?Language=E&Page=pmarchive&Sub=Speeches&Doc=convention20031113_e.htm, 2003.

2. Source: http://www.gg.ca/media/doc.asp?lang=e&DocID=4039.

Credits

Index